SYSTEMIC SEX THERAPY

This comprehensive textbook, intended for graduate students in couple and family therapy programs as well as for clinicians of diverse orientations, offers descriptive discussions of sex therapy based on the Intersystem Approach, as developed by Gerald R. Weeks.

The Intersystem Approach considers the biology, psychology, couple dyad, family-of-origin, and larger contextual factors of any sexual disorder or issue. It is grounded in systems theory and represents a new understanding of human sexuality and sexual problems. Appropriate for anyone who wants to progress to a more comprehensive and integrative understanding of sexual dysfunctions, this text will teach the reader how to treat the couple, rather than the individual.

Now in a second edition, *Systemic Sex Therapy* presents 12 updated chapters and two new chapters, bringing the material up-to-date with the *DSM-5*. Each chapter examines the definition and description of a disorder, its etiology, assessment, treatment, research, and future directions. Experts in the field discuss issues ranging from pharmacology, sexual compulsivity, and therapy with lesbian and gay couples, to chapters on male and female lack of desire.

A standard text in the field, *Systemic Sex Therapy* integrates couple and sex therapy to inform the treatment of sexual problems, and to give beginning and experienced clinicians the abilities and confidence they need to produce viable change in their patients' lives.

Katherine M. Hertlein, Ph.D., is an associate professor and Program Director of the Marriage and Family Therapy program at the University of Nevada, Las Vegas. She has published over 50 articles, six books, and 25 book chapters over the course of her career. She presents nationally and internationally on sex, technology, and couples.

Gerald R. Weeks, Ph.D., ABPP, is a certified sex therapist with 30 years of practice experience, and is a professor at the University of Nevada, Las Vegas. He is among a handful of individuals to be given the "Outstanding Contribution to Marriage and Family Therapy" award in 2009 from the American Association of Marriage and Family Therapy, and was named the "2010 Family Psychologist of the Year." He has published over 20 books in the fields of individual, couple, family, and sex therapy.

Nancy Gambescia, Ph.D., is a certified sex therapist with 35 years of practice experience, and is the Director of the Postgraduate Sex Therapy Program at Council for Relationships in Philadelphia, Pennsylvania. She also maintains a private practice specializing in relationship and sex therapy in Rosemont, Pennsylvania. Dr. Gambescia has published numerous book chapters, journal articles, and five books on couple and sex therapy.

SYSTEMIC SEX THERAPY

Second Edition

Edited by
Katherine M. Hertlein,
Gerald R. Weeks, and
Nancy Gambescia

Routledge
Taylor & Francis Group

NEW YORK AND LONDON

Second edition published 2015
by Routledge
711 Third Avenue, New York, NY 10017

and by Routledge
27 Church Road, Hove, East Sussex BN3 2FA

*Routledge is an imprint of the Taylor & Francis Group,
an informa business*

© 2015 Taylor & Francis

First edition published by Routledge 2008

Library of Congress Cataloging-in-Publication Data
Systemic sex therapy / [edited] Katherine M. Hertlein, Gerald R.
   Weeks, Nancy Gambescia. — Second edition.
      p. ; cm.
   Preceded by: A clinician's guide to systemic sex therapy / Katherine
M. Hertlein, Gerald R. Weeks, Shelley K. Sendak. c2009.
   Includes bibliographical references and index.
 I. Hertlein, Katherine M., editor.   II. Weeks, Gerald R., 1948– ,
editor.   III. Gambescia, Nancy, editor.   IV. Hertlein, Katherine M.
Clinician's guide to systemic sex therapy. Preceded by (work):
   [DNLM: 1. Couples Therapy—methods.   2. Marital Therapy—
methods.   3. Sexual Dysfunction, Physiological—therapy.   4. Sexual
Dysfunctions, Psychological—therapy. WM 430.5.M3]
   RC488.5
   616.89′1562—dc23
   2014037579

ISBN: 978-0-415-73821-7 (hbk)
ISBN: 978-0-415-73824-8 (pbk)
ISBN: 978-1-315-81752-1 (ebk)

Typeset in Sabon
by Apex CoVantage, LLC

TO ERIC HERTLEIN
—KH

TO NANCY LOVE
—GW

TO MICHAEL, MATT, AND LAUREN—WITH LOVE
—NG

CONTENTS

CONTENTS

CONTENTS

ABOUT THE EDITORS

Katherine M. Hertlein, Ph.D., is an associate professor and the Program Director of the Marriage and Family Therapy Program at the University of Nevada, Las Vegas. She received her master's in marriage and family therapy from Purdue University Calumet and her doctorate in human development with a specialization in marriage and family therapy from Virginia Tech and is an AAMFT Approved Supervisor. Across her academic career, she has published over 50 articles, six books, and over 25 book chapters. She has co-edited a book on interventions in couples treatment, interventions for clients with health concerns, and a book on infidelity treatment. Dr. Hertlein has also produced the first multitheoretical model detailing the role of technology in couple and family life published in her latest book, *The Couple and Family Technology Framework*. She presents nationally and internationally on sex, technology, and couples. Dr. Hertlein has won numerous awards including the 2008 and 2014 Greenspun College of Urban Affairs Outstanding Teaching Award, the 2010 Greenspun College of Urban Affairs Outstanding Research Award, the 2013 Supervisor of the Year Award from the Nevada Association for Marriage and Family Therapy, the 2013 Outstanding Mentor Award from UNLV's Graduate and Professional Student Association, the 2014 Nevada System of Higher Education's Regent's Rising Researcher Award, and the 2014 Barrick Scholar Award from the University of Nevada, Las Vegas.

Gerald R. Weeks, Ph.D., ABPP, is a professor in the Marriage and Family Therapy Program at the University of Nevada-Las Vegas. For over 30 years, he has published, conducted research, practiced, taught, and supervised sex, couple, and family therapy. Dr. Weeks is a licensed psychologist, Approved-Supervisor, and Clinical Fellow of the American Association of Marriage and Family Therapy, a Diplomate and Senior Examiner of the American Board of Family Psychology, and a member of the American Board of Sexology. He has published 20 books, including one or more classic texts in the fields of individual, sex, couple, and family therapy. Several of his texts are widely used in Marriage and Family Therapy Programs. In 2009, he was the 16th member to receive the "Outstanding Contribution the Marriage and Family Therapy" award from the American Association of Marriage and Family Therapy in its 60 year history. In 2010, the American Psychological Association awarded "Family Psychologist of the Year" to Dr. Weeks. One of his major contributions to the field of couple and sex therapy is the development of a new paradigm of therapy known as the Intersystem Approach. Dr. Weeks has lectured and conducted intensive training in couple and sex therapy throughout North America, Europe, and Australia.

Nancy Gambescia, Ph.D., CST, is the Director of the Postgraduate Program in Sex Therapy at the Council for Relationships, Philadelphia, PA. The Program is one of very few in the U.S. that provides AASECT (American Association of Sex Educators Counselors and Therapists) approved post-graduate training in sex therapy. Also, she is a clinical associate in Psychiatry at the Perelman School of Medicine at the University of Pennsylvania. Dr. Gambescia has over 30 years of experience in teaching, supervising and working with individuals and couples. Dr. Gambescia is a Clinical Fellow and Approved Supervisor in the American Association of Marriage and Family Therapy (AAMFT). She is also a Clinical Member, Certified Sex Therapist, and Approved Supervisor of Sex Therapy in AASECT. Dr. Gambescia is a member of the Society for Sex Therapy and Research (SSTAR), and a certified sexologist and diplomate of the American Board of Sexology. She has coauthored six books (two in press) that emphasize the Intersystem Approach to couple and sex therapy and written numerous journal articles and textbook chapters, which focus on relationship and sexual issues. She has presented a number of refereed and invited lectures and workshops in The United States and Europe on couple and sex therapy.

CONTRIBUTORS

Stephen J. Betchen, D.S.W., L.M.F.T., is an AAMFT Approved Supervisor and AASECT Certified Supervisor with a full-time private practice specializing in couples and sex therapy. He is also a clinical assistant professor in the graduate program for couples and family therapy at Thomas Jefferson University, and a senior supervisor in the post-graduate sex therapy program at the Council for Relationships. Dr. Betchen has published three books and several scholarly articles on relationships.

David L. Delmonico is a professor at Duquesne University in Pittsburgh, Pennsylvania. Dr. Delmonico is a graduate of Kent State University's Counseling and Human Development Services Program. He conducts research, consultation, and training on topics such as cybersex, cyberoffense, and cybersafety. Dr. Delmonico also lectures on topics such as general Internet psychology and sexually addictive and compulsive behaviors. Dr. Delmonico is co-author of *In the Shadows of the Net, Cybersex Unhooked, Cybersex Unplugged*, and his latest book, *Illegal Images*. He has published numerous scholarly articles on a variety of addiction and sexuality topics. Dr. Delmonico is Director of the Online Behavior Research and Education Center (OBREC) at Duquesne University and Associate Editor of the Sexual Addiction & Compulsivity journal.

Evan Fertel is a Ph.D. student in the clinical psychology program at the University of Nevada, Las Vegas. His research investigates the role of self-focus in sexual desire and arousal and sex differences therein.

Sallie Foley, LMSW is the director of the Center for Sexual Health at the University of Michigan Health Systems and teaches at the University of Michigan. She has a private practice in psychotherapy and consultation in Ann Arbor. She is on the medical advisory board for the Intersex Society of North America and is an AASECT certified sex therapist. She writes and lectures frequently on the subject of human sexuality.

Elizabeth J. Griffin, M.A., is a licensed marriage and family therapist with over 27 years of experience treating individuals with sexually problematic behaviors, especially those that involve the Internet. She has worked in out-patient, in-patient, military, and prison settings. Ms. Griffin lectures nationally on the assessment and treatment of sexual offenders and those with sexually compulsive behavior, as well as issues related to cybersex. She is currently a consultant for the Minnesota Civil Commitment Program. She has written numerous professional articles on these topics, and is co-author of four books—*In the Shadows of the Net, Cybersex Unhooked, Cybersex Unplugged*, and *Illegal Images*. Ms. Griffin is the founder of Internet Behavior Consulting, a company focused on issues related to problematic online behavior.

Kathryn Hall, Ph.D., is a clinical psychologist in private practice in Princeton, New Jersey. She has conducted research on a variety of sex-related topics and has presented at national and international conferences. Her current interest is in the cultural variations in the experience and treatment of sexual problems. Dr. Hall is coeditor of the *Cultural Context of Sexual Pleasure and Problems: Psychotherapy with Diverse Clients*. She is the author of *Reclaiming Your Sexual Self: How You Can Bring Desire Back Into Your Life*.

Ruth Hallam-Jones now works as an independent clinician providing sexual and relationship assessment, psychotherapy, and sexual medicine resources. She uses retreats based on systemic residential sex therapy. She also provides individual and group training for professionals. She has worked as a nurse and sexual and relationship therapist for over 30 years. An experienced and creative clinician, Ruth has gained her understanding of systemic work with patients with sexual and relationship problems not just from her training but also from working in community and residential psychiatry and psychotherapy settings in Sheffield, Rotherham, and the Maudsley, London, and from the residential sex therapy used by Restoration-Therapy. She has also worked for ten years in outpatient sexual medicine services. Until recently she co-ordinated training and was the senior psychotherapist at Porterbrook Clinic, Sheffield.

Ashley Blackmon Jones, M.D., is a board certified adult psychiatrist. She is an assistant clinical professor and the director of Adult Resident Outpatient Clinics in the Department of Neuropsychiatry and Behavioral Science at the University of South Carolina School of Medicine. Dr. Jones is also the assistant program director for the General Psychiatry Residency Training Program at Palmetto Health/University of South Carolina School of Medicine. In professional psychiatric practice she has worked in the areas of emergency psychiatry, consultation-liaison, outpatient psychiatry, the department of corrections, and in the division of biological research. She currently supervises an integrated care clinic in the Department of Obstetrics and Gynecology, which provides psychiatric care to pregnant and postpartum women. She is a member of the American Psychiatric Association, South Carolina Psychiatric Association, and American Association of Directors of Psychiatric Residency Training and serves as a board member for Mental Health America of South Carolina. Dr. Jones is an active presenter in the community, medical school, and within the Palmetto Health residency programs of psychiatry, internal medicine, family medicine, and obstetrics and gynecology. Presentations, lectures, and posters include topics on women's mental health, resident wellness, psychopharmacology, emergency psychiatry, brief psychotherapies, psychiatric interviews, and biological-psychological-social formulation.

Peggy J. Kleinplatz, Ph.D., is professor of medicine and clinical professor of psychology at the University of Ottawa. She is a clinical psychologist, certified in sex therapy, in sex education, and has a diplomate in and is a supervisor of sex therapy. Since 1983, she has been teaching human sexuality at the School of Psychology, University of Ottawa, where she received the Prix d'Excellence in 2000. She is currently chair of ethics and former chair of certifications for the American Association of Sexuality Educators, Counselors and Therapists. Kleinplatz has edited three books, most recently, *New Directions in Sex Therapy: Innovations and Alternatives* (Routledge, 2nd edition), winner of the AASECT 2013 Book Award. Her clinical work focuses on eroticism and transformation. Her current research focuses on optimal sexuality, with a particular interest in sexual health in the elderly, disabled, and marginalized populations.

Arlene Istar Lev, LCSW-R, CASAC, is a social worker, family therapist, educator, and writer whose work addresses the unique therapeutic needs of lesbian, gay, bisexual, and transgender people. She is part-time lecturer at the University at Albany, School of Social Welfare and is the project director of the *Sexual Orientation and Gender Identity Project (SOGI)*. She is also an adjunct professor at Smith School of Social Work, Empire College, Excelsior College, and the Rockway Institute, California School of Professional Psychology at Alliant International University. Ms. Lev is the founder and clinical director of Choices Counseling and Consulting and The Training Institute for Gender, Relationships, Identity, and Sexuality (TIGRIS), in Albany, New York (www.choicesconsulting.com). She has authored numerous journal articles and essays including authoring two books: *The Complete Lesbian and Gay Parenting Guide* and *Transgender Emergence*, winner of the APA (Division 44) Distinguished Book Award, 2006.

Desa Markovic, DPsych, holds the post of program director for psychotherapy and counselling at Regent's University London. Her clinical practice has spanned over 30 years and is currently based at Covent Garden Counselling in London where she specializes in systemic and psychosexual therapy and supervision. After studying clinical psychology in Belgrade, Yugoslavia, she continued with post graduate training in systemic family therapy at Kensington Consultation Centre in London subsequently obtaining a clinical doctorate in psychotherapy from the University of London. She has taught on systemic and sexual therapy courses at various institutions including the Institute of Family Therapy in London and the Porterbrook Clinic in Sheffield. Her most recent publications and international conference presentations relate to her current area of interest being the development of a Multidimensional Model integrating systemic approach and sexology.

Caroline Maykut is a Ph.D. student in the clinical psychology program at the University of Nevada, Las Vegas. Her research centers on the investigation of how men and women self-assess their own sexual desire levels and the extent to which these assessments are related to sexual function and well-being.

Marita P. McCabe, Ph.D., is a professor of psychology and the foundation director of the Health and Well Being Research Priority Area at Deakin University in Melbourne, Australia. She is an associate editor for the *Journal of Sexual Medicine and Body Image*, and is on the editorial board of the *Journal of Sex Research*. As well as her clinical experience, she has over 400 refereed articles and book chapters. Professor McCabe has obtained research grants and supervised postgraduate students conducting studies on sexual dysfunction, sex and disability, sexual harassment, sexual abuse, rape, extramarital affairs, and adolescent sexuality. In particular, she has conducted a series of studies that have investigated aetiology and most effective method of treatment for sexual dysfunction. She has recently devised and evaluated an Internet based treatment program for the treatment of erectile dysfunction and also for the treatment of female sexual dysfunction.

Marta Meana, Ph.D., is professor of psychology, dean of the Honors College at the University of Nevada, Las Vegas, and is past president of the Society for Sex Therapy and Research. The author of numerous books, peer-reviewed publications, chapters, and conference presentations on sexuality and women's health, her early work was instrumental in the reconceptualization of dyspareunia as a pain disorder. Her current research on female sexual desire also seeks to deconstruct traditional notions of desire and its relationship to behavior. Dr. Meana's work has been featured widely in national and international media, including in the *New York Times*, the *Charlie Rose* show, and the *Oprah Winfrey Show*. She currently serves on the editorial boards of the *Archives of Sexual Behavior* and the *Journal of Sex Research* and she is a Fellow of the Society for the Scientific Study of Sexuality. She was also an advisor to the *DSM-5* Sexual Dysfunctions Workgroup and is a licensed clinical psychologist in the state of Nevada.

Margaret Nichols, Ph.D., is a psychologist, sex therapist, and executive director of the Institute for Personal Growth, a psychotherapy organization in New Jersey specializing in sex therapy and other clinical work with the sex and gender diverse community. She has been active in community mental health for many years, helping to start one of the first shelters for victims of domestic violence in the 1970s and the Hyacinth Foundation, New Jersey's largest HIV support and service agency, in 1985. She is an international speaker on LGBTQ issues and author of many articles and papers on LGBTQ sexuality. Her current primary clinical areas of interest are transgender and gender nonconforming young people, and those who make up the 'Q' in LGBTQ, e.g., kinky, polyamorous, and queer people. She is also working on developing a queer theory of sex therapy and sex science.

Rebecca Ann Payne, M.D., is board certified in general and addiction psychiatry. She is an assistant clinical professor in the Department of Neuropsychiatry and Behavioral Science at the University of South Carolina School of Medicine. Dr. Payne primarily functions as a clinician-educator, treating inpatients and outpatients with comorbid psychiatric and substance use disorders, supervising medical students and psychiatry residents, and educating the community about co-occurring disorders.

Kenneth Wayne Phelps, Ph.D., LMFT is an assistant clinical professor and outpatient clinic director in the Department of Neuropsychiatry and Behavioral Science at the University of South Carolina's School of Medicine. Dr. Phelps has a doctorate in medical family therapy from East Carolina University, specializing in treating youth, adults, and couples navigating medical illness. He is a member of the American Association of Sexuality Educators, Counselors, and Therapists and American Association for Marriage and Family Therapy through which he has attained the designation of AAMFT Approved Supervisor. Dr. Phelps completed a predoctoral internship at Dartmouth Family Practice Residency Program associated with Concord Hospital in New Hampshire. He has presented and published on the topics of sexual health, relational health, diabetes, tic disorders, autism, and residency education.

Jane Ridley, B.A. PQSW, trained originally as a social worker at the London School of Economics and at the University of Newcastle and as a mature student at the Institute of Psychiatry. She ran the Richmond Fellowship training in residential care of the recovering mentally ill, for 7 years and joined Dr. M. Crowe in 1983 at the Marital and Sexual Therapy Clinics. She was instrumental in developing the course in relationship and sexual therapy, which offered both MSc and Diploma at the Maudsley and Institute of Psychiatry. She further developed her work in supervision, running courses for experienced therapists. She has also been chair of the Family, Marital and Sexual Section of UKCP and a member of the Governing Board of UKCP. She currently works privately. Her writing includes joint authorship of *Therapy with Couples*, a behavioral-systems approach to relationship and sexual problems (Blackwell Science 2000, 2nd ed.), and authorship of *Intimacy in Crisis* (Pub Whurr 1999). In 2007 she contributed chapters 17 and 18 to *The Handbook of Clinical Adult Psychology* (eds. Stan Lindsay and Graham Powell, 3rd ed.).

Kevan R. Wylie, FRCP FRCPsych FRCOG FECSM, is a consultant in sexual medicine for the NHS in Sheffield, UK, and leads the Sexual Therapy, Sexual Medicine, and Andrology (Urology) services. His academic appointments include honorary professor at The University of Sheffield, visiting professor at Sheffield Hallam University, and course director of the Sheffield MSc program on Sexual & Relationship Psychotherapy. Kevan was awarded the EFS Gold Medal in 2008 for his work into sexual medicine, sexology, and sex education across Europe, has published in excess of 140 peer reviewed papers and 15 book chapters, and is the current president of the World Association for Sexual Health.

PREFACE

Authors are motivated to write texts because they wish to make a significant contribution to a field of study or they perceive a theoretical gap in the existing literature. The first edition of *Systemic Sex Therapy* represented our attempt to provide a book that would serve as an introduction to the field of sex therapy from a systems perspective. The first edition outperformed our expectations and has been adopted in a number of marriage and family therapy programs in the United States and other countries. We were encouraged by our colleagues and editors to produce a second edition of this popular book.

Target Audience

There are two target audiences for this book. Graduate students in marriage and family therapy programs, who are knowledgeable in systems thinking, wanted a book that was written from a systems perspective. The other target audience is the many clinicians who want to progress to a more comprehensive and integrative understanding of sexual dysfunctions. Some sex therapists have had some training in systems thinking and will gravitate toward our Intersystem theoretical position. Others, unfortunately, have had no training in systems thinking and although interested in a systems approach will, by default, continue to think and practice from an individually oriented framework. One only has to attend professional sex therapy conferences or read the literature to observe the theoretical divide that exists within the field. Some of the more senior members of the field of sex therapy are unfamiliar with systemic thinking and will have limited interest in changing their theoretical approach.

Purpose and Theoretical Framework

Our objective is to present a highly focused and comprehensive text that promotes understanding of the etiology and treatment of sexual problems from a systemic perspective. We believe that the second edition of *Systemic Sex Therapy* continues to be very comprehensible, offering descriptive discussions of sex therapy without using a great deal of professional and/or technical jargon. This edition will be helpful to both graduate students and practitioners desiring a greater understanding of the current literature in the field of sex therapy within a systemic framework.

This book's main purpose is to accomplish what we believe no other book in the field of sex therapy has ever fully done. It is based on a unique approach to systems theory (called the Intersystem Approach; Weeks, 1989), one that involves the partner and treats the couple, rather than the individual, as a unit. Most published books in the field of sex therapy are behaviorally grounded and/or medically driven. This circumstance is not surprising since the field of sex therapy has been clearly dominated by behaviorists and physicians. Moreover, in some of the more recent works on sex therapy, the emphasis is still on the individual with the sexual problem rather than an inclusion of the context within which the individual lives such as the relationship, environment, and culture in addition to medical and psychological contributors to sexual problems.

We do not, however, intend to discard the invaluable work of behaviorally informed therapists. Our framework is broad enough to embrace this perspective and many more within the much larger theoretical framework. We believe the systemic view of couple dynamics is the essential unit of therapy, but not in the limited view of the behavioral tradition. One of our major assumptions is that many sexual dysfunctions reflect difficulties in the couple relationship. This basic supposition has many implications for sex therapy that are highlighted in this volume:

1. sexual problems may reflect problems at many different levels in the couple ranging from lack of communication to underlying intimacy problems;
2. the resolution of the couple's problems are necessary to remedy many sexual problems;
3. unconscious factors in the couple's relationship may impede or sabotage the couple's ability to develop a more satisfying sexual relationship;
4. a sexual problem in one partner may "mask" a sexual and/or relational problem in the other;
5. the sexual problem may be unconsciously maintained by the couple;
6. assignments to be performed at home are designed to be reciprocal; thus, each partner is given respect and benefits from treatments that enhance their relationship on multiple levels;
7. sexual problems may exacerbate couple issues or create new challenges for the couple. A systemic perspective considers all of the major abovementioned factors and the more subtle and less common links between the couple's sexual relationship and their overall relationship.

The systems framework used in this text was initially developed by Weeks (1977) in a paper that was formative in the development of the Intersystem Approach. Subsequent publications refined this approach and applied it to numerous clinical issues (Weeks, 1989; Weeks & Fife, 2014; Weeks & Hof 1987, 1994, 1995; Weeks, Odell, & Methven, 2005; Weeks & Treat, 2014). The theory that informs this book is called the Intersystem Approach (Weeks, 1989). It is a quantum leap over traditional systems theory as described in Gurman and Kniskern's (1991) edited *Handbook of Family Therapy* in which most contributors disregarded the importance of the individual within the larger system. The Intersystem Approach has been successfully demonstrated in the treatment of erectile dysfunction, the lack of sexual desire (Weeks & Gambescia 2000, 2002), and infidelity (Weeks, Gambescia, & Jenkins, 2003) and all the major sexual dysfunctions described in the first edition of this book.

The Intersystem Approach encompasses the simultaneous consideration of the individual-biological/medical, individual-psychological, couple dyad, family-of-origin, and larger contextual factors such as religion, culture, etc. The purpose of this approach is to gain as comprehensive an understanding of the problem as possible in order to treat all the factors involved in the creation and continuation of the problem. *Systemic Sex Therapy* (2nd ed.) follows this approach in that it is integrative, examining multiple domains of behavior such as that of the individual (including individual psychopathology and biological or medical concerns), couple issues from multiple levels, and the influence of the family of origin on couple development, functioning, and dysfunction in all aspects of the relationship. In summary, we believe this book has several unique features not found in any other texts on sex therapy:

- **Grounded in Systems Theory.** This text is the first that truly takes a systems perspective; the couple is viewed as the unit of treatment. This view transcends the traditional view of the partner as an informant and useful homework surrogate. The theoretical basis for this volume extends traditional systems theory to an Intersystem Approach.
- **Intersystem Approach.** Specifically, this volume uses a meta-framework known as the Intersystem Approach. This approach transcends traditional (cognitive)-behavioral and medical sex therapy approaches to a much broader systemic framework where individual, couple, and intergenerational factors are considered in both the etiology and treatment. This process is inclusionary and comprehensive rather than exclusionary and myopic.
- **Theory Development.** The field of sex therapy has been devoid of any new theory development since the late 1990s. This volume presents a new theory in understanding human sexuality and sexual problems. It is a broad and all-encompassing theory that could produce the development of other theories within the various domains of behavior.
- **Clinical Innovation.** Advances in the field of sex therapy have been primarily medical for the past couple of decades. Theory development leading to new treatment strategies and techniques has been virtually non-existent. This text not only renders a new theoretical framework, but encourages clinical innovation in the understanding and treatment of sexual problems.
- **Integration of Sex and Couple Therapy.** We view sex and couple therapy as inseparable fields; the unit of treatment has always been focused on the couple. Prior to this volume, the couple was not viewed from a systems framework and sexual and couple issues were viewed as largely non-intersecting phenomena leading to an artificial division in these two fields in theory, research, and practice.
- **Greater Focus on Implementation than Competing Works.** Many books give the reader the techniques and expect the clinician to automatically know how to implement the technique. Techniques are relatively easy to learn. We will describe the technique, discuss the implementation of the technique, and provide some case material to illuminate the use of the technique in the second edition of *Systemic Sex Therapy* and the second edition of the companion volume.

The theory also includes a number of integrational constructs that organize the various domains of behavior. For reasons beyond our comprehension, behaviorally-oriented writers have not incorporated the concept of a theoretically based approach to integration into their writings. Perhaps part of the reason is discussed in our last chapter on the lack of theory in the field of sex therapy in general.

Chapter Outline

The contributors to this text were asked to follow a standard outline for the core treatment chapters. These are the chapters that describe the traditionally defined sexual problems. Of course, some variation will exist depending on how much literature and insight we currently have into the role each factor plays in the etiology and treatment of the disorders. Additionally, some of the chapters not dealing with the sexual disorders do not follow this outline.

- **Definition and Description of Disorder.** The definition should reflect the material regarding definition and clinical criteria in the *Diagnostic and Statistical Manual of Mental Disorders (DSM-5)* (APA, 2013). Authors were asked to include reviews of other descriptions in the literature and any other information on the development of the classification.
- **Etiology.** What are the known or suspected causes of this disorder from the multiple domains of behavior in the Intersystem Approach (e.g., individual-medical-psychological, couple, intergenerational, and contextual influences)?
- **Assessment.** How this disorder is assessed using the Intersystem framework?
- **Treatment.** Treatment is discussed from the perspective of the Intersystem Approach (e.g., individual/medical, couple, intergenerational, contextual). It is important to take the clinician from the beginning to the end of treatment focusing on stages of treatment, techniques, implementation of techniques, examples of how to implement techniques, homework exercises, how to deal with non-compliance or homework failure, etc.
- **Research and Future Directions.** Our authors provide a brief review of research supporting the treatment, and if possible, directions for future development (e.g., new medical treatments for ED, PE, and FOD, new therapeutic techniques, etc.).

Changes From the Previous Edition

The reader will note three significant changes from the first edition. In the *DSM-5* male and female lack of desire is divided into two different classifications. Thus, we have chapters on each disorder. It should be noted that very little has been written about lack of desire in men and a great deal has been written about lack of desire in women. We believe many of the etiological factors for men and women are the same and the principles of treatment would be the same or similar. We have also deleted the chapter on sensate-focus from this volume. This chapter will appear in the companion volume (*A Clinician's Guide to Systemic Sex Therapy*). We also deleted the chapter on infidelity because we view that as primarily a couple problem, and a revised and updated chapter on infidelity has been published in *Couples in Treatment* by Weeks and Fife (2014).

Organization of the Text

The book is organized into several sections. The first section provides an overview of some of the basics of sex therapy, and serves to orient the new professional to the field. It is composed of three chapters: "What Every Sex Therapist Needs to Know" by Jane Ridley, "The Current Profession of Sex Therapy" by Peggy Kleinplatz, and "Toward a New Paradigm in Sex Therapy" by Gerald R. Weeks and Nancy Gambescia.

Ridley's chapter outlines the resilience, personal attributes, and competencies required of aspiring sex therapists. It focuses on the interconnected and interdependent nature of sexuality through providing a brief introduction to diagnosis and prevalence of sexual difficulties. The chapter contains a discussion of the questions raised about *DSM-5* and the implications for the sex therapist. It covers anatomy and physiology, and information about sexual response cycles. Areas of controversy are highlighted, in particular the problem of musicalizing the personal sexual experiences of individuals.

The chapter "The Current Profession of Sex Therapy" by Peggy J. Kleinplatz describes the history of sex therapy, current trends in the field including the medicalization of sexual dysfunction, and the shift toward systemic/behavioral approaches, the various sex therapy organizations, the personal and professional process of becoming a sex therapist, and ethical principles of sex therapy.

Finally, the chapter by Weeks and Gambescia presents the paradigm shift in sex therapy by providing an integrative, comprehensive model, the Intersystem Approach. In a departure from eclectic approaches, this framework synthesizes information from the fields of healthcare, couples therapy, psychology, sexuality, and communication to inform the treatment of sexual problems.

The second section is comprised of chapters describing how the Intersystemic Approach can be utilized for the treatment of specific sexual dysfunctions. Gerald R. Weeks and Nancy Gambescia have provided a chapter on the treatment sexual interest/arousal disorder in women and general information about the lack of sexual desire from an intersystem perspective, given desire problems are caused by any number of bio-psycho-social factors. Chapter 4 is about hypoactive sexual desire disorder. This disorder has been split from low/absent sexual desire in woman. In the past, women were also given the same diagnosis. There is now enough research to suggest that the etiology and treatment of female and male low/absent desire may be different.

In chapter 5, "Systemic Treatment of Erectile Disorder," Nancy Gambescia and Gerald R. Weeks discuss how erectile dysfunction adversely affects a man's self-esteem, quality of life, his partner's enjoyment of sexual intimacy, and the overall interpersonal relationship. The Intersystem method is presented as a comprehensive, intimacy-based, and integrative approach to assessing and treating erectile dysfunction. The desired outcome of the Intersystem Approach is the restoration of sexual satisfaction for the couple, not just erectile capacity.

Stephen J. Betchen has included a chapter on using the Intersystem Approach with couples struggling with premature ejaculation. This chapter depicts how premature ejaculation and relational dynamics are intertwined, and also presents a systemic and integrative model designed to treat the disorder, attending to medical issues, and combining aspects of psychoanalytic conflict theory and psychodynamic family-of-origin work with basic sex therapy principles and exercises.

The chapter on delayed ejaculation, written by Sallie Foley and updated for this edition by Nancy Gambescia, outlines the multitude of biopsychosocial factors that contribute to the emergence of delayed ejaculation and describes how the Intersystem Approach is applied to the treatment of this presenting problem.

Gerald R. Weeks and Nancy Gambescia wrote the chapter on low/absent desire in women. They reviewed the issues with definition and the multiple etiological and treatment strategies and techniques.

Although arousal disorders in women are comingled in the *DSM-5* with the lack of sexual interest, the authors decided to retain an updated version of arousal disorders for the current volume. In this chapter, Kevan R. Wylie, Desa Markovic, and Ruth Hallam-Jones discuss the use of metaphor as a treatment modality. They also provide a wealth of resources for the assessment and treatment of this problem.

Marita McCabe contributed the chapter on anorgasmia in women, one that maps out the complex factors contributing to the development of this condition. She focuses on Intersystemic etiology and outlines specific treatment for each of these factors.

In Chapter 11 on painful intercourse, Marta Meana, Caroline Maykut, and Evan Fertel propose a multidisciplinary Intersystem Approach to etiology, assessment, and treatment of dyspareunia and vaginismus. Within this chapter, Meana also proposes an integrative approach as the optimal standard of care, with the collaboration of sex therapy, gynecology, and physical therapy.

The final section of the book details information on the future of sex therapy as well as contemporary issues. Arlene Istar Lev and Margaret Nichols have contributed a chapter on sexual issues in lesbian and gay couples, which outlines the historical, cultural, social, and familial factors influencing lesbian and gay male couples. Differences and similarities between same sex and mixed sex couples are reviewed and discussed, including the ways in which different types of couples function relationally and sexually.

Additionally, a chapter on sexual compulsivity is included as it represents an increasingly prevalent sexual issue affecting many couples and families. David Delmonico and Elizabeth Griffin review the complex etiology of the development of a sexual compulsivity and outlines treatment from an integrative model. In addition, the evolution of the concept of sexual "addiction," from its historical roots, to present day theory and the future of the construct is included.

Kenneth Wayne Phelps, Ashley Blackmon Jones, and Rebecca Ann Payne have contributed a chapter discussing the medicalization of sex, discussing the impact certain drugs have on relationship and sexual functioning, and exploring sexual pharmacology from a systemic perspective.

Finally, in "Sex Therapy: A Panoramic View" by Gerald R. Weeks, Nancy Gambescia, and Katherine M. Hertlein, the authors review where the field of sex therapy has been, where it is now, and where it is going. Topics include the predominantly behavioral focus, the need for integration, the medicalization of sex therapy, working with special populations, and gaps in theory.

The second edition of *Systemic Sex* is not intended to be a stand-alone volume. Just as with the first edition, we will be updating and revising *A Clinician's Guide to Systemic Sex Therapy*. This companion volume extends the concepts in *Systemic Sex Therapy* in a practical book that the therapist can refer to for direct application of diagnoses, assessment, techniques, and other practice-oriented material. The major strength of the companion volume is explicating the process of developing a treatment plan that guides the clinician in deciding which problem(s) to treat first and how to sequence treatment when multiple problems are presented. We believe the beginning sex therapist will need both volumes in order to understand the practice of sex therapy from a systemic perspective.

We sincerely hope that students, clinicians, and academics will benefit greatly from this book. It is our firm belief that this book will become the standard text in our field as well as move the field to the next stage of its development theoretically while giving the students practical information.

Gerald R. Weeks
Katherine M. Hertlein
Nancy Gambescia

References

American Psychiatric Association (APA). (2013). *Diagnostic and statistical manual of mental disorders.* (5th ed.) Arlington, VA: American Psychiatric Publishing.

Gruman, A., & Kniskern, D. (Eds.). (1991). *Handbook of family therapy (Vol. 2).* New York: Brunner Mazel.

Weeks, G. R. (1977). Toward a dialectical approach to intervention. *Human Development, 20,* 277–292.

Weeks, G. R. (Ed.). (1989). *Treating couples: The intersystem model of the Marriage Council of Philadelphia*. New York: Brunner/Mazel.

Weeks, G. R. & Fife, S. (2014). *Couples in treatment* (3rd ed.). New York: Routledge.

Weeks, G. R., & Gambescia, N. (2000). *Erectile dysfunction: Integrating couple therapy, sex therapy and medical treatment*. New York: W.W. Norton.

Weeks, G. R., & Gambescia, N. (2002). *Hypoactive sexual desire: Integrating couple and sex therapy*. New York: W.W. Norton.

Weeks, G. R., Gambescia, N., & Jenkins, R. (2003). *Treating infidelity*. New York: W. W. Norton.

Weeks, G. R. & Hof, L. (Eds.). (1987). *Integrating sex and marital therapy: A clinician's guide*. New York: Brunner/Mazel.

Weeks, G. R. & Hof, L., (Eds.). (1994). *The marital-relationship therapy casebook: Theory and application of the intersystem model*. New York: Brunner/Mazel.

Weeks, G. R. & Hof, L. (1995). *Integrative solutions: Treating common problems in couples' therapy*. New York: Brunner/Mazel.

Weeks, G. R., Odell, M., & Methven, S. (2005). *If only I had known: Common mistakes in couple therapy*. New York: W.W. Norton.

ACKNOWLEDGMENTS

There have been many people who have helped us in the creation of this book. First, we would like to thank the numerous contributors who have made this book a success. We consider ourselves very lucky to work with such an esteemed class of authors. Their insights, writing, and dedication to this project will surely shape the field of sex therapy, and we are appreciative of their significant efforts. We would also acknowledge the support from our family and friends throughout this endeavor. Thank you to Eric Hertlein, Nancy Love, and Michael Chenet for providing us support during the completion of this project. I (K.H.) would like to extend a huge thank you to my husband, Eric, as without his support of my career and insane writing schedule, this book (or many things I do) would not be possible. Thank you for allowing me to spread my wings and fly. To Adam— thank you for being the most amazing son. I look forward to many more years teaching you about the world. And finally, to good friends—those who have supported me and given me strength to do amazing things.

We thank the staff at Taylor and Francis for their support of this project, specifically the work of Marta Moldvai for giving us this opportunity to revise. Finally, we would also like to acknowledge the hard work of our graduate assistants in preparation of this manual, including Jenna DiLauro, Paige Espinosa, Lauren McCoy, and Claire Wertz.

Section 1

THE BASICS OF SEX THERAPY

1

WHAT EVERY SEX THERAPIST NEEDS TO KNOW

Jane Ridley

Introduction: Resilience of the Therapist

When considering training as a sex therapist, it is essential to understand the fluid nature of life today. Rapid changes have resulted from the pressure of new technologies, such as web, cameras, mobile phones, iPads®, and the consequent alternative communication styles. As these technological systems of communication (e.g. Skype™) are developed, relationships are also adjusting and changing. Sex and sexuality are more open to public gaze and discussion, thus affecting codes of behaviour. Medicine, too, is changing attitudes to sexual difficulties; drugs (Viagra®, Cialis®) are available for problems previously perceived as individual or relationship problems. For example, more men now discuss their erectile difficulties and seek help from their general practitioners or the Internet. In addition, neuroscience, biology, and genetics are pushing the boundaries of knowledge affecting how we think about the mind and body. Within today's social context, becoming a sex therapist is an increasingly demanding professional role.

In such a changing world, a sex therapist needs to be resilient and flexible, able to adjust to new learning, and at the same time be firm about his/her own and others' boundaries. The demands are not just academic as challenges occur legally, ethically, and personally. An inevitable aspect of increasing knowledge regarding sexuality is the challenge this provides to each trainee and their sense of self. Questioning will occur in a variety of contexts: of yourself, your motivation, sexual orientation, moral and social code, your prejudices and excitements. As you respond to these challenges with courage and growing insight, this will be a maturing experience. New thoughts, feeling, and fantasies are likely to emerge, which may be troubling to you (Giami, 2001). Feelings of guilt, excitement, or shame may emerge, as well as powerful sexual thoughts or wishes. Your current moral or ethical code will be questioned, and you may occasionally feel overwhelmed by these unfamiliar experiences.

This is the point in your career at which your ability to become a competent and professional sex therapist is tested. It is essential that you allow yourself to monitor your reactions and share these with your supervisor and trainers. Learning to respond to the clients' world with empathy and without judgement is stretching and enriching. A central aspect of becoming a sex therapist is your own curiosity, openness, and preparedness to learn, without prejudice. Being open to the client's reaction to you may also be a new experience; it encompasses the clients' reactions, attitudes, feelings, or fantasies towards you. Your age, dress, ethnicity, gender orientation, voice tone, choice of language, social or religious attitudes, likes and dislikes, and prejudices will be observed, noted, and judged by your clients. Since you rapidly become part of the client's system, how clients

3

perceive you will influence the outcome of your work together. This too is stretching but enriching.

A sex therapist is also a citizen and as such is constrained by the laws relating to sexual behaviour, and the Code of Ethics set by the Profession and/or set by the employing Agency. Rape, sexual abuse, the use of the web for grooming of children, or downloading explicit sexual material relating to children is now more public. This presents the therapist with increasingly difficult personal, moral, ethical, and therapeutic dilemmas. Ethical, religious, or social attitudes towards sexual behaviours, such as masturbation, pornography, homosexuality, or pre-marital sex, can conflict with "therapeutic interventions" considered to help the client. In addition, guidelines designed to assist the therapist can cause concerns. For example, there has been considerable debate regarding the accuracy of the *DSM-5 (Diagnostic and Statistical Manual of Mental Disorders* (APA, 2013) in its description of disorders as emphasis is turning toward acknowledging the new scientific developments within neuroscience. Any new classification system, however, is likely to take 10 years to define (Grohol, 2013). Meanwhile, the sex therapist needs to understand the current definitions of normal sexual behaviour or characterizations of sexual difficulties or dysfunctions, as defined by *DSM-5* (APA, 2013). These are still central to the work and such discussions will continue and enrich the world of therapy.

Less controversially, the therapist must have a clearer knowledge of the anatomy and physiology of male and female sexuality and the sexual response cycle. The impact of life events and ageing upon sexuality must be understood within an historical context of the individual, couple, family, or social network, as well as their ethnic or religious affiliations. Physical and mental health, the use of drugs or alcohol, domestic violence, previous sexual or emotional abuse, and traumatic experiences all have an impact upon an individual and, consequently, a couple's sexual life. Specialist knowledge and skills may need to be learned to work with these client groups. The pressure to seek evidence-based approaches means that Cognitive-Behavioural Therapy (CBT), Eye Movement Desensitisation and Reprocessing (EMDR), and mindfulness-based therapies are emerging as significant, well-researched therapies, which can target traumatic experiences effectively. These need to be understood and integrated into any approach to sexual therapy, providing yet again a challenge to the sex therapist to be adaptable but clear. The recent discussion in preparation for *DSM-5* (APA, 2013) regarding rape as a crime and not a mental disorder is significant for sexual therapists and demonstrates how volatile some aspects of our knowledge base can be (Frances, 2013).

Disentangling the interaction between organic, physical, individual, relational, social, or environmental factors can make you feel part of a tangled web with few boundaries (Heiman, 2002). Developmentally, however, these skills depend upon an awareness of the complex interaction between the physical and organic aspects of sexuality and the individual's internal and external psychological world as well as the social network surrounding the individual or couple. Thinking and working systemically greatly facilitates this process (Weeks & Hof, 1987). The current helpful focus on mindfulness seems to be a creative response to this complexity (Brady, 2013; Burch & Penman, 2013).

Historically, therapy has developed down separate theoretical routes (Ridley, 2006). More recently there has been a movement towards an integrative approach enabling therapists to select, from the rich range of theoretical options, the approach most suited to each particular client. Crowe and Ridley (2000) describe a hierarchy of alternative interventions which offer the therapist guidelines on why and when to choose which approach, and when it may be useful to move up or down the hierarchy during therapy to an alternative intervention. Weeks and Hof (1994, 1995) develop the Intersystem Approach for this purpose. The impact of newer knowledge regarding biology and genetics, imaging, and the research into cognition are adding layers which, as the information becomes more concrete, can be included within an integrative and systemic approach (Kraly, 2006). It may also be sensible to tread softly within this area.

Clarity about the therapist's use of theory, and the ability to move between theories, is an essential skill. "A good postulate here is: fire your theory before you fire your client, or your client fires you" (Weeks, Odell, & Methven, 2005, p. 9). Throughout this book the Intersystem Approach is used when assessing the impact upon the individual's sexual function, the interplay between his/her psychological makeup, and the interpersonal and social environment one inhabits. This parallels Crowe and Ridley's (2000) assessment framework.

As sex therapists learn more about clients, difficult moral or legal issues can arise. Conflict between loyalty to the client, or client confidentiality, may seem at odds with society's requirements. Knowing the limits of therapy and working within the professional codes of practice and the legal framework are essential and challenging (AAMFT, 2012; COSRT, 2012). Both of these organisations have good web pages which outline their codes and offer help and guidance to therapists. The highly professional AAMFT website states, "The next time you are faced with an ethical dilemma, consult with an Ethics case manager by phone or email BEFORE you act." This highlights the stark fact that therapists are increasingly faced with ethical and legal questions. We therapists do not work outside the legal and social framework of the country in which we work (even though, occasionally it may feel that way). Working together with other professionals and knowing the limits of sexual therapy, as well as knowing when to seek help from other co-professionals and when to refer on, are basic requirements. Working together with specialist therapists, psychiatrists, doctors, social workers, probation, prison, or other welfare agencies then becomes a support for both therapist and client. These personal attributes and rich knowledge base are essential requirements for the sex therapist who wishes to learn the intervention skills described throughout this book and developed during clinical practice under professional supervision.

Sexuality and Sexual Behavior: Social Norms

If one accepts that society is experiencing rapid change, then the concept of norms becomes increasingly complex, particularly when focussing on specific individuals, couples, or families. One learns from clinical experience that sexual behavior is affected by changing family values and social or religious beliefs, taboos, and anxieties; but also by the stress which change brings. Clinically clients may say "I am no longer a Catholic/Muslim/Jew," but the social norms, e.g., habits, customs, beliefs, or taboos which they rejected, are often deeply ingrained in their psyche and do still affect their behavior (Sneider & Rieder, 1994; Michael et al., 1998; Pariera, 2013). A strange mixture of change and stability co-exist in this uncertain world. Gender and gender issues, such as whether lesbian, gay, bisexual, or transgender individuals have similar experiences of sexuality as heterosexual men and women; whether men's and women's approach to sex is different will affect the way sexuality is understood (Basson, 2002; Komisaruk, Beyer-Flores, & Whipple, 2006; Ridley, 1999). Over time, however, attitudes about sexuality have been slowly changing. For example, Mercer et al. (2013) noted that acceptance of same sex behaviour is increasing in the general population.

Sexual Minorities

Kinsey and co-workers (1948; 1953) were amongst the first to study and publish material regarding the sexual behaviour of Americans between 1938 and 1952 and opened up sexual behaviour as an appropriate area for study. Newport (1997), examining the concept of "norms," writes, "The concept of a norm is mysterious because it refers to a concept which exists 'out there' as part of culture, but is something which generally, unlike laws, for example, is never written down or codified formally" (p. 1).

In 1973, the American Psychiatric Association ceased to consider homosexuality as pathological. "It is hard to overestimate the impact of this decision. First declaring homosexuals as 'normal', or at least as normal as heterosexuals, undermined laws, civil commitment procedures and the practice of therapy itself" (Nichols & Shernoff, 2007, p. 393). The legal acceptance of gay and lesbian long-term relationships in the United Kingdom through the Civil Partnerships Act 2004 implemented in December of 2005 allowed for changes in the perceptions of sexual behavior in Britain. The gay, lesbian, and bisexual community are now requesting the legal status of marriage, which is being implemented piecemeal in several parts of the world.

Much of the resistance to the acceptance of anal or oral sexual contacts between consenting adults in private tend to come from church organizations or affiliations. Both American and British data indicate that around 25% of heterosexual couples have had anal intercourse, and suggest that, "oro-genital contact may be experienced by increasing proportions of those who have not yet had vaginal intercourse . . . as a risk reduction strategy in the face of AIDS" (Wellings & Johnson, 2013, p. 157). It is noteworthy that "stimulating the rectum, could add to the quality of orgasm" for women, and may account for the "experience of orgasm in men receiving mechanical stimulation of the prostate during anal intercourse" (Komisaruk, Beyer-Flores, & Whipple, 2006, pp. 7–8). This is one of many aspects of sexual behaviour demonstrating that norms are complex, difficult to define, and constantly changing with blurred boundaries (Popovic, 2006).

Professional organizations can also be at odds with what society accepts. Paraphilias for example, as defined by the American Psychological Association (APA) are "intense and persistent sexual interest other than sexual interest in genital stimulation or preparatory fondling with phenotypically normal, physically mature, consenting human partners." This behavior must cause "distress or impairment" (American Psychiatric Association, 2013, p. 685). Are we therefore to assume that unless there is clinically significant distress, paraphilias can be placed within the normal spectrum of human behavior? The same question can be raised regarding *DSM-5* where "significant distress" is a defining characteristic.

The Ageing Population

By the year 2030, nearly 20% of people in the United States will be 65 years or older (Bradford & Meston, 2007). Worldwide adults 60 and over are the most rapidly growing population (World Health Organization, 2002). Many myths and misconceptions inhibit the understanding of the norms of sexual needs and desires of this population (Hodson & Skeen, 1994). Contrary to some myths, the sexual life of the older couple may slow down but continues into late age. It is understandably dependent upon factors such as the availability of a partner, illness, and the impact of some medications. The changes that do occur affect men and women slightly differently.

Although erectile functioning tends to decline from mid-life into old age, erectile failure is not inevitable. Typical changes include a delay in gaining a full erection, less rigidity of the erect penis, a lessening of sensitivity of the penis, and fewer erections during sleep (Wespes, 2002). The orgasmic responses may change, taking longer to achieve orgasm with a less forceful ejaculation and less volume of semen (Schiavi, 1999). For women, there is a difference between desire and arousal, as there seems to be a steep decline in sexual desire (DeLamater & Sill, 2005) but sexual satisfaction may remain higher in older women than in men, particularly if the physical changes associated with ageing, such as the need to use lubricants, can be accepted (AARP, 2005; National Surveys of Sexual Attitudes and Lifestyles [Natsal], 2013). Myths about sexuality and ageing and a lack of awareness of the needs of the older person can compromise the therapeutic alliance.

Sexual Abuse, Rape, Domestic Violence

Until the 1960s, sexual abuse of girls and its impact on their future sexual selves and sexuality was rarely discussed (Jehu, 1989). Greater awareness, often through clinical experience, enabled the issue of the abuse of males to be raised. Within the context of a discussion about norms, what does this mean? Was sexual abuse seen as an acceptable aspect of family life until the 20th century? Do rape and domestic violence fall into this same category? Such dilemmas are part of becoming a sex therapist and can be difficult to resolve.

The *DSM-5* (APA, 2013) has clarified that rape is not a mental disorder but is a crime (Frances, 2013). There are those who still do not wish to accept that rape is a crime, and others who do not report for a myriad of reasons, despite recognizing that it is a crime. Genital mutilation is illegal within Britain, but is still performed within some British cultural groups and is often understood as a necessary religious or "circumcision ritual" providing the therapist with real ethical dilemmas within therapy.

Tiefer (2004) questions the way sexuality has been understood and corralled by "experts who know a lot about the body mechanics rather than those who understand learning, culture and imagination" (p. 134). She prefers to understand sex as an aspect of human potential, but its interpretation within each society as a social construct. She also wonders whether sex is a talent such as music or mathematics and writes, "to insist that everyone is equally talented at sex is fraudulently democratic" (p. 156). Her view of normality is challenging and well worth thinking through. The sex therapist working with clients whose norms are not their own requires a sensitivity, which is respectful of the client, without being overwhelmed.

Conceptualizing Sexual Difficulties

Following publication of *DSM-5*, criticism has emerged from several authorities, notably Thomas R. Insel, Director of the National Institute of Mental Health, the American government's leading agency on mental health illness research and prevention, who attacked the manual's validity. In Britain the Division of Clinical Psychology, representing 10,000 practitioners and part of the British Psychological Society, has called for the abandonment of psychiatric diagnosis and the development of alternatives which do not use the language of "illness" or "disorder" (Doward, 2013).

The relevance of this debate to the sexual therapist is twofold. First, that the issue of "clinically significant distress" has been re-emphasized as a crucial element in the "diagnosis

7

and treatment" of sexual difficulties. Secondly, the importance of "clinical judgment" is a key piece in understanding and diagnosing dysfunctions (APA, 2013, p. 3). "It is not sufficient to simply check off the symptoms in the diagnostic criteria . . . the relative severity and valence of individual criteria and their contribution to a diagnosis require clinical judgement" (APA, 2013, p. 3). In an extreme example, where a woman is not distressed by her lack of interest in a sexual relationship, but her husband is, what judgement does the therapist make? Komisaruk, Beyer-Flores, and Whipple (2006) noted that 43% of women and 31% of men in the United States are affected by sexual problems. The researchers, however, did not ask about the level of distress, now seen as a defining characteristic. This type of conceptualization has implications for both diagnosis and treatment.

For women, the *DSM-5* (American Psychiatric Association, 2013) has combined sexual desire and arousal disorders as female interest/arousal disorders; genito-pelvic pain/penetration disorder now combines vaginismus and dyspareunia. Binik, Meana, Berkeley, and Khalifé (1999) argue cogently that these are not sexual problems but problems of pain and fear of pain and should be treated as such. Low or absent desire in men, termed Male Hypoactive Sexual Desire Disorder (*DSM-5*; APA, 2013) has been questioned, as is the issue of rapid ejaculation, or premature ejaculation (Althof, 2007), now described as premature (early) ejaculation by *DSM-5*. Delayed ejaculation remains a little understood sexual difficulty, and is less prevalent, the rates range widely from 1%–10% (Spector & Carey, 1990) with a possible increase with age. Erectile dysfunction is described as Erectile Disorder, and is considered to be a common and distressing aspect of male sexuality with possibly 50% of the over-60s expressing concerns (Rosen, 2005). Again, rates seem to vary from 5%–20% in one study to 1% for those under age 50, 5% for ages 50–59, and 16% for over 60s (Read & Mati, 2013).

A thorough assessment and proper diagnosis of the client, or client system, is essential. It is the basis of the treatment plan and therapeutic approach chosen. The present discussions are invigorating, if also confusing. For the new recruit into sex therapy, *DSM-5* and its surrounding controversy reemphasizes the importance the therapist must place upon the client(s) and the client system without medicalizing the problem.

The Anatomy and Physiology of Sexuality

An appreciation of the anatomy and physiology of sexuality is necessary, but undue emphasis has led to a mechanistic view of sexuality, largely resulting from Masters and Johnson's approach. Focusing upon the context and complexity of sexuality helps to avoid this. Sexuality cannot be separated from the total context within which the individual or couple inhabit. Their social, religious, ethical, community, and familial systems and individual makeup will all have an important influence upon their understanding of and response to sexuality. The meaning given to dancing, music, eating, clothing, scents, setting, and ambiance; the meaning of a glance, the movement of a hand, or the wiggle of a bottom will all have a personal and social context within which the individual or couple respond. The anatomy and physiology of the individual must be set and understood within these interconnecting systems.

The Impact of the Internet

Good factual information is available by searching the web. Yet at the same time, attempts to describe the whole person are missing. Sites for teen or adult porn are easily accessible and give a distorted picture of interpersonal relational sex. Individuals are highly affected by life experiences; social networking, electronic communication, and web-based informa-tion are now central to most of the younger generations, which will also affect their view of sexuality. It is difficult to assess the impact of these forms of communication upon the sexual life but is thought to have a distorting influence. The National Coalition to Prevent Child Sexual Abuse and Exploitation (2013) is concerned that watching "abusive and demeaning acts" via the web is likely to encourage young boys to think this behavior is part of a "normal" relationship. Inappropriate sexual touching in childhood, for example, of the breast, may mean that touching of the breast in adult relationships becomes a "sen-sitive issue," because of these earlier experiences. The position of the light, odors, sounds, and music may all have powerful positive or negative associations affecting the respon-siveness of the individual to touch or sensuality. Unless these are seen as powerful aspects of the sensual or sexual experience, the therapist will miss much.

The Sexual Response Cycle

Masters and Johnson's (1966) study of Human Sexual Response is a landmark in the understanding of male and female sexual responses, built upon by succeeding clinicians and researchers. They set the direction that sex therapy would travel for many years. How they presented their material and succeeding professionals interpreted the research may be responsible for over emphasizing the physical to the exclusion of others. Nevertheless, their research formed the basis for ongoing work and is worth considering in some detail.

The Four Phases and Two Physiological Changes

Masters and Johnson (1966) divided the sexual cycle into four specific phases, through which the individual progresses from excitement, to plateau, orgasm, and finally resolu-tion. Significantly they described this as a "purely arbitrary design" (p. 7), which "is inad-equate for evaluation of finite psychogenic aspects of elevated sexual tensions." Women are described as "having the response potential of returning to another orgasmic experi-ence from any point in the resolution phase" which they describe as the "multiple orgas-mic expression" (p. 65). Although aware of male/female differences, these tend to get lost in their excitement at discovering "similarities, not the differences" (p. 8) between the male and female sexual response cycle. These differences are addressed (Basson, 2007; Ridley, 1999) while Petersen and Hyde (2011) suggest we may be making too much of these differences. Masters and Johnson described the sexual responses as the result of two principal physiological changes; increase in blood flow to various parts of the body (vaso-congestion), and an increase in muscle tension (myotonia). Detailed physiological changes in the female or male were noted as they moved through the phases of the cycle.

Male/Female Similarities and Differences

While the clitoris and penis are anatomically similar, the clitoris does not respond as quickly as the penis to stimulation whether direct or indirect, and to only think that the clitoris and penis respond the same is an error in thinking about female sexual responses. Additionally, they challenge the notion of the clitoris having an erection paralleling the male erection. The clitoris is a unique organ. The different rates of excitement and engorgement between male and female responses are emphasized, as is the need for the clitoris to be stimulated to enable female orgasm. The vagina was studied with similar intensity.

In describing the female orgasm, there are three key areas, which interact upon the female orgasm: the physiological, psychological, and sociological. Sociologically, Masters and Johnson recognize that female orgasmic attainment has never achieved the undeniable status afforded the male ejaculation. They predict that the human female now has an undeniable opportunity to develop realistically her own sexual response levels. The male sexual arousal cycle, as described by Masters and Johnson, is simpler than the female's. Again the four phases of excitement, plateau, orgasm, and resolution are noted. The whole body, as with the female, shows physical evidence of sexual tension, following the two basic patterns—first widespread vasocongestion and second myotonia, both widespread and specific. The male orgasm and ejaculation is described using three areas as with the female, of physiologic, psychologic, and sociologic.

They comment that sociological pressures have played a trick upon the two genders; fears of performance in the female have been directed towards gaining an orgasm, and in the male towards erection.

An important contribution of Masters and Johnson was their detailed study of the impact of ageing upon sexuality. Crucially they were able to challenge the myths of the death of sexual activity with age but describe a slowing down of the sexual arousal system and accompanying minor changes. Their work focused exclusively on the functions and dysfunctions of the genitalia. They identified erectile and ejaculatory problems for men and women with problems relating to penetration and orgasm. These became categories established within *DSM-III* (American Psychiatric Association, 1980). This had the twofold impact of having sexual problems taken seriously, while emphasizing the medical and physical aspects as dominant.

The Significance of Desire

Kaplan (1976, 1995) challenged Masters and Johnson's focus on the genitalia, adding the crucial dimension of sexual desire. She believed, as a result of her clinical experience, that Masters and Johnson had missed this essential element and thus ignored sexual problems relating to desire. As a result Hypoactive Sexual Desire (HSD) disorders were included in *DSM-III* (American Psychiatric Association, 1980). She believed that "the pathological decrease of these patients' libido is essentially an expression of normal regulation of sexual motivation gone awry" (Kaplan, 1995).

Kaplan's (1995) treatment approach included *erotic techniques* and their accompanying emotional impact upon the client/couple. She was concerned about the unconscious conflicts, fears, and desires which she felt may cause or exacerbate sexual difficulties and are evident within the therapeutic process between clinician and clients/patients. Kaplan (1995) draws attention to the "wider psychic matrix of which sexuality is an integral and beautiful part" (p. 7). Her contribution added greatly to the understanding of the emotional and social aspects of sexuality.

Paradoxically, the inclusion of hypoactive sexual desire as a disorder within *DSM-III* (American Psychiatric Association, 1980) added significantly to the medicalization of female sexuality.

The Analytic Contribution

The psychoanalytic field has tended to take a very separate perspective on female and male sexuality, within which a fascinating and often fierce dialogue continues (Bassin, 1999). Students should be aware of these debates and their impact on theories regarding female and male development. Karen Horney (in Bassin, 1999), aptly describes the skeleton around which such dialogues rage. Seen from the analytic perspective she lists the **growing boys** ideas, as follows: naïve assumptions that girls as well as boys possess a penis; realization of the absence of the (female's) penis; belief that the girl has suffered punishment which also threatens him: the girl is regarded as inferior; the boy is unable to imagine how the girl can ever get over this loss or envy; the boy dreads her envy. She then lists ideas about the development of the **female** as follows: for both sexes it is only the male genital which plays any part; sad discovery of the absence of the penis; belief of the girl that she once possessed a penis and lost it by castration; castration is conceived of as the infliction of punishment; the girl regards herself as inferior, penis-envy; the girl never gets over the sense of deficiency and inferiority and has constantly to master afresh her desire to be a man; the girl desires throughout life to avenge herself on the man for possessing something which she lacks. Concepts such as penis envy or the castrating woman, from the psycho-analytic field, have entered popularly accepted wisdom.

Cognitive Behavior Therapy (CBT); Eye Movement Desensitization and Reprocessing (EMDR) and Mindfulness

Emphasis is increasingly being placed on "evidence-based practice" in both Britain and America. Within Britain The National Institute for Clinical Excellence is setting standards for which therapy is most effective for specific problem areas. Cognitive Behavior Therapy (CBT) and Eye Movement Desensitization and Reprocessing (EMDR) are recommended for acute stress disorders and post-traumatic stress disorders (Ehlers et al., 2010). Acute stress often follows rape, sexual abuse, or violence for which these therapies are being found to be valuable. Both therapies require some additional training and are often included within training for sex therapists. If not included within the basic training it is helpful to include these specialities within the experienced sex therapist's tool kit. Clinical experience suggests however, that they are only valuable within an empathic therapeutic relationship that emphasizes the uniqueness of the individual or couple and the system to which they belong. The therapist can become too much of a technician, when the approach is less likely to be effective. Integrating mindfulness within a therapeutic approach is also gaining respect and can be seen as an antidote to the pressurized world around us (Burch & Penman, 2013).

The Complex Female

An intense and fascinating debate is occurring, largely in America, regarding the complexity of female sexuality. Beverly Whipple has carried out detailed research into the nature of the female orgasm, best summarized in Komisaruk, Beyer-Flores, and Whipple (2006). Emphasis is placed upon women being asked about the level of distress they experience, as this is now believed to be a key component in the diagnosis of sexual disorder. They also challenge the linear sequence derived from the Masters and Johnson (1966) four phases of excitement, plateau, orgasm, and resolution, and believe it to be "unhelpful in assessing and managing women's sexual problems and disorders" (p. 64). Basson (2002, 2007) and Basson et al. (2003) seek to redefine the nature of female sexuality because interests and pleasure are experienced differently for men and women (Leiblum, 2007, 2010). While emphasizing the complex nature of female sexuality, there is also the danger of objectifying and medicalizing this very personal aspect of femininity.

11

The Dual Control Model for Men

Bancroft and colleagues (2005) have sought to clarify the nature of male sexuality. A concept of an inhibitory factor, which operates against an excitatory factor, the "dual control model" provides a useful theoretical model with which to examine male sexuality, in particular erectile difficulties. Within this model, the Sexual Inhibition/Sexual Excitation Scales (SIS/SES) are used (Janssen et al., 2002a, 2002b). The propensity for sexual inhibition, due to the threat of performance failure (SIS 1), or the propensity for sexual inhibition, due to the threat of performance consequences (SIS 2), is measured. The propensity for sexual excitation (SES) is also measured. According to this theoretical model, sexual arousal, including genital response, depends upon both an active excitation response plus reduction of inhibitory tone together with the relative absence of inhibitory response to the sexual situation. Further research is obviously necessary, but the concepts of an inhibitory system, which may work against the excitatory system, certainly resonate with clinical experience. Gender differences are now recognized in intimacy needs, desired levels of closeness in a relationship, and other areas of partnership (Popovic, 2005; Ridley, 1999).

Balancing Medical Aspects of Sexuality

An over-emphasis upon the physical and medical aspects of sexuality can develop in both the client and practitioner (Hart & Wellings, 2002; Tiefer, 2002). When sexual difficulties are viewed as an illness or purely physical, a medical solution is usually sought. The arrival of Viagra® and similar drugs has provided such an opportunity (Ashton, 2007; Finger, 2007) and has improved some men's sexual lives. Additionally, personal difficulties can be highlighted, and addressed when prescriptions do not solve the difficulties. A search for a similar drug for women is underway. This, while helpful, also adds to depersonalizing a very personal aspect of women's sexuality (Tiefer, 2002).

Read and Mati (2013) draw attention to the notion that drug companies use their financial power to manipulate public opinion, which they describe as a development following the introduction of Viagra® in 1998. Companies who produce the drugs that are said to be effective for erectile dysfunction are then able to advertise and sell via the web, thus "manipulating" the public to seek pharmaceutical answers to sexual, and often interpersonal, difficulties.

Both mental and physical illnesses should also be taken seriously and where necessary treated medically. Many seek medication via the web, which can cause additional problems if the medication is not monitored or may be impure. Illnesses such as depression, diabetes, or heart problems have a serious impact upon the quality of life including the sexual life. Essential medication can treat the illness but may impact negatively upon sexual abilities. Working with clients to find an appropriate balance between these conflicting elements requires an ability to take seriously the physical and medical circumstances faced by each client, and the impact medication may have on sexuality (Gill & Hough, 2007; Read & Mati, 2013).

Conclusion

This chapter has emphasized the fluid nature of society today, with many changes occurring at a rapid pace. When considering a career as a sex therapist, you may want to ask yourself if you can accept the personal and professional challenges this presents.

Wanting to help is not good enough. A wide spectrum knowledge base must be learned during which your value system and prejudices will be challenged. As new knowledge emerges, you will again be asked to review your previous knowledge and assumptions. This requires an openness to new experiences while retaining the ability to be both flexible and boundaried. The easy availability of sexual knowledge or behaviour via videos and the web often mean that clients have "new experiences" which can be unsettling for them and for you. This may test your ability to be empathic. Examining your own emotional and sexual responses under supervision will become part of your regular routine. Understanding the multi-layered interaction between the inner/outer world of the client, client system, modern technology, and the wider social context will involve you setting aside previously held perspectives. Knowing the limits of one's knowledge and skill will mean that seeking advice or referring on to other specialists may be necessary.

Being prepared to question attitudes to what is normal, to value others whose way of life is different to your own, to learn from good research and evidence-based practice, to practice within the law, however complex, to co-work with medical and psychiatric specialists while continuing to value the whole person, can test us all, but these are essential requirements of a sex therapist.

References

Althof, S. E. (2007). Treatment of rapid ejaculation: Psychotherapy, pharmacotherapy, and combined therapy. In S. Lieblum (Ed.), *Principles and practice of sex therapy* (4th ed., pp. 212–240). New York: Guilford Press.

American Association of Marriage and Family Therapy (AAMFT). (2012, July 1). Code of ethics. Retrieved from http://www.aamft.org/imis15/content/legal_ethics/code_of_ethics.aspx.

American Association of Retired Persons. (2005). *Sexuality at mid-life and beyond: 2004 update of attitudes and behaviour.* Retrieved from http://assets.aarp.org/rgcenter/general/2004_sexuality. pdf.

American Psychiatric Association. (1980). *Diagnostic and statistical manual of mental disorders* (3rd ed.). Washington, DC: Author.

American Psychiatric Association. (2013). *Diagnostic and statistical manual of mental disorders* (5th ed.). Arlington, VA: American Psychiatric Publishing.

Ashton, A. K. (2007). The new sexual pharmacology. In S. Lieblum (Ed.), *Principles and practice of sex therapy* (4th ed., pp. 509–541). New York: Guilford Press.

Bancroft, J., Herbenick, D., Barnes, T., Hallam-Jones, R., Wylie, K., Janssen, E., & Members of BASRT*. (2005). The relevance of the dual control model to male sexual dysfunction: The Kinsey Institute/BASRT Collaborative Project. *Sexual and Relationship Therapy, 20*(1), 13–30.

Bassin, D. (1999). *Female sexuality, contemporary engagements.* Northvale, NJ: Jason Aronson.

Basson, R. (2002). Are our definitions of women's desire, arousal and sexual pain disorders too broad and our definition of orgasmic disorder too narrow? *Journal of Sex & Marital Therapy, 28*(4), 289–300. doi: 10.1080/00926230290001411

Basson, R. (2007). Sexual desire/arousal disorders in women. In S. Lieblum (Ed.), *Principles and practice of sex therapy* (4th ed., pp. 84–123). New York: Guilford Press.

Basson, R., Leiblum, S., Brotto, L., Derogatis, L., Fourcroy, J., Fulg-Meyer, K., . . . & Schultz, W. (2003). Definitions of women's sexual dysfunction reconsidered: Advocating expansion and revision. *Journal of Psychosomatic Obstetrics and Gynecology, 24*(4), 221–229. doi: 10.1503/cmaj.102017

Binik, Y. M., Meana, M., Berkley, K., & Khalifé, S. (1999). The sexual pain disorders: Is the pain sexual or is the sex painful? *Annual Review of Sex Research, 10*(1), 210–235.

Bradford, A., & Meston, C. M. (2007). Senior sexual health: The effects of aging on sexuality. In L. VandeCreek, F. L. Petertson, Jr., & J. W. Bley (Eds.), *Innovations in clinical practice: Focus on sexual health* (pp. 35–45). Florida: Professional Resource Press.

Brady, D. (2013). *Mindfulness, neurobiology, and gestalt therapy.* Scotts Valley, CA: On-Demand Publishing, LLC.

Burch, V., & Penman, D. (2013). *Mindfulness for health (enhanced edition): A practical guide to relieving pain, reducing stress and restoring wellbeing.* Hachette, UK: Piarkus.

COSRT (College of Sexual and Relationship Therapy). (2012). *Code of practice.* Retrieved from http://www.cosrt.org.uk/wp-content/uploads/2012/10/3_code_ethics_members.pdf.

Crowe, M., & Ridley, J. (2000). *Therapy with couples: A behavioral-systems approach to couple relationship and sexual problems.* Oxford: John Wiley & Sons.

DeLamater, J. D., & Sill, M. (2005). Sexual desire in later life. *Journal of Sex Research, 42*(2), 138–149. doi: 10.1080/00224490509552267

Doward, J. (2013). Medicine's big new battleground: Does mental illness really exist? *The Guardian.* Retrieved from http://www.theguardian.com/society/2013/may/12/medicine-dsm5-row-does-mental-illness-exist.

Ehlers, A., Bisson, J., Clark, D., Creamer, M., Pilling, S., Richards, D., . . . Yule, W. (2010). Do all psychological treatments really work the same in posttraumatic stress disorder? *Clinical Psychology Review, 30*(2), 269–276.

Finger, W. W. (2007). Medication and sexual health. In L. VandeCreek, F. L. Petertson, Jr., & J. W. Bley (Eds.), *Innovations in clinical practice: Focus on sexual health* (pp. 47–62). Florida: Professional Resource Press.

Frances, A. (2013). DSM 5 Confirms that rape is a crime, not a mental disorder. *DSM-5 in Distress.* Retrieved from http://www.psychologytoday.com/blog/dsm5-in-distress/201302/dsm-5-confirms-rape-is-crime-not-mental-disorder.

Giami, A. (2001). Counter-transference in social research: George Devereux and beyond. *Papers in Social Research Methods, Qualitative Series no. 7.* Methodology Institute, London School of Economics and Political Science.

Gill, K. M., & Hough, S. (2007). *Sexual health of people with chronic illness and disability.* In L. VandeCreek, F. L. Petertson, Jr., & J. W. Bley (Eds.), *Innovations in clinical practice: Focus on sexual health* (pp. 223–244). Florida: Professional Resource Press.

Grohol, J. M. (2013). Did the NIMH withdraw support for the DSM-5? Retrieved from http://psychcentral.com/blog/archives/2013/05/07/did-the-nimh-withdraw-support-for-the-dsm-5-no/.

Hart, G., & Wellings, K. (2002). Sexual behavior and its medicalisation: In sickness and in health. *BMJ, 324*(7342), 896–900. doi: http://dx.doi.org/10.1136/bmj.324.7342.896

Heiman, J. R. (2002). Sexual dysfunction: Overview of prevalence, etiological factors, and treatments. *Journal of Sex Research, 39*(1), 73–78. doi: 10.1080/00224490209552124

Hodson, D. S., & Skeen, P. (1994). Sexuality and aging: The hammerlock of myths. *Journal of Applied Gerontology, 13*(3), 219–235.

Janssen, E., Vorst, H., Finn, P., & Bancroft, J. (2002a). The sexual inhibition (SIS) and sexual excitation (SES) scales: I. Measuring sexual inhibition and excitation proneness in men. *Journal of Sex Research, 39*(2), 114–126.

Janssen, E., Vorst, H., Finn, P., & Bancroft, J. (2002b). The sexual inhibition (SIS) and sexual excitation (SES) scales: II. Predicting psychophysiological response patterns. *Journal of Sex Research, 39*(2), 127–132.

Jehu, D. (1989). Mood disturbances among women clients sexually abused in childhood. *Journal of Interpersonal Violence, 4,* 164–184.

Kaplan, H. S. (1976). *Illustrated manual of sex therapy.* New York: A&W Publishing.

Kaplan, H. S. (1995). *The sexual desire disorders: Dysfunctional regulation of sexual motivation.* New York: Psychology Press.

Kinsey, A., Pomeroy, W., & Martin, C. (1948). *Sexual behavior in the human male.* Philadelphia: Saunders.

Kinsey, A., Pomeroy, W., Martin, C, & Gebhard, P. (1953). *Sexual behavior in the human female.* Philadelphia: Saunders.

Komisaruk, B. R., Beyer-Flores, C., & Whipple, B. (2006). *The science of orgasm* (Vol. 1). Baltimore: Johns Hopkins University Press.

Kraly, F. S. (2006). *Brain science and psychological disorders: Therapy, psychotropic drugs, and the brain.* New York: W. W. Norton.

Leiblum, S. R. (2007). Sex therapy today, current issues and future perspectives. In S. Lieblum (Ed.), *Principles and practice of sex therapy* (4th ed., pp. 3–25). New York: Guilford Press.

Leiblum, S. R. (2010). *Treating sexual desire disorders: A clinical casebook.* New York: Guilford.

Masters, W. H., & Johnson, V. E. (1966). *Human sexual response* (Vol. 1). Boston: Little, Brown & Co.

Mercer, C. H., Tanton, C., Prah, P., Erens, B., Sonnenberg, P., Clifton, S., . . . Johnson, A. M. (2013). Changes in sexual attitudes and lifestyles in Britain through the life course and over time: Findings from the National Surveys of Sexual Attitudes and Lifestyles (Natsal). *The Lancet, 382*(9907), 1781–1794. doi: 10.1016/S0140–6736(13)62035–8

Michael, R. T., Wadsworth, J., Feinleib, J., Johnson, A. M., Laumann, E. O., & Wellings, K. (1998). Private sexual behavior, public opinion, and public health policy related to sexually transmitted diseases: A US-British comparison. *American Journal of Public Health, 88*(5), 749–754.

National Coalition to Prevent Child Sexual Abuse and Exploitation. (2013). Impact of exposure to sexually explicit materials. *Child Sexual Abuse & Exploitation: Facts for Prevention.* Retrieved from http://preventtogether.org/Resources/Documents/Impact%20of%20Exposure%20to%20Sexually%20Explicit%20and%20Exploitative%20Materials.pdf.

National Surveys of Sexual Attitudes and Lifestyles (Natsal). (2013). *Natsal-3.* Retrieved from http://www.natsal.ac.uk/natsal-3.

Newport, F. (1997). *Gallup poll review from the poll editors—Sexual norms: Where does America stand today?* New York: Gallup Organization.

Nichols, M., & Shernoff, M. (2007). Therapy with sexual minorities: Queering practice. In S. Lieblum (Ed.), *Principles and practice of sex therapy* (4th ed., pp. 379–415). New York: Guilford Press.

Pariera, K. L. (2013). Misperceived social norms about taboo sexual behaviors. *Electronic Journal of Human Sexuality, 16*, 1–9. doi: 10.1037/0022–3514.76.1.129

Petersen, J. L., & Hyde, J. S. (2011). Gender differences in sexual attitudes and behaviors: A review of meta-analytic results and large datasets. *Journal of Sex Research, 48*(2–3), 149–165. doi: 10.1080/00224499.2011.551851

Popovic, M. (2005). Intimacy and its relevance in human functioning. *Sexual and Relationship Therapy, 20*(1), 31–49. doi: 10.1080/14681990412331323992

Popovic, M. (2006). Psychosexual diversity as the best representation of human normality across cultures. *Sexual and Relationship Therapy, 21*(02), 171–186. doi: 10.1080/14681990500358469

Read, J., & Mati, E. (2013). Erectile dysfunction and the internet: Drug company manipulation of public and professional opinion. *Journal of Sex & Marital Therapy, 39*(6), 541–559. doi: 10.1080/0092623X.2012.736922

Ridley, J. (1999). *Intimacy in crisis: Men and women in crisis through the life cycle and how to help.* London: Whurr Publishers.

Ridley, J. (2006). The subjectivity of the clinician in psychosexual therapy training. *Sexual and Relationship Therapy, 21*(3), 319–331.

Rosen, R. C. (2005). Reproductive health problems in ageing men. *The Lancet, 366*(9481), 183–185. doi: 10.1016/S0140–6736(05)67318

Schiavi, R. C. (1999). *Aging and male sexuality.* Cambridge, UK: Cambridge University Press.

Sneider, S. N., & Rieder, R. O. (1994) A review of sexual behaviour in the United States. *The American Journal of Psychiatry, 151*, 330–341.

Spector, I. P., & Carey, M. P. (1990). Incidence and prevalence of the sexual dysfunctions: A critical review of the empirical literature. *Archives of Sexual Behavior, 19*(4), 389–408.

Tiefer, L. (2002). Sexual behaviour and its medicalisation: Many (especially economic) forces promote medicalisation. *BMJ, 325*(7354), 45. doi: 10.1136/bmj.324.7342.896

Tiefer, L. (2004). *Sex is not a natural act* (2nd ed). Boulder, CO: Westview Press.

Weeks, G. R. & Hof, L. (Eds.). (1987). *Integrating sex and marital therapy: A clinician's guide.* New York: Brunner/Mazel.

Weeks, G. R., & Hof, L. (Eds.). (1987). *Integrating sex and marital therapy: A clinician's guide.* New York: Brunner/Mazel.

Weeks, G., & Hof, L. (1994). *The marital relationship therapy casebook: Theory and application of the intersystem model.* New York: Brunner/Mazel.

Weeks, G., & Hof, L. (1995). *Integrative solutions: Treating common problems in couples therapy.* New York: Brunner/Mazel.

Weeks, G., Odell, M., & Methven, S. (2005). *Common mistakes in couple therapy.* New York: W. W. Norton.

Wellings, K., & Johnson, J. (2013). Study of sexual health and lifestyles in Britain reveals changing sexual attitudes and behaviour. *The Lancet.* Retrieved from http://www.thelancet.com/themed/natsal.

Wespes, E. (2002). The ageing penis. *World Journal of Urology, 20*(1), 36–39. doi: 10.3978/j.issn.2223–4683.2011.12.01

World Health Organization. (2002). Active ageing: A policy framework. *Ageing and life course.* Retrieved from http://whqlibdoc.who.int/hq/2002/WHO_NMH_NPH_02.8.pdf?ua=1.

2

THE CURRENT PROFESSION
OF SEX THERAPY

Peggy J. Kleinplatz

This chapter will review the history of sex therapy and recent trends in the field including the medicalization of sexual dysfunction and responses to medicalization. The professional life of the sex therapist will be described, highlighting the various sex therapy
organizations, the personal and professional process of becoming a sex therapist, and the
ethical principles of sex therapy. Finally, the controversy over the distinctiveness of sex
therapy—or lack thereof—and therefore, whether or not certification of sex therapists is
warranted, will be considered.

The History of Sex Therapy

Throughout the twentieth century until the development of sex therapy, sexual problems
were either unspoken or the province of religion, philosophy, and, to a minor extent,
medicine. They were often discussed in "marriage manuals," which had some nifty little
ideas about how much sex was desirable, which kinds were appropriate, and for that matter what constituted sex (Van de Velde, 1926). Whatever ideas they put forth were based
on the values and beliefs of the era, with no basis in sexology, that is, the scientific study
of sexuality. In addition, sexuality was a major focus of the work of psychoanalysis, which
dealt with the whole person and his/her development rather than targeting sexual problems for treatment. Although psychoanalysis had the advantage of aiming for substantive
personality change (Freud, 1917/1963), it was time-intensive, hardly cost-effective, and
dealt with the individual alone rather than the couple or society, that is, the context in
which sexual difficulties tend to arise and be manifest.

In the late 1940s and early 1950s, the work of Kinsey and his colleagues helped to
revolutionize what could be studied by sexologists by seeking to describe and categorize
the spectrum of normal sexual behaviors. The popularity of Kinsey's work, even though it
was highly controversial, helped to pave the way for the study of the physiology of sexual
response in the laboratory by Masters and Johnson (1966). Their findings mapped out the
sequence of the four stages of what they termed the "Human Sexual Response Cycle,"
consisting of excitement, plateau, orgasm, and resolution. This laboratory research in turn
laid the foundations—and provided the credibility—for Masters and Johnson's 1970 text,
Human Sexual Inadequacy, which described the sexual disorders and their treatment.
This seminal book essentially created the field of sex therapy. Sexual problems came to be
defined largely in terms of deviations from the physiological norms found among subjects
engaging in sexual acts in the lab. Deviations from Masters and Johnson's model of the
Human Sexual Response Cycle later came to be reified as the criteria for defining sexual

disorders in the American Psychiatric Association's various editions of the *Diagnostic and Statistical Manual of the Mental Disorders* (DSM).

The evolution of sex therapy and the current status of sexual problems and their treatment cannot be understood without further attention to the basic precepts and concepts elucidated by Masters and Johnson. William Masters, a gynecologist, became interested in the scientific study of sexuality and specifically, the treatment of sexual disorders. He was joined in his investigations and in the development of a treatment paradigm by social scientist Virginia Johnson. The foundation of their work was consistent with Masters' training as a physician. One of their major precepts was that sex is a biological function, not unlike urination, defecation, or respiration (1986). Much of their clinical work was aimed at eliminating psychosocially imposed obstacles (e.g., ignorance, fear, guilt, and shame) to sexual function so that "natural" functioning could re-assert itself. They stated that 90% of sexual problems were likely to be psychogenic and the remaining 10% of organic origin. (Although the discourse popular in the current Zeitgeist is reversed and would suggest that 90% of sexual problems are of organic etiology and only 10% are psychogenic, the mind-body dualism prevails/endures.)

A second major precept proposed by Masters and Johnson was that the relationship should be the focus of treatment rather than targeting only the symptomatic patient. Regardless of which individual presented the problem, the couple would be required in therapy to achieve a solution. Ironically, they have been criticized for giving only lip-service to the importance of the relationship in maintaining the problem (Weeks, 2004, 2005); the use of surrogates as part of their treatment paradigm betrays their belief that although two people may be necessary to effect symptom amelioration, the interchangeability of the partners suggests a neglect in this model of the role of the *intimate* relationship and the couple *system* in sexual problems. In short, the early pioneers talked about working with the couple, but did not conceptualize or intervene systemically.

The treatment approach they developed consisted of brief, behaviorally oriented couples therapy with a strong educational component intended to target the symptoms of sexual dysfunction. The success of Masters and Johnson's approach as first reported in 1970 led to great interest in sex therapy and laid the groundwork for the entire field over the next decades. Unfortunately, the paradoxical effect of this "success" led to widespread acceptance of their methods without due consideration of underlying theoretical foundations—or lack thereof—allowing the prevailing assumptions to remain unexplored (Kleinplatz, 2001, 2003; Wiederman, 1998).

During the 1970s and 1980s, Masters and Johnson's work began to be critiqued for ignoring subjective aspects of sexual response such as desire, psychological arousal during sex, and satisfaction thereafter (Kaplan, 1977, 1979; Lief, 1977; Zilbergeld & Ellison, 1980) as well as for unorthodox reporting of outcome data, making it difficult either to interpret their findings or to replicate them. Helen Singer Kaplan, trained in psychoanalysis, emphasized the need to assess for not only "immediate" factors blocking sexual response but also "remote," developmental factors which might affect personality and relationships. Ironically, despite her insight as to the role of historical factors, she emphasized that "fortunately," it was easy enough to remediate symptoms without needing to deal with underlying dynamics except in recalcitrant cases (Kaplan, 1974). In 1977, both Kaplan and Harold Lief described the desire disorders as particularly common and vexing. The desire disorders were more complex than could be accounted for by studying the physiology of sexual response alone.

In the years that have ensued, sex therapy has consisted primarily of brief, directive couples therapy and often, individual therapy blended with psychoeducational counseling and using "homework" assignments. Sex therapy has historically been rather effective in treating the symptoms of sexual dysfunctions, at least as compared with mainstream psychotherapy's track record in treating its most prevalent presenting problems, e.g., depression and anxiety. As such, sex therapy assumed brand name proportions, becoming the "Kleenex™" of psychotherapy, without much attention to the ill-defined, poorly explored assumptions implicit in our treatment methods (Kleinplatz, 1996). A variety of sex therapists have attempted to articulate, broaden, and integrate treatment paradigms to focus more extensively on a wider and deeper array of issues, particularly relationship and systemic factors, including Weeks (1977, 1994; Hertlein, Weeks, & Gambescia, 2009; Weeks & Hof, 1987) in formulating the Intersystem model, Schnarch (1991, 1997) the Crucible model, Metz and McCarthy (2005, 2011a, 2011b) the Biopsychosocial Approach to Sex Therapy, Ogden (2006, 2012) the ISIS [Integrating Sexuality and Spirituality] model, Kleinplatz (1996, 1998, 2004, 2007, 2010a, 2010b, 2013) and the Experiential model developed by Mahrer (1996, 2012).

Recent Trends in the Field

The burgeoning attention that was starting to be focused on the need to integrate sexual and couples therapy was suddenly deflected by the introduction of Sildenafil citrate (i.e., Viagra ™) in March 1998. The introduction of a pharmacological intervention for treatment of a sexual dysfunction was not new, in and of itself; however, the ease of administration combined with a curiously, sex-negative, socio-cultural environment and the relative theoretical void with which to make sense of this option provided a perfect opportunity for media spotlight on quick-fix solutions for sexual problems.

Some history is useful to situate "the Viagra™ moment" in context: In a society that has long been ambivalent, at best, about sex education, let alone comprehensive sexuality education, the pull toward dealing with sexual problems as if they are somehow separate from the rest of our lives is irresistible. It is as if the people with sexual difficulties, the surrounding society, the pharmaceutical industry, and clinicians collectively entered into a silent pact: Let's just conspire to keep our sexual difficulties sealed off from the rest of the context in which they come into existence, are perceived as problematic and require "fixing." Let us collude to treat the symptoms of sexual dysfunctions as if the symptoms are the (possibly underlying) problems themselves. Let us prop up the sagging penis as if that alone will take care of his (and his partner's) deflated spirits, as if hard penises are all we need for sex, and as if sex equals intercourse. Let's talk about our genitals—if we must talk about them at all—as if they are mechanical objects in need of repair rather than parts of whole persons silently asserting their discontent at unfulfilling intimate relations (Loe, 2004; Goldstein et al., 1998).

Such a pact was not so easy for as long as the treatment itself was unduly painful or cumbersome, as was the case with the biomedical treatment of erectile dysfunction prior to Viagra™. Throughout the 1990s, my practice (and that of many colleagues) was replete with men who reported being diagnosed with "leaky blood vessels" (Kleinplatz, 2004). The major medical treatment for erectile dysfunction at that time had been the use of intracavernosal injections of papaverine, phentolamine, and prostaglandin E_1 to produce rapid, firm, and long-lasting erections. (It remains the treatment of choice for many men who cannot use the PDE5 inhibitors, for example, because of potentially dangerous interactions with nitrates). The popularity of this treatment, however, was limited by the queasiness engendered by having to inject oneself in the penis (Althof et al., 1989; Althof & Turner, 1992; Irwin & Kata, 1994). It was hardly pleasant and difficult to administer inconspicuously. (Even more so, it violated the belief system that proclaimed sex, defined as intercourse, was supposed to be "natural and spontaneous.") I was struck by how quickly this epidemic of "leaky blood vessels" disappeared at precisely the same time that the little blue pills appeared on the market (Kleinplatz, 2004). The latter were much easier to swallow.

The field of sex therapy was forced to react to the easy availability of a new, relatively safe, and effective non-intrusive method for treating erectile dysfunction without the theoretical foundations with which to conceptualize this innovation. It was as though the field was thrust into a collective (albeit silent) identity crisis (Giami, 2000), attempting to ascertain how to deal with this new option (e.g., as merely another intervention, adjunct, rival, ally, diagnostic tool) while unsure of our own clinical and professional objectives. How were we to deal with the new kid on the block while still unclear on who we want to be when we grow up (Maurice 1999)?

In 1994, Schover and Leiblum warned of the encroaching medicalization of sex therapy. Long before the field had begun to grapple with its theoretical lacunae, "the Viagra™ moment" had arrived. In the interim, we had neglected to identify the basic questions a science of psychotherapy practice must encounter, while continuing to act as if we had all the answers (Kleinplatz, 2003, 2012). Here are just a few fundamental questions: What is sexuality? How are we to understand sexual experience? What is the basis/origin of sexual desire? Why do some things seem powerfully erotic to some people, abhorrent to others and irrelevant to still others, leaving them cold? Are all people capable of some kind of sexual feeling? What is "normal" sexuality? What is the relationship between "normal" and "abnormal/dysfunctional" sexuality and what can we learn about one from the other? What is optimal sexuality? What kinds of sex do we want to promote? How are we to conceptualize sexual problems? What is the context in which certain things come to be defined and come into existence as sexual problems? What are the meanings of those difficulties for the individual, the couple, and the system? What should our goals be in dealing with sexual problems? Whereas it had been simple enough to ignore our own assumptions when we were the only game in town, with the introduction of Viagra™, the time was well overdue for us to (re-)consider the provisional principles underlying sex therapy praxis.

The Medicalization of Sexual Problems

Over the last 15 years, the lacunae in our fundamental theoretical underpinnings allowed "sex therapy" to devolve increasingly into treatment of *symptoms* of sexual dysfunctions and disorders. Correspondingly, there was a loss of focus on the men and women who deserved our attention to the complex intrapsychic, systemic, and psychosocial meanings of their suffering. In this void, the increasing medicalization of sex therapy emerged in the forms of new pharmacological treatments, new organizations, and conferences designed to teach non-sex therapist physicians the rudiments of prescribing these drugs, and the marketing of not only the drugs but a new discourse on sexual difficulties. Advertisements blanketed American television, magazines, and other media announcing first Pfizer's Viagra™ and later, two other PDE5 inhibitors, Lilly's tadalafil (Cialis™) and Bayer's vardenafil (Levitra™). Each ad exhorted the audience or reader to "Ask your doctor." Unfortunately, since 2000, the increasingly sex negative atmosphere has led to funding cutbacks for teaching in sex therapy and even basic training in medical schools about human sexuality and its problems has **declined**. Shindel and Parish (2013) have described the current training as "scant or absent" in many medical schools. The majority of medical students in the U.S. and Canada feel uncomfortable talking about sex with patients, unprepared to do so, inadequately trained to do so, or in most cases, all of the above (Malhotra, Khurshid, Hendricks, & Mann, 2008; Shindel et al., 2010; Wittenberg & Gerber, 2009.) Thus, prospective patients have been instructed to contact physicians who were increasingly ill-equipped to handle the newly created demand for their services. The pharmaceutical industry funded conferences that taught physicians about urological aspects of erectile dysfunction with little attention to the sexological or relational dimensions. This fit quite well with the marketing of the discourse touting that 90% of erectile dysfunction was of organic etiology while only 10% was psychogenic or relational in origin. That notion, in turn, was especially appealing to individuals and couples who preferred to blame the malfunctioning penis rather than be forced to delve too deeply into the possibility of personal or interpersonal problems. Thus, the drugs, the industry, the clinicians, and the social discourse managed to jointly create a situation in which the patient's penis was working while the man attached—or detached—was ignored.

In addition, the off-label prescription of other drugs for sexual difficulties was promoted increasingly in the 1990s and thereafter. Selective serotonin reuptake inhibitors (SSRIs) were recommended increasingly as a treatment for rapid ejaculation. Drugs such as Paxil™ (GlaxoSmithKline), intended originally as anti-depressants, demonstrated an adverse impact on sexual desire and response, diminishing or even preventing orgasm in many patients. The SSRIs succeeded in slowing down men's ejaculations and were therefore used as an adjunct to or instead of conventional sex therapy for treatment of rapid ejaculation (Althof, 2007; Waldinger, 2003). The SSRIs are also used in combination with anti-androgens to control paraphilic behavior.

The phenomenal amount of attention garnered by Viagra™ led to great interest in the development of a female equivalent (Hartley, 2006) and the introduction into the clinical lexicon of the new phrase, "Female Sexual Dysfunction" [FSD]. Pharmaceutical companies began to lay the foundations for a biomedical discourse of the nebulous FSD. Hypothesis after hypothesis was put forth as to the etiology and treatments of FSD. First came the mechanics and hydraulics hypothesis of FSD, suggesting that just like men, women needed more blood flow to their genitalia. In 2004, after 8 years of research on the effects of Sildenafil with women, Pfizer withdrew Viagra from further clinical trials with females claiming that women, unlike men, were just too complicated (Harris, 2004). Thereafter, the hormonal hypothesis was promoted (Hartley, 2006; Moynihan & Mintzes, 2010). Ubiquitous "experts" spoke in the media as if it were a given that desire or lack thereof was a direct result of levels of testosterone. It came as a surprise to the lay public in December, 2004 when the FDA rejected unanimously Proctor and Gamble's bid to seek approval for Intrinsa, their proposed testosterone patch for low desire in women. Two studies released shortly thereafter affirmed the *lack* of correlation between androgen levels and female sexual desire (Davis, Davison, Donath, & Bell, 2005; Wierman et al., 2006). Next, the notion that desire is all in the brain was popularized just as Palatin Technologies undertook clinical trials for their Bremelanotide nasal spray while Boehringer Ingelheim sought FDA approval for their prospective desire drug, Flibanserin—both unsuccessfully. Given the scale of enormous potential profits, new drugs such as "Libigel" (Biosante), Androgel (Solvay, off label), and Lybrido/Lybridos remain in the pipeline though at present, the search for pharmaceutical solutions leaves much to be desired.

The emphasis on biomedical interventions for sexual problems was also apparent in the mechanical treatment of Female Sexual Arousal Disorder with the EROS-CTD™ (Billups et al., 2001) and the use of Botox injected into the vaginal opening in combination with dilators for the treatment of vaginismus (Pacik, 2010).

New professional organizations, often sponsored by the pharmaceutical industry, were formed and began to provide continuing education for physicians, especially gynecologists and urologists in treating sexual dysfunctions (see below). Although there is a serious need for physicians to be trained in the comprehensive care of patients' sexual difficulties (Frank, Coughlin, & Elon, 2008; Moser, 1999; Shindel et al., 2010), the instruction in many of these instances was largely about the high prevalence of sexual dysfunction and the need to be on the lookout for them, checklists to evaluate for their symptoms, and pharmacological information. The psychosocial and interpersonal contexts in which problems are generated were largely overlooked.

A new organization was established in 1998 with Irwin Goldstein (the urologist who first introduced sildenafil citrate [1998]) at the helm. It was known initially as the Female Sexual Function Forum (FSFF) and made up primarily of physicians, rather than clinicians trained/identifying as sex therapists. It is now known as the International Society for the Study of Women's Sexual Health (ISSWSH). (It had followed the establishment in 1982 of the International Society for Impotence Research, which changed its name in 2000 to the International Society for Sexual and Impotence Research and subsequently to the International Society for Sexual Medicine [ISSM]. The vast majority of its members are urologists.) New journals, notably the *Journal of Sexual Medicine* (published by ISSM) were established. In 2013, three more journals devoted to medical aspects of sexual problems began publication: *Sexual Medicine, Sexual Medicine Reviews* and *Current Sexual Health Reports*. By contrast, the unfortunate demise in 2000 of the *Journal of Sex Education and Therapy* further illustrated the shift since the 1990s towards fragmentation of the field.

Responses to Medicalization

As the medicalization of sex therapy grew, so too did the developing resistance to and backlash against it. During the early 1990s, sociologists (e.g., Irvine, 1990; Jeffries, 1990; Reiss, 1990) had begun to criticize the field of sex therapy. They stated that the treatment of clients' problems, one-on-one without attempting to change the social environment in which these problems are generated, maintained, and treated, allows clinicians to make a profit by helping individuals adjust to a troubled norm while sustaining the dysfunctional status quo intact. In the successive years, sex therapists, too, began to question openly the tenuous, tacit assumptions built into our beginnings (Kleinplatz, 1996, 1998, 2003, 2012; Schnarch, 1991, 1997; Tiefer, 1991, 1996, 2001, 2012; Weeks & Hof, 1987). These shaky foundations made it easier for the field to be co-opted by reductionistic, biomedical models; correspondingly, they made it easy for the pharmaceutical industry to market treatments for sexual dysfunctions to clinicians and the lay public and to achieve "buy-in."

In 2000, in response to the growing medicalization of sexuality and sexual problems, a group of sexologists coalesced under the leadership of Leonore Tiefer and proffered an alternate diagnostic framework for conceptualizing sexual difficulties. The Working Group for a New View of Women's Sexual Problems (Alperstein et al., 2002) recommended that all women's (and later, men's) sexual problems be assessed in terms of sociocultural, political, or economic factors; problems relating to partner and relationships; psychological and medical factors. The call for multi-dimensional approaches to assessing and dealing with human sexuality has been welcomed in some quarters (e.g., Ogden, 2012) and been dismissed as regressive, outmoded, "feminist" complaints by others.

As a result of these trends, the field has moved increasingly to splintering of the profession(s) (Kleinplatz, 2003, 2012). Although the demand for help with sexual problems continues unabated, the nature of the services provided often depends on which type of clinician with what type of training the client/patient happens to see. Perhaps more often, particularly in the United States, it is less a matter of happenstance and related instead to health insurance coverage (or lack thereof, a situation that will hopefully improve under "Obamacare"). It has been particularly disturbing that much health insurance will not reimburse consumers for couples therapy. Although the increasing emphasis on "empirically supported treatments" and "best practices" seems logical enough, the most expedient treatment with the most clear-cut effectiveness in reducing symptoms of sexual dysfunctions may not be in the patient's best interests in an area as complex as sexuality. Studies of pharmaceutical interventions may show impressive results when criteria for effective outcome are "more restricted and unidimensional" (Heiman, 2002, p. 74) than in studies of individual or couples therapy. However, most couples are seeking more than "erections firm enough for penetration" or to be free of "vaginal spasms preventing intercourse"; they are hoping for sex that is desired and worth wanting, a feeling of connection with their partners during sex and feelings of shared contentment thereafter (Kleinplatz, 2010a, 2010b).

At this time, the treatment of sexual problems and concerns often occurs in a fragmented fashion, with a need for richer paradigms and more integrated clinical care. Although there have been calls for inter-disciplinary training for decades (c.f., Moser, 1983) numerous institutional obstacles, real or perceived turf wars, and the lack of a coherent, cohesive, and multi-dimensional theoretical framework have impeded comprehensive care. The increased attention to symptoms of sexual problems in recent years presents clinicians with a remarkable opportunity to broaden the discourse around sexuality itself, to consider anew what men and women truly aspire towards as sexual beings, as partners and how we can help them attain their goals.

Professional Sex Therapy Associations

The oldest of the major North American sexology organizations is the Society for the Scientific Study of Sexuality (http://www.sexscience.org/), founded in 1957, which focuses primarily on research into sexuality broadly rather than being limited to sex therapy alone. Its interdisciplinary membership of 700 or so sexologists consists largely of academics. The Society for Sex Therapy and Research (http://www.sstarnet.org/) was founded in 1975 and has maintained a relatively constant membership of approximately 275 sex therapist/researchers whose primary focus is on sexual difficulties and treatment of them. The primary, international, credentialing body for sex therapists is the U.S.-based American Association of Sexuality Educators, Counselors and Therapists (AASECT at www.aasect.org). AASECT was founded in 1967 and currently has approximately 2,100 members with an applied focus, of whom roughly 550 are certified as sex therapists. In addition, sex therapists in Ontario, the most populous Canadian province, can be certified by the Board of Examiners in Sex Therapy and Counselling of Ontario (BESTCO; see www.BESTCO.info), founded in 1975. There are approximately 35–40 BESTCO certified sex therapists at any given time. Although their model of training and evaluation and certification is not renowned outside Ontario, it probably deserves to set the standard for the profession (see below). As stated above, both ISSWSH and ISSM are comprised overwhelmingly of physicians who may treat sexual disorders in male or female patients respectively but who are not trained as nor identify as sex therapists.

The Personal and Professional Process of Becoming a Sex Therapist

Many students are curious about the process of becoming a sex therapist. Some assume that it must be a very glamorous field, with regular appearances on talk shows or in Cosmo. Others assume that becoming a sex therapist mostly requires a hearty appreciation for the joys of sex. The reality is neither so gilt-edged nor so simple. Becoming a sex therapist requires first and foremost that one become skilled at individual and couples therapy. That is, the process of becoming a sex therapist presupposes prior training and expertise in psychotherapy per se. Only those adept at psychotherapy (and licensed accordingly within their jurisdictions as discussed below, at least if they are seeking to be certified by AASECT or BESTCO) will qualify for training in sex therapy. This requires graduate or doctoral level training in one of the fields that licenses psychotherapists, typically, clinical psychology, social work, marital and family therapy, or medicine. (Others are possible, too, e.g., graduate degrees in counseling, depending on the jurisdiction and possibility of licensure.)

Above and beyond one's qualifications and license to practice psychotherapy, prospective sex therapists require fundamental knowledge of sexology and advanced training in sex therapy. AASECT (see http://aasect.org/certification.asp) requires that candidates for certification as sexuality educators, counselors, and therapists acquire at least 90 hours of course work covering such basics as the history of sexology, knowledge of sex research and literature, the anatomy and physiology of sexual response, developmental, sociocultural, and medical factors affecting sexual values and expression, gender roles, relationship issues, sexually transmitted infections and prevention issues, sexual abuse and its consequences, sexual orientation, sexual minorities, etc. In addition, prospective sex therapists require a minimum of 60 graduate course hours on sexual difficulties and how to deal with them in therapy. Among other things, this includes knowledge of the DSM sexual dysfunctions, gender disorders, and paraphilias as well as the more common problems (e.g., sexual desire discrepancy, disappointment with sex, lack of "connection") that bring individuals and couples into the offices of sex therapists; the major intrapsychic, interpersonal, psychosocial, and organic causes of sexual problems; theory and methods of assessment, diagnosis, and clinical intervention (i.e., psychotherapeutic and medical) with sexual problems; models and methods of couples/systemic sex therapy; knowledge of the role of the sex therapist in working with other health professionals, whether generalists or specialists; ethical issues and decision-making in sex therapy; and techniques for assessment of outcome. In addition, the sex therapist requires specialized knowledge of how other clinicians' interventions (e.g., treatment of depression, diabetes, cardiovascular disease, cancer) affect, engender or exacerbate sexual problems. My own therapy practice is sometimes dominated by the need to sort through the overlay/underlay of iatrogenic disorders that complicate and can even distract from the work of individual and relational sex therapy. The role of the sex therapist today increasingly requires skill at advocating for one's clientele with other health care practitioners who often have diminished time to investigate sexual problems or concerns. Sex therapists are also situated to advocate for sexual minorities within other systems.

Above and beyond didactic information, sex therapists are expected to complete several years of supervised, (via direct observation or audio/video recording) clinical training (generally at the post-graduate level) in the practice of sex therapy with a wide array of clients. These are to include therapy with individuals, couples, and, sometimes, groups, men and women, sexual minorities and learn to deal with a broad range of DSM disorders and other sexual concerns.

Both AASECT and BESTCO require that all certified members engage in a process of personal reflection and sexual values clarification. Sexual Attitude Reassessment (SAR) workshops, generally lasting a weekend or so, challenge participants to examine their own feelings, attitudes, and previously untested beliefs about sexuality in all its diversity and complexity. SARs involve experiential learning processes in small groups led by trained leaders who encourage participants to become aware of their own philosophies of sexuality and sexology. Therapists are to be become aware of their own personal and professional limits and of the kinds of situations or clients they may not be ideally suited to serving well.

In addition to the requirements above, BESTCO requires a three-year period of clinical training, supervision, and attendance at all, twice yearly, two-day meetings, to become certified as a sex therapist. Thereafter, attendance at all meetings is a requirement for maintaining one's certification. Much of the sex therapy literature refers to a "biopsychosocial approach" or conversely, a "psychobiosocial approach" (Metz & McCarthy, 2003). Unfortunately, this is often merely lip service. By contrast, BESTCO meetings are truly inter-disciplinary and are characterized by a remarkable atmosphere of mutual respect, collegiality, and desire to learn from one another's experience and expertise. Approximately half of BESTCO members are physicians while the other half holds graduate/doctoral degrees in the social sciences. All BESTCO members must be full, clinical members of the American Association of Marital and Family Therapists or must otherwise document and demonstrate competence in couples therapy before being allowed to enter the three-year apprenticeship period. The primacy of skill in couples therapy and the heavily, interdisciplinary component make BESTCO unique within sex therapy associations. Although the primary theoretical orientation is systemic, there are psychodynamic, experiential and cognitive behavioral approaches, too. BESTCO also has the distinction of requiring a series of examinations, at least one of which entails a case presentation in front of the entire BESTCO membership, with written synopsis and bibliography, before one can be certified as a sex therapist.

Some practitioners are trained and certified as sex counselors rather than sex therapists. The major distinction is that sex counseling tends to be rather brief and focused on problem-solving around time-limited concerns (e.g., choice of contraceptives, safer sex practices, dealing with sexual assault) rather than more intensive psychotherapy. Sex counselors tend to be employed in such agencies as Planned Parenthood or work in the community as nurses, guidance counselors, etc., rather than in psychotherapy practice as such.

Ethical Principles of Sex Therapy

Sex therapists are expected to study and follow the codes of ethics of their respective disciplines. AASECT members are also required to adhere to the organizations' code of ethics for sex therapists (see http://aasect.org/codeofethics.asp). Issues such as integrity, confidentiality, clients' autonomy, dealing with therapist-client power differentials, and avoiding dual relationships are particularly salient in sex therapy, given the vulnerability that clients generally feel in revealing highly taboo and often hidden material. Similarly, ethical principles such as respect for diversity in values, sexual orientations, gender, and sensitivity to human rights issues—each important in all psychotherapy—take on added dimension and importance in sex therapy.

Some lay people wonder if sex therapy entails talk therapy only or whether treatment will involve sexual contact with the therapist or even between the partners while in the therapist's office. In fact, no sexual contact between therapist and clients is permissible. While clients are often given "homework" assignments (e.g., sensate focus exercises) for the couple to share at home and then discuss during the following session, it would be unethical to have clients engage in sexual activity with the therapist present.

Some confusion may be a remnant of the sensationalistic publicity surrounding the early days of Masters and Johnson's work with surrogate partners. (The confusion and controversy were re-ignited by the 2012 film "The Sessions," which depicted an actual 1980s case of surrogate partner therapy with a severely disabled man.) Masters and Johnson believed strongly that effective therapy required a couple present and refused to offer individual therapy. When men presented for therapy alone, a surrogate partner was provided in order for these clients to engage in the accompanying homework. (Single women were presumed able to find their own sex therapy partners.) Masters and Johnson eventually gave up their work with surrogates out of fear of legal threats and possible repercussions. The use of surrogate partners has continued as an adjunctive component of some sex therapy although it is not widespread. Surrogate partners are now trained and regulated by the International Professional Surrogates Association (IPSA), see www.SurrogateTherapy.org. These individuals are trained to work with sex therapists and their clients and have their own code of ethics. In all instances, they are to use touch appropriate to the client's needs as assessed by the sex therapist; it is incumbent whenever physical contact is used as any component of treatment for the therapist to justify the use of whatever touch is prescribed in terms of the standards of care and clinical goals appropriate to the case.

Is Sex Therapy a Distinct Modality? The Case for Certifying Professionals

Controversy has simmered over whether or not sex therapy is a distinct modality and therefore, whether certification of sex therapists should continue. In 2009, Binik and Meana called for the abolition of sex therapy certification. They argued that the theoretical basis of sex therapy was negligible and therefore the study of it, presumably the foundation for professional development in any field, was nonsensical. On this point there can be little dispute (Kleinplatz, 2003, 2012; Wiederman, 1998). Binik and Meana then argued that the psychotherapy techniques used in the treatment of sexual dysfunctions are hardly unique to sex therapy: The major interventions, including psychoeducational counseling, cognitive-behavioral homework assignments, learning of communication skills, and bibliotherapy are used rather extensively for a wide array of purposes by other varieties of psychotherapists. There is no technique used by sex therapists that is unique to sex therapy alone. This reasoning too, is solid. Then what, if anything, makes sex therapy special? Binik and Meana would say that the time is well overdue to strip away the illusion of distinctiveness.

What makes sex therapy unique is the knowledge about human sexuality and sexology that practitioners must acquire during the training process. Unfortunately, this knowledge is increasingly difficult to obtain while misleading and flat out erroneous information about sexuality is ubiquitous, especially on the Internet. In North America, public and graphic discussion (and sometimes, display) of sex is omnipresent and paradoxically, individuals feel increasingly alone with their sexual difficulties. The misinformation found on television, the Internet, and the magazines we see at check-out stands and in physicians' waiting rooms continue to scare people and leave them feeling sexually defective (Kim & Ward, 2004; Kleinplatz et al., 2009). The media are replete with misleading stories about the role of technique in sexual fulfillment, gender differences in arousal, sexuality and aging, "normal" levels of desire, hormones, sexual orientation, etc. Ignorance and myths combined with the resulting fear, shame, and sense of inadequacy are precisely why so many of us continue to have extensive waiting lists. Unfortunately, the same lack of knowledge found in the lay public pervades the ranks of clinicians; none of us is immune to the consequences of being raised in a sex-negative culture. It is precisely in order to counter these effects that it is compulsory for certified sex therapists to undertake the aforementioned coursework in the study of human sexuality and to attend a SAR.

In an ideal world, such course training would be unnecessary. Our childhood and adolescent years would prepare us for adult sexual relations, thus curtailing somewhat the need for help with sexual problems. Family or school-based sexuality education could be relied upon to combat the entertaining but fictitious and ludicrous images of sexuality that pervade Internet pornography. Or failing that, given the crucial role of sexuality in personal well-being, all mental and medical health care providers would naturally receive considerable training in sexology in the course of their undergraduate and graduate schooling; they would then be prepared to help clients/patients deal with their sexual difficulties. Not only is that not the case at present, but the cutbacks to training in human sexuality in recent years have made the required knowledge increasingly and abysmally inaccessible within medical schools and within clinical psychology programs (Millers & Byers, 2009, 2010). That means that we cannot rely on the garden variety mental health or medical professional to know much about human sexuality and its problems. Such a clinician cannot be expected to be comfortable or skilled in responding to and dealing with the full array of complex clients'/patients' sexual problems or concerns, let alone broaching them in therapy.

As such, the major purpose of sex therapy certification remains consumer protection. Most certified sex therapists can rattle off a series of horror stories, where we have been brought in to take care of the casualties produced by other, duly licensed health care providers: the woman who is told she will need long-term therapy because she is unable to reach orgasm during intercourse; the "impotent" man who is treated for the childhood origins of his fear of women when he has not been assessed until too late for diabetes mellitus; the woman who is given some lubricant for her lack of arousal when in fact, her relationship is so filled with vitriol she should be advised to listen to the wisdom of her dry vagina; the couple who are distressed about their sexual desire discrepancy are told to "just compromise," when sex is merely the battleground for far more complex power dynamics; the infertile couple who are told to "just relax" when they find themselves paralyzed by the rigors of infertility treatment, and the list continues. . .

More frighteningly, because "sex therapist" is not generally a registered title—with only two notable exceptions in North America, that is, in the state of Florida and the province of Quebec—anyone can advertise him/herself as having an interest/expertise in treating sexual problems or even claim to be a sex therapist. In such instances, clients/patients assume they are in competent hands when there is no assurance of any skill, knowledge base, or clinical training to correspond with the clinician's claims. (And of course sometimes, those advertising their willingness to deal with sexuality are not clinicians at all and are offering an entirely different service.) Thus, whereas we should hope with Binik and Meana that certification in sex therapy will ultimately become unnecessary, at this time, certification serves to protect the public from ignorant, incompetent and unscrupulous "health care" providers.

Conclusions

[handwritten margin note: clients who are seeking]

Sex therapy provides a wonderful and deeply meaningful professional life. Sex therapists serve clients/patients who are searching for more sexual pleasure, fulfillment, and intimacy. Given that sexual wishes, hopes, and fantasies touch the core of human existence, sex therapy can prove profoundly rewarding. We serve the public uniquely, in that few mainstream, individual, and couples therapists have the knowledge base, skill, training, and especially comfort level to deal in depth with complex sexual problems. More importantly, sex therapists are privileged with the opportunity to help people attain their most cherished and unspoken dreams, working not only to alleviate sexual disorders and dysfunctions but to allow couples to experience their own erotic potentials (Kleinplatz, 1998, 2004, 2006, 2010a, 2010b; Kleinplatz et al., 2009).

[handwritten margin note: alleviate and experience potential]

Resources

To locate a Certified Sex Therapist

The Board of Examiners in Sex Therapy and Counselling of Ontario: www.BESTCO.info
American Association of Sex Educators Counselors and Therapists: www.AASECT.org

Major Sexology Associations and Opportunities for Continuing Education

The Society for the Scientific Study of Sexuality (SSSS): http://www.sexscience.org/
Society for Sex Therapy and Research: www.sstarnet.org
American Association of Sex Educators Counselors and Therapists: www.AASECT.org
Canadian Sex Research Forum: www.csrf.ca
The British Association for Sexual and Marital Therapy: www.basrt.org.uk

Distributors of Sex Toys and Educational-Sexually Explicit Videos

Come As You Are (An especially useful resource for sex toys and aids for the disabled as well as the able-bodied): www.comeasyouare.com
Good Vibrations: www.goodvibes.com

References

Alperstein, L., Ellison, C.R., Fishman, J.R., Hall, M., Handwerker, L., Hartley, H., . . . Tiefer, L. (2002). A new view of women's sexual problems. *Women and Therapy, 24* (1/2), 1–8. doi: 10.1300/J015v24n01_01

Althof, S.E. (2007). Treatment of rapid ejaculation: Psychotherapy, pharmacotherapy, and combined therapy. In S.R. Leiblum (Ed.), *Principles and practice of sex therapy* (4th ed., pp. 212–240). New York: Guilford Press.

Althof, S.E., & Turner L.A. (1992). Pharmacological and vacuum pump techniques: Treatment methods and outcome. In R. Rosen & S. Leiblum (Eds.), *Erectile disorder: Assessment and treatment* (pp. 283–312). New York: Guilford Press.

Althof, S.E., Turner, L.A., Levine, S.B., Risen, C., Kursh, E., & Bodner, D. (1989). Why do so many people drop out from auto-injection therapy for impotence? *Journal of Sex and Marital Therapy, 15,* 121–129.

Billups, K.L., Berman, L., Berman, J., Metz, M.E., Glennon, M.E., & Goldstein, I. (2001). A new non-pharmacological vacuum therapy for female sexual dysfunction. *Journal of Sex & Marital Therapy, 27* (5), 435–441. doi: 10.1080/713846826

Binik, Y.M., & Meana, M. (2009). The future of sex therapy: Specialization or marginalization? *Archives of Sexual Behavior, 38* (6), 1016–1027. doi: 10.1007/s10508-009-9475-9

Davis, S.R., Davison, S.L., Donath, S., & Bell, R.J. (2005). Circulating androgen levels and self-reported sexual function in women. *Journal of the American Medical Association, 294* (1), 91–96. doi: 10.1097/01.AOG.0000177770.40155.92

Frank, E., Coughlin, S. S., & Elon, L. (2008). Sex-related knowledge, attitudes, and behaviors of U.S. medical students. *Obstetrics and Gynecology, 112,* 311–319. doi: 0.1097/AOG.0b013e3181809645

Freud, S. (1917/1963). Introductory lectures on psychoanalysis. *The Standard Edition of the Complete Psychological Works of Sigmund Freud,* Volumes XV and XVI (trans. James Strachey). London: Hogarth Press.

Giami, A. (2000). Changing relations between medicine, psychology and sexuality: The case of male impotence. *Journal of Social Medicine, 37,* 263–272.

Goldstein, I., Lue, T., Padma-Nathan, H., Rosen, R., Steers, W., & Wicker, P. (1998). Oral sildenafil in the treatment of erectile dysfunction. *New England Journal of Medicine, 338,* 1397–1404.

Harris, G. (2004, February 28). Pfizer gives up testing Viagra on women. *New York Times,* Section C, page 1, column 5.

Hartley, H. (2006). The "pinking" of Viagra culture: Drug industry efforts to create and repackage sex drugs for women. *Sexualities, 9,* 363–378. doi: 10.1177/1363460706065058

Heiman, J. (2002). Sexual dysfunction: Overview of prevalence, etiological factors, and treatment. *Journal of Sex Research, 39* (1), 73–78. doi: 10.1080/00224490209552124

Hertlein, K.M., Weeks, G.R., & Gambescia, N. (2009). *Systemic sex therapy.* New York: Routledge.

Irvine, J. M. (1990). *Disorders of desire: Sex and gender in modern American sexology.* Philadelphia: Temple University Press.

Irwin, M. B., & Kata, E.J. (1994). High attrition rate with intra-cavernous injection of prostaglandin E1 for impotency. *Urology, 43,* 84–87.

Jeffries, S. (1990). *Anticlimax: A feminist perspective on the sexual revolution.* London: The Women's Press.

Kaplan, H.S. (1974). *The new sex therapy.* New York: Brunner/Mazel.

Kaplan, H. S. (1977). Hypoactive sexual desire. *Journal of Sex & Marital Therapy, 3*(1), 3–9.

Kaplan, H.S. (1979). *Disorders of sexual desire and other new concepts and techniques in sex therapy.* New York: Brunner/Mazel.

Kim, J.L., & Ward, L.M. (2004). Pleasure reading: Associations between young women's sexual attitudes and their reading of contemporary women's magazines. *Psychology of Women Quarterly, 28,* 48–58. doi: 10.1111/j.1471–6402.2004.00122.x

Kleinplatz, P.J. (1996). Transforming sex therapy: Integrating erotic potential. *The Humanistic Psychologist, 24* (2), 190–202.

Kleinplatz, P.J. (1998). Sex therapy for vaginismus: A review, critique and humanistic alternative. *Journal of Humanistic Psychology, 38*(2), 51–81.

Kleinplatz, P. J. (2001). A critique of the goals of sex therapy or the hazards of safer sex. In P. J. Kleinplatz (Ed.), *New directions in sex therapy: Innovations and alternatives* (pp. 109–131). Philadelphia, PA: Brunner-Routledge.

Kleinplatz, P.J. (2003). What's new in sex therapy: From stagnation to fragmentation. *Sex and Relationship Therapy, 18*(1), 95–106. doi: 10.1080/1468199031000061290

Kleinplatz, P.J. (2004). Beyond sexual mechanics and hydraulics: Humanizing the discourse surrounding erectile dysfunction. *Journal of Humanistic Psychology, 44*(2), 215–242. doi: 10.1177/0022167804263130

Kleinplatz, P.J. (2006). Learning from extraordinary lovers: Lessons from the edge. *Journal of Homosexuality, 50*(3/4), 325–348.

Kleinplatz, P.J. (2007). Coming out of the sex therapy closet: Using Experiential Psychotherapy with sexual problems and concerns. *American Journal of Psychotherapy, 61*(3), 333–348.

Kleinplatz, P.J. (2010a). "Desire disorders" or opportunities for optimal erotic intimacy. In S.R. Leiblum (Ed.), *Treating sexual desire disorders: A clinical casebook* (pp. 92–113). New York: Guilford.

Kleinplatz, P. J. (2010b). Lessons from great lovers. In S. Levine, S. Althof, & C. Risen (Eds.), *Handbook of clinical sexuality for mental health professionals* (2nd ed., pp. 57–72). New York: Brunner-Routledge.

Kleinplatz, P. J. (2012). Advancing sex therapy or is that the best you can do? In P. J. Kleinplatz (Ed.), *New directions in sex therapy: Innovations and alternatives* (2nd ed., pp. xix–xxxvi). New York: Routledge.

Kleinplatz, P. J. (2013). The paraphilias: An experiential approach to "dangerous" desires. In I. Binik & K. Hall (Eds.), *Principles and practice of sex therapy* (5th ed., pp. 195–218). New York: Guilford.

Kleinplatz, P. J., Ménard, A. D., Paquet, M.-P., Paradis, N., Campbell, M., Zuccarini, D., & Mehak, L. (2009). The components of optimal sexuality: A portrait of "great sex." *Canadian Journal of Human Sexuality*, 18(1–2), 1–13.

Lief, H. I. (1977). Inhibited sexual desire. *Medical Aspects of Human Sexuality*, 7, 94–95.

Loe, M. (2004). *The rise of Viagra: How the little blue pill changed sex in America*. New York: NYU Press.

Mahrer, A. R. (1996). *The complete guide to Experiential Psychotherapy*. New York: Wiley.

Mahrer, A. R. (2012). Goodbye sex therapy, hello undergoing my own transformation. In P. J. Kleinplatz (Ed.), *New directions in sex therapy: Innovations and alternatives* (2nd ed., pp. 231–252). New York: Routledge.

Malhotra, S., Khurshid, A., Hendricks, K. A., & Mann, J. R. (2008). Medical school sexual health curriculum and training in the United States. *Journal of the National Medical Association*, 100, 1097–1106.

Masters, W. H., & Johnson, V. E. (1966). *Human sexual response*. Boston: Little, Brown.

Masters, W. H., & Johnson, V. E. (1970). *Human sexual inadequacy*. New York: Bantam Books.

Masters, W. H., & Johnson, V. E. (1986). *Sex therapy on its twenty-fifth anniversary: Why it survives*. St. Louis: Masters and Johnson Institute.

Maurice, W. L. (1999). *Sexual medicine in primary care*. St. Louis: Mosby.

Metz, M. E., & McCarthy, B. W. (2003). *Coping with premature ejaculation: How to overcome P.E., please your partner & have great sex*. Oakland, CA: New Harbinger.

Metz, M. E., & McCarthy, B. W. (2005). Erectile dysfunction: An integrative, biopsychosocial approach to evaluation, treatment, and relapse prevention. *Contemporary Sexuality*, 39(5), i–viii.

Metz, M. E., & McCarthy, B. W. (2011a). *Enduring desire: Your guide to lifelong intimacy*. New York: Routledge.

Metz, M. E., & McCarthy, B. W. (2011b). The "good enough sex" (GES) model: Perspective and clinical applications. In P. J. Kleinplatz (Ed.), *New directions in sex therapy: Innovations and alternatives* (2nd ed., pp. 213–230). New York: Routledge.

Miller, S., & Byers, E. (2009). Psychologists' continuing education and training in sexuality. *Journal of Sex & Marital Therapy*, 35(3), 206–219.

Miller, S., & Byers, E. (2010). Psychologists' sexual education and training in graduate school. *Canadian Journal of Behavioural Science*, 42(2), 93–100.

Moser, C. (1983). A response to Reiss' "Trouble in Paradise." *Journal of Sex Research*, 19(2), 192–195.

Moser, C. (1999). *Health care without shame: A handbook for the sexually diverse and their caregivers*. San Francisco: Greenery Press.

Moynihan, R., & Mintzes, B. (2010). *Sex, lies and pharmaceuticals: How drug companies plan to profit from female sexual dysfunction*. Vancouver: Greystone Books.

Ogden, G. (2006). *The heart and soul of sex: Making the ISIS connection*. Boston: Trumpeter.

Ogden, G. (2012). *Expanding the practice of sex therapy*. New York: Routledge.

Pacik, P. T. (2010). *When sex seems impossible: Stories of vaginismus and how you can achieve intimacy*. Manchester, NH: Odyne Publishing.

Reiss, I. L. (1990). *An end to shame: Shaping our next sexual revolution*. New York: Prometheus Books.

Schnarch, D. (1991). *Constructing the sexual crucible: An integration of sexual and marital therapy*. New York: Norton.

Schnarch, D. (1997). *Passionate marriage.* New York: Norton.

Schover, L. R., & Leiblum, S. R. (1994). Commentary: The stagnation of sex therapy. *Journal of Psychology and Human Sexuality*, 6(3), 5–30.

Shindel, A. W., Ando, K. A., Nelson, C. J., Breyer, B. N., Lue, T. F., & Smith, J. F. (2010). Medical student sexuality: How sexual experience and sexuality training impact U.S. and Canadian medical students' comfort in dealing with patients' sexuality in clinical practice. *Academic Medicine*, 85(8), 1321–1330. doi: 10.1097/ACM.0b013e3181e6c4a0

Shindel, A. W., & Parish, S. J. (2013). Sexuality education in North American medical schools: Current status and future directions. *Journal of Sexual Medicine*, 10(1), 3–18.

Tiefer, L. (1991). Historical, scientific, clinical and feminist criticisms of "The Human Sexual Response Cycle" model. *Annual Review of Sex Research*, 2, 1–24.

Tiefer, L. (1996). The medicalization of sexuality: Conceptual, normative, and professional issues. *Annual Review of Sex Research*, 7, 252–282.

Tiefer, L. (2001). The selling of "female sexual dysfunction." *Journal of Sex & Marital Therapy*, 27(5), 625–628.

Tiefer, L. (2012). The "New View" campaign: A feminist critique of sex therapy and an alternate vision. In P. J. Kleinplatz (Ed.), *New directions in sex therapy: Innovations and alternatives* (2nd ed., pp. 21–36). New York: Routledge.

Van de Velde, Th. H. (1926). *Ideal marriage: Its physiology and technique.* New York: Random House.

Waldinger, M. D. (2003). Rapid ejaculation. In S. B. Levine, C. B. Risen, & S. Althof (Eds.), *Handbook of clinical sexuality for mental health professionals* (pp. 257–274). New York: Brunner-Routledge.

Weeks, G. (1977). Toward a dialectical approach to intervention. *Human Development*, 20, 277–292.

Weeks, G. (1994). The intersystem model: An integrative approach to treatment. In G. Weeks & L. Hof (Eds.), *The marital-relationship therapy casebook: Theory and application of the intersystem mode, 1* (pp. 3–34). New York: Brunner/Mazel.

Weeks, G. R. (2004, May). *Integration in sex therapy.* Presented as the opening plenary speaker at the European Sexology Conference, Brighton, England.

Weeks, G. R. (2005). The emergence of a new paradigm in sex therapy: Integration. *Sexual and Relationship Therapy*, 20, 89–104.

Weeks, G., & Hof, L. (Eds.). (1987). *Integrating sex and marital therapy: A clinical guide.* New York: W. W. Norton.

Wiederman, M. (1998). The state of theory in sex therapy. *Journal of Sex Research*, 35(1), 88–99.

Wierman, M. E., Basson, R., Davis, S. R., Khosla, S., Miller, K. K., Rosner, W., & Santoro, N. (2006). Androgen therapy in women: An Endocrine Society Clinical Practice guideline. *Journal of Clinical Endocrinology & Metabolism*, 91(10), 3697–3710. doi: 10.1210/jc.2006–1121

Wittenberg, A., & Gerber, J. (2009). Recommendations for improving sexual health curricula in medical schools: Results from a two-arm study collecting data from patients and medical students. *Journal of Sexual Medicine*, 6(2), 362–368. doi: 10.1111/j.1743–6109.2008.01046.x

Zilbergeld, B., & Ellison, C. R. (1980). Desire discrepancies and arousal problems in sex therapy. In S. R. Leiblum & L. A. Pervin (Eds.), *Principles and practice of sex therapy* (pp. 65–101). New York: Guilford Press.

3

TOWARD A NEW PARADIGM
IN SEX THERAPY

Gerald R. Weeks and Nancy Gambescia

The Intersystem Approach involves the *integration* of various models of psychotherapy, each containing specific theoretical foundations and techniques (Weeks & Cross, 2004; Norcross, 2005). Integration is different from the practice of eclecticism, which is an ad hoc selection of theoretical approaches applied to a specific situation. Fundamentally, integrative psychotherapy involves a clearly articulated framework that informs diagnosis and treatment (Van Kaam, 1969). The concept of integration is not new to the field of couple and family therapy (Gurman & Fraenkel, 2002; Lebow, 1997) as it is consistent with a systems approach to the complex issues that one encounters in working with family structures (Stricker & Gold, 1996).

The Lack of Integration in Couple and Sex Therapy

Regrettably, sex therapy emerged and grew as a parallel yet separate domain from couple and family therapy; each field associated itself with independent philosophical approaches and treatment modalities. Considering the fact that couple and sex therapy concentrate on relational issues involving intimacy and sexuality, one would expect them to be conjoined theoretically and practically. Each should have an integrated framework, systemic orientation, and comingled theoretical approaches to treatment. Although the two fields are beginning to overlap, the intersection is small and somewhat inconsistent (Gurman, 2008). Moreover, it is our assertion that the two fields remain unnecessarily bifurcated. The following discussion will focus on the issues that result, directly or indirectly, from the lack of integration in the professional domains of couple and sex therapy:

1. Traditional sex therapy is non-systemic
2. There is a lack of theory in sex science, research, and practice
3. Professional organizations for couple and sex therapy are distinct
4. The actual practice of sex and couple therapy are often performed by different practitioners

Traditional Sex Therapy Is Non-systemic

While family and couple therapy fields have accepted a family systems approach to treatment, a fundamental systemic methodology has traditionally been absent in the field of sex therapy. For example, Masters and Johnson (1966, 1970) provided the original accounts of the physiology of the sexual response and treatment of sexual dysfunctions;

their approach was not systematic, even though the couple, rather than the individual, was the unit of treatment. The partners were not viewed as the client-system. As such, the ostensibly asymptomatic partner often acted as an assistant to the therapist in carrying out assignments that focused on the symptomatic partner. A few years later, Kaplan (1974) attempted to bridge the gap between traditional psychodynamic and more contemporary behavioral approaches. Although Kaplan (1974) recognized the importance of resolving relational conflict in promoting sexual satisfaction, her approach was not systemic or truly integrative. In fact, it was suggested the therapist circumvented relational problems using the "bypass" technique in order to focus on sexual symptoms from an individually oriented behavioral perspective. LoPiccolo and LoPiccolo (1978) incorporated the element of mutual responsibility in their sex therapy approach, approximating what we now know as systemic sex therapy. They recognized the reciprocal nature of sexual dysfunctions and, accordingly, treated the couple as a unit. The next generation of sex therapy models promoted a greater emphasis on medical, cognitive, behavioral, and psychodynamic approaches yet did not significantly contribute to a systemic, integrative theoretical framework (Leiblum, 2007; Leiblum & Rosen, 1989, 2000).

The Intersystem Approach engendered the greatest paradigm shift in the field of sex therapy. It united behavioral, biological, cognitive, and affective constituents (Weeks, 1989). This systemic and truly integrative theoretical approach is utilized in sex therapy and also for the treatment of any individual, couple, or family problem. Moreover, it naturally intersects the domains of couple and family therapies because it is systemic and integrative. This theoretical approach was implemented in texts concentrating on erectile disorder (Weeks & Gambescia, 2000), sexual desire disorders (Weeks & Gambescia, 2002), infidelity (Weeks, Gambescia, & Jenkins, 2003), and sex therapy (Hertlein, Weeks, & Gambescia, 2009).

The Lack of Theory in Sex Science, Research, and Practice

Another major problem in the field of human sexuality and sex therapy is the lack of theory and theory-informed research. In 1998, *The Journal of Sex Research* highlighted this problem in a special issue on theory. One of the articles was a review of *The Use of Theory in Research and Scholarship on Sexuality* (Allgeier, 1998). This issue of *The Journal of Sex Research* includes a number of mini-theories in the field of human sexuality and very few in the area of sex therapy, none of which attempted to offer an integrative perspective. The lack of theory in sex therapy means most of the articles published are about data and therefore do not provide theory-based or theory-driven research. As the reader will shortly see, this special issue had virtually no effect on the field of human sexuality and sex therapy. It is clear this part of the field is grossly underdeveloped and stagnant.

Standard sex therapy treatment is largely unsupported by underlying theoretical principles of behavior theory, couple therapy, systems theory, and the other elements that would constitute a theoretically integrative model. Rarely is the underlying theory even discussed in the treatment of sexual disorders. As stated, more often than not, sex therapy trends toward eclecticism, frequently resembling a "cookbook" approach, listing elements and techniques for customizing therapy with expected outcomes. In fact, *The Illustrated Manual of Sex Therapy (Second Edition)* is an example of such an approach. This text presents sketches used to demonstrate various techniques, and a formulaic list of steps to follow in treating various problems; however, it lacked a stated theoretical framework that informs treatment (Kaplan, 1988).

Through the publication of *Integrating Sex and Marital Therapy: A Clinical Guide*, Weeks and Hof (1987) presented an approach, which specifically recognized the need for the integration of sex and couple therapy as a minimal requirement for the fields of sex and couple therapy. In a recent publication, Weeks and Fife (2014) further refine the integrative approach, which significantly enhanced these domains. Other theorists have argued for the integration of sex therapy into other fields of psychotherapy; for instance, Wiederman (1998), in the *Journal of Sex and Research*, advocated that human sexuality and sex therapy concepts, treatment approaches, and research be integrated into the more broader fields of psychology, psychiatry, social work, nursing, and other health care and social sciences.

Ruppel (1994) examined articles published in the *Archives of Sexual Behavior* and the *Journal of Sex Research* between 1990 and 1997. He found about three-fourths of the articles published were primarily about data. Only 6% of the articles published in the *Archives of Sexual Behavior* were classified as theory development and about 25% of those published in the *Journal of Sex Research* were classified as theory development. Likewise, Dubois and Wiederman (1997) coded articles published in the *Journal of Sex and Marital Therapy*, which were theory-based between the years of 1974–1995, and found that none of the articles actually identified a true theoretical framework in sex therapy.

In researching the revision of this book we examined several sex therapy journals over the course of the past 6 years. There were many articles devoted to definitional issues, etiology of sexual problems, new medical therapies; nonetheless, we found very little on new sex therapy protocols, sex therapy research, or theory development. This finding is, to us, indicative that the field is severely lacking in a theoretical framework for understanding sexuality and developing new approaches to sex therapy.

Essentially, our approach acknowledges a connection between an individual's inner and outer worlds and the numerous processes that influence and are impacted by these domains. We identify constructs that help to tie together the different systems involved, and the elements common to each system. *Integrational* constructs cut across the major domains of the framework (individual, couple, family, outside influences). Furthermore, our integrative psychotherapy involves a clearly articulated theoretical method and conceptual framework that informs diagnosis and treatment (Van Kaam, 1969). This framework enables us to synthesize our knowledge about systems theory, couple therapy, sex therapy, medical therapy, psychology, and knowledge about larger systemic contexts.

The Lack of Integration in Professional Organizations

The standards of training for the professional organizations devoted to couple and sex therapies are needlessly fragmented. For example, organizations such as AAMFT (American Association for Marriage and Family Therapy) and ACA (American Counseling Association) require only minimal training in the areas of human sexuality, sexology, or sex therapy. In fact, COAMFTE-accredited programs (Commission on Accreditation for Marriage and Family Therapy Education) do not delineate a specified amount of sexuality training in their programs' requirements. COAMFTE-accredited programs should include in their clinical knowledge component content issues including "gender, sexual functioning, sexual orientation, [and] sex therapy . . . in the treatment of individuals, couples, and families from a relational/systemic perspective" (Commission on Accreditation for Marriage and Family Therapy Education, 2005, p. 1). The lack of specificity in this standard means that the curricula of COAMFTE-accredited programs offer very little training in human sexuality and sex therapy.

Another accrediting organization for counseling programs, CACREP (Council Accreditation of Counseling and Related Educational Programs) requires some focus aimed at "human sexuality (e.g., gender, sexual functioning, sexual orientation) and its impact on family and couple functioning" (Council for Accreditation of Counseling and Related Educational Programs [CACREP], 2009, p. 37). We believe the requirement for sexuality topics should be quantified, not just mentioned.

In brief, both accreditation bodies mentioned above set standards for couple therapy training as a significant part of their accredited programs, but essentially fail to adequately address sexuality and sexual problems. This is unfortunate as couple and family therapists and general counselors are ineffectively prepared to assess and treat sexual intimacy issues, which are so commonly associated with individual, couple, and family problems. Likewise, the two most prominent sex therapy organizations, AASECT (American Association of Sex Educators, Counselors, and Therapists) and SSSS (Society for the Scientific Study of Sexuality), have accentuated training in human sexuality and sex therapy, but only minimally emphasized couple therapy in their process to becoming a certified sex therapist.

This makes no sense since sexual and relationship problems are typically intermingled. The standard to become a certified sex therapist through AASECT is that the applicant has training in the theory and methods of intervention dealing with couple systems; yet there is no specific requirement for the amount of training. In our experience, many ASSECT certified sex therapists do not have any systemic training in how to work with a couple, nor have they had any intensive training in couple therapy. Additionally, the AASECT supervisor must be an experienced sex therapist, not necessarily a practitioner who has a working knowledge of couple and family systems, systems theory, and systemic therapy (American Association of Sexuality Educators, Counselors and Therapists, 2004). To date, the sex therapy organizations establishing training standards essentially have not set requirements for systems thinking or intensive and systematic training in couple therapy.

In summary, the organizations which establish the training standards for couple and sex therapy each suggest training in the "other" field but do not support such a suggestion in requiring a specific curriculum. On the other hand, each accrediting body does set rigorous standards for training within their own respective field. For those who attend national conferences in both fields it is obvious how little the two arenas intersect. Simply examining the lectures and workshops offered by AAMFT and AASECT over the past couple of decades shows that AAMFT rarely offers any training in sexuality or sex therapy and AASECT rarely offers any training in couple therapy.

The Lack of Integration of Sex and Couple Therapy Practice

As a consequence of historically poor integration of couple and sex therapy theory, the lack of a systemic sex therapy metatheory, fragmented training, bifurcated teaching programs, and segregated professional organizations, etc., there exists the problem of couple therapists referring clients with sexual issues to sex therapy practitioners. We have attempted to remedy this difficulty by offering an integrated approach to couple and sex therapy in our publications, education, and supervision. We dissuade making a referral of a couple with a sex problem to another therapist who treats only the sexual problem. The referral could send a message that the sexual problem is too complicated, serious, and untreatable, etc. These clients are feeling hopeless and often the recommendation to the "expert" reinforces their sense of pessimism. Alternately, unrealistic expectations for a "cure" can be generated by the fragmentation of treatment. The couple could construe that seeing a therapist just for a sexual problem will ensure that the specialist will be able to resolve their sexual disorder. Moreover, the couple therapist already knows the couple's issues and is in a good position to make the links between the sexual and relational problems. Financial issues should also be considered. Instead of staying within their confined areas of training despite feeling deskilled, couple and sex therapists could welcome collaboration, supervision, and training in order to learn how to integrate the two fields. We strongly believe that sex and couple therapy should be performed by the same practitioner. Sexual and relational satisfactions are correlated, each promoting and resulting from the other. Similarly, sexual and relational dissatisfaction perpetuate each other (Monteiro, Narcisco, & Pereira, 2014). Sexual issues are embedded in the relationship and relationship concerns express themselves in sex. Since these areas are interconnected relationally, why treat them in isolation?

The Intersystem Approach

Our approach was generated from various metatheoretical concepts and utilizes major domains of behavior in which to conceptualize human behavior and therapy. A metatheory is a theory about theories and often considered a branch of epistemology. Metatheory provides some of the rules, principles, and integrational concepts that allow us to understand and treat behavior from a larger perspective. The Intersystem Approach balances attention to the individual, couple, and family system, as well as the larger systems in which we live. This framework integrates five specific domains of behavior:

1. Individual/biological/medical
2. Individual/psychological
3. Dyadic relationship or couple dynamics
4. Intergenerational influences (patterns, values, attachment style, etc.)
5. Society/culture/history/religion

This paradigm is now being embraced by systems thinkers as reflected in the number of marriage and family programs that use the first edition of this text. Nonetheless, the traditional sex therapy practitioners still appear to be wedded to the individual, behaviorally oriented approach as evidenced by the lack of integrative workshops at sex therapy conferences and publications and the lack of attention to theory in sex therapy. The Intersystem Approach provides the foundation for the therapist developing a comprehensive case formulation, which will be described in our forthcoming revised companion volume, *A Clinician's Guide to Systemic Sex Therapy, Second Edition* and was described in the first edition. Additionally, treatment is organized around individual, couple, intergenerational, and the larger elements of the environmental system as described above. The major components of systems should be simultaneously considered when treating any client systems.

Major Domains of the Intersystem Approach

Individual/Biological. A couple is composed of two individuals, each with distinct biological and medical backgrounds. Since biological features differ for each partner, it is critical for the therapist to consider the influences of each individual's biology and medical concerns on the relationship and its effect on a couple's sexual problems. For example, in the treatment of erectile dysfunction, therapists are well advised to consider any medical problems potentially contributing to the dysfunction as well as hormonal issues that may be affecting the condition. In addition, certain medications can also impact one's sexual function. SSRIs (selective serotonin reuptake inhibitors) can have significant sexual side effects including diminished libido and delayed/absent orgasm. It is imperative for therapists to acquire a list of all medications, dosages, action of the medications, and duration of medication treatment. Once the therapist identifies how medications, drugs, or medical conditions might impact sexual functioning, the treating physicians should be contacted in order to collaborate about available alternatives.

Individual/Psychological. The therapist then assesses the individual psychological structures of each partner. Psychological make-up is composed of personality (including personality disorders), psychopathology, intelligence, temperament, developmental stages and deficits, attitudes, values, and defense mechanisms, etc. It is through our psychological composition that we learn to understand sexuality and develop personal ways to experience and express it. For example, a person suffering with depression may not feel desire to engage in sexual activity, particularly if the depression is related to the relationship in some way. One's sexual intelligence may also have been acquired in such a way that elicits guilt about particular sexual activities, thus inhibiting the sexual response. The individual client's psychological temperament is evaluated through inquiry about both a sexual history and familial history. There may be a history of depression, anxiety, or other psychological issues as well as covert messages about sexuality impacting the current relationship. In some cases the therapist may want to conduct traditional psychological testing.

Dyadic/Couple Relationship. As stated, traditional sex therapy did not assess and treat sexual problems from a systems perspective as proposed by Weeks (2005). Although it is important to assess the individual patterns of each partner, our approach goes one step further and addresses how these individual influences manifest within the couple by affecting how the partners manage such issues as conflict, communication, intimacy, etc. (see Weeks & Fife, 2014). For example, in cases involving low desire, one partner may not feel desire nor consider the lack of desire to be problematic to the relationship while the other partner is greatly distressed by it. A therapist working from a systemic perspective may identify the partner who is indifferent to the lack of interest/desire as having some fears toward intimacy. In some cases, the higher desire partner might also have underlying fears of intimacy, which predisposes a tolerance for the lack of desire or sexual activity on the part of the lower desire partner. In other words, there can be an unconscious collusion that is expressed by both partners to avoid sexual intimacy. In understanding these dynamics, the therapist recognizes and addresses the individual and couple domains in sustaining a sexual problem.

Family-of-Origin Factors. Individuals learn about relationships and sexuality in their families. Internalized messages about sexuality can be obvious or covert yet they find expression within the intimate relationship. For example, some families do not discuss sexuality openly. Consequently, children in these families may conclude that sexuality is inherently unspeakable and, thus, bad. In such cases, future expression of sexuality is often minimized. This can be problematic as these children become adults and begin to struggle with their emerging sexual feelings. They may in turn tell themselves that they are "bad" for having sexual feelings, thus impacting their self-esteem and inevitably their relationships. Some parents are overt in their condemnation of sexual behavior, again creating internal struggles for their children as they grow into adulthood and develop intimate relationships. Evidence of this impact is documented in research demonstrating that children from dysfunctional families with or without sexual abuse can lead to sexual dysfunctions such as low desire or interest in sex (Kinzl, Mangweth, Traweger, & Biebl, 1996; Kinzl, Traweger, & Biebl, 1995). Therapists can assess for information about family history via a relationship/sexual genogram (see Belous, Timm, Chee, & Whitehead, 2012; Berman, 1999; Berman & Hof, 1987). For more detailed information about this approach, consult DeMaria, Weeks, and Hof (1999).

Society/Culture/History/Religion. Sexuality is viewed through the lens of one's culture (Graham & Hall, 2013) and other environmental factors such as race, ethnicity, socio-economic status, and physical environment. Couples need to understand that sexual beliefs, expectations, preferences, and behaviors are based on their background; the culture and history in which they were raised and are psychologically embedded in the individual partners and seek expression in the relationship. These environmental influences shape one's customs, and values around sexuality and sexual expression. As norms change, couples should work to understand the extent to which culture and contemporary society have played into their decision-making, values, and behaviors as a couple. See McGoldrick, Loonan, and Wohlsifer (2007) and Hall and Graham (2012) for further elaboration on these concepts.

In short, the Intersystem Approach was designed to integrate the individual, couple dyad, intergenerational (family-of-origin), and environmental domains, which may be affecting sexual functioning. Integration begins during the assessment phase with a case conceptualization of the couple based on the Intersystem Approach. Treatment follows from the case formulation. Therapists using this approach should be knowledgeable in the areas of systems theory, couple and family therapy, sex therapy, and individual therapy. Each of these therapeutic modalities would be reflected in the way the therapist thinks about the problem and intervenes in a particular case. Because attention is needed in so many different systems, the therapist must have mastery of multiple therapeutic modalities. Of course this task is a difficult framework to master, especially for therapists who have not been trained extensively in all these treatment modalities.

Integrational Constructs of the Intersystem Approach

In the previous discussion, we explained that a metatheory provided rules, principles, and integrational concepts that allow us to understand and treat behavior from a larger perspective; thus, a metatheory needs to have integrational constructs that unify many differential theories of behavior (VanKaam, 1969). In the Intersystem Approach, the integrational constructs described below allow the therapist to transcend the limits of the differential theories because these concepts are universal or cut across all domains of behavior and specific theories. In other words, the theory has multiple domains to which the therapist must simultaneously attend (individual, couple, family-of-origin, outer influences). There are specific theories within each domain such as cognitive therapy within the individual domain and so on. The integrational concepts are not specific to any one sphere, but apply in each domain thus helping us to see or tie together the different domains of behavior. We will now discuss three sets of integrational constructs: theory of interaction, theory of love, and attachment theory.

Theory of Interaction

We will begin with a theory of interaction that serves as one set of integrational constructs. Grounded in a social-psychological model, the theory of interaction posits that there are intrapsychic (individual/psychological) and interactional (relational) components active in every relationship (Strong & Claiborn, 1982). We apply the theory of interaction to working with couples within the context of sex therapy. Below we will review the integrational components and discuss their implications in sex therapy treatment. We consider the six components of their theory to be one of the three sets of integrational constructs of the Intersystem Approach. In Figure 3.1 (below), we did not include the fact that for each integrational construct it may be important to view it from a behavioral, affective, and cognitive perspective nor do we include the integrational construction. The figure is designed to show the major components of approach.

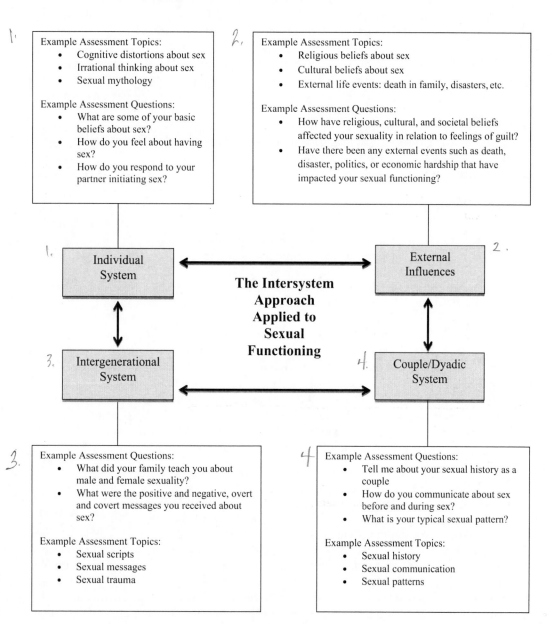

Figure 3.1 The Intersystem Approach showing the four systems and examples for sex therapy (adapted from Weeks, 1994).

how can you integrate this w/ your fam sys. theory

Intrapsychic Components of the Theory of Interaction

There are three intrapsychic components: interpretation, definition, and prediction. The first component of the theory of interaction is interpretation.

Interpretation. Interpretation refers to the meaning that is ascribed to an event, behavior, or problem. This is relevant to couples in that they may interpret their partner's behavior inaccurately or may not understand the intent of the behavior. One's understanding of another's behavior is often grounded in previous experiences and learning histories. A partner who suffers from low desire may have a partner who interprets their behavior as unloving, uncaring, or withholding. This attribution, though potentially incorrect, will be that which underlies the partner's future behavior and views about the relationship.

Definition. The second intrapsychic component is definition. The reciprocal or circular nature of how the relationship defines each partner and how each partner defines the relationship is called definition. Sager (1976) indicated definitions and expectations can be conscious and articulated, conscious and not articulated, or unconscious (and therefore not articulated). These definitions and expectations can infiltrate our view of our relationship, without our knowledge, and influence our cognitions, affect, and behavior. Partners might have discrepant expectations about the frequency of sexual activity and the range of acceptable sexual behaviors. If these expectations are articulated, partners can come to some agreement on the frequency and behaviors, which will constitute part of their relationship. If these expectations are not articulated or are unconscious, communication problems or conflict may develop between the couple and it then becomes incumbent upon the therapist to help the couple address the unspoken disappointments in expectations. This means the partners must become aware of their unconscious expectations, articulate them to each other, and then reach some consensus. Each partner will try to define the relationship and the relationship will define the partner's behavior. For example, each partner may believe they should be more experimental sexually, but as a couple they agree that they will have sex in a routine way.

Prediction. The third intrapsychic component, prediction, addresses the notion that to some degree, we have a tendency to try to predict one's behavior, thoughts, or a particular outcome. Couples in sex therapy may not complete homework assignments, for example, because they anticipate failure. Unfortunately, when couples evade homework or sexual contact, sexual avoidance becomes a self-perpetuating pattern. It is quite common to prescribe a sensate focus exercise only to find that the couple circumvented doing it. If one partner avoided the homework, then the other partner may begin to predict they will continue to avoid the homework and not progress in therapy.

Interactional Components of the Theory of Interaction

The three interactional components address the systemic aspects of relationships; these include congruence, interdependence, and attributional strategy.

Congruence. This integrational component refers to the degree to which a couple can share or agree about how events are defined. A husband may consider his wife's online chatting with other men as a form of infidelity while the wife does not. The perceptions of the event may be incongruent, but the couple can also agree that they define infidelity differently, thus being congruent in that aspect of the definition. Another example is where one partner believes that sexual frequency is adequate and their partner disagrees. This could be considered as incongruence in their perceptions or behaviors. In general, couple's with a higher sense of congruence will have fewer problems because they tend to agree about more areas of the relationship.

Interdependence. The extent to which a partner depends on and trusts the other will determine the level of reliance that the other will meet their needs. This can include how one meets the other's emotional as well as sexual requirements. For example, a husband may believe that he is meeting his wife's sexual needs, but the wife does not agree. In fact, she believes that her husband will never be able to meet her sexual needs. Couples who have relatively high levels of interdependence typically proceed through treatment quicker and with a lower frequency of dropping out than couples with lower levels of interdependence because they have a tendency to view the relationship as one where they will be able to have their needs fulfilled. They believe they will eventually get what they need from their partner. In couples with lower levels of interdependence, discussion of commitment may accompany a conversation about how each fulfills the other or is perceived as not being willing or able to meet their partner's needs. Low level interdependence couples may also be more vulnerable to infidelity as one or both partners may believe that their needs are best met or can only be met outside of the primary relationships (Weeks, Gambescia, & Jenkins, 2003). Therapists should be attuned to the couple's interdependence level and assess whether a conversation about commitment is warranted. Further, therapists should also address whether the need fulfillment the partners have identified is realistic and help the couple develop realistic expectations or needs.

Attributional strategy. This third interactional component refers to the manner in which partners ascribe meaning to an event. It is similar to the concept of interpretation discussed earlier, and, in this context, specifically means whether a couple relates in a linear or circular fashion to one another. In a linear attribution strategy, couples attribute their partner's behavior (effect) to a stimulus (cause). A husband, for instance, might report that his wife "makes" him angry when she nags him about household chores; a wife might state that she cannot achieve orgasm because her husband's so called premature ejaculation does not permit her to do so. Blaming is the hallmark of negative linear attribution and is highly correlated with relational dissatisfaction (Gottman, 1994). In circular attribution strategies, partners examine the impact of their behavior on the other. They understand the interlocking nature of the relationship and the reciprocal influence that each has on the other. In this case, the wife might state overtly that sex with her partner is not something she enjoys, thus sustaining her partner's premature ejaculation. The male partner might agree that he knows his wife does not enjoy sex with him and tries to complete the act of intercourse as quickly as possible.

Reframing is one technique sex therapists can use to help the couple move from linear and blaming statements to a circular, positive view. Weeks and Fife (2014) discuss reframing in its application to all types of problems. Weeks and Gambescia (2000, 2002) discuss reframes for sexual problems. The therapist might reframe the wife's displeasure in the above example and the manifestation of premature ejaculation in the relationship as each partner trying desperately to protect one another so hard that they end up failing sexually, which paradoxically reflects how much they care about each other. He protects her by having sex quickly because he knows she doesn't enjoy it, and she protects him from having to confront his premature ejaculation by having no or little desire, which leads to an avoidance of sex. This shifts the focus of the problem from a linear, individually focused problem to a relationship problem.

41

commitment (cognitive)

GERALD R. WEEKS AND NANCY GAMBESCIA

intimacy
(closeness)

passion

2. Triangular Theory of Love

Another integrational construct that we use in the Intersystem Approach is Sternberg's (1986) triangular theory of love. Sternberg, a social psychologist, believed that there are three components of love: (1) commitment, (2) intimacy, and (3) passion, and that each of these components interact with one another in our relationships. The first component of the triangle, commitment, refers to the cognitive element of love; that is, the determination of whether couples stay together. Intimacy, the second component, describes the amount of closeness partners feel toward one another. This includes the extent of trust in the relationship, feelings of mutual respect, and the bond each would describe they have to the other partner. The final component of the triangle is passion or the affection, feelings of longing to be together, and the sexual attraction a couple demonstrates in a relationship.

While Sternberg (1986) advanced the idea of the triangle to be used as a whole rather than utilizing the parts individually (all three components are necessary for adult loving relationships), this model has often been used in isolated components. Sex therapists might traditionally focus on the passion element, while traditional couple therapists might focus on intimacy and commitment. This division of this theory can have significant treatment implications. For example, underlying fears of intimacy or varying levels of commitment might impact one's level of passion toward their partner. Therapists who do not address all aspects of the triangle may be vulnerable to treating one or two of three elements by focusing on the etiology deriving from just that/those elements. Addressing a problem from all three perspectives gives us a more complete picture of how sexuality functions within their system. A therapist working from an integrative stance will consider the interlocking nature of all three components of the triangle. Sexual problems do not just occur in the passion segment of the triangle, but stem from other parts, as we will demonstrate in subsequent chapters, especially the chapter on low sexual desire.

3. Attachment Styles

The Intersystem Approach also incorporates attachment theory, specifically attachment styles, as an integrational construct. Bowlby (1973, 1982) conceptualized attachment as a fundamental component of human nature. The patterns of emotional connection between people are established in the family-of-origin and remain fixed or become modified in subsequent dyadic relationships, such as the choice of a life partner, how one relates to their significant other, and manner of connecting to one's children.

A number of theorists have written about attachment styles, often describing the same concepts using inconsistent language and labeling. The most common terminology used to refer to adult attachment styles is: secure, fearful-avoidant, preoccupied, and dismissive (Locke, 2008). The attachment styles are as follows:

1. Secure (low anxiety and low avoidance)
2. Fearful-Avoidant (high anxiety and high avoidance)
3. Preoccupied: (high anxiety and low avoidance)
4. Dismissive: (high avoidance and low anxiety)

Within the last decade, researchers have begun to consider how attachment style affects sexual functioning. This application of attachment theory has not created a significant volume of research, but we expect that it will in the future. Nonetheless, we suggest that in treating sexual problems it is essential to consider the attachment style of each partner.

Actually, Laschinger et al. (2004) recommended that human sexuality could not be separated from attachment style, social, and cultural contexts based simply on their clinical experience. Additionally, Burchell and Ward (2011) considered how attachment style predicted a person's reaction to spousal infidelity. They noted that previous research has generally found that women were more threatened by emotional infidelity and men by sexual infidelity. However, they found that preoccupied men were more likely to be threatened by emotional affairs and avoidant women more likely to be distressed by sexual infidelity. The effect was modest yet illustrated that attachment style can override the typical pattern of jealously.

Attachment style can also affect sexual and emotional satisfaction. Individuals with a preoccupied-insecure attachment style were found to be less satisfied sexually due to inhibited communication. Additionally, this subgroup used sex as a barometer of their status within the relationship, monitoring partners for availability; partner sexual availability reduced anxiety in the preoccupied-insecure attachment. Conversely, partner unavailability precipitated sexual avoidance. See Brassard et al. (2012), Birnbaum et al. (2006), and Mikulincer and Shaver (2007) for a greater elaboration of attachment styles on sexual and relationship.

Johnson and Zuccarini (2010) developed an integrated theory of attachment and human sexuality and provided a comprehensive review of studies on the relationship between the two. They found there is growing evidence between attachment styles, engagement in sexuality, and types of problems that might occur. In general, their review of the research showed that attachment styles are associated with different reasons for engaging in sex. Partners with a secure attachment style wanted to increase their sense of closeness while anxious-insecure partners wanted to have sex to feel reassured or avoid feelings of rejection. Based on their clinical experience, anxious-insecure partners were hypersensitive to any deficiency in their companion's response to them. Insecure-avoidant partners tend to focus on their own pleasure and not focus on the emotional connection between partners. Avoidant partners dislike affection. No research was reviewed involving insecure-dismissive partners. The theory is fairly general thus specific hypothesis were not formally proposed. There is certainly enough exploration to show that attachment theory affects how partners relate to each other in general and sexually. The specific relationship between attachment style and adult loving, sexual engagement, and sexual problems will require additional empirical inquiry and produce much more clarification in the future.

Bringing It Together: An Integrative Paradigm

We discussed that the field of sex therapy has been tightly wedded to the behavioral model (i.e., Kaplan, 1974; Leiblum & Rosen, 1988, 2000; Leiblum, 2007; Masters & Johnson, 1970) and more recently to cognitive-behavioral approaches and medical interventions. Our framework provides a balanced effort toward understanding sexual problems from multiple perspectives as well as addressing the cognitive, behavioral, and emotional components of sexual problems. This distinction is critical because cognition in sexual problems is typically significantly overlooked (see chapter on low desire in this text for research in this area).

The negative thoughts accompanying sexual behavior should always be identified and countered by promoting the use of positive thoughts. This cognitive modality should be a focus of diagnosis and treatment because it helps both the couple and therapist understand how negative thought patterns can have a negative impact on sexual functioning and the relationship (Weeks & Gambescia, 2000). For example, Weeks and Gambescia (2002) presented ideas for addressing cognitive and affective elements in the treatment of low desire and sexual dysfunction. Also, we encourage therapists to be purposeful in providing assignments to the couple, and assessing the couples feelings and thoughts related to their problem and their feeling and thoughts about the homework given, which is one of the hallmarks of sex therapy. This attention to thoughts and feeling would communicate the therapist's warmth, genuineness, and caring attitude toward the clients. The joining relationship is enhanced and leads to greater compliance on the part of the clients when thought and feeling are not ignored.

The case example below shows how the Intersystem Approach can be applied. All the various components of the model are addressed and the reader will note that the therapist asked them about their thoughts and feelings as reflected in what each one said.

Case Example[1]

Randy and Martha, each in their mid 40s, have been married for 15 years and have two children. Randy works as an executive for a software company and Martha is a manager of a retail store. Martha is attending treatment at her husband's insistence due to her lack of interest and desire in sex. This case is analyzed from the perspective of the major domains of the approach and the three major integrational constructs, which involve more specific constructs.

Intersystem Domains

Individual

Martha reported while she had been experiencing lack of desire for several years, it was really within the last few years that she noticed it had worsened. In addition to the lack of sexual appetite, she noted that she felt more angry and depressed over the past few years. Prescribed Effexor three months ago by her physician, she noted that her lack of desire further deteriorated along with her ability to orgasm. She cited her relationship with Randy as a main source of her anxiety and depression and expressed significant concern about wanting to feel desire for Randy's sake but not being able to do so. Randy noted that he had been feeling hopeless over the last few months, especially since Martha indicated things became worse after taking Effexor. Randy viewed Martha's lack of desire as intentionally withholding and had initially been angry with her. He was now filled with resignation and resentment. Finally, while the couple agreed that Martha was depressed, Randy saw no part that he played in her depression.

Couple

Randy and Martha had little time together based on job schedules and household responsibilities. Martha reported that Randy often agreed to "help" with things around the house, but rarely if ever followed through with such promises. Further, reported anger and resentment toward Randy when he would offer to "help," as she saw this as still placing her in the role of household manager. Randy, who had narcissistic personality traits, overtly defined Martha to be deliberately sexually withholding. Martha tried desperately to comply with his requests, as she had a dependent personality. Martha unconsciously used sexuality as one way to gain an upper hand in the relationship. Because the conflict between the couple was, for the most part, expressed covertly, there was tension between the couple.

44

Family-of-Origin

Randy and Martha indicated they remained connected to one another over the years because of their common familial background and perceived similarities due to the dynamics related to their respective alcoholic families. Randy stated that his mother treated him as an equal rather than a child. He saw himself as a parentified child. Martha shared a similar role in her family, as a caretaker. As an attempt to seek love and acceptance in their extra-familial lives, each had experienced sex at an early age, and still had yet to resolve the guilt over this issue. Further, Martha's family was highly religious and she expressed guilt about having sex at all in addition to experiencing it early in life.

External Factors

Despite the degree of dysfunction in Martha and Randy's families of origin, divorce was a rare phenomenon in their family histories. Only one uncle on Randy's side was divorced, and the circumstances were that he had married young and was divorced within a short time. As mentioned above, Randy and Martha are active in their local religious organization and believe in intact families. The couple also indicated that there were few people within their social network who were divorced.

Sternberg's Triangular Theory of Love Constructs

Commitment

Martha suggests that despite her lack of desire in the last few years, she is still very committed to her marriage and her family. Randy, too, reports that he is loyal to Martha. Further, both believe in negative spiritual implications for divorced couples.

Intimacy

While both Martha and Randy worked long hours at their respective jobs, Martha resented that she was primarily in charge of the household tasks and custodian to the children. Also, she felt that she was taking on increasing responsibilities in the household while Randy's tasks remained the same. As a result, the couple had difficulty setting aside time for togetherness. As such, they failed to take responsibility for enjoyment, recreation, and socializing together. Martha had been socialized from a young age to be more nurturing than sexual while Randy learned to suppress vulnerabilities in order to preserve his self-worth and competence. His impassiveness made it difficult for Martha to connect with Randy on an intimate level as that side of him is more guarded. Over time, Martha learned to be more selective about the vulnerabilities she shared with Randy because she had been hurt in the past by his limited expression of feelings.

Passion

The couple agreed that, while both loved one another, their sexual relationship, which manifested the most significant amount of passion in their relationship, was largely absent as a result of Martha's lack of interest and avoidance of sex. She did not view sexuality as an important of an aspect in the relationship, and with the problems mentioned above, nothing was happening to foster sexual desire. Thus she did not feel individual distress over her lack of desire but wanted to feel desire for the sake of the relationship; Randy did express concern about their discordant levels of sexual desire.

Theory of Interaction Constructs

Interpretation

Martha believes that her lack of desire toward Randy is a response to how she is treated by him (i.e., resents his controlling behavior, so she controls their sex life). Randy interprets her lack of desire as something that she is intentionally doing to punish him and does not believe that his attitude toward her has any influence on her actions.

Definition

Both Randy and Martha define the problem as significantly impairing their relationship but are not willing to divorce. Thus, they are stuck in a gridlock of resentment and misattribution. They are unable to view the lack of desire in terms of their own behavior and differ on how they define the level of desire each should have: Randy simply says Martha has too little, while Martha says Randy has too much.

Prediction

Randy indicated that he feels hopeless, and predicts that nothing will change in the future until Martha gets some help. Martha believes that Randy's behavior or attitude toward her will not change in the future, thus resulting in more of the same for both. Though both are hopeful that therapy may improve the desire issue, they are unable to see how it might have a larger impact on their relationship.

Congruence

Randy believes the problem is that Martha has too little desire and Martha sees Randy as having too much desire. Thus, the couple's definitions of the problem are incongruent. As a result, the couple has difficulty agreeing on goals for treatment.

Interdependence

While both partners are extremely frustrated and pessimistic, they do not recognize how their personalities balance one another in the perpetuation of their stalemate. At an unconscious level, Martha vicariously experiences Randy's narcissism and control as something she lacks and is therefore drawn toward it. Randy sees Martha's dependence as a good match to his controlling personality because she is willing to comply with most of his sexual needs.

Attribution

As discussed earlier, Martha blames her lack of desire on Randy (linear), just as Randy blames her lack of desire on her unwillingness or withholding (linear). Neither party entertains the notion that each might have some influence on the other's behavior, affect, and cognitions.

Once this assessment across multiple areas is made, the therapist can develop a comprehensive case conceptualization. The therapist has multiple areas of intervention and can develop a treatment plan that prioritizes and sequences the goals of treatment. Some problems in the couple's relationship must be attended to prior to other problems. In general, relationship problems take priority over sexual problems. A couple with relationship problems will not be able to progress in sex therapy if they are in conflict, have difficulties in communication, intimacy, etc.

Attachment Style Constructs

Randy grew up in a family where the parents were uninvolved in his life. He developed an avoidant attachment style. Randy desperately wanted Martha to have more desire so he could have his sexual needs fulfilled. His controlling behavior was an attempt to get her to give him what he wanted. When he was unable to get the response he wanted from her, he suppressed his vulnerability and became even more controlling. Martha grew up in a family where her parents' love, attention, and approval were contingent on her doing what they wanted. She wanted their love and approval so she became anxious about doing the "right" thing and tried to conform to their wishes. Martha demonstrated dependent personality traits; however, she did not like being controlled. She felt she had been controlled growing up and now wanted freedom and unconditional love, but unconsciously chose someone who would not be able to give her the love and affection she desired. The hurt and rejection she suffered in her early years was being replayed in the current relationship. Her typical response to Randy's demands was to withdraw in order to protect herself from feeling further rejection.

Suggestions for Moving Toward Greater Integration

As sex therapy moves from a fragmented to more integrated framework, changes at multiple levels can help us achieve this goal. These modifications cannot all be implemented immediately; however, the spirit of the following suggestions is to continue to push the field of sex therapy into developing a comprehensive theoretical framework.

Envision Sexual Problems From an Expansive, Multivariate Framework

The etiology of sexual problems must be conceptualized by using multiple perspectives as described above. Then, integrative theories can be developed for assessment and treatment. For example, sex therapists should consider the impact of medications or organic conditions on sexual functioning. These factors can have significant implications for the couple's relationship. Essentially, organic factors, including medication effects, can create complications, which increase performance anxiety regarding sexual functioning. Additionally, individual issues such as personality problems and major mental illnesses, like depression, can affect one's sexual functioning. Finally, a conflicted couple or a couple with other relationship problems will be more vulnerable to sexual problems.

Expand the Context of Treatment Beyond the Use of Medications

A strictly medical conceptualization can be problematic because medications have rarely been effective for the treatment of a majority of sexual difficulties, as will be demonstrated throughout this book. The medical agenda is driven by pharmaceutical companies and does not address the variety of other comorbid etiologies. Likewise, therapists need to recognize that there may be an organic component to a sexual dysfunction that is primarily psychogenic. In fact, mixed organic and psychogenic etiologies are common in sexual issues, especially among older couples. A medical evaluation will address any organic issues that might be best served through medical intervention; however, collaboration with the medical team is always most beneficial when medications or organic problems are known to affect sexuality. The therapist can provide education regarding the potential multiple causes of sexual problems to physicians, therapists, and their clients. Clients seem predisposed to want simple explanations for complex sexual issues. Even when the etiology is primarily organic, the sexual symptoms produce anxiety in each partner and stress in the relationship.

Expand Clinical and Research Realms by the Use of: (1) Comprehensive Conceptual Frameworks, (2) Theoretical Models, and (3) Metatheoretical Issues

The field of sex therapy is in need of additional theories that explain the relationship between factors and can be verified through scholarly research. We promote and encourage more theory building in our field. Journal editors and reviewers should be more aware of the inclusion and integration of theory in scholarly articles and must encourage theory-based submissions. Also, sex therapy must have a significant position within the larger context of medical and psychological healthcare. Presently it is viewed as a small separate discipline and profession, which involves discussing issues that many couples as well as therapists are uncomfortable approaching. Graduate training programs in marriage and family therapy, psychology, counseling, psychiatry, medicine, nursing, and other healthcare programs should integrate sex therapy more extensively and intensively in their training. Once included, sex therapy can be integrated with the knowledge in that particular area rather than discussed as a separate and distinct topic.

We invite professional organizations such as AAMFT, ACA, and AASECT to bridge the gap between the fields with a commitment to treating sexual problems. These organizations could consistently work to integrate their fields as a way to provide the most comprehensive education about sex therapy treatment. Yet, these organizations appear to be completely disinterested or opposed to such cooperation. Currently clinical training is limited to the curriculum standards relevant to each discipline, with minimal focus on other disciplines. The focus on sexuality could be strengthened in many disciplines. In reality, we do not see any circumstance where this is likely and only a few theorists in each discipline are advocating for better training standards and integration.

Facilitate Movement Away From Theoretical Purism

As stated, the current emphasis on cognitive-behavioral and medical approaches is too narrow. What then happens is the client must conform to the treatment rather than the treatment being tailored to the client. We believe integrative theorists who consider multiple views in their approach to sex therapy should receive more attention and be more active in submitting articles for publication. The integrative theorists could be invited to give talks at the major sex and couple therapy conferences and journals editors could encourage submission of articles that will further enhance the field. What would be absolutely astounding is if one of the conferences had, as it major theme, the integration of sex and marital therapy that Weeks described in his 1987 text.

tailor the treatment to the client.

The gap between research and practice in sex therapy must be eliminated, allowing for exploration of the ways in which sex therapy is informed by research and generating research questions based on treatment. Bridging this gap will inspire therapists to employ best practices and limit the risk of considering only one theoretical approach. While this idea is promoted within the field of psychotherapy in general, little ever seems to happen. Special forums at conferences could be established bringing together researchers and therapists and journal editors could invite a dialogue between leading researchers and clinicians as they have done with other topics.

Conduct More Research on the Interface Between Diversity and Sexual Problems

Diversity research in psychotherapy has been advancing over the past decade, but inadequate attention is given to diversity in sex research and therapy. Little is known about how different ethnic groups and cultures view their sexuality. We see numerous clinical presentations of the impact of specific cultural scripts on sexuality yet the research, especially empirical research, is lagging behind leaving a void in the field.

The Future of Theory in Sex Therapy

In the past 20 years, sex therapists have been virtually silent in the production of better psychotherapeutic treatment methodologies. Many of the developments in the field have been driven by improvements in the medical community. Some of the medical advances have produced successful treatments while others have not; nonetheless, researchers are quite energetic in finding new ways to intervene medically. The medicalization of sex therapy has promoted the view that some sexual problems, mostly ED, should be treated in a medical framework, virtually ignoring the importance of recognizing and treating psychological factors. Moving forward, we trust that the partnership between therapists and physicians will continue to develop and promote more comprehensive treatment of sexual problems.

Another major issue in the field of sex therapy is the conspicuous absence of theoretical integration of the many sexual and psychological modalities. With few exceptions, the field lacks the necessary coordination of areas such as couple and sex therapies, medical, and individual treatments. An integrative paradigm shift, such as the one proposed in this text, encourages sex therapists to develop a unified case formulation, which then leads to an integrative approach to treatment, and a more comprehensive perspective on sexual problems and sex therapy.

We advocate a paradigm shift, which encourages therapists and researchers to consider etiology and interventions from multiple perspectives. Also, we anticipate this goal to be a work in progress. Justifiably, we are cautious of approaches that are offered as "complete" theoretical models. The field of sex therapy is still quite young. For instance, we continue to expand our understanding of some of the basics of human sexuality such as the definition of desire and the gender differences related to sexual interest. As we acquire more information about sexuality, we can better understand how it relates to sexual problems.

As stated, researchers are strongly inclined to study various aspects of sexual behavior without a theoretical framework; thus, new discoveries do not necessarily facilitate the development of new therapies. Many of the studies reviewed in this volume reveal various etiologies for sexual problems, but fail to integrate them into existing treatments or offer very few new approaches to psychotherapeutic treatment. We are encouraged when reading recent empirical research that moderately supports the Intersystem Approach. For instance, Monteiro, Narcisco, and Pereira (2014) investigated the meaning of sexual satisfaction for couples in exclusive relationships. They revealed a two-dimensional model, consistent with systems theory, that best explained their data. The two main dimensions were personal sexual well-being (e.g., positive feelings, pleasure, openness, and arousal/desire) and dyadic process (e.g., creativity, frequency of sex, romance, expression of feelings, and mutuality). They asserted these two dimensions were inseparable in understanding sexual satisfaction. This study links individual and couple domains of the system. Our model is even more inclusive.

In summary, the goal of this volume is to organize research and theories in order to present an integrative approach to understanding and treating the various sexual disorders. Currently, much more research is needed to answer fundamental questions regarding the definition and clinical criteria for some problems, especially low desire. Each chapter in this volume is organized around four domains of behavior; therefore, the reader is helped to consider etiologic contributions that stem from the individual, the couple, family-of-origin, and socio-cultural factors. Without a comprehensive assessment, the clinician will not know what contributed to the problem and not be able to develop a sequenced and comprehensive treatment plan. The Intersystem Approach is our effort to promote the best treatment possible for sexual/relational issues now and in the future.

Note

1. This case represents a typical composite of low sexual desire clients.

References

Allgeier, E. R. (Ed.). (1998). The use of theory in research and scholarship on sexuality [Special Issue]. *Journal of Sex and Research*, 35(1), 1–9.

American Association of Sexuality Educators, Counselors and Therapists. (2004). AASECT home page. Retrieved from http://www.aasect.org

Belous, C., Timm, T., Chee, G., & Whitehead, M. (2012). Revisiting the sexual genogram. *The American Journal of Family Therapy*, 40, 281–296. doi: 10.1080/01926187.2011.627317

Berman, E. (1999). Gender, sexuality, and romantic love genograms. In R. DeMaria, G. Weeks, & L. Hof (Eds.), *Focused genograms: Intergenerational assessment of individuals, couples, and families* (pp. 145–176). New York: Brunner/Mazel.

Berman, E., & Hof, L. (1987). The sexual genogram—Assessing family-of-origin factors in the treatment of sexual dysfunction. In G. Weeks & L. Hof (Eds.), *Integrating sex and marital therapy: A clinical guide* (pp. 37–56). New York: W. W. Norton.

Birnbaum, G. E., Reis, H. T., Mikulincer, M., Gillath, O., & Orpaz, A. (2006). When sex is more than just sex: Attachment orientations, sexual experience, and relationship quality. *Journal of Personality and Social Psychology*, 91(5), 929–943. doi: 10.1080/00224490609552332

Bowlby, J. (1973). *Attachment and loss: Vol. 2. Separation, anxiety and anger*. New York: Basic Books.

Bowlby, J. (1982). *Attachment and loss: Vol. 1. Attachment* (2nd ed.). New York: Basic Books.

Brassard, A., Peloquin, K., Dupuy, E., Wright, J., & Shaver, P. (2012). Romantic attachment insecurity predicts sexual dissatisfaction in couples seeking marital therapy. *Journal of Sex & Marital Therapy*, 38(3), 245–262. doi: 10.1080/0092623X.2011.606881

Burchell, J., & Ward, J. (2011). Sex drive, attachment style, relationship status and previous infidelity as predictors of sex differences in romantic jealously. *Personality and Individual Differences*, 51(5), 657–661. doi: 10.1016/j.paid.2011.06.002

Commission on Accreditation for Marriage and Family Therapy Education. (2005). COAAMFT educational guidelines. Retrieved from http://www.aamft.org/imis15/Documents/COAMFTE_MFT_Educational_Guidelines.pdf

Council for Accreditation of Counseling and Related Educational Programs (CACREP). (2009). CACREP 2009 standards. Retrieved from http://www.cacrep.org/doc/2009%20Standards%20with%20cover.pdf

DeMaria, R., Weeks, G., & Hof, L. (1999). *Focused genograms: Intergenerational assessment of individuals, couples, and families.* New York: Brunner/Mazel.

Dubois, S. L., & Wiederman, M. W. (1997, June). The journal of sex and marital therapy: A content analysis of articles from 1974–1995. Paper presented at the annual meeting of the Mid-continent Region Society for the Scientific Study of Sexuality, Chicago.

Gottman, J. (1994). *What predicts divorce: The relationship between marital processes and marital outcomes.* Hillsdale, NJ: Lawrence Erlbaum.

Graham, C. A., & Hall, K. (Eds.). (2013). *The cultural context of sexual pleasure and problems: psychotherapy with diverse clients.* New York: Routledge.

Gurman, A. (2008). Integrative couple therapy: A depth-behavioral approach. In A. Gurman (Ed.), *Clinical handbook of couple therapy* (4th ed., pp. 383–423). New York: Guilford.

Gurman, A., & Fraenkel, P. (2002). The history of couple therapy: A millennial review. *Family Process, 41*(2), 199–260.

Hall, K., & Graham, C. (Eds.). (2012). *The cultural context of sexual pleasure and problems.* New York: Routledge.

Hertlein, K. M., Weeks, G. R., & Gambescia, N. (Eds.). (2009). *Systemic sex therapy.* New York: Routledge.

Johnson, S., & Zuccarini, D. (2010). Integrating sex and attachment in emotionally focused couple therapy. *Journal of Marital and Family Therapy, 36,* 431–445. doi: 10.1111/j.1752-0606.2009.00155.x

Kaplan, H. S. (1988). *The illustrated manual of sex therapy* (2nd ed.). New York: Brunner/Routledge.

Kaplan, H. S. (1974). *The new sex therapy.* New York: Brunner/Mazel.

Kinzl, J., Mangweth, B., Traweger, C., & Biebl, W. (1996). Sexual dysfunction in males: Significance of adverse childhood experiences. *Child Abuse and Neglect, 20*(8), 759–766.

Kinzl, J., Traweger, C., & Biebl, W. (1995). Sexual dysfunctions: Relationship to childhood sexual abuse and early family experiences in a nonclinical sample. *Child Abuse and Neglect, 19*(7), 785–792.

Laschinger, B., Purnell, C., Schwartz, J., White, K, & Wingfield, R. (2004). Sexuality and attachment from a clinical point of view. *Attachment and Human Development, 6*(2), 151–164. doi: 10.1080/14616730410001688194

Lebow, J. (1997). The integrative revolution in couple and family therapy. *Family Process, 36*(1), 1–17. doi: 10.1111/j.1545-5300.1997.00001

Leiblum, S. R. (Ed.). (2007). *Principles and practice of sex therapy* (4th ed.). New York: Guilford Press.

Leiblum, S. R., & Rosen, R. C. (1988). *Sexual desire disorders.* New York: Guilford Press.

Leiblum, S., & Rosen, R. (1989). *Principles and practice of sex therapy: An update for the 1990s* (2nd ed.). New York: Guilford Press.

Leiblum, S. R., & Rosen, R. C. (Eds.). (2000). *Principles and practice of sex therapy* (3rd ed.). New York: Guilford Press.

Locke, K. (2008). Attachment styles and interpersonal approach and avoidance goals in everyday couple interactions. *Personal Relationships, 15,* 359–374. doi: 10.1111/j.1475–6811.2008.00203.x

LoPiccolo, J., & LoPiccolo, L. (Eds.). (1978). *Handbook of sex therapy.* New York: Plenum.

Masters, W. H., & Johnson, V. (1966). *Human sexual response.* Boston: Little Brown.

Masters, W. H., & Johnson, V. (1970). *Human sexual inadequacy.* Boston: Little, Brown.

McGoldrick, M., Loonan R., & Wohlsifer, D. (2007). Sexuality and culture. In S. R. Leiblum (Ed.), *Principles and practice of sex therapy* (4th ed., pp. 416–441). New York: Guilford Press.

Mikulincer, M., & Shaver, P. R. (2007). *Attachment in adulthood: Structure, dynamics, and change.* New York: Guilford Press.

Monteiro, P., Narcisco, I., & Pereira, N. (2014). What is sexual satisfaction? Thematic analysis of lay people's definitions. *Journal of Sex Research, 51*, 22–30. doi: 10.1080/00224499.2013.815149

Norcross, J. (2005). A primer on psychotherapy integration. In J.C. Norcross & M.R. Goldfried (Eds.), *Handbook of psychotherapy integration* (2nd ed., pp. 3–23). New York: Oxford.

Ruppel, H.J., Jr. (1994). Publications trends in the sexological literature: A comparison of two contemporary journals. (Unpublished doctoral dissertation). Institute for the Advanced Study of Human Sexuality, San Francisco.

Sager, C. (1976). *Marriage contracts and couples therapy.* New York: Brunner/Mazel.

Sternberg, R. (1986). A triangular theory of love. *Psychological Review, 93*(2), 119–135.

Stricker, G., & Gold, J.R. (1996). Psychotherapy integration: An assimilative, psychodynamic approach. *Clinical Psychology: Science and Practice, 3*(1), 47–58. doi: 10.1037/11436–005

Strong, S., & Claiborn, C. (1982). *Change through interaction: Social psychological processes of counseling and psychotherapy.* New York: Wiley.

Van Kaam, A. (1969). *Existential foundations of psychology.* New York: Basic Books.

Weeks, G.R. (Ed.). (1989). *Treating couples: The intersystem model of the marriage council of Philadelphia.* New York: Brunner/Mazel.

Weeks, G. (1994). The intersystem model: An integrative approach to treatment. In G. Weeks & L. Hof (Eds.), *The marital-relationship therapy casebook: Theory and application of the intersystem model* (pp. 3–34). New York: Brunner/Mazel.

Weeks, G. (2005). The emergence of a new paradigm in sex therapy: Integration. *Sexual and Relationship Therapy, 20*(1), 89–103.

Weeks, G., & Cross, C. (2004). The intersystem model of psychotherapy: An integrated systems approach. *Guidance and Counselling, 19*(2), 57–64.

Weeks, G., & Fife, S. (2014). *Couples in treatment.* New York: Routledge.

Weeks, G., & Gambescia, N. (2000). *Erectile dysfunction: Integrating couple therapy, sex therapy, and medical treatment.* New York: W.W. Norton.

Weeks, G., & Gambescia, N. (2002). *Hypoactive sexual desire: Integrating couple and sex therapy.* New York: W.W. Norton.

Weeks, G., Gambescia, N., & Jenkins, R. (2003). *Treating infidelity.* New York: W.W. Norton.

Weeks, G., & Hof, L. (Eds.). (1987). *Integrating sex and marital therapy: A clinical guide.* New York: W.W. Norton.

Wiederman, M. (1998). The state of theory in sex therapy. *Journal of Sex Research, 35*(1), 88–99.

Section 2

TREATMENT OF SPECIFIC DISORDERS

4

MALE HYPOACTIVE SEXUAL DESIRE DISORDER

Kathryn Hall

> The basic conflict between men and women, sexually, is that men are like fire-
> men. To men, sex is an emergency, and no matter what we're doing we can be
> ready in two minutes. Women, on the other hand, are like fire. They're very
> exciting, but the conditions have to be exactly right. . . .
>
> (Seinfeld, 2013).

This joke, and others like it, reflects the cultural belief that men's sex drive is a biological juggernaut unimpeded by emotional or psychological factors. Many men believe this to be true and are ill prepared when reality differs.

While the experience of sexual desire may seem to be straightforward, a closer exami-nation reveals that desire is a complex phenomenon. It is variously described as a moti-vational state, a physiological reaction, an emotional or cognitive condition, or some combination of the above (Regan & Berscheid, 1996). Levine (1987) described desire as the energy brought to sexual behavior that not only precedes sexual arousal but also accompanies arousal throughout sexual activity. Levine notes that male desire is depen-dent on contextual cues, situational and relationship factors, and level of stress. Men's sexual desire is often purported to be stronger in intensity and frequency than women's desire (Baumeister, Catanese, & Vohls, 2001) but others have argued that male and female desire, while sharing many similarities (Janssen et al., 2008) may also be qualitatively dif-ferent (Wallen, 2000).

Perhaps one of the difficulties in defining and understanding sexual desire is that desire is often experienced (or not) in the context of a relationship and yet our diagnostic systems are based on individual psychopathology. Men who have little or no desire for sex may be diagnosed with Hypoactive Sexual Desire Disorder, or HSDD. According to the fifth edition of the Diagnostic and Statistical Manual (*DSM-5*) (APA, 2013) the following four conditions must be met for a diagnosis of HSDD:

1. Deficient or absent sexual thoughts or fantasies
2. Deficient or absent desire for sexual activity
3. Must be of six months duration or longer
4. Must cause clinically significant distress

Interestingly, the severity of this disorder is classified not by the deficiency of the desire, but by the level of distress the disorder produces—mild, moderate, or severe. HSDD may be of lifelong duration or acquired, which presupposes a period of 'normal' sexual desire. HSDD is further divided into generalized or situational subtypes, the latter referring to men who experience desire in some situations (e.g., masturbation, internet pornography, extra-marital relationship) but not in others (e.g., with spouse or long term partner). HSDD that is both acquired and situational is generally considered to be the most common subtype of the disorder (Brotto, 2010; Maurice, 1999), leading Meana and Steiner (2014) to suggest another meaning for HSDD—hidden sexual desire disorder. They coined this term to refer to men who have high levels of sexual interest for partners or sexual activities that are outside the bounds of their committed relationship and which are kept secret from their partners. An example of acquired and situational HSDD would be a preference for masturbating to internet pornography, or an extra marital affair. McCarthy and McDonald (2009) describe a similar pattern for primary (lifelong) HSDD in which they note: "The core issue is usually a sexual secret. By order of frequency, this includes; (1) a variant arousal pattern (deviant arousal is much less common); (2) a preference for masturbatory sex rather than intimate couple sex; (3) a history of poorly processed sexual trauma; or (4) a conflict about sexual orientation" (p. 59). Low frequency of sexual activity is not considered a diagnostic marker for HSDD as sexual activity, especially partnered sex, is affected by factors other than desire (religious beliefs, partner availability, relationship factors, health). Not much, if anything is known about low desire in gay or bisexual men. The majority of research and clinical reports are specific to heterosexual men.

Prevalence

In epidemiological surveys a surprising number of men report a lack of sexual desire. However, there is a great deal of variation in estimated prevalence with figures that range from 3–41% of the population (Brotto, 2010). Conservative estimates place the overall prevalence of low desire in men between 15% and 25% (Lewis et al., 2010; Meana & Steiner, 2014). Lack of desire is clearly related to age, with older men more frequently reporting problems (Laumann, Paik, & Rosen, 1999; Fugl-Meyer & Sjogren Fugl-Meyer, 1999; Eplov et al., 2007; Hyde et al., 2012). The increased prevalence of erectile dysfunction (ED) in older men (Rosen, Miner, & Wincze, 2014) is associated with decreased sexual desire (Corona et al., 2013). Health (physical and psychological) and the health of one's partner are also factors as are individual and relationship stress (Christensen et al., 2011; Corona et al., 2004; Štulhofer, Træen, & Carvalheira, 2013). When surveying men from the same country or culture, no difference is found between ethnic groups in reports of desire problems (Brotto, 2010). It is unclear whether there are cultural variations in the experience of sexual desire as the very few cross-cultural studies suffer from methodological problems that preclude definitive conclusions (Hall & Graham, 2014).

Most if not all of the above mentioned epidemiological surveys do not specifically address duration of low desire or the distress caused by it, so it is unknown how many of the men reporting low desire would actually meet the criteria for a diagnosis of HSDD. Indeed, more men report low desire than seek treatment for the problem (Laumann, Glasser, Neves, & Moreira, 2009; Najman et al., 2003). One might conjecture either that the prevalence estimates are grossly inflating the actual number of men that suffer from HSDD or that shame might cause men to hide the problem rather than seek help. Men are also less likely to be referred to sex therapy clinics if their complaint is first made to a medical practitioner (Kedde, Donker, Leusink, & Kruijer, 2011). Men who do present for sex therapy often do so because of the distress of their partner and so again, the low prevalence in clinical samples may reflect the fact that low desire in men is not problematic in all relationships. Furthermore, it is also possible that men with low desire are more likely to suffer from related sexual dysfunctions, which then become the presenting complaint.

Comorbidity With Other Sexual Dysfunctions

Sexual desire problems in men have long been known to be associated with erectile difficulties with over 45% of men reporting both (Fugl-Meyer & Fugl-Meyer, 2002; Segraves & Segraves, 1991). Fugl-Meyer and Fugl-Meyer noted that men with low sexual interest also suffered from early ejaculation (26%) and that in heterosexual relationships partner sexual dysfunctions were also concurrently experienced (39% had partners with lubrication difficulties and 24% had anorgasmic partners). Apfelbaum (2000) makes a compelling case for HSDD being a precipitating factor in some cases of delayed ejaculation where the preference is for solo masturbation over partnered sex. Although there is a coincidence of desire and arousal/orgasm problems in men, there is still sufficient evidence that HSDD in men and erectile dysfunction represent separate diagnostic categories (Brotto, 2010). Therefore, in the most recent version of the *DSM* (APA, 2013) women's problems with sexual desire have been integrated into one diagnostic category with arousal disorders, leaving HSDD a dysfunction of male sexuality. In clinical practice, however, it may be difficult to disentangle male sexual desire and arousal.

The linear model of sexual responding first outlined by Masters and Johnson (1966), with desire later added as a preliminary and prerequisite phase (Kaplan, 1979; Lief, 1977) has been criticized for not adequately capturing sexual experiences (Tiefer, 1991). Desire and arousal are often entwined in a reciprocally enhancing pattern—desire fuels arousal, which increases desire—and this pattern repeats until orgasm or some other end of sexual activity. Basson (2001) noted that many women have a responsive pattern of sexual responding (in other words they don't initiate sex, but are receptive when their partner does), leading her to propose a circular model of female sexual responding that specifically addresses the observation that desire sometimes follows arousal. While the applicability of this model to men's sexual responding is unclear, male responsive desire appears to be an infrequent pattern and has been associated with sexual boredom (Štulhofer, Carvalheira, & Træen, 2013).

Etiology

Individual Medical Factors

Some endocrine disorders such as hyperprolactinemia (excessive levels of prolactin) and hypogonadism (low levels of testosterone) have direct and negative effects on male sexual desire (Bancroft, 2009; Khera et al., 2011). Among the other medical conditions that can contribute to low sexual desire hypothyroidism, cardiovascular disease, cancer, depression, and anxiety disorders rank high (Clayton & Ramamurthy, 2008). In addition, the medications used to treat these and other problems may also be implicated in HSDD. Most notably, SSRIs (selective serotonin reuptake inhibitors) have been found to reduce desire in men (Clayton, 2013). Given the comorbidity of HSDD and other sexual dysfunctions it may be assumed that medications that negatively affect other sexual functions (erections, ejaculation) will also have an indirect effect of lowering sexual desire. When a substance or medication is known or presumed to be responsible for low desire, the diagnosis is not one of low sexual desire but of Substance/Medication-Induced Sexual Dysfunction. When low desire is attributable to a medical condition, a diagnosis of HSDD would not be made according to the *DSM-5* (APA, 2013). Nevertheless, in clinical practice it is often difficult to separate out the contributions of physical and psychological factors. Men with physiological risk factors for low desire will still present for sex therapy treatment. HSDD, even when attributed to a physiological condition will inevitably have psychological and relational consequences. Psychological, relational, and physiological factors thus become intertwined and mutually reinforcing.

Recently there has been a marketing push by pharmaceutical companies describing a syndrome they have labeled "low T." According to advertisements, low testosterone is responsible for lethargy, low sex drive, and modest weight gain (Singer, 2013). As a result of this marketing campaign many people now believe that the lowered testosterone levels that come with healthy aging are responsible for men's reduced interest in sex, which can then be reversed with the administration of testosterone (Van Anders, Goldey, & Bell, 2014). Consequently there has been a sharp increase in the number of prescriptions written for testosterone, without any evidence that the recipients of these prescriptions have abnormally low testosterone levels (Baillargeon et al., 2013). Indeed in healthy men testosterone is not linked to level of sexual desire. Testosterone may show a threshold effect such that only men with atypically low or high testosterone levels may demonstrate concomitant differences in sexual desire. However, behavioral rather than hormonal variables appear to be key in understanding desire in otherwise healthy men. Specifically frequency of masturbation appears to be not only an outcome of desire, but is important for the maintenance of sexual desire in men. Frequency of masturbation may reflect the degree to which a man has an open attitude towards sex, sexual pleasure, and his genitals (Van Anders, 2012).

Individual Psychological Factors

Anxiety, especially that resulting from poor body image or inaccurate beliefs about sex may be related to HSDD (Weeks, Hertlein, & Gambescia, 2009; Wiederman & Sarin, 2014). Stress is another important variable—often men who work long hours, have stressful jobs, commutes, or money problems have difficulty maintaining an interest and desire for sex (Corona et al., 2004). As mentioned above, depression can result in low desire, even if the depression is situational and not biologically based (George et al., 2014).

Other sexual dysfunction. Low sexual desire can often be secondary to another sexual dysfunction (Fugl-Meyer & Fugl-Meyer, 2002) and may even be secondary to worry about another sexual dysfunction. For example, Brad, a 24-year-old medical student, was worried about his sexual performance after his former girlfriend ridiculed him for having premature ejaculation. It was not clear diagnostically that Brad suffered from premature ejaculation, but the thought that he was a poor sexual partner decreased his desire as sexual thoughts and fantasies now invoked anxiety.

Intergenerational Factors

Child sexual abuse. A history of child sexual abuse (CSA) might well fit under the etiological heading of personal factors. However, since CSA occurs in the context of a child's life, which is intertwined with his family, it is important to include it in this category. The effects of CSA are strongly correlated with the family's response to the abuse (Lalor & McElvaney, 2010). Although they are often victims of incest, boys are more often abused by someone outside the home, including family friends, coaches, teachers, and other older adults (Stoltenborgh, van IJzendoorn, Euser, & Bakermans-Kranenburg, 2011). Intergenerational sexual contact is not always experienced as abuse (even if it is criminally defined as such) and CSA does not inevitably lead to sexual dysfunction in adulthood (Hall, 2008). For example, Carl was 12 years old when his 19-year-old cousin masturbated him. Carl was grateful for the experience and years later when he was suffering from sexual difficulties with his wife, he wished for someone to teach him how to have sex the way his cousin had taught him to masturbate. On the other hand, Mike was 15 when he was molested by his high school wrestling coach. It was a traumatic experience that left Mike feeling depressed and suicidal throughout his adolescence. Years later Mike had low desire for his wife, whom he loved very much. He could not bear the thought that his sexual advances would ever be unwanted, so he had muted his own desires to the point that he was unaware of having them.

Religiosity and culture. While most, if not all, religions proscribe certain sexual behaviors or privilege some sexuality (usual heterosexual, marital, procreative sex), the degree to which a family interprets and adheres to their religious injunctions can influence sexual reactions later in life (Hall & Graham, 2012). The negative impact of transgressing cultural dictates regarding sex has been linked to guilt and sexual dysfunction in women (Woo, Morshedian, Brotto, & Gorzalka 2012). The same may apply for men.

Interactional/Relationship Factors

Relationship conflict. Sometimes desire wanes in committed and intimate relationships. It has been theorized that domesticity and the attendant feelings of safety and familiarity may often diminish desire, which is fueled by excitement, danger, and distance (Morin, 1995; Perel, 2007). However, it is perhaps more often the case that the reverse is true (Corona et al., 2004). A high degree of conflict within a relationship, as well as chronic or repeated feelings of anger and resentment, are often factors that men cite for their lack of desire towards their partner. In these cases, the loss of desire is situational and men may then find another outlet for their sexual interests (e.g., internet pornography, another partner).

A rigid adherence to a sexual script (e.g., men must initiate, men don't need foreplay) is associated with reduced sexual desire (Sanchez, Crocker, & Boike, 2005), especially if the man does not identify with the role as defined in the script (e.g., macho, dominant) (Katz & Farrow, 2000). Couples who are anxious about sex do not deviate from standard sexual scripts, even if these scripts are no longer, or never were, entirely satisfying. Often poor communication (in general and regarding sex in particular) is part of this clinical picture, making it even less likely that the couple can improve the sexual aspect of their relationship. It makes little sense to desire unsatisfying sex.

Partner Sexual Dysfunction. Male HSDD can also be secondary to sexual dysfunction in his partner. Partners of women who experience pain during sexual activity may lose desire for sex because they have no wish to hurt their partner (Bergeron, Rosen, & Pukall, 2014). This same issue—the wish not to inflict suffering on a partner—is also relevant for partners with chronic illness (Enzlin, 2014) or disability (Mona, Syme, & Cameron, 2014). Men may lose interest in sex if their partner is disinterested and/or fails to become aroused or is not orgasmic. Men want to please their partners, and men's desire is often contingent upon the pleasure they are able to give (Morgentaler, 2013).

Assessment

The stigma attached to low desiring men may result in the problem being hidden behind another sexual disorder or complaint. The possibility of HSDD should be investigated in all cases presenting for sex therapy, but may be especially relevant in the following situations:

1. couples presenting with low frequency or no sex in their marriage
2. other male sexual dysfunction, including erectile dysfunction and delayed ejaculation
3. a single man complaining of difficulty engaging in romantic relationship.

Even when patients self diagnose: "I just don't have any desire for sex" a thorough assessment is necessary for a diagnosis of HSDD. The *DSM-5* (APA 2013) makes it clear that clinical judgment is used to determine whether sexual desire is deficient, or whether low desire is an expected adaptation to stress or other life situation (age, health status). This requires the diagnosing clinician to be aware of research regarding these factors and not to rely on supposition (e.g., a belief that older men lose desire).

Diagnostic Dilemmas

Sexual desire versus sexual motivation. It is important to distinguish between sexual desire and sexual motivation. Many men, even men with low desire, are motivated to be sexual. Basically they want to want to have sex. Most men coming to therapy, even if "dragged" by their partner, want to be sexual. The reasons may range from "I want to be normal", "I don't want to disappoint or hurt my partner", to "sex is a healthy part of a relationship." The difference between desire and motivation is the difference between craving that chocolate cake and thinking: "It's noon, I should have lunch".

Sexual desire versus sexual arousal. Some men may complain of a lack of desire, when in reality they are failing to become aroused and attain an erection. Some men believe that they should have an erection before any sexual activity begins. While this may have been the case for many of these men in their younger years, the lack of erection does not necessarily indicate a lack of desire (Janssen, 2011). When assessing for sexual desire problems, there is an opportunity to educate men and their partners about normative age-related changes in sexual functioning. It is helpful for men and their partners to know that as men age they require physical stimulation to achieve erections, when once visual stimuli or fantasy would suffice.

Asexuality. While asexuality and lifelong, global HSDD may have much in common, the distinguishing feature is the lack of distress among asexuals. Asexuality is considered to be rather rare, with estimates placing it at roughly 1% of the general population (Bogaert, 2004). However, since asexuals may experience discord in their intimate relationships, relational distress may be mistaken for distress about absent sexual desire leading some asexuals to be misdiagnosed with HSDD.

Desire discrepancy. In order to diagnose HSDD, desire has to be deficient or absent, not simply lower than his partner's level of desire. Differences in level of desire between partners can cause a great deal of interpersonal distress and relationship discord. Concern about the adequacy of sexual performance, including level of desire, can lead to a cycle of worry and worsening of sexual functioning. Desire discrepancies are not uncommon among couples, not only in overall levels of desire (she wants sex more often than he does), but also on particular occasions (she wants sex tonight and he does not). The myth that real men want sex all the time can leave a man who does not want to have sex with his interested partner feeling inadequate. Most sexual activity in committed long term relationships takes place because one person (the one who desires sex in that moment) successfully initiates the activity. Individual or relationship distress due to sexual asynchrony may indicate unreasonable expectations of self or other (he should always be interested in sex), relationship problems (including power imbalance), or inadequate or inept initiation (he doesn't know his partner is signaling an interest in sex). Because there are no standard definitions of what constitutes deficient desire, clinical judgment is paramount in making the differential diagnosis regarding deficient or discrepant desire.

Assessment Tools

Questionnaires can sometimes be helpful in the evaluation process. While they should never be used in place of an in depth clinical interview they may supplement or inform the interview. The *International Index of Erectile Function* (IIEF; Rosen, Cappelleri, & Gendrano, 2002) is a validated measure that assesses erectile function, orgasmic function, sexual desire, intercourse satisfaction, and overall sexual satisfaction in men. It can be used to help determine whether there are co-morbid sexual dysfunctions and then the clinician can follow up to determine whether these other dysfunctions are the result of low desire or have contributed to the deterioration of desire. The *Female Sexual Function Index* (FSFI; Rosen et al., 2000) assesses desire, as well as arousal, lubrication, orgasm, satisfaction, and pain in women. Again it can be used to determine whether there exist concomitant sexual problems in the female partner and whether these problems contribute to the HSDD, are the result of being with a partner who has little desire or whether they are independent of the HSDD. For a measure of the overall quality of the sexual and intimate relationship in a heterosexual couple, the *Golombok-Rust Inventory of Sexual Satisfaction* (GRISS; Rust & Golombok, 2007) can provide the starting point for more in-depth exploration. While not an assessment tool per se, the sexual genogram (Hof & Berman, 1986) provides a way of diagramming and therefore clarifying intergenerational dynamics.

It is strongly recommended that any evaluation of HSDD include a medical evaluation. If the medical evaluation accomplishes nothing else besides assuring the man that he is healthy, it will have accomplished something. Many men worry that they have low testosterone (T), and a simple blood test performed by the patient's general practitioner will usually suffice to allay concerns, or on rare occasions indicate a problem. Free or bioavailable T is the measurement of most interest since it indicates the amount of T available to travel through the blood and bind to receptors (Van Anders et al., 2014). However, even an estimate of overall T is useful. A preliminary test indicating low T will often require replication. If there is a concern, a referral to an endocrinologist for further evaluation or treatment is necessary. It is important to note that a prescription for testosterone in a man with normal T levels will not increase sex drive (Rajfer, 2000). An urologist can also investigate testosterone deficiency and may need to be consulted in cases where there is a question of low desire secondary to sexual dysfunction. For example, an urologist can rule out an organic basis for erectile dysfunction. Furthermore, the potential impact of medications and medical conditions can be reviewed with the patient's physician to determine which, if any, medications may be modified or changed in the event that they are contributing to the desire disorder.

Clinical interview. The clinical interview will be the cornerstone of the evaluation of HSDD. It is strongly recommended that the initial assessment follow a format involving four meetings; first seeing the couple together, then seeing each member of the couple alone and then discussing the assessment with the couple together again. In this way relationship dynamics can be observed and detailed histories of the individual can be obtained, as well as investigating for the presence of sexual secrets. However, patients are not always comfortable divulging sexual secrets in the first few sessions with a therapist. The evaluation will be ongoing with treatment and the savvy therapist will remain alert and open to the possibility of further disclosures. Individual sessions interspersed in ongoing couples' therapy should be considered.

In the first session, the couple is present. This reinforces the relational context of the desire problem. At this time it is possible to see how the couple relates to each other and to assess their level of intimacy, hostility, attraction, and commitment to each other. In this first meeting the therapist can provide some education about the relational nature of sexual desire and reduce the shame that the male partner may be feeling (I'm not a *real* man). While reducing shame may be a goal for therapy, treatment begins from the first contact with the couple and in this way is difficult to separate from assessment.

In the couple's session the history of the relationship, a detailed exploration of their sexual experiences together and the course of the problem should be explored. Questions may include:

- When was the last time the two of you were sexual together?
- Why did you have sex on that occasion? (e.g., felt close, wanted to try to fix things, wanted to conceive, to avoid a fight)
- (Given the time lag to the present session) Is that (e.g., 3 weeks) typical in the past 6 months? In other words, in the past 6 months is the frequency of sex about once every 3 weeks?
- When did you first notice a problem (this may differ depending on who is answering the question)?
- What, if anything, have you tried to do to fix the problem?
- Tell me about the last time you had sex together-

  ◦ Ask specifically about who initiated, how, what the response was, what sexual activities occurred, was there orgasm for one or both? (Ask the couple if this is a typical or usual pattern, in this way the therapist can determine how rigidly the couple adheres to a sexual script).

- What are your expectations or goals for therapy? What would your sexual life look like if therapy is successful?

The goal of individual sessions is to assess for individual factors that might be relevant to the problem, especially sexual secrets, but also dissatisfaction with the current sexual repertoire, which the individual client may not have felt comfortable discussing with his or her partner present. In cases where there is a sexual secret, the goal is to destigmatize the secret, to bring it out in the open where it can become part of the treatment. While individuals should rightfully expect confidentiality about their disclosures during their individual session, discussion should be initiated into how the material that was privately discussed can be integrated into the treatment of the couple. If an ongoing extra-dyadic sexual or emotional relationship is revealed, this would be a contraindication to couples' therapy, which would have to await resolution of the conflict (e.g., the involved person would have to end the extra-dyadic relationship). In all cases, it is essential that both members of the couple understand the rules of confidentiality before proceeding with the individual evaluation sessions. All parties should complete signed informed consents at the initial meeting.

As part of the detailed individual sexual history in which intergenerational and developmental factors are explored, levels of desire in other circumstances (e.g., a preference for swinging, solo rather than dyadic sex, fetish, or bondage interests) as well as desire in past and other concurrent relationships, fantasy, masturbation, and pornography should be investigated. Lack of physical attraction to the current partner is also best explored individually, especially if the partner has changed physically in some way (e.g., illness, disability, serious weight gain). The individual session is the time to ask detailed questions regarding cognition during sexual activity, and to assess for distraction or negative thoughts that may interfere with sexual desire. Men with sexual dysfunction have negative and distracting thoughts more often than do men without sexual problems including; concern about erections ("I must get an erection"), anticipation of failure ("this is not going anywhere"), and lack of erotic thoughts (Nobre & Pinto-Gouveia, 2008).

McCarthy and McDonald (2009), noting the probability of sexual secrets in cases of HSDD, suggest asking about orgasms—how many in the last month, and by what means? This can lead to inquiry regarding masturbation (how often do you masturbate?), fantasy, or other variant arousal such as a fetish. (What do you think about when you masturbate, or when you have a sexual daydream? What type of pornography catches your attention? What websites have you visited?) These questions also open up the possibility of inquiring about the mismatch of sexual orientation (e.g., a man realizes that he is primarily attracted to other men but wishes he was attracted to his wife). The paucity of research on sexual desire disorders in gay or bisexual men makes empirically based assessment recommendations for same sex couples difficult. At a minimum, a heterosexual therapist treating men in same sex relationships must not apply heterosexual standards of normal, ideal or healthy sexuality. Therapists need to be aware of the variance in sexual behavior and attitudes inherent in the gay community and be open to learning from their gay (and other sexually variant) clients (Nichols, 2014).

Other questions that may be asked in the individual session include:

- In what ways is this sexual relationship different from other relationships (assess for attraction, intimacy, relationship satisfaction)?
- When you are having sex, what are you thinking about? What thoughts are going through your mind?
- How often do you have sexual thoughts, for example when you see an attractive person, or look at erotic material online?
- How often do you masturbate or pleasure yourself when you are alone, whether to orgasm or not?
- Do you feel that it is more pleasurable having sex on your own (masturbating) than having sex with your partner? If so, why do you think this is the case?

Note that the above questions regarding masturbation, fantasy, and pornography use all assume that the individual is engaging in those activities. It is easier for a man to correct a misperception in the direction of saying "No, I don't use pornography" than to admit to something he may fear will be negatively judged.

Treatment

Sexual desire disorder in men is complex. Therefore, as Weeks, Hertlein, and Gambescia (2009) aptly note, treatment "cannot follow a short protocol-based model but must be comprehensive, flexible, and tailored to each couple" (p. 83). The goal of systemically based sex therapy is an improvement in the sexual relationship, and so sexual symptoms will always be the primary focus of treatment. Nevertheless, concurrent intervention regarding etiological factors (e.g., relational conflict, stress, intimacy problems) is almost always a necessary part of treatment for the majority of sexual complaints. If relationship distress is high, reducing marital or relationship conflict prior to initiating sex therapy interventions is crucial to the success of treatment. Concurrent medical intervention may be required if physiological factors are contributing to desire problems.

Sex therapy interventions that are particularly helpful for HSDD will include some or all of the following:

1. Distress-reduction.

Given the stigma often associated with low desire in men, the first therapeutic task should be to prepare the couple for therapy by reducing the distress they have been experiencing and improving motivation for treatment, for both partners. It is often important to educate the couple about sexual desire and HSDD, highlighting the fact that low desire is not an uncommon problem for men. Using information gleaned from the assessment, the problem is then reframed. Instead of "He has a sexual dysfunction" the couple now agree: "*We* have a sexual problem that *we* need to work on." The techniques of motivational interviewing (Miller & Rose, 2010) may be very helpful at this point in therapy. Motivational interviewing increases readiness for change and emphasizes the collaborative nature of therapy.

2. Proscribing the problem.

In the beginning stages of treatment, sex therapists often prohibit problematic sexual activities (e.g., intercourse). In the case of HSDD, all sexual contact is prohibited except for that prescribed in therapy. This alleviates the need for sexual desire and allows the low desiring partner to stop trying to regain his desire for sex. Desire is a wish for something one does not currently have and the obligation—for example, "I have to have sex"—diminishes desire (Hall, 2004). This also alleviates the stress and anxiety his partner may feel, as the partner may otherwise wonder: "Will we have sex tonight?" This is often referred to as response anxiety.

3. Sensate focus exercises.

Sensate focus involves a hierarchy of structured touching exercises designed to assess and redress problems with sexual skills, communication, and the experience of pleasure. Importantly, sensate focus exercises are aimed at reducing performance demand (arousing one's partner or getting aroused oneself) concentrating instead on being able to stay in the present and attending to one's own experience of being touched (Weiner & Avery-Clark, 2014). The couple is encouraged first to use non-verbal communication during sensate focus to indicate the kinds of touching that they really enjoyed. The emphasis is on the positive, what he or she enjoyed, which helps not only improve the quality of the sensate focus exercises but also to repair the hurt one partner may have experienced from feeling undesired. The therapist purposefully times the exercises to proceed at a slow pace (sensate focus I which is non genital touching, may occur 4–6 times over a period of two months), so that the low desiring partner will have the opportunity to *want* more activity rather than feeling burdened by having to perform. Desire is reframed as a positive state that can be enjoyed rather than as a feeling that must be immediately satisfied and therefore disappears.

4. Positive anticipation, curiosity, and improving the sexual repertoire.

In addition to the anticipation felt as a result of the sensate focus exercises, desire can be rekindled by encouraging the couple to explore and develop their sexual interests. A homework assignment may involve browsing through sex books or manuals, shopping (even if not buying), sex toys, lingerie, etc. During the exercise the clients are prompted to be curious—"What would this be like? What would this feel like? Would I enjoy this?" Each member of the couple is encouraged to keep a list of things they would like to introduce to their sexual relationship. This can be shared in therapy. Not only is desire increased by this exercise, but also improvements may be made to the couple's sexual repertoire, which may have become stagnant at this point in time. It is incumbent upon the therapist to normalize the sexual interests shared by the individual members of the couple and to facilitate the sharing of ideas in a respectful and supportive manner.

5. Simmering.

Essentially simmering works on the notion that a pot of water set to simmer will come to a boil more quickly. This technique was first described by Zilbergeld and Ellison (1980) and is especially relevant for the low desiring man, but may also be helpful to his partner. Essentially the client is advised to pay attention to any sexual feelings that occur throughout the day. Then he is encouraged to develop the fantasy further, in essence "to run his own x-rated movie" (p. 312). He does this for a few minutes, then he lets the image fade. Later, he is advised to recall the fantasy and to re-engage with it several times a day if possible. After he can do this exercise successfully, he is advised to incorporate his partner into his fantasy, essentially fantasizing about his partner and then ultimately initiating some sexual activity (letting his partner know in advance that he would like to be sexual).

A variation on simmering involves the couple engaging in a required number of small activities each day such as; flirting, complementing each other, affectionate touches, kisses that linger longer than the proverbial peck on the cheek, and romantic texts or emails. This improves the overall tone of the relationship and makes for a smoother transition to sex. In essence this sex therapy technique builds on the work of John Gottman, who in a series of prospective longitudinal studies of married couples, found that happy couples had a ratio of 5:1 positive to negative behavioral interactions (Gottman, 1994).

6. Cognitive behavioral therapy (CBT).

Directly challenging irrational thoughts that may interfere with sexual desire is an important component of sex therapy for HSDD. Often the challenge is enough to get clients to rethink and therefore to change their behavior. Some common myths and misperceptions include:

a. You can only initiate sex if you already feel desire.
b. Men are responsible for initiating sex.
c. Men are always ready for sex and only refuse an unattractive or undesirable partner.
d. An erection is a necessary sign of desire, and the lack of an erection means a lack of desire.

Therapists should be familiar with the literature that refutes many of these myths, but may also simply challenge these beliefs by asking why? Often when clients reflect on these beliefs they come to understand that the beliefs are irrational, or are based on outmoded ideas. In addition to challenging irrational beliefs, some coaching may be necessary to help clients with behavior change necessitated by the change in belief systems (e.g., coaching on how to initiate sex if you are not feeling sexual desire, but have the thought that it is time to reconnect sexually with your partner).

7. Cognitive refocusing, mindfulness.

Men who have low desire are often distracted during sex and have nonerotic thoughts (Nobre & Pinto-Gouveia, 2008). Mindfulness meditation provides the skills to stay focused on present experiences and may be a helpful adjunct to sex therapy (Brotto & Heiman, 2007). For clients who are not predisposed to meditation, the directive to focus on what they are doing and experiencing, without criticism, is often sufficient. This technique can be enhanced by adding positive commentary: "I am caressing my partner's skin. I like this, her skin feels smooth, I am enjoying this. . . . "

8. Jump start desire by bypassing it.

Many of the techniques described above bypass desire. However, when it is apparent that sexual desire is present during sex, but does not precede sex ("I never feel like having sex, but when I do I always enjoy it and wonder why I don't want to have sex more often") the couple can be encouraged to have sex without first having desire. Explaining the circular model of sexual responding (Basson, 2001) is helpful. The low desiring partner can also use fantasy (see the simmering technique described above) to become aroused prior to initiating partnered sex. This will help his partner regain a feeling of being desired. In terms of using internet or other forms of pornography to jump start desire, it must first be determined whether pornography can be used to bridge the desire gap or whether it has been used in the past to distance a man from his partner. If so, it would likely be used for the same purpose again (McCarthy & McDonald, 2009). In this case, couples may be advised that sharing erotica (such as reading erotic stories) is an activity to be done together and never separately. Erotica is here used to refer to less graphic portrayals of sex when compared to pornography, and reading material together is less likely to result in the emotional distancing that might occur when viewing pornography.

Clinical challenges are presented when the problem is lack of attraction to one's partner. If the lack of attraction can be mediated (for example a man with a shoe fetish may persuade his wife to wear high heels and she may oblige) the therapist may help the couple negotiate this change. If the lack of attraction is due to a physical feature that is unchanging (e.g., age) the dual control model (Bancroft & Janssen, 2000) is helpful conceptually. Very basically this theory posits that men experience both sexually excitatory and sexually inhibitory signals. Sexual desire and arousal will result if the number of excitatory signals is greater than the number of inhibitory factors. Sex therapy can be utilized to improve the balance in favor of the excitatory signals. For example, Jake was married late in life to a lovely woman his age. He felt that she was a wonderful companion to him, but since his sexual experiences had for a long time been limited to pornography, he was turned off to his wife's graying pubic hair and other signs of her age. He began to obsess about these features and soon lost desire for sex with her. In therapy he learned to focus on the positive physical features he enjoyed, the sensations he experienced from being touched and the emotional attachment he felt to his wife, which then increased his desire and sexual pleasure.

Case Vignette

Paul and Marie met in college and were very attracted to each other. They had each independently decided to wait until marriage before having sex and thus they felt that they shared similar values. Once married however, Marie was disappointed in the low frequency of sexual interaction with Paul. Having been raised in a strict Catholic household, she was uncomfortable with her own sexuality and reluctant to initiate sex with Paul, believing that the timing of sex was the man's prerogative. Paul was raised in a working class family that struggled financially. Prioritizing his academics and later his professional responsibilities over sex was Paul's path to the middle class life he greatly wanted. Unfortunately, Paul continued to prioritize work over sex long after he achieved professional and financial success. Paul was apologetic and felt sad and guilty about letting his wife down. He just didn't think about sex if he had work obligations. When Marie would timidly raise the subject of sex, he would initiate, but then Marie would refuse thinking Paul was only initiating because of her complaint and not because he desired her sexually. When this relationship dynamic was uncovered in the assessment, it highlighted the shared nature of the sexual problem (he did not prioritize his own desires, while she adhered to a gendered script—men must initiate sex). A ban on any sexual activity outside of that prescribed during therapy helped alleviate the difficulty this couple faced with initiating sex. They were advised to make dates to spend time together and during these dates they did sensate focus exercises to help with their communication regarding sex and to build desire and pleasure. Sensate focus exercises were slowly paced (they had to do four exercises at each stage and feel comfortable doing so before they could advance to the next step). This slow pace allowed Paul and Marie to enjoy feeling desire for more sexual contact with each other. Once the couple was having sex (activity that involves orgasm and/or intercourse) they found it difficult to maintain the practice of making dates, believing that "sex should be spontaneous." Marie continued to worry that Paul did not desire her given that they only had sex during date times. When asked if they only went out to dinner when they spontaneously felt hungry they agreed that they enjoyed a romantic dinner together even though it was planned in advance, and sex could be like that for them too. Since Marie was responsible for planning and implementing 50% of the dates from the beginning of therapy, she had become more comfortable initiating. From doing the sensate focus exercises Paul learned how to pay focused attention to his own sexual feelings including his desires and became more willing to make his sexual relationship a priority. Simmering was especially helpful to Paul and allowed him to initiate sex with Marie because he felt desire and arousal. At the end of therapy, Paul was spontaneously initiating sex the majority of the time, but Marie would occasionally initiate, especially when she saw Paul getting distracted by work obligations. Although they originally expected that they would be having sex at least two to three times per week, at the end of therapy the frequency of sex was about three times per month. However both were satisfied with the quality and quantity of sex.

Treatment Efficacy—Research and Future Directions

There is a dearth of research into the effectiveness of psychological interventions for sexual dysfunctions in general, and for male HSDD in particular (Fruhauf, Gerger, Schmidt, Munder, & Barth, 2013). Indeed, research on emotional factors in men's sexual happiness has also lagged behind that for women (Træen, Štulhofer, & Carvalheira, 2013) reflecting perhaps the cultural bias that men's sexual desire is almost purely a function of biology. Despite millions being spent in pursuit of an effective drug for desire, none has yet been approved for use in the United States by the Federal Drug Administration. While research is proceeding apace on testosterone, other hormones such as cortisol, estradiol, and progesterone, as well as other androgens (DHEA, DHEAS) are gathering more attention and are increasingly implicated in understanding the complexity of sexual desire. There is a growing awareness that when it comes to sex, biological, relational, emotional, and cultural context is essential to understanding and improving sexual health and happiness (Heiman, 2013; Van Anders et al.,2014).

References

American Psychiatric Association. (2013). *Diagnostic and statistical manual of mental disorders* (5th ed.). Washington, DC: Author.

Apfelbaum, B. (2000). RE; a much-misunderstood syndrome. In S. Lieblum & R. Rosen (Eds.), *Principles and practice of sex therapy* (2nd ed.). New York: Guilford Press.

Baillargeon, J., Urban, R. J., Ottenbacher, K. J., Pierson, K. S., & Goodwin, J. S. (2013). Trends in Androgen prescribing in the United States, 2001 to 2011. *JAMA Internal Medicine. 173*(15), 1465–1466. doi: 10.1001/jamainternmed.2013.6895

Bancroft, J. (2009). *Human sexuality and its problems* (3rd ed.). London: Churchill Livingstone.

Bancroft, J., & Janssen, E. (2000). The dual control model of male sexual response: A theoretical approach to centrally mediated erectile dysfunction. *Neuroscience & Biobehavioral Reviews, 24*(5), 571–579. doi: 10.1016/S0149-7634(00)00024-5

Basson, R. (2001). Using a different model for female sexual response to address women's problematic low sexual desire. *Journal of Sex and Marital Therapy, 27,* 395–403. doi: 10.1080/713846827

Baumeister, R. F., Catanese, K. R., & Vohls, K. D. (2001). Is there a gender difference in strength of sex drive? Theoretical views, conceptual distinctions, and a review of relevant evidence. *Personality and Social Psychology Review, 5,* 242–273. doi: 10.1207/S15327957PSPR0503_5

Bergeron, S., Rosen, N. O., & Pukall, C. F. (2014). Genital pain in women and men: It can hurt more than your sex life. In Y. M. Binik & K. S. Hall (Eds.), *Principles and practices of sex therapy.* New York: Guilford.

Bogaert, A. F. (2004). Asexuality: Prevalence and associated factors in a national probability sample. *Journal of Sex Research, 41,* 279–287. doi: 10.1080/00224490409552235

Brotto, L. A. (2010). The DSM diagnostic criteria for Hypoactive Sexual Desire Disorder in men. *Journal of Sexual Medicine, 7,* 2015–2030. doi: 10.1111/j.1743-6109.2010.01860.x

Brotto, L. A., & Heiman, J. H. (2007). Mindfulness in sex therapy: Applications for women with sexual difficulties following gynecologic cancer. *Sexual and Relationship Therapy, 22*(1), 3–11. doi: 10.1080/14681990601153298

Christensen, B. S., Grønbæk, M., Osler, M., Pedersen, B. V., Graugaard, C., & Frisch, M. (2011). Associations between physical and mental health problems and sexual dysfunctions in sexually active Danes. *Journal of Sexual Medicine, 8,* 1890–1902. doi: 10.1111/j.1743-6109.2010.02145.x

Clayton, A. (2013). The impact of antidepressant-associated sexual dysfunction on treatment adherence in patients with major depressive disorder. *Current Psychiatry Reviews, 9,* 293–301. doi: 10.2174/15734005113096660007

Clayton, A., & Ramamurthy, S. (2008). The impact of physical illness on sexual dysfunction. *Advances in Psychosomatic Medicine, 29,* 70–88. doi: 10.1159/000126625

Corona, G., Mannucci, E., Petrone, L., Giommi, R., Mansani, R., Fei, L., . . . Maggi, M. (2004). Psycho-biological correlates of hypoactive sexual desire in patients with erectile dysfunction. *International Journal of Impotence Research, 16,* 275–281. doi: 10.1111/j.1743-6109.2010.01812.x

Corona, G., Rastrelli, G., Ricca, V., Jannini, E. A., Vignozzi, L., Monami, M., . . . Maggi, M. (2013). Risk factors associated with primary and secondary reduced libido in male patients with sexual dysfunction. *Journal of Sexual Medicine, 10*(4), 1074–1089. doi: 10.1111/jsm.12043

Enzlin, P. (2014). Sexuality in the context of chronic illness. In Y. M. Binik & K. S. Hall (Eds.), *Principles and practices of sex therapy*. New York: Guilford.

Eplov, L., Giraldi, A., Davidsen, M., Garde, K., & Kamper-Jurgensen, F. (2007). Sexual desire in a nationally representative Danish population. *Journal of Sexual Medicine, 4*, 47–56. doi: 10.1111/j.1743–6109.2006.00396.x

Frühauf, S., Gerger, H., Schmidt, H. M., Munder, T., & Barth, J. (2013). Efficacy of psychological interventions for sexual dysfunction: A systematic review and meta-analysis. *Archives of Sexual Behavior, 42*, 1–19. doi: 10.1007/s10508–012–0062–0

Fugl-Meyer, A. R., & Fugl-Meyer, K. S. (2002). Sexual disabilities are not singularities. *International Journal of Impotence Research, 14*, 487–493. doi: 10.1038/sj.ijir.3900914

Fugl-Meyer, A. R., & Sjogren Fugl-Meyer, K. (1999). Sexual disabilities, problems and satisfaction in 18–74 year old Swedes. *Scandinavian Journal of Sexology, 2*, 79–105. doi: 10.1176/appi.ajp.2008.08050714

George, W. H., Norris, J., Nguyen, H. V., Masters, T., & Davis, K. C. (2014). Sexuality and health. In D. L. Tolman & L. M. Diamond (Eds.), *APA handbook of sexuality and psychology*. Washington, DC: APA Books.

Gottman, J. M. (1994). *What predicts divorce: The relationship between marital processes and marital outcomes*. Hillsdale, NJ: Lawrence Erlbaum Associates.

Hall, K. (2004). *Reclaiming your sexual self: How to bring desire back into your life*. New York: John Wiley and Sons.

Hall, K. S. (2008). Childhood sexual abuse and adult sexual problems: A new view of assessment and treatment. *Feminism and Psychology, 18*, 546–556. doi: 10.1177/0959353508095536

Hall, K. S., & Graham, C. (2012). Introduction. In K. S. Hall & C. A. Graham (Eds.), *The cultural context of sexual pleasure and problems: Psychotherapy with diverse clients*. New York: Routledge.

Hall, K. S., & Graham, C. A. (2014). Culturally sensitive sex therapy: The need for shared meanings in the treatment of sexual problems. In Y. M. Binik & K. S. Hall (Eds.), *Principles and practices of sex therapy*. New York: Guilford.

Heiman, J. (2013). Introduction. In D. L. Tolman & L. M. Diamond (Eds.), *APA handbook of sexuality and psychology*. Washington DC: APA Books.

Hof, L., & Berman, J. (1986). The sexual genogram. *Journal Marital & Family Therapy, 12*(1), 39–47.

Hyde, Z., Flicker, L., Hankey, G. J., Almeida, O. P., McCaul, K. A., Chubb, S. A. P., & Yeap, B. B. (2012). Prevalence and predictors of sexual problems in men aged 75–95 years: A population-based study. *Journal of Sexual Medicine, 9*, 442–453. doi: 10.1111/j.1743–6109.2011.02565.x

Janssen, E. (2011). Sexual arousal in men: A review and conceptual analysis. *Hormones and Behavior, 59*, 708–716.

Janssen, E., McBride, K. R., Yarber, W., Hill, B. J., & Butler, S. M. (2008). Factors that influence sexual arousal in men: A focus group study. *Archives of Sexual Behavior, 37*, 252–265.

Kaplan, H. S. (1979). *Disorders of sexual desire*. New York: Brunner Mazel.

Katz, J., & Farrow, S. (2000). Heterosexual adjustment among women and men with non-traditional gender identities: Testing predictions from self-verification theory. *Social Behavior and Personality: An International Journal, 28*(6), 613–620.

Kedde, H., Donker, G., Leusink, P., & Kruijer, H. (2011). The incidence of sexual dysfunction in patients attending Dutch general practitioners. *International Journal of Sexual Health, 23*(4), 269–277.

Khera, M., Bhattacharya, R. K., Blick, G., Kushner, H., Nguyen, D., & Miner, M. M. (2011). Improved sexual function with testosterone replacement therapy in hypogonadal men: Real-world data from the Testim Registry in the United States (TRiUS). *Journal of Sexual Medicine, 8*, 3204–3213. doi: 10.1111/j.1743–6109.2011.02436.x

Lalor, K., & McElvaney, R. (2010). Child sexual abuse, links to later sexual exploitation/high-risk sexual behavior, and prevention/treatment E.T. programs. *Trauma, Violence, & Abuse, 11*(4), 159–177. doi: 10.1177/1524838010378299

Laumann, E. O., Glasser, D. B., Neves, R. C. S., & Moreira, D. C. J. (2009). GSSAB Investigators' Group: A population based survey of sexual activity, sexual problems and associated help-seeking behavior patterns in mature adults in the United States of America. *International Journal of Impotence Research, 21,* 171–178. doi: 10.1038/ijir.2009.7

Laumann, E. O., Paik, A., & Rosen, R. (1999). Sexual dysfunction in the United States: Prevalence and predictors. *Journal of the American Medical Association, 281,* 537–544.

Levine, S. B. (1987). More on the nature of sexual desire. *Journal of Sex and Marital Therapy, 13,* 35–44.

Lewis, R. W., Fugl-Meyer, K. S., Corona, G., Hayes, R. D., Laumann, E. O., Moreira, E. D., Jr., . . . Segraves, T. (2010). Definitions/epidemiology/risk factors for sexual dysfunction. *Journal of Sexual Medicine, 7,* 1598–1607. doi: 10.1111/j.1743–6109.2010.01778.x

Lief, H. (1977). Inhibited sexual desire. *Medical Aspects of Human Sexuality, 7,* 94–95.

Masters, W., & Johnson, V. (1966). *Human sexual response.* New York: Little Brown & Co.

Maurice, W. L. (1999). Low sexual desire in men and women. In *Sexual medicine in primary care* (pp. 159–191). St. Louis: Mosby.

McCarthy, B., & McDonald, D. (2009). Assessment, treatment, and relapse prevention: Male hypoactive sexual desire disorder. *Journal of Sex and Marital Therapy, 35,* 58–67. doi: 10.1080/00926230802525653

Meana, M., & Steiner, E. T. (2014). Hidden disorder/hidden desire: Presentations of low sexual desire in men. In Y. M. Binik & K. S. Hall (Eds.), *Principles and practice of sex therapy.* New York: Guilford.

Miller, W. R., & Rose, G. S. (2010). Motivational interviewing in relational context. *American Psychologist, 65*(4), 298–299. doi: 10.1037/a0019487

Mona, L. R., Syme, M. L., & Cameron, R. P. (2014). A disability-affirmative approach to sex therapy. In Y. M. Binik & K. S. Hall (Eds.), *Principles and practices of sex therapy* (5th ed.). New York: Guilford.

Morgentaler, A. (2013). *Why men fake it: The totally unexpected truth about men and sex.* New York: Henry Holt & Co.

Morin, J. (1995). *The erotic mind: Unlocking the inner sources of sexual passion and fulfillment.* New York: Harper Collins.

Najman, J. M., Dunne, M. P., Boyle, F. M., Cook, M. D., & Purdie, D. M. (2003). Sexual dysfunction in the Australian population. *Australian Family Physician, 32,* 951–954.

Nichols, M. (2014). Therapy with LGBTQ clients: Working with sex and gender variance from a Queer Theory perspective. In Y. M. Binik & K. S. Hall (Eds.), *Principles and practices of sex therapy* (5th ed., pp. 309–333). New York: Guilford.

Nobre, P. J., & Pinto-Gouveia, J. (2008). Differences in automatic thoughts presented during sexual activity between sexually functional and dysfunctional men and women. *Cognitive Therapy and Research, 32*(1). doi: 10.1007/s10608–007–9165–7

Perel, E. (2007). *Mating in captivity: Unlocking erotic intelligence.* New York: Harper Perennial.

Rajfer, J. (2000). Relationship between testosterone and erectile dysfunction. *Reviews in Urology, 2*(2), 122–128. doi: 10.1371/journal.pone.0039234

Regan, P. C., & Berscheid, E. (1996). Beliefs about the state, goals and objects of sexual desire. *Journal of Sex and Marital Therapy, 22,* 110–120.

Rosen, R., Brown, C., Heiman, J., Leiblum, S., Meston, C., Shabsigh, R., & D'Agostino, R., Jr. (2000). The Female Sexual Function Index (FSFI): A multidimensional self-report instrument for the assessment of female sexual function. *Journal of Sex and Marital Therapy, 26,* 191–208.

Rosen, R. C., Cappelleri, J. C., & Gendrano, N. (2002). The international index of erectile function (IIEF): A state-of-the-science review. *International Journal of Impotence Research, 14,* 226–244. doi: 10.1038/sj.ijir.3900857

Rosen, R. C., Miner, M. M., & Wincze, J. P. (2014). Erectile dysfunction: Integration of medical and psychological approaches. In Y. M. Binik & K. S. Hall (Eds.), *Principles and practice of sex therapy* (5th ed., pp. 61–85). New York: Guilford Press.

Rust, J., & Golombok, S. (2007). *The handbook of the Golombok Rust inventory of sexual satisfaction (GRISS).* London: Pearson Assessment.

Sanchez, D.T., Crocker, J., & Boike, K.R. (2005). Doing gender in the bedroom: How investment in gender norms affects the sexual experience. *Personality and Social Psychology Bulletin, 31,* 1445–1455. doi: 10.1177/0146167205277333

Segraves, K.B., & Segraves, K.R.T. (1991). Hypoactive sexual desire disorder: Prevalence and comorbidity in 906 subjects. *Journal of Sex and Marital Therapy, 17,* 55–58.

Seinfeld, J. (2013). *Jerry Seinfeld quotes.* Retrieved from http://www.goodreads.com/author/quotes/19838.Jerry_Seinfeld?page=2

Singer, N. (2013, November 13). Selling that new man feeling. *New York Times,* p. B1.

Stoltenborgh, M., van IJzendoorn, M.H., Euser, E.M., & Bakermans-Kranenburg, M.J. (2011). A global perspective on child sexual abuse: Meta-analysis of prevalence around the world. *Child Maltreatment, 16*(2), 79–101. doi: 10.1177/1077559511403920

Štulhofer A., Carvalheira A., & Træen B. (2013). Is responsive sexual desire for partnered sex problematic among men? Insights from a two-country study. *Sexual and Relationship Therapy, 28,* 246–258. doi: 10.1080/14681994.2012.756137

Štulhofer A., Træen B., & Carvalheira, A. (2013). Job-related strain and sexual health difficulties among heterosexual men from three European countries: The role of culture and emotional support. *Journal of Sexual Medicine, 10,* 747–756. doi: 10.1111/j.1743-6109.2012.02967.x

Tiefer, L. (1991). Historical, scientific, clinical and feminist criticisms of "the human sexual response cycle" model. *Annual Review of Sex Research, 2,* 1–23.

Træen, B., Štulhofer, A., & Carvalheira, A. (2013). The associations among satisfaction with the division of housework, partner's perceived attractiveness, emotional intimacy, and sexual satisfaction in a sample of married or cohabiting Norwegian middle-class men. *Sexual and Relationship Therapy, 28*(3), 215–229. doi: 10.1080/14681994.2013.808323

Van Anders, S.M. (2012). Testosterone and sexual desire in healthy women and men. *Archives of Sexual Behavior, 41*(6), 1471–1484. doi: 10.1007/s10508-012-9946-2

Van Anders, S.M., Goldey, K.L., & Bell, S.N. (2014). Measurement of testosterone in human sexuality research: Methodological considerations. *Archives of Sexual Behavior, 43*(2), 231–250. doi: 10.1007/s10508-013-0123-z

Wallen, K. (2000). Risky business: Social context and hormonal modulation of primate sexual drive. In K. Wallen & J.F. Schneider (Eds.), *Reproduction in context: Social and environmental influences on reproductive physiology and behavior* (pp. 289–323). Cambridge: Massachusetts Institute of Technology.

Weeks, G.R., Hertlein, K.M., & Gambescia, N. (2009). The treatment of hypoactive sexual desire disorder. In K.M. Hertlein, G.R. Weeks, & N. Gambescia (Eds.), *Systemic sex therapy* (pp. 81–106). New York: Routledge.

Weiner, L., & Avery-Clark, C. (2014). Clarifying Masters and Johnson's sensate focus. *Sexual and Relationship Therapy, 29*(3), 307–319.

Wiederman, M.W., & Sarin, S. (2014). Body image and sexuality. In Y.M. Binik & K.S. Hall (Eds.), *Principles and practices of sex therapy.* New York: Guilford.

Woo, J.S.T., Morshedian, N., Brotto, L.A., & Gorzalka, B.B. (2012). Sex guilt mediates the relationship between religiosity and sexual desire in East Asian and Euro-Canadian college-aged women. *Archives of Sexual Behavior, 41*(6), 1485–1495. doi: 10.1007/s10508-012-9918-6

Zilbergeld. B., & Ellison, C.R. (1980). Desire discrepancies and arousal problems in sex therapy. In S.R. Leiblum & L.A. Pervin (Eds.), *Principles and practice of sex therapy* (pp. 65–101). New York: Guilford.

5

SYSTEMIC TREATMENT OF ERECTILE DISORDER

Nancy Gambescia and Gerald R. Weeks

Erectile disorder (ED) is the persistent inhibition of a man's sexual arousal and erectile capacity, precluding his ability to engage in satisfying sexual experiences. The psychological consequences of ED are considerable, impeding self-esteem, confidence, and overall quality of life (Feldman et al., 1994). In fact, depression, anxiety, and other psychiatric symptoms are often experienced in men with ED (Simopoulos & Trinidad, 2013). Over time, this disorder can contribute to relationship dissatisfaction and the avoidance of sexual intimacy (McCabe & Matic, 2008). Partners of men with ED are affected by the recurrent interruption of sexual gratification; often they report diminished sexual interest, confidence and satisfaction (Chevret et al., 2004; Hart & Schwartz, 2010; Fisher et al., 2005a). Additionally, the psychological distress caused by ED can adversely affect the man's overall state of health (Bocchio et al., 2009; Thompson et al., 2005). The etiology of ED can include multiple layers of psychogenic, relational, and situational elements. Moreover, as the man ages, organic factors progressively influence the clinical presentation; thus, a comprehensive bio-psycho-social assessment is essential. The Intersystem Approach, used throughout this volume, proposes that all aspects of the man's life, including his intimate relationship, need to be considered when treating ED.

Diagnostic Criteria

ED is described as a sexual dysfunction in the *Diagnostic and Statistical Manual of Mental Disorders, fifth edition (DSM-5)* (American Psychiatric Association, 2013). In order for the psychiatric diagnosis of ED to be used, at least one of following three diagnostic criteria must be present on almost all or all (75–100%) occasions of sexual activity:

- Distinct difficulty in obtaining an erection during sexual activity
- Noticeable difficulty in maintaining an erection until the completion of sexual activity
- A marked decrease in erectile rigidity

Additionally, the symptoms will have persisted for a minimum duration of six months approximately (American Psychiatric Association, 2013).

- Lifelong ED is an extremely rare presentation in which the man has always had this problem.
- Acquired ED occurs in men who have previously had satisfactory sexual activity and is more typical.

- The onset of acquired ED can be gradual or sudden.
- Generalized ED occurs in all situations, partnered or alone.
- Situational ED is more common, occurring only with certain partners, situations, or during particular types of stimulation.

In the *DSM-5*, the term severity is used to categorize the degree of psychological distress about the abovementioned symptoms. While psychological distress usually persuades the man to seek treatment for ED, it is a subjective phenomenon and must be assessed within the context of his age, relationship, and other physical and psychological variables.

The associated features supporting the diagnosis of ED in the *DSM-5* encompass a number of factors, which are consistent with the risk factors identified in the Intersystem Approach (American Psychiatric Association, 2013).

- Underlying medical influences in the man
- The sexual status and health of the partner
- Relational problems such as poor communication or discord
- Psychological influences and situational stressors in the man
- Cultural, religious, and environmental considerations

Differential Diagnosis

In order to accurately diagnose ED, the therapist must determine that the man's sexual symptoms are not caused by another problem such as:

- Major depressive disorder
- Substance or medication abuse
- Another medical condition that fully explains the ED
- Other sexual dysfunctions

The man could have a co-existing medical condition, such as diabetes mellitus, which might not necessarily cause ED; however, under stressful conditions, erectile symptoms can occur. It must not be concluded that, in this example, ED is caused by the diabetes mellitus and not psychological factors (American Psychiatric Association, 2013).

Prevalence

As stated, ED becomes more common as the man ages. Lewis et al. (2010) performed an extensive analysis of published worldwide studies describing the epidemiology of sexual dysfunction in men and women using evidence-based criteria. The prevalence of ED was reported:

- 1–10% in men younger than 40 years
- 2% to 9% in men between the ages of 40 and 49 years
- 20–40% in men aged 60–69 years
- 50% to 100% in men older than 70 years of age

There are few studies of sexual dysfunction in men who have sex with men (MSM). Often, the data are obtained from convenience samples and Internet questionnaires. Sometimes, a single question is used to attain information about ED. Nonetheless, in one study,

ED was reported 12% more frequently in MSM than heterosexually identified men (Bancroft et al., 2005). The conclusions were based on a sample of 2,937 MSM with a mean age of 35. Alternately, an online survey of 2,640 predominantly American respondents found that there were statistical similarities in sexual dysfunction between MSM and non-MSM respondents, particularly with respect to ED (Shindel, Vittinghoff, & Breyer, 2012). This study also determined that in MSM, ED is statistically related to HIV seropositive status and lack of a stable sexual partner in addition to other correlates. It is difficult to generalize prevalence statistics based on the information available; however, it is reasonable to assume that the medical and psychosocial needs of gay men with ED may differ from heterosexually identified men.

The Intersystem Approach

The Intersystem Approach is a therapeutic framework used in treating individuals, couples, and families. It is a comprehensive method that systematically integrates many theoretically based treatment modalities. It is particularly useful in the assessment and treatment of sexual dysfunctions, providing the lenses necessary for viewing all facets of ED and the valuable tools needed for treatment. The five major components of the Intersystem framework include:

1. Individual biological issues
2. Individual psychological factors
3. Interactional (relational) dynamics
4. Intergenerational (family-of-origin) influences
5. Environmental (society, culture, history, religion, etc.) considerations

The desired outcome of the Intersystem Approach is the restoration of sexual satisfaction for the man or the couple and not merely a concentration on erectile capacity (Gambescia, Sendak, & Weeks, 2009).

Intersystemic Assessment

Individual Biological Issues

The first component of the assessment involves the man's medical history, health status, physical strengths, illnesses, and physical changes throughout the lifespan. ED is a common sexual ailment that becomes more prevalent as the man ages due to the increasing occurrence of underlying organic disease processes in men 40 and older (Lewis et al., 2010). In the last 5 years, evidence supporting the empirically significant relationship between medical conditions and ED is rising (Kloner & Schwartz, 2011). Currently, organic ED is regarded as a known marker for cardiovascular diseases, diabetes, and morbidity (Chung, Chen, Lin, & Lin, 2011). ED can also result from modifiable lifestyle factors such as obesity, smoking, poor dietary choices, and the lack of exercise.

Some of the more common medical conditions that cause or are associated with ED include:

*   Vascular changes resulting from diabetes and hypertension, accounting for 75–80% of organic ED (Simopoulos & Trinidad, 2013)
*   Structural abnormalities, including Peyronie's disease and atherosclerosis, producing fibrous plaque deposits in penile tissues diminishing blood supply during arousal

- Endocrine malfunctions including diabetes mellitus and hypogonadism; the latter is a condition in which the testes do not produce sufficient testosterone (Stief, 2002)
- Systemic illnesses creating general physical debilitation, which include: liver, renal, respiratory, and cardiovascular disease (Shamloul & Ghanem, 2013)
- The use of certain types of medications, including antihypertensives, antiandrogens, and major tranquillizers; up to 60% of patients taking selective serotonin reuptake inhibitors report some form of treatment-emergent sexual dysfunction (Clayon, Keller, & McGarvey, 2006)
- Neurological disorders associated with ED comprise Alzheimer's disease, Parkinson's disease, and injuries to the spinal cord
- Iatrogenic factors involving tissue damage from operative procedures or radiotherapy to the prostate
- Injury to the spinal cord, brain, blood vessels, ligaments, or nerves which provide pathways for erection (Awad et al., 2011)

Even when the etiology is mostly organic, the man and his partner will need assistance in discussing the relational impact of such medical conditions and the various treatments for ED (Weeks & Gambescia, 2000).

Individual Psychological Factors

The next component of the Intersystem Approach involves the psychological nature of the man and his partner, including: psychological traits, tendencies, diagnoses, strengths, disorders, developmental stages, etc. The emotional issues of each partner will influence and be impacted by the other in a reciprocal manner, driving their unique system. Regardless of sexual preference or orientation, in ED, apprehension is expressed sexually and typically manifests as performance anxiety. Performance anxiety causes the man to perceive that he is not getting an erection fast enough, that the erection is not firm enough, or that it does not seem to last long enough. Once a man experiences even a single case of ED, a vicious cycle may become established whereby he anticipates erectile problems, and increasingly uses negative thinking, which skews perceptions of self-worth and partner attributes (Gambescia, Sendak, & Weeks, 2009; Dean et al., 2006). Additionally, men tend to use their sexual functioning at a younger age as a baseline for erectile capacity. The fact that getting the erection takes longer and is not immediate may be interpreted as a sexual performance problem rather than a predictable change in sexual functioning. This misinterpretation can significantly increase performance anxiety and pessimism about erectile ability.

Additionally, depression, anger, anxiety, low self-esteem, lack of confidence, poor body image, and adherence to rigid gender ideals can interfere with both sexual interest and arousal (Fisher et al., 2005; Lourenco, Aevedo, & Gouveia, 2010). Notably, depression is commonly seen in men with ED. Several studies have documented this correlation independent of physical etiologies (Araujo et al., 2000) and also in men with cardiovascular disease (Mulat et al., 2009). The empirical evidence does not always document bidirectional causality between the aforementioned psychological correlates and ED; yet, our clinical observations confirm that depression, shame, guilt, negative cognitions, and performance anxiety are major contributors to, as well as consequences of, ED.

Men with ED also report a lack of assurance that they can control the outcomes of sexual interactions; this risk factor perpetuates their lack of self-worth (Abdo, Afif-Abdo, Otani, & Machado, 2008). It is understandable that men with ED feel saddened or depressed by the perceived loss of masculinity, partner disappointment, lack of control, etc. Additionally, ED can perpetuate or result from other sexual dysfunctions such as male hypoactive sexual desire disorder and early ejaculation. Mental illnesses, such as schizophrenia and bipolar disorder, can impair relationship stability and sexual arousal (Simopoulos & Trinidad, 2013). Finally, the therapist must also be vigilant for sexual secrets resulting from undisclosed emotional or sexual trauma, sexually compulsive behaviors, or infidelity as these factors can interrupt sexual functioning at all phases of the sexual response cycle (Maltz, 2012; Weeks, Gambescia, & Jenkins, 2003).

ED often occurs within the context of partnered sex; thus, the Intersystem Approach views the couple, not just the man, as an integral part of the sexual problem and solution (Weeks & Fife, 2014). Relationship factors must be explored as they are often associated with ED. These include but are not limited to: strengths, vulnerabilities, communication patterns, conflict resolution modes, and the couple's capacity for intimacy. We have found that the symptoms of ED are often a cause or consequence of relationship dissatisfaction or conflicting expectations; therefore, consideration is given to each partner's view of the predicament and how it is systemically maintained. Additionally, communication problems, power struggles, or unmet intimacy needs can contribute to the progression of ED and interfere with seeking treatment (Althof, 2002). The therapist must also assess for conscious or unrecognized fears of intimacy, dependency, rejection, or being controlled (Weeks & Gambescia, 2000). ED can be a contributor to and consequence of infidelity, a lack of partner trust, and changes in perception of partner's physical attractiveness (Gambescia, Sendak, & Weeks, 2009). When a sexual problem such as ED exists, partners become goal-oriented, losing focus of the pleasurable sexual and sensual aspects of intimacy. Lastly, we have often found that it is not unusual to find that both partners are experiencing sexual dissatisfaction or dysfunction when the man suffers from ED.

Intergenerational Influences

Much of what is learned about affection, love, intimacy, masculinity, and femininity is acquired, overtly or covertly, within the family-of-origin. Through the transgenerational learning process, messages about sexuality often comingle with emotions and expectations regarding intimacy and sexuality. In many instances, accurate sex information is not acquired within the family or through structured educational channels; misinformation can be highly detrimental to healthy sexual functioning. In fact, the belief system of the man with ED often contains sexual mythology, negative automatic thinking, sexual guilt, and anxiety (Mosher, 1979). Sexual misinformation can be transmitted through a legacy of secrecy-the fact that sex is not discussed in the family-of-origin, or through other family secrets regarding pregnancies, abortions, affairs, and sexual orientation of family members. Sexual secrecy, ignorance, internalized sex-negative messages, boundary violations, family dysfunction, and sexual abuse have profound negative effects on sexual functioning (Kinzl, Mangweth, Traweger, & Biebl, 1996). Understanding a man's internalized belief system will ensure a more comprehensive appraisal of his sexual system, ED, his transgenerational dynamics, and expectations.

Environmental Considerations

Sexuality is understood within the context of sociocultural norms, beliefs, preferences, customs, and values. These environmental factors contribute to a person's sexual script, which provides guidelines for the development of sexual attitudes, expectations, and

The scripts can get calcified

behavior (Kimmel, 2007). If sexual partners follow similar scripts, expectations and perceptions should be compatible and distress relatively low (Wiederman, 2005). Typically, however, various overlapping environmental factors can be contradictory within the individual and between partners, creating difficulties in ascribing meaning to and understanding of sexual interactions (McGoldrick, Loonan, & Wohlsifer, 2007). To practice effective sex therapy in the treatment of ED, the clinician must grasp the meaning of diverse environmental issues for the man and his partner and help them make sense of the conflicts related to culture, religion, social class, ethnicity, sexual practices, etc. (Hall & Graham, 2012). Moreover, the clinician is obligated to demonstrate insight and sensitivity with respect to these factors.

The Sex History

The foundation of Intersystemic treatment of ED is the comprehensive sex history, beginning with the personal background, mental status, and the medical history of each partner. Thorough attention is given to the presenting problem, allowing for discussion of feelings and thoughts about the causes and consequences of the sexual symptoms. It is helpful to ask what measures the couple has taken to correct the situation on their own. This question allows discussion of feelings of pessimism, often because they have tried to remedy the problem, have been unsuccessful, and fear they are beyond hope. Encourage dialogue about a sexual time line, beginning with their first intimate experience together, including qualitative and quantitative information. Be attentive for the presence of additional sexual problems in the man with ED and the presence of sexual dysfunction in the partner. Through individual or conjoint sessions, explore their cognitive scripts, and the potential disjuncture between individual and relational schemas (Masters, Casey, Wells, & Morrison, 2013). Intergenerational factors can be accessed through the use of a sexual genogram (see DeMaria, Weeks, & Hof, 1999).

Attempt to determine the extent to which the ED is organic, psychogenic, or of combined etiology. ED cannot be viewed as a binary phenomenon; typically, organic, psychogenic, relational, and environmental factors influence each other in the development and maintenance of the symptom. If a man awakens from sleep with firm erections, the cause, most likely, is predominantly psychogenic. The most useful question to obtain this information is to ask about awakening from sleep with erections and the quality of morning erections (Segraves, Segraves, & Schoenberg, 1987). In organic etiology, the onset of erectile difficulty is typically gradual and the duration is long term (Montorsi et al., 2010). ED with a sudden onset and short duration suggests a psychogenic etiology according to Shamloul and Ghanem (2013). Also, it is imperative to understand the technique, frequency, and fantasy used in masturbation to determine etiology. Is the partner able to replicate the physical and psychological stimulation he requires? Does the man have erectile difficulty with a partner and not during masturbation?

Flexibility is essential in terms of what is asked, pacing questions to the tolerance of the couple, and pausing to clarify their emotional responses. Open-ended questions are useful at first, with subsequent progression to more specific queries about the problem. Clarify the rationale for questions used in order to increase compliance and reduce anxiety. It is beneficial to normalize a question, placing it in a greater context of occurrence, such as "many people experience periods of anxiety during sexual activity, when does this happen to you?" With any sex history, it is important to permit opportunity for sensitive material to be shared in individual sessions. Since ED can occur only during certain acts, such as fellatio or anal penetration, if the therapist maintains an exclusive focus on coitus, this information could be unseen.

Include a relational assessment of the couple's history, sexual and sensual styles, expectations, strengths, and positive and negative coping strategies. As stated previously, sexual problems become embedded in the relationship dynamics, each impacting the other. Relational risk factors, such as anger, resentment, or power struggles can predispose the man and his partner to experience sexual problems.

The following questions, specific to erectile capacity, will aid the clinician in determining the etiology and severity of ED:

- How long have you had problems with erections?
- Describe the erectile difficulty.
- How often are you able to get an erection during sexual activity?
- How confident are you that you can get and keep an erection to the completion of sex?
- Do you have erectile difficulty in particular situations?
- Are you satisfied with the hardness of your erection?
- Are you satisfied with the overall sexual experience?
- How difficult is it to maintain your erection to completion of sexual activity?
- Are your erections hard enough for penetration?
- Is sexual stimulation with your partner adequate?
- Was the onset of problems sudden or gradual?
- Do you have erections in the morning, upon awakening or during sleep?
- Do you have erectile difficulties during solo sexual activity?
- During penetration, how difficult is it to maintain the erection to completion?
- Are you sometimes able to get a firm erection but then lose it shortly after penetration?

Intersystemic Treatment

The treatment for ED is tailored to the unique needs of the man and his partner. The goal of treatment is to reduce psychological distress, recover self-esteem, improve quality of life, and enhance sexual functioning and satisfaction. Partner distress and concern about the relationship are often strong motivators for pursuing treatment of ED, in addition to the personal distress discussed previously (McCabe & Matic, 2008; Swindle, Cameron, Lockhart, & Rosen, 2004); thus, we believe that inclusion of the partner and addressing relational needs is an important factor in treatment outcome (Conaglen & Conaglen, 2008). Moreover, the advances in medical managements for ED often require the comingling of medical and psychological therapies. The therapist must have a working knowledge of all treatment modalities and comfort with integrating numerous treatment options.

The Intersystemic treatment of ED, therefore, involves clarification of the meaning of the dysfunction for the couple, expansion of the couple's definition of sex and intimacy, and establishing a wider repertoire of sexually pleasurable activity. For many couples, treatment facilitates a return to sexual activity after a period of abstinence. In such instances, the couple must be given the opportunity to process thoughts about past sexual experiences as well as apprehension about their future. Additionally, treatment provides an occasion for the man and his partner to discuss how and when to use medical options, lifestyle modifications, and relationship concerns that contribute to or result from ED. Thus, the therapist supports the couple in establishing and working toward goals that promote physical health as well as sexual satisfaction (Gupta et al., 2011; Weeks & Gambescia, 2000).

Medical Treatments

It is the responsibility of the Intersystemic therapist to:

- Conduct a comprehensive sex history
- Require that the man undergo a physical examination
- Discuss lifestyle modifications
- Review the advantages and risks associated with all medical treatments

Lifestyle modifications, (smoking cessation, weight reduction, and increasing physical activity) in conjunction with oral medical treatments discussed below, have been found to reduce the severity of ED (Horasanli, Boylu, Kendirci, & Miroglu, 2008).

Oral medications. Phosphodiesterase type 5 (PDE5) inhibitors are considered the first line medical treatment for ED (Shamloul & Ghanem, 2013). Essentially, these medications promote genital tumescence through a series of complex physiologic mechanisms that regulate smooth muscle tone and increase blood flow into the corpora cavernosa of the penis; these oral agents do not stimulate libido or desire. See Raina et al., (2010) for a more detailed explanation. PDE5 inhibitors vary in the dosage, onset, and duration of action. Recently daily dosing regimens and sublingual administration have been approved for use. The man and his partner should be helped to consider these factors in the selection of the best medication for the specific situation. Often, physicians do not have sufficient time to teach and include the partner. Sometimes, the man is given a few different oral agent samples and is told to try them.

The therapist should be mindful that side effects, while generally mild and well tolerated, could include headache, reddening of the face and neck (flushing), indigestion, and nasal congestion. Cialis® may cause muscle aches and back pain, which usually resolve within 48 hours. Priapism (a persistent and usually painful long-lasting erection) is rarely associated with oral agents. PDE5 inhibitors are contraindicated when taking nitrates because the blood pressure could drop to an unsafe level. Excessive amounts of alcohol when taking PDE5-I inhibitors should be avoided because the interaction can cause a drop in blood pressure. Up to 35% of men taking oral agents fail to respond to this treatment due to underlying medical conditions (Shamloul & Ghanem, 2013). For purposes of brevity, we will discuss the three most commonly prescribed drugs in this group:

1. Cialis® (tadalafil)

   Dosage: 2.5, 5, 10, and 20 mg.
   Onset of action: 20–45 minutes (not affected if taken with food)
   Duration: up to 36 hours

2. Levitra® (vardenafil)

   Dosage: 2.5, 5, 10, and 20 mg.
   Onset of action: 30 minutes (delayed if taken with food)
   Duration 4–6 hours

3. Viagra® (sildenafil)

   Dosage: 25, 50, and 100 mg
   Onset of action: 30–60 minutes (delayed if taken with food)
   Duration: 4–6 hours

The use of oral agents in treating ED has been found to improve sexual and relationship satisfaction in many men (Rosen et al., 2006). Several new drugs in this group are under investigation or recently released.

The following therapies for ED can be used in conjunction with the oral therapies or used alone if the man does not respond to first line oral therapies. They are considered the second line of medical treatments for ED.

Vacuum constriction device. This noninvasive device applies continuous negative pressure to the shaft of the penis, creating a vacuum. It involves placing a clear plastic cylinder over the penis and drawing air from the cylinder. Reduced air pressure within the cylinder helps draw blood into the cavernous tissue of the penis, causing an erection. Blood is trapped through the use of an adjustable tourniquet applied around the base of the penis that is removed after sexual relations. Although some men and their partners are satisfied with this appliance, less than half discontinue use because of the mechanical issues, inconvenience, and inhibition of sexual spontaneity (Glina & Porst, 2006; Wessels, 2006).

Tourniquet. A tourniquet alone can be used to help maintain erectile tumescence. A soft adjustable loop device can be placed at the base of the penile shaft in order to enhance erection by retaining the blood in the penis during arousal and orgasm. The device is then removed after the completion of sexual activity. The best product we have seen is called the ACTIS® venous flow controller (Vivus.com) and requires a prescription from a physician.

Intracavernosal Injection. Penile injections are used to introduce a single or combination of vasodilators directly into the erectile tissue of the penis with a small needle prior to anticipated sex. The erection is immediate and predictable although unrelated to sexual desire. Each man requires an individualized dosing regimen. Proper education about administration is necessary. The most common side effect is penile pain. Also, the injection cannot be used every day to avoid penile fibrosis. Over half of the men successfully using this method discontinue due to inconvenience and apprehension about injecting the penis (Hatzimouratidis & Hatzichristou, 2005; Soderdahl, Thrasher, & Hansberry, 1997).

Intraurethral medication. A tiny pellet is inserted into the penile urethra with a thin plastic applicator approximately 15 minutes prior to sexual relations. The pellet contains a vasodilator, which dissolves within the urethra and is absorbed into the erectile tissue, promoting tumescence. Theoretically, a resulting erection can last for an hour; however, efficacy is often more limited than the injection mentioned above and many men experience burning after insertion. Success rates are between 43% and 69% (Shamloul & Ghanem, 2013). Many men discontinue intraurethral treatment due to an inadequate response or side effects.

Penile Prosthesis. Penile implants, the third line of medical treatment, are recommended as a last resort for the treatment of ED. Flexible rods or inflatable tubes are surgically inserted into the erectile tissue of the penis enabling tumescence sufficient for sexual activity. The flexible implant can be manipulated into different positions for sexual relations or for rest. However, it cannot produce a fully erect penis, and the device is difficult to conceal (Shamloul & Ghanem, 2013).

The inflatable implant involves more working components. The hydraulic prosthesis can be inflated or deflated through activation of a pump controlling the flow of water from a reservoir in the lower abdomen to the cylinders placed inside the corpora cavernosa of the penis.

When an erection is desired, the man pumps the fluid from the reservoir to the cylinders within the penis (Mulcahy et al., 2004). Surgical, mechanical, and financial risks should be carefully considered; infection occurs in 2–4% of cases (Selph & Carson, 2011). Bettocchi et al. (2010) report high rates of satisfaction for the man and his partner with this method; however once the penile prosthesis is implanted, the erectile tissue is permanently altered, and it is impossible to achieve an erection if it is removed.

Noncompliance With Medical Therapies

Despite efficacy, second line treatments for ED are often discontinued (Soderdahl, Thrasher, & Hansberry, 1997). The drop-out rate can be explained by numerous burdensome logistic problems with the vacuum apparatus and unpleasant methods of administration of pellets and injections. First line oral medications, however, also carry surprisingly high discontinuation rates of roughly 50% according to Carvalheira, Pereira, Maroco, and Forjaz (2012). A combination of factors can lead to discontinuation of PDEI-5s such as non-effectiveness, embarrassment about drug-assisted erections, fears about physical safety, and relationship factors. As Althof (2006) explains, the man's psychological comfort and relationship with his partner must be considered and addressed when making decisions about treatments for ED. Our clinical observations are supported by research findings that, despite seeking treatment to improve sexual functioning, many men who discontinued oral therapy reported relationship problems and partner sexual disinterest (Klotz, Mathers, & Sommer, 2005). Sometimes resuming sexual interest after a period of inactivity can disturb the delicate yet fragile emotional or intimate homeostasis maintained by the couple. Perhaps the intimacy fears of one or both partners hinder their motivation to be sexually intimate, or other preexisting relationship problems can influence noncompliance. Additionally, oral agents introduce pressure/expectation to engage in a greater quantity of sex than is desired by one or both partners. It is plausible that the prior focus on the ED symptoms distracted the couple from the now obvious dysfunction in the "asymptomatic" partner such as lack of desire. The couple might have become so burdened by ED symptoms and the concomitant performance anxiety that the motivation for satisfying sexual activity is low. Occasionally there is little or no prior discussion about using an oral agent and the unsuspecting partner is surprised or unprepared for sexual activity. We often hear that medically augmented erections are artificial and, thus, not about true attraction to the partner. Conceivably there can be inadequate sexual interest, desire, or attraction in either partner to seek a higher level of sexual engagement. Less frequently, discontinuation is related to sexual preferences that have not been articulated or agreed upon by the couple such as fetishistic or sadomasochistic preferences. Finally, environmental and situational stressors such as work pressure, finances, and concerns about family members might present obstacles to treatment.

Psychological Treatments

We believe the Intersystem Approach provides the best theoretical model for the treatment of ED since it is comprehensive and integrative; however, the therapist must be comfortable and flexible in using a number of psychological treatments concurrently. Moreover, the aforementioned medical therapies are often used in combination with psychotherapy in the treatment of ED. It has been well substantiated in the literature that the combined approach is more efficacious in promoting sexual satisfaction and compliance than the use of either psychotherapy or medical treatments alone (Abdo, Afif-Abdo, Otani, & Machado, 2008; Melnik, Soares, & Nasello, 2008).

In the following sections, we will review some of the abundant cognitive, behavioral, and dynamic treatment strategies that can help the man and his partner overcome obstacles to sexual arousal.

Promoting Systemic Thinking

The first goal of treatment is to support the understanding that ED is a problem for the couple, not just the man. Each partner is helped to see their role in the development and maintenance of sexual symptoms and in overcoming obstacles to intimacy and sexual satisfaction, regardless of the etiology (Weeks & Gambescia, 2000). The therapist involves the couple in discussions about the connection between sexual fulfillment and relational satisfaction, helping them to see how ED may stem from relational causes not previously expressed or considered. Conversely, experiencing ED might have contributed to relationship dissatisfaction. Sometimes preexisting sexual problems or those in response to ED, such as the lack of sexual desire, may surface during treatment. The couple is aided in discussing how they felt about their sexual relationship prior to and during the emergence of ED, the concerns that they may currently have, and other expectations. When psychotherapy and medical treatments are combined, all components must be understood and negotiated by the couple.

Reframing the Symptom

The technique of reframing is often used in the Intersystemic treatment of ED. It is a way to help the man and his partner to change the cognitive or perceptual meaning of the symptom from something that is purely negative; for instance, ED can be viewed as a way to maintain a safe and comfortable distance both emotionally and physically. Additionally, it protects the partners from encountering conflict within themselves or between them. The couple can eventually be helped to comprehend some of the unseen obstacles that have contributed to and maintained the erectile difficulty, and, therefore, they can feel that resolution is tangible (Weeks & Gambescia, 2000).

Supporting Realistic Expectations

The medicalization of ED treatment has contributed to the notion that sexual disorders are purely physical and easily corrected with medication alone. This overly simplistic misconception can generate pessimism and noncompliance with psychological therapies. The man and his partner are helped to comprehend that ED is a physical symptom with layers of potential etiologies. The therapist helps the couple to identify and correct the underlying individual and relational risk factors that maintain the sexual symptom. Frequently, the couple with ED has avoided physical intimacy for months or years. They may have tried to remedy the difficulty on their own, hoped that it would go away, and found that the more they tried, the more they failed. The man and his partner often share feelings of skepticism and a sense of urgency to correct the situation. The therapist can lead them to construct realistic expectations of sexual enjoyment given their preferences, ages, and physical ability. This process is interactive with the therapist continuously offering accurate information about normative sexuality. Optimism is encouraged through repeated small successes that result in measurable and steady progress (Gambescia, Sendak, & Weeks, 2009; Weeks & Gambescia, 2000).

Changing Cognitions

Couples dealing with ED obsess and worry about sexual performance. Additionally, the anticipation of a problem (anticipatory anxiety) and the self-monitoring that occurs during sexual activity interferes with pleasure and perpetuates ED. Yet, it is not performance anxiety alone that produces the sexual difficulty, but the dysfunctional catastrophic thinking associated with it (I am going to lose my erection again? My partner will leave me. I am not a man. I am a failure). Female partners often experience negative cognitions related to their self-worth or attractiveness (Is it my fault? He does not find me attractive? He does not love me.) or they entertain misattributions about the ED (He must be having an affair? Is he gay?). The therapist helps them to recognize irrational thoughts, stop them, and replace them with factual cognitions about sex, and the relationship. Additionally, men with ED often report that the penis has a mind of its own. They fail to make the connection between the real situational stressors that can interfere with sexual arousal such as relationship discord and occupational concerns. Cognitive restructuring helps the couple to expand their focus beyond sexual performance to consider that ED does not just happen; it is a consequence of life distress, relationship problems, individual traits, and perhaps, organic factors.

Reducing Anxiety

The relationship between anxiety and sexual dysfunction is well documented in the clinical literature (Dèttore, Pucciarelli, & Santarnecchi, 2013). Sexual anxiety is common and can manifest in various ways, but two forms are particularly damaging with respect to ED: performance anxiety and response anxiety. The former appears in anticipation of sex or during sexual intimacy. For instance, in ED the couple focuses on the man's penis and awaits erectile failure rather than concentrating on pleasurable sensations. Response anxiety is the belief that one should feel more desire for the partner than they currently experience or to force the feeling of desire. Cognitive interventions, sensate focus, and psychoeducation promote recognition and reduction in sexual anxiety (Epstein & Baucom, 2002). Additionally, the partners learn to appreciate the damaging effect of anxiety on pleasure and intimacy. Generally, the therapist prescribes and promotes conditions that focus on relaxation and pleasurable sensations and illustrates the connection between sexual and relational satisfaction.

Correcting Mythology

We often find that our couples, despite obvious intelligence, are uninformed about normative sexual functioning and fail to challenge internalized sexual misconceptions and mythology. Misunderstandings about sex perpetuate unrealistic performance expectations and ultimately foster disappointment and sexual dissatisfaction. A particularly destructive belief is that sexual arousal should be automatic and unrelated to feelings, desires, and preferences (Bullough & Bullough, 1995; Camacho & Reyes-Ortiz, 2005). Additionally, it is crucial to challenge the equation of erection with self-worth (Althof & Wieder, 2004), a common misconception in men with ED. Other heterosexual cognitive distortions involve beliefs about what a woman wants and needs: the size and firmness of the erect penis alone will satisfy a female partner; women prefer intercourse to other non-coital sex; and, it is the obligation of the man to satisfy the woman. An extremely user-friendly book, *The New Male Sexuality* (Zilbergeld, 1999), continues to be a non-threatening psychoeducational tool for men and their partners. Correcting mythology in addition to other therapeutic strategies reduces sexual anxiety and cognitive distortions and ultimately fosters sexual satisfaction.

Enriching Communication Skills

Communication is an imperative mediating variable between relationship and sexual satisfaction (Byers, 2005; Purnine & Carey, 1997). We find that our couples often have difficulty expressing feelings about life stressors, worries, concerns, etc. They seem to believe that if a problem is not discussed, it will disappear. They do not appreciate that unexpressed feelings can and will interfere with sexual arousal. Moreover, they are embarrassed to discuss sexual preferences and desires due to internalized negative messages about intimacy and sexuality. Another factor contributing to poor sexual communication is the lack of comprehension of normal sexual structures and functioning. With specific relevance to ED, some couples fear that speaking about it will worsen the symptoms; thus, the therapist must carefully guide them to release the underlying fears and apprehensions tied to the sexual symptom (Gambescia, Sendak, & Weeks, 2009). Additionally, many men may construe genuine support from their partners as humiliating and as evidence of a profound problem. The therapist's role is to correct such misattributions, noting that motivations and intentions are frequently misunderstood, especially in sexual matters (Fisher et al., 2005).

It is necessary to explain that clear communication about sex improves sexual fulfillment and overall relationship satisfaction (MacNeil & Byers, 1997; Schwartz & Young, 2009). Direct, unambiguous communication is demonstrated by the therapist and validated during sessions. We encourage speaking for oneself in an honest and non-judgmental way, and reflective listening, an active process in which the receiver restates the content and reflects back the feeling tone of the sender's message. In sexual communication, the therapist corrects misinformation, clarifies ambiguous language used by the partners, and provides strategies for using correct terminology in sessions and at home.

Psychoeducation

Through recommending readings (bibliotherapy), and other technological modalities, accurate information about sexuality is discussed in session and at home. Psychoeducation serves to correct sexual mythology, provide permission to discuss sexual material, and encourage communication about sex. The therapist is responsible to read and review the assigned material with the couple, exploring their reactions and ideas in subsequent sessions (see Gambescia & Weeks, 2006).

Homework

Homework has always been the hallmark of sex therapy and is a strategic constituent of the Intersystem Approach. While many do not like the term or concept, at-home assignments serve countless beneficial functions such as reinforcing what the partners have already learned in session and applying these skills to new situations. Ultimately homework reduces the anxiety and dysphoria associated with ED by introducing concrete methods to interrupt negative thinking and behavior, and by promoting success instead of failure. Homework extends the learning experience from the office to the home, augmenting overall therapeutic efficacy (see Gambescia & Weeks, 2006). Typically, assignments for treating ED contain basic components of: psychoeducation, bibliotherapy, communication skills, sensual touch, and sensate focus exercises. Creating and discussing a sexual genogram elucidates internalized misinformation, sexual scripts and related expectations, familial intimacy patterns, and other barriers to sexual arousal (Hof & Berman, 1986). Constructing and deconstructing assignments is a collaborative process although the therapist clearly takes the lead.

Promoting Sensuality

Sensate focus is a specific application of systematic desensitization in which partners are helped to overcome anxiety and negative associations to sexual intimacy (Lazarus, 1971).

The couple is gradually and judiciously exposed to situations that once made them anxious; however, they learn to use relaxation techniques in such circumstances. Each exercise must be designed so that it is a small step in the direction of a specific goal. The graduated increments must be so small that each step is experienced as a success, not a failure. Since the emphasis is on feeling sensations, rather than sexual performance, success is much more likely. Additionally, sensate focus exercises interrupt the cycle of avoidance that is so destructive to relational satisfaction. See Weeks and Gambescia (2000) for more elaboration about the systemic approach to sensate focus.

Expansion of the Sexual Repertoire

Unlearning old self-defeating expectations and patterns is a challenge to the man with ED and his partner. A goal of Intersystem treatment is to re-educate the couple and reset expectations about normative age-related sexual function and frequency. We emphasize that levels of desire may vary and do not have to be synchronous; noncoital, non-demand touch can be satisfying; and that enjoyable sex does not necessarily focus on a solitary goal of coitus. Often, mindfulness techniques are recommended to help the man and his partner relax and experience pleasurable sensations *in the moment* (Lazaridou, & Kalogianni, 2013; Rosenbaum, 2013; Sommers, 2013). Mindfulness interventions promote empathy, compassion, affection, and connection (Kozlowski, 2013). Intersystemic treatment encourages sensuality as a goal in itself rather than a performance orientation (Lousada & Angel, 2011).

Relapse Prevention

Relapses are an expected part of treatment, especially in states of negative emotion, interpersonal conflict, social pressure, etc. Identifying and anticipating the negative connection between stress and sexual arousal will help the couple to remain optimistic in the presence of a setback. They can be reminded to use the cognitive-behavioral skills they have acquired previously (McCarthy & Fucito, 2005) while the therapist works to uncover other issues that might be triggering relapse (Gambescia, Sendak, & Weeks, 2009). Terminating treatment too soon can trigger setbacks. Determine that goals have been successfully accomplished, underlying concomitant factors are addressed, and the couple has a plan to return for future sessions as needed and as scheduled.

Avoiding Common Mistakes

As with relapses in treatment, therapeutic errors should be anticipated and corrected immediately. Dealing with complex sexual/relational issues can be taxing and challenging. Psychotherapy involves trying many approaches, continuing the ones that work and eliminating those that prove unproductive. Since the Intersystemic therapist wears many hats, errors are unavoidable; thus, early detection and correction is essential. Common therapeutic mistakes include but are not limited to:

- Ill timed interventions
- Overlooking commitment issues
- Faulty reframes
- Failing to make process interventions
- Mismatched interventions

- Forced pacing
- Overlooking spiritual, cultural, and other environmental considerations
- Confidentiality traps
- Unrecognized therapist biases
- Losing control of the structure or process
- Not remaining neutral
- Inadequate assessment of concomitant factors

As Weeks (2005; Weeks, Odell, & Methven, 2005) suggests, perfect therapy is unrealistic; yet, it is in everyone's best interests that the therapist is productive rather than perfect.

References

Abdo, C.H., Afif-Abdo, J., Otani, F., & Machado, A.C. (2008). Sexual satisfaction among patients with erectile dysfunction treated with counseling, sildenafil, or both. *Journal of Sexual Medicine*, 5(7), 1720–1726. doi: 10.1111/j.1743–6109.2008.00841.x

Althof, S.E. (2002). Quality of life and erectile dysfunction. *Urology*, 59(6), 803–810. doi: 10.1016/S0090–4295(02)01606–0

Althof, S.E. (2006). Sexual therapy in the age of pharmacotherapy. *Annual Review of Sex Research*, 17, 1–16.

Althof, S.E., & Wieder, M. (2004). Psychotherapy for erectile dysfunction: Now more relevant than ever. *Endocrine*, 23(2–3), 131–134.

American Psychiatric Association. (2013). *Diagnostic and statistical manual of mental disorders* (5th ed.). Arlington, VA: American Psychiatric Publishing.

Araujo, A.B., Johannes, C.B., Feldman, H.A., Derby, C., & McKinlay, J.B. (2000). Relationship between psychosocial risk factors and incident erectile dysfunction: Prospective results from the Massachusetts male aging study. *American Journal of Epidemiology*, 152(6), 533–541. doi: 10.1093/aje/152.6.533

Awad, A., Alsaid, B., Bessede, T., Droupy, S., & Benoit, G (2011). Evolution in the concept of erection anatomy. *Surgical & Radiologic Anatomy*, 33, 301–312. doi: 10.1007/s00276–010–0707–4

Bancroft, J., Carnes, L., Janssen, E., Goodrich, D., & Long, J. (2005). Erectile and ejaculatory problems in gay and heterosexual men. *Archives of Sexual Behavior*, 34(3), 285–297. doi: 10.1007/s10508–005–3117–7

Bettocchi, C., Palumbo, F., Spilotros, M., Lucarelli, G., Palazzo, S., Battaglia, M., . . . Ditonno, P. (2010). Patient and partner satisfaction after AMS inflatable penile prosthesis implant. *Journal of Sexual Medicine*, 7(1), 304–309. doi: 10.1111/j.1743–6109.2009.01499.x

Bocchio, M., Pelliccione, F., Mihalca, R., Ciociola, F., Necozione, S., Rossi, A., . . . Francavilla, S. (2009). Treatment of erectile dysfunction reduces psychological distress. *International Journal of Andrology*, 32(1), 74–80. doi: 10.1111/j.1365–2605.2007.00820.x

Bullough, V.L., & Bullough, B. (1995). *Sexual attitudes: Myths and realities*. New York: Prometheus Books.

Byers, E. (2005). Relationship satisfaction and sexual satisfaction: A longitudinal study of individuals in long-term relationships. *The Journal of Sex Research*, 42(2), 113–118.

Camacho, M.E., & Reyes-Ortiz, C.A. (2005). Sexual dysfunction in the elderly: Age or disease? *International Journal of Impotence Research*, 17(1), 52–56. doi: 10.1038/sj.ijir.3901429

Carvalheira, A.A., Pereira, N.M., Maroco, J., & Forjaz, V. (2012). Dropout in the treatment of erectile dysfunction with PDE5: A study on predictors and a qualitative analysis of reasons for discontinuation. *Journal of Sexual Medicine*, 9(9), 2361–2369. doi: 10.1111/j.1743–6109.2012.02787.x

Chevret, M., Jaudinot, E., Sulllivan, K., Marrel, A., & De Gendre, A.S. (2004). Impact of erectile dysfunction (ED) on sexual life of female partners: Assessment with the Index of Sexual Life (ISL) questionnaire. *Journal of Sex & Marital Therapy*, 30(3), 157–172. doi: 10.1080/00926230490262366

Chung, S.D., Chen, Y.K., Lin, H.C., & Lin, H.C. (2011). Increased risk of stroke among men with erectile dysfunction: A nationwide population-based study. *Journal of Sexual Medicine, 8*(1), 240–246. doi: 10.1111/j.1743-6109.2010.01973.x

Clayon, K., Keller, A., & McGarvey, E. (2006). Burden of phase-specific sexual dysfunction with SSRIs. *Journal of Affective Disorders, 91*(1), 27–32. doi: 10.1016/j.jad.2005.12.007

Conaglen, H.M., & Conaglen, J.V. (2008). The impact of erectile dysfunction on female partners: A qualitative investigation. *Sexual and Relationship Therapy, 23*(2), 147–156. doi: 10.1080/14681990801918680

Dean, J., deBoer, B., Graziottin, A., Hatzichristou, D., Heaton, J., & Tailor, A. (2006). Partner satisfaction and successful treatment outcomes for men with erectile dysfunction. *European Urology Supplements, 5*(13), 779–785. doi: 10.1016/j.eursup.2006.06.006

DeMaria, R., Weeks, G.R., & Hof, L. (1999). *Focused genograms: Intergenerational assessment of individuals, couples, and families.* Philadelphia, PA: Brunner/Mazel.

Dèttore, D., Pucciarelli, M., & Santarnecchi, E. (2013). Anxiety and female sexual functioning: An empirical study. *Journal of Sex & Marital Therapy, 39*(3), 216–240. doi: 10.1080/0092623X.2011.606879

Epstein, N., & Baucom, D.H. (2002). *Enhanced cognitive-behavioral therapy for couples: A contextual approach.* Washington, DC: American Psychological Association.

Feldman, H.A., Goldstein, I., Hatzichristou, D.G., Krane, R.J., & McKinlay, J.B. (1994). Impotence and its medical and psychosocial correlates: Results of the Massachusetts Male Aging Study. *Journal of Urology, 151*(1), 54–61.

Fisher, W., Rosen, R., Eardley, I., Sand, M., & Goldstein, I. (2005a). Sexual experience of female partners of men with erectile dysfunction: The female experience of men's attitudes to life events and sexuality (FEMALES) study. *The Journal of Sexual Medicine, 2*(5), 675–684.

Fisher, W.A., Derogatis, L.R., Sand, M., Rosen, R.C., Mollen, M. Brock, G., . . . Bandel, T.J. (2005). Improving the sexual quality of life of couples affected by erectile dysfunction: A double-blind, randomized, placebo-controlled trial of vardenafil. *The Journal of Sexual Medicine, 2*(5), 699–708. doi: 10.1111/j.1743-6109.2009.01222.x

Gambescia, N., Sendak, S., & Weeks, G. (2009). The treatment of erectile dysfunction. *Journal of Family Psychotherapy, 20*(2–3), 221–240.

Gambescia, N. & Weeks, G. (2006). Sexual dysfunction. In N. Kazantizis & L. L'Abate (Eds.), *Handbook of homework assignments in psychotherapy: Research, practice, and prevention* (pp. 351–368). Norwell, MA: Kluwer Academic Publishers.

Glina, S., & Porst, H. (2006). Vacuum erection devices. In H. Porst & J. Buvat (Eds.), *Standard practice in sexual medicine.* Malden, MA: Blackwell.

Gupta, B.P., Murad, M.H., Clifton, M.M., Prokop, L., Nehra, A., & Kopecky, S.L. (2011). The effect of lifestyle modification and cardiovascular risk factor reduction on erectile dysfunction: A systematic review and meta-analysis. *Archives of Internal Medicine, 171*(20), 1797–1803. doi: 10.1001/archinternmed.2011.440

Hall, K., & Graham, C. (Eds.). (2012). *The cultural context of sexual pleasure and problems.* New York: Routledge.

Hart, T., & Schwartz, D. (2010). Cognitive-behavioral erectile dysfunction treatment for gay men. *Cognitive and Behavioral Practice, 17,* 66–76. doi: 10.1016/j.cbpra.2009.04.009

Hatzimouratidis, K., & Hatzichristou, D.G. (2005). A comparative review of the options for treatment of erectile dysfunction: Which treatment for which patient? *Drugs, 65*(12), 1621–1650. doi: 10.2165/00003495-200565120-00003

Hof, L., & Berman, E. (1986). The sexual genogram. *Journal of Marital and Family Therapy, 12,* 39–47.

Horasanli, K., Boylu, U., Kendirci, M., & Miroglu, C. (2008). Do lifestyle changes work for improving erectile dysfunction? *Asian Journal of Andrology, 10*(1), 28–35. doi: 10.1111/j.1745-7262.2008.00363.x

Kimmel, M. (2007). *The sexual self: The construction of sexual scripts.* Nashville, TN: Vanderbilt University Press.

Kinzl, J., Mangweth, B., Traweger, C., & Biebl, W. (1996). Sexual dysfunction in males: Significance of adverse childhood experiences. *Child Abuse and Neglect, 20*(8), 759–766.

Kloner, R., & Schwartz, B. (2011). Clinical cardiology: Physician update: Erectile dysfunction and cardiovascular disease. *Circulation, 123*(1), 98–101.

Klotz, T., Mathers, M., & Sommer, F. (2005). Why do patients with erectile dysfunction abandon effective therapy with sildenafil (Viagra)? *International Journal of Impotence Research, 17*, 2–4. doi: 10.1038/sj.ijir.3901252

Kozlowski, A. (2013). Mindful mating: Exploring the connection between mindfulness and relationship satisfaction. *Sexual and Relationship Therapy, 28*(1–2), 92–104. doi: 10.1080/14681994.2012.748889

Lazaridou, A., & Kalogianni, C. (2013). Mindfulness and sexuality. *Sexual and Relationship Therapy, 28*(1–2), 29–38. doi: 10.1080/14681994.2013.773398

Lazarus, A. (1971). *Behavior therapy and beyond*. New York: McGraw-Hill.

Lewis, R. W., Fugl-Meyer, K. S., Corona, G., Hayes, R. D., Laumann, E. O., Moreira, Jr., E. D., . . . Segraves, T. (2010). Definitions/epidemiology/risk factors for sexual dysfunction. *Journal of Sexual Medicine, 7*(4pt2), 1598–1607.

Lourenco, M., Aevedo, L. P., & Gouveia, J. L. (2010). Depression and its impact on sexual desire. *European Psychiatry, 26*, 1549. doi: 10.1111/j.1743–6109.2011.02582.x

Lousada, M., & Angel, E. (2011). Tantric orgasm: Beyond Masters and Johnson. *Sexual and Relationship Therapy, 26*(4), 389–402. doi: 10.1080/14681994.2011.647903

MacNeil, S., & Byers, E. S. (1997). The relationship between sexual problems, communication, and sexual satisfaction. *The Canadian Journal of Human Sexuality, 6*(4), 277–289.

Maltz, W. (2012). *The sexual healing journey* (3rd ed.). New York: Harper Collins.

Masters, N. T., Casey, E., Wells, E. A., & Morrison, D. M. (2013). Sexual scripts among young heterosexually active men and women: Continuity and change. *Journal of Sex Research, 50*(5), 409–420. doi: 10.1080/00224499.2012.66110

McCabe, M. P., & Matic, H. (2008). Erectile dysfunction and relationships: Views of men with erectile dysfunction and their partners. *Sexual and Relationship Therapy, 23*(1), 51–60. doi: 10.1080/14681990701705559

McCarthy, B., & Fucito, L. (2005). Integrating medication, realistic expectations and therapeutic interventions in the treatment of male sexual dysfunction. *Journal of Sex & Marital Therapy, 31*(4), 319–328. doi: 10.1080/00926230590950226

McGoldrick, M., Loonan R., & Wohlsifer, D. (2007). Sexuality and culture. In S. R. Leiblum (Ed.), *Principles and practice of sex therapy* (4th ed., pp. 416–441). New York: Guilford Press.

Melnik, T., Soares, B., & Nasello, A. (2008). The effectiveness of psychological interventions for the treatment of erectile dysfunction: Systematic review and meta-analysis, including comparisons to sildenafil treatment, intracavernosal injection, and vacuum devices. *Journal of Sexual Medicine, 5*(11), 2562–2574. doi: 10.1111/j.1743–6109.2008.00872.x

Montorsi, F., Adaikan, G., Becher, E., Giuliano, F., Khoury, S., Lue, T. F., . . . Wasserman, M. (2010). Summary of the recommendations on sexual dysfunctions in men. *Journal of Sexual Medicine, 7*(11), 3572–3588.

Mosher, D. (1979). Sex guilt and sex myths in college men and women. *Journal of Sex Research, 15*(3), 224–234.

Mulat, B., Arbel, Y., Mashav, N., Saar, N., Steinvil, A., Heruti, R., . . . Justo, D. (2009). Depressive symptoms and erectile dysfunction in men with coronary artery disease. *Urology, 75*(1), 104–107.

Mulcahy J. J., Austoni, E., Barada, J. H., Hyung, K., Choi, H. K., Hellstrom, W. J., Krishnamurti, S., . . . Wessells, H. (2004). The penile implant for erectile dysfunction. *British Journal of Sexual Medicine, 1*(1), 98–109. doi: 10.1016/j.urology.2009.09.041

Purnine, D. M., & Carey, M. P. (1997). Interpersonal communication and sexual adjustment: The roles of understanding and agreement. *Journal of Consulting and Clinical Psychology, 65*(6), 1017–1025.

Raina, R., Pahlajani, G., Agarwal, A., Jones, S., & Zippe, C. (2010). Long-term potency after early use of a vacuum erection device following radical prostatectomy. *British Journal of Urology International, 106*, 1719–1722. doi: 10.1111/j.1464–410X.2010.09360.x

Rosen, R., Janssen, E., Wiegel, M., Bancroft, J., Althof, S., Wincze, J., . . . Barlow, D. (2006). Psychological and interpersonal correlates in men with erectile dysfunction and their partners: A pilot study of treatment outcome with sildenafil. *Journal of Sex & Marital Therapy*, 32(3), 215–234. doi: 10.1080/00926230600575314

Rosenbaum, T. Y. (2013). An integrated mindfulness-based approach to the treatment of women with sexual pain and anxiety: Promoting autonomy and mind/body connection. *Sexual and Relationship Therapy*, 28(1–2), 28–28. doi: 10.1080/14681994.2013.764981

Schwartz, P., & Young, L. (2009). Sexual satisfaction in committed relationships. *Sexuality Research & Social Policy*, 6(1), 1–17. doi: 10.1525/srsp.2009.6.1.1

Segraves, K. A., Segraves, R. T., & Schoenberg, H. W. (1987). Use of sexual history to differentiate organic from psychogenic impotence. *Archives of Sexual Behavior*, 16(2), 125–137.

Selph, J. P., & Carson, C. C. (2011). Penile prosthesis infection: Approaches to prevention and treatment. *Urologic Clinics of North America*, 38(2), 227–235. doi: 10.1016/j.ucl.2011.02.007

Shamloul, R., & Ghanem, H. (2013). Erectile dysfunction. *The Lancet*, 381(9861), 153–165.

Shindel, A., Vittinghoff, E., & Breyer, B. (2012). Erectile dysfunction and premature ejaculation in men who have sex with men. *Journal of Sexual Medicine*, 9(2), 576–584. doi: 10.1111/j.1743–6109.2011.02585.x

Simopoulos, E. F., & Trinidad, A. C. (2013). Male erectile dysfunction: integrating psychopharmacology and psychotherapy. *General Hospital Psychiatry*, 35(1), 33–38. doi: 10.1016/j.genhosppsych.2012.08.008

Soderdahl, D. W., Thrasher, J. B., & Hansberry, K. L. (1997). Intracavernosal drug-induced erection therapy versus external vacuum devices in the treatment of erectile dysfunction. *British Journal of Urology*, 79, 952–957.

Sommers, F. G. (2013). Mindfulness in love and love making: A way of life. *Sexual and Relationship Therapy*, 28(1–2), 84–91. doi: 10.1080/14681994.2012.756976

Stief, C. (2002). Is there a common pathophysiology for erectile dysfunction and how does this relate to the new pharmacotherapies? *International Journal of Impotence Research*, 14(Suppl. 1), 11–16.

Swindle, R. W., Cameron, A. E., Lockhart, D., & Rosen, R. C. (2004). The psychological and interpersonal relationship scales (PAIRS): Assessing psychological and relationship outcomes associated with erectile dysfunction and its treatment. *Archives of Sexual Behavior*, 33(1), 19–30. doi: 10.1023/B:ASEB.0000007459.48511.31

Thompson, I. M., Tangen, C. M., Goodman, P. J., Probstfield, J. L., Moinpour, C. M., & Coltman, C. A. (2005). Erectile dysfunction and subsequent cardiovascular disease. *Journal of the American Medical Association*, 294(23), 2996–3002. doi: 10.1001/jama.294.23.2996

Weeks, G. R. (2005). The emergence of a new paradigm in sex therapy: Integration. *Sexual and Relationship Therapy*, 20, 89–104.

Weeks, G., & Fife, S. (2014). *Couples in treatment*. New York: Routledge.

Weeks, G. R., & Gambescia, N. (2000). *Erectile dysfunction: Integrating couple therapy, sex therapy and medical treatment*. Dunmore, PA: W. W. Norton.

Weeks, G. R., Gambescia, N., & Jenkins, R. (2003). *Treating infidelity*. New York: W. W. Norton.

Weeks, G., Odell, M., & Methven, S. (2005). *If only I had known: Avoiding common mistakes in couples therapy*. New York: W. W. Norton & Company.

Wessels, H. (2006). Vacuum erection devices. In J. Mulcahy (Ed.), *Male sexual function: A guide to clinical management* (pp. 323–329). Totowa, NJ: Humana Press.

Wiederman, M. (2005). The gendered nature of sexual scripts. *The Family Journal: Counseling and Therapy for Couples and Families*, 13(4), 496–502. doi: 10.1177/1066480705278729

Zilbergeld, B. (1999). *The new male sexuality*. New York: Bantam.

6

PREMATURE EJACULATION

An Integrative, Intersystems Approach for Couples

Stephen J. Betchen

Premature ejaculation (PE), sometimes referred to as early ejaculation, is now considered the most common male sexual disorder in every country (Namavar & Robati, 2011). Studies from all over the globe support this assertion: Africa (Amidu et al., 2010), Australia (Palmer & Stuckey, 2008), Brazil (Busato & Galindo, 2004), China (Liang et al., 2010), Italy (Littara, Palmieri, Rottigni, & Iannitti, 2013), the United Kingdom (Linton & Wylie, 2010), and the United States (Serefoglu, 2013), to name a few. Still, PE remains difficult to measure with any great certainty primarily because of a lack of a universal consensus regarding the definition, differences in methodology, and the reluctance of men to report it because "a taboo on PE still exists" (Waldinger, 2013a, p. 19). While rates range from 20–30% (Andersson & Abdel-Hamid, 2011), Serefoglu (2013) believes that the prevalence rates are inflated due to reports of men who sometimes, but not always, experience PE. He believes that the actual percentage of persistent PE is approximately 8–10%.

It is believed that PE is a result of sexual inexperience and youth; thus, it is anecdotally considered to be widespread in adolescents, young adults, and other sexually naïve males. This assumption was confirmed in a sample of 755 Italian patients attending an outpatient clinic for sexual dysfunction (as cited in Jannini & Lenzi, 2005). The prevalence of PE younger than 40 years of age was greater than 40%. In men aged 70 and older, reported PE was less than 10% (Jannini & Lenzi, 2005, pp. 399–400). Additionally, advancing age does not appear to be a risk factor for PE (Carson & Gunn, 2006, p. 7).

Regarding men who have sex with men (MSM), as compared to heterosexually identified men, the prevalence estimates of PE are mixed (Carson & Gunn, 2006). Clearly, more empirical research in this area is necessary in order to draw any substantial conclusions. For instance, Rosser, Metz, Bockting, and Buroker (1997) found that PE was a "lifetime" problem for MSM. An incidence of 44% was reported, a rate far greater than for the general population. Conversely, Bell and Weinberg (1978) related the prevalence of PE is 27% in gay men, which is consistent with the prevalence estimates of the general population. In a study of 1,379 MSM and an age-matched sample of heterosexually identified men, PE was reported significantly more frequently in MSM (Bancroft et al., 2005).

PE Defined

Searching for an empirically derived definition of PE, many sexologists have embraced the use of a stopwatch to measure the intravaginal ejaculatory latency time (IELT), or the time between the start of vaginal penetration and the onset of intravaginal ejaculation. Studies utilizing this method have repeatedly found that 90% of men with lifelong PE (present since sexually active) ejaculated within 1 minute of intromission (Janssen et al., 2009; Waldinger et al., 2005). In a continuing attempt to find a universally acceptable definition for PE, The International Society of Sexual Medicine (ISSM) approved the following criteria for a definition of lifelong PE in 2008 (as cited by Waldinger, 2010, p. 273):

- Ejaculation always or nearly always happens prior to or within approximately 1 minute of vaginal penetration
- An inability to delay ejaculation on all or almost all vaginal penetrations
- Negative personal consequences, such as distress, bother, frustration, or the avoidance of sexual intimacy

Studies on acquired PE (after a period of normal sexual functioning) have not yielded sufficient enough data to merit definition based on empirical evidence (McMahon, 2013); however, the research did indicate that it could be successfully treated by medical or psychological interventions. Lifelong PE cannot be treated by medication or psychotherapy; because of the depth of its nature, it can only be controlled or postponed (Waldinger, 2010).

The *DSM-5* (American Psychiatric Association, 2013) defined PE as "a persistent or recurrent pattern of ejaculation occurring during partnered sexual activity within approximately 1 minute following vaginal penetration and before the individual wishes it" (p. 443). The disorder must be present on all sexual occasions for at least 6 months, cause significant distress, and not better explained by a nonsexual emotional disorder, relationship issue, or substance/medication or another medical condition. The *DSM-5* made further distinctions between lifelong and acquired types, generalized and situational types, and severity. The idiosyncratic nature of the sexual partner, relationship dynamics, vulnerability, psychiatric comorbidity, stressors, cultural/religious factors, medical factors, age, genetic factors, and drug use were also included in the evaluation process.

Etiology of PE

Masters and Johnson (1966) described a physiologic linear response cycle with four phases: arousal, plateau, orgasm and resolution. PE is considered a disorder of the orgasm phase of the male sexual response cycle. In the first phase of this cycle, sexual arousal/excitement, vasocongestion occurs (increased blood supply to the tissues of the genitals) and culminates in an erection. Kaplan (1979) later added a psychological component to the sexual response, sexual desire, which was believed to precede sexual arousal. A plateau phase follows in which arousal basically intensifies, sexual pleasure increases, and sexual tension peaks. There are two stages to the male orgasm: First, rhythmic contraction of the genital musculature and internal reproductive structures occurs and the man experiences a sense of ejaculatory inevitability (the point during arousal when the man can no longer prevent ejaculation). In effect, the ejaculate is moving through the internal structures, and thus, the orgasm has commenced and cannot be stopped even though the ejaculate has not yet been expelled. In the second phase of the male orgasm, the ejaculate is released from the penis in a series of rhythmic contractions. A state of resolution completes the cycle, as the body gradually returns to a non-aroused state. When a male cannot sustain a sufficient period of time engaged in the plateau stage, PE is the result.

Individual Biological/Physiological Factors

PE can sometimes be attributed to an individual man's biological predispositions. Jern et al. (2009) reported a significant moderate genetic effect (28%) for PE. Janssen et al. (2009) found IELT in lifelong PE sufferers to be associated with a diminished neurotransmission of serotonin. While not all neurological studies contended that penile hypersensitivity is a causal agent in PE (Abdel-Hamid, Abdel-Razek, & Anis, 2013), Jannini and Lenzi (2013) wrote: "The sensitivity of the glans penis, the organ triggering ejaculatory reflex, undoubtedly has an important role in the ejaculatory mechanism, and possibly in some forms of PE" (p. 85). Other neurological risk factors for PE include cerebral diseases such as traumatic brain injury, cerebrovascular disease, Parkinson's disease, and epilepsy (Abdel-Hamid et al., 2013).

Studies of the endocrine system and its impact on the ejaculatory process have yielded some valuable results. Corona et al. (2011) confirmed that all hormonal parameters: testosterone, thyroid stimulating hormone (TSH), and prolactin (PRL) significantly and independently contributed to IELT variation. The authors also confirmed that PE and DE (delayed ejaculation) are two ends of a single continuum; high testosterone levels were characteristic of PE while (DE) was associated with lower levels.

Urological problems have long been linked to PE. Diseases of the prostate are common correlates. Liang et al. (2010) found a high prevalence of PE in Chinese men with chronic prostatitis and chronic pelvic pain syndrome (CP/CPPS). Some of the symptoms of these disorders include pain in the perineum (the area between the anus and the posterior part of the external genitalia), penis and testicles, ejaculatory pain, and urinary urgency and frequency. Varicocele (the abnormal dilation of veins in the pampiniform plexus in the scrotum due to retrograde venous flow) and monosymptomatic enuresis (inability to control urination) have also been found to be associated with PE (Boonjindasup, Serefoglu, & Hellstrom, 2013, p. 163).

Type II diabetes mellitus (El-Sakka, 2003) and cardiovascular disease have been associated with PE, particularly if the PE was associated with erectile disorder (ED) (Palmer & Stuckey, 2008). In fact, PE was found to correlate significantly with ED. For example, in an attempt to control the ejaculatory process, some men attempt to distract themselves from the excitement of the sexual process and suffered erectile loss. Conversely, in an effort to achieve a firmer erection others increased stimulation and inadvertently incited PE (Rowland et al., 2010).

It was determined that PE can develop from the chronic use of or withdrawal from certain substances, particularly opiates. Some users reported that opiate use had alleviated their PE, and that they were afraid to stop using for fear their PE would return (Chekuri, Gerber, Brodie, & Krishnadas, 2012). Arackal and Benegal (2007) found that men who are alcohol dependent can develop PE. The authors noted that the amount of alcohol consumed was the best predictor: the heavier the drinker the greater the risk. It was reported that PE can also occur following withdraw from alcohol (American Psychiatric Association, 2013). Many alcohol abusers have avoided PE through courtesy of alcohol, but once they adjusted their drinking habits their PE often returned (Betchen, 2009).

Individual Psychological Factors

PE could also be a consequence of individually oriented emotional issues such as anxiety, depression, vulnerability to embarrassment and guilt, social phobia, low self-confidence, negative body image, and psychosocial stress (American Psychiatric Association, 2013; Rowland

& Cooper, 2013). Michetti et al. (2007) found that PE sufferers experienced more severe alexithymia, a disorder characterized by an inability to recognize, interpret, and verbalize signs of emotional arousal in oneself or others (Rowland & Cooper, 2013, pp. 102–103).

Cognitive-behavioral sexologists viewed PE primarily from a behavioral and social learning perspective (Metz & McCarthy, 2003). Abdo (2013) noted that some men who experience lifelong PE "appear to lack dating or interpersonal skills as well as specific sensual and sexual physiologic knowledge and skills" (p. 213). I have treated several men in my clinical practice who have suffered from PE, in part, because they had little to no sexual experience. As a result they were unable to control their ejaculatory reflex.

According to psychoanalytic theory, PE is the consequence of a man's unconscious conflicts with women. Abraham (1917/1949) believed the disorder, which he termed *ejaculatio praecox*, to be anchored in a repressed sadistic struggle against the mother, which in real time manifested in a desire to give a female partner something of himself that he values (i.e., his semen), but also a need to exact revenge (i.e., PE). The conflict was believed to be symptomatic of "…the disappointments of love to which as a child his mother subjected him, and which he finds repeated again in later years" (p. 297).

Couple/Dyadic Factors

Partners must cooperate with one another to create a healthy sex life. Cognitive-behavioral and psychodynamic systems therapists believe that PE, particularly the acquired type, can be symptomatic of relational problems. Power or control struggles, poor communication, fear of commitment, fear of intimacy, and the pressure generated by a non-symptomatic partner's unrealistic expectations of the symptomatic partner to perform sexually have been cited (Abdo, 2013; Betchen, 2001; Metz & McCarthy, 2003). While dyadic factors have been attributed to PE, conversely, the disorder was also found to have a negative impact on a couple's overall relationship (Althof, 2013).

A power or control struggle may ensue when partners differ in their sexual demands. A man suffering from acquired PE sought couple's therapy because his longtime girlfriend became critical of his sexual style. She preferred to have intercourse "fast and hard," with no let up until she achieved a vaginal orgasm. If her boyfriend ejaculated before she reached her goal, she would disparagingly compare him to her past lovers. The boyfriend "hated fast sex." He soon became less caring about his girlfriend's needs and in turn, gave up control of his ejaculatory reflex. A full blown control struggle emerged.

Effective communication is an important factor in a couple's sex life. The wife of a middle-aged man gave her husband an ultimatum to attend couple's/sex therapy or she would divorce him. Apparently, the husband could only delay his ejaculation for several seconds during intercourse, an acquired problem. When he was finally able to communicate his anger and hurt regarding his wife's threat to divorce him, she apologized and told him that his PE made her feel that he didn't care about her. The husband's ejaculatory control soon returned.

PE can emerge out of a sexual atmosphere wrought with pressure and anxiety. A woman 20 years her husband's junior presented with him for couples/sex therapy because he was exhibiting PE. For many years the husband functioned well sexually but as the relationship began to deteriorate, because of other factors such as age and value differences, the wife became more and more demanding in bed until her husband could last no more than a few seconds following penetration. On more than one occasion he ejaculated before penetration because his wife had insisted on prolonged foreplay. While his solid erection was attributed to his sustained attraction to his wife, his PE was symptomatic of the enormous pressure he was under.

Family-of-Origin Factors

PE has been found to be symptomatic of internalized emotional conflicts emanating from the family-of-origin (Betchen, 2001, 2009). Conflicts can be passed down from generation to generation and manifest in the same or different symptoms. Bowen (1978) referred to this as the *multigenerational transmission process*. He believed that the greater the influence an individual's family-of-origin wielded the lower the individual's *differentiation of self* (or level of emotional autonomy), and the greater the odds of the individual becoming symptomatic. In this model, greater differentiation is required from the couple in order to maintain balance and control over the internalized conflicts that are closely connected to their sexual disorders. DeMaria, Weeks, and Blumer (2014) employed the genogram to assess sexual influences.

A man with lifelong PE presented for treatment at his wife's insistence. It was determined that his PE was symptomatic of a cruel and erroneous message he received repeatedly in his family-of-origin: He was told by his father and older brothers that he had a "little penis." His father also told him that he would have a hard time satisfying a woman someday. Carrying this devastating message from his family-of-origin, the man didn't attempt intercourse until he was in college, and even then he needed the help of alcohol or drugs to allay his anxiety. Once he married and cut back on the substance use, the PE became evident. His PE symptom was believed to be a metaphor for his feelings of inferiority, which his wife reinforced every time he ejaculated too quickly and "robbed her of a vaginal orgasm."

Sociocultural Factors

PE is a geographic and culture-dependent symptom (Namavar & Robati, 2011). Studies utilizing data from the Global Study of Sexual Attitudes and Behaviors (GSSAB) found that rates in Non-European West (27.4%), Central/South American (28%), East Asia (29.1%), and Southeast Asia (30.5%) were similar; rates in Northern Europe (20.7%) and Southern Europe (21.5%) were lower (Laumann et al., 2005). PE rates in Middle Eastern countries (12.4%), however, were found to be significantly lower. One possible explanation is that circumcision, a procedure that actually diminishes the sensitivity of the glans, is common among Jews and Muslims in this region (Namavar & Robati, 2011).

Prevalence rates of PE across ethnic groups in the United States are generally mixed. The only consistent finding is that Afro American men have a higher prevalence of PE than white men. While socioeconomic status and PE have not been found to correlate, men with lower educational levels were reported to be more prone to PE (Carson & Gunn, 2006; Laumann et al., 2005).

Growing up in a home with rigid religious values or a strict moral code can produce internal sexual conflicts; negative attitudes towards sex (e.g., sex is dirty) can do the same (American Psychiatric Association, 2013). I have treated men with PE who grew up in households that either failed to mention a word about sex, or did so in a negative manner. Even if marital sex was sanctioned, the anti-sexual messages received in their youth often-times made it difficult for these grown men to enjoy sexual activity to its fullest. As a compromise, they allowed themselves to have sex, and in many cases to procreate, but hastened the activity in an attempt to circumvent the pleasure of orgasm.

Even religious groups that encourage sex between spouses in a relatively positive manner can, because of their laws, create sexual skill deficits leading to PE and other sexual disorders. In treating Hassidic Jews, I found the concept of refraining from premarital sex in conjunction with isolating from the popular culture/media to be important factors in their inability to control the ejaculatory reflex.

The Treatment Model

A systemic model has been found to be particularly effective with those couples who suffer from sexual disorders such as PE (Betchen, 2001, 2009). The model proposed herein combines aspects of psychoanalytic conflict theory (Freud, 1910/1957) and psychodynamic family-of-origin work (Bowen, 1978) with basic sex therapy principles and exercises (Kaplan, 1989). The objective of this approach is to help couples uncover and resolve any unconscious conflicts, rooted in their families of origin, which are responsible for sexual symptoms. In order to achieve this resolution, each partner must appropriately differentiate (i.e., increase his/her level of emotional autonomy) from the deleterious influences of their respective families of origin.

A conflict is defined as a predominantly unconscious, internalized fight or duality within each partner that, if unbalanced, can produce relational and sexual symptoms. For example, if each partner has a *success versus sabotage* (i.e., big vs. small) conflict (see Betchen, 2010, pp. 60–62 for list of conflicts) one side of each of them wants to achieve their goals and the other side resists. When a conflict is unbalanced or tipped too far for too long a period of time, the homeostasis of the dyadic system is disturbed and symptoms may emerge. In this case, if one partner becomes too successful, the other partner may then attempt to rebalance the conflict (e.g., sabotage that partner's success), escalate the imbalance (e.g., increase his/her own level of resistance to succeed), or end the relationship (e.g., choose loss over the discomfort of a newly balanced conflict). It is not hard to imagine why conflicts regarding success can show up in the bedroom.

Behavioral sex therapy exercises (Kaplan, 1989) are employed at the discretion of the clinician. They may be deemed unnecessary if the clinician believes the couple can resolve their symptoms without behavioral intervention, or viewed as inappropriate given the depth and intensity of the underlying conflict. Exercises may be assigned simultaneously with psychodynamic work or follow it after certain resistances have been removed.

A medical evaluation is usually mandatory but some of the PE sufferers I've treated completed a urological evaluation prior to seeking sex therapy. This issue presents a paradox: Men with PE tend to avoid seeking medical help because of embarrassment (Shabsigh, 2006); but because our society is far more medically focused than psychologically oriented, most men seek medical attention for sexual disorders first. Sex therapy is oftentimes perceived as a last option.

Assessment

The assessment process is usually performed with both partners in attendance. The first question asked is what brings them to treatment. Partners are allowed equal opportunity to present their perspective. If one partner attempts to dominate, the therapist is to gently intervene in order to maintain therapeutic balance, a key ingredient in couple's therapy.

After forming a clear understanding of what each partner perceives as the chief complaint, the therapist assumes control and begins by asking each partner a series of questions about their individual, relational, and sexual lives. Many of these questions regarding each partner's sexual history and current sexual status can be found in Risen's (2007) *How to Do a Sexual Health Assessment*. The genogram is used as a tool to record what the therapist deems as significant information (DeMaria, Weeks, & Blumer, 2014). The evaluation can be completed in one or two sessions, depending on the complexity and cooperation of the couple. However, the genogram process is ongoing as the clinician can, at any time, add new information or make adjustments to his/her initial hypothesis.

Medical/Pharmacological Treatment

Immediately following the assessment the man should be referred for a physical examination (if he has not had one recently). Preferably, the examination should be performed by a urologist with a background in working with sexual dysfunctions. Ideally the partner will be present during the discussion that follows the physical evaluation. While there is still no universally approved medication to treat PE, many physicians rely on the off-label use of antidepressant selective serotonin reuptake inhibitors (SSRIs). The decision to consider medications for the treatment of PE should be made by the man and his partner. Although the man is being treated, PE is a relational problem. It is more likely that the partner will be receptive if the rationale for treatment is explained and medication related issues are discussed.

SSRIs block axonal reuptake of serotonin from synapse by 5-HT transporters, resulting in enhanced 5-HT neurotransmission, stimulation of postsynaptic membrane 5-HT2C receptors and ejaculatory delay (McMahon, 2013). The most commonly used SSRIs are paroxetine (Paxil), fluoxetine (Prozac), sertraline (Zoloft), and citalopram (Celexa) (Linton & Wylie, 2010), although fluvoxamine (Luvox) and escitalopram (Lexapro) are used as well (McMahon, 2013; Waldinger, 2013b).

Recent outcome studies on these drugs prompted Waldinger (2013b) to write: "Without doubt, daily SSRI treatment is effective in delaying ejaculation" (p. 231). While Waldinger did not claim that SSRIs work for every man, he reported that an adequate ejaculation delay occurs in approximately 70–80% of PE sufferers within a 1–3 week period. He also felt that patients should be informed of the potential side effects of these medications which have been consistently reported by many studies: anejaculation, reduced libido as well as erectile dysfunction, dizziness, dry mouth, depression, fatigue, nausea, constipation, diarrhea, insomnia, a negative effect on semen parameters, weight gain, and in very rare occurrences, priapism (i.e., a painful medical condition in which an erect penis fails to return to a flaccid state (Koyuncu et al., 2011; Linton & Wylie, 2010; Waldinger, 2013b) Linton and Wylie (2010) warned that abrupt cessation or discontinuation of these drugs may also cause dizziness, nausea, vomiting, fatigue, headaches, lethargy, anxiety, agitation, and insomnia.

The SSRI that is generating the most promise is dapoxetine (Priligy). Dapoxetine is the first drug specifically developed to treat PE. While it has yet to receive final approval by the United States Food and Drug Administration (USFDA), agencies have sanctioned it in countries such as Austria, Finland, Germany, Italy, Mexico, New Zealand, Portugal, South Korea, and Sweden. Additionally, the drug is currently in its last phases of testing in many European countries. It is in Phase III of the USFDA testing and is expected to be approved (McMahon, 2012).

Similar to other SSRIs, dapoxetine is a very strong inhibitor of the serotonin reuptake transporter. But because of its short half-life, it was found to be better suited as an on demand treatment of PE (Linton & Wylie, 2010; Waldinger, 2010). Unlike the long-acting SSRIs, dapoxetine has also been found to produce a lower incidence of undesirable sexual side-effects, including discontinuation syndrome, (McCarty & Dinsmore, 2010; McMahon et al., 2011).

Pryor et al. (2006) reported the results of two double-blind, randomized-controlled studies of the efficacy and tolerability of dapoxetine in the treatment of PE. In both studies, dapoxetine was found to significantly improve IELT compared to baseline and placebo times. In another double-blind, randomized, placebo-controlled phase three clinical trial, incorporating participants from 22 countries, similar results were reported (Buvat et al., 2009). All participants reported significant improvement in their PE symptoms after using dapoxetine for 24 weeks. In addition to being effective, this drug is also well tolerated.

Off-label use of other antidepressants such as tricyclic antidepressants (TCAs) particularly clomipramine (Anafranil), have also proven effective. Clomipramine was the first antidepressant medication prescribed to treat PE (McCarty & Dinsmore, 2010). Commonly used to treat obsessive-compulsive disorders, clomipramine inhibits the reuptake of noradrenaline and serotonin (Linton & Wylie, 2010). While proven to significantly extend IELT, clomipramine did evoke a higher incidence of side effects when compared to SSRIs (Linton & Wylie, 2010; McCarty & Dinsmore, 2010). Side effects included sleeplessness, nausea, and dry mouth (Powell & Wylie, 2009).

Tramadol is an oral opioid analgesic that inhibits activity against serotonin and norepinephrine. Studies have shown that the drug has been safely and successfully used to treat PE (Safarinejad & Hosseini, 2006; Salem et al., 2008), but there is insufficient evidence regarding long-term outcome and tolerance. There is also some concern that users of this medication may be exposed to potential abuse, dependence, and addiction (Palmer, 2009). Topical anesthetics (e.g., creams and sprays) have been effective in treating PE. According to Dinsmore and McCarty (2013), these anesthetics are particularly attractive because they can be used on an as-needed basis with little systemic side effects. They can, however, produce localized side effects such as associated penile hypoanesthesia (decrease in sensitivity), vaginal numbness, and female anorgasmia, which require a condom to prevent (Rowland et al., 2010).

Severance-secret (SS) cream is a mixture of nine traditional medicines including Korean ginseng, bufonoid venom, and cinnamon. The cream is applied to the glans penis approximately 1-hour before intercourse and washed off right before penetration. While studies in Korea have found the cream effective in treating PE, negative side effects were reported as well such as pain and burning, delayed ejaculation, anejaculation (failure to ejaculate), and erectile dysfunction (Choi et al., 2000). SS-cream is not legally available outside of Korea (Dinsmore & McCarty, 2013).

EMLA (eutectic mixture of local anesthetic) is a local anesthetic cream that contains 2.5% each of lidocaine and prilocaine. Lidocaine-prilocaine cream has proved effective in treating PE when applied 20–30 minutes prior to intercourse (Hellstrom, 2010). The largest scale study to date reported IELT from 1.49 minutes to 8.45 minutes (Busato & Galindo, 2004). The medication was also found to be messy, slow acting, and associated with hypoesthesia (Dinsmore & McCarty, 2013).

TEMPE (topical eutectic mixture for PE) is a formulation of lidocaine and prilocaine spray that delivers 7.5 mg lidocaine and 2.5 mg of prilocaine. It is fast-acting and well-tolerated by both partners (Dinsmore & McCarty, 2013). Another spray found useful in treating PE is Lignocaine 9.6% spray (i.e., Stud 100 or Premjact). Available for some time, this spray consists of local anesthetic lignocaine, which can be bought over the counter without a prescription (Linton & Wylie, 2010).

Dyclonine 0.5%, an aesthetic used in dentistry, and the vasodilator alprostadil 0.4% have been combined and formulated into a topical cream to treat PE. The cream is applied to the tip of the penis in the region of the meatus (Linton & Wylie, 2010). More research is needed to definitively prove its efficacy.

As noted earlier, many times PE is often comorbid with ED. The PE may be the cause of, or result from ED (Linton & Wylie, 2010). Phosphodieterase type 5 (PDE5) inhibitors—which were originally developed to treat ED, such as sildenafil citrate (Viagra), vardenafil HCI (Levitra, Staxyn), and tadalafil (Cialis) are sometimes employed to treat PE (Hellstrom, 2010). While several studies have demonstrated the efficacy of PDE5s in treating men with acquired PE and associated ED, the drugs were not effective in treating those with lifelong PE who did not have erection problems (Palmer, 2009). However, Gökçe, Halis, Demirtas, and Ekmekcioglu (2010) found that PDE5s prolonged IELT and that penile rigidity was also better in post-ejaculatory period. The authors suggested that their findings support the usage of PDE5s to treat lifelong PE. Asimakopoulos et al. (2012) specifically studied the impact of PDE5s on PE sufferers without erectile disorder. The authors found that the PDE5s served to enhance IELT as monotherapy or in combination with other drugs.

Hyaluronic acid is a natural compound used in aesthetic surgery and for the treatment of osteoarthritis. Littara, Palmieri, Rottigni, and Iannitti (2013) found that delivered by injection, hyaluronic acid can safely and significantly lengthen IEFT and serve as an effective approach for glans penis augmentation.

Male clients with PE should be informed that the body sometimes adjusts to medication or a spontaneous remission of any drug-related sexual problem may occur. This may be the case for SSRIs and MAOs, but the anorgasmia that TCAs produce does not remit spontaneously (Haberfellner & Rittmannsberger, 2004; Komisaruk, Beyer-Flores, & Whipple, 2006).

Sex Therapy Exercises: The Stop-Start Method

Kaplan's (1989) use of the stop-start method (see Semans, 1956) to treat PE is replicated in this model. This method allows the PE sufferer to become aware of his pre-monitory sensations (i.e., the feelings that warn him that he may be on the verge of ejaculating) in order to control ejaculatory latency while enjoying sexual activity. Based on the general principle of systematic desensitization (Wolpe, 1982), stop-start exercises are gradually introduced to the man beginning with the least stimulating and fear evoking to those that replicate the desired behavior, in this case, ejaculatory control. Gay male couples can adjust the exercises to meet their specific needs.

Exercise #1: The man is asked to lie on his back and have his partner stroke his penis with a dry hand while he pays attention to the erotic feelings in his penis. When he feels orgasm is approaching but not inevitable (the point it is too late for the male to stop himself from ejaculating) the partner is to stop stroking and allow the man's erotic feelings to dissipate without loss of erection. Couples are to do the stop-start exercises 3 to 5 times per week. When the man achieves enough control that he only has to stop 2 to 3 times in a 10 minute period, the couple may move on to the next exercise. If the man does not have a partner he can practice the stop-start technique on his own, but the clinician should warn him that this may result in limited gains.

Exercise #2: The first exercise is repeated, but this time the partner is to stroke the male using a water-based lubricant. The man may want to consider adding Kegel exercises to his practice regimen (Kegel, 1952). By contracting his pelvic floor muscles at the point before ejaculatory inevitability he may help to delay ejaculation. The man should be forewarned, however, that Kegels can cause early ejaculation in some men.

Exercise #3: In the third exercise, slow-fast penile stimulation, the partner is to stroke the man until he reaches a high level of sexual excitement. The partner is to then slow down rather than come to a complete stop.

Exercise #4: The partner is to continuously stroke the man at a high level of arousal without adjustment or interruption and to stop just prior to ejaculation.

Exercise #5: The partner is to mount the man (i.e., female superior position) and use the man's penis to caress her vaginal area. The partner must stop the caressing just before the point of ejaculation.

Exercise #6: During the sixth exercise, the partner remains on top and inserts the man's penis. She only moves when there is a need to maintain the erection (quiet vagina or non-demand coitus).

Exercise #7: The sixth exercise can be repeated with partners lying side by side. I offer this exercise as an option for those couples that prefer this position during intercourse.

Exercise #8: In this final exercise, the man mounts his partner (i.e., male superior position or missionary position) and practices speeding up and slowing down his thrusting. This better simulates intercourse. Thrusts should be slow and deep to avoid stimulation received from friction.

Sensate Focus exercises (Masters & Johnson, 1970) can be assigned to anxious couples as a primer for stop-start exercises. They may also be offered to couples who insist on being assigned exercises. Kaplan (personal communication, September, 1987) claimed that if a clinician is prematurely pressured by clients to assign exercises, Sensate Focus will do little damage, if unsuccessful.

It is quite common for one or both partners to sabotage exercises. Many partners refuse to cooperate in performing them; some leave little or no time to practice; others make up their own exercises despite the clinician's instructions. The clinician should be as clear and detailed about the exercises assigned. Insisting that the couple agree on the time, place frequency of the assignments, as well as who is to initiate and for how long, may avert confusion and preempt conscious or unconscious sabotage. To avoid a partner feeling taken advantage of by the exercise process, the clinician might want to discuss whether the partner wishes to be satisfied prior to beginning each exercise.

The behavioral bent of sex therapy makes it easy for the clinician to assign exercises as if reading a cookbook. However, because couples differ in introspective ability, motivation, levels of resistance, degree of experience, and degree of sexual difficulty, the exercise regimen offered should be considered a general framework for treatment and not one automatically applied in the same way to all couples.

Uncovering Conflicts: Interactional Level

In order to uncover any individual conflicts that may be responsible for the PE symptom, the clinician must carefully examine a couple on two levels: *Interactional* and *Psychodynamic*. On the interactional level, the clinician observes the couple's interactional style and searches for contradictory patterns indicative of conflicts and collusions that are symptomatic of their sexual symptom. For example, during the treatment process a wife was threatening to leave her husband if he didn't get his PE under control. She has asked him numerous times over the years to seek treatment and he only recently acquiesced. After many attempts to sabotage his exercises, the husband began to gain ground but the closer he got to success, the less cooperative his wife became.

This contradictory behavior begs the question: Does or doesn't the wife want her husband to function better sexually? According to theory put forth in this model, the answer is: She does and she doesn't want her husband to gain control over his PE. She allowed him to avoid treatment for years and now that he is progressing she is sabotaging the process. One can ask the same question of the husband. He procrastinated long enough before he sought treatment and he sabotaged his exercises numerous times before he got on track.

Uncovering Conflicts: Psychodynamic Level

Some couples may be fully aware that their interactional style is a contributing factor to their PE, but few realize that underlying conflicts may be operating as well. The clinician may use the genogram to help the couple bring their conflicts into consciousness by probing each partner's family-of-origin. The objective is to help the couple to see the connection that exists between the past and the present, that is, between the conflicts, their current relational interactions, and the associated PE symptom. This process persists throughout the therapy.

The genogram of a male client with acquired PE helped him to see that he was unconsciously replicating the pattern of never being able to satisfy the women in his life. His mother was very critical of him, and his father was too passive a man to intervene on his son's behalf. The man's first wife was a materialistic woman. She demanded that he shower her with gifts and allow her an open checkbook. Although the client functioned well sexually with her, she nevertheless left him for another man as soon as the client could no longer afford to keep her in the manner to which she had become accustomed. The client was traumatized.

Another man presented for treatment of PE at the insistence of his second wife who refused to attend sessions. It was determined that he was so anxious about losing his wife and experiencing another divorce that he couldn't perform. The more sexually disabled the husband became the more he upset his wife. While she didn't leave her husband, as he neared gaining control over his PE, she told him that she was never attracted to him and that she didn't want to have sex with him ever again. He needed medication to deal with this news. There was also some concern that he might harm himself. Part of the man wanted to be loved and accepted and the other part seemed to have an unconscious desire to be rejected. This dynamic indicated an *acceptance versus rejection* conflict (Betchen, 2010).

With the aid of the genogram, the man was able to track his conflict pattern back to his family-of-origin. He soon realized that he was playing his father's somewhat helpless role and marrying rejecting women, like his mother. The genogram also depicted this conflict in the client's relationship history as far back as high school; a discovery that was instrumental in convincing the PE sufferer that he has had this problem for a long time, and that it was causing him a great deal of pain.

Resolving Conflicts

In order to resolve a conflict, both partners must accept the fact that gain on one side means a loss on the other. However, most partners are unaware of this concept as made evident by the vast amounts of time they will often spend trying to find a way to "have it all." They do so even after their conflicts are made clear to them. People fear change no matter how tough their situation is. The ability to choose a different way of life usually depends on the degree of anxiety partners can tolerate, and their ability to bear frustration.

The previously mentioned client felt that he was being mistreated by his second wife; he knew full well that she would never have sex with him again. But he was also afraid of challenging her for fear she would leave him. He had a big decision to make: challenge his wife and risk another divorce or live on her terms. He came to grips with the fact that he would suffer a loss either way. The question is would the gains outweigh the losses.

While going through the differentiation process (i.e., the process by which one increases the level of emotional autonomy from his /her family-of-origin), the client eventually realized that if he decided to become more assertive in his relationships and demand to be accepted for who he was, he would have to admit that his father's passivity might have been just as detrimental to him as his mother's rejection, maybe more so. He would have to feel more comfortable internalizing a more masculine presence rather than view this as "behaving like his mother." Ultimately, it is each partner's choice as to whether they want change. It is the clinician's job to show them the conflicts, discover where they've come from, and to help them to explore their options. If the client decided to stay with his wife on her terms, it was his choice.

Termination

According to Betchen (2009, 2010), treatment success is dependent on the alleviation of the PE symptom. While improved individual differentiation and a more functional couple interactional style are often prerequisites for success, if the PE is found to be solely organic in origin and is treated successfully with medication, treatment will obviously be brief (unless the partner actually wants brief sex or if the issue of medication is a problem for the partner). In most cases, however, the PE symptom will not dissipate until psychodynamic conflicts have improved; this often takes longer. In other instances, the PE symptom is alleviated but the underlying conflicts may produce another symptom. In this situation, the clinician should warn the couple that their underlying problem lives and gently encourage them to continue treatment. They should also know that their PE symptom could return if they end prematurely. The termination of a case is usually a decision made by the couple and the clinician together. The termination process may take one or several sessions to accomplish. The couple should be made aware that they can return for treatment anytime they feel the need.

Case Study

Bill and Lynn were married and in their middle 40s. Bill presented with lifelong PE. He first experienced it as a late teen while losing his virginity to a girlfriend; the results were similar in subsequent encounters in college up to and including intercourse with his wife. Bill reported that he can last as long as 20 minutes during manual and oral stimulation but would usually lose control within 10–15 seconds during intercourse. Bill's urologist could not find an organic cause for his PE, but he did see Bill as very anxious and recommended that he follow up with his internist. Bill's internist prescribed Paxil. He believed that this medication could curb Bill's anxiety as well as help him with his PE. Because it wasn't enough, the internist decided to refer Bill and his wife for marital/ sex therapy.

Both Bill and Lynn were frustrated by their situation in part, because Lynn was capable of achieving intravaginal orgasms. While Bill often brought her to orgasm prior to intercourse, it was clear that both partners wanted him to last somewhat longer. It was also evident that the partners were frustrated and angry with one another. Bill felt Lynn was too critical of him in general, and partly responsible for his anxiety.

101

"I'm afraid of her," he said. Lynn felt Bill's PE was another sign of his incompetence. She complained, "I always have to make the decisions or clean up his messes (e.g., financial and organizational). I'm really tired of living this way. He can run a company but not a family."

The interactional dynamic consisted of Lynn on the offensive: She consistently challenged Bill's adequacy and complained that she was routinely victimized by his incompetence. Bill was on the defensive: He often made excuses for himself and complained that Lynn picked on him. During the course of the treatment it became obvious that each partner was right about the other. Bill had trouble making decisions and when he did, he failed to think them through. His poor judgment often set him up for failure and subsequent feelings of inadequacy. If that wasn't shameful enough, Lynn would reluctantly intervene and attempt to straighten things out—something she wasn't that good at anyway.

Lynn claimed that she wanted to trust Bill and to perceive him as a competent man. She continuously stated how much she wanted him to overcome his PE. But her perception of Bill as incompetent rendered her critical of him, thereby exacerbating his feelings of inadequacy. Bill's anxiety grew to the point that he needed to add a condom to his regimen of Paxil, and he still experienced PE. The more anxious and incompetent Bill grew, the angrier and more powerless Lynn became, in part because she couldn't fix him, or the situation.

Because the couple was at odds, PE exercises were put on hold in favor of psychodynamic work. It was already suspected that an *adequacy versus inadequacy* conflict (Betchen, 2010) was internally operating. In this conflict each partner feels both adequate and inadequate simultaneously. Bill was a very good financial provider. But as Lynn aptly pointed out, he seemed at a loss as to how to please his wife and organize his family. On more than one occasion he forgot to pick one of his children up after a sporting event. Lynn felt superior to Bill and to the therapist at times. She seemed to think that her way was best, but the other part of her knew she didn't have the skills to clean up many of Bill's problems and to fix his PE.

As their conflicts became apparent, Bill and Lynn realized they were similar in a very important way—they both had conflicts about being "adequate" that were anchored in their respective families of origin. Bill's mother was extremely controlling and domineering; his father was a quiet, passive man who never intervened to protect Bill from his wife. As a result, Bill longed to be free to make his own decisions and to prove his adequacy. But, he also lacked confidence and looked to a woman to help him. It certainly wasn't in his favor that his father failed to serve as a strong and confidant male role model.

Lynn experienced a similar dynamic. Her mother was the strong, competent figure and her father was irresponsible. Even though she saw her mother as a critical perfectionist, Lynn grew to distrust a man's decision-making. She came to believe her mother's motto: "If you want to get something done right don't depend on a man; do it yourself." The flip side of Lynn's confidence, however, is that her "take-charge" mother thwarted her development.

This insight helped the couple to empathize with one another and to decide to be adequate together, a sign of increased differentiation. Once there was sufficient movement in the differentiation process and the interactional dynamic de-escalated, stop-start exercises were employed. Although the couple colluded to sabotage several of these exercises (e.g., Bill would fail to initiate, placing the burden on Lynn to follow through; Lynn would criticize Bill's technique), they eventually succeeded in gaining adequate control over their PE symptom. The treatment took approximately 1 year.

Future Considerations

In recent years, medical science has made some progress in the treatment of PE, particularly with regards to the lifelong type. Dapoxetine, for example, is the first drug specifically developed to treat PE. Although it has yet to receive final approval by the USFDA, this is widely considered to be imminent. The drug has already been sanctioned in several countries (McMahon, 2012). Researchers continue to explore off-label medication use to treat PE. But because studies have consistently indicated that the disorder returns soon after stopping drug use; Waldinger (2103c) suggested that a more realistic goal would be to continue to develop new drugs that not only delay ejaculation, but produce more tolerable side effects, if any side effects at all.

Pharmacological progress is encouraging, but it also presents the danger of relying too heavily on a medical solution to treat PE. In their efforts to alleviate discomfort, many physicians still prescribe medications without asking about their patients' relationships. As a consequence, many patients continue to suffer from troubling systemic dynamics and their associated sexual symptoms. Those with acquired PE are more likely to fall victim to a purely pharmacological approach because this type is more likely to emanate from relational and psychological origins.

The model presented herein is integrative and systemic, reflecting the author's conflict theory approach to treating couples with sexual disorders. It contends that exposing a couple's internalized conflicts, determining the origins of these conflicts, and helping the couple differentiate from the deleterious influences of their families of origin, from which these conflicts have emanated, can result in their resolution. The alleviation of any accompanying sexual symptoms such as PE is expected to be a byproduct of this process.

Ultimately, this chapter calls for clinicians to be broad-minded in the treatment of couples with PE. It is particularly important for clinician's to consider the causal factors that may be behind the disorder as well as the treatment options available to help couples achieve greater overall intimacy and a higher level of sexual functioning.

References

Abdel-Hamid, I. A., Abdel-Razek, M. M., & Anis, T. (2013). Risk factors in premature ejaculation: The neurological risk factor and the local hypersensitivity. In E. Jannini, C. McMahon, & M. Waldinger (Eds.), *Premature ejaculation: From etiology to diagnosis and treatment* (pp. 167–185). Italy: Springer-Verlag.

Abdo, C. H. N. (2013). Treatment of premature ejaculation with cognitive therapy. In E. Jannini, C. McMahon, & M. Waldinger (Eds.), *Premature ejaculation: From etiology to diagnosis and treatment* (pp. 213–220). Italy: Springer-Verlag.

Abraham, K. (1917/1949). Ejaculatio praecox. In D. Bryan & A. Strachey (Trans.), *Selected papers of Karl Abraham, M.D.* (pp. 280–298). London: Hogarth Press and the Institute of Psychoanalysis.

Althof, S. (2013). Risk factors in premature ejaculation: The relational risk factor. In E. Jannini, C. McMahon, & M. Waldinger (Eds.), *Premature ejaculation: From etiology to diagnosis and treatment* (pp. 133–139). Italy: Springer-Verlag.

American Psychiatric Association. (2013). *Diagnostic and statistical manual of mental disorders* (5th ed.). Washington, DC: Author.

Amidu, N., Owiredu, W. K. B. A., Woode, E., Addai-Mensah, O., Gyasi-Sarpong, K. C., & Alhassan, A. (2010). Prevalence of male sexual dysfunction among Ghanaian populace: Myth or reality? *International Journal of Impotence Research, 22*, 337–342. doi: 10.1038/ijir.2010.24

Andersson, K. E., & Abdel-Hamid, I. A. (2011). Therapeutic targets for premature ejaculation. *Maturitas, 70*, 26–33. doi: 10.1016/j.maturitas.2011.06.007

Arackal, B.S., & Benegal, V. (2007). Prevalence of sexual dysfunction in male subjects with alcohol dependence. *Indian Journal of Psychiatry, 49*, 109–112. doi: 10.4103/0019-5545.33257

Asimakopoulos, A., Miano, R., Agro, E. F., Vespasiani, G., & Spera, E. (2012). Does current scientific and clinical evidence support the use of phosphodiesterase type 5 inhibitors for the treatment of premature ejaculation? A systematic review and meta-analysis. *Journal of Sexual Medicine, 9*, 2404–2416. doi: 10.1111/jsm.2012.9.issue-9/issuetoc

Bancroft, J., Carnes, L., Janssen, E., Goodrich, D., & Long, J. S. (2005). Erectile and ejaculatory problems in gay and heterosexual men. *Archives of Sexual Behavior, 14*, 285–297. doi: 10.1007/s10508-005-3117-7

Bell, R. R., & Weinberg, M.S. (1978). *Homosexualities: A study of diversity among men and women*. New York: Simon & Schuster.

Betchen, S. (2001). Premature ejaculation as symptomatic of age difference in a husband and wife with underlying power and control conflicts. *Journal of Sex Education and Therapy, 26*(1), 34–44.

Betchen, S. (2009). Premature ejaculation: An integrative, Intersystem Approach for couples. In K. Hertlein, G. Weeks, & N. Gambescia (Eds.), *Systemic sex therapy* (pp. 131–152). New York: Routledge.

Betchen, S. (2010). *Magnetic partners: Discover how the hidden conflict that once attracted you to each other is now driving you apart*. New York: Free Press.

Boonjindasup, A. G., Serefoglu, E. C., & Hellstrom, W. J. G. (2013). Risk factors in premature ejaculation: The urological risk factor. In E. Jannini, C. McMahon, & M. Waldinger (Eds.), *Premature ejaculation: From etiology to diagnosis and treatment* (pp. 159–197). Italy: Springer-Verlag.

Bowen, M. (1978). *Family therapy in clinical practice*. New York: Aronson.

Busato, W., & Galindo, C.C. (2004). Topical anaesthetic use for testing premature ejaculation: A double-bind, randomized, placebo-controlled study. *Brazilian Journal of Urology, 93*, 1018–1021. doi: 10.1111/j.1464–410X.2004.04773x

Buvat, J., Tesfaye, F., Rothman, M., Rivas, D. A., & Giuliano, F. (2009). Dapoxetine for the treatment of premature ejaculation: Results from a randomized, double blind, placebo-controlled phase three trial in 22 countries. *European Urology, 55*, 957–968. doi: 10.1016/J.eururo.2009.01.025. Epub2009Jan21

Carson, C., & Gunn, K. (2006). Premature ejaculation: Definition and prevalence. *International Journal of Impotence Research, 18*, S5–S13. doi: 10.1038/sj.ijir.3901507

Chekuri, V., Gerber, D., Brodie, A., & Krishnadas, R. (2012). Premature ejaculation and other sexual dysfunctions in opiate dependent men receiving methadone substitution. *Addictive Behaviors, 37*, 124–126. doi: 10.1016/j.addbeh.2011.08.005.Epub2011Aug.25

Choi, H.K., Jung, G.W., Moon, K.H., Xin, Z.C., Choi, Y.D., Lee, W.H., . . . Kim, D.K. (2000). Clinical study of SS-cream in patients with lifelong premature ejaculation. *Urology, 55*(20), 257–261.

Corona, G., Jannini, E.A., Lotti, F., Boddi, V., De Vita, G., Forti, G., . . . Maggi, M. (2011). Premature and delayed ejaculation: Two ends of a single continuum influenced by hormonal milieu. *International Journal of Andrology, 34*, 41–48. doi: 10.1111/j.1365–2605.2010.01059.x

DeMaria, R., Weeks, G., & Blumer, M. (2014). *Focused genograms* (2nd ed.). New York: Routledge.

Dinsmore, W., & McCarty, E. (2013). Use of local anesthetics in the treatment of premature ejaculation. In E. Jannini, C. McMahon, & M. Waldinger (Eds.), *Premature ejaculation: From etiology to diagnosis and treatment* (pp. 263–288). Italy: Springer-Verlag.

El-Sakka, A.I. (2003). Premature ejaculation in non-insulin-dependent diabetic patients. *International Journal of Andrology, 26*, 329–334. doi: 10.1111/j.1365–2605.2003.00433.x

Freud, S. (1910/1957). Five lectures on psycho-analysis. In J. Strachey (Ed. and Trans.), *The standard edition of the complete psychological works of Sigmund Freud* (Vol. 11, pp. 9–55). London: Hogarth Press and the Institute of Psychoanalysis.

Gökçe, A., Halis, F., Demirtas, A., & Ekmekcioglu, O. (2010). The effects of three phosphodiesterace type 5 inhibitors on ejaculation latency time in lifelong premature ejaculators: A double-bind laboratory setting study. *BJU International, 107*, 1274–1277. doi: 10.1111/j.1464–410X.2010.09646.x

Haberfellner, E.M., & Rittmannsberger, H. (2004). Spontaneous remission-induced orgasm delay. *Pharmacopsychiatry, 37*, 127–130. doi: 10.1055/s-2004–818991

Hellstrom, W. J. G. (2010). Update of treatments for premature ejaculation. *International Journal of Clinical Practice, 65*, 16–26. doi: 10.1111/jcp.2010.65.issue-1/issuetoc

Jannini, E. A., & Lenzi, A. (2005). Epidemiology of premature ejaculation. *Current Opinion in Urology, 15*(6), 399–403.

Jannini, E. A., & Lenzi, A. (2013). Pathophysiology of acquired premature ejaculation. In E. A. Jannini, C. G. McMahon, & M. D. Waldinger (Eds.), *Premature ejaculation: From etiology to diagnosis and treatment* (pp. 81–97). New York: Springer.

Janssen, P. K., Bakker, S. C., Réthelvi, J., Zwinderman, A. H., Touw, D. J., Olivier, B., & Waldinger, M. (2009). Serotonin transporter promoter region (5-HTTLPR) polymorphism is associated with the intravaginal ejaculation latency time in Dutch men with lifelong premature ejaculation. *Journal of Sexual Medicine, 6*, 276–284. doi: 10.1111/j.1743–6109.2008.01033.x

Jern, P., Santtila, P., Johansson, A., Varjonen, M., Witting, K., von der Pahlen, B., & Sandnabba, N. K. (2009). Evidence for a genetic etiology to ejaculatory dysfunction: Genetic effects on ejaculatory dysfunction. *International Journal of Impotence Research, 21*, 62–67. doi: 10.1038/ijir.2008.61

Kaplan, H. S. (1979). *Disorders of sexual desire.* New York: Brunner/Mazel.

Kaplan, H. S. (1989). *PE: How to overcome premature ejaculation.* New York: Brunner/Mazel.

Kegel, A. (1952). Sexual functions of the pubococcygeus muscle. *Western Journal of Surgery in Obstetrics and Gynecology, 60*(10), 521–524.

Komisaruk, B., Beyer-Flores, C., & Whipple, B. (2006). *The science of orgasm.* Baltimore: The Johns Hopkins Press.

Koyuncu, H., Serefoglu, E. C., Yencilek, E., Atalay, H., Akbas, N. B., & Sanca, K. (2011). Escitalopram treatment for premature ejaculation has a negative effect on semen parameters. *International Journal of Impotence, 23*, 257–261. doi: 10.103/ijir.2011.35

Laumann, E. O., Nicolosi, A., Glasser, D. B., Palik, A., Gingell, C., Moreira, E., & Wang, T. (2005). Sexual problems among women and men aged 40–80 years: Prevalence and correlates identified in the Global Study of Sexual Attitudes and Behaviors. *International Journal of Impotence, 17*, 39–57.

Liang, C. Z, Hao, Z. Y., Li, H. J., Wang, Z. P., Xing, J. P., Hu, W. L., . . . Tai, S. (2010). Prevalence of premature ejaculation and its correlation with chronic prostatitis in Chinese men. *Urology, 76*, 962–966. doi: 10.1016/j.urology.2010.01.061

Linton, K., & Wylie, K. (2010). Recent advances in the treatment of premature ejaculation. *Drug Design, Development and Therapy, 4*, 1–6.

Littara, A., Palmieri, B., Rottigni, V., & Iannitti, T. (2013). A clinical study to assess the effectiveness of a hyaluronic acid-based procedure for treatment of premature ejaculation. *International Journal of Impotence, 25*, 117–120. doi: 10.1038/ijir.2013.13

Masters, W., & Johnson, V. (1966). *Human sexual response.* Boston: Little, Brown & Company.

Masters, W., & Johnson, V. (1970). *Human sexual inadequacy.* Boston: Little, Brown & Company.

McCarty, E. J., & Dinsmore, W. W. (2010). Premature ejaculation: Treatment update. *International Journal of STD & AIDS, 21*, 77–81. doi: 10.1258/ijsa.2009.009434

McMahon, C. (2012). Dapoxetine: A new option in the medical management of premature ejaculation. *Therapeutic Advances in Urology, 4*(5). 233–251

McMahon, C. (2013). Taxonomy of ejaculatory disorders and definitions of premature ejaculation. In E. Jannini, C. McMahon, & M. Waldinger (Eds.), *Premature ejaculation: From etiology to diagnosis and treatment* (pp. 53–69). Italy: Springer-Verlag.

McMahon, C., Althof, S., Kaufman, J., Buvat, J., Levine, S., Aquilina, J., . . . Porst, H. (2011). Efficacy and safety of dapoxetine for the treatment of premature ejaculation: Integrated analysis of results from five phase 3 trials. *Journal of Sexual Medicine, 8*, 524–539. doi: 10.1111/j.1743–6109.2010.02097.x

Metz, M., & McCarthy, B. (2003). *Coping with premature ejaculation: How to overcome PE, please your partner and have great sex.* Oakland, CA: New Harbinger Publications.

Michetti, P. M., Rossi, R., Bonanno, D., De Dominicis, C., Lori, F., & Simonelli, I. F. (2007). Dysregulation of emotions and premature ejaculation (PE): Alexithymia in 100 outpatients. *Journal of Sexual Medicine, 4*, 1462–1467. doi: 10.1111/j.1743–6109.2007.00564.x

Namavar, M. R., & Robati, R. (2011). Removal of foreskin in remnants in circumcised adults for treatment of premature ejaculation. *Urology Annals, 3*, 87–92. doi: 10.4103/0974–7796.82175

Palmer, N. (2009). Tramadol for premature ejaculation. *Journal of Sexual Medicine*, 6, 299. doi: 10.1111/j.1743–6109.2008.00916.x/full

Palmer, N., & Stuckey, B.G.A. (2008). Premature ejaculation: A clinical update. *Medical Journal of Australia*, 188(11), 662–666.

Powell, J.A., & Wylie, M.G. (2009). "Up and coming" treatment for premature ejaculation: Progress towards an approved therapy. *Journal of Impotence Research*, 21, 107–115. doi: 10.1038/ ijir.2008.67

Pryor, J., Althof, S., Steidle, C., Rosen, R., Hellstrom, W. J. G., Shabsigh, R., . . . Kell, S. (2006). Efficacy and tolerability of dapoxetine in treatment of premature ejaculation: An integrated analysis of two double-blind, randomized controlled trials. *The Lancet*, 368, 939–947.

Risen, C. (2007). How to do a sexual health assessment. In L. Vandecreek, F. Peterson, & J. Bley (Eds.), *Innovations in clinical practice: Focus on sexual health* (pp. 18–33). Sarasota, FL: Professional Resource Press.

Rosser, B.R., Metz, M., Bockting, W.O., & Buroker, T. (1997). Sexual difficulties, concerns, and satisfaction in homosexual men: An empirical study with implications for HIV prevention. *Journal of Sex & Marital Therapy*, 23(1), 61–73.

Rowland, D., & Cooper, S. (2013). Risk factors for premature ejaculation: The intrapsychic risk factor. In E. Jannini, C. McMahon, & M. Waldinger (Eds.), *Premature ejaculation: From etiology to diagnosis and treatment* (pp. 99–109). Italy: Springer-Verlag.

Rowland, D., McMahon, C., Abdo, C., Chen, J., Jannini, E., Waldinger, M., & Ahn, T.Y. (2010). Disorders of orgasm and ejaculation in men. *Journal of Sexual Medicine*, 7, 1668–1686. doi: 10.1111/j.1743–6109.2010.01782.x

Safarinejad, M., & Hosseini, S. (2006). Safety and efficacy of citalopram in the treatment of premature ejaculation: A double-bind placebo-controlled, fixed-dose randomized study. *International Journal of Impotence Research*, 18, 164–169. doi: 10.1038/sj.ijir.39011384

Salem, E.A., Wilson, S.K., Bissada, N.K., Delk, J.R., Hellstrom, W.J., & Cleves, M.A., (2008). Tramadol HCl has promise in an on-demand use to treat premature ejaculation. *Journal of Sexual Medicine*, 5(1), 188–193.

Semans, J. (1956). Premature ejaculation: A new approach. *Southern Medical Journal*, 49, 353–358.

Serefoglu, E.C. (2013). Epidemiology of premature ejaculation. In E. Jannini, C. McMahon, & M. Waldinger (Eds.), *Premature ejaculation: From etiology to diagnosis and treatment* (pp. 45–52). Italy: Springer-Verlag.

Shabsigh, R. (2006). Diagnosing premature ejaculation: A review. *Journal of Sexual Medicine*, 3, 318–323. doi: 10.1111/j.1743–6109.2006.00307.x

Waldinger, M. (2010). Premature ejaculation and delayed ejaculation. In S. Levine, C. Risen, & S. Althof (Eds.), *Handbook of clinical sexuality for mental health professionals* (pp. 267–292). New York: Routledge.

Waldinger, M. (2013a). History of premature ejaculation. In E. Jannini, C. McMahon, & M. Waldinger (Eds.), *Premature ejaculation: From etiology to diagnosis and treatment* (pp. 5–24). Italy: Springer-Verlag.

Waldinger, M. (2013b). Treatment of premature ejaculation with selective serotonin re-uptake inhibitors. In E. Jannini, C. McMahon, & M. Waldinger (Eds.), *Premature ejaculation: From etiology to diagnosis and treatment* (pp. 229–240). Italy: Springer-Verlag.

Waldinger, M. (2013c). Future treatments of premature ejaculation. In E. Jannini, C. McMahon, & M. Waldinger (Eds.), *Premature ejaculation: From etiology to diagnosis and treatment* (pp. 359–369). Italy: Springer-Verlag.

Waldinger, M., Quinn, B., Dileen, M., Mundayat, R., Schweitzer, D., & Bodell, M. (2005). A multinational population survey of intravaginal ejaculation latency time. *Journal of Sexual Medicine*, 2, 492–497. doi: 10.1111/j.1743–6.2005.00070.x

Wolpe, J. (1982). *The practice of behavior therapy* (3rd ed.). New York: Pergamon.

7

THE COMPLEX ETIOLOGY OF DELAYED EJACULATION

Assessment and Treatment Implications

Sallie Foley and Nancy Gambescia[1]

Defining Delayed Ejaculation

Delayed ejaculation (DE) is also referred to as inhibited ejaculation, retarded ejaculation, ejaculatory incompetence, male orgasmic disorder, impaired ejaculation, impaired orgasm, delayed orgasm, inhibited orgasm, anejaculation, and ejaculatory inhibition (Althof, 2012). The numerous ways to refer to delayed ejaculation give some indication of the difficulties in coming to agreement about not only what it is, but how to effectively treat it (Richardson & Goldmeier, 2006). Of all the male sexual disorders, DE relies most on clinical and anecdotal observations for treatment. Virtually no empirical studies for treatment are available (Hartmann & Waldinger, 2007; McMahon et al., 2010; McMahon, Jannini, Waldinger, & Rowland, 2013).

Delayed ejaculation is the least common and least understood of male sexual difficulties, occurring in less than 1% of American men (American Psychiatric Association, 2013); yet, it is one of the most challenging to treat (McMahon, 2013). DE is defined as the marked delay or inability to achieve ejaculation despite the presence of adequate sexual stimulation and the desire to ejaculate (American Psychiatric Association, 2013). For DE to be classified as a sexual dysfunction, it must be experienced during almost all of occasions of partnered or solo sexual activity (75–100% of the time). The delay in ejaculation is distressful for the man and not within his control. Although the *DSM-5* recognizes that DE usually occurs during partnered sexual activity, the distress described in the diagnostic criteria pertains only to the man. Nonetheless, the clinical research is replete with evidence that DE can have a significant negative bearing on the man's sexual relationship and on his partner (Althof, 2012). This is especially impactful if the couple is attempting to procreate.

As with other sexual dysfunctions, it is important to accurately ascertain whether DE is lifelong or acquired. Lifelong DE is extremely rare. Most cases are acquired after a period of normal functioning. Another distinction to be made is if the DE is generalized (all situations) or situational (occurring only under certain conditions or with specific individuals). Approximately 25% of men with DE suffer from the generalized type (McMahon, 2013). When assessing for DE, it is also important to determine the level of distress for the man suffering with this disorder. Is it mild, moderate, or severe?

Regarding associated features of DE, five general areas are discussed in the *DSM-5* as potentially contributory to this disorder (American Psychiatric Association, 2013). These contributory factors are consistent with the Intersystem Approach to DE:

1. Relationship problems such as partner sexual problems or partner health status
2. Relationship factors such as poor communication or desire discrepancies
3. Individual vulnerabilities such as history of sexual abuse or other psychiatric comorbidities such as anxiety depression or situational stressors
4. Cultural religious factors that serve as inhibitors against sexual activity, negative attitudes toward sexuality
5. Medical factors relevant to the prognosis

From the description in the *DSM-5* (American Psychiatric Association, 2013), one sees problems in this diagnosis. The clinician is put in the position of having to judge whether the technique is adequate, stimulation has been sufficient, and excitement has been normal. If DE is situational or intermittent, for instance only occurs in the presence of a partner when trying to have intercourse, the clinician is also going to address that partner's reactions to the problem, as well as any interpersonal dynamics contributing to the DE (Waldinger, 2010). Intermittent DE increases in likelihood as men age (McMahon, 2013), usually due to a physical breakdown in the processes necessary for orgasm. Theoretically, the *DSM-5* has a separate classification for sexual disorders caused by medication or drug abuse, called Substance/Medication Induced Sexual Dysfunction. DE can be a consequence of the initiation, increase, or discontinuation of a substance or medication (American Psychiatric Association, 2013).

Physiology of Orgasm

In order to understand DE, we will briefly review the physiology of the male orgasm. For a more detailed description, see Rowland (2010). It is important to understand and distinguish the two phases of the male orgasm: emission and ejaculation. These processes typically occur simultaneously but in reality, they are distinct activities, regulated by separate neural pathways (Waldinger & Schweitzer, 2005). Emission begins after physical/psychological stimulation with the closure of the urethra at the bladder neck to prevent the release of urine from the bladder during orgasm. The internal structures such as the vas deferens, seminal vesicles, prostate, and ejaculatory ducts contract and deposit seminal fluid (sperm, semen, & prostatic fluid) into the penile urethra. The man experiences ejaculatory inevitability; thus, the orgasm cannot be stopped during the emission phase because it is already in process (Komisaruk, Beyer-Flores, & Whipple, 2006). Ejaculation encompasses the continued movement of seminal fluid into the penile urethra and expulsion of fluid from the penis. The contractions of the pelvic floor and bulbospongiosus musculature enable ejaculation. The processes of emission and ejaculation involve complex central nervous system activities, adequate nerve transmission from the spinal cord to the internal and external genital structures, and brain stimulation.

As such, any psychological condition, medical disease such as diabetes, medications such as serotonin-based antidepressants and major tranquilizers, or surgical procedures that interfere with the brain or the nerve supply to and from the genitals can cause DE (see McMahon, 2013). Orgasm is a physical and emotional process that primarily originates in the brain and central nervous system and has significant personal variation. The time it takes for a man to ejaculate is variable and believed to be influenced by both physical and psychological factors (Perelman, 2009). While orgasm is usually associated with ejaculation, it is not essential to orgasm. Hence, pleasurable orgasms may still occur in men who no longer have a prostate (the organ that produces most of the seminal fluid) or who have had injuries to the spinal cord. Appreciating both the mental and physical factors involved in these important processes allows us to understand ejaculatory disorders, as disruptions of these phases.

The Etiology of DE

A contemporary approach to diagnosis that is more straightforward is the one developed by Metz and McCarthy (2007) who prefer the term ejaculatory inhibition. They suggest that proper diagnosis and treatment depends on knowledge of the 10 types of delayed ejaculation differentially caused by five physiological types of problems (physical system conditions, physical illness, physical injury, drug side-effects, and lifestyle issues), four psychological types of problems (psychological system, psychological distress, relationships distress, and psychosexual skills deficits), and a tenth "mixed" type of problem where the delayed ejaculation co-occurs with another sexual dysfunction like low sexual desire or a partner's dyspareunia (Metz & McCarthy, 2007).

Clinicians treating delayed ejaculation will need to approach it as a couple's problem to solve (Apfelbaum, 2000), understanding that it will often be a mix of psychological and organic causes, and that pharmacologic agents, like antidepressants and antihypertensives, often play an expanding role in the causes of delayed ejaculation (McMahon, 2013). The partner's reactions always need to be considered. The lack of empirical data, the varying theories about cause and the different algorithms for treatment, all point to a sexual dysfunction that is not well understood requiring an eclectic approach to treatment (Althof, 2012). In many ways, it is the counterpart of inhibited sexual desire. While some people cannot develop enough desire and interest to have sexual arousal, others—in biology, psychology, or both—cannot fully enjoy the sexual arousal they have (Perelman, 2006). Ultimately, individuals with delayed ejaculation feel like the song from the Rolling Stones, they "can't get no satisfaction." A good working definition of delayed ejaculation is that "a man finds it difficult or impossible to ejaculate despite the presence of adequate sexual stimulation, erection, and conscious desire to achieve orgasm" (Hartmann & Waldinger, 2007).

The problem of arousal without ejaculation is further complicated by two myths in dominant culture—one that frustrates the therapist, the other the client. The first myth is that many clinicians do not seek skill development in treating delayed ejaculation because they think that it is so unusual that they'll rarely see it in their practices (Metz & McCarthy, 2007). Primary (lifelong) DE is indeed rare, but acquired DE is increasingly common due to medications (i.e., antidepressants) and because of an aging population (Perelman, 2006). With aging there is often an increase in chronic illness; more changes in blood flow, neuroperception, and medication usage (Perelman, 2014). This may lead to intermittent delayed ejaculation, or increasing difficulty with ejaculation associated with partner intimacy arousal.

Situational delayed ejaculation may also result from the over-reliance on the partner's arousal and resultant inability to describe one's own arousal trajectory. Additionally, an over-reliance on a very specific, idiosyncratic, high-frequency masturbation pattern that must be followed inflexibly may contribute to situational DE (Althof, 2012). Finally, it is believed that another factor in the development and persistence of DE is the inability to replicate the masturbatory fantasy in real life sexual partners (Perelman, 2014).

The other myth that bedevils clients more than therapists is the urban legend that in sexual interaction, the man who can "go longer" is the gold standard for sexual satisfaction (Zilbergeld, 1999). In fact, partners are usually dissatisfied and frustrated with delayed ejaculation, and often feel personally rejected (Althof, 2012). For men with delayed ejaculation, there can be feelings of inadequacy both in sexual function and in self-image (Robbins-Cherry, Hayter, Wylie, & Goldmeier, 2011). Due to frustration and low self-esteem, a man may avoid intimate communication and sexual interaction rather than engage in problem solving with his partner. It is quite possible that many years may elapse before getting help (Apfelbaum, 2000).

To summarize, it is not easy to treat delayed ejaculation, and to ignore any part of the biopsychosocial interaction is a mistake. However, DE can be treated successfully for some and managed more hopefully for others. The sex therapist should expect treatment to be integrated and comprehensive. The most useful approach to treating DE is to integrate rather than separate the biological, relational, psychological, social, intergenerational, environmental, and cultural factors. The partner must be included as DE is the couple's problem and affects the interpersonal relationship. Additionally, the therapist must be flexible in the use of individual, couple, and intergenerational understandings and include both systemic and behavioral approaches.

Prevalence

In the United States (U.S.), the prevalence of delayed ejaculation is 8% of men aged 18–59 in the last year (Laumann, Gagnon, Michael, & Michaels, 1994). More recently, the prevalence in the U.S. is reported to be less than 1% in the *DSM-5* (American Psychiatric Association, 2013). Please note that prevalence rates range from less than 1% to 10% depending on age of participant and the country in which the study was conducted (Perelman & Rowland, 2006; Waldinger, 2010).

DE may be underreported because it can co-occur with other sexual dysfunctions like erectile dysfunction or low sexual desire. In fact, Apfelbaum (2000; 2001) believes that DE is often a manifestation of low sexual desire. Unfortunately, prevalence data are in short supply, but it is estimated that 7% to 15% of men over the age of 50 will cope with secondary delayed ejaculation. This form of sexual dysfunction is characterized by intermittent problems and is correlated with aging (Waldinger, 2010).

Prior and Current Treatments

Past therapies have included medications especially for SSRI induced delayed ejaculation. Richardson, Nalabanda, and Goldmeier (2006) report that amantadine, cyproheptadine, yohimbine, bupropion, bethanechol, and buspirone have all been used with varying degrees of success, but none of the studies were placebo-controlled stopwatch studies.

In the past, psychological therapy has included meditative relaxation with psychotherapy (Delmonte, 1984), increased sexual play (Shaw, 1990), behavioral therapy with increased manual stimulation or vibratory stimulation to penis, and increased sensory awareness (Bancroft, 1989; Hawton, 1989) increased self-awareness and partner communication (Apfelbaum, 2000). The "sexual tipping point" devised by Perelman in the treatment of delayed ejaculation (Perelman, 2009); the use of integrated treatment combining systemic, psychodynamic, and cognitive-behavioral modalities described by Hartmann and Waldinger (2007); and the integration of couples therapy and psychosexual skills training advocated by Metz and McCarthy (2007) illustrate the most current treatments available for delayed ejaculation. There are no research studies comparing the use of medication treatment with the use of psychotherapy treatment in delayed ejaculation.

The Intersystem Approach to Treatment

The Intersystem Approach to treating sexual dysfunctions is useful in addressing the known or suspected causes and subsequent treatment of delayed ejaculation. Weeks (1994) describes the Intersystem Approach as a framework with five components: individual/biological/medical, individual/psychological, dyadic relationship, family-of-origin, and society/culture/history/religion. The therapist's case formulation comprises information organized in all five components and treatment that include the individual, interactional, and intergenerational aspects in each component. The Intersystem Approach is particularly useful in sex therapy because it is integrative, guards against the clinician's neglect of any component, and assures systematic formulation and interventions that are replicable and consistent. In fact, even when assessment points to only one causative agent, i.e., biological causes within the individual, all components must be explored with the client. There are too many times when a hasty conclusion prevents a full understanding of the person/dyad and also of the person's or couple's unique abilities to change based on the interaction of these systems (Weeks & Gambescia, 2000; Weeks & Gambescia, in press).

Individual Causes of Delayed Ejaculation—Physiological and Psychological

The etiology of delayed ejaculation is not well understood and is thought to be a complex mix of the individual/biological/psychological, couple, and intergenerational. There are a number of possible biological causes for DE. Some researchers hypothesize that delayed ejaculation is caused, at least in part, by slower bulbocavernous reflexes (slower reflexes), less sensitivity in the penis, and a too-high penile sensory threshold (the opposite of premature ejaculation) (Lipsith, McCann, & Goldmeier, 2003). There may also be congenital anomalies or abnormalities due to pelvic trauma or surgery. Common surgical procedures that have been associated with delayed orgasm or ejaculation are radical prostatectomy, transurethral resection of the prostate, and bladder neck surgery (McMahon, 2013).

As stated, medications are often associated with delayed ejaculation (Rowland, 2010). Common medications that can cause delayed ejaculation include anticholinergics, anti-adrenergics, antihypertensives, psychoactive drugs, selective serotonin reuptake inhibitors (SSRIs) and other antidepressants, antipsychotics, and medications associated with the treatment of obsessive compulsive disorder (Corona et al., 2011). Alcohol can also cause delayed ejaculation although a review of research indicates that alcohol and delayed ejaculation have not been systematically studied (Richardson, Nalabanda, & Goldmeier, 2006). Again, the clinician relies on clinical case reports since there is a lack of empirically based study of causation. Delayed ejaculation may also result from spinal cord injury, multiple sclerosis, and diabetes (DasGupta & Fowler, 2002; LoPiccolo, 1994; Richardson, Nalabanda, & Goldmeier, 2006; Rowland et al., 2010).

Psychological causes are so varied that almost any psychological experience has been named the culprit for delayed ejaculation (Althof, 2012). The client's history should include a thorough assessment of the individual's psychosocial development, major life events, cultural and religious beliefs related to sexual attitudes and functioning, body image, gender identity, general self-esteem, and history of relationships (Metz & McCarthy, 2007; Richardson, Nalabanda, & Goldmeier, 2006; Hertlein, Weeks, & Sendak, 2009). Additional hypotheses of causative factors include specific fears of being hurt, castration anxiety, fear of pregnancy or committing in a relationship, performance anxiety, religious proscriptions against sexual behavior, and anger at the self or the partner (Wincze & Carey, 2001).

The absence of carefully controlled research to understand psychological causes for delayed ejaculation has been documented (Hartmann & Waldinger, 2007). Apfelbaum (2000) theorizes that delayed ejaculation results from an individual being out of touch with his own sensory experience in the presence of another person. He cannot "let go of control" and "selfishly" attend to his own pleasure. Further, there may be fears about being inadequate that lead to being overly goal directed. A man can objectify his penis and become driven by a compulsion to reach orgasm (Apfelbaum, 2001). Since lack of orgasm during intercourse is the most common type of delayed ejaculation, Apfelbaum (2000) also suggests that delayed ejaculation is really a form of a desire/arousal dysfunction—the man is not orgasmic with his partner, but can self-stimulate to orgasm. He prefers his own auto-arousal and is not able to fully relax and be reciprocal with his partner. He maintains an erection, but it is automatic and not pleasurable.

If a man has delayed ejaculation that is situational and he is able to masturbate to orgasm by himself, but cannot orgasm with a partner, it is hypothesized that he may have difficulty with loss of control in front of another person or have fears of hurting or being hurt by the other (Hartmann & Waldinger, 2007). Delayed ejaculation leads to performance anxiety thereby increasing the possibility of further sexual problems (Metz & McCarthy, 2007). Men with delayed ejaculation report feelings of shame, loss of control, and helplessness as a result of their problem (Zilbergeld, 1999).

The feature of idiosyncratic masturbation styles associated with DE may be a contributor to this dysfunction as a result of nonspecific inherent biological mechanisms, which cause the man to be "hardwired" for DE (McMahon, 2013). Perelman (2006) observes that both idiosyncratic masturbatory styles and high frequency masturbation may lead to difficulty in comfort or communication with a partner about the stimulation pattern needed for ejaculation. Often, the man is unable to replicate his masturbatory technique with a partner, particularly if it involves rough stimulation or the glans or the shaft of the penis. Additionally, he might be too embarrassed to accurately convey his preferences to his partner.

Anxiety disorders present special challenges in sex and relationship therapies (Barlow, 2002). Bancroft and Janssen (2000) propose a theory of erectile dysfunction related to centrally mediated anxiety in either the fear of performance or anxiety related to outcome of performance. The individual with delayed ejaculation may be similarly challenged, resulting either in over control of his sexual response or his relationship (Baucom, Stanton, & Epstein, 2003). A clinician must remember the role of anxiety in delayed ejaculation and question, "Is there underlying anxiety that may have been present well before the event of delayed ejaculation or is there underlying anxiety that has been created by the event of delayed ejaculation?" Intermittent delayed ejaculation, often experienced by men over 50, may cause increased anxiety and relationship stress (Foley, 2005).

Relational Causes of Delayed Ejaculation and Treatment Approaches

Relationship factors often play a role in both generalized and situational delayed ejaculation. Causative influences can include insufficient pleasure in the interaction, the man's holding back as a way of gaining power, ambivalence about commitment, over-concern about "pleasing the partner," difficulties the couple may have in facilitating his communicating of necessary and adequate stimulation, disparity between fantasied partner and the real partner, and idiosyncratic masturbatory patterns that prevent arousal in partnership (Apfelbaum, 2000; Perelman & Rowland, 2006).

The partner of the man with delayed ejaculation often feels that she or he is to blame for not being attractive enough or skilled enough to facilitate ejaculation (Robbins-Cherry, Hayter, Wylie, & Goldmeier, 2011). There can be a degenerative, spiraling effect when both people experience feelings of failure and inadequacy, leading to a couple's avoidance of sex. Sometimes the man with delayed ejaculation will fake orgasms in order to please his partner. The sexual interaction thus becomes mechanical and disconnected, performance oriented without pleasure, serious not playful (McCarthy & McCarthy, 1998). Eroticism, sexual playfulness, intimacy, mutuality, and spontaneity—central to a couple's sexual pleasure—are usually absent.

Metz and McCarthy (2007) point out delayed ejaculation often leads to reduced motivation and interest in sex, lowered sexual desire, and sexual avoidance. Secondary sexual dysfunction of inhibited sexual desire or erectile dysfunction can occur. Situational delayed ejaculation can result from relationship dissatisfaction and problems the couple are experiencing outside the bedroom. A man who is conflicted about his relationship may not experience pleasurable relaxation and sensation necessary for orgasm (Weeks & Gambescia, in press).

Intergenerational Causes of Delayed Ejaculation

Intergenerational causes include faulty or nonexistent sexual education and overly critical, strict religious orthodoxy (Wincze & Carey, 2001). Hypotheses about intergenerational influences abound and there is no empirical data to support the theories (Hartmann & Waldinger, 2007). It is possible that early experiences of punitive shaming either if caught masturbating or being sexually curious can lead to difficulties with delayed ejaculation. Some men report feeling conflicted about aggression, either because of overly aggressive parental figures or because of severe restriction of any form of normal aggressive activity. These men may become anxious about showing "aggression" or "selfishness" during sexual activity with a partner (Hartmann & Waldinger, 2007). Men may receive messages and sexual scripts that run the gamut from thinking that real men ejaculate easily and every time, to thinking of sex as sport and that real men should be detached and not intimate. These messages coupled with a lack of sexual education can spell disaster for some men (Metz & McCarthy, 2007). A past history of trauma can also create conflicts that can manifest in delayed ejaculation (Lew, 2004), including the confusion of arousal and aggression, or association of shame with pleasurable arousal.

Sociocultural Factors Affecting Delayed Ejaculation

Culture and socialization contribute to a person's formation of sexual identity and influence sexual functioning. In North America, men are taught to be independent, self-sufficient, and protective of partner and family. Advertising also has a stake in promoting this 'mighty man' sexual performance image since it sells sexual enhancement products. Zilbergeld (1999) calls this predominant image of male sexuality the "fantasy model," observing that North American culture views the penis as "two feet long, hard as steel" and can go all night. This prevalent cultural model is constrictive and can make real men into anxious performers who have difficulty staying connected with their own sensations, partner intimacy, and a realistic understanding of what sexual responsivity looks and feels like (Apfelbaum, 2000; Metz & McCarthy, 2004). The cultural paradigm stressing these characteristics is a potent socializer. Men may be hesitant to admit they have a problem with delayed ejaculation and feel even more shame if they must seek help.

Assessment—Establishing Openness and Safety in Sex Therapy

Assessing delayed ejaculation may occur in individual or couples treatment. The process of asking questions and seeking information about the problem will be interwoven with information that the therapist provides to the client both about the processes and about the dynamics of interaction between the therapist and the client (Hertlein et al., 2009). At the beginning of treatment, the therapist explains how the psychotherapy proceeds and gains the client/couple's agreement to participate in this process. The assessment questions in Table 7.1 outline the process of assessing delayed ejaculation, but the clinician must also be attuned to creating an environment of safety and openness. In the absence of empirically based algorithms for treatment, the clinician must rely on skillful piecing together of individual, couple, and intergenerational contributors to the problem. The client and the therapist will collaborate in treatment planning and increasing the client's insight and awareness (Hartmann & Waldinger, 2007).

As the clinician moves through the assessment questions, the clinician will clarify to the client what a sex therapist is—many people are referred and have no idea what they will encounter when meeting a sex therapist or what will happen in a sex therapy session. The clinician then proceeds to ask how the individual or couple was referred for therapy, if either has ever sought sex therapy or psychotherapy before and if so, what that experience was like for him or them. Following the client's line of reasoning for choosing a specific therapist will provide information about how this client assesses his own situation, fantasies he may have about "instant cures" or pace of treatment, and general level of awareness of how psychotherapy works. It is useful to explore how long the client knew about the possibility of sex therapy but waited to begin.

It is important to discuss the gender of the therapist with the client and if this was an important consideration in selecting the therapist. If the client is assigned a therapist at a clinic and has not chosen the therapist, the therapist will need to ask the client how the client feels about having a same gender or different gender therapist. For some, the therapist's gender is not an important issue. But most clients will have feelings one way or the other about the effect their therapist's gender has on their comfort level in talking about sexual concerns (Maurice, 1999). Clients may feel strongly that they do not wish to discuss their sexual problems with a woman either due to embarrassment or due to feelings that she "could never understand" what he is going through. Conversely, the client may feel that talking to a woman is easier because a male therapist would make the client feel more inadequate, less masculine. In fact, in a research study involving 65 couples randomly assigned to a man, a woman, or a dual sex-therapy team, there was no significant difference in treatment outcomes (LoPiccolo, Heiman, Hogan, & Roberts, 1985).

The therapist may predict that at times the client/couple will feel frustrated or experience a loss of hope. The therapist may even request that if the client/couple becomes so frustrated that they are considering terminating that they will first come in and talk with the therapist before ending treatment. The therapist's prediction of frustration and despair and the invitation to discuss even matters of disappointment with the therapist serves as a parallel process mirroring the way that the couple will eventually learn to talk constructively with each other about disappointments without disengaging from sexual interaction. Finally, in the treatment of delayed ejaculation, it is especially important to discuss the need for an individualized treatment plan (Maurice, 1999). Some clients expect a standard protocol. It is useful to contrast physical therapy and psychotherapy (of which sex therapy is a subset) in order to highlight the differences in procedure in the two practices. In physical therapy, there is often a specific set of exercises set out in stepwise

Table 7.1 The Intersystem Assessment: Individual and Couple Structure of assessment process: Couple session, individual session with each partner, then return to couple sessions

- Couple, first session: Presenting problem/concern
  - History of problem
  - Precipitants
  - Communication about problem to others, including partner and professionals
  - Solutions previously tried

- Individual and interactional information during couple session:
  - Age
  - Developmental history and family-of-origin observations
  - Social interests/friends
  - Present home/family life
  - Relationship status
  - General capacity to experience pleasure in life
  - Work and meaning of work to person
  - Current partnership: length of relationship
  - Past crises in the relationship and how the couple solved them
  - How does the couple handle disagreements and anger
  - How does the couple divide up work/roles/financial responsibilities/parenting

- Individual session, general
  - Health data
  - General health
  - Relaxation/stress—self-awareness
  - History of serious illness and family-of-origin history
  - Current medications—this is especially important because of effect on delayed ejaculation
  - Alcohol and substance use, including marijuana, cocaine—effect on delayed ejaculation
  - Thought and mood: i.e, ruminations, anxiety, depression, obsessions/compulsions, thought disorders, prior mental health challenges—effect on delayed ejaculation

- Individual session, orientation/gender/relationship history
  - Sexual orientation
  - Age of awareness of sexual orientation
  - Shame about sexual orientation or sexual habits from earlier development?
  - Gender—self-esteem and body image
  - Relationships: length, satisfaction, changes over time, upsetting events in relationship

- Individual session, sexual history with intergenerational and sociocultural focus
  - Earliest remembered sexual experiences and general attitude about these experiences.
  - How learned about sex: What did family teach about male and female sexuality?
  - What were the positive and negative, overt and covert messages received about sex?
  - What cultural messages are believed about male sexuality? For instance, how would the client finish the phrase: "A real man should. . ."
  - How would the client's father or grandfather have answered the above question?
  - How was the client introduced to, or socialized to, these cultural messages?
  - Childhood, adolescent, and early adult sexual development and sexual experiences
  - Sexual mistreatment or trauma. Note: It is normal for people to initially downplay trauma history. Often a client will provide more detail about past history of trauma later in the session or later in sex therapy

(Continued)

Table 7.1 (Continued)

- Individual session, sexual history with individual focus:
  - Any difficulty with erections—important to differentiate from delayed ejaculation?
  - Any pain during erection?
  - When did difficulty with ejaculation begin?
  - Does the person have retrograde ejaculation due to prior surgeries?
  - Does the person experience orgasm even though they cannot experience ejaculation?
  - Difficulty with infertility or having children?
  - If have children, how have children affected sense of sexual self and sex life?
  - General current attitude about sex and its importance in life: What are beliefs about sex?
  - Self-concept as a sexual person
  - Is sexual behavior ever enjoyable? When?
  - Decisions about safer sex and birth control.
  - Current feelings about masturbation and does masturbation lead to ejaculation?
  - If ejaculation occurs with masturbation, what are the specific actions, thoughts, fantasies that he relies on to assure ejaculation?
  - Current feelings about partner initiating sex and how does he respond?

- Couples session, interactional information:
  - What is this couples' history of sexual interaction together?
  - How do they communicate about sex?
  - What is their motivation for sexual interaction at this time?
  - How frequent is sexual activity?
  - Who initiates and what happens: What is their typical sexual pattern? Range of sexual behaviors and comfort level.
  - With regard to delayed ejaculation, what is a typical situation where this occurs? Are either aware if he is under pressure to perform, experiences "spectatoring," or is mechanical or detached in approach?
  - When does he lose his erotic focus and feel pressure?
  - Does the person with delayed ejaculation avoid intense sensory experience with his partner during sexual activity, i.e., avoid wetness in kissing or genital contact, or avoid increased sensory intensity like heavy breathing or moaning?
  - Can he have a subjective feeling of pleasure, enjoy stimulation from his partner, and direct his partner in ways to stimulate him?
  - Is he able to ejaculate to manual stimulation from his partner?
  - How does the couple handle the partner's desire for orgasm?
  - If the partner has an orgasm, does sexual interaction continue?
  - Is either partner comfortable with masturbation in front of the other?
  - How well do they know each other's bodies and what "works" in sexual pleasure?
  - What happens when things don't "work"? Does either partner get frustrated or accusatory? If so, how does the couple handle these difficulties?
  - Does intercourse take place? If so, does he sometimes ejaculate during intercourse? How long does this take?

- Discussion of sex therapy
  - Assess their motivation for treatment.
  - Are they able to plan sexual interactions?
  - Do they hold the myth that good sex equals spontaneous sex?

fashion. Physical therapy often uses a "carrot on a stick" approach—certain exercises will produce certain results. The therapist in sex therapy must create a tone of positive hope for improvement but cannot promise a specific outcome by following a stepwise program. Sex therapy, however, should make sense to clients and time will be needed to explain interventions (Metz & McCarthy, 2007).

The assessment takes several sessions and usually includes one individual session with each partner. In individual sessions, a greater emphasis can be placed on developmental history; social, cultural, and religious influences; and any concerns that may be difficult for the individual to raise with the partner present.

Treatment of Delayed Ejaculation

Treatment of delayed ejaculation must proceed flexibly, integrating the individual, couple, and intergenerational approaches characteristic of Intersystem sex therapy.

Treatment techniques routinely rely on three things:

- Cognitive behavioral therapy (CBT) implementing homework (sometimes referred to as homeplay) assignments that increase competence
- Insight-oriented strategies that reduce self-blame and judgment and increase feelings of self-acceptance
- Couple-focused strategies that promote intimacy and mutuality as well as further sexuality education and positive sexual interaction for the couple

Competence, self-acceptance, and furthering mutuality are the base for a more successful resolution to the problem of delayed ejaculation.

The treatment of delayed ejaculation may take only a few months when the problem is primarily the result of sexual misinformation and mild anxiety and the person is able to engage in specific behavior change—like more direct stimulation and personal focus on pleasure. Delayed ejaculation, however, is more often a treatment of behavior accommodation, where longer term issues are uncovered and certain aspects of personality "are what they are," meaning resistant to change. Then ejaculation may be accomplished occasionally, but delayed ejaculation remains intermittently and must be accommodated and "lived with" at least some of the time. In these situations, the couple will need to reinforce that their friendship and mutual acceptance are vital parts of their sexual life (Metz & McCarthy, 2007).

Medication/Biological Approaches and the Individual

Individual approaches include a respect for possible biologic and genetic precursors of delayed ejaculation. At this time, there are no medications that specifically treat lifelong or acquired delayed ejaculation. In the future some medication may be developed that would involve stimulation of the dopamine, noradrenalin, and oxytocin receptors in the brain (Waldinger, 2010).

It is possible for some individuals, whose delayed ejaculation is associated with not reaching adequate sensory thresholds, to be helped by the use of vibratory stimulation. In one presentation of lifelong delayed ejaculation, the individual purchased a small battery-operated vibrator which he learned to use and found stimulation pleasurable against his upper inner thigh, on his perineum, and at the base of the shaft of his penis. He used the vibrator to successfully achieve sensory thresholds to orgasm while masturbating alone. He was not currently in a partnership so it is not possible to tell if he was able to successfully ejaculate with a partner. He was cautioned by the sex therapist about "idiosyncratic masturbation" and learned to masturbate to ejaculation without the vibrator.

If the individual is taking any medication that may contribute to delayed ejaculation, it is recommended that the clinician work with the treating physician to alleviate medication interference whenever possible (McMahon, 2013). This may include, for instance in the case of some SSRIs, the possibility of reducing the dosage, switching to another medication with fewer side effects, or possibly adding a medication (for instance, buproprion) where appropriate. Explaining to the client that medication dosing/switching/adding will require teamwork, an inquisitive attitude, and patience is important in the client's tolerance of this sometimes long and frustrating road of treatment.

It is often possible that an individual with delayed ejaculation develops erectile dysfunction. In these cases, the person may be helped by treatment with medications used to treat erectile dysfunction. There are some clients who do not have erectile dysfunction, but experience a positive placebo effect from taking sildenafil while treating delayed ejaculation. Developing patience in treatment is not easy for clients and some clients respond more positively when they feel they are "doing something." The benefits of this must always be weighed against the drawbacks that may include the client thinking that medicines are the preferred route of treatment, a commonly held belief in the United States.

Sensory Defensiveness or Anxiety Treatments and the Individual

Having noted the central role that anxiety or obsessiveness plays in either helping to create or further problems of delayed ejaculation, the introduction of anxiety reduction techniques is a significant part of sex therapy for delayed ejaculation. These techniques are essentially cognitive behavioral techniques and begin with teaching the individual mindfulness and breathing techniques, progressive relaxation, and increasing sensory tolerance (Metz & McCarthy, 2007).

For many individuals with delayed ejaculation, there may be problems with sensory defensiveness—a condition in which normal sensory input, like certain smells, tastes, sounds, or touch, may be experienced as overwhelming and anxiety producing by a person with sensory defensiveness (Curtis, 2001). For instance, an individual who is mucus averse and dislikes open mouth kissing or the sensation of vulvovaginal "wetness" may have difficulty reaching the necessary sensory threshold for ejaculation in the presence of a partner because the normal wetness or slipperiness of sex is uncomfortable for the individual. In these situations, it is necessary to teach techniques of increasing sensory tolerance through progressive desensitization to not only touch and wetness, but also to the amount or intensity of the experience, focusing on intimacy and closeness rather than on performance (Metz & McCarthy, 2007). A client may select the homework assignment of exploring different types of kissing without further sexual demand (often referred to in sex therapy as "nondemand"), increasing tolerance for open mouth kissing and tongue exploration. Or a client who is unable to ejaculate during intercourse may experiment with the sensation of nondemand "wetness" and "closeness" by taking showers with a partner and learning to explore genitals, use lubrications, even rub his penis against his partner's body while they are both "wet all over" in the shower.

Masturbation Flexibility and the Individual

Many individuals with delayed ejaculation have strong idiosyncratic masturbation patterns that have been in place a long time. Using an educational approach, the sex therapist encourages the individual to reconsider the inflexible masturbation pattern and begin to slowly branch out both in stimulation—by using different positions and different intensities of touch when self-stimulating—and by using different fantasies or visualizations when self-stimulating. The technique is especially useful when the delayed ejaculation is situational and involves a partner but is not present when the person is masturbating alone. The sex therapist explains to the individual that increasing his flexibility in masturbation will translate into being more capable of openness to partner touch and flexible response to arousal in partnership.

Resistance is a therapeutic term indicating that the client is avoiding insight, behavior change, or communication change with partner (Goldstein, 1995). Resistance to changing, or more accurately, *trying* to change idiosyncratic masturbation patterns, should be pointed out to the client. The client's resistance to trying new things needs to be explored with the client so that he can use insight into his own behavior as a part of his treatment.

For some clients, resistance can be framed as a way of really staying in place with his partner. Clinicians often observe that a client may become aware that he does not like his partner and is using delayed ejaculation to get his body to speak for him. In some cases, this has been the beginning of the end for the relationship and has led the client to explain he has no real sexual interest in the partner, which has, in turn, led to the couple's decision to separate. However, other couples have used this awareness to address the reasons why there is no sexual interest and rededicate themselves to creating a positive and playful relationship with the hope that this will lead to more positive interactions in the sexual relationship. For many with motivation and mutual generosity, this is the case.

Increasing Awareness of Outside Influences

Sex therapy often reduces anxiety and self-criticism by exploring the sources of external messages that have influenced the client and encouraging new perspectives about the meanings of those messages. Often a process of reframing takes place. Weeks (1994) points out that exploring the real intentions and realistic assessment of behavior can help the client reach different conclusions about the meaning of a sexual behavior like delayed ejaculation. If he has considered himself to be "inadequate," "withholding," "uncaring," or "over the hill," it will be helpful to explore with this individual the other meanings that delayed ejaculation can carry. Notably, a therapist can remind the client that many individuals with delayed ejaculation are very caring and are actually being overly responsive or attentive to their partners. They are committed to not being aggressive, selfish, or overwhelming their partner with their own sexual needs. They may suffer from a lack of sex education and are self-conscious about sexuality information. And they may just be trying too hard, not having pleasure, pressing on because they feel the demand to perform. Hopefully, the client can begin to see the ways in which he has been burdened by these negative beliefs that often stem from either faulty intergenerational messages or social expectations he has inculcated. He may advance this insight orientation by using the therapy to understand the background family history that helped create those intergenerational messages about sexuality that were so negative about sexual involvement. Some clients realize that early messages about sex being dirty, immoral, or shameful have contributed to anxiety in sexual interaction. At times, the insight may include a memory of having been caught masturbating as a child—memories that are inevitably connected with having displeased the adult and memories that led to negative feelings about sexual pleasure. A client may also reflect on the cultural messages he learned about his own sexuality and sexual performance, messages from television, magazines, the Internet, that stress performance not pleasure, and disconnection of the man from his penis and his partner. He may also recognize that he was socialized not to seek help from others for his problems.

Finally, sex therapy may stimulate awareness of grief and loss for the individual who has struggled with the problem. Understanding that he has a right to grieve and that sexual dysfunction is a loss that "no one brings over a casserole for" can create an environment of openness and therapeutic alliance. The very process of talking in sex therapy, grieving, and gaining new information about sexual function can lead to decreased performance anxiety and increased self-esteem.

Couple Techniques

If a client with delayed ejaculation has a partner, it is crucial to include that person in the treatment if at all possible. The partner will need an opportunity to dispel myths, grieve the presence of the problem, and engage positively in finding more successful ways to interact. The couple will be helped through increasing psychosexual skills with graduated homework assignments, decreasing performance pressure, and increasing comfort and playfulness (Metz & McCarthy, 2007). Couples who are capable of relaxing and playing together may be helped by the therapist introducing the concept of "borrowing competencies" from other parts of their relationship. The therapist asks the couple to discuss when and how they relax and play together. For instance, if this couple enjoys playing cards, hiking together, or any other shared activity, the therapist can point out that the couple knows how to experience pleasure and playfulness that can be borrowed over into the now "too serious" sex life. This can contribute to a more comfortable focus on nondemand physical playfulness including non-genital massage—touch that is not sexually or genitally focused. The therapist continues to point out that playfulness requires a focus on one's own sensory experience, i.e., being selfish at the same time one is engaged in partnership.

Treatment is often linear, beginning with nondemand playfulness, building pleasurable experiences and then proceeding on to nondemand physical playfulness and sensate focus exercises. The couple learns to increase comfort with increased erotic stimulation, thereby decreasing self-consciousness. Couples need to be reminded that trust in being physical, erotic, and sensual takes time.

The therapist may find that there is disappointment on the partner's part to the "slow" pace of therapy or therapeutic interventions. It is important to "hear the partner out" when concerns arise as well as continue to assess how the couple sustains friendship and intimacy. The therapist encourages the partner and person with delayed ejaculation to see themselves as a team engaging in desensitizing techniques, reducing performance anxiety, and increasing sensuality. The partner may need to be encouraged to continue to understand her/his own sexual response as separate and important.

Work with couples should include intergenerational messages about sexuality for both individuals. When suggesting the couple try any technique, it is important that the couple feels they have the choice to do the assignment. The sex therapist can offer a range of two or three different possible assignments and the couple makes the decision which one they will try (Weeks & Fife, 2014). The couple should also decide who will be in charge of initiating homework and may need to establish day/time/place for the homework to take place. Grieving the idealization that sex should be spontaneous may be a part of the treatment for the couple as well.

In addition, couples can each create their own "desire" checklist of behaviors/interactions that they enjoy. They can work together to create pleasant and pleasurable places in which to enjoy sex (Foley, 2005). Some couples have sexual scripts of how they want sexual interaction to proceed and these scripts may need discussion and modification in sex therapy. Establishing the expectation that sexual interaction will be about mutual pleasure while decreasing the focus on perfect performance is an important part of modifying sexual scripts (Foley, Kope, & Sugrue, 2002). Some couples need to work on "reading" each other's body cues and use massage, dance, or exercises to learn to mirror each other's movements, increasing comfort in being together.

If an individual with delayed ejaculation has avoided intercourse for some time and he is partnered to a post-menopausal woman, she may have some vaginal atrophy if she has not been engaging in penetrative sex (Foley, 2005). If intercourse is resumed after a time of no sex, a woman may have dyspareunia (Foley, Kope, & Sugrue, 2002). She may need to investigate the use of a localized estrogen replacement (like Vagifem, Estrace cream, or Estring), as well as practice penetration with fingers, a penis-shaped vibrator, or vaginal dilators (vaginal inserters) before resuming sexual intercourse. Discussion of lubrications should be included in the sex therapy as well (Foley, 2005).

Intersystem Approaches in Three Therapeutic Situations

If a man with delayed ejaculation does not have a partner, the sex therapist might recommend he use a vibrator with masturbation, encourage further sexuality education, increase his understanding about intergenerational messages from his childhood, and recommend flexibility in masturbation techniques so that the client does not become overly dependent on "one way." Clients can also learn to "pleasure to arousal" for 10 or 15 minutes without focusing on or attempting orgasm, followed by shifting their focus to other things and allowing arousal and erection to abate. Practicing this emphasis on pleasure over performance often helps with intermittent delayed ejaculation and spectatoring.

If a client with delayed ejaculation also has anxiety or sensory defensiveness with his partner, the sex therapist will need to predict a longer course of treatment, addressing the client's tendency to retreat to self-stimulation, educate about the role of anxiety and sensory defensiveness, and help his partner to address reactivity or disappointment in sexual situations. Encouraging nondemand pleasurable touch, increasing intimacy behaviors and language, and encouraging focus on the couple's friendship and other resiliencies may provide the necessary ingredients for change. This approach may also work for couples with the intermittent delayed ejaculation that many men experience with aging.

In more complex presentations, especially for those clients who must overcome trauma or untangling pleasurable sexual responsivity from fear about intimacy or vulnerability, the course of therapy must include that discussed above as well as help the individual or couple work to integrate insights about their individual and shared histories, reducing feelings of shame or isolation. A flexible use of both individual and couples sessions may be needed where traumatic experiences or histories of childhood neglect have resulted in an adult tendency to too rapidly withdraw from connection to partner. Homework assignments must be flexible and slowly paced. A coherent narrative of the trauma experience may need to be developed piece by piece (Naparstek, 2004; Scaer, 2001; Solomon & Siegel, 2003). Finally, the couple will need to be reminded to reduce idealizations of "perfect sex" and become more accepting of sex that is "good enough" most of the time (Metz & McCarthy, 2007).

Future Directions

The diagnosis and treatment of delayed ejaculation is an area that needs further study and collaboration between disciplines to develop a more definitive diagnosis—even if it is a complex diagnosis. The diagnosis of delayed ejaculation will be affected by both the rising numbers of aging men in the boomer generation and the increasing numbers of men using medications that may affect ejaculation and orgasm. This will add pressure to look for better ways to research the treatment of delayed ejaculation, both medically and psychologically. The Intersystem treatment approach is currently viewed as the most relevant. Continued research is needed about the effectiveness of this treatment technique and the characteristics of clients who tend to benefit from this approach. At this time, there is no medical treatment for delayed ejaculation. In fact, it responds best to Intersystem Approaches combined with motivation, flexibility, and patience on the part of both the client and the sex therapist.

Note

1   The original chapter written by Sallie Foley was updated by Nancy Gambescia for this edition

References

Althof, S. E. (2012). Psychological interventions for delayed ejaculation/orgasm. *International Journal of Impotence Research, 24,* 131–136.

American Psychiatric Association. (2013). *Diagnostic and statistical manual of mental disorders* (5th ed.). Washington, DC: Author.

Apfelbaum, B. (2000). Retarded ejaculation: A much misunderstood syndrome. In S. Leiblum & R. Rosen (Eds.), *Principles and practice of sex therapy* (3rd ed., pp. 205–241). New York: Guilford Press.

Apfelbaum, B. (2001). What the sex therapies tell us about sex. In P. Kleinplatz (Ed.), *New directions in sex therapy: Innovations and alternatives* (pp. 5–28). New York: Brunner-Routledge.

Bancroft, J. (1989). *Human sexuality and its problems* (2nd ed.). Edinburgh: Churchill Livingstone.

Bancroft, J., & Janssen, E. (2000). The dual control model of male sexual response: A theoretical approach to centrally mediated erectile dysfunction. *Neuroscience and Biobehavioral Reviews, 24,* 571–579. doi: 10.1016/S0149-7634(00)00024-5

Barlow, D. H. (2002). *Anxiety and its disorders: The nature and treatment of anxiety and panic.* New York: Guilford Press.

Baucom, D. H., Stanton, S., & Epstein, N. B. (2003). Anxiety disorders. In D. K. Snyder & M. A. Whisman (Eds.), *Treating difficult couples: Helping clients with co-existing mental and relationship disorders* (pp. 57–87). New York: Guilford Press.

Corona, G., Jannini, E. A., Lotti, F., Boddi, V., De Vita, G., Forti, G., . . . Maggi, M. (2011). Premature and delayed ejaculation: Two ends of a single continuum influenced by hormonal milieu. *International Journal of Andrology, 34,* 41–48. doi: 10.1111/j.1365-2605.2010.01059.x

Curtis, V. (2001). Dirt, disgust, and disease: Is hygiene in our genes? *Perspectives in Biology and Medicine, 44*(1), 17–31.

DasGupta, R., & Fowler, C. J. (2002). Sexual and urological dysfunction in multiple sclerosis: Better understanding and improved therapies. *Current Opinion Neurology, 5,* 271–278.

Delmonte, M. M. (1984). Case reports on the use of meditative relaxation as an intervention strategy with retarded ejaculation. *Biofeedback & Self Regulation, 9,* 209–214.

Foley, S. (2005). *Sex and love for grownups: A no-nonsense guide to a life of passion.* New York: Sterling.

Foley, S., Kope, S. A., & Sugrue, D. (2002). *Sex matters for women: A complete guide to taking care of your sexual self*. New York: Guilford Press.

Goldstein, E. G. (1995). *Ego psychology and social work practice*. New York: The Free Press.

Hartmann, U., & Waldinger, M. (2007). Treatment of delayed ejaculation. In S. Leiblum & R. Rosen (Eds.), *Principles and practice of sex therapy* (4th ed., pp. 241–276). New York: Guilford Press.

Hawton, K. (1989). *Sex therapy: A practical guide*. Oxford: University Press.

Hertlein, K., Weeks, G., & Sendak, S. (2009). *Clinician's guide to systemic sex therapy*. New York: Routledge.

Komisaruk, B., Beyer-Flores, C., & Whipple, B. (2006). *The science of orgasm*. Baltimore: The Johns Hopkins University Press.

Laumann, E. O., Gagnon, J. H., Michael, R. T., & Michaels, S. (1994). *The social organization of sexuality: Sexual practices in the United States*. Chicago: University of Chicago Press.

Lew, M. (2004). *Victims no longer: The classic guide for men recovering from sexual child abuse* (2nd ed.). New York: Quill.

Lipsith, J., McCann, D., & Goldemier, D. (2003). Male psychogenic sexual dysfunction: The role of masturbation. *Sexual and Relationship Therapy, 18*(4), 447–471. doi: 10.1080/1468199031000099442

LoPiccolo, J., Heiman, J. R., Hogan, D. R., & Roberts, C. W. (1985). Effectiveness of single therapists versus cotherapy teams in sex therapy. *Journal of Consulting Clinical Psychology, 53*, 287–294.

Lopicollo, T. A. (1994). Sexual function in persons with diabetes: Issues in research, treatment and education. *Clinical Psychology Review, 14*, 1–86.

Maurice, W. L. (1999). *Sexual medicine in primary care*. St. Louis, MO: Mosby.

McCarthy, B., & McCarthy, E. (1998). *Male sexual awareness*. New York: Carroll & Graf.

McMahon, C. (2013). Taxonomy of ejaculatory disorders and definitions of premature ejaculation. In E. Jannini, C. McMahon, & M. Waldinger (Eds.), *Premature ejaculation: From etiology to diagnosis and treatment* (pp. 53–69). Italy: Springer-Verlag.

McMahon, C. G., Rowland, D. L., Abdo, C., Jannini, E., Chen, J., Waldinger, M. (2010). Disorders of orgasm and ejaculation in men. In F. Montorsi, R. Basson, G. Adaikan et al. (Eds). *Sexual medicine: Sexual disorders in men and women*, Paris: Health Publication LTD.

McMahon, C. G., Jannini, E., Waldinger, M., & Rowland, D. (2013). Standard operating procedures in the disorders of orgasm and ejaculation. *The Journal of Sexual Medicine, 10*(1), 204–229.

Metz, M. E., & McCarthy, B. W. (2004). *Coping with erectile dysfunction: How to regain confidence and enjoy great sex*. Oakland, CA: New Harbinger Publications.

Metz, M. E., & McCarthy, B. W. (2007). Ejaculatory problems. In L. Vandecreek, F. L. Peterson, & J. W. Bley (Eds.), *Innovations in clinical practice: Focus on sexual health* (pp. 135–155). Sarasota, FL: Professional Resource Press.

Naparstek, B. (2004). *Invisible heroes: Survivors of trauma and how they heal*. New York: Bantam.

Perelman, M. (2006). A new combination treatment for premature ejaculation: A sex therapist's perspective. *Journal of Sexual Medicine, 36*, 104–112.

Perelman, M. A. (2009). The sexual tipping point: A mind-body model for sexual medicine. *Journal of Sexual Medicine, 63*, 629–632. doi: 10.1111/j.1743–6109.2008.01177.x

Perelman, M. A. (2014). Delayed ejaculation. In Y. M. Binic & K. S. Hall (Eds.), *Principles and practice of sex therapy* (5th ed., pp. 138–158). New York: Guilford Press.

Perelman, M. A., & Rowland, D. L. (2006). Retarded ejaculation. *World Journal of Urology, 24*(6), 645–652.

Richardson, D., & Goldmeier, D. (2006). Recommendations for the management of retarded ejaculation: BASHH special interest group for sexual dysfunction. *International Journal of STD and AIDS 2006, 17*, 7–13. doi: 10.1258/095646206775220450

Richardson, D., Nalabanda, A., & Goldmeier, D. (2006). Retarded ejaculation—A review. *International Journal of STD & AIDS 2006, 17*, 143–150.

Robbins-Cherry, S., Hayter, M., Wylie, K., & Goldmeier, D. (2011). The experiences of men living with inhibited ejaculation. *Sexual and Relationship Therapy, 26*(3), 242–253. doi: 10.1080/14681994.2011.62193

Rowland, D. (2010). *Sexual dysfunction in men*. Cambridge, MA: Hogrefe.

Rowland, D., McMahon, C. G., Abdo, C., Chen, J., Jannini, E., Waldinger, M. D., & Ahn, T. (2010). Disorders of orgasm and ejaculation in men. *Journal of Sexual Medicine*, 7, 1668–1686. doi:10.1111/j.1743–6109.2010.01782.x

Scaer, R. (2001). *The body bears the burden: Trauma, dissociation, and disease*. New York: Haworth.

Shaw, J. (1990). Play therapy with the sexual workhorse: Successful treatment with twelve cases of inhibited ejaculation. *Journal of Sex and Marital Therapy*, 16, 159–164.

Solomon, M., & Siegel, D. (2003). *Healing trauma: Attachment, mind, body, and brain*. New York: Norton.

Waldinger, M.D. (2010). Premature ejaculation and delayed ejaculation. In S.B. Levine, C. Risen, & S. Althof (Eds.), *Handbook of clinical sexuality for mental health professionals* (2nd ed.). New York: Routledge.

Waldinger, M.D., & Schweitzer, D.H. (2005). Retarded ejaculation in men: An overview of psychological and neurobiological insights. *World Journal of Urology*, 23, 76–81. doi: 10.1007/s00345–004–0487–8

Weeks, G. (1994). The intersystem model: An integrative approach to treatment. In G. Weeks & L. Hof (Eds.), *The marital-relationship therapy casebook: Theory and application of the intersystem model, 1* (pp. 3–34). New York: Brunner/Mazel.

Weeks, G., & Fife, S. (2014). *Couples in treatment* (3rd ed.). New York: Routledge.

Weeks, G., & Gambescia, N. (2000). *Erectile dysfunction: Integrating couple therapy, sex therapy, and medical treatment*. New York: W.W. Norton.

Weeks, G., & Gambescia, N. (in press). Couple therapy and the treatment of sexual problems: The Intersystem Approach. In A. Gurman, J. Lebow, & D. Snyder (Eds.) *Clinical handbook of couple therapy* (5th ed.). New York: Guilford.

Wincze, J.P., & Carey, M.P. (2001). *Sexual dysfunction: A guide for assessment and treatment* (2nd ed.). New York: Guilford Press.

Zilbergeld, B. (1999). *The new male sexuality*. New York: Bantam.

8

DEFINITION, ETIOLOGY, AND TREATMENT OF ABSENT/LOW DESIRE IN WOMEN

Gerald R. Weeks and Nancy Gambescia

Since the publication of *Systemic Sex Therapy* in 2009, there has been an explosion of research on lack of, deficient, or absent desire in women. Our review of the research uncovered dozens of articles and chapters written about women and the lack of desire, but only a handful about men. We also found that two topics seemed to dominate the investigation landscape in sex therapy. These were articles about the definition of the lack of desire and models of desire containing a medical focus on hormonal or pharmacological treatment of lack of desire. Before we begin our discussion of low desire, we would like to challenge the notion that sexual desire is the prime motivation for having sex. Meston and Buss (2007) surveyed over 1,500 undergraduate students using a list of 237 reasons for having sex. Twenty of the top twenty-five reasons for having sex were identical for men and women. Most of the reasons had little to do with sexual desire, which may include both the lack of interest in sexual activity as well as the lack of interest or arousal in erotic cues and extermal simuli (Basson, 2014). A factor analysis revealed four main factors and 13 subfactors. These included: (1) physical reasons such as stress reduction, pleasure, physical attractiveness, and seeking a new experience; (2) attaining goals, for example, increasing social status, revenge, utilitarian goals, and obtaining resources; (3) emotional reasons such as love, commitment, and expression of emotion; and (4) insecurity factors such as boosting self-esteem, duty or pressure from partner, mate guarding. A few gender differences were noted in the paper and unfortunately the sample was young and mostly unmarried. A study of individuals of a wide age range might have produced markedly different results.

The Meston and Buss (2007) study raises many questions about the role of desire in having a sexual interaction. Moreover, placing this study in a broader context, there is the general assumption that desire leads to sex and sex leads to pleasure. The role of sexual motivation and pleasure are rarely discussed in the sex therapy literature. Clearly, desire may or may not lead to sex, and if it does we cannot simply assume the outcome is pleasurable or satisfying.

A Goal Response Model of Sex developed by Boul Hallam-Jones and Wylie (2008) is a good fit for the empirical findings reviewed above. According to this model, sex may be for hedonistic reasons or to enjoy the moment (pleasure) or it can be for eudemonic reasons that are more practical in nature such as maintaining a relationship or acquiring material security. The Goal Response Model incorporates cognitive, physiological and emotional components. Basically, there is a stimulus, which creates sensory processes, which in turn leads to cognitive processes. The authors propose this as a general model of sexual functioning and specifically point to an idea that is unique in considering

125

happiness

desire. They propose that engaging in a sexual activity can produce a positive emotion, even if the goal is eudemonic or not for pleasure. Thus, sexual activity with low desire can have a positive emotional outcome such as strengthening a relationship. On the other hand, it may not necessarily have a positive emotional outcome. In fact, we discuss later that having sex without desire can beget the lack of desire (Hubin, De Sutter, & Reynaert, 2011).

Prevalence

Low/absent sexual desire is one of the most common presenting problems in the practice of sex and couple therapy; approximately 20% of men and 33% of women are affected by low or absent sexual desire (Laumann, Palik, & Rosen, 1999). Laumann et al. (2005) analyzed the data from the Global Study of Sexual Attitudes and Behaviors and found that women experienced low desire in the range of 26–43%. Brotto (2010) has provided an extensive review and critique of many studies on prevalence, definitional issues, and other research to support a revision of DSM diagnostic criteria. One of the most interesting findings of this review was that about half of women reporting low desire were distressed by not having as much desire as they would like. Since distress has historically been one of the defining characteristics of low desire, removing it from the diagnostic criteria would have meant that, by definition, a significantly reduced number of women would be diagnosed with low desire.

While low desire is prevalent, it is also among the most complex and difficult sexual problems to treat because it can be caused by any number of bio-psycho-social factors. For instance, the source of low/absent desire is often a combination of factors such as: the woman's feelings and beliefs about sexual intimacy, relationship issues, and in some cases, family-of-origin difficulties and traumas. Hormone imbalances and other physical factors might also be contributory. Further, low/absent desire can occur in conjunction with other sexual dysfunctions in either partner (Weeks & Gambescia, 2002). For example, a woman who experiences pain with intercourse may gradually lose her desire for sex. Treatment, therefore, cannot follow a short protocol but must be comprehensive, flexible, and tailored to each couple based on the etiological factors that are uncovered for the client-system.

Definition

In *DSM-5*, (American Psychiatric Association, 2013) the definition and diagnostic criteria for low/absent desire are significantly different than in the previous edition of the diagnostic manual. In the prior edition of *DSM-IV-R* (American Psychiatric Association, 2000) men and women were combined under one diagnostic category. In the current edition of *DSM-5*, (American Psychiatric Association, 2013) the general diagnostic category for women is called female sexual interest/arousal disorder. There is a separate diagnostic category for men called male hypoactive sexual desire disorder. This chapter is based on data that utilized the diagnostic criteria of *DSM-IV-R* (American Psychiatric Association, 2000) since we are writing just after the release of the new *DSM-5* and there are no available data utilizing the current diagnostic categories and criteria for women.

Female sexual interest/arousal disorder is the current diagnostic label in the *DSM-5*. *For the sake of brevity, we will hereafter call the disorder that of low desire.* The reduced or lack of sexual interest and arousal must manifest in at least three of six diagnostic criteria (American Psychiatric Association, 2013):

DSM-IV

1. Absent or reduced interest in sexual activity
2. Absent or reduced sexual or erotic thoughts or fantasies
3. Absent or reduced initiation of sexual activity and typically being non-responsive to the partner's attempts to initiate sexual activity
4. Absent or reduced sexual excitement or pleasure during sexual activity 75% to 100% of the time during sexual activity
5. Absent or reduced sexual interest or arousal in response to internal or external sexual or erotic stimuli (e.g., written, verbal, visual)
6. Absent or reduced genital or non-genital sensations during sexual activity 75–100% of sexual encounters.

Additionally, the symptoms will have persisted for a minimum duration of six months approximately and the problem must cause significant distress to the individual. In order to accurately diagnose low desire, the therapist must determine that the woman's sexual symptoms are not caused by another problem such as:

1. A non-sexual mental disorder, for example depression
2. A consequence of severe relationship problems leading to distress
3. The presence of other major life stressors
4. A result of medication side effects, substance abuse, or a medical condition, which has the potential to affect desire/arousal.

There are newly added additional specifying criteria related to the degree of distress (mild, moderate, or several distress) over the abovementioned diagnostic criteria.

The diagnosis is further specified according to the following identifying characteristics: lifelong, acquired, generalized, and situational. Low desire can be a *lifelong* condition in which absence of sexual desire is a typical state for the woman. Alternately, when an individual has experienced a change of her sexual appetite, the term *acquired* is used; desire has been present, normally for a period of several years, but there has been a noticeable decline in desire over time. The change can be gradual or precipitous (American Psychiatric Association, 2013). An individual with *generalized* lack of desire does not have a sexual appetite under any circumstance regardless of the partner or situation. Typically, this individual does not engage in sexual fantasy or any type of self-pleasuring. The *situational* type, on the other hand, is marked by selective desire, in certain situations or with specific partners (American Psychiatric Association, 2013). For example, the woman might feel desire when alone, but not with a spouse, or one might feel desire toward an affair partner, but not with one's established partner.

A great deal of literature has been published about the definition of sexual desire. The new criteria mentioned above will satisfy some clinicians/researchers and not others. Further, much more has been written about female sexual desire than male sexual desire. For that reason, the definition of low desire in women may be based on more empirical and theoretical work than that of men. Meana (2010) has written the most comprehensive, scholarly researched, and intellectually penetrating analysis of this issue. Her analysis revealed the multifaceted nature of desire and showed the complexity of the concept. She suggests that the benchmark for desire has been more male-oriented toward what is known as spontaneous desire. This is desire that just happens. Many other theorists and researchers have emphasized the responsive nature of desire, or desire which is in reaction to the initiation of some kind of sexual activity. Meana (2010) suggests that rather than a dichotomy between the two, there may be a continuum of desire, all of which may

spontaneous

responsive

Continuum
of desire

be responsive, but individuals with what is labeled spontaneous desire may have a low threshold for sexual stimuli, whether internal or external, and those with the label of responsive desire may have a high threshold for sexual stimuli. She does not believe the research at this point is strong enough to make a distinction between the two, but states that the spontaneous-responsive distinction is merely code for desire, which is triggered by undetectable stimuli. Finally, she proposed nine areas of research needed before a good conceptual and operational definition of desire can be made. The readers who are troubled by the definitions and/or criteria in *DSM-5* (American Psychiatric Association, 2013) or want to put these definitions in perspective are urged to read this article.

Models of Sexual Desire

Over the years a number of models of sexual desire have been proposed. The models have strongly influenced the way in which low sexual desire was defined. See Bitzer, Giraldi, and Pfaus (2013) for a thorough examination of all the major models of sexual desire. In this chapter, we will review the models that have received the most attention in the literature and exerted the most influence on the understanding of desire.

Levine (1992) developed a model consisting of three components: (1) drive or the biological dimension that leads to spontaneous desire, (2) expectations or the social dimension, and (3) motivation or the psychological dimension. The three components work together in determining whether or how much sexual desire occurs. Another study found that in a sample of 142 college students, about 87% thought desire was a motivational state, 26% an emotional state, and only 7% thought it was a cognitive state (Regan & Berscheid, 1996).

Masters and Johnson (1966), pioneers in research in sexuality, proposed a model based on four stages of the physiological sexual response. During the first three stages (excitement, plateau, and orgasm) there is ever increasing arousal and, by implication, increasing desire. In the fourth stage, there is resolution or relaxation and reduction in arousal and, by implication, decreased desire. Kaplan (1977) built on the Masters and Johnson model (1966) by adding desire as a distinct psychological phase at the beginning of the sexual response cycle. These models were simply descriptive of what happens during the sexual response cycle, but did not explain what produces desire.

Basson proposed the latest and most controversial model (Basson 2001a; 2001b; 2007; Basson, Wiermann, van Lankveld, & Brotto, 2010) that is circular and complex with reciprocal influences among various components. Sexual drive, motivation, and responsivity to sexual stimuli are integrated. Moreover, men are viewed as experiencing spontaneous desire more frequently than women. With women, sexual activity, arousal, or erotic stimuli are usually required to trigger sexual desire. Basson proposes that a woman is lacking in desire only if confronted with effective sexual stimuli (never actually defined) and does not then experience desire. Thus, her argument is that women, for the most part, experience responsive sexual desire (a response to sexual stimuli) rather than spontaneous desire, which is more common in men. Interestingly, Sand and Fisher (2007) conducted a survey of over 500 nurses using a 58-item questionnaire that asked women which model of desire best fit their experience of sex. The women were about equally split among the Masters and Johnson, Kaplan, and Basson models. The women who endorsed the Basson model were the most likely to have the lowest level of desire.

Realistically, there is no grand model that can account for sexual desire in men and women given all the variables that have been found to both increase and decrease sexual desire. However, it should be noted that in Brotto's (2010) review of the empirical

128

literature on diagnostic criteria found increasing support for a model of sexual desire which suggests that sexual desire in both men and women is triggered by a "competent sexual stimulus" (p. 2025). These stimuli may be consciously recognized or unconsciously experienced. Thus, Brotto is arguing against the idea of spontaneous desire, proposing that there is always a trigger for the experience of desire. Brauer et al. also reached the same basic conclusion in another review of the literature in 2012.

In the future, we may have a model of sexual desire that is more related to brain functioning. Bancroft (2010) proposed a Dual Control Model, which consists of sexual excitation and sexual inhibition with each one intrinsically related to neurophysiology. In short, he is relating sexual activity or lack thereof to anatomically discrete brain structures. Much more research on the brain is needed with regard to which structures within the brain respond to excitory or inhibitory stimuli and why. As the field of neuropsychology develops, we may eventually gain a biologically based model for sexual desire.

Theoretical Model of Treatment

Weeks developed a model for the assessment and treatment of low desire based on the theoretical structure called the Intersystem Approach (1994; 2005). This meta-theoretical framework represents a new way of conceptualizing sexual diagnosis and treatment from a systemic perspective. We will not discuss this theory here except to note that assessment and treatment must involve consideration of multiple systems. These include

1. Individual biological issues
2. Individual psychological factors
3. The couple relationship
4. Intergenerational (family-of-origin) influences
5. Environmental (society, culture, history, religion, political, economic, etc.) considerations

Clinical Assessment

Preliminary Assessment. Treating low desire involves a comprehensive assessment that begins with the first telephone contact through the early sessions. The therapist notes which partner ostensibly has the problem, the duration of the problem, and what the couple hopes to gain from treatment. Is the symptomatic partner taking the initiative for treatment or placating the significant other? In the next few sessions, the therapist begins to generate hypotheses regarding the causes of the problem. Initial impressions and reactions are gathered about the individual partners and their relationship, including recent significant changes in each partner's life. Early in treatment, the therapist begins to establish treatment goals by exploring and identifying the couple's expectations of treatment.

Focused Appraisal. Next, the therapist directs the assessment to the sexual relationship by asking focused questions in the session and also suggesting that the couple think about them at home as part of a deeper exploration:

- How often do you have sex? What are the main reasons you have sex?
- How often do you feel like having sex based on your desire? If you don't feel desire how much do you miss it?
- When you do have sex are you able to get in the mood or feel desire, if so, how much? (We use a subjective scale from 1–10)

- Do you feel that your desire is more spontaneous or a reaction/response to your partner's behavior?
- Do you believe your desire level is too low?
- When did you first notice losing desire for sex? What was happening at that time?
- Did you lose desire rapidly or slowly?
- What was your level of sexual desire earlier in your relationship and over the course of your relationship?
- Who usually initiates sex? Is it due to desire or another reason?
- Any changes in your health? What medications are you taking now?
- On a scale of 1 to 10 how much desire do you feel in general? Prior to sex? During sex?
- How often do you think about sex or fantasize about romantic scenarios?
- What is your theory about why you no longer feel as much desire as you would like?

Individual Partners

The clinical assessment also includes individual sessions to determine level of desire, extent of sexual thoughts and fantasies, solo sexual activity and related fantasies, preferred forms of erotic stimulation, ease in articulating erotic desires, and fantasies that make the individual comfortable or uncomfortable. Individual sessions provide a forum for discussing secrets that can later be shared, atypical sexual preoccupations, or if there is an extramarital affair. The therapist also considers aspects of the low desire that will require medical evaluation.

The Couple

Throughout the duration of the assessment process the therapist evaluates the couple's emotional contracts, styles of communication, level of discord, conflict resolution style, and ways of defining problems. Another focal point of an ongoing dyadic assessment is the capacity for intimacy of each partner. Thus, sexual and non-sexual relational parameters are evaluated.

The Intergenerational System

Intergenerational factors are assessed through the use of a genogram, which examines different aspects of familial functioning (DeMaria, Weeks, & Hof, 1999). Also, the clinician evaluates for incest, parentification, triangulation, and other dysfunctional patterns of familial relating that impact intimacy and sexuality. Sexual misinformation generated within the family-of-origin can negatively influence intellectual and emotional understanding of sexuality and interfere with the enjoyment of sexual intimacy in adult relationships.

Environmental Factors

Environmental factors often contribute directly or indirectly to the lack of desire; thus, it is the obligation of the clinician to assess for sociocultural beliefs, customs, and values, affecting the ability to form nourishing sexual relationships. Additionally, issues of finance, politics, religion, ethnicity, race, social class, gender, and other socio-cultural issues affecting the partner or the couple are evaluated.

Empirical Tools. The assessment procedures mentioned above are all clinical in nature. The clinician or researcher who wishes to conduct an evaluation that includes psychometric devices may also use instruments that have been empirically validated for female clients. For general sexual dysfunction, the clinician could use the Female Sexual Function Index (FSFD) (Meston, 2003; Wiegel, Meston, & Rosen, 2005). A new inventory that has been developed to assess low desire is the Sexual Interest and Desire Inventory-Female (SIFI-F) (Sills et al., 2005; Clayton et al., 2007). For a recent review of standardized self-report questionnaires with good reliability and validity for a number of sexual problems, the reader can consult Leiblum (2010a pp. 16–17). The reader should keep in mind that most clinicians prefer to conduct a clinical history rather than use a survey. Also, the questionnaires that are currently available were based on the definition and clinical criteria before the publication of *DSM-5* (American Psychiatric Association, 2013).

Etiology

The Intersystemic framework is used to assess the risk factors for low desire arising from four major areas: the individual partners (physical and psychological factors), the couple's relationship, intergenerational factors, and environmental stressors.

Physical Risk Factors in the Individual

There are many normative physical states that can produce fluctuations in desire and arousal in women. Fatigue, hormone imbalances during phases of the menstrual cycle, breastfeeding, and menopause, for example, can affect the level of interest or sexual desire. Typically these states are transient, self-stabilizing, and do not produce persistent lack of desire. Some medical risk factors are more continuing, such as postmenopausal estrogen deficiency and persistently low testosterone levels; these states will chronically interfere with sexual desire. Various other medical conditions can continually affect interest in sex and arousal; the most common are diabetes and thyroid dysfunctions. Others include chronic arthritis, which makes sex painful, and surgeries or medical procedures, which may have interfered with normal sexual functioning such as removal of the ovaries (see Crenshaw & Goldberg, 1996; Maurice, 2007; Weeks & Gambescia, 2002). These conditions need to be addressed through medical referrals and collaborative therapy; however, they do not constitute the diagnostic criteria for psychogenic lack of desire.

Most therapists treating low desire are not physicians, yet they must assess for physical disorders that could cause or contribute to the lack of desire. Often, a medical consultation is a necessary part of treatment. The therapist must be comfortable interfacing with medical professionals such as neurologists, urologists, endocrinologists, and gynecologists. Also, the therapist must be familiar with the role of testosterone and other hormones in sexual desire and the medical conditions that could create deficiencies of various hormones.

Psychological Risk Factors in the Individual

Psychological risk factors in the individual partners can be expressed within the context of sexual intimacy, thus giving rise to the development of low sexual desire. These involve but are not limited to: anxiety, depression, negative cognitive distortions, inaccurate beliefs about sex, poor body image, a tendency to fuse sex and affection, career

131

overload, and related sexual problems. In such cases, the therapist may be tempted to turn the focus of treatment to the partner with the lack of desire, but it is imperative that a systemic stance is maintained (Weeks & Gambescia, 2002). For example, depression can reduce desire and is often related to the quality of a couple's relationship. In other words, a relationship that is problematic can produce depression in an individual, (Kouros & Cummings 2011; Rosand, Slinning, Eberhard-Gran, Roysamb, & Tambs, 2012; Whitton & Whisman 2010).

intimacy

Fears of intimacy or other interpersonal fears in one or both partners could place a couple at risk for the development of low sexual desire since emotional and physical intimacies are closely related. Working on sexual desire may be hampered by one partner's fear of intimacy anger, rejection, abandonment, exposure, or dependency (Weeks & Treat, 2001). As noted previously, psychiatric factors such as anxiety, depression, obsessive-compulsive disorder, and sexual orientation conflicts can contribute to the development of low desire. Further, historical factors such as sexual abuse and emotional trauma can inhibit desire. It is important for the therapist to assess in all of these areas.

Cognitive considerations. Weeks (1987) and Weeks and Gambescia (2002) were the first sex therapists to argue that the presence of negative cognitions (about the self, partner relationship, family-of-origin, etc.) will directly affect sexual desire. We also believe that the individual who is able to experience sexual desire is actually having positive sexual thoughts while the individual who lacks desire has an absence of sexual thoughts or has a number of negative sexual thoughts. In many cases these thoughts are unconscious or simply not noticed by the individual. From the onset of treatment, negative sexual cognitions are observed and recorded in writing regarding the self, the partner, the relationship, the family-of-origin, etc. This aspect of the assessment helps to determine which of the thoughts can be changed through cognitive therapy techniques, and to further gauge other problems in the relationship that must be addressed through couple therapy or the reprocessing of early family dysfunction and trauma.

Notwithstanding the clinical observations made by the authors of this chapter, researchers have ignored the role cognitions play in lack of desire until recently. A study of individuals with sexual dysfunctions, not necessarily low desire, revealed that individuals with sexual problems had significantly more negative cognitive schemas when exposed to vignettes of negative sexual events (Nobre & Pinto-Gouveia, 2009). Much more research has now been done on cognitive schemas and low desire. Carvalho and Nobre (2011) found that the best predictors of lack of desire were negative cognitive factors or beliefs and automatic thoughts, as they are called in cognitive behavior therapy. The participants in this study experienced restrictive attitudes, concerns or anxiety about performance, and a lack of erotic thoughts in an erotic or sexual context. All subjects were men, but we believe the same negative cognitions about sex could adversely affect sexual desire and arousal in women. The treatment model proposed by Carvalho and Nobre (2011) for assessing and treating low desire for men and women involved examining negative sexual cognitions, changing those negative cognitions to positive cognitions where appropriate, and using the other cognitions as a guide to assessing other factors that needed to be changed.

In another review of the literature, Geonet, Sutter, and Zech (2013) came to the conclusion that negative cognitions play a central role in low desire in both men and women. They noted that negative automatic thoughts might be linked to the partner and the relationship or to oneself, as the authors of this chapter had proposed many years earlier. They also suggested that negative thoughts, sexual schemas, and beliefs should be therapeutic targets.

Cognitive distraction. The research on cognitive distraction is similar to the research mentioned above but involves thinking about non-sexual things that reduce sexual desire. A review of the literature on cognitive distraction showed that men *and women* might be diverted from sexual cues leading to cognitive interference that decreases desire. Two recent studies using female subjects also support the role of cognitive distraction or attentional mechanisms or focus. Female sexual feeling could be manipulated by shifting instructions regarding attentional focus. In addition, women experienced diminished sexual feelings with repeated erotic stimulation, but increased sexual feeling when a novel sexual stimulus was introduced. Both, Laan, and Everaerd, (2011) and Alvarez and Garcia-Marques (2011) also found that cognitive and contextual variables are related to desire.

In the most recent study to examine this phenomenon, Brauer et al. (2012) suggested it was not the attentional focus alone that determined desire, but the positive associations attributed to the stimuli. Sex-positive associations produced stronger desire. However, the authors indicate that in clinical practice the lack of sex-positive associations may be either the cause or the result of low sexual desire. The direction of causality has not conclusively been demonstrated. Brauer et al. (2012) suggested a therapeutic strategy of strengthening sex-positive associations such as the rewards of a sexual experience (whether it is a feeling of closeness to one's partner or an orgasm) could help to increase desire (Katz & Jardine, 1999).

The reader who is interested in surveys to measure schema activation in men and women in a sexual context can find them in Nobre and Pinto-Gouveia (2009). These questionnaires can be used for empirical studies or to indirectly assess some of the factors leading to low desire. Nevertheless, a thorough clinical evaluation should be done over time in order to capture all the negative cognitions associated with low desire.

Interactional Risk Factors

Research indicates that marital satisfaction is related to sexual fulfillment (Morokoff & Gilliland, 1993). Conversely, problems with sexual interest and arousal are often associated with relationship dissatisfaction (American Psychiatric Association, 2013). For example, women with low desire tend to report greater degrees of marital distress and less relational cohesion (Trudel, Ravart, & Matte, 1993). For women, sexual satisfaction is associated with factors such as the manner in which sex was initiated, level of arousal, and the behaviors present in that interaction. Also, disinterest or lack of initiation on the part of the partner plays a significant role in lack of desire; if one person becomes habitually disinterested, the partner may also become disinterested. Other relational risk factors include contemptuous feelings, criticism, defensiveness, power struggles, and toxic communication (Gottman, 1994). The etiological factors mentioned above are presented in a highly compressed form. Readers interested in doing a thorough assessment of this disorder should consult our text on this subject (Weeks & Gambescia, 2002).

Intergenerational Risk Factors Including External Risk Factors

Many of the aforementioned risk factors, such as anti-sexual beliefs, are learned within the social and familial contexts of each partner, including the experience of sexual abuse (Rellini & Meston, 2011). It is essential that the therapist explore intergenerational legacies and other environmental messages regarding sexual intimacy. In one example, the couple presented for treatment of the woman's lifelong low desire. She was raised in an extremely religious household and learned that sex was for procreation and not personal enjoyment. Although she recognized that her beliefs did not make sense, she found it

GERALD R. WEEKS AND NANCY GAMBESCIA

difficult to observe her own body, engage in erotic thoughts or solo sex, and enjoy sexual intimacy with her husband. Treatment required a flexible format of individual and conjoint sessions, psychoeducation, bibliography, correcting mythological cognitions, and ultimately acceptance of her right to enjoy all of the intimate benefits of marriage. Weeks and Gambescia (2002) clinically observed that parentification can have a detrimental effect on sexual functioning, and reviewed the literature on the sexual effects of sexual trauma for both men and women on loss of desire and overall sexual functioning.

Environmental Risk Factors

Intersystemic sex therapy recognizes that culture is central to a person's life.

Sexuality is interpreted through sociocultural beliefs, customs, values, and norms, all of which affect the ability to develop sexual desire in relationships (Hyde, 2010; Kimmel, 2007; Money, 1986). Internalized messages about sexuality are frequently distorted through culture, religion, racism, and sexism (McGoldrick, Loonan, & Wohlsifer, 2007; Hall & Graham, 2013).

Often, unrealistic messages about romantic love and sexual behavior are perpetuated through all forms of media. These messages and images can lead the woman to feel less feminine, attractive, and desirable, compared to social norms. Negative feelings about falling short or the lack of sexual perfection can decrease sexual desire.

Comprehensive Studies Consistent With the Intersystem Approach

Hubin, De Sutter, and Reynaert (2011) conducted a broad analysis of clinical and empirical accounts of low desire and constructed a model based on five general categories of contributors to lack of interest/arousal in women: cognitive, physiological, behavioral, emotional, and environmental factors. We cite this analysis because it is so closely aligned to our own Intersystem Approach. We will reflect upon salient themes that predominate the clinical picture of low sexual interest/arousal as presented by the authors.

Hubin, De Sutter, and Reynaert (2011) empirically demonstrated that women who lack desire often have negative cognitions in anticipation of sexual intimacy. Over time they have learned that sex is more of an obligation than a pleasurable activity; consequently, the motivation to have sex is more about pleasing the partner than personal enjoyment. The systemic response to the woman with low desire is for the partner to continue to request sex or to abandon sex altogether. The woman anticipates that her partner will either ask her to have sex when she's not interested or fail to show any interest in her at all. The state of negative cognitive anticipation perpetuates the lack of interest and arousal. Eventually these negative cognitions will lead to a pattern of sexual avoidance. If the woman avoids a sexual interaction, and the partner becomes more driven to seek sexual connection, her need to avoid sexual intimacy is strengthened (Hubin, De Sutter, & Reynaert, 2011).

Although they do not enjoy sex, women with low desire continue to hold perfectionistic expectations about sex and intimacy and, thus, consider themselves to have failed. Understandably, depressive thinking is correlated with the lack of interest or desire for sex; the relationship is bidirectional and self-perpetuating. Also, Hubin, De Sutter, and Reynaert (2011) present empirical research validating the clinical observation that women who lack interest also tend to lack accurate sex education and often subscribe to misinformation about sexuality. Moreover, low desire women are often clueless about the physical responses within their own bodies to erotic stimuli. They tend to underutilize sexual fantasies and, consequently, do not allow themselves to experience auto arousal in situations where desire is asynchronous or routine. When sexual thoughts occur, they are almost reflexively rejected. The authors also present an interesting description of feelings of repugnance about sexual jokes, touching, or sexuality itself.

Women who lack sexual interest or arousal are typically in partnerships that suffer from poor regulation of intimacy needs, with too much attention to children, hobbies, work, etc., instead of focusing on the relationship. Also, such couples often report relational dissatisfaction, lack of sexual attraction, and poor communication skills (Hubin, De Sutter, & Reynaert, 2011).

Sims and Meana (2010) conducted open-ended interviews with 19 highly educated women in marriages with an average length of 6.52 years with an average age of 31.5. They identified three major themes that the women believed lead to reduced desire. The first theme was the institutionalization of the relationship in marriage. This theme included feelings of de-eroticization of the relationship, the over-availability of sex, too much responsibility, and a sense of lack of "transgression" which had earlier lead to sexual desire or excitement. The second theme was over-familiarity, which fosters a loss of romance and sexual advances that become too routine. Also, a lack of sense of self and lack of attention to physical care were reported. The third theme was that of desexualized roles. This topic had to do with the feeling of sex as a chore or obligation, the partners having rigid roles in the relationship, and not feeling desirable due to other roles they played.

In each of the two studies mentioned, the authors reported salient features of the individual and the couple system in which the woman experienced low sexual desire. While the empirical findings are consistent with our clinical observations, a therapeutic model and treatment strategies were not offered.

Treatment Strategies

In this section, we will provide an overview of some basic treatment strategies. These strategies are driven by the etiological factors and other more general factors we have found useful in clinical practice. Some of the treatment strategies are more individually oriented while others deal with the couple, family-of-origin, or medical issues. As an introduction to the basic treatment strategies for treating sexual problems, we would like to point out some general indications and contraindications for moving into the treatment of sexual problems immediately.

Indications and Contraindications

Favorable conditions. We expect that other individual and relational issues will surface during treatment because low desire does not occur in a vacuum. Most concerns are treatable, although their position of importance may vary during the duration of treatment. Often, the clinician must balance the pressure to treat the low desire against the obvious problems that must be addressed first. It is always important to elucidate the relationship between the low desire and the other emotional and relational concerns in order to promote compliance. Even when the low desire is caused by physical problems, psychotherapy can help the couple to address their intimacy needs. We consider the following conditions to be favorable for treatment:

- Partners have positive sex beliefs and want to experience desire again
- Both partners are relatively free from psychiatric problems that can impede treatment
- There is an inability to break the cycle of negative sexual cognitions and obsessive thoughts that interfere with building sexual desire

- If a partner has withheld historical information about physical, sexual, or emotional abuse or sexual addiction, and is willing to share and work on this information
- Negative sexual attitudes based on religious beliefs, internalized negative sex messages from the family-of-origin, and the resulting sexual guilt
- Stress from situational life stressors that affect one partner such as severe work stress, or death of a loved one
- Unrealistic expectations, the normal physiological changes of aging, and the willingness to accept accurate information
- Treatable relational difficulties in negotiating issues of power, control, inclusion, and autonomy
- The couple's sexual script has not been successfully negotiated or the partners may have different preferences or misinformation
- Treatable discord in other areas of the relationship, such as ineffective communication, unresolved anger, and unmet expectations
- When low desire can be related to other sexual difficulties in either partner such as erectile disorder, genito-pelvic pain, etc.
- The presence of response anxiety (discussed later in this chapter)
- Presence of a medical condition known to lower sexual desire

Unfavorable conditions. The systemic treatment for low desire is *not* appropriate when:

- The low desire partner does not wish for or care about sexual desire or has sexual aversion
- If the problem is viewed as solely belonging to the partner who lacks desire and the other partner is unwilling to participate in the therapy
- A great deal of untreatable discord in the relationship or the inability to work together cooperatively
- A lack of commitment to treatment
- A lack of commitment to the marriage such as an undisclosed affair, covert sexual compulsivity or active addiction in one or both parties.
- Presence of a significant psychopathology in either partner

Addressing Pessimism and Skepticism

In most cases, our couples have struggled with low desire for months or years before seeking treatment. Often, they have attempted to change the problem on their own, have failed, and then resigned themselves to a passionless relationship. Consequently, they enter treatment with a sense of pessimism and skepticism because they cannot imagine how talking about a sexual problem could possibly alleviate it. Lack of sexual desire is a complex phenomenon and difficult for a person to change. Explaining that pessimism is a natural response to a difficult situation should help to normalize the couple's failed attempts. Support them for their efforts to correct the problem even if these strategies have failed.

Using Sensate Focus

In the sections to follow we will describe a variety of treatment techniques. We almost always combine these techniques with the use of sensate focus. As soon as we think the couple is ready and they are willing to begin sensate focus exercises, we commence by prescribing incremental touch exercises to be performed at home. Not only is it important for the couple to begin to connect in some way physically, but also many of the psychotherapy techniques work best when combined with sensate focus. For example, negative sexual cognitions are almost always associated with low desire. A woman might be able to articulate some of these thoughts from the beginning of therapy. However, when sensate focus is combined with identifying sexual cognitions, the woman is likely to uncover more and more negative thoughts as the touching progresses. The combination of many of the techniques to follow addresses the multiple etiologic factors and creates a synergy that a single technique would not produce.

sensate focus

Reframing

Maintaining a Systemic Focus

Couples often view the symptomatic partner or the one with low desire as the one with the problem. They must be educated to think systemically. This involves helping them to recognize that low desire is a relationship problem. One systemic technique is the *therapeutic reframe* in which the therapist helps to conceptualize the low desire in a different way (Weeks & Treat, 2001). The therapist reframes the low desire by asking focused questions that become more and more directed in order to help the couple appreciate how relational problems may have contributed to the lack of desire, helped to maintain it, or created another layer to the lack of desire which is systemic. For example, one reframe would be to say that the low desire partner has created distance in the relationship because the couple could not tolerate too much closeness. The therapist emphasizes that the couple struggles together and will need to work together to resolve how they will relate to each other sexually. For a more detailed discussion of reframing the reader is directed to our text (Weeks & Gambescia, 2002). In those cases where the lack of desire is an individual medically related problem, the way the couple copes with the situation may influence the degree of desire felt and the way sexuality is expressed. A possible reframe for this situation would be to suggest that the couple has had to struggle to find others ways of relating and being close which has in turn helped them develop more intimacy than ever before in spite of the desire problem.

Responsibility for Sexual Intimacy

Many women feel powerless with respect to owning and controlling their sexual feelings. They believe that sexual gratification is something that happens to them. Throughout the process of therapy, the woman and the couple gradually learn that sexual desire and satisfaction are created, fostered, practiced, and nurtured by the self and the partner (Gambescia & Weeks, 2007). Sensate focus exercises and other cognitive behavioral assignments promote responsibility for sensual and sexual enjoyment. Ultimately, the woman needs to recognize that she has control over her feelings, behavior, and sexual satisfaction.

Setting Priorities

The systemic treatment of low desire should not be generic or predetermined. Usually, the therapist commences by focusing on the presenting problem. During the course of treatment, however, other individual or relational issues might take precedence. These often include: anxiety, anger, sexual ignorance, or lack of communication. The therapist prioritizes the order in which each issue is treated. Some problems may overlap or be addressed concurrently. Moreover, it is important for the couple to understand that the format of treatment must be flexible, and that modifications do not indicate failure. In one instance, individual issues in the wife contributed to her lifelong low desire. During treatment, she revealed that as a child she had been sexually abused; this fact surprised her husband of 20 years. The couple required time to discuss and understand this aspect of her childhood experience and the impact of early trauma on adult sexual functioning. The wife needed to do some individual therapy to help her cope with the trauma. Then, the focus of treatment returned to the low desire as the couple gained a better understanding of the genesis of the problem.

Establishing Treatment Goals

The fundamental goal of treatment is to restore sexual desire or some form of physical connection to the couple's relationship; however, other objectives can be accomplished in the process. A lack of sexual desire can be tied to other elements of the couple's relationship, specifically those that diminish the sexual experience such as anger, resentment, poor communication, and many of the etiological factors mentioned earlier in this chapter. Thus, treatment of low desire addresses relationship problems, thereby improving overall relationship satisfaction. Moreover, effectively working together to solve their sexual problem will foster greater improvements in the overall emotional relationship.

Implementing Goals

Since the treatment of low desire also addresses the relational problems that contributed to or were an effect of the low desire, it is essential that the therapist is qualified and knowledgeable about couples and sex therapy techniques and knows the circumstances under which the techniques will be most effective. Furthermore, we suggest that couples must be active participants in their treatment; thus, they should be aware of why a strategy is being used and what the outcome is expected to be. This collaborative effort will increase compliance (Weeks & Treat, 2001).

Correcting Unrealistic Expectations

Couples enter a relationship with expectations of themselves, each other, and what it means to be in a loving relationship. The expectations are often unstated and partners are left feeling disappointed upon the realization that hopes and dreams will not come to fruition. Some ideas are unrealistic from the start, such as believing that if your partner loved you, s/he would know automatically what you want. In cases where expectations are not met, one partner may misattribute this idea to their partner not caring about them enough and, as a result, withhold sex or not feel desire. The therapist should help the couple to develop realistic perceptions of themselves, what each can offer, and a reasonable perception of love and all that it involves.

Lowering Response Anxiety

A woman may continuously monitor and worry about her lack of sexual desire rather than enjoying sensual or sexual activity. Response anxiety is the belief that one should experience more desire for their partner than they currently feel at any point of time in their relationship. This could occur when they are simply together, when she is being touched non-sexually, during sharing of affection, when the partner suggests something sexual, or during sexual activity. The focal point of sexual intimacy turns into anxiety rather than pleasure or the fulfillment of some other need to have sex. As response anxiety increases, the likelihood of sexual desire decreases, thereby increasing anxiety, and so on. One critical component to the treatment of low desire is lowering the response anxiety and to do so, we use several techniques. First, the therapist educates the couple by explaining the concept. Cognitive strategies such as thought-stopping and thought substitution are also useful (Beck, 1976; 1995). Another approach is to confront irrational ideas that foster response anxiety, such as the equation of sex and intercourse. In this case, the definition of sex is broadened to include behaviors that are less likely to cause response anxiety, such as non-coital sensual or sexual touching. Next, the low desire partner is given permission to feel whatever they feel without the need to think they should feel more desire. Brotto and Woo (2010) discussed the combination of CBT with mindfulness therapy. Mindfulness therapy incorporates an awareness of one's thoughts, feeling, and sensations without judgment (Sipe & Eisendrath, 2012). Basically, we give the woman permission to feel whatever she is feeling without trying to force a feeling or judging a feeling or herself.

Addressing Affect

Another focus of treatment is the emotional processes that occur within the session. As such, the couple will learn to communicate about feelings rather than staying fixed on content. The therapist will need to attend to the level of affect expressed by each partner. For instance, the woman may appear to have a lack of motivation for sex, a lack of affect, and seem withdrawn, especially in the sexual area. Conversely, the higher desire partner is often more emotional, frustrated, and pessimistic. As stated previously, the unpleasant feelings expressed by the higher desire partner may have the effect of causing avoidance of any situations that might lead to sex. In these instances, the therapist should help the partners attend to and discuss their style of expressing emotion. Also, they are helped to inquire rather than ascribe motives for each other's feelings. This process helps the couple become more aware of their patterns of interaction, and the emotional barriers to expressing and experiencing feeling of desire. This work is ongoing throughout all stages of treatment.

Cognitive Work

Cognitive therapy is indispensable in the treatment of low desire. Negative cognitions about sexual intimacy, the self, and the partner directly contribute to the lack of desire by preventing the emergence of enjoyable sexual thoughts and fantasies. This cognitive mental mechanism is powerful; it has strong behavioral consequences as shown earlier in this chapter. Further, couples develop interlocking sets of irrational beliefs that perpetuate sexual problems; these beliefs need to be explored, interrupted, and changed conjointly. A woman with low desire might think, "I'm just not interested in sex." Her partner might also think, "She isn't interested in sex, so why initiate anything." These two interlocking thoughts help to perpetuate sexual avoidance.

The partners are helped to identify interlocking irrational sexual beliefs and to replace them with more positive, factual cognitions. Also, they are encouraged to engage in erotic thoughts and fantasies to promote prosexual cognitions and feelings. Each partner learns to monitor his or her thoughts or behaviors in order to determine when the nonproductive thought has started again. The negative thought needs to be stopped (thought stopping) and consciously replaced (thought substitution) with a positive thought. As such, the woman and her partner are rehearsing positive sexual thoughts such as replaying a positive sexual encounter, having a sexual fantasy, or thinking some "sexy" thoughts. This process creates a state of positive anticipation for the next experience. Eventually, erotic thoughts become more natural and automatic (Beck, 1976; 1995; Weeks & Hof, 1987; 1994). Some of the negative thoughts probably have a basis in reality. For example, if a woman says my partner approaches me for sex in a crude way, then the issue becomes one for the couple. In addition to changing the negative thoughts and schemes, it is also useful to have them shift their attention toward sexual cues and contexts and to ascribe positive meaning to those attentional factors. For example, if a woman notices a sexual cue from her partner she could think about or remember the sexual pleasure or some other positive experience of having some kind of affectional, sensual, or sexual encounter.

Communication

Another aspect of treatment involves helping the woman to discuss her sexual needs, wishes, preferences, and concerns. Since most of our clients find it difficult to talk about sex, the therapist might start by fostering communication about less threatening topics and gradually move into sexual intimacy. Other areas of effective communication include: using "I" statements, validating each other, reflective listening, and learning to edit what one says (Weeks & Treat, 2001). In addition, Gottman (1994) recommends that a 5:1 ratio of positive to negative exchanges promotes relational satisfaction which may facilitate more sexual desire.

Psychoeducation

The therapist wants to correct as much misinformation as possible about sexual desire, the lack of desire, and sexuality in general. The revision of some misconceptions may take time and repeated discussions, whereas others seem to evaporate the moment the conversation is over. Some mythological beliefs are not revealed until they are uncovered through an individual discussion with the therapist. Bibliotherapy reinforces the psychoeducational process by providing accurate information about sexual functioning. Also, we recommend readings that normalize aspects of sexual intimacy such as fantasy and solo sexual activity (Barbach, 1982; Comfort, 1994; Friday, 1998a; 1998b; Zilbergeld, 1992; Mintz, 2009). We suggest that the couple should investigate accurate information about human sexuality and erotic literature to find material that suits their taste. We notice that women often internalize cultural notions about not being sexual by suppressing sexual fantasies and solo sexual activity.

Systemic Homework

The therapist treating low desire must play a directive role in session and beyond the therapy hour through the prudent use of assignments to be performed at home. Homework assignments address individual, relational, and intergenerational issues associated with the lack of sexual desire. For instance, homework for the individual partner(s) includes prescriptions regarding physical exercise, guided imagery, gradual exposure to sexual material, directed masturbation, and exposure to fantasy through bibliotherapy or selected visual materials (Martin, 1997; Bright, 2000; Gambescia & Weeks, 2007). Homework for the couple includes sensate focus, communicating sensual and sexual wishes and needs, and conflict resolution exercises (Weeks & Gambescia, 2002). The couple is also directed to explore intergenerational messages regarding sexual intimacy, pleasure, and entitlement to sexual satisfaction. Additionally, the continued use of homework assignments will promote compliance and prevent relapse of the sexual symptoms, particularly with desire phase disorders (McCarthy & Breetz, 2010).

Treating Other Sexual Dysfunctions

It is not unusual for a woman and her partner to have more than one sexual problem; thus, it is possible that low desire might be related to another sexual difficulty such as physical discomfort during sex, erectile dysfunction, or trouble with orgasm. Sometimes, the higher desire partner also has sexual difficulties that can make intercourse less desirable, such as erectile dysfunction, thereby increasing the possibility of low desire (Segraves & Segraves, 1991; Feldman, Goldstein, Hatzichristou, Krane, & McKinlay, 1994). In fact, Corona et al. (2004) found that 43.3% of men with erectile dysfunction also experienced a lack of sexual desire. As we discussed earlier, men more often than women initiate a sexual interaction. If a woman needs a competent sexual stimulus from her husband, she is not going to receive it, thereby reducing her opportunity to experience responsive sexual desire. The role of the therapist is to educate the couple in how other sexual dysfunctions in either partner might contribute to the development and maintenance of low desire. Further, the couple is encouraged to make a commitment to working on all elements of the dysfunction, not just the low desire.

A couple, married for 30 years, sought treatment for the woman's disinterest in sex for the past few years. The therapist learned that she had experienced some degree of discomfort or pain for several years, but she did not want to "let her husband down." Assessment revealed that she occasionally engaged in masturbation and fantasy when alone. The husband was unaware that she felt discomfort or pain, but knew that something was different about their sex life. She wanted sex to be routine, quick, and did not seem to enjoy it. She began habits that blocked sexual activity such as going to bed after her husband and staying busy throughout the evening or any time she suspected her husband might be interested in sex. Through psychoeducation, cognitive therapy, and behavioral homework, the couple gradually resumed sexual intimacy. In addition, they began treatment for the wife's undiagnosed vaginismus, which improved over three months. She was then able to enjoy intercourse, not anticipate pain, and her level of desire began to increase.

Promoting Sexual Intimacy and Erotocism. The topic of sexual intimacy is a central focus of systemic treatment of low desire. The couple shares their ideas about what it means to be sexually intimate, identifies discrepancies in their definitions, and work toward a common meaning (Weeks & Treat, 2001). Next, the therapist helps the couple to understand that intimacy and sex are not distinct entities. This concept is reinforced during the treatment as intimacy within their sexual relationship is encouraged. Additionally, the therapist works with the couple to expand their definition of sexuality to include other intimate, sexual, and erotic behaviors that do not include physical sexual activity. For example, reading erotic stories to each other from a book or creating stories brings eroticism back into the relationship in a safe way.

Working With Fears of Intimacy

Fears of intimacy and closeness, whether conscious or unconscious, are often exhibited through one's behavior. Of all the etiological factors mentioned earlier, not one study identified unconscious fears of intimacy as a factor in low desire. However, our clinical experience has shown us time and time again how important this factor is in some cases of low desire. The therapist assumes that the fear of intimacy may be an unconscious motivator in cases of low desire; thus, this hypothesis should be shared with the couple. Then the therapist helps the partners identify their fears through the use of a genogram that focuses on elements of one's upbringing that have an effect on intimate behavior (DeMaria et al., 1999). Also, the therapist educates the couple about the many reasons why individuals might fear intimacy so that they understand the concepts and will be willing to discuss the related issues as they apply to them (see Weeks & Fife, 2014). In some cases, the clinician can begin to infer their underlying fear of intimacy from their behavior as well as the information obtained about their early years.

In low desire cases, a few factors related to underlying fears of intimacy are seen more frequently than others. For example, the fear of losing control or of being controlled (loss of identity and autonomy) is something we have seen in women a number of times. It may be manifested in the relationships through a power imbalance that is so severe that one partner is perceived as a parent and the other as a child. This issue has the potential to make sex feel nearly incestuous (Weeks & Gambescia, 2002). When there is a fear of losing control for a woman she may unconsciously turn off sexually as a way to say symbolically that "this is my body and I am ultimately in control of my sexuality."

There are several guidelines for treating intimacy fears. First, it is important to identify the fear. The most common fears of intimacy have been described by Weeks and Treat (2001). Next, the therapist uses cognitive therapy to help neutralize the negative thoughts associated with the fear and then replace the negative thoughts with appropriate and adaptive cognitions. The therapist and clients then work to disrupt the pattern of avoidance that results from the fears generated by the negative thoughts. It is important for each partner to validate the fearful partner's emotions without agreeing with them, as agreeing would lead to continued avoidance of the feared stimuli and, consequently, the behavior. The historical basis for the fear can also be explored. Once the client understands the origin of the fear they may see that it was adaptive when they were younger, but the fear is now unnecessary. For example, women are taught to be the gatekeepers of sex when they are teenagers. If a woman had pre-marital sex at a young age she may fear being exposed for her "immoral" or "misbehavior." Moving past fears that are deeply embedded and emerged from childhood is a long term challenging therapeutic task.

It is essential that the therapist and couple explore the ways in which each person in the relationship contributes to the problem rather than placing the blame solely on the person with the low desire or the fear. When one partner has a strong underlying fear of intimacy the other partner usually has a strong fear of intimacy too. It is no accident they are together. The underlying fears of intimacy on both sides are interlocking and usually deeply entrenched and require extended work ranging from cognitive therapy to intergenerational work.

Working With Conflict and Anger

Many of our low desire women have experienced anger and frustration over a protracted period of time. For some, the anger has become chronically suppressed or circumvented, making it very difficult to feel desire toward one's partner. Eventually, the woman avoids all emotional contact in order to avoid stirring up her chronically suppressed anger. Additionally, sexual feelings become suppressed and fused with the noxious emotions of anger, frustration, disappointment, helplessness, etc. The woman must be helped to understand that anger, if expressed, need not destroy the partner or the relationship (Lerner, 2005).

A variety of techniques can be implemented to promote appropriate expression of anger (Weeks & Gambescia, 2002).

In one case, the wife, in her mid-30s, suffered from situational low desire and avoidance of sex for a year after the birth of their first child. Her husband was frustrated and angry about her apparent lack of attention to him and the ailing sexual relationship. His anger was uncensored, which caused her to withdraw from him. The more he raged, the more unreceptive she became. By the time they presented for treatment, they were prepared for divorce. The therapist used techniques to regulate the affect of both partners. As the woman began to discuss her feelings of frustration, being blamed, sadness, etc., her husband was able to respond more empathically. He accepted her feelings; consequently, she became interested in getting closer to him, and so on. He also learned how to control his feelings of neglect, anger, and rage by expressing his underlying feelings of feeling hurt and rejected. The therapeutic outcome was positive after 6 months.

Creating an Erotic Environment

The study mentioned earlier by Sims and Meana (2010) illustrated why women in longer term relationships may begin to feel a lack of desire. Weeks and Gambescia (2002) recognized the need to create a sexual environment in working with low desire couples by creating realistic expectations, developing an ego-syntonic view of sexuality, being responsible for one's own sexual desire, and expressing desire through solo sex. Considering the results of the Sims and Meana study (2010) it would also seem important to focus on some of the following therapeutic goals: defining what is erotic and enacting erotic scenarios, building romantic/sexual fantasies, being more creative and experimental, viewing oneself as a sexual being with many sexually positive attributes, making a date night that may or may not lead to sex, share equally in household responsibilities, learn the difference between making sex and making love, trying different ways to initiate, showing more affection just for the sake of showing affection or unlink it from sex, communicate more about sexual needs, wants, and desires, maintain good self-care, stay active and exercise, have a clear sense of self, view lovemaking and sex as a pleasure, accept compliments, compartmentalize time to be a sexual being rather than mother, employee, or chore-doer, and think of other ways to re-vitalize desire and a sexual relationship.

Family-of-Origin

We have exemplified a number of factors that can contribute to low desire from the family-of-origin. In treatment, we might do a sexual genogram (DeMaria et al., 1999) and ask about what the partners observed in their parents relationship regarding affection and intimacy, and the overt and covert messages that were passed on to the clients as a child and teenager about sexuality. The woman must begin to understand the origin of some of these old deeply embedded beliefs and learn how to differentiate herself from these internalized observations and beliefs. We promote self-awareness and changing these beliefs, and we use a technique that helps the woman affirm her sexuality. We call this technique her "Sexual Bill of Rights." She is asked to write the most powerful and compelling statements about what she is entitled to sexually. In most cases, the initial few drafts do not represent sexual autonomy and ownership of her sexuality. The therapist provides feedback and asks the woman to keep working on it, sometimes with the assistance of her partner, until she has embraced her right to experience desire and express her sexual freedom.

Medical Therapies

The use of medical therapies is beyond the scope of this chapter. We are therapists and will want to treat the problem from a psychotherapeutic perspective. However, some knowledge of medical therapies is useful in understanding how various treatments may be combined. A variety of prosexual remedies is currently available to enhance the sexual appetite. Most of these preparations are nutritional supplements and remain unregulated by the FDA (Food and Drug Administration). Some prescription medications are used off-label for prosexual purposes. For example, Bupropion SR (sustained release), an anti-depressant, has been found to enhance desire in non-depressed women (Ashton, 2007; Segraves, Clayton, Croft, Wolf, & Warnock, 2004; Segraves et al., 2001). However, a couple of recent studies show the limitations of these treatments. Bupropion (Wellbutrin) was used in one study to show whether non-depressed women might benefit from an increase in desire. Ten women participated in the study for a period of 20 weeks. Of the 10 women, about half reported subjective improvement in desire and arousability, but these feelings could not be transferred to the sexual relationship with their partners (Hartmann, Ruffer-Hesse, Kruger, & Philippsohn, 2012). Based on this finding imagine what might happen if a drug could be developed that produced drug induced desire. Nappi et al. (2010) examined both psychological and medical therapies in the treatment of sexual problems. They found the best predictors of overall sexual functioning (not just desire) was prior level of sexual functioning, a change in partner status, feeling toward the partner, and the level of estradiol. Once again the psychological and relational factors proved to be more important than the hormonal system and medical therapies. For the reader interested in the biological aspects of desire, the authors also proposed a biological model of desire (pp. 168–169).

The iatrogenic effects of many commonly used prescription medications can be another factor in low desire (Ballon, 1999; Kennedy, Dickens, Eisfeld, & Bagby, 1999; Rosen, Lane, & Menza, 1999; Saks, 2010). Treatment strategies for overcoming the sexual side effects of medications, especially anti-depressants, include waiting to see if the symptoms remit, lowering the dose, substituting another antidepressant, adding a supplementary medicine to act as an antidote which is quite questionable, or discontinuation for brief periods (a brief drug holiday) (Fava, Rankin, Alpert, Nierenberg, & Worthington, 1998).

Testosterone is recognized as an important component of the sexual appetite in men and women as it promotes sexual desire, curiosity, fantasy, interest, and behavior (Crenshaw & Goldberg, 1996; Krapf & Simon, 2009; Rako, 1996). Testosterone deficiency in men can be treated with an assortment of products and with varying results; however, testosterone deficiency in women remains a mystery when all the research is examined. Moreover, the relationship between testosterone and sexual desire in women is complicated. Davis, Davison, Donath, and Bell (2005) found that low desire in women could not be diagnosed through assessing the level of circulating sex hormones such as testosterone. Specifically, some women with low testosterone levels do not experience desire problems and most women with low desire have normal testosterone levels. Brotto, Bitzer, Laan, Leiblum, and Luria (2010) have written the most comprehensive and critical review of medical therapies for low desire in women. The studies they reviewed showed inconclusive, contradictory, or marginally significant findings. Overall, a thorough assessment by a well-trained physician, who has expert knowledge of how all the hormones interact, is needed. The only treatment which consistently proved to be useful was testosterone therapy for estrogen-replete naturally menopausal women and only marginally effective for premenopausal women. Much more research clearly needs to be done. Pharmaceutical companies appear to believe low desire will be as easy to treat and as lucrative as the medications used for erectile dysfunction. In recent years Gepirone-ER, an antidepressant, was shown to have a prosexual effect but only with depressed women. Thus, the finding of this study cannot be applied to non-depressed women (Fabre, Smith, & DeRogatis, 2011). Flibanserin was a drug that showed promise in increasing the level of desire in non-depressed women (DeRogatis et al., 2012); however, the drug was not approved by the FDA (Jones, 2010).

The medical and psychological treatments can work in combination as proposed in the Intersystem Approach (Weeks & Gambescia, 2000; 2002). However, we do not believe that medications will override the effects of adverse relationship factors in low desire, but interventions to change, reduce, or take a brief holiday from the drug may prove useful where certain medical and drug side effects are present. A drug may eventually be developed that serves as a basic "energizer" of sexual desire thus making it easier to experience desire when the suppressive individual, relational, and family-of-origin factors are worked through therapeutically and there is a desire to feel sexual desire for one's partner.

Relapse Prevention

The therapist should help the couple to understand that sexual desire is maintained through active sensual and sexual contact with one another. Thus, the therapist assists the woman in relapse prevention by including strategies in the repertoire which involve the couple making affectionate statements, erotic talk, and sensual touching and caressing. One of the signs that a couple is relapsing during therapy is their non-completion of the homework assignments. Therefore, the couple is reminded to plan a schedule including sexual dates to spend with one another. A thorough discussion needs to take place in order to uncover the possible reasons for a relapse and the strategies mentioned above may be used again to help the woman and couple move forward.

Paradoxical strategies can also prevent relapses (Weeks & Gambescia, 2002; Weeks & L'Abate, 1982). One strategy is to ask the couple to identify and predict the ways that they might sabotage their progress during and post-therapy. Therapists can also ask the couple to predict the factors that might provoke the recurrence of low desire. Asking the couple to think about these factors will increase the likelihood that these problems will not arise. Finally, mediocre sex is better than no sex. Once the couple starts to avoid sex, the pattern become self-perpetuating and low desire may return. If a coupe agrees to have sex on a regular basis and accept the fact that variability will exist in the degree of desire and satisfaction experience, they have the opportunity to improve the quality of their sexual interaction over time.

Research

Given the number of articles written about lack of desire and its prevalence one would suspect that equal attention might be given to the development of treatment programs and research. In addition, there are few recent books on the topic with the exception of Leiblum (2010b). Only a few research studies could be found for improving desire in women (Heiman, 2002). Hurlbert (1993) conducted an eight-session marital and sex therapy group study with 63 women, along with their partners. One group received what they termed standard treatment. This group received training in a variety of techniques to increase positive marital interactions and decrease negative marital interactions. The other group received the standard treatment plus orgasm consistency training. Women in both groups reported greater arousal and desire. The women in the orgasm consistency group also reported greater sexual satisfaction and sexual assertiveness. Trudel et al. (2001) investigated cognitive-behavioral couple group therapy with 74 couples over a period of 12 sessions. These researches confirmed that negative thinking was a factor in low desire. The therapy was delivered weekly in a couple's group format. At the end of 12 weeks the participants reported a modest improvement in their desire. A 1-year follow up showed that participants had lost some of the improvement but were still functioning at a level better than their baseline. They suggested much more research needed to be done on cognitive therapy with low desire. Brotto, Basson, and Luria (2008) provided only a three session trial of treatment for 26 women, over 6 weeks using a combination of techniques (education, sex and relationship therapy, cognitive-behavioral therapy, and mindfulness therapy). Multiple measures were taken before and after the study. There were significant increases in the subjective awareness of vaginal wetness and positive affect to erotic stimuli. Women who had been sexually abused showed much more significant improvement. These three studies show positive results for increased desire.

In the most recent study, 19 women read a self-help book on sex over a period of 6 weeks. They also showed an improvement in their level of desire. However, it is difficult to say these gains would persist over time (Mintz, Balzer, Zhao, & Bush, 2012). In our opinion, this problem is severely under-researched and the efforts to develop new programs that are sophisticated and flexible enough to accommodate the multifactorial nature of the problem are abysmal.

Conclusion

Treating low desire can be complex, as it involves many factors related to the individual partner, the couple's relationship, intergenerational influences, and other factors such as biology medical conditions, medications, and the socio-sexual environment. The Intersystem Approach can guide the therapist to decode and address many problem areas in couples presenting with this complex dilemma (Weeks, 2005). The therapy is characterized by a number of apparent contradictions. First, although one partner ostensibly expresses the symptom, low desire is a relational problem in some form. Next, low desire is not simply a sexual problem; often, the lack of desire is a reflection of other problems in the relationship. Also, the woman may appear unemotional; yet, the sexual symptom is often a way of indirectly expressing strong emotions related to the partner. The woman might appear to be totally disinterested in sex. In effect, she is often distressed and wants to feel desire for her partner, yet this desire cannot be forced or it will further diminish the sexual appetite. The therapist must be equipped with a variety of techniques that are used judiciously; patience and flexibility are critical. Moreover, the therapeutic strategies must be shared with the partners in order to ensure their cooperation. The research studies suggest that brief therapy might be productive. However, no long-term follow up has been conducted. The approach developed by Weeks and Gambescia (2002) has a number of treatment components that are congruent with the various common etiologies reported. Unfortunately, this approach would be difficult to investigate empirically and we have found that given the multifactorial nature of low desire, the treatment can last anywhere from 6 months up to 2 years. In order to keep a couple interested in therapy for this length of time, they need to see the relationship between her lack of desire, the factors contributing to it, and some progress in alleviating those factors. Ideally, the couple would be able to re-connect physically through some sensate focus exercises (Hertlein, Weeks, & Gambescia, 2009; Weeks & Gambsicia, 2009) which gives them more hope that the problem can be resolved.

146

References

Alvarez, M., & Garcia-Marques, L. (2011). Cognitive and contextual variables in sexual partner and relationship perception. *Archives of Sexual Behavior*, 40(2), 407–417. doi: 10.1007/s10508–011–9725–5

American Psychiatric Association. (2000). *Diagnostic and statistical manual of mental disorders* (4th ed., text rev.). Washington, DC: Author.

American Psychiatric Association. (2013). *Diagnostic and statistical manual of mental disorders* (5th ed.). Washington, DC: Author.

Ashton, A.K. (2007). The new sexual pharmacology: A guide for the clinician. In S.R. Leiblum (Ed.), *Principles and practice of sex therapy* (4th ed., pp. 509–541). New York: The Guilford Press.

Ballon, R. (1999). Sildenafil and sexual dysfunction associated with antidepressants. *Journal of Sex & Marital Therapy*, 25(4), 259–264.

Bancroft, J. (2010). Sexual desire and the brain revisited. *Sexual and Relationship Therapy*, 25(2), 166–171. doi: 10.1080/14681991003604680

Barbach, L. (1982). *For each other: Sharing sexual intimacy*. New York: Doubleday.

Basson, R. (2001a). Are the complexities of women's sexual function reflected in the new consensus definitions of dysfunction? *Journal of Sex & Marital Therapy*, 27(2), 105–112.

Basson, R. (2001b). Using a different model for female sexual response to address women's problematic low sexual desire. *Journal of Sex and Marital Therapy*, 27(5), 395–403.

Basson, R. (2007). Sexual desire/arousal disorders in women. In S.R. Leiblum (Ed.), *Principles and practice of sex therapy* (4th ed., pp. 25–53). New York: The Guilford Press.

Basson, R. (2014). On the definition of Female Sexual Interest/Arousal Disorder. *Archives of Sexual Behavior*. doi: 10.1007/s10508–014–0324–0

Basson, R., Wiermann, M.E., van Lankveld, J., & Brotto, L. (2010). Summary of the recommendations on sexual dysfunction in women. *Journal of Sexual Medicine*, 7, 314–326.

Beck, A.T. (1976). *Cognitive therapy and the emotional disorders*. New York: International Universities Press.

Beck, J. (1995). *Cognitive therapy: Basics and beyond*. New York: Guilford.

Bitzer, J., Giraldi, A., & Pfaus, J. (2013). Sexual desire and hypoactive sexual desire disorder in women. Introduction and overview. Standard operating procedure (SOP part 1). *Journal of Sexual Medicine*, 10(1), 36–49. doi: 10.1111/j.1743–6109.2012.02818.x

Both, S., Laan, E., & Everaerd, W. (2011). Focusing "hot" or focusing "cool": Attentional mechanisms in sexual arousal in men and women. *Journal of Sexual Medicine*, 8(1), 167–179. doi: 10.1111/j.1743–6109.2010.02051.x

Boul, L., Hallam-Jones, R., & Wylie, K.R. (2008). Sexual pleasure and motivation. *Journal of Sex & Marital Therapy*, 35(1), 25–39. doi: 10.1080/00926230802525620

Brauer, M., van Leeuwen, M., Janssen, E., Newhouse, S.K., Heiman, J.R., & Laan, E. (2012). Attentional and affective processing of sexual stimuli in women with hypoactive sexual desire disorder. *Archives of Sexual Behavior*, 41(4), 891–905. doi: 10.1007/s10508–011–9820–7

Bright, S. (Ed). (2000). *Best American erotica 2000*. New York: Touchstone.

Brotto, L.A. (2010). The DSM diagnostic criteria for hypoactive sexual desire disorder in men. *Journal of Sexual Medicine*, 7(6), 2015–2030. doi: 10.1111/j.1743–6109.2010.01860.x

Brotto, L.A., Basson, R., & Luria, M. (2008). A mindfulness-based group psychoeducational intervention targeting sexual arousal disorders in women. *Journal of Sexual Medicine*, 5(7), 1646–1659. doi: 10.1111/j.1743–6109.2008.00850.x

Brotto, L.A., Bitzer, J., Laan, E., Leiblum, S., & Luria, M. (2010). Woman's sexual desire and arousal disorders. *Journal of Sexual Medicine*, 7, 586–614.

Brotto, L. & Woo, J. (2010). Cognitive-behavioral and mindfulness-based therapy for low sexual desire. In S. Leiblum (Ed.), *Treating sexual desire disorders* (pp. 149–164). New York: Guilford Press.

Carvalho, J., & Nobre, P. (2011). Biopsychosocial determinants of men's sexual desire: Testing an integrative model. *Journal of Sexual Medicine*, 8(3), 754–763. doi: 10.1111/j.1743–6109.2010.02156.x

Clayton, A. H., Segraves, R. T., Leiblum, S., Basson, R., Pyke, R., Cotton, D., . . . Wunderlich, G. R. (2007). Reliability and validity of the sexual interest and desire inventory-female (SIDI-F), a scale designed to measure severity of female hypoactive sexual desire disorder. *Journal of Sex & Marital Therapy*, 32(2), 115–135.

Comfort, A. (1994). *The new joy of sex: A gourmet guide to lovemaking in the nineties*. New York: Crown Publishing.

Corona, G., Mannucci, E., Petrone, L., Giommi, R., Mansani, R., Fei, L., . . . Maggi, M. (2004). Psycho-biological correlates of hypoactive sexual desire in patients with erectile dysfunction. *International Journal of Impotence Research*, 16(3), 275–281.

Crenshaw, T., & Goldberg, G. (1996). *Sexual pharmacology*. New York: W. W. Norton.

Davis, S., Davison, S., Donath, S., & Bell, R. (2005). Circulating androgen levels and self-reported sexual function in women. *Journal of the American Medical Association*, 294(1), 91–96.

DeMaria, R., Weeks, G., & Hof, L. (1999). *Focused genograms: Intergenerational assessment of individuals, couples, and families*. Philadelphia: Brunner/Mazel.

DeRogatis, L. R., Komer, L., Katz, M., Moreau, M., Kimura, T., Garcia, M., . . . Pyke, R. (2012). Treatment of hypoactive sexual desire disorder in premenopausal women: Efficacy of flibanserin in the VIOLET study. *Journal of Sexual Medicine*, 9(4), 1074–1085.

Fabre, L. F., Smith, L. C., & DeRogatis, L. R. (2011). Gepirone-ER treatment of low sexual desire associated with depression in women as measured by the DeRogatis inventory of sexual function (DISF) fantasy/cognition (desire) domain-A post hoc analysis. *Journal of Sexual Medicine*, 8(9), 2569–2581. doi: 10.1111/j.1743–6109.2011.02330.x

Fava, M., Rankin, M., Alpert, J., Nierenberg, A., & Worthington, J. (1998). An open trial of oral sidenafil in antidepressant-induced sexual dysfunction. *Psychotherapy and Psychosomatics*, 67(6), 328–331.

Feldman, H. A., Goldstein, I., Hatzichristou, D. G., Krane, R. J., & McKinlay, J. B. (1994). Impotence and its medical and psychosocial correlates: Results of the Massachusetts male aging study. *Journal of Urology*, 151(1), 54–61.

Friday, N. (1998a). *Forbidden flowers: More women's sexual fantasies*. New York: Pocket.

Friday, N. (1998b). *Men in love*. New York: Dell.

Gambescia, N., & Weeks, G. (2007). Sexual dysfunction. In N. Kazantzis & L. L'Abate (Eds.), *Handbook of homework assignments in psychotherapy: Research, practice, and prevention* (pp. 351–368). Norwell, MA: Kluwer Academic Publishers.

Geonet, M., De Sutter, P., & Zech, E. (2013). Cognitive factors in women hypoactive sexual desire disorder. *Sexologies*, 22(1), e9–e15. doi: 10.1016/j.sexol.2012.01.011

Gottman, J. (1994). *What predicts divorce: The relationship between marital processes and marital outcomes*. Hillsdale, NJ: Lawrence Erlbaum.

Hall, K., & Graham, C. (Eds.). (2013). *Cultural context of sexual pleasure and problems*. New York: Routledge.

Hartmann, U. H., Ruffer-Hesse, C., Kruger, T. H. C., & Philippsohn, S. (2012). Individual and dyadic barriers to a pharmacotherapeutic treatment of hypoactive sexual desire disorders: Results and implications from a small-scale study with bupropion. *Journal of Sex & Marital Therapy*, 38(4), 325–348. doi: 10.1080/0092623X.2011.606495

Heiman, J. R. (2002). Psychologic treatments for female sexual dysfunction: Are they effective and do we need them? *Archives of Sexual Behavior*, 31(5), 445–450.

Hertlein, K. M., Weeks, G. R., & Gambescia, N. (Eds.). (2009). *Systemic sex therapy*. New York: Routledge.

Hubin, A., De Sutter, P., & Reynaert, C. (2011). Etiological factors in female hypoactive sexual desire disorder. *Sexologies*, 20(3), 149–157. doi: 10.1016/j.sexol.2010.12.003

Hurlbert, D. F. (1993). A comparative study using orgasm consistency training in the treatment of women reporting hypoactive sexual desire. *Journal of Sex and Marital Therapy*, 19(1), 41–55. doi: 10.1080/00926239308404887

Hyde, J. (2010). *Understanding human sexuality* (11th ed.). New York: McGraw Hill.

Jones, J. (2010, June 21). Female viagra ineffective. *Psych Central*. Retrieved from http://psychcentral.com

Kaplan, H.S. (1977). Hypoactive sexual desire disorder. *Journal of Sex and Marital Therapy, 3*(1), 3–9.

Katz., R.C., & Jardine, D. (1999). The relationship between worry, sexual aversion, and low sexual desire. *Journal of Sex & Marital Therapy, 25*(4), 293–296.

Kennedy, S.H., Dickens, S.E., Eisfeld, B.S., & Bagby, R.M. (1999). Sexual dysfunction before antidepressant therapy in major depression. *Journal of Affective Disorders, 56*(2–3), 201–208.

Kimmel, M. (2007). *The sexual self: The construction of sexual scripts.* Nashville, TN: Vanderbilt University Press.

Kouros, C.D., & Cummings, E.M. (2011). Transactional relations between marital functioning and depressive symptoms. *American Journal of Orthopsychiatry, 81*(1), 128–138. doi: 10.1111/j.1939–0025.2010.01080.x128

Krapf, J., & Simon, J. (2009). The role of testosterone in the management of hypoactive sexual desire disorder in postmenopausal women. *Maturitas, 63,* 213–219.

Laumann, E.O., Nicolosi, A., Glasser, D.B., Paik, A., Gingell, C., Moreira, E., & Wang, T. (2005). Sexual problems among women and men aged 40–80 y: Prevalence and correlates identified in the Global Study of Sexual Attitudes and Behaviors. *International Journal of Impotence Research, 17*(1), 39–57.

Laumann, E.O., Palik, A., & Rosen, R.C. (1999). Sexual dysfunction in the United States: Prevalence and predictors. *Journal of the American Medical Association, 281*(6), 537–544.

Leiblum, S.R. (2010a). Introduction and overview: Clinical perspectives on and treatment of sexual desire disorders. In S.R. Leiblum (Ed.). *Treating sexual desire disorders: A clinical casebook* (pp. 1–22). New York: Guilford Press.

Leiblum, S. (Ed.) (2010b). *Treating sexual desire disorders: A clinical casebook.* New York: Guilford Press.

Lerner, H. (2005). *The dance of anger: A woman's guide to changing the patterns of intimate relationships.* New York: HarperCollins.

Levine, S.B. (1992). *Sexual life: A clinician's guide.* New York: Plenum Press.

Martin, R. (Ed). (1997). *Dark eros: Black erotic writings.* New York: St. Martin.

Masters, W.H., & Johnson, V.E. (1966). *Human sexual response.* New York: Bantam Books.

Maurice, W.L. (2007). Sexual desire disorders in men. In S.R. Leiblum (Ed.), *Principles and practice of sex therapy* (4th ed., pp. 181–211). New York: The Guilford Press.

McCarthy, B., & Breetz, A. (2010). Confronting male hypoactive sexual desire disorder. In S. Leiblum (Ed.), *Treating sexual desire disorders: A clinical casebook* (pp. 75–91). New York: Guilford Press.

McGoldrick, M., Loonan, R., & Wohlsifer, D. (2007). Sexuality and culture. In S. Leiblum (Ed.). *Principles and practice of sex therapy* (4th ed., pp. 416–441). New York: Guilford Press.

Meana, M. (2010). Elucidating women's (hetero)sexual desire: Definitional challenges and content expansion. *Journal of Sex Research, 47*(2–3), 104–122. doi: 10.1080/00224490903402546

Meston, C.M. (2003). Validation of the female sexual function index (FSFI) in women with female orgasmic disorder and in women with hypoactive sexual desire disorder. *Journal of Sex & Marital Therapy, 29*(1), 39–46.

Meston, C.M., & Buss, D.M. (2007). Why humans have sex. *Archives of Sexual Behavior, 36*(4), 477–507.

Mintz, L.B. (2009). *A tired woman's guide to passionate sex: Reclaim your desire and reignite your relationship.* Avon, MA: Adams Media.

Mintz, L.B., Balzer, A.M., Zhao, X., & Bush, H.E. (2012). Bibliotherapy for low sexual desire: Evidence for effectiveness. *Journal of Counseling Psychology, 59*(3), 471–478. doi: 10.1037/a0028946

Money, J. (1986). *Lovemaps: Clinical concepts of sexual/erotic health and pathology, paraphilia, and gender transposition in childhood, adolescents, and maturity.* New York: Irvington Publishers.

Morokoff, P., & Gilliland, R. (1993). Stress, sexual functioning, and marital satisfaction. *The Journal of Sex Research, 30*(1), 43–53.

Nappi, R.E., Martini, E., Terreno, E., Albani, F., Santamaria, V., Tonani, S., Polatti, F. (2010). Management of hypoactive sexual desire disorder in women: Current and emerging therapies. *International Journal of Women's Health, 2,* 167–175.

149

Nobre, P. J., & Pinto-Gouveia, J. (2009). Cognitive schemas associated with negative *sexual* events: A comparison of men and women with and without sexual dysfunction. *Archives of Sexual Behavior, 38*(5), 842–851. doi: 10.1007/s10508–008–9450-x

Rako, S. (1996). *The hormone of desire: The truth about sexuality, menopause and testosterone.* New York: Haworth.

Regan, P. C., & Berscheid, E. (1996) Beliefs about the state, goals, and objects of sexual desire. *Journal of Sex and Marital Therapy, 22*(2), 110–120.

Rellini, A. H., & Meston, C. M. (2011). Sexual self-schemas, sexual dysfunction, and the sexual responses of women with a history of childhood sexual abuse. *Archives of Sexual Behavior, 40*(2), 351–362. doi: 10.1007/s10508–010–9694–0

Rosand, G. B., Slinning, K., Eberhard-Gran, M., Roysamb, E., & Tambs, K., (2012). The buffering effect of relationship satisfaction on emotional distress in couples. *BMC Public Health, 12*(66). doi: 10.1186/1471–2458–12–66

Rosen, R., Lane, R., & Menza, M. (1999). Effects of SSRIs on sexual function: A critical review. *Journal of Clinical Pharmacology, 19*(1), 67–85.

Saks, B. (2010). Sexual psychopharmacology and treatment of sexual desire. In S. Leiblum (Ed.). *Treating sexual desire disorders: A clinical casebook* (pp. 219–233). New York: Guilford Press.

Sand, M., & Fisher, W. A. (2007). Women's endorsement of models of female sexual response: The nurses' sexuality study. *Journal of Sexual Medicine, 4*(3), 708–719.

Segraves, R. T., Clayton, A., Croft, H., Wolf, A., & Warnock, J. (2004). Bupropion sustained release for the treatment of hypoactive sexual desire disorder in premenopausal women. *Journal of Clinical Psychopharmacology, 24*(3), 339–342.

Segraves, R. T., Croft, H., Kavoussi, R., Ascher, J. A., Batey, S. R., Foster, V. J., & Metz, A. (2001). Bupropion sustained release (SR) for the treatment of hypoactive sexual desire disorder (HSDD) in nondepressed women. *Journal of Sex & Marital Therapy, 27*(3), 303–316.

Segraves, K., & Segraves, R. (1991). Hypoactive sexual desire disorder: Prevalence and comorbidity in 906 subjects. *Journal of Sex & Marital Therapy, 17*(1), 55–58.

Sills, T., Wunderlich, G., Pyke, R., Segraves, R. T., Leiblum, S., Clayton, A., & Evans, K. (2005). The sexual interest and desire inventory-female (SIDI-F): Item response analyses of data from women diagnosed with hypoactive sexual desire disorder. *The Journal of Sexual Medicine, 2*(6), 801–818.

Sims, K. E., & Meana, M. (2010). Why did passion wane? A qualitative study of married women's attributions for declines in sexual desire. *Journal of Sex & Marital Therapy, 36*(4), 360–380. doi: 10.1080/0092623X.2010.498727

Sipe, W., & Eisendrath, S. (2012). Mindfulness-based cognitive therapy: Theory and practice. *Canadian Journal of Psychiatry, 57*(2), 63–69.

Trudel, G., Marchand, A., Ravart, M., Aubin, S., Turgeon, L., & Fortier, P. (2001). The effect of a cognitive-behavioral group treatment program on hypoactive sexual desire in women. *Sexual and Relationship Therapy, 16*(2), 145–164. doi: 10.1080/14681990120040078

Trudel, G., Ravart, M., & Matte, B. (1993). The use of the mutliaxial diagnostic system for sexual dysfunctions in the assessment of hypoactive sexual desire. *Journal of Sex & Marital Therapy, 19*(2), 123–130.

Weeks, G. (1987). Systemic treatment of inhibited sexual desire. In G. Weeks & L. Hof (Eds.), *Integrating sex and marital therapy* (pp. 183–201). New York: Brunner-Routledge.

Weeks, G. (1994). The intersystem model: An integrative approach to treatment. In G. Weeks & L. Hof (Eds.), *The marital-relationship casebook: Theory and application of the intersystem model* (pp. 3–34). New York: Brunner/Mazel.

Weeks, G. (2005). The emergence of a new paradigm in sex therapy: Integration. *Sexual and Relationship Therapy, 20*(1), 89–103.

Weeks, G., & Fife, S. (2014). *Couples in treatment: Techniques and approaches for effective practice* (3rd ed.). New York: Routledge.

Weeks, G., & Gambescia, N. (2000). *Erectile dysfunction: Integrating couple therapy, sex therapy, and medical treatment.* New York: W. W. Norton.

Weeks, G., & Gambescia, N. (2002). *Hypoactive sexual desire: Integrating sex and couple therapy.* New York: W.W. Norton.

Weeks, G., & Gambescia, N. (2009). A systemic approach to sensate focus. In K. Hertlien, G. Weeks, & N. Gambescia (Eds.), *Systemic sex therapy* (pp. 341–362). New York: Routledge.

Weeks, G., & Hof, L. (Eds.). (1987). *Integrating sex and marital therapy: A clinical guide.* New York: Brunner/Mazel.

Weeks, G., & Hof, L. (Eds.). (1994). *The marital-relationship therapy casebook.* New York: Brunner/Mazel.

Weeks, G., & L'Abate, L. (1982). *Paradoxical psychotherapy: Theory and practice with individuals, couples, and families.* New York: Brunner/Mazel.

Weeks, G., & Treat, S. (2001). *Couples in treatment: Techniques and approaches for effective practice* (Rev. ed.). New York: Brunner/Mazel.

Whitton, S.W., & Whisman, M.A. (2010). Relationship satisfaction instability and depression. *Journal of Family Psychology, 24*(6), 791–794. doi: 10.1037/a0021734

Wiegel, M., Meston, C., & Rosen, R. (2005). The female sexual function index (FSFI): Cross-validation and development of clinical cutoff scores. *Journal of Sex & Marital Therapy, 31*(1), 1–20.

Zilbergeld, B. (1992). *The new male sexuality.* New York: Bantam.

9

INHIBITED AROUSAL IN WOMEN

Kevan R. Wylie, Desa Markovic, and Ruth Hallam-Jones

Female sexual interest/arousal disorder is a common condition frequently presented to sexual medicine clinics and psychosexual therapy practitioners. The definition of this disorder has recently changed with the introduction of the *Diagnostic and Statistical Manual of Mental Disorders* (*DSM-5*) (APA, 2013) but is still referred to as female sexual arousal disorder in the 10th edition of the World Health Organization's international classification of disease (1992). Before summarizing the main areas of change, we will present the definitions proposed in *DSM IV-TR* (APA, 2000).

Definitions

The *DSM IV-TR* (APA, 2000) classification of sexual disorders is derived from phases of a linear sexual response cycle as first described by Masters and Johnson (1966) and then Kaplan (1979). *DSM IV-TR* (APA, 2000) classification system separated Female Sexual Arousal Disorder (FSAD) and Hypoactive Sexual Desire Disorder (HSDD) into different categories. For the diagnosis of FSAD, the following criteria were established:

1. Persistent or recurrent inability to attain or to maintain, until completion of the sexual activity, an adequate lubrication-swelling response of sexual excitement.
2. The disturbance causes marked distress or interpersonal difficulty.
3. The sexual dysfunction is not better accounted for by another Axis I disorder (except another sexual dysfunction) and is not due exclusively to the direct physiological effects of a substance (e.g., drug abuse, medication) or a general medical condition.

Specify type: Lifelong type or acquired type
Specify type: Generalized type or situational type
Specify type: Due to psychological factors or due to combined factors

It has been argued that there are a number of serious problems with the classification criteria of *DSM IV-TR*. Clarity and evidence of normal arousal from sufficient sexual stimulation based on age, life circumstances and sexual experience is lacking. In addition, the complexity of establishing adequacy of sexual stimulation is difficult to quantify. Furthermore, each of the four primary *DSM IV-TR* diagnoses (Sexual desire disorders; Sexual arousal disorders; Orgasmic disorders; Sexual pain disorders) is not necessarily independent. Finally, there is increasing evidence that physiological response does not necessarily coincide with subjective experience. The revision by the International Committee of the American Foundation of Urological Disease (Basson, Berman, & Bernett, 2000), incorporates medical risk factors and divides arousal disorders into primary, secondary and situational, as well as including the concept of personal distress. Basson, Wierman, van Lankveld, and Brotto (2010) emphasized a lack of subjective arousal as a principal cause of distress for women, rather than a lack of genital response, as defined in the *DSM IV-TR*. They recommended subtypes of sexual arousal disorder: subjective sexual arousal disorder; genital sexual arousal disorder; combined genital and subjective arousal disorder; and persistent genital arousal disorder. They also regarded the *DSM IV-TR* definition of HSDD as highly problematic in its emphasis on sexual fantasies and desire for sexual activity and recommended that desire be regarded as the result of an incentive (sexually competent stimulus) that activates the sexual system. Brotto et al. (2010) criticized compartmentalized treatment of women's sexual desire, arousal, and orgasmic disorders. They referred to studies that found co-morbidity between desire and arousal and like Basson, Wierman, van Lankveld, and Brotto (2010) stressed the importance of subjective sexual experience for establishing the diagnosis. Brotto et al. (2010) also found emphasis on sexual fantasies and desire for sexual activity for the diagnosis of HSDD problematic, given this does not apply to all women. More recently, Giraldi, Rellini, Pfaus, and Laan (2013) commented on the exclusive focus on genital response in the *DSM IV-TR* diagnosis of FSAD and its failure to include the subjective components. They also drew attention to an oversight in *DSM-IV-TR* regarding the variety of ways in which women can become aroused and the types and intensity of stimulation needed. Their findings stress the following risk factors for FSAD: co-morbidity of FSAD with other sexual problems, the increase of arousal problems with age, the influence of cultural factors on the prevalence of arousal disorders, the partner's depression, and relationship problems.

Following research and critique of *DSM IV-TR*, some of which is referred to above, the *DSM -5* combines female sexual desire and arousal disorders into one disorder: female sexual interest/arousal disorder (FSI/AD). The distinction between sexual desire and arousal has been argued as being artificial in spite of *DSM-5* (APA, 2013). The term "hypoactive sexual desire disorder" is abandoned. The proposed criteria for FSI/AD are (Brotto, 2013):

A. Lack of sexual interest/arousal for at least 6 months duration as manifested by at least three of the following indicators:
   1. Absent/reduced frequency or intensity of interest in sexual activity
   2. Absent/reduced frequency of intensity of sexual/erotic thoughts or fantasies
   3. Absent/reduced frequency of initiation of sexual activity and is typically unreceptive to a partner's attempts to initiate
   4. Absent/reduced frequency or intensity of sexual excitement/pleasure during sexual activity on all or almost all (approximately 75%) sexual encounters
   5. Sexual interest/arousal is absent or infrequently elicited by any internal or external sexual/erotic cues (e.g., written, verbal, visual, etc.)
   6. Absent/reduced frequency or intensity of genital and/or nongenital sensations during sexual activity on all or almost all (approximately 75%) sexual encounters

B. The problem causes clinically significant distress or impairment.
C. The sexual dysfunction is not better accounted for by another disorder (except another sexual dysfunction) and is not due to the effects of a substance (e.g., drug abuse, medication) or a general medical condition.

Subtypes of FSI/AD are specified as lifelong vs. acquired and generalized versus situational.

Additional factors to consider are:

- Intergenerational Factors, such as: psychiatric history in the family, early relationship with caregivers, childhood stressors, history of abuse experience
- Relational Factors, such as: poor communication, relationship discord, discrepancies in desire for sexual activity; partner factors (partner's sexual problems, partner's health status)
- Environmental Factors, such as: cultural/religious (e.g., inhibitions related to prohibitions against sexual activity)

Furthermore, *DSM-5* acknowledges variability in how sexual interest and arousal are expressed. Finally, subjectivity of sexual experience has been given prominence (APA, 2013; Brotto, 2013).

We wish to emphasize early on in our description that, as well as there being co-morbidity between sexual problems, there may also be a number of ways in which they may present. Sexual arousal has both psychological and physiological correlates. The emphasis of each of these, and in particular, the individual clinician's determination of the importance of these correlates can have a profound impact on both the understanding and the management of the condition.

Working Paradigms

Separation between the fields of couple therapy and sex therapy has been observed and commented on by many authors and practitioners in both these fields. A leading example, Weeks (2005) offered a new paradigm for treating sexual problems, integrating sex therapy, couple therapy, and biological interventions into a comprehensive Intersystem model of five dimensions: individual biological; individual psychological; couple; family; and cultural/environmental. McCarthy and Thestrup (2008) offered a Psychobiosocial Model advocating that couple therapists should not treat sexuality with "benign neglect" (p. 141). Furthermore, they encouraged couple therapists to integrate sexual permission—giving, scientifically and clinically relevant sexual information and guidelines, and specific sexual suggestions/interventions into their couple work (p. 139). McCarthy and Thestrup (2008) provided guidelines for revitalizing and maintaining sexual desire, which comprised a list of questions and statements for therapists to give to their clients as a useful tool during the course of treatment. Bradley and Fine (2009) and Markovic (2013) discussed the importance of an inclusive approach, holding both the medical and the systemic psychotherapy perspectives for the most effective treatment of sexual dysfunctions. Bradley and Fine (2009) emphasized the lack of evidence-based outcome research in sex therapy and appealed both to psychotherapists and medical practitioners to "look beyond traditional classifications to fully understand the complexity of sexual dysfunctions" (p. 77). They called for therapists' wider involvement in treating sexual issues rather than allowing medical and pharmaceutical solutions to dominate treatment. Markovic (2013) offered a model for an integrated assessment and treatment of sexual issues, combining the scientific and medical base of sexology with a systemic social constructionist perspective, focusing on six dimensions of human lived experience: emotional; rational; physical; behavioral; relational; and cultural. Case studies providing detailed illustrations of theoretical and practical integration of sex therapy with the postmodern systemic therapy approach were recently published (Bulow, 2009; Markovic, 2010). Through a couple case study, Bulow (2009) illustrated the need for integration of sex therapy and couples therapy in order to best meet the clients' needs. This approach incorporated family-of-origin history, intrapsychic and cognitive issues, relational dynamics, and medical concerns into a treatment combining couple therapy and behavioral interventions. Markovic (2010) demonstrated the challenges and possibilities of working on a sexual relationship with an individual, illustrating an integration between systemic approach and sex therapy by way of a case example of a female client presenting problems with sexual arousal and orgasm. The treatment combined systemic therapy with psycho-educational interventions and behavioral tasks.

For the purposes of this chapter, we are using the Intersystem model (Weeks, 2005) as an overarching framework for dealing with the specific problems of FSI/AD. The Model comprises of five components, the first of which is to understand what the woman brings into the relationship as well as what her partner brings into the couple. Each will have their own physiological and biological background, and it is important to remember that the man or lesbian partner may have their own contributory causes of dysfunction. The second component is the woman's psychological make-up, which is something that incorporates the individual's values, attitudes, opinions, intelligence, and any psychopathology however "soft" that may be. The third component is the relational aspects of the couple, and for this to be dealt with adequately a systemic perspective must be taken. The fourth element deals with family-of-origin for both individuals in the relationship, since both families and upbringing within particular environments (e.g., education, religion, society, culture) can all have an impact on individuals' perspective of sexuality. The final component in the Intersystem model is how the environmental, societal, cultural, religious, and historical factors seem to have a marked influence on both decision making and judgments (Weeks, 2005).

Individual Biological Components

The physiological correlates that accompany genital arousal can include genital swelling around the introitus, sensory change including tingling and heightened sensitivity, clitoral body prominence, protuberance and firmness, and a general awareness of moisture or actual oozing of fluid from the vagina. Genital arousal is a combination of increased blood flow in both the vagina (causing the transudate of lubrication) and the clitoral bulbs and body (which brings about many of the other signs and experiences).

A number of important co-morbid conditions may be associated with FSI/AD, and it is likely that there are common risk-factor categories associated for sexual dysfunctions of arousal in both men and women (Lewis et al., 2004). The principal areas of concern involve cardiovascular status and neurological conditions. One of the commonest cardiovascular conditions is diabetes mellitus, which is increasingly regarded to have a similar impact on genital blood flow in women as in men. Hypertension, dyslipidemia, and smoking cigarettes are also risk factors (Lewis et al., 2004).

Endocrinological contributions towards inhibited sexual arousal include conditions bringing about the hypo-oestrogenism states natural menopause and surgically induced menopause. The contribution of reduced androgens is less clear but is considered by many as a contributory factor. Neurological conditions include multiple sclerosis and conditions that bring about autonomic neuropathy. Women who are prescribed medications for cardiovascular or psychiatric conditions are particularly prone to the sexual side effects secondary to these conditions.

In summary, physiological changes of inhibited sexual arousal include damage or disease of the blood vessels or nerves of the pelvic region and generalized vascular disease (e.g., peripheral vascular disease, hypertension, diabetes mellitus). Medical conditions may bring about hormonal change such as hypothyroidism, hypo-oestrogenism, and hypoandrogenism (e.g., menopause) as may the effect of prescribed medications.

Individual Psychological Components

There are many psychological components to sexual arousal, which can occur independently of genital arousal. Psychological excitation, sexual anticipation, emotional longing, and related anticipatory and preparatory sexual behaviors are just some of these. These must be differentiated from the lack of sexual fantasy and desire to engage in sexual activity seen with inhibited arousal and a lack of sexual interest. Common psychiatric conditions include anxiety, depression, and anorexia nervosa (Maurice, 2003), the consequences of sexual trauma and abuse, bereavement, relational problems, and major psychiatric conditions (e.g., posttraumatic stress disorder, major depression, psychosis) .

Couple Components

The consequences of sexual dysfunction on relationships are far reaching and are a frequent presenting problem in sexual and relationship therapy. The interpersonal context must be always considered when assessing and treating sexual dysfunctions. Inhibited sexual arousal, like so many other sexual problems, can have a negative impact on the general well-being and emotional well-being of the woman. This can affect her overall quality of life and have a substantial impact on the relationship with her partner.

Even today the precise relationship between sexual satisfaction and relationship satisfaction is hard to measure, though in general the literature suggests that individuals with greater relationship satisfaction may also report improved sexual satisfaction (Byers, 2005; Yeh et al., 2006).

Family Components

We propose a comprehensive treatment that includes exploration of the family-of-origin and caretakers' influences that may have predisposed the sexual dysfunction. Treatment involves exploration of the early messages about sex, affection and intimacy, and a challenge of any strong negative attitudes related to sexual desire and sexual expression. Typical factors contributing to FSI/AD include: internalized family messages leading to shame and guilt related to sexual behavior; lack of affection in the family and between the parents/carers; psychiatric history in the family.

Cultural Components

DSM-5 (APA, 2013) acknowledges marked variability in prevalence rates of FSI/AD across different cultures. An important point is made in relation to the necessity of considering cultural and religious factors in order to avoid pathologizing. Research available to date suggests lower rates of sexual desire in East Asian female population compared to Euro-Canadian women (Yule, Woo, & Brotto, 2010). In fact, psychophysiological research has shown that East Asian women demonstrated lower level of arousal than Euro-Canadian Women. In our experience, women's religious beliefs may contribute to her developing

156

sexuality as a young person, causing confusion and guilt, particularly when strong sexual urges were experienced, which conflicted with religious ideals.

It is important that the psychosexual therapist and sexual medicine clinician undertakes a thorough assessment of each of these components. Whether these are addressed either by one or both of the co-therapists or by an assisting general medical practitioner or physician will depend on local policy. Treatment models that focus on identified symptoms, or identified partners, fail to provide a holistic and integrative understanding of the various contributory factors. It is our belief that such treatment plans that remain grounded in an individualistic and genital perspective are both inadequate and less helpful than viewing matters in a holistic and systemic way by identifying how the physical, psychological, relational, gender, and cultural issues impact on the woman, her partner, and their general well-being and relatedness.

Assessment of FSI/AD

Nearly half of men and women in a survey done in 2005 had experienced at least one sexual problem but only 19% sought help from their physicians (Moreira et al., 2005). It should be emphasized again that FSI/AD must have a thorough assessment, particularly as the detail given by the referrer may be minimal or misleading. However, the complexity and associated comorbidity of the individual and the partner found in FSI/AD means that the therapists must repeatedly review the state and progress of assessment. Therapeutic interventions may also act as diagnostic tools to demonstrate ongoing assessment needs. As such, there may be a blurred distinction between when assessment ends and treatment begins. For many couples, sensate focus has served this dual purpose.

As part of the initial assessment in our clinic, a brief questionnaire is sent to patients that collects the epidemiological data and brief outline of their previous medical and psychosexual history. Obtaining this information in advance saves time during the therapeutic sessions and to a degree ameliorates the possibility of one person being presented as the specific person holding the problem (and so meriting referral). Both partners are invited to complete and return the questionnaire in advance of their appointment, which needs to accommodate the needs of both partners so that both members of the couple are able to attend together from the outset. This can then be perused by both clinicians and any supervising team so that some basic information, at least according to the reality of the individual completing the form, is obtained. Initial hypotheses and formulations can therefore be established (see http://www.porterbrookclinic.org.uk/publicdocs/CouplesQ. pdf for the questionnaire).

Part of working systemically is to be engrossed in what is happening in the session and in the current reality of the couple rather than being allowed to be "indoctrinated" with the "story according to" either or both partners who attempt to assist the clinician in understanding the basis of a problem. We recognize and appreciate the importance of establishing any organic contribution toward the problem. This is crucial because not only can steps be taken to prevent deterioration of any biological processes, but also any litigious issues which may follow a failure to diagnose such issues is addressed. Notwithstanding this, as explained already, a number of factors must be addressed in any attempt to understand the individual and couple issues. We cannot stress enough that an initial perusal of these completed comprehensive forms is often extremely revealing and helps the co-therapist and supervisory team to make a formulation and progress in the first therapeutic session thereafter.

Preliminary Assessment

The Intersystem Approach developed by Weeks (1994) pertaining to individual, couple, and intergenerational components is extremely helpful in resolving couple related problems. One of the difficult decisions for clinicians is whether to proceed with sessions when one partner fails to appear. This is particularly complicated during the preliminary assessments. Questionnaires may be used for assessment with the woman alone or in couple's sessions as well. One such is the Sexual Interest and Desire Inventory—Female (SIDI-F) (Sills et al., 2005). The Profile of Female Sexual Function (PFSF) is specifically for women with suspected HSDD in postmenopausal women (DeRogatis et al., 2004). The Female Sexual Function index is established for self-report and can discriminate between clinical and non-clinical populations (Rosen et al., 2000) but it only asks about function in the past four weeks and does not ask about the degree of distress related to symptoms. It has been specifically validated in women with HSDD and orgasmic disorders (Meston, 2003).

Key Area of Questions. One of the key issues to address is the extent of the relational etiology in causing this disorder. The vital question when working with couples is who (the woman or her partner) is distressed about the inhibited arousal and what are they distressed about. This question needs asking and reviewing as the therapeutic relationship develops with the woman. Why has she sought help? In other words, does the woman want to feel more arousal for herself or does she want to feel more arousal because her partner wants her to feel it?

As reported by Dennerstein, Koochaki, Barton, and Graziottin (2006), women who suffer from arousal difficulties and secondary desire disorder, may nonetheless seek assistance to improve unsatisfying sex, typically in order to retain relationship due to their partner's distress. This is a difficult starting point for a therapy that needs motivation to succeed. If the woman has the need to establish motivation for sexual activity, then this is the key not only to the therapeutic approach but also to the possible outcome. Exploring relational issues leads to understanding the possibility of change both in the woman's sexual attitude and behavior and in the adaptability of the couple relationship to other styles of behavior. For example, if her loss of arousal is linked to a very different sexual timetable with her partner and the partner is not able to change their cycle of need for sexual activity, then this may prevent any therapeutic work, despite the woman's actual motivation to change herself. A variety of specific assessment activities can be used with a couple to try to help them understand how they function together at a sexual level and some of the reasons. These activities can be part of the session work (structural intervention), or they may be set as tasks (strategic intervention) for the couple to carry out at home to bring back to a later session. Systemically, activities rather than "heavy discussion" can be more useful, acting as creative interventions, than reflection or reviewing of the past.

A decision as to whether the woman can be offered a physical treatment without going through an extended assessment may happen when there is a clear temporal recollection of physical symptoms that precedes other complaints or difficulties (Althof et al., 2005)

Sex Therapy Assessment Activities

We have chosen to describe a horticultural view of therapy, with the goal of a *green, organic garden* being representational of the healthy couple relationship. We have therefore described the process in a gardening concept to draw on this easily understood and commonly appreciated metaphor. For example, the woman with a physical aetiology may need to nurture the garden plants already growing by pruning, feeding, and strengthening her arousal skills that are still functioning. The concept of sexual activity being considered natural only if it is spontaneous is usually unhelpful. Activity can be reframed as needing to be chosen, grown, nurtured, and worked for by the individual and couple and is used through our assessment and thereafter within the treatment options. A number of these assessment activities can be carried out during the session together or may be given to carry out at home as a task. The following concepts of therapeutic tools available to therapists for use can be viewed as helping the woman to nurture any available sexual arousal that is still present or to develop and grow new arousal ability where she has not experienced it before.

Diagnostic check of the garden's ability to grow. This introductory work may benefit by checking the different individual goals held, and this can be linked to level of priorities for other areas of the relationship that appear to need work or change.

Complex tools to measure garden growth. In order to ascertain the changes in growth, we need to use adequate outcome measures for changes in relational and sexual activity in terms of satisfaction and confidence for each individual, and to gage how they decrease couple inhibition and behavioral skills.

All of these activities and topics may be vital to explore and investigate to ascertain some of the reasons why the couple has come and to identify their individual motivation for improving arousal issues in the relationship. However, after the initial issues other problems may be identified that may be more complex or deep-seated.

Case Example (Assessment)

Alice, age 36, with two children aged seven and five, attended a couple therapy session and was obviously distressed by the situation she had described on her assessment sheet as relationship deterioration due to her problems with lack of excitement and sensation and now lack of desire as well. She discussed this more fully in the session, especially the anxiety that she had about the relationship that in the past had also been a problem for her, resulting in separation from her first husband. Only a year ago Alice and her partner, Andrew, had separated for a month. The issue that led to repeated friction was usually her low desire for sexual activity, lack of satisfaction with any activity she engaged in, and her unhappiness at her genitalia being so unresponsive because they were dry and often sore after any lovemaking with Andrew.

Alice felt the problem had been present since the birth of her second child, who was now aged five. The low desire seemed continuous since that time; however, there seemed to have been a 5-year history of poor arousal with very little evidence of physical arousal on stimulation. She could recall two occasions when she had experienced sexual interest and had initiated sexual activity with Andrew, but with little sexual satisfaction. Therefore, this had not led to an increase in desire but had caused confusion, and she often reviewed these two occasions, trying to find the clue to what had gone wrong. On exploring more closely her reason for her attending the appointment, it became clear that her motivation for attending was not straightforward. She felt well in herself, and she would be quite happy to never engage in a sexual relationship again. However, although she was sad at her partner's distress over this lost dimension of their lives, she did not appear to wish to improve her sexual activity just for his benefit. Alice said that she had tried often to do this, and it just upset her more as she was so dry and unsatisfied. As the therapist's understanding of the woman deepened, the therapist realized that the woman's main aim was to correct the poor couple image that her daughters were receiving from them. "They never see us being warm," she commented. "They don't know how parents should be.

They are getting old enough to comment on couple behavior on TV and compare it with their experience at home." All of her children's attitudes seemed to reflect what was not normal in her relationship and what she was failing as a mother to do in giving them better guidelines and standards.

The therapeutic work remained difficult even when the patient had high motivation, but Alice was not aware of any personal reason for her to engage in the therapy. Alice appeared willing to work at improving the arousal disorder in order to give her children a better appreciation of couple's relationships. Her priority was to give the best to her children. The main gain for her was to know that the children see both her and Andrew as a more warm and affectionate couple and to experience an ability to include affection as a family activity.

Physical Examination and Physiological Assessments (Tests)

A general examination of the cardiovascular, neurovascular, and endocrine status should be carried out. A focused physical examination of the gynecological system includes examination of the external genitalia. This will include looking at skin turgor and thickness and any abnormalities in the distribution and amount of pubic hair, which may all signify a degree of atrophy. The vaginal mucosa on inspection and the pH may change with atrophic changes, and other pathologies may be identified. The physical examination will often provide the opportunity for the physician to educate the patient about anatomy and sexual function.

In specific cases where it is deemed appropriate to assess genital arousal, several options are possible including intravaginal photoplesmography, the Gold Sheffield Electrode, and measurement of labial temperature (see Goldstein, Meston, Davis, & Traish, 2006). Doppler ultrasonography is a further investigation that may be useful to assess clitoral blood flow. Pressure stimulation along the lower third of the vagina increased blood velocity and flow into the clitoral arteries in 9 out of the 10 women. Blood flow increases at 4 to 11 times baseline pre-stimulation level were noted (Lavoisier, Aloui, Schmidt, & Watrelot, 1995).

Treatment Options in Couples Sex Therapy

These can be summarized as reducing response anxiety; reframing the problem to become couple oriented rather than specific end organ focused; attending to any comorbid affective, cognitive, emotional, and behavioral aspects of the FSI/AD, including those that may be exacerbated by the response and behavior of the partner; normalizing the commonality of the condition.

Though we may advocate a multi-factorial and interdisciplinary approach to dealing with any problems of FSI/AD that may be multi-etiological in causation, it is important to try to present this to the individual and to the couple as succinctly and as simply as possible. By doing so, the likelihood of instilling faith and confidence will be improved. Identifying treatment priorities and making incremental and gradual changes are beneficial. Most of the work is done in a strategic sense insofar as therapeutic interventions suggest activities outside the session (i.e., maneuvers and exercises outside of the therapeutic session rather than within ("structural").

Sexual intimacy is promoted by encouraging the couple to share their ideas about what it means to be intimate, identifying discrepancies in their definitions, and working towards a common meaning (Weeks, Hertlein, & Gambescia, 2009). The therapist helps the couple to understand that intimacy and sex are not distinct entities and that as they create obstacles to intimacy, these barriers may inhibit sexual desire. In addition, the inevitability of "disaster days" and "relapse inevitability" must be addressed. We encourage the couple to define the problem in simple terms and by identifying these specific concerns and breaking down the components into their most reducible and definable form. The aim should be to provide the opportunity for the couple to explore these without any immediacy or threat of scrutiny by focusing not just on these intensely investigated sequences of the courtship ritual. We strongly encourage couples to become as intimate as they feel comfortable, and, if necessary, we will encourage them to find ways of deepening their relationship, starting initially with the sensate focus program and encouraging regularity of the process on the basis that "practice makes perfect." Fears of intimacy, the consequences of sexual activity (e.g., pregnancy, infection), and the need to ensure commitment to a prolonged (yet fruitful) relationship together may need substantial exploration.

Some simple maneuvers that are important in the early stages include ensuring adequate education about sexual response and setting boundaries for what is acceptable and unacceptable behavior, whether this is arguments between the couple or their sexual activities with each other. We always encourage couples to have time together, including quality time in the evening where childcare facilities may be necessary. See Box 9.1 for resources.

It is our belief that treatment is most effective and efficacious in terms of time and therapist-patient involvement if an Intersystem Approach is used for the management of this complex and often difficult-to-treat clinical scenario. Time spent during the initial assessment can glean valuable information that allows for a substantial collection of information about the woman and, where relevant, her partner or partners. By offering an inclusive assessment that asks about physical, psychological, and relationship issues, the woman will be afforded the opportunity to reflect on the importance of why each of these areas is being examined and why information is being gathered as part of the holistic assessment. It should therefore be much less of a surprise when a package of care and intervention is presented that has more than one treatment modality.

Box 9.1 Patient Educational Material

Title	Author	Publisher
New Male Sexuality	Bernie Zilbergeld	Bantam 1999 ISBN 0553 38042-7
Perfectly Normal	Sandra Perfot	Rodale 2005
She Comes First	Ian Kerner	PerfectBound 2004 ISBN: 0060729678
Becoming Orgasmic	Julia Heiman and Joseph LoPiccolo	Platkins 1999
The Mirror Within	Anne Dickson	Quartet Books 1999 ISBN 0704 33474-7
Integrating Sex Therapy Interventions with Couple Therapy	Barry McCarthy and Maria Thestrup	*Journal of Contemporary Psychotherapy*, 38(3), 139–149. doi: 10.1007/ s10879-008-9083-3

Early on in therapy, we want to understand clearly what it is that both partners are hoping to achieve whilst attending the clinical service. For some, this is no more than a restoration of clinical function, and any attempt to identify psychological or "head originated" issues will be rejected, sometimes forcefully by one or both partners. Some example tools are listed in Table 9.1, Table 9.2, and Table 9.3.

Table 9.1 Assessment Checklist

- Previous medical and psychosexual history sent to clients and obtained from each partner
- Five different components of Intersystem Approach assessed for
  - What does each partner bring into the relationship; psychosexual histories
- Women's psychological makeup (values, attitudes, opinions, general intelligence, general upbringing, and any psychopathology)
- Relational aspects of the couple
- Family-of-origin
- Environmental, societal, cultural, religious, and historical factors
- Preliminary assessment
  - Assessment for both partners attending treatment
  - Discussion of how treatment works with both partners
  - Assess for who is distressed about the inhibited arousal and details surrounding that
- Cultural assessment activities
  - Initial review of motivation to grow
  - Diagnostic introductory check of ability to grow
  - Complex tools to measure or assess garden growth
    - Tree climbing
    - Reviewing the relational roots
    - Genogram of growth
    - Body image or plant diagrams
    - Beliefs about sexual issues and reasons for healthy growth
    - Reviewing past storm damage
    - Knowledge of gardening
    - Relooking at the flowerbed

Case Example—Continued (Treatment)

Physical treatment and couples sex therapy were offered in an integrated manner (Daines & Hallam-Jones, 2007). What did Alice and Andrew choose? Alice initially appeared to be more interested in the assessment process than the treatment. She was keen to find out what had caused the problem and to understand it. However, as the sessions progressed and she realized that there were a variety of causes and treatment options, she shared that she had previously expected that there would be no actual successful treatment. She had felt that, by coming to the clinic, the most useful thing she would achieve was a chance to talk about it and to share how difficult it had been. By being given the option of discussing physical treatments she became much more interested in the possibility of there being real choices to make. She did want to discuss the problems that she and Andrew were having in further detail and valued the opportunity to choose couple therapy. At the same time she wanted to be assessed for whether any physical treatment options were suitable or available for her. Alice had her blood hormone levels measured, which revealed borderline testosterone levels. However, Alice was eager to try an unlicensed medical option concurrent with the couple therapy.

Table 9.2 Couple Sex Therapy Treatment Tools

Objectives	Activities
Behavioral This can be viewed as the patient pruning and training the plants to grow in the chosen direction. Need to understand the couple changes needed and see why and what training is required. Often the initial training needed is sexual education physical, anatomy and physiology, and psychological and cognitive and emotional education, which may take longer to absorb and understand the complex issues.	It may be useful to make a list of the changes needed in the order of difficulty. Then, starting with the priorities at the lowest level of difficulty, work towards changing the behavior that is relevant to the sexual dysfunction. This may utilize an individual sexual growth program and may use the "Becoming Orgasmic" focus (Heiman & LoPiccolo, 1999). For example, for Alice and Andrew the level of physical intimacy was experienced as limited so the list of suitable physical contacts was made. The easiest was set first, to regularly increase physical intimacy. This is vital to improve the physical contact needs to begin to gain physical and psychological arousal. Newly gained behavioral skills must be rehearsed regularly and the skills must continue to be developed to prevent the skills stagnating again.
Systemic 1. Multiple Nutrients The interdependence of the (garden) couple means that by changing the interdependence of plant nutrients and feed material (i.e., hormonal chemical intake) the structure can be altered.	Medication prescribed is not only a sexual medicine issue; it may also be a systemic intervention as one change (e.g., resolving an anemic state) may bring about becoming more alert, energized, and so more interested to work and improve her ability for physical arousal.
Systemic 2. Breaking the Weed Power Chain This can be achieved by regular weeding, reviewing, decreasing, and removing couple problem areas, friction, and misunderstanding or by keeping the area full, growing other plants (e.g., more couple time together, more opportunity to feed back and review events together).	This may involve the use of sensate focus as a means of encouraging intimacy but without allowing the problem areas of higher arousal (later stages). Banning this higher level of arousal to prevent anxiety and failure may, of course, systemically produce more desire and even activity from them both. This stage involves keeping the watering system functioning, the need to ensure the "love" water barrels are kept topped up, and the need to assist the couple and ensure that they supply and obtain adequate love and support from the partner and their friends, often not from the family. This adequate supply enables them to share warmth, support, and encouragement with each other— love tanks.
Systemic 3. Complex Integration Work	Growth in different areas needs to be achieved. Options for treatment are often more successful, particularly in the short term, if a behavioral systemic integrated approach is used. Behavioral work can include sex education, by adding an increased range of possible sexual behaviors or by altering the attitude of the couples to differing acceptability behavior. The therapist will need to establish a directory of what activities the couple find more helpful and how they want to re-engage in intimacy. So, what choices do couples often make for treatment?
Systemic 4. Replanting the Healthy Growth	Couple activities that she is working on with her partner are encouraged. Because Alice had chosen this combined integrated approach there was of necessity a very important need for communication between the different clinicians involved. The couple therapist, for example, needed to understand what physical treatment options were being utilized and when changes in treatment occurred.

Table 9.3 Couple Sex Therapy Treatments (2)

Systemic 5. *Retraining the Vine* Package of individual sexual growth (ISG) program.	At this point there will be other activities that will be important to begin to integrate into this pattern using the body (color) mapping discussed earlier in the assessment. This now becomes part of the individual sexual growth (ISG) program where we look at the areas that were seen as green and acceptable and encourage more personal time and attention to be lavished on those areas whilst moving into the yellow areas to allow these areas more opportunity to be sensuous and acceptable to the individual. As time progresses and these areas are covered and improved, the therapist will suggest a move towards including the least red of the red areas (i.e,. the least difficult) and gradually then move towards the more difficult areas, which tend to be either areas of high sexual connotation or areas linked to abuse or negative experience.
Systemic 6. *Re-planning* *the Touch* Vulval massage and desensitization of the vulval area.	What is meant by vulval massage? The concept of touching the genitalia could have been a negative experience, for instance, all touch of the vulval area may have been viewed as a painful experience, preventing the patient being open to re-focusing on sexual touch. By increasing touch of sexual tissue via a clinical exercise the therapist can help to open up alternative ways of experiencing touch—this may not rapidly move the sensations from negative to positive but, for example, the use of vulval massage may initially just provide the patient with a system to allow a small area of vulval tissue to be touched without discomfort. This neutral experience can be increased in area, frequency, and intensity to, hopefully, work towards altering one's beliefs about the impossibility of touch being a positive activity and to allow experimentation of possible tissue arousal.
Systemic 7. *Wake Up the New* *Growth Buds* Versatile vibrators.	This area of new growth of arousal may lead to the possibility of using specific appropriate sexual toys and aids to increase sensitivity and variety of sensation to improve arousal. The new highly versatile vibrators can be very successful at providing alternative stimulation of the nervous systems' responsiveness. This also needs to be linked to the use of an adequate lubrication to ensure that the new growth of sensitive tissues is encouraged with this protective aid.
Systemic 8. *Connecting the* *Vines Together* Sensate focus—SFO and ISG	These areas then become integrated as they are more sensually perceived into the sensate focus with the partner so the process is desensitizing the areas, moving them into the individual sexual growth program and then moving them into the sensate focus. This is a complicated piece of work made more difficult by the fact that one continually needs to look not only at the patients' needs but also at the needs of the partner, including the sexual needs of the partner. He or she is not a mere bystander but is actively involved in this and may need to be helped to support his partner and needs to feel that his own issues are regularly reviewed and supported. Time needs to be given to helping him engage in his own sexual satisfaction, either by him or with his partner's support and this can be helped by a variety of ways.
Systemic 9a. *Feeding Both Plants* Male related activities	It is important to give plenty of support to the couple as they learn more about their sexual needs. By helping Andrew to be able to voice his sexual needs and say how he would like them met, adds balance to the work carried out. This raises the huge issue of allowing space for the partner, as well as encouragement and a chance to develop their own sexual and masturbation practices. This needs to be seen by the couple as part of the learning experience of the couple, and the therapist will be working toward helping the couple understand and accept the need for Andrew to have a much wider repertoire of sexual activity and to understand his own body better. This will need to be working within the context of the individual and couple's religious, ethnic, and cultural beliefs and lifestyle.

Systemic 9b. *Feeding Both Plants* Male related activities	Finding what Andrew's other needs are is important, and ensuring that in the concentration on sexual issues we have not colluded with Alice to ignore these needs such as social time with his own peers and other activities that enhance his lifestyle. This is a period of intense growth for both partners in the relationship, and the therapist will be working hard with the couple, holding them emotionally as they try these new tasks. Often this can be difficult as their lifestyle will still have other stressors which may occur and may appear to be taking priority again.
Systemic 9c. *Feeding Both Plants* Male related activities	In addition, often couples systemically hold to the stuck position by bringing in new stressors so as to prevent the changes from occurring. An example of this would be a couple that start therapy and then decide they want to do the kitchen extension. It is important to discuss before commencing and during therapy, the need for this to be a priority area and the building projects, etc., need to be allowed to wait until therapy has achieved its goals. Other members of the family, including the children, may also join in this prevention of movement and maintenance of the status quo, by creating their own crises, so as "to help" the parents to remain the same.
Systemic 10. *Attaching the* *Walkways or Talking* *to Flowers*	All of these discussions on therapy issues are going to raise the therapist and couples' awareness of any communication issues that exist between them. Any changes that a couple make in their relationship also demonstrate, because of the possible friction involved, the weak spots in terms of how well they explain what they want, how well they listen to each other, and how well they are able to adapt their thinking to new ideas. It is, therefore, vital that this part of the therapy assesses and provides treatment options to improve communication skills. These communication skills can be taught during therapy or may again be set as activities that can be carried out at home (see Crowe and Ridley, 2000). Non-verbal communication may also be important, and this is not only touch (SFO and ISG). For example, a positive effect of male fragrance on genital arousal during erotic fantasy was noted in one study but only during the follicular phase (Graham, Janssen, & Sanders, 2000) with the effect not being mediated by any effects of fragrance on mood.
Systemic 11. *Re-establishing the* *Plants*	Sex growth in individuals cannot occur without permission giving to change. Not changing and staying with the status quo is usually much easier. Some individuals can use self-motivation and insight to aid the growth and re-rooting in new behaviors but often it requires partner encouragement which is difficult to achieve when they are trapped in the same cycles. The couple therapist may be used or seen as an agent for change and re-establishment of the plant by "giving permission" to move, or alter growth. Giving suggestions of possible growth behavior, prescribing changed activities, or modeling acceptance of new actions, roles, and diversity may all be useful and may help to decrease the power of previous familial models (e.g., by parents and family), or unhelpful patterns of relating and arousal.
Systemic 12. *Limiting Movement* Restricting the sexual activity	Constricting or preventing movement may help to encourage or strengthen growth. Often the systemic action of restricting the couples' sexual activity may increase their confidence in the area they are already inhabiting/using but it could lead to the combining of the couples' energy to resist the constriction and lead to more powerful couple strength to resist the therapist's ideas and become more independent. Placing a ban on arousal may make her more relaxed about it occurring or make her more determined to work at experiencing it again.

(Continued)

Table 9.3 (Continued)

Systemic 13. Prescribing or Alternating Symptoms	Giving one individual the chance to live with, practice, and gain understanding how it is to live with the other partner's symptoms can be helpful to both members of the couple relationship. For instance, having no desire or experiencing jealousy can isolate and prevent understanding or support from a partner as they are often reactive to those situations. Imagining experiencing the "other's" symptoms of inhibited arousal for a short period of time may be helpful. How much more quickly can a patient gain insight into a partner's response once they have felt the reality of the symptoms?
Systemic 14. Spelling out the Cost of No Growth	Growth takes effort and time, and couples who put in the energy or cost to enable them to reframe or change will need to give rewards to each other for that change to occur. However, no growth or change also has a more negative cost to the system. Seeking help for the sexual issues can enable a stuck system to be reviewed and the consequences considered such as divorce, separation, or remaining in an entrenched stance.
Systemic 15. Reversing Plant Positions Roles	The situations we occupy allows for our view of the present situation— changing positions in the plot allow a couple to see the world from a different (partner's) perspective—tasks swapped can allow a different appreciation of the role taken in the relationship and the pressures and lack of support that may be available for that role. Giving Andrew the role for a week of never achieving arousal made him feel left out and deprived. This helped him afterwards to spend time and effort to include Alice in differing ways of experiencing warmth.
Systemic 16. Accepting the Stunted Plant Adapting to reality or loss—or using it as a new focus	The inability to change may be the focus for anger and sadness but a reframe, if considered, can allow this stuckness to be a new stability to base other change on. For example, Alice may not experience high levels of sexual arousal, but she can learn not to worry about arousal and work on her ability to relax and enjoy the time we give to lovemaking as valuable couple space. A more common difficulty experienced with women with inhibited arousal is that their motivation for intimacy may come from a very different source then their partners. The concept of differing sexual languages and differing intimacy languages is probably important to explain why men with their activity-orientated language demonstrate their love by being sexual (e.g., "I care about you. The proof that I care about you is that I physically desire you and initiate sexual activity towards you"). The woman's language may be much more emotional and verbal and says, "Because I care about you and I love you I then am willing to be sexual as evidence of my emotion." This is difficult because when the woman does not choose to be sexual, the result may be a perception by the male partner, that this means that she does not love him. It is difficult for a man in such a situation to understand that his partner does not necessarily link her ability to be sexual with her ability to show love. This can be divisive and source of confusion for many couples. It can become the cause of secondary desire disorder because a woman who does not wish to be sexual may still want the intimacy of cuddles and hugs and may want to know that it will not lead any further and so she need not be worried about the consequences. However, the male activity language may suggest that: "If I can't do it properly it is better not to start," and therefore the couple's inability to carry out his concept of a full sexual range of behaviors may mean his withdrawal and lack of intimacy. The woman with "desire disorder" may actually crave intimacy and yet not "desire" penetrative sexual activity. This can make the diagnosis even more difficult, as she may express distress at the lack of intimacy and no distress at the lack of sexual activity.

In couple therapy, the sensate focus is used not only as a diagnostic tool but also as a treatment option. Often the therapist will integrate into the couple's behavioral work an individual sexual growth program as a separate individual piece, and a series of exercises that the patient can commit to that will aid the other behavioral activities that can be introduced.

To assess these issues, the therapist has to understand the differing languages the couple are using and help them to understand their different meanings. The therapist should help the couple identify what intimacy means to them and what it is that they have lost or want to regain. This can be achieved from a behavioral standpoint by asking the couple to list the 10 things that they would want to regain in the relationship and then to systematically work through how to achieve those in the therapy program. From a systemic point of view, the therapist could look at how the couple can break the current stuck pattern of non-intimacy by inducing intimacy from a different standpoint and seeing whether this had any effect of changing the whole of the intimacy relationship—for example, "I don't want sex but I do want a holiday in April. I will have sex three times in March and we will then have a holiday in April." The concept of female plasticity may be useful for women to understand that women can change their minds and enjoy different sexual activities if they allow a positive attitude to accompany the new experiences (see Baumeister, 2001).

Finally, to understand the whole system before commencing a therapy program it is vital that the therapists spend adequate time assessing which sexual activities the couple have actually carried out between sessions. It is hard to have sexual desire if you have only ever learnt to do one kind of sexual activity in one particular way and that particular way is now removed from you due to illness or body discomfort or change in situations. An example of this is the couple that have only ever had limited foreplay and sex in the missionary position, which becomes impossible if the position becomes too painful for an individual. Adaptability is fairly difficult to achieve with no alternatives; therefore, assessment includes ascertaining exactly which behaviors they use, have tried, and have found helpful in the past. This may give some excellent starting points or clues as to how to progress in therapy and some insights into possible outcome levels.

Physical Treatments. Currently, there are no licensed agents for the treatment of desire or arousal problems in women. Research and development of potential molecules continues with limited success although use of existing agents is also under review. Recent studies have identified that low sexual desire in women may result from a relative insensitivity of the brain for sexual cues. Administration of sublingual testosterone increases the sensitivity of the brain to sexual cues. Sexual stimulation in the brain is necessary for phosphodiesterase type 5 inhibitor (PDE5i)-mediated increases in genital sexual response. On demand use of both testosterone and a PDE5i, particularly in women with low sensitivity for sexual cues, is reported as a potentially promising treatment combination for women with desire and arousal problems (Poels et al., 2013).

Estrogen delivered locally into the vagina as low dose natural estrogens (estradiol tablet or ring or estradiol pessaries) improves both menopausal vaginal atrophy and symptoms of dryness, pain, and discomfort (Simunic et al., 2003; Tan, Bradshaw, & Carr, 2012).

A study showed that tibolone, a synthetic steroid hormone drug that influences the synthesis and metabolism of estrogen, was associated with significant improvement in sexual function in postmenopausal women.

Significant increase in vaginal blood flow in response to erotic fantasy but not to visual material suggests two possible pathways of female sexual response (Laan, Van Lunsen, &

Everaerd, 2001). This follows previous work by Laan, Everaerd, van Bellen, and Hanewald (1994) showing that the largest contribution to female sexual excitement resulted in the processing of stimulus content and stimulus meaning in video material—especially when the film was made by women, since those made by men evoked more feelings of shame, guilt, and aversion. Sexuality around menopause is an area that needs much more attention, for there is considerable ignorance both at clinician and patient level. This matter is addressed further by Wylie (2006b) and Wylie et al. (2007). In addition, the need to optimize clinical interventions for sexual difficulties of any type within a relationship may require considerable psychosexual and psychological maneuvers (Wylie, 2006a).

Prognostic Planning. Before concluding, we need to consider prognostic factors that may be positive for therapy to be experienced as supportive, the primary of which must be the intention to experience positive sexual arousal. This may be inhibited or ameliorated by patients who have a number of comorbid conditions—particularly patients with psychiatric conditions. Reduced situational life stresses are inevitably a positive indicator of success of any type of intervention, whether this is physiological or pharmacological or psychological. Of primary importance is ensuring that any anxiety that may be present, however real to the individual or couple, is addressed, and suitable maneuvers to manage this are established early on. In addition, sharing the problem and accepting and recognizing as well as acknowledging this to be the case is important. Exploring these problems, including any intergenerational legacies and environmental messages that may affect or interfere with sexual intimacy, may well improve the likelihood of positive response to any subsequent therapeutic exercises.

Conclusion

We emphasize that the complexity of female sexual interest/arousal disorder requires a thorough assessment to identify the possible multiple issues that are contributing to the etiology. However, the patient can expect the therapists to have an array of tools to use for these issues and, where necessary, to integrate the physical, relational, and psychological interventions into the change process and growth work that the couple are encouraged to commence.

References

Althof, S. E., Dean, J., Derogatis, L. R., Rosen, R. C., & Sisson, M. (2005). Current perspectives on the clinical assessment and diagnosis of female sexual dysfunction and clinical studies of potential therapies: A statement of concern. *Journal of Sexual Medicine*, 2(S3), 146–153.

American Psychiatric Association (APA). (2000). *Diagnostic and statistical manual of mental disorders* (4th ed., text rev.). Washington, DC: Author.

American Psychiatric Association (APA). (2013). *Diagnostic and statistical manual of mental disorders* (5th ed.). Arlington, VA: Author.

Basson, R., Berman, J., & Bernett, A. (2000). Report of the international consensus development conference on female sexual dysfunction: definitions and classifications. *Journal of Urology*, 163(3), 888–893. doi: 10.1097/00005392-200003000-00043

Basson, R., Wierman, M. E., van Lankveld, J., & Brotto, L. (2010). Summary of the recommendations on sexual dysfunctions in women. *Journal of Sexual Medicine*, 7, 314–326. doi: 10.1111/j.1743-6109.2009.01617.x

Baumeister, R. (2001). *Social psychology and human sexuality*. Philadelphia, PA: Taylor and Francis.

Bradley, P. D., & Fine, R. W. (2009). The medicalization of sex therapy: A call to action for therapists. *Journal of Systemic Therapies*, 28(2), 75–88. doi: 10.1521/jsyt.2009.28.2.75

Brotto, L. (2013). *Classifying sexual dysfunction*. Vancouver: UBC Sexual Health Lab. University of British Columbia Department of Obstetrics and Gynaecology. Retrieved from http://www.obgyn.ubc.ca/SexualHealth/sexual_dysfunctions/index.php

Brotto, L. A., Bitzer, J., Laan, E., Leiblum, S., & Luria, M. (2010). Women's sexual desire and arousal disorders. *Journal of Sexual Medicine, 7*, 586–614. doi: 10.1111/j.1743–6109.2009.01630.x

Bulow, S. (2009). Integrating sex and couples therapy: A multifaceted case history. *Family Process, 48*(3), 379–389. doi: 10.1111/j.1545–5300.2009.01289.x

Byers, E. S. (2005). Relationship satisfaction and sexual satisfaction: A longitudinal study of individuals in long-term relationships. *Journal of Sex Research, 42*, 113–118. doi: 10.1080/00224490509552264

Crowe, M., & Ridley, J. (2000).*A behavioural-systems approach to couple relationship and sexual problems: Therapy with Couples*. Hobooken, NJ: Wiley-Blackwell.

Daines, B., & Hallam-Jones, R. (2007). Multifaceted intervention sex therapy. *Sexual and Relationship Therapy, 22*(3), 339–350. doi: 10.1080/14681990701413766

Dennerstein, L., Koochaki, P., Barton, I., & Graziottin, A. (2006). Hypoactive sexual desire disorder in menopausal women: A survey of Western European women. *Journal of Sexual Medicine, 3*, 212–222. doi: 10.1111/j.1743–6109.2006.00215.x

DeRogatis, L. R., Rust, J., Golombok, S., Bouchard, C., Nachtigall, L., Rodenberg, C., . . . McHorney, C. A. (2004). Validation of the profile of female sexual function (PFSF) in surgically and naturally menopausal women. *Journal of Sex and Marital Therapy, 30*, 25–36.

Giraldi, A., Rellini, A. H., Pfaus, J., & Laan, E. (2013). Female sexual arousal disorders. *Journal of Sexual Medicine, 10*, 58–73. doi: 10.1111/j.1743–6109.2012.02820.x

Goldstein, I., Meston, C. M., Davis, S. R., & Traish, M. A. (2006). *Women's sexual function and dysfunction*. Philadelphia, PA: Taylor and Francis.

Graham, C. A., Janssen, E., & Sanders, S. A. (2000). Effects of fragrance on female sexual arousal and mood across the menstrual cycle. *Psychophysiology, 37*(1), 76–84. doi: 10.1111/1469–8986.3710076

Heiman, J., & LoPiccolo, J. (1999). *Becoming orgasmic*. London: Piatkus Books.

Kaplan, H. (1979). *Disorders of sexual desire*. New York: Brunner/Mazel.

Laan, E., Everaerd, W., van Bellen, G., & Hanewald, G. (1994). Women'ss sexual and emotional responses to male- and female-produced erotica. *Archives of Sexual Behavior, 23*(2), 153–169.

Laan, E., Van Lunsen, R. H., & Everaerd, W. (2001). The effects of tibolone on vaginal blood flow, sexual desire and arousability in postmenopausal women. *Climacteric, 4*(1), 28–41. doi: 10.1080/cmt.4.1.28.41

Lavoisier, P., Aloui, R., Schmidt, M., & Watrelot, A. (1995). Vaginal stimulation increases clitoral blood flow. *Sexologies, 2*(8), 30–33.

Lewis, R. W., Fugl-Meyer, K. S., Bosch, R., Fugl-Meyer, A. R., Laumann, E. O., Lizza, E., & Martin-Morales, A. (2004). Epidemiology/risk factors of sexual dysfunction. *Journal of Sexual Medicine, 1*(1), 35–39. doi: 10.1111/j.1743–6109.2004.10106.x

Markovic, D. (2010). A case of enhancing sexual confidence: Both the client and the therapist are the experts. *The Australian and New Zealand Journal of Family Therapy, 31*(1), 13–24. doi: 10.1375/anft.31.1.13

Markovic, D. (2013). Multidimensional psychosexual therapy: A model of integration between sexology and systemic therapy. *Sexual and Relationship Therapy, 28*(4), 311–323. doi: 10.1080/14681994.2013.845656

Masters, W. H. & Johnson, V. E. (1966). *Human sexual response*. Boston: Little, Brown.

Maurice, W. L. (2003). Sexual medicine, mental illness and mental health profession. *Sexual and Relationship Therapy, 18*, 7–12.

McCarthy, B., & Thestrup, M. (2008). Integrating sex therapy interventions with couple therapy. *Journal of Contemporary Psychotherapy, 38*, 139–149. doi: 10.1111/j.1545–5300.2009.01289

Meston, C. M. (2003). Validation of the Female Sexual Function Index (FSFI) in women with female orgasmic disorder and in women with hypoactive sexual desire disorder. *Journal of Sex and Marital Therapy, 29*, 39–46. doi: 10.1080/713847100

Moreira, E. D. Jr., Brock, G., Glasser, D. B., Nicolosi, A., Laumann, E. O., Paik, A., . . . GSSAB Investigators' Group. (2005). Help seeking behaviour for sexual problems: The global study of sexual attitudes and behaviors. *International Journal of Clinical Practice, 59*(1), 6–16. doi: 10.1111/j.1742–1241.2005.00382.x

Poels, S., Bloemers J., van Rooij, K., Goldstein, I., Gerritsen, J., van Ham, D., . . . Tuiten, A. (2013). Toward personalized sexual medicine (part 2): Testosterone combined with a PDE5 inhibitor increases sexual satisfaction in women with HSDD and FSAD, and a low sensitive system for sexual cues. *Journal of Sexual Medicine, 10,* 810–823. doi: 10.1111/j.1743–6109.2012.02983.x

Rosen, R., Brown, C., Heiman, J., Leiblum, S., Meston, C., Shabsigh, R., . . . D'Agostino, R., Jr. (2000). The Female Sexual Function Index (FSFI): A multidimensional self-reported instrument for the assessment of female sexual function. *Journal of Sex and Marital Therapy, 26,* 191–208. doi: 10.1080/009262300278597

Sills, T., Wunderlich, G., Pyke, R., Segraves, R. T., Leiblum, S., Clayton, A., . . . Evans, K. (2005). The Sexual Interest and Desire Inventory-Female (SIDI-F): Item response analyses of data from women diagnosed with hypoactive sexual desire disorder. *Journal of Sexual Medicine, 2,* 801–818.

Simunic, V., Banovic, I., Ciglar, S., Jeren, L., Pavicic Baldani, D., & Sprem, M. (2003). Local oestrogen treatment in patients with urogenital symptoms. *International Journal of Gynaecology and Obstetrics, 82*(2), 187–197.

Tan, O., Bradshaw, K., & Carr, B.R. (2012). Management of vulvovaginal atrophy-related sexual dysfunction in postmenopausal women: An up-to-date review. *Menopause, 19,* 109–117. doi: 10.1097/gme.0b013e31821f92df

Weeks, G. (1994). The intersystem model: An integrative approach to treatment. In G. Weeks & L. Hof (Eds.), *The marital-relationship casebook: Theory and application of the intersystem model* (pp. 3–34). New York: Brunner/Mazel.

Weeks, G. (2005). The emergence of a new paradigm in sex therapy: Integration. *Sexual and Relationship Therapy, 20*(1), 89–103.

Weeks, G. R., Hertlein, K. M., & Gambescia, N. (2009). The treatment of hypoactive sexual desire disorder. In K. M. Hertlein, G. R. Weeks, & N. Gambescia (Eds.), *Systemic sex therapy.* New York: Routledge.

World Health Organization. (1992). *The ICD-10 classification of mental and behavioural disorders: Clinical descriptions and diagnostic guidelines.* Geneva: World Health Organization.

Wylie, K. R. (2006a). Sexuality and the menopause. *Journal of the British Menopause Society, 12*(4), 149–152.

Wylie, K. R. (2006b). Optimising clinical interventions for sexual difficulties within a relationship. *Journal of Men's Health and Gender, 4,* 650–655.

Wylie, K. R., Daines, B., Jannini, E. A., Hallam-Jones, R., Bould, L., Wilson, L., . . . Kristensen, E. (2007). Loss of sexual desire in the postmenopausal woman. *Journal of Sexual Medicine, 4,* 395–405. doi: 10.1111/j.1743–6109.2006.00419.x

Yeh, H. C., Lorenz, F. O., Wickrama, K. A., Conger, R. D., & Elder, G. H., Jr. (2006). Relationships among sexual satisfaction, marital quality and marital instability at midlife. *Journal of Family Psychology, 20,* 339–343. doi: 0.1037/0893–3200.20.2.339

Yule, M., Woo, J, & Brotto, L. (2010). Sexual arousal in East Asian and Euro-Canadian women: A psychophysiological study. *The Journal of Sexual Medicine, 7,* 3066–3079.

10

FEMALE ORGASMIC DISORDER

Marita P. McCabe

Definition and Description of Disorder

Female orgasmic disorder is defined as either "marked delay in, marked infrequency of, absence of orgasm or markedly reduced intensity of orgasmic sensations" (APA, 2013, p. 429). The symptoms need to be present for a minimum of about 6 months, cause distress, and not be better explained by another psychological disorder, severe relationship problems, or be due to the effects of a substance/medication or a medical disorder.

Current diagnostic criteria of female sexual dysfunction (FSD) vary across diagnostic categories. The *Diagnostic and Statistical Manual of Mental Disorders*, 5th ed. (*DSM-5*, APA, 2013) categories are limited to psychiatric disorders and reflect the traditional linear models of sexual response (Kaplan, 1979; Masters & Johnson, 1966). Having said this, the latest *DSM* has combined desire and arousal disorders for women, reflecting the high level of comorbidity between those two disorders. The *DSM-5* classifies female orgasmic disorder as one of a number of sexual dysfunctions for women. This diagnostic category is further specified as lifelong or acquired or generalized or situational. Lifelong refers to cases in which the woman has never been able to be orgasmic where acquired refers to cases where the woman has had the ability in the past to be orgasmic. Generalized cases are diagnosed when a women does not have the ability to orgasm in any situation (i.e., not with any partner or even in masturbation or fantasy) whereas situational orgasm disorder refers to cases where the woman can experience orgasm in certain contexts but not in others. Additional criteria require that the dysfunction causes the subjective experience of marked distress. However, specification of the occurrence of the dysfunctional (frequency, settings, activities, and encounters) is not taken into account.

There are also different ways to experience orgasms. While some literature discusses the types as either being a clitorial or vaginal orgasm (i.e., Brody & Weiss, 2010; Komisaruk et al., 2004), "The names don't actually indicate different types of orgasms, but indicate the type of genital stimulation triggering the orgasm" (Wallen & Lloyd, 2010, p. 781). Likewise, Laan and Rellini (2011) have questioned this ability to feel this difference because of the anatomical structure of the clitoris. Outside of whether orgasms are vaginal or clitoral, orgasms have been classified into one of four categories: high pleasure/high sensation, high pleasure/medium sensation, medium pleasure/medium sensation, low pleasure/low sensation (King, Belsky, Mah, & Binik, 2011). At the same time the authors caution that these types of orgasms were in response to items the authors listed as being part of an orgasm and may not directly measure all of the qualities related to sensation and satisfaction involved in an orgasm.

Adegunloye and Ezeoke (2011) found the prevalence of female orgasmic disorder was 40% among secondary school teachers in Nigeria. Similar findings were obtained by Giles and McCabe (2009) in their large sample from the general population in Australia. Other reports indicate 40–60% of women do not experience orgasms reliably, with 10% never having had experienced them (Graham, 2010). Recently, Basson (2001) has highlighted the overlapping nature of the different phases of the female sexual response cycle among women. A review of clinical and empirical research has indicated that women may experience orgasm before maximum arousal, during peak arousal, and further orgasms may occur during the gradual resolution phase of sexual arousal (Basson, 2005). It is interesting to note that only about half of the women who experience orgasm difficulties report associated distress (Laan & Rellini, 2011). Although orgasms are important to sexual satisfaction, this lack of distress may be associated with the expectation among women that they will not consistently experience orgasm during partnered sexual intercourse.

This overlap between the sexual response phases has implications for treatment, which are discussed later in this chapter. However, the above discussion suggests that many of the same strategies that are useful for treating arousal disorders would also be useful in the treatment of orgasmic disorder.

Intersystemic Etiology

A broad range of factors have been related to the development of anorgasmia in women. McCabe (1991) developed a model of sexual dysfunction that incorporated factors from intergenerational, individual, and relationship influences. The contribution of these factors to anorgasmia are outlined below.

Intergenerational Influences

Difficulties in the process of socialization during childhood have been considered an important predictor of adult sexual dysfunction. The development of misconceptions about sex, negative attitudes towards sexual pleasure, and problems with sexual orientation or gender identity may result from the family-of-origin and may negatively influence sexual functioning in adulthood (Basson, Althop, et al., 2004; Graziottin & Leiblum, 2005). Such historical factors are particularly salient in the development of lifelong sexual problems (Basson, Leiblum, et al., 2004). Hof and Berman (1986) also attributed adult attitudes and behaviors to sexual scripts which are developed during childhood as a result of parental attitudes towards sex. In reviews of the literature, it has been claimed that one of the causes of sexual dysfunction in adulthood is sexual abuse during childhood (Chaill, Llewelyn, & Pearson, 1991; Talmadge & Wallace, 1991). However, both these reviews based their conclusions on studies that were largely clinical explorations, with little or no attempt to sample representative groups of adults. Although these studies have demonstrated that a large proportion of dysfunctional adults have experienced sexual abuse during childhood, without corresponding data from non-dysfunctional samples, causative statements cannot be made.

The contribution of experiences or attitudes during adolescence to adult sexual dysfunction has received little attention. Heiman, Gladue, Roberts, and LoPiccolo (1986) found that the type of relationship in which first intercourse occurred had an impact on adult sexual functioning for women but not for men, specifically in that women with sexual dysfunction noting less arousal and sexual satisfaction. In addition, women who engaged in intercourse for the first time at an older age experience sexual dysfunction in later life such as sexual aversion and lower self-efficacy (Reissing, Andruff, & Wentland, 2012). However, Leitenberg, Greenwald, and Tarran (1989) found that the frequency of sexual experiences during adolescence had no impact on adult levels of sexual satisfaction, sexual arousal, or sexual dysfunction.

It is difficult from the literature on intergenerational factors to determine the manner in which they may impact on female anorgasmia. Much of the literature talks about links between events in childhood and adolescence and overall levels of sexual dysfunction in adulthood, without specifying specific sexual dysfunctions. A recent study on a large sample of both sexually functional and dysfunctional women found that child sexual abuse did not predict sexual functioning for either the functional group or any of the dysfunctional groups (hypoactive sexual desire arousal disorder or orgasmic dysfunction) (McCabe & Giles, 2012). Further the authors found that although negative parental attitudes to sex predicted level of hypoactive sexual desire disorder, there was no relationship between this variable and orgasmic dysfunction. Further research, with the inclusion of a range of sexual dysfunctions as well as a control group, is necessary in order to better understand the impact on sexual functioning of events in childhood. Given the overlapping nature of sexual disorders among women that was discussed earlier, it is likely that childhood events that negatively impact on one phase of the sexual response cycle are also likely to have a negative impact on other phases.

Individual Influences

There has been little investigation of the individual factors that are associated with female anorgasmia. Obstfeld, Lupfer, and Lupfer (1985) found that sexual identity had no impact on sexual functioning, but the influence of lifestyle factors as well as sexual attitudes on sexual dysfunction, in particular, female anorgasmia, requires further exploration. It has been suggested that stress, levels of fatigue, sexual identity, health, and other individual attributes and experiences may alter sexual desire or response. Morokoff and Gillilland (1993) investigated the impact of life stressors (for example unemployment, stressful life events, and daily hassles) on sexual functioning. Unemployment was shown to predict lower levels of sexual desire. Women with mood disorders have been shown to consistently demonstrate lower levels of sexual functioning in all phases of the sexual response cycle compared to normal controls (e.g., Clayton, McGavery, Calvet, & Piazza, 1997; Cyranowski, Frank, Cherry, Houck, & Kupfer, 2004). However, McCabe (2005) demonstrated that performance anxiety (i.e., concern about one's performance in a sexual interaction) was associated with high levels of anorgasmia. This would suggest that the more a woman focuses on and becomes anxious about her arousal levels and whether or not she is likely to experience an orgasm, the less likely she is to be orgasmic. McCabe and Giles (2012) have recently demonstrated that high levels of stress are also associated with orgasmic dysfunction among women. Other factors are related to the education of women and sexuality such as fear, sexual misinformation and ignorance, lack of interest, guilt, concerns about attractiveness, and shame (Birnbaum, 2003; Ramage, 2004). Finally, Costa and Brody (2011) discovered anxious attachment styles were correlated with less consistency in vaginal orgasms. Finally, in addition to the psychological influences, a number of studies have confirmed that medical issues such as heart disease and conditions, hypertension, asthma, thyroid problems, as well as medications can have a pronounced impact on orgasm (Basson, Rees, Wang, Montejo, & Incrocci, 2010; Shifren, Monz, Russo, Segreti, & Johannes, 2008). Further research is necessary to explore the role of individual influences in the development and maintenance of anorgasmia in women.

Relationship Factors

There is a substantial body of research that has explored the contribution of relationship factors to sexual functioning. For example, Pascoal, Narciso, and Pereira (2014) have identified two key ingredients to sexual satisfaction: personal sexual well-being (character- ized by such factors as positive feelings, arousal, openness, individual sexual experience, to name a few) and dyadic process (characterized by such factors as romance, expression of feelings, frequency of sex, and ability to act out desires, to name a few). Such studies focusing on the value of relationships in sexual functioning have focused on the role of the quality of the relationship on the sexual functioning of the partners. Snyder and Berg (1983) found that the major causes of sexual problems in men and women related to their interactions with their partner. The general level of enjoyment of sexual activities as well as satisfaction with the frequency of sexual activities was associated with sexual distress. Lack of affection for the partner was also an important predictor of sexual satisfaction.

Communication between partners seems to play an important part in both the quality of the marital relationship and level of sexual dysfunction. A general lack of communica- tion and difficulty in communicating preferences for various types of sexual interactions has been demonstrated among sexually dysfunctional couples (McCabe, 1999). Empiri- cal studies have consistently demonstrated that anorgasmic women reported experiencing significantly greater discomfort with communication about sexual activities (Kelly, Strass- berg, & Kircher, 1990; Kelly, Strassberg & Turner, 2004; McCabe & Giles, 2012). Roffe and Britt (1981) found evidence for high levels of hostility among couples seeking sexual dysfunction therapy. However, they also found that a lack of expressiveness and low lev- els of affection within the relationship contributed to sexual dysfunction. Hulbert (1991) found that sexually assertive women were more likely to experience high sexual desire, arousal, and sexual satisfaction. On the other hand, Heiman, Gladue, Roberts, and LoPic- colo (1986) found no difference in the communication patterns of sexually functional and dysfunctional couples. It is difficult to interpret these conflicting results. Perhaps it is the way in which the sexual interaction and lack of communication within the relation- ship is viewed that relates to anorgasmia, rather than the objective interaction and com- munication patterns. For example, couples who report higher levels of general relational satisfaction also reported having a higher level of communication on both sexual and non- sexual topics, which, in turn, was positively associated with sexual satisfaction (Mark & Jozkowski, 2013).

Pietropinto (1986) and McCabe and Cobain (1998) found that relationship factors were strongly associated with sexual dysfunction for women but not as strongly for men. Global deficits in the current relationship (for example relationship quality), as well as lower levels of sexual experience were more likely to occur among sexually dysfunctional women. Whether the sexual dysfunction led to relationship difficulties or vice versa is not clear. Regardless of which set of problems occurred first, both were now in place. Surpris- ingly, there were no differences between the functional and dysfunctional groups in their levels of communication, sexual communication, or arguments. But this does not mean that the relationships of the sexually dysfunctional responders were of the same quality as those of the functional respondents; women who have poor relationships, and who are unable to communicate, may express their lack of satisfaction with their relationship by avoiding sexual interactions with their partner and so restricting their range of sexual experiences. Specific to anorgasmia, women are often unable to communicate their spe- cific desires regarding physical stimulation, intensity, focus of stimulation, etc. In addition, partner variables, such as lack of experience, knowledge about sexual stimulation, or indifference to her arousal can contribute to anorgasmia. Also, dysfunction in the partner can play a role. Levels of sexual satisfaction showed a particular deterioration among the anorgasmic groups (McCabe & Cobain, 1998). Examining the data from a different perspective, it may be that the negative attitudes to sex impede the development of sexual intimacy, causing not only sexual dysfunction by also a breakdown in other aspects of the relationship. According to Travis and Travis (1986), intimacy is developed through a range of sexual and sensual contracts. A discomfort with non-genital and genital touching impedes the development of intimacy which, in turn, leads to a breakdown in relationship functioning and on to sexual dysfunction in one or both partners. Consistent with this proposal, McCabe and Giles (2012) found that both relationship satisfaction and sexual intimacy predicted higher levels of sexual functioning among women with orgasmic dysfunction.

Sociocultural Factors

Ramage (2004) asserts that information and miseducation can be key factors in the development and maintenance of sexual problems in women, and this can certainly affect orgasm problems. For women in the 1960s and 1970s, the "myth of the vaginal orgasm" dominated their view of sexuality until it was challenged in the late 1960s by Koedt (Gerhard, 2000). While many of the clients we see with orgasm problems may have been born after the challenge presented by Koedt such myths of women and sexuality may persist. In addition, the fact that women experience single or multiple orgasms as well as the lack of clarity in where in each woman the most sensitive area to being an orgasm is located further adds to the mythology (Colson, 2010). It may be this type of mentality that reinforces women's sexual scripts and, in part, underscores women's tendencies to fake orgasms (approximately 48% of women report having faked an orgasm as compared to 18% of men) (Muehlenhard & Shippee, 2010).

Assessment

Intersystemic evaluation of anorgasmia in women should include a detailed psychological, relational, social, and medical history (Walsh & Berman, 2004). In order for treatment approaches to address the psychological factors that contribute to anorgasmia, it is important to have a clear understanding of the manner in which they contribute to this sexual dysfunction. There have been major changes in the treatment of female sexual dysfunction in the last 10 years, with an increase in the use of centrally acting agents (e.g., serotonin agonists) to peripheral localized treatment (e.g., vasodilating creams) (Walsh & Berman, 2004). However, these medical approaches are not based on a clear physiological cause for these disorders, and have been shown to be largely ineffective. The following discussion considers the factors that need to be evaluated among women with anorgasmia prior to treatment.

It is important that the role of intergenerational, individual, and relationship factors that may have precipitated or be maintaining the sexual dysfunction are evaluated. These factors are likely to vary from one woman to another. However, it would appear that a central factor to the development of anorgasmia that needs to be evaluated is the nature of communication in the relationship. Kelly, Strassberg, and Turner (2006) found that there were behaviorally assessable differences in the communication pattern of couples experiencing female anorgasmia when compared to functional couples, specifically the negative interactional dynamics of blame and lack of receptivity to interactions by their partner.

It is also important that the clinician has a clear understanding of the nature of the sexual dysfunction. To this end, the clinician needs to assess the frequency of orgasm, the situation in which anorgasmia occurs, whether or not anorgasmia is primary or secondary, if anorgasmia is partial or complete and the length of time the problem has been in place. An additional piece of information that I have found useful in therapy is to determine if there were other events that occurred at the time that the anorgasmia developed. It is also useful to question the woman and her partner on why she is seeking treatment at this point in time, and what expectations/goals she has for therapy. In addition, it may be the case that a woman is unsure that she had an orgasm, thus warranting education. Finally, the lack of orgasm may be the result of lack of stimulation, too much stimulation, or related to the fact that the clitoris is dynamic and stimulation in one position does not mean the stimulation will remain the same.

Treatment

Treatment programs for sexual dysfunction frequently lack adequate research methodology, which makes it difficult to evaluate their effectiveness. There is often no clear definition of the problem; the target variables for treatment are not clearly specified and so evaluation of treatment success is inadequate; there are no pre- and post-measures of target variables; outcome measures, if used, are lacking in adequate information on their psychometric properties; the treatment program is not clearly described; and sample sizes are too small for adequate statistical analysis (Heiman & Meston, 1997). These flaws make it difficult to evaluate which treatment programs for female anorgasmia are most successful and cost effective (O'Donohue, Dopke, & Swingen, 1997; O'Donahue, Swingen, Dopke, & Roger, 1999).

A further factor that may relate to the success of therapy is the length of time the problem has been in place. When a problem has been present for an extended period of time, it may have become incorporated into the person's view of themselves, and the relationship may have adjusted to incorporate the dysfunction. As a result, a number of changes need to occur if the dysfunction is no longer present, and so the person with the dysfunction or the partner may be resistant to these changes.

Some educational content would appear to be useful for women with anorgasmia. Teaching effective techniques of stimulation may well improve the orgasmic response of anorgasmic women. This process involves masturbatory training in order to achieve orgasmic consistency via masturbation (Heiman & LoPiccolo's early book *Becoming Orgasmic*). However, the transfer of the ability to reach orgasm through masturbation to an ability to reach orgasm in intercourse is problematic. Directed masturbation has been shown to be an effective strategy for women with primary anorgasmia (Heiman & Meston, 1997). This process involves providing education to the woman about the ways to achieve orgasm, and then providing her with strategies and permission to explore her body. This process of self-exploration allows the woman to discover what is sexually arousing for her, what feels pleasant, and what is difficult or unpleasant. The woman is encouraged to use a mirror to examine her genitals in the early stages of this exercise. She is also encouraged to tune into her sensations, to alter her cognitions regarding masturbation, and to use sexual fantasies to enhance her sexual response (Heiman, 2007).

Directed masturbation (teaching one to self-stimulate) has been shown to be particularly effective among women who experience primary anorgasmia, with a success rate reported of between 80–90% (LoPiccolo & Stock, 1986; Meston, Hull, Levin, & Sipski, 2004; Riley & Riley, 1978). This is especially true for women who differ from lifelong,

generalized anorgasmia. For women with secondary anorgasmia, the directed masturbation appears to be less effective, with success rates of 10–75% being reported (Kilmann,
Boland, Norton, Davidson, & Caird, 1986; Kuriansky, Sharp, & O'Connor, 1982). In
addition, vibrators might be helpful in assisting a woman with identifying whether the
issue is one of stimulation. The coital alignment technique has also been shown to demonstrate positive effects (i.e., frequency and intensity of orgasm) in women with anorgasmia
(Eichel, Eichel, & Kule, 1988; Hurlbert & Apt, 1995).

For women to transfer her orgasmic response in masturbation to sexual interaction with
her partner, she and her partner may need to use additional stimulation of the woman's
genitals during sexual intercourse. The woman needs to learn to communicate her sexual
needs to her partner, and guide the partner on how to stimulate her. During sexual intercourse, it is important that the coital alignment technique (Heiman, 2007) is used, which
increases the level of clitoral contact as well as the orgasmic frequency among women
with secondary anorgasmia (Heiman, 2007). This technique positions the man's pelvis in
alignment with the woman's pelvis and moves his pelvis rather than thrusting (Taublieb &
Lick, 1986).

The above discussion demonstrates the difficulties encountered in comparing studies designed to increase sexual education to treat secondary anorgasmia. Non-treatment
control groups are rarely included, outcome measures are not clearly defined (and may
be unrealistic), and the differential effect of sex education is difficult to isolate due to
combination treatment strategies. However, it seems that ignorance of the best techniques, reluctance about using them, and/or an inability to communicate preferences for
sexual stimulation to the partner contribute to low orgasmic frequency during sexual
interaction.

Medical treatment strategies for anorgasmia are not considered in detail in this chapter.
This is primarily because the focus is on psychological interventions, but also because
hormone replacement and other pharmaceutical approaches have not been shown to be
effective in the treatment of this dysfunction (see Kope, 2007 for a summary of medical
approaches to the treatment of anorgasmia). Further, there is no currently approved medication for the treatment of female sexual dysfunction, including orgasmic dysfunction.

Studies seem to demonstrate that psychological interventions for anorgasmia are most
effective if they utilize cognitive and behavioral strategies and focus on intergenerational,
intrapersonal, and interpersonal factors that may contribute to the women's sexual dysfunction. Heiman (2007) reviewed a range of treatment approaches for anorgasmia in
women, including pharmacotherapy, psychoanalytic, cognitive behavioral, and systems
theory. She noted that research studies support the adoption of cognitive behavioral
approaches, although the strategies employed in systems approaches in sex therapy may
be useful. However these approaches have yet to be adequately evaluated in research studies. McCabe (2001) implemented a psychologically focused treatment program for 95 sexually dysfunctional men and 54 sexually dysfunctional women, 36 of whom experienced
anorgasmia. The treatment program was based on cognitive behavioral principles. It was
a 10 session program that focused on enhancing communication between the partners,
increasing sexual skills, and lowering sexual anxiety and performance anxiety. Both cognitions and behaviors that impeded functioning in these areas were addressed. Homework
exercises comprised cognitive strategies and behavioral exercises to enhance communication between partners, as well as sensate focus exercises. During therapy sessions, there
was discussion of blocks to sexual performance, and strategies to overcome these blocks
were developed by addressing cognitions and behaviors that impeded sexual performance
and enjoyment of sexual activities. The first two therapy sessions occurred weekly, and the

subsequent session occurred fortnightly. Success is defined differently for each couple—in some cases, it would be orgasm through intercourse; in other couples, coital intercourse.

Therapy was successful for 44.4% of women and was most likely to be effective for women who experienced anorgasmia and sexual arousal disorder; it was least effective among women who experienced a lack of sexual interest. In fact, of the 36 women who presented with anorgasmia pre-therapy, only 6 women experienced problems in this area post-therapy. A more detailed description of this treatment program is presented later in this chapter.

The results of this study demonstrated that a large proportion of participants experienced sexual dysfunction less frequently post-therapy, but many of them still experienced some level of sexual dysfunction. Does this constitute successful therapy, or does successful therapy only entail a complete absence of sexual dysfunction post-therapy? This dilemma demonstrates the difficulty of defining success in therapy, and the importance of a complete description of pre-therapy and post-therapy levels of sexual dysfunction, as well as other associated measures of sexual functioning.

Effective Strategies From Previous Research

Hucker and McCabe (2012) conducted a review of the most effective treatments of a range of female sexual dysfunctions. From this review, it was clear that for orgasmic dysfunction, masturbation training, which resulted in women having a greater comfort with their body, was an important ingredient in successful therapy. However, communication skills training and couple therapy were also shown to be effective in improving the orgasmic response of women. In fact, using these strategies, the results of the studies demonstrated an improvement in marital functioning as well as orgasmic response. These findings are consistent with results obtained by Hucker and McCabe (2013) that found that a mindfulness-based online treatment for female sexual dysfunction led to improvements in sexual and emotional intimacy as well as communication in the treatment group compared to the control group.

As noted earlier, there has been limited research that has examined the effectiveness of treatment strategies for anorgasmia. However, levels of both communication and performance anxiety appear to be important factors to address in the treatment of this sexual dysfunction.

Communication

A lack of communication between partners about their sexual relationship appears to be a factor related to anorgasmia in women. Everaerd and Dekker (1982) compared the relative effectiveness of sex therapy and communication skills training on the treatment of secondary orgasmic dysfunction. Both therapies were assessed as equally effective in improving orgasmic experience, although the extent of the improvement was not reported. In this study, sex therapy consisted of sensate focus and sexual stimulation exercises, with a ban on intercourse. The communication training included exercises for active and passive listening, verbalization and reflection of feelings, productive conflict management, and assertive behavior.

Both communication and sexual skills training, together with measures to reduce anxiety, were used in the treatment of primary and secondary anorgasmia by McGovern, McMullen, and LoPiccolo (1978). Women with primary anorgasmia improved markedly in orgasmic responsiveness whereas the women with secondary anorgasmia did not. This led the researchers to suggest that martial therapy might be more appropriate for the latter, since these women reported more dissatisfaction with their marital relationships than did the women experiencing primary anorgasmia.

More recently, Weeks (1994; 2004) developed the Intersystem Approach to the treatment of sexual problems. This approach focuses on the couple in the resolution of sexual problems, and the dynamic that operates in the couple relationship. Although Weeks develops strategies to work with the genetic makeup, values, family-of-origin, and cultural setting within which the dysfunction was occurring, an overriding systemic approach to the resolution of the problem means that effective communication patterns are central to the resolution of the sexual dysfunction.

Performance Anxiety

Performance anxiety can arise from various sources and is not reserved just for men with erectile disorder. Past failure to achieve orgasm can elicit self-defeating and distracting thoughts about whether she will be able to achieve orgasm this time. The enthusiasm of an insecure partner, who regards her orgasmic response as an assurance of his or her own competence, can be perceived by the woman as a pressure on her to achieve orgasm. Fear of rejection or feelings of obligation towards the partner may lead her to accept her partner's sexual overtures, despite apprehension about her ability or desire to respond fully. As sexual activity continues, she tries to will her response, wanting to become so aroused that orgasm will be triggered, but afraid she might "turn-off" or that her partner might become impatient or irritated at her slowness. She mentally monitors her own and her partner's response, unable to allow herself to relax and enjoy the sexual stimulation for its own sake. She can no longer trust her own natural sexual responsivity to maintain and intensify the arousal process through to orgasm, but rather, as spectator, demands her body's response. At the same time, her partner is also a spectator as he or she physically attempts to bring her to orgasm, wondering what he or she is doing wrong when she does not respond (Masters & Johnson, 1970). This view is reinforced by Kaplan (1974; 1983) who regarded obsessive self-observation arising out of fear of failure to be the single most immediate cause of female anorgasmia. In other words, this is the "fear of fear response": In short, the woman fears that she will experience the fear of not being able to orgasm.

The original proponents of performance anxiety, Masters and Johnson (1970), attempted to deal with this problem by counseling couples on the nature of performance anxiety and by temporarily placing a ban on orgasm and intercourse until permitted by their sensate focus program. The partners engaged in a graduated series of tasks from general body massage through to intercourse. Although this program purported to address performance anxiety, it also involved assertion training, modeling, behavioral rehearsal, and education. By focusing on sexual activities other than intercourse, subjects explored a wide range of sexual activities other than intercourse; participants explored a wide range of sexual activities which may well have lengthened the time involved in sexual play before intercourse occurred. Elements of this program are still evident in treatment programs for anorgasmia, and are an essential element in the program described below.

Systemic Treatment Framework

As noted at various points of this chapter, female anorgasmia is likely to be caused, precipitated, and maintained from a range of intergenerational, individual, and relationship factors. After an adequate assessment of the nature of the anorgasmia and the factors that relate to this sexual dysfunction, it is important that treatment address the multitude of factors that currently maintain this dysfunction. Consistent with the systemic treatment framework, the following program has been implemented for the sexual dysfunction of women with anorgasmia (McCabe & Delaney, 1991; Purcell & McCabe, 1992). We have found that these aims are best addressed in therapy by the use of three interrelated treatment strategies; communication exercises, sensate focus exercises, and guided fantasy.

Communication exercises. Communication exercises were devised to both improve the quality of the marital relationship and develop and explore emotional responses of the woman. Questions were developed that were designed to address all aspects of the relationship, both sexual and nonsexual. Both partners were instructed to share their feelings with their partner about a particular issue. Each day a different issue was discussed and feelings were expressed. Examples of early questions were, "What do I like best about us as partners and how does that make me feel?" and "How do I feel about differences between us in desire for sexual contact?" As other aspects of the treatment program were pursued, the communication exercises continued to encourage the development of the emotional side of the woman by exploring her reaction to the program, and sharing this reaction with her partner. For example, when partners were physically exploring their responses to body massage and genital stimulation, one of the communication questions was "How do I feel when you caress me intimately? What body feelings occur?"

Sensate focus exercises. The Masters and Johnson (1970) sensate focus program was outlined in therapy and implemented at home by the client. The program was commenced two weeks after the commencement of therapy. These exercises comprised of non-genital, then genital pleasuring, and finally intercourse in a graduated pattern. A detailed description of sensate focus strategies is outlined in a chapter in the first edition of this book and will be refined in a chapter in the *Clinician's Guid to Systemic Sex Therapy*. Weeks and Gambescia (2009) described a more sophisticated and client friendly approach to sensate focus.

Fantasy. We have found that the use of sexual fantasy was an important aspect of therapy. The purpose of sexual fantasy seems to be different for men and women. Some women may have difficulty accepting themselves as sexual persons and experience a high level of guilt in association with their sexual functioning. Therefore, they may experience difficulties in accepting the physical aspects of the sexual encounter. Men may also experience guilt in association with sexual expression, but this guilt is accompanied by a lack of emotional involvement in the actual relationship. Fantasies were aimed at enhancing the acceptance of oneself as a sexual person. Sexual fantasies are also very useful for women experiencing anorgasmia to distract them from their actual performance, and so lower levels of performance anxiety. Early fantasies employed in the program for anorgasmia emphasized the romantic, interpersonal aspects of the relationship. This allowed for sexual arousal within a romantic setting. Once arousal in this setting was tolerated and then enjoyed, the fantasies used during progressive therapy sessions became more sexually implicit so as to counteract the feelings of guilt associated with the experience of physical sexual pleasure and enhance the acceptance of oneself as a sexual being. Within these fantasies both the emotional and physical aspects of sex were presented so that the development of both types of involvement could be explored in order to foster sexual functioning. Fantasies are also tied to increases in sexual arousal (Dekker & Everaerd, 1988). The therapist should normalize the experience of fantasies for women and can direct the client to resources to assist her in building an active fantasy life, as fantasy can be more powerful for women in becoming aroused than viewing erotic films (Youn, 2006).

Research and Future Directions

A promising area for the treatment of female orgasmic disorder is the use of online treatment approaches. Jones and McCabe (2011) found that an online treatment strategy that focused on masturbation training in combination with communication skills training and sexual exercises to enhance the relationship were extremely effective in reducing levels of all types of sexual dysfunction, including orgasmic problems. Hucker and McCabe (2013) incorporated mindfulness into the Internet program, and found that the addition of mindfulness enhanced treatment effectiveness. Although the attrition from these Internet based programs is high (McCabe & Jones, 2013), it is not substantially higher than attrition from face-to-face therapy. This is certainly an approach that should be considered for women with orgasmic problems who are geographically isolated, who do not have time in work hours, or who are reluctant for other reasons to engage in face-to-face therapy.

Further research is required on the development and evaluation of integrated treatment programs for anorgasmia in women. A combination of both psychotherapy and pharmacotherapy should also be evaluated in future research. With the advent of readily available medications for erectile disorder in men, combination therapies may also be affective for female on its own. Future research, therefore, needs to focus on whether outcomes are improved by the use of more focused integrated psychological interventions or combination therapies. In this way the most efficacious treatment for anorgasmia can be determined.

In a paper that provided a comprehensive review of pharmacotherapy for sexual dysfunction in women, Basson (2004) proposed that there is still too little known about the mode of action, effectiveness, and long term consequences of utilizing medical interventions for female sexual dysfunction, in particular, anorgasmia. It is likely that there will continue to be research studies to attempt to isolate a safe, effective medical intervention for sexual dysfunction in women. However, given the nature of the factors that contribute to sexual dysfunction in women, it is unlikely that a medical intervention alone is likely to be effective. It is possible that, as for a number of sexual dysfunctions in men, a combined psychological and medical approach to sexual dysfunction in women may be the treatment of choice in the next 10 years.

Case Study

Client

A husband and wife, aged 31 and 29 years, respectively, were referred by a family planning agency. They had been married for 18 months, having lived together for 12 months prior to the marriage. Both tertiary-educated professional people, they had met while working together and became friends. The wife at this time was just emerging from a broken first marriage and subsequent divorce. The sexual relationship in this first marriage was not good, but she had had several affairs in which she had enjoyed sex, experiencing orgasm during sexual interaction but not during intercourse. Currently she still enjoyed sex and became sexually aroused, but her frequency of orgasm was reported as having fallen to 25% during sexual activity. She had not experienced orgasm during intercourse at all. As a consequence, she claimed that she was beginning to lose interest in sex and came to therapy looking for more enjoyment for her. She reported her loss of interest in sex as beginning when she and her now-husband had begun living together. Up until then, their sexual relationship had been good from both their points of view. She also reported

181

no anxiety about sex and a rather neutral attitude towards it in the original family home, with other repressive influences. The husband, who came from a very religious background, described family attitudes as neutral towards sex. He reported no other sexual relationships, either past or present. There was a concern about premature ejaculation but questioning revealed his concern to be unfounded. He enjoyed sex and seemed to function well. There was no admission of any anxiety about sex, just enthusiasm for his wife to enjoy it more and experience orgasm during intercourse. Both husband and wife were currently working in demanding jobs. In the coming months they planned to start a family.

Treatment Program

The program involved nine sessions with the therapist.

Session 1. Pre-therapy. Specific information was given about the program. Both partners were present, with joint and separate interviews being conducted. This was followed by the counselling of both partners together on the nature of secondary orgasmic difficulties. The concept of performance anxiety was introduced and its effects on the sexual response of both men and women were explained. The cooperation of the male partner in being neither too enthusiastic nor ambivalent about his wife's sexual response was elicited. A temporary ban on any sexual activity, until allowed by the therapist in the context of the sensate focus program, was prescribed. The communication exercises were introduced and the time commitment required by these and the sensate focus program made clear. The format of the individual therapy sessions was briefly outlined as: review of the preceding week, relaxation with guided imagery based on each phase of the sensate focus program, then brief discussion of how the guided imagery was experienced. Guided imagery could be characterized as guided fantasy, where people may be instructed to recall a previous experience where they enjoyed self-pleasuring and were aroused.

Important features that emerged in this session with the couple were that both lived busy professional lives, often with meetings of further study outside of working hours. They did not think of themselves as having a sexual problem in their relationship, but thought that the wife's diminishing enjoyment of sex could become a problem if not addressed. Their main aim in coming to therapy was to increase the wife's enjoyment. She currently experienced orgasm during 25% of their sexual interactions but had never experienced it during intercourse either in this or in previous relationships. Also noted was the husband's enthusiasm for his wife to enjoy sex more and his disappointment that he would not be coming to all the sessions with her. Both partners commented that their sexual relationship had been very good and non-problematic before they began living together. Both partners admitted to having difficulty resolving conflict, being more likely to withdraw into silence rather than express feelings. The husband also expressed some concern about the possibility that he was ejaculating too early during intercourse. Further inquiry into what was happening enabled the therapist to reassure him that he was not a premature ejaculator.

Both husband and wife came from similar lower middle class socio-economic backgrounds. Both had grown up in intact families with one or more siblings of the opposite sex. Religion was an important factor in the early life of both partners. The wife had a Protestant background, the husband, Catholic. In both homes, the children were allowed to ask questions and talk about sex but discussion was not encouraged and parental attitudes were described as neutral. There was no display of physical affection either to spouse or children in either household.

The wife had a steady boyfriend at 17 years and this developed into a sexual relationship, although she felt both guilt and anxiety about intercourse and regarded it as unpleasant. Otherwise there were no other unpleasant or traumatic sexual experiences during this time. She was sexually responsive and orgasmic with her present partner before they formed a permanent relationship. Currently, she felt negative about sexual fantasy, sexual secretions, and masturbation but positive about foreplay and manual orgasms when her husband provided the stimulation. She also regarded sex as important in their relationship and looked for a certain equality in both sexual and non-sexual activities. Within this present relationship, however, there were conflicts not satisfactorily resolved about the division of household labour and time spent at the work place. Concerning her present problem, she thought that previous negative experiences and lack of sexual knowledge had contributed to it. She also recognized that fatigue, mood, and duration of foreplay influenced her ability to become aroused.

Session 2–7. Therapy. These sessions were for the woman alone and occurred at weekly intervals, except for a 2-week break between Sessions 5 and 6. In session 6 it was necessary to repeat much of the content of the previous session since the home assignments had been somewhat neglected in the interval. The first half of each session was devoted to a review of the past week and its prescribed activities. It included counselling on any relationship and sexual issues that had surfaced as a result of the communication or sensate focus homework. Ways of dealing with self-monitoring and performance concerns were described, i.e., by thought-stopping, focusing on bodily sensations and feelings, and by incorporating the latter into concurrent fantasies, either self-generated or based on the fantasy imagery presented during the therapy sessions. The experiences that were brought to therapy were used to discuss cognitive, behavioural, and relationship enhancing strategies to address any negative thoughts or responses. Only one fantasy was presented in each session. The fantasy was presented following brief relaxation instructions. Fantasies were drawn from Nin's book of fantasies (Nin, 1978; 1979). At the conclusion, the woman was invited to talk of her response, of aspects she found sexually arousing or maybe troubling in some way. Progressively each of the stages of sensate focus was introduced during these six sessions.

Session 2. The communication exercises were reported as going well, with additional relationship issues being spontaneously raised. One such issue concerned working late, in that, while it was accepted that the husband did, it was not acceptable to him that the wife should work late. All but two of the communication questions were completed. The guided imagery session was found enjoyable, relaxing, and non-threatening. During this session the woman was encouraged to explore her own body. She was told to use a mirror to help her examine her genitals, and to touch her breasts and genitals while engaging in sexual fantasy to see what types of touching she found pleasurable.

Session 3. The communication exercises continued to bring forward issues for discussion that had not been broached by the couple before. All the questions were tackled. The importance of the wife's work to her had been clarified between them. The couple found that listening to each other's expression of feeling, with no attempt to problem-solve, was a new and refreshing experience. During the session, the communication of sexual feelings in a positive and non-rejecting way was discussed, with some modelling by the therapist in the use of appropriate phrases. The woman revealed anxiety both about undressing in front of her male partner and about being aware of his sexual arousal. She was encouraged to explore, at home, in fantasy and in practice, aspects of undressing she might find sexually arousing to herself. She was also encouraged to explore her own body and when she felt comfortable, masturbate using a vibrator in order to enhance her sexual pleasure, and become familiar with the types of stimulation that she found pleasurable. These techniques were important for her to experience sexual arousal, and also to discover how to guide her husband in techniques to increase her arousal and orgasmic response.

Session 4. The sensate focus sessions prescribed for the previous week had at first been just relaxing, but now the woman was finding them sexually arousing as well. Her husband was reported as finding the massage enjoyable. The communication exercises continued to open up discussion between the couple in such a way that they were able to resolve misunderstandings that had arisen. They had come to realize that the woman liked to plan ahead whereas her husband preferred more spontaneous activities. An association between her tendency to plan ahead and her sexual difficulties was explored and found relevant. At the same time, it was also recognized that the therapy program necessitated some planning of sexual activity which would work against the desired spontaneity of normal sexual activity even to the extent of inducing anticipatory performance anxiety. Another issue arising through the communication questions concerned the woman's poor body image. It was suggested that she ask her husband what he liked about her body as he massaged her and that later she repeat these phrases to herself while standing naked in front of a mirror.

Session 5. By using the sensate focus exercises they had been discovering enjoyable ways of touching each other. The husband was encouraged to respond to the guidance provided by his wife in terms of what she found pleasurable in both the general as well as genital body pleasure. In particular, the wife needed to provide guidance on pleasurable techniques for clitoral stimulation. Despite this, the woman said she was beginning to feel under some pressure from the program and the expectation that she should enjoy the activities, and proceeded to describe sensitivity to being touched on nipples or clitoris. This called for reassurance that the aim of the sensate focus exercises was to explore different ways of touching and being touched, and that sometimes only a very gentle indirect approach might be pleasurable—or it might not. There seemed to be no pattern of masturbation at all, so it was suggested that she might like to explore herself what she found pleasurable then she could guide her husband's touch when they were together. She was encouraged to engage in the suggested activities out of a sense of curiosity and desire to know her own body, and then only when she was ready. At no time was anything to be tried just because she felt she "had" to because of the program.

Session 6. Career issues continued to be a focus of discussion for the couple. The husband had been able to voice his concern that, because she went to evening committee meeting, of a professional nature, this might indicate she did not need him. Another area of concern was the woman's plans for improving the house. Her husband was not able to tell her that he found this prospect of more work at home a real burden. Through the communication exercises the role expectations that the couple had of husband and wife were now emerging and being discussed and negotiated. With the sensate focus, the woman was finding a re-awakening of her sexual feelings and discovering there was very little she didn't enjoy. She was even discovering that being touched around the nipple area could be pleasurable. Her use of fantasy during sexual interaction was only occasional, and it was used to ward off distracting thoughts. However, she had been reading erotic stories 'to get in the mood' before their mutual sexual activities.

Session 7. Their commitment to the communication exercises was evident again, with five of the seven questions being completed, with seemingly a good level of self-disclosure on both sides. With the allowing of non-demand intercourse, old anxieties returned as the woman felt under pressure to perform on the two occasions that the couple had intercourse. She did not like manual concurrent stimulation of her clitoris, finding it almost painful. Again she was encouraged to explore this more slowly, at first on her own, and then guiding her partner's hand in any way that she found pleasurable.

In the preceding week the use of fantasy had not been sufficient to allay her anxieties. The woman was encouraged to continue with the non-demand (i.e. non-orgasmic) inter-course phase of the program, putting no pressure on herself to be orgasmic, but focusing on any pleasurable sensations that arose. Only when she could relax and enjoy this, she was advised, should she allow the possibility of orgasm. A further therapy session was considered but decided against. The couple seemed to need time to assimilate what had been happening and to explore the new techniques in their own time, without the pressure of reporting back to the therapist.

Session 8. The aim of this session was to review progress and problems and assess the readiness to terminate therapy or need to extend it. An appointment was made for a follow-up session 2 months later. This session reviewed the influence of the program on both sexual activity and the overall relationship. In the preceding week, the communica-tion question on clitoral stimulation had provoked discussion between the partners and it came up again in this session. It was explained by the therapist that this form of stimula-tion during intercourse was, for many women, the only way they were able to experience orgasm during intercourse. Husband and wife differed over the idea of self-stimulation during intercourse and compromises were discussed. During the joint session the woman herself made a connection between her ambivalence about expressing her own sexuality and her sexual difficulties and said this was something she planned to work on. She said she felt more relaxed about their sexual relationship, but was finding that constantly hav-ing to decide what she liked or didn't like during their sexual activity was a distraction. This suggested that she was still feeling some performance pressure from the program.

In the separate interview the woman again reported little use of fantasy. She was disap-pointed she had not accomplished more during the program and reported that orgasm happened on less than 25% of their sexual encounters. However, she was finding sex more relaxing and enjoyable and felt hopeful of future improvement. She expressed some concern that her husband seemed depressed but she did not know why.

In the interview with the husband it became clear that for him the relationship had reached a crisis point over the issue of beginning a family and that his wife was unaware of this. He had been unable to share with her his feelings of inadequacy about supporting her and a child. Indeed these feelings had affected his commitment to the program, fearing the possibility of impregnating his wife each time they had intercourse. He was encour-aged to raise this issue as a communication question in the following week, the urgency of doing so being stressed.

Session 9. Follow-up (2 months later). The aim of this session was primarily a review of what had been happening since the couple had attended the post-therapy session and to note any changes that had occurred since that time. The issue of parenting had been raised and some resolution reached. The woman had been surprised at her husband's concern and ambivalence about becoming a father. The husband had now become more amenable to the idea and even talked of some positive aspects of having a child. The relationship seemed to have stabilized at a new level of understanding. Both husband and wife, when asked separately, commented that everything was going well. The partners seemed to have confronted and come to terms with some of the role pressures each was facing.

The woman remarked on feeling much more relaxed and happy about their relation-ship, and her own sexuality. She said they had bought two popular sex manuals and that she was reading and enjoying the stories of Anais Nin. She was also now finding fantasy useful and enjoyable, both before and during lovemaking. She was experiencing orgasm more often, about 50% of the time but not during intercourse.

Telephone follow-up (6 months post-therapy). The woman reported that the improvement in their sexual relationship had been maintained, that she was experiencing orgasm in about 50% of sexual interactions, but not during intercourse.

Discussion

The eventual increase in the woman's orgasmic frequency from 25% to 50%, combined with a fall in performance anxiety, and the overall rise in sexual satisfaction for the woman suggests that the therapeutic focus on performance anxiety was appropriate. The finding that the effects of therapy were not fully realized until after the end of therapy gave credence to the client's comment that therapy was itself perceived as imposing performance demands. The focus on sexual arousal led to the uncovering of areas of anxiety about particular sexual activities and a deeper ambivalence about female sexuality. This, in turn, led to the recognition that both sexual anxiety and performance anxiety can co-exist in the one client, expressing both the demand to be non-sexual and the demand to be orgasmically sexual. On the behavioral level these demands can make a woman reluctant to express her sexual preferences. On the other hand, they can lead to performance pressures, with associated fears of failure, from both the woman and her spouse to experience orgasm more often. All the components of therapy—counselling, the use of fantasy, sensate focus, and communication exercises—were too well-integrated to allow any assessment of individual contributions. The communication exercises were found invaluable in allowing marital issues to surface and find some resolution. Had this not happened, marital therapy may have replaced sex therapy so that the problems in the relationship that were impacting on the sexual problems could be addressed.

The goal of the program was remission of the symptoms of secondary orgasmic dysfunction by reducing performance anxiety and intensifying sexual arousal. For the woman in this case study, some symptom remission was achieved in conjunction with a reduction in performance anxiety. Whether there was intensification of arousal is unclear. There appeared to be an increase in sexual communication and decrease in performance anxiety which seemed to be associated with an increase in relationship factors, sexual satisfaction, and orgasmic response. Sexual anxiety, as measured by the questionnaire, persisted at a relatively low but stable level. Anxiety about particular sexual activities and female sexuality, however, did surface during therapy sessions. Some attitudinal change towards various sexual activities was achieved, along with reports of increased sexual enjoyment and feelings of relaxation about sex.

References

Adegunloye, O., & Ezeoke, G. (2011). Sexual dysfunction-a silent hurt: Issues on treatment awareness. *Journal of Sexual Medicine, 8*, 1322–1329. doi: 10.1111/j.1743–6109.2010.02090.x

American Psychiatric Association. (2013). *Diagnostic and statistical manual of mental disorders* (5th ed., rev). Washington, DC: Author.

Basson, R. (2001). Female sexual response: The role of drugs in the management of sexual dysfunction. *Journal of Obstetrics and Gynaecology, 98*, 350–353. doi: 10.1016/S0029–7844(01)01452–1

Basson, R. (2001). Human sexual response cycles. *Journal of Sex and Marital Therapy, 27*, 33–43.

Basson, R. (2004). Pharmacotherapy for sexual dysfunction in women. *Expert Opinion on Pharmacotherapy, 5*, 1045–1059. doi: 10.1517/14656560903004184

Basson, R. (2005). Women's sexual dysfunction: Revised and expanded definitions. *Canadian Medical Association Journal, 172*, 1327–1333. doi: 1 0.1503/cmaj.1020174

Basson, R., Althop, S., Davis, S., Fugl-Meyer, K., Goldstein, I., Leiblum, S., . . . Wagner, G. (2004). Summary of recommendations on sexual dysfunction in women. *Journal of Sexual Medicine, 1*, 24–34. doi: 10.1111/j.1743–6109.2010.01889

Basson, R., Leiblum, S., Brotto, L., Derogatis, L., Fourcoy, J., Fugl-Meyer, K., . . . Schultz, W. W. (2004). Revised definitions of women's sexual dysfunction. *Journal of Sexual Medicine, 1*, 40–48. doi: 10.1111/j.1743–6109.2004.10107.x

Basson, R., Rees, P., Wang, R., Montejo, A. L., & Incrocci, L. (2010). Sexual function in chronic illness. *Journal of Sexual Medicine, 7*(1 Pt 2), 374–388. doi: 10.1111/j.1743–6109.2009.01621.x

Birnbaum, G. E. (2003). The meaning of heterosexual intercourse among women with female orgasmic disorder. *Archives of Sexual Behavior, 32*(1), 61–71. doi: 10.1023/A:1021845513448

Brody, S., & Weiss, P. (2010). Vaginal orgasm is associated with vaginal (not clitoral) sex education, focusing mental attention on vaginal sensations, intercourse duration, and a preference for a longer penis. *Journal of Sexual Medicine, 7*, 2774–2781.

Chaill, C., Llewelyn, S. P., & Pearson, C. (1991). Long term of sexual abuse which occurred in childhood: A review. *British Journal of Clinical Psychology, 30*, 117–130.

Clayton, A. H., McGarvey, E. L., Clavet, G. J., & Piazza, L. (1997). Comparison of sexual functioning in clinical and nonclinical population using the changes in Sexual Functioning Questionnaire (CSFQ). *Psychopharmacology Bulletin, 33*, 747–753.

Colson, M. H. (2010). Female orgasm: Myths, facts, and controversies. *Sexologies, 19*(1), 8–14. doi: 10.1016/j.sexol.2009.11.004

Costa, R. M. & Brody, S. (2011). Anxious and avoidant attachment, vibrator use, anal sex, and impaired vaginal orgasm. *Journal of Sexual Medicine, 8*, 2493–2500. doi: 10.1111/j.1743–6109.2011.02332.x

Cyranowski, J. M., Frank, E., Cherry, C., Houck, P., & Kupfer, D. J. (2004). Prospective assessment of sexual function in women treated for recurrent major depression. *Journal of Psychiatric Research, 38*, 267–273. doi: 10.1016/j.jpsychires.2003.08.003

Dekker, J., & Everaerd, W. (1988). Attentional effects on sexual arousal. *Psychophysiology, 25*, 45–54.

Eichel, E. A., Eichel, J., & Kule, S. (1988). The technique of coital alignment and its relation to female orgasmic response and simultaneous orgasm, *Journal of Sex & Marital Therapy, 14*(2), 129–141.

Everaerd, W., & Dekker, J. (1982). Treatment of secondary orgasmic dysfunction: A comparison of systematic desensitization and sex therapy. *Behaviour Research and Therapy, 20*, 269–274.

Gerhard, J. (2000). Revisiting "the myth of the vaginal orgasm": The female orgasm in American sexual thought and second wave feminism. *Feminist Studies, 26*(2), 449–476.

Giles, K., & McCabe, M. P. (2009). Conceptualising women's sexual function: Linear vs. circular models of sexual response. *Journal of Sexual Medicine, 6*, 2761–2771. doi: 10.1111/j.1743–6109.2009.01425.x

Graham, C. A. (2010). The DSM diagnostic criteria for female orgasmic disorder. *Archives of Sexual Behavior, 39*, 256–270.

Graziottin, A., & Leiblum, S. R. (2005). Biological and psychosocial pathophysiology of female sexual dysfunction during the menopausal transition. *Journal of Sexual Medicine, 2, Suppl 35*, 133–145.

Heiman, J., & LoPicclo, J. (1988). *Becoming orgasmic: A sexual and personal growth program for women.* New York: Prentice Hall.

Heiman, J. R. (2007) Orgasmic disorders in women. In S. R. Leiblum (Ed.), *Principles and practice of sex therapy* (4th ed., pp. 84–123). New York: Guilford Press.

Heiman, J. R., Gladue, B. A., Roberts, C. W., & LoPiccolo, J. (1986). Historical and current factors discriminating sexually functional from sexually dysfunctional married couples. *Journal of Marital and Family Therapy, 12*, 163–174.

Heiman, J. R., & Meston, M. (1997). Empirically validated treatment for sexual dysfunction. *Annual Review of Sex Research, 8*, 148–194.

Hof, L., & Berman, E. (1986). The sexual genogram. *Journal of Marital and Family Therapy, 12*, 39–47.

Hucker, A., & McCabe, M. P. (2012). Manualized treatment programs for FSD: Research challenges and recommendation. *Journal of Sexual Medicine, 9*, 350–360. doi: 10.1111/j.1743–6109.2011.02573.x

Hucker, A., & McCabe, M.P. (2013). An online, mindfulness-based cognitive-behavioral therapy for female sexual difficulties: Impact on relationship functioning. *Journal of Sexual Medicine*, *40*(6), 561–576. doi: 10.1080/0092623X.2013.796578

Hulbert, S.F. (1991). The role of assertiveness in female sexuality: A comparative study between sexually assertive and sexually non-assertive women. *Journal of Sex and Marital Therapy*, *17*, 183–190.

Hurlbert, D.F., & Apt, C. (1995). The coital alignment technique and directed masturbation: A comparative study on female orgasm. *Journal of Sex and Marital Therapy*, *21*(1), 21–29.

Jones, L., & McCabe, M.P. (2011). The effectiveness of an internet-based psychological treatment program for female sexual dysfunction. *Journal of Sexual Medicine*, *8*, 2781–2792. doi: 10.1111/j.1743-6109.2011.02381.x

Kaplan, H.S. (1974). *The new sex therapy: Active treatment of sexual dysfunctions*. New York: Brunner/Mazel.

Kaplan, H.S. (1979). *Disorders of sexual desire*. New York: Brunner/Mazel.

Kaplan, H.S. (1983). *The evaluation of sexual disorders: Psychological and medical aspect*. New York: Brunner/Mazel.

Kelly, M.P., Strassberg, D.S., & Kircher, J.R. (1990). Attitudinal and experimental correlates of anorgasmia. *Archives of Sexual Behavior*, *19*, 165–177.

Kelly, M.P., Strassberg, D.S. & Turner, C.M. (2004). Communication and associated relationship issues in female anorgasmia. *Journal of Sex and Marital Therapy*, *30*, 263–276. doi: 10.1080/00926230490422403

Kelly, M.P., Strassberg, D.S., & Turner, C.M. (2006). Behavioral assessment of couples' communication in female orgasmic disorder. *Journal of Sex and Marital Therapy*, *32*, 81–95.

Kilmann, P.R., Boland, J.P., Norton, S.P., Davidson, E., & Caird, C. (1986). Perspectives of sex therapy outcome: A survey of AASECT providers. *Journal of Sex and Marital Therapy*, *12*, 116–138.

King, R., Belsky, J., Mah, K., & Binik, Y. (2011). Are there different types of female orgasm? *Archives of Sexual Behavior*, *40*(5), 865–875. doi: 10.1007/s10508-010-9639-7

Komisaruk, B.R., Whipple, B., Crawford, A., Grimes, S., Liu, W.C., Kalnin, A., & Mosier, K. (2004). Brain activation during vaginocervical self-stimulation and orgasm in women with complete spinal cord injury: fMRI evidence of mediation by the vagus nerves. *Brain Research*, *1024*(1–2), 77–88.

Kope, S.A. (2007) Female sexual arousal and orgasm: Pleasures and problems. In L. VanderCreek, F. Peterson, & J. Bley (Eds.), *Innovations in clinical practices: Focus on sexual health* (pp. 93–106). Sarasota, FL: Professional Resource Press.

Kuriansky, J.B., Sharp, L., & O'Connor, D. (1982). The treatment of anorgasmia: Long-term effectiveness of a short-term behavioral group intervention. *Journal of Sex and Marital Therapy*, *8*, 29–43.

Laan, E.H., & Rellini, A.H. (2011). Can we treat anorgasmia in women? The challenge to experiencing pleasure. *Sexual & Relationship Therapy*, *26*, 329–341. doi: 10.1080/14681994.2011.649691

Leitenberg, H., Greenwald, E., & Tarran, M.J. (1989). The relation between sexual activity among children during preadolescence and/or early adolescence and sexual behavior and sexual adjustment in young adulthood. *Archives of Sexual Behavior*, *18*, 299–313.

LoPiccolo, J., & Stock, W.E. (1986). Treatment of sexual dysfunction. *Journal of Consulting and Clinical Psychology*, *54*, 158–167.

Mark, K.P., & Jozkowski, K.N. (2013). The mediating role of sexual and nonsexual communication between relationship and sexual satisfaction in a sample of college-age heterosexual couples. *Journal of Sex & Marital Therapy*, *39*(5), 410–427. doi: 10.1080/0092623X.2011.644652

Masters, W.H., & Johnson, V. (1966). *Human sexual response*. Oxford, England: Little, Brown.

Masters, W.H., & Johnson, V. (1970). *Human sexual inadequacy*. Boston: Little, Brown.

McCabe, M.P. (1991). The development and maintenance of sexual dysfunction: An explanation based on cognitive theory. *Sexual and Marital Therapy*, *6*, 245–260.

McCabe, M.P. (1999). The interrelationship between intimacy, relationship functioning, and sexuality among men and women in committed relationships. *The Canadian Journal of Human Sexuality*, *8*, 31–38.

McCabe, M. P. (2001). De we need a classification system for female sexual dysfunction? A comment on the 1999 Consensus Classification System. *Journal of Sex and Marital Therapy*, 27, 175–178.

McCabe, M. P. (2005). The role of performance anxiety in the development and maintenance of sexual dysfunction in men and women. *International Journal of Stress Management*, 12, 379–388. doi: 10.1037/1072-5245.12.4.379

McCabe, M. P., & Cobain, M. (1998). The impact of individual and relationship factors on sexual dysfunction among males and females. *Sexual and Marital Therapy*, 13, 131–143.

McCabe, M. P., & Delaney, S. M. (1991). An evaluation of therapeutic programs for the treatment of secondary inorgasmia in women. *Archives of Sexual Behavior*, 21, 69–89.

McCabe, M. P. & Giles, K. (2012). Differences between sexually functional and dysfunctional women in psychological and relationships domains. *International Journal of Sexual Health*, 24, 181–194. doi: 10.1080/19317611.2012.680686

McCabe, M. P., & Jones, L. (2013). Attrition from an internet-based treatment program for female sexual dysfunction: Who is best treated with this approach? *Psychology, Medicine & Health*. doi: 10.1080/13548605.2013.764460

McGovern, K. B., McMullen, R. S., & LoPiccolo, J. (1978). Secondary orgasmic dysfunction. 1. Analysis and strategies for treatment. In J. LoPiccolo & L. LoPiccolo (Eds.), *Handbook of sex therapy*. New York: Plenum Press.

Meston, C. M., Hull, E., Levin, R. J., & Sipski, M. (2004). Disorders of orgasm in women. *Journal of Sexual Medicine*, 1(1), 66–68.

Morokoff, P. J., & Gillilland, R. (1993). Stress, sexual functioning and sexual satisfaction. *Journal of Sex Research*, 30, 43–53.

Muehlenhard, C. L., & Shippee, S. K. (2010). Men's and women's reports of pretending orgasm. *Journal of Sex Research*, 47(6), 552–567. doi: 10.1080/00224490903171794

Nin, A. (1978). *Delta of venus*. London: Allen.

Nin, A. (1979). *Little birds*. London: Allen.

O'Donohue, W. T., Dopke, C. A., & Swingen, D. N. (1997). Psychotherapy for female sexual dysfunction: A review. *Clinical Psychiatry Review*, 17, 537–566.

O'Donahue, W. T., Swingen, D. N., Dopke, C. A., & Roger, L. G. (1999). Psychotherapy for male sexual dysfunction. *Clinical Psychiatry Review*, 19, 591–630.

Obstfeld, L. S., Lupfer, M. B., & Lupfer, S. L. (1985). Exploring the relationship between gender identity and sexual functioning. *Journal of Sex and Marital Therapy*, 11, 248–258.

Pascoal, P.M., Narciso, I., & Pereira, N. M. (2014). What is sexual satisfaction? Thematic analysis of lay people's definitions, *Journal of Sex Research*, 51(1), 22–30. doi: 10.1080/00224499.2013.815149

Pietropinto, A. (1986). Male contribution to female sexual dysfunction. *Medical Aspects of Human Sexuality*, 20, 84–91.

Purcell, C., & McCabe, M. P. (1992). The impact of imagery type and imagery training on the subjective sexual arousal of women. *Sexual and Marital Therapy*, 7, 251–260.

Ramage, M. (2004). Female sexual dysfunction. *Women's Health Medicine*, 3(2), 84–88.

Reissing, E. D., Andruff (Armstrong), H. L., & Wentland, J. J. (2012). Looking back: The experience of first sexual intercourse and current sexual adjustment in young heterosexual adults. *The Journal of Sex Research*, 49(1), 27–35. doi: 10.1080/00224499.2010.538951

Riley, A. I., & Riley, E. J. (1978). A controlled study to evaluate directed masturbation in the management of primary orgasmic failure in women. *British Journal of Psychiatry*, 133, 404–409.

Roffe, M. W., & Britt, B. C. (1981). A typology of marital interaction for sexually dysfunctional couples. *Journal of Sex and Marital Therapy*, 7, 207–222.

Shifren, J. L., Monz, B. U., Russo, P. A., Segreti, A., & Johannes, C. B. (2008). Sexual problems and distress in United States women: prevalence and correlates. *Obstetrics and Gynecology*, 112(5), 970–978. doi: 10.1097/AOG.0b013e3181898cdb

Snyder, D. K., & Berg, P. (1983). Determinants of sexual dissatisfaction in sexually distressed couples. *Archives of Sexual Behavior*, 12, 237–246.

Talmadge, L. D., & Wallace, S. C. (1991). Reclaiming sexuality in female incest survivors. *Journal of Sex and Marital Therapy*, 17, 163–182.

Taublieb, A. B., & Lick, J. R. (1986). Female orgasm via penile stimulation: A criterion of adequate sexual functioning? *Journal of Sex and Marital Therapy, 12*, 60–64.

Travis, R. P., & Travis, P. Y. (1986). Intimacy based sex therapy. *Journal of Sex Education and Therapy, 12*, 21–27.

Wallen, K., & Lloyd, E. A. (2010). Female sexual arousal: Genital anatomy and orgasm in intercourse. *Hormones and Behavior, 59*(5), 780–792. doi: 10.1016/j.yhbeh.2010.12.004

Walsh, K. E., & Berman, J. R. (2004). Sexual dysfunction in the older woman—An overview of the current understanding and management. *Drugs & Aging, 21*, 655–675. doi: 10.2165/00002512-200421100-00004

Weeks, G. (1994). The intersystem model: An integrative approach to treatment. In G. Weeks & L. Hof (Eds.), *The marital relationship casebook: Theory and application of the Intersystem Model* (pp. 3–34). New York: Brunner/Mazel.

Weeks, G. (2004). The emergence of a new paradigm in sex therapy: Integration. *Sexual and Relationship Therapy, 20*, 89–103.

Weeks, G., & Gambescia, N. (2009). A systemic approach to sensate focus. In K. Hertlein, G. Weeks, & N. Gambescia, *Systemic sex therapy* (pp. 341–362). New York: Routledge.

Youn, G. (2006). Subjective sexual arousal in response to erotica: effects of gender, guided fantasy, erotic stimulus, and duration of exposure. *Archives of Sexual Behavior, 35*(1), 87–97. doi: 10.1007/s10508-006-8997-z

11

PAINFUL INTERCOURSE
Genito-Pelvic Pain/Penetration Disorder

Marta Meana, Caroline Maykut, and Evan Fertel

Genito-Pelvic Pain/Penetration Disorder (GPPPD) is a disorder of pain and of sex. The pain wreaks havoc on the sex. It sets the stage for the development or reinforcement of co-morbid sexual dysfunctions, negative sexual attitudes, avoidant and damaging behaviors, relationship discord, and declines in self-esteem and mood. These, in turn, augment the experience of pain. Despite significant overlap, pain may require certain interventions while sexual problems may require others. An Intersystem or integrative approach (Hertlein & Weeks, 2009) is thus the way to maximize effectiveness in the treatment of GPPPD. In fact, a sex therapist alone is unlikely to comprehensively assess or effectively treat the painful intercourse without the concurrent (rather than sequential) collaboration of one or more other health professionals (Binik & Meana, 2009). A sex therapist, however, may be ideally suited to coordinate the effort, if he/she has an understanding of the multidimensionality involved. The effort is a considerable one, as GPPPD can be a difficult problem to resolve.

[handwritten margin note: Collaboration]

Definition and Description

GPPPD is a new diagnosis in the recently published fifth edition of the Diagnostic and Statistical Manual of Mental Disorders (*DSM-5*; American Psychiatric Association [APA], 2013) that applies only to women (Öberg, Fugl-Meyer, & Fugl-Meyer, 2004). In the prior edition of the DSM (*DSM-IV TR*; APA, 2000), women who experienced pain or difficulties with penile-vaginal intercourse were diagnosed with dyspareunia or vaginismus. A diagnosis of dyspareunia required recurrent or persistent genital pain with sexual intercourse and was applicable to men also; a diagnosis of vaginismus required a recurrent or persistent involuntary spasm of the outer third of the vagina sufficiently intense to interfere with intercourse. Women with dyspareunia presented with pain but women with vaginismus presented with what they perceived to be the impossibility of penetration (e.g., "it can't go in"). The rationale for collapsing these two disorders under a new classification and set of criteria emanates from 20 years of research that (1) supported a conceptualization of dyspareunia as a pain disorder that interfered with sex rather than as a psychosexual disorder that resulted in pain, and (2) found little evidence for the vaginal spasm that purportedly distinguished vaginismus from dyspareunia; vaginal hypertonicity is found in both *DSM-IV* disorders; anxiety and avoidance appeared to be the more reliable distinguishing factors. The rationale for excluding men from the diagnosis of GPPPD appears to lie in a lack of research on male dyspareunia (Binik, 2010a; 2010b).

A diagnosis of GPPPD requires the persistence of one of four symptoms (1) difficulty with vaginal penetration during sexual intercourse, (2) marked genital or pelvic pain during intercourse attempts, (3) significant fear of pain as a result of vaginal penetration, (4) tensing or tightening of the pelvic floor muscles during attempted vaginal penetration (APA, 2013). The difficulty has to have lasted for a minimum duration of approximately 6 months, cause clinically significant distress, and not be better explained by a non-sexual mental disorder or as a consequence of severe relationship distress or other significant stressors, or attributable to the effects of a substance/medication or another medical condition.

In addition, GPPPD has two specifiers: whether the dysfunction is *lifelong* (present since the individual became sexually active) or *acquired* (the problem began after a period of normal sexual function) and the level of distress experienced (*mild, moderate, severe*). Finally, the text of the *DSM-5* emphasizes the importance of assessing five potential influences on GPPPD: (1) partner factors, such as partner sexual dysfunction and health status; (2) relationship factors, such as desire discrepancies and poor communication; (3) individual vulnerabilities, such as history of abuse or body image concerns, psychiatric comorbidity, or stressors such as socio-economic difficulties or caretaking; (4) cultural or religious factors that impinge on sexual expression or pleasure; (5) medical factors relevant to etiology and treatment (APA, 2013).

Given the new set of criteria, the prevalence of GPPPD has not yet been ascertained. Epidemiological studies on the old diagnoses of dyspareunia and vaginimus, however, provide a good sense of how common this problem is. Prevalence estimates for dyspareunia have ranged from 14–34% in younger women and 6.5–45% in older women (van Lankveld et al., 2010). Vaginismus, diagnosed primarily via its characteristic intercourse-related anxiety and intense avoidance of the activity rather than by vaginal hypertonicity, is substantially rarer with estimates ranging from .4–6% (ter Kuile & Reissing, 2014).

Etiology

The etiological literature here reviewed is based on the old diagnoses of dyspareunia and vaginismus as there have yet to be studies on the etiology GPPPD. As dyspareunia and vaginismus are encompassed within GPPPD, the reader can simply consider them to be different presentations of GPPPD.

Individual Physiological Factors

There are many physiological factors that can result in pain with intercourse. Acute and chronic diseases, such as pelvic inflammatory disease, endometriosis, urinary tract, yeast infections, and dermatosis have been linked to pain with intercourse, as have changes in vaginal structure, elasticity, and lubrication associated with menopause-related reductions in estrogen. Episiotomies, other genital surgeries/procedures, and chemotherapy can also result in painful intercourse (Meana, 2012; van Lankveldt et al., 2010). The most common type of intercourse pain, however, appears to be genital (rather than pelvic) pain and the most common cause for that pain appears to be provoked vestibulodynia (PVD) (Harlow, Wise, & Stewart, 2001). PVD is characterized by a burning pain experienced on the vulvar vestibule (entry of the vagina) when pressure is placed on it by any stimulus (e.g., penis, tampon, speculum) (Moyal-Barracco & Lynch, 2004). PVD appears to involve nociceptor proliferation and sensitization and has been linked to recurrent vaginal infections, and early and prolonged use of oral contraceptives (Bergeron, Rosen, & Pukall, in press;

van Lankveld et al., 2010). Pelvic floor abnormalities (hypertonicity or hypotonicity) also have a strong association with genital pain and difficulties with penetration (ter Kuile & Reissing, 2014). Sometimes, the extent to which hypertonicity is a cause or a consequence of painful intercourse can be unclear, although making this distinction may not be that important to treatment efforts.

Individual Psychological Factors

There is little support for any one psychological etiology in the development of painful intercourse. Most women with GPPPD do not differ from controls on psychological factors other than pain-related expectancies, cognitions, and affect. Although these alone are unlikely to cause pain, their mediating effect is sufficiently substantial to consider them the equivalent of etiologic factors. In fact, research has repeatedly shown that the following factors are associated with higher pain intensity in women who have pain with intercourse (Desrochers, Bergeron, Landry, & Jodoin, 2008; Meana, 2012):

- Somatic hypervigilance
- Pain catastrophizing
- Fear of pain
- Negative attitudes about sexuality
- Distraction from sexual cues
- Anxiety
- Negative causal attributions for the pain
- Feelings of low self-efficacy in coping with pain
- Depressive symptoms

Increasingly, the fear-avoidance model of chronic pain is being invoked to illustrate the negative feedback loop in women with GPPPD (Vlaeyen & Linton, 2000). Intercourse pain produces fear and catastrophic cognitions, which lead to a somatic hypervigilance that magnifies sensations, ultimately resulting in a woman avoiding sexual intercourse as much as possible. A history of sexual, physical, and psychological abuse is more common in women with GPPPD symptoms, although the vast majority report no abuse (Harlow & Stewart, 2005; Landry & Bergeron, 2011; Reissing et al., 2003). Additionally, it is essential to assess for other comorbid psychological conditions in the woman or her partner as these individual factors can complicate the clinical picture.

Couple Factors

Research on the role of relational factors in the experience of pain with intercourse is in its nascence, but findings are pointing to promising avenues for intervention. General relationship adjustment has not been linked to painful intercourse. This may be, in part, because couples whose relationship does not survive the experience simply do not present to research studies or to therapy. On the other hand, partner reactions to the problem of PVD are now being repeatedly associated with pain intensity in the woman, as well as with well-being and sexual function in both partners (Rosen et al., 2014; Smith & Pukall, 2011). The determining reactions appear to be whether the partner is highly solicitous, negative, or facilitative. Partners who score high on solicitousness generally halt all sexual activity at the first hint of the woman's discomfort, thus reinforcing avoidance and precluding experimentation with the possibility that the discomfort may be tolerable or even overpowered by increasing arousal. Negative partner responses (e.g., hostility, anger) also predictably have negative outcomes. Alternately, facilitative partner responses characterized by encouraging the woman and positively reinforcing her attempts to have sex are associated with lower pain reports and greater well-being and sexual function in both the woman and her partner.

Intergenerational Factors

There is no research directly investigating family-of-origin factors related to the onset of painful intercourse, other than the possibility that there may be a genetic component. Independent studies have found approximately 30% of sufferers reporting to have relatives with the same complaint, and a susceptibility to inflammatory disorders have been identified for PVD (Burri, Cherkas, & Spector, 2009; Gerber, Bongiovanni, Ledger, & Witkin, 2002). On the other hand, the implication of negative sexual attitudes and childhood sexual abuse or victimization as possible risk factors for sexual pain indirectly suggest that family-of-origin factors may be involved in some cases. Lack of education about sexuality may also emanate from a particularly restrictive upbringing or one in which sexuality was considered a taboo subject. These links, however, are only speculative as there is currently insufficient data to indicate that the sexual pain disorders have a familial component.

Societal/Cultural Factors

It is difficult to determine empirically the impact of societal/cultural factors on painful intercourse. There is some suggestion that religious orthodoxy may be a risk factor for the development of vaginismus (ter Kuile & Reissing, 2014), which has also been found to be more prevalent in less educated women and in first-generation immigrants to Western Europe (Öberg et al., 2004). Research emanating from Turkey suggests a higher prevalence of vaginismus than is generally found in North America and Western Europe and this may be a function of the fact that Turkey is at a crossroads between a religious culture that is generally sex-negative and a more secular culture in which sex research into such culturally delicate issues is actually being conducted (see Sungur, 2012).

More generally, women continue to be socio-politically disempowered in comparison to men and their sexuality remains central to their socio-culturally defined sense of worth. This can translate into the stigmatization of women who encounter problems with their sexual function. Indeed, in a qualitative study of young American women with dyspareunia, Donaldson and Meana (2011) found embarrassment and fear of stigma to be primary reasons given for not reporting the problem or seeking help. Historically, women who have resisted sexual activity for one reason or another have been denigrated and had their femininity questioned. Against this backdrop, it would not be surprising if many women with intercourse pain experience a sense of inadequacy and unspoken pressure to persist with partnered sex, sometimes silently, despite significant pain. This societal overlay on a distressing set of symptoms can contribute to their exacerbation.

Assessment

Although GPPPD is a female sexual dysfunction, it is essentially a couple dysfunction. Sometimes the couple will present for therapy; however, often, women assume they will be engaging in individual therapy. They believe they are the ones with "the problem."

Correcting this misattribution is the first important therapeutic intervention. Most partners can be persuaded to participate, as they are generally motivated to resolve the sexual dilemma. There are, however, exceptions and the therapist has to do his/her best under the circumstances.

Involving a gynecologist is essential, but will require the therapist to identify gynecologists in their community who have a special interest and expertise in genital pain. Women with these problems have traditionally been considered difficult patients because of the elusiveness of a cure. There are, thus, many physicians who are reluctant to treat them. The involvement of a gynecologist who is interested and invested in both assessment and treatment of painful intercourse can be an important factor in the outcome. Some women with the symptoms of vaginismus will never have had a gynecological examination and believe that it is not possible. However, gynecologists familiar with this disorder usually succeed in performing the examination. It may require that the therapist be present to help the client with relaxation.

Lastly, it is not unusual for primary presenting problems to end up being secondary to more serious ones that are disclosed or discovered well after the initial intake. This is especially true in Intersystem therapy, as the interactions between the systems may take a long time to reveal themselves clearly. It is thus essential that the therapist retain a hypothesis-testing attitude throughout the treatment, integrate assessment at all stages and not become overly attached to initial case conceptualizations. This attitude also requires that the therapist have the flexibility to change treatment course, if ongoing assessment indicates a re-direction in treatment.

Preliminary Assessment and Consultation

Pain is the primary presenting complaint in GPPPD and thus it should be assessed first. Essential questions include:

- Where exactly does it hurt when you have or attempt sexual intercourse? (A diagram or model of the genital and pelvic region will be very helpful here).
- Describe the pain in terms of intensity (1–10 scale) and quality (descriptors like "burning" or "tearing").
- When does the pain start (before, during, or after penetration)?
- How long does the pain last?
- Do you always have pain with intercourse or does it depend on certain conditions (e.g., fatigue, menstrual cycle, level of arousal)?
- Do you have genital or pelvic pain with other sexual or non-sexual stimulation (e.g., finger insertion, oral sex, tampon insertion, gynecological exam)? By genital pain, we mean pain felt directly in the vulvar or vaginal area; by pelvic pain, we mean pain in your lower abdomen.
- Do you ever have genital or pelvic pain spontaneously, without any stimulation?
- In your lifetime, when did you start having pain with intercourse (from the first time you had intercourse or did it start later)?
- Is the pain at the opening of the vagina (intriotus)?
- Is the pain deep in the pelvis? Do you feel it in the lower abdomen?
- To what extent do you or your partner anticipate pain during intercourse?
- To what extent do you or your partner engage in efforts (direct or indirect) to avoid having sexual intercourse?

195

This pain assessment should also be followed up with a referral to a gynecologist who is knowledgeable about this disorder and who can investigate the location of the pain with a vulvar cotton swab test (to assess for painful conditions of the inner folds of the vulva) and digital exploration. The gynecologist needs to determine if the client has any of the physiological risk factors covered in the physiological etiology section of this chapter. The therapist should ask the client to obtain a release of information from the gynecologist so as to facilitate consultation.

The sexual function of both the client and her partner should be the immediate next target of assessment. Most important to cover are the perceived impact of the pain on their sexual life (frequency of intercourse and other sexual activity, desire, arousal, orgasm, satisfaction), as well as the existence of co-morbid sexual dysfunctions. Additionally, it is useful to determine if the couple continues to be sexual non-coitally or if they have abandoned attempts to be sexually intimate. For the purposes of the latter, it may be expedient to administer the *Female Sexual Function Index* (FSFI: Rosen et al., 2000) to women and the *International Index of Erectile Function* (IIEF; Rosen et al., 1997) to men. Treatment may need to address multiple sexual problems simultaneously. For therapists interested in developing a client-administered assessment protocol as an adjunct to the clinical interview, Pukall, Meana, and Fernandez (2010) provide a comprehensive review of the most psychometrically sound measures of sexual dysfunction.

The cognitive and coping styles of both partners are also important to assess. Why do they think they have this problem? What do they fear? What do they think it means, if anything? How do they cope with it? Self-administered measures can also be useful at this point. Of particular relevance would be the *Pain Catastrophizing Scale* (PCS; Sullivan, Bishop, & Pivik, 1995) and the *Vaginal Penetration Cognition Questionnaire* (VPCQ; Klaassen & ter Kuile, 2009), which assesses maladaptive cognitions about sexual intercourse.

Given recent data on the importance of partner reactions, it is also important to assess the extent to which partners are engaging in solicitous, negative and/or facilitative responses. Asking the couple to keep a diary of their intercourse attempts that includes perceived and actual partner responses, as well as pain intensity and other sexual outcomes of interest can be very helpful. More generally, it is imperative that the temperature of the relationship be taken at this stage, in part because treatment will rely to a great extent on the ability of the relationship to navigate the challenges of treatment.

Treatment-Integrated Assessment

The Intersystem Approach places a significant burden on assessment, as it broadens the playing field substantially. It is neither reasonable nor productive to attempt to assess all possible contributors to the problem before starting treatment. The preliminary assessment provides a current snapshot of pain, sexual function, coping style, and relationship distress/reactions. There is some urgency, though, for treatment to commence. Further assessment can be integrated throughout the treatment. Sexual history, developmental and familial factors of relevance, general ideology about sexuality and gender, and the role that the pain problem plays in the relationship will more slowly become manifest as trust and rapport between the therapist and the couple grow. The treatment itself will raise issues of which clients were unaware at intake. That is how assessment and treatment are inseparable in an Intersystem Approach to GPPPD.

Treatment

1. Initial Stage: Education, Goal Setting, Anxiety Reduction

Education is an integral part of the initial stage of therapy. Most clients will know close to nothing about GPPPD and even less about its treatment. Moreover, they may not know anything about the anatomy and constituents of the vulva. It is essential that the therapist be well-versed in the outcome research on diseases of the vulva, medications and procedures, which may include anti-fungals, anti-allergens, topical estrogen, topical steroids, anti-depressants, or even the recommendation of surgery. In addition to imparting his/her knowledge, the therapist can provide clients with reading materials, as appropriate.

In the context of the initial assessment and gynecological findings, it is time to calibrate expectations and set reasonable treatment goals (Curtin, Ward, Merriwether, & Allison, 2011). At the beginning of therapy, clients are often filled with hope that this problem will finally be resolved. The literature, however, indicates that the complete resolution of genital pain is often difficult to attain. While hope is integral to treatment, expectations also need to be realistic. Aligning client expectations with the empirical data and setting goals that aim at pain reduction and increases in sexual function and satisfaction are central to the therapeutic effort.

Although most clients are hopeful as they start therapy, they are also understandably anxious. They believe treatment will be focused on the one activity they have been avoiding or fearing for a long time. It is also the activity that has often resulted in arguments, fears of abandonment, and feelings of inadequacy. The therapist can help allay the anxiety in the initial stage of therapy by starting to address some of the less threatening aspects of the pain problem. The following are a number of techniques that can be instrumental in the first stages of therapy:

Reinforcing help-seeking. The client and her partner should be commended for addressing the problem. They should be informed that failing to address the issue would likely only have made it further degenerate—that confronting the pain problem indicates strength and will, both of which auger well for treatment outcome.

Validating the experience of pain. Many women experiencing pain with intercourse have been told that or wonder if the pain is "in their heads" or a somatic manifestation of intra-psychic or relational conflict. Emphasizing that their pain is real is crucial. It is also important to explain that the exploration of well-being, sexual function, and/or their relationship reflects an understanding that these issues can have an impact on the pain, not that they are the "real" problem.

Demystifying pain. Even seemingly inexplicable pain has its patterns. One way of transforming the pain from a mysterious tormentor to a more controllable force is to train the client to explore the conditions under which the pain is minimized and maximized. A pain diary can be very helpful in this regard, as clients monitor conditions when the pain occurred (e.g., emotions, thoughts, behaviors, arousal level, and relationship interactions before, during, and after the pain). For women who have stopped attempting sexual intercourse, this demystification may simply involve a retrospective analysis of factors that made it worse or better.

Demystifying anxiety. Anxiety is not an inevitable reaction to the pain problem. It can be targeted and reduced or eradicated. Starting to do so using relaxation therapy techniques (e.g., imaging, breathing exercises, progressive muscle relaxation, mindfulness), cognitive re-structuring, and de-catastrophization can be important steps.

Genital self-exploration. Many women who experience intercourse pain have developed an avoidance of their genitalia. They usually have not tried to explore and locate where it hurts. Getting women re-acquainted with their genitalia can be useful for a number of reasons: (1) they can locate painful areas, (2) they can experiment with muscle exercises, (3) they develop self-efficacy, whereby they come to control certain aspects of their genitalia (muscle flexing).

Giving the woman control over penetration. Because penetration is painful, it is essential at the beginning of treatment to emphasize that the woman "calls the shots" in terms of whether penetration happens and in terms of its pacing. This intervention will immediately help with the pain experience as it will be her who agrees to it rather than her who is subjected to it. The distinction is crucial.

De-emphasizing intercourse. Letting the client know that much of the work ahead will focus on increasing desire, arousal, and relational connectedness rather than on increasing intercourse frequency will relieve anxiety. Discouraging or even banning intercourse until a later stage in the treatment may be indicated. Clients often experience these interventions as significant stress reducers that help them concentrate on the other aspects of the treatment.

Emphasizing affection and sensuality. Directing clients to increase their non-sexual demonstrations of physical affection is an important step. It is common for couples who have stopped having sex or greatly curtailed it to avoid all forms of physical contact. This damages their connectedness and alienates them from each other, both psychologically and physically.

2. Core Stage of Treatment: Connecting the Dots of Pain, Sex, Self, and Partner

The treatment of GPPPD targets the interrelated domains of pain, sex, individual factors, and couple dynamics concurrently. This does not necessarily mean that every session has to cover these four domains. Some sessions will focus more on the sexual aspects than on the relational ones. Other sessions might fall exclusively into the domain of individual beliefs. That is perfectly natural and desirable. Treatment plans need to be responsive to snags along the way, as well as to the primacy of one domain over others in contributing to the disorder. But pain, sex, individual concerns, and couple dynamics all need to be juggled throughout the treatment. The neglect of any one of them can impact outcome negatively.

Pain and Physiological Processes

Addressing the gynecological consult. If the gynecologist consult has resulted in a recommendation for either a medical or surgical treatment component, the sex therapist is well-advised to further familiarize him/herself with the details of that recommendation. There is controversy about some of the medical and surgical options, and clients may not know this. The therapist is well-positioned to educate the client about these treatment options so that she can make an informed decision. If the client chooses to undergo a certain procedure or medical regimen, the therapist can also help the client adhere to the treatment and adjust to its effects.

Coordinating with physical therapy. Following the gynecological consult, it is often appropriate for the client to be assessed and treated by a physical therapist who specializes in pelvic floor dysfunction (Rosenbaum, 2007). Such physical therapists can be found by accessing the national database of the American Physical Therapy Association (www.apta.org). Individual states also have their own physical therapy association with referral directories. Research indicates that physical therapy can result in pain reduction and improved sexual function (Bergeron et al., 2002; Gentilcore-Saulnier, McLean, Goldfinger, Pukall, & Chamberlain, 2010; Goldfinger, Pukall, Gentilcore-Saulnier, McLean, & Chamberlain, 2009; Reissing, Armstrong, & Allen, 2013).

The number of physical therapy sessions can vary from a couple to several, and they focus on education about musculature and its role, manual therapy, and home exercises. Physical therapy can also include pelvic floor biofeedback and electrical stimulation. Rosenbaum (2007) provides a detailed description of the physical therapy regimen. Ideally, the sex therapist collaborates with the physical therapist, especially in the planning and execution of vaginal dilatation. Vaginal dilatation is, in part, a form of systematic desensitization whereby the woman is instructed to insert dilators of increasing size into her vagina over a period of time. These dilators can be bought from a number of sources easily accessible through the Internet. Although the involvement of a physical therapist is optimal, circumstances (financial difficulty or lack of local professionals) can sometimes preclude this team approach. In those cases, carefully guided vaginal dilatation exercises are still worth attempting, even without physical therapy involvement. They work as a type of systematic desensitization that will be particularly effective with women who have the fear and anxiety associated with the former diagnosis of vaginismus. When the woman moves beyond her own insertion of the dilators to penile insertion, it is also important, as aforementioned, that the woman initially be in charge of the rate, extent, and movement during these first penile penetration attempts.

Addressing influences on pain. In the initial stage of therapy, women are asked to monitor influences on the pain experience, using a pain diary. This identification of exacerbating and alleviating factors can now be translated into specific interventions to improve the conditions under which sex takes place. The point is to learn from the diary and then try to instate the best possible conditions for sexual interactions, conditions that minimize the pain experience.

Sexual Interactions

Making quality time. Even couples who are not dealing with painful sex often fall into the trap of neglecting their sexual life. The multiple demands of busy professional lives and a laundry list of childcare activities can easily push couple-focused activities to the very bottom of the priority list. Many couples present to therapy saying that by the time they get to bed after a long day of obligations, they are exhausted. The result is that they either do not have sex at all or they have a routine, disengaged, and uninspired version of it. If you add pain to this scenario, the situation worsens considerably. Thus, the first change the couple needs to enact is to reserve quality time for sexual interactions. Some couples find it useful to set aside special times during the week for their sexual encounters. Other couples find this overly staged and lacking in spontaneity. Scheduled or not, sex cannot be neglected. It requires quality time and attention.

Building desire and arousal. It is well known that painful intercourse impacts all stages of the sexual response: desire, arousal, and orgasm. It is difficult for a woman to desire what hurts and/or to get aroused when she is anticipating pain. It may also be challenging for her partner to feel desire and become or stay aroused to an activity he knows she finds aversive. Difficulties with desire and arousal may also predate the onset of the pain. In most cases, reinstating desire and arousal is likely to be an essential part of any treatment plan for dyspareunia and vaginismus. There are a number of ways to target desire and arousal. The following are some suggested strategies, although not all of these will be appropriate for all clients and their partners.

Enhancing self-perceptions of desirability. In order for most women to feel sexy, they have to believe in their own desirability. They have to find themselves attractive before they believe anybody else's assessment. Partner compliments about physical attractiveness are often dismissed as thinly veiled attempts to get sex. It is thus important to build a woman's sense of her own attractiveness. This can be a challenge considering the idealized images of beauty that the media bombards us with. The therapist can, however, work individually with each woman to heighten her sense of desirability, both cognitively and behaviorally. Most women have ideas about realistic things they can do to make themselves feel more attractive.

Use of erotica (books or videos). These materials can be used in anticipation of a sexual interaction, as part of one, or privately by the woman alone. They are "getting in the mood" strategies than can be instrumental, as long as the client chooses materials that are tasteful to her.

Directed solitary masturbation. Women who experience pain with intercourse have often stopped engaging in any sexual activity, even masturbation. Re-introducing masturbation may be useful to build desire and arousal, as well as to reacquaint the client with her genitalia. Some women will never have masturbated at all and a discussion about their desire to do so is indicated.

Heightening awareness of arousal. Because arousal is a relatively concealed phenomenon in women, many fail to attend to its physiological signs, such as lubrication and genital swelling. Heightening their awareness of these signs can serve two functions. First, the physiological feedback may increase subjective arousal. Second, since intercourse is likely to be less painful when the woman is aroused, it is useful for her (and her partner) to recognize the signs of arousal (e.g., lubrication, genital swelling) so that intercourse is not attempted until these signs are present.

Mindfulness. Related to heightening awareness of arousal is the more general principle of mindfulness which involves focusing on what is happening in the present in a non-evaluative way. Much of the anxiety that occurs during sex involves imagining negative outcomes. A mindfulness approach can help to focus the woman and her partner on immediately current sensations without the interfering anticipation of next steps (see Rosenbaum, 2013).

Expanding the sexual repertoire. Many people define sex exclusively as intercourse. The rest is considered foreplay and thus demoted to the status of preparations for the main event. It is thus not surprising that when couples have difficulties with intercourse, they have a tendency to drop all sexual interactions. What is the point of preparing for something that is not going to happen or that is going to feel bad anyway? Changing that focus is a good strategy for all couples and an essential one for couples who have painful intercourse. As stated in several chapters of this text, sex includes many acts that provide intense pleasure and orgasm. A couple who deprives themselves of these experiences because intercourse is problematic is missing out on a potentially very satisfying sex life. Furthermore, increasing the emphasis on non-intercourse sexual acts can also have the effect of raising arousal levels, which in turn decreases the intensity of pain. Finally, expanding the repertoire can also result in more exciting and less mechanistic sex. Rather than playing out the same script every time in the same order, sex can be open to variations and spontaneity. The expansion of the sexual repertoire has traditionally been implemented through sensate focus exercises designed to shift the attention from the performance of intercourse

200

and its attendant anxiety to the experience of sensual pleasure. Sensate focus exercises are used for multiple reasons; including, helping the woman become more aware of her own sensual and sexual pleasure and getting the couple re-connected physically. Sensate focus was first developed by Masters and Johnson (1970) but the technique was not further developed and make client-friendly until a chapter was written by Weeks and Gambescia (2009). But expanding the sexual repertoire is also about branching out in terms of locations and situations. Sex does not always have to happen in the bedroom with the lights out at 11 pm. It can happen in the kitchen, fully clothed at 2 pm! This may be challenging for some couples with children and hectic work schedules, but arrangements can be made to facilitate these interludes if the couple has the will. They should be encouraged to think outside their box to the extent they find acceptable. There are a number of books that couples may find helpful in their attempts to expand their sexual repertoire. Three of these are *The Guide to Getting it On! A Book About the Wonders of Sex* (Joannides, 2012), *The Joy of Sex: The Ultimate Revised Edition* (Comfort, 2009), and *The Good Vibrations Guide to Sex: The Most Complete Sex Manual Ever Written* (Winks & Semans, 2002).

Communicating preferences and corrective feedback. Even couples who claim to be very connected emotionally will often report that communicating directly about sex is difficult. They struggle with the best way to say things and are afraid to hurt each other's feelings, more so than in other aspects of their shared lives. The unfortunate result of this can be enduring unpleasant sexual experiences and missing out on other experiences that could easily be introduced or increased. Couples can be taught to communicate about sex in non-hurtful productive ways. Many are uncomfortable vocalizing preferences during sex, but there are other ways to communicate. They can do so verbally after sex and they can do so with their bodies during sex. Below are three strategies, although the therapist should ask couples directly if they have any other ideas about how they can communicate sexual preferences in ways that are acceptable to them. When on task, couples can be quite creative in their problem-solving about these matters.

Corrective feedback. After a sexual interaction, each person can identify two things the partner did that were real "turn-ons" and two things that were less than desirable. Requiring that both of them engage in this exercise removes the feared elements of blame and hurt. This feedback will then be incorporated into the next love-making session to enhance the next experience.

Body shifts. The body can be a terrific communicator if the partner is "listening". Often, a very minor shift or repositioning in one direction or another can be just the adjustment to enhance pleasure and/or to communicate that something does not feel good.

Hand-guiding. Another technique is for one person to gently take their partner's hand and model for them the stimulation desired. This can be done quite seamlessly as part of the lovemaking. It can also be very arousing as both partners' hands together make the same motion.

Introducing levity into sex. For the couple who wants to maintain a sexual connection, sex needs to be taken seriously enough to prioritize it and to work on maintaining its vibrancy. On the other hand, many couples take what happens in any one sexual episode far too seriously. Clumsy attempts at arousing the partner are interpreted as reflections of personal inadequacy. Failure to "perform," as in the case in GPPPD, is often considered a disastrous event. Introducing a healthy sense of lightness and even humor into sex can be very liberating, as it relieves pressure and can also increase intimacy. Even highly satisfied couples report frequent episodes when the sex did not rock anybody's world. These less than perfect interactions do not have to signal doom. They can be opportunities to laugh and to feel close in these valiant but not always spectacular attempts.

Individual Proclivities

Challenging sexual and relationship schema. Each member of the couple comes to therapy with a set of beliefs or schema about pain, sex, and relationships. These beliefs may have their origins in personal experiences, familial upbringing, religion, culture of origin, or in broad societal messages about sexuality and gender. It is not uncommon to find generally sex-negative beliefs or specific beliefs about painful intercourse that are rooted in sexist notions of femininity as intrinsically linked to receptivity. While some of these beliefs need to be respected, others may be open to discussion and challenge. The therapist needs to explore which are which. Sometimes, clients are eager to be disabused of certain notions they find repressive, even when they have lived with them since childhood. Other clients are resistant to belief challenges. In every case, the therapist needs to remain sensitive to cultural values and not impose their world view on clients. Even within very restrictive sexual and relationship schema, the creative and culturally competent therapist can usually find room to work and improve the couple's situation.

Cognitive reframing. There are two cognitive styles that have been empirically identified in women who experience pain with intercourse: hypervigilance and catastrophization (Payne, Binik, Amsel, & Khalifé, 2005). In relation to painful intercourse, hypervigilance refers to a cognitive style in which there is acute attention to and monitoring of pain cues and of sensation in the genitalia that could signal the onset of pain. Catastrophization refers to a cognitive style that infers the worst possible outcome (Sullivan, Lynch, & Clark, 2005). A minor discomfort becomes an indication of irreversible physical damage. An insignificant argument signals the end of the relationship. The magnification characteristic of both hypervigilance and catastrophization can make the problem of painful intercourse much worse than it is. Challenging these distortions is an important part of therapy for women who experience painful intercourse. This can be accomplished with (1) education about the actual physiological consequences of pain with intercourse, (2) reality testing with the partner and the therapist, (3) exercises in which the client lists the evidence that supports and does not support her thoughts regarding what might happen when she has these sensations.

Coping reconstruction. Ineffective coping strategies also tend to be either avoidant or emotionally based. Avoidance is a dead-end. A classic example is negative reinforcement. It entails either denial of the problem or resignation to it. Although seeking therapy signals that the client has decided to address the problem, the therapist needs to keep in mind that the partner may have insisted on the therapy and/or the client will resist subsequent treatment steps as they approach the feared stimulus. Using a lay explanation of a classical conditioning paradigm, the therapist can explain why avoidance is highly reinforcing, yet ultimately counterproductive. The problem will not fix itself without direct confrontation. As a matter of fact, there is a very good chance that it will worsen. If resistance arises at different points in the treatment (and it usually does), it may be helpful to remind the client about the seductiveness and self-destructiveness of avoidance.

The emotionally-focused coping of many women who experience pain with intercourse (and their partners) can result in anger, hostility, depression, anxiety, shame, and sexual aversion. These emotional states damage the client's (and partner's) well-being and their relationship. However, these destructive emotional states are not inevitable, even when the pain persists. Therapists can teach their clients how to regulate emotions. The client can learn that pain does not have to result in an emotional reaction, especially considering that the emotional reaction is likely to increase pain. Emotional regulation involves the realizations that: (1) emotional reactions are often within a person's control—one can decide to submit to a feeling or not, (2) feeling something does not make it true, (3) it is not always useful to give free reign to a feeling, and (4) one can choose to feel something slightly different and more constructive. Emotional regulation is not about emotional repression. It is about not giving emotions more than their due.

Relationship Dynamics

schema

Bridging sexual and relationship schemas. Most individuals are unaware that they have sexual and relationship schema. A schema is an internalized pattern of thoughts, feelings, and behaviors organized around a particular topic. It is thus not surprising that couples rarely discuss their respective sexual and relationship belief differences about sex, gender, and relationships (Dattilio & Beck, 2013). The therapist can facilitate this discussion. Often couples are surprised to discover that they are working under substantially different assumptions. In the process of therapy, a wife may discover that her husband's beliefs about masculinity include the imperative to sexually satisfy his wife and that the GPPPD feels emasculating to him. A husband may discover that his wife believes the pain is some kind of divine retribution for past "promiscuity." Although the aim of this exploration is not necessarily to change anybody's views in particular, the discovery of different world views and their familial or cultural origins can help depersonalize conflicts and contextualize differences. This de-personalization and contextualization can also soften world views and make room for compromise positions and the discovery of common ground.

Encouraging individuation. In a relationship, it can sometimes be difficult to distinguish an individual problem from a relational one. Yet it might be the single most important skill to learn, both in terms of individual well-being and relationship adjustment. From the perspective of object relations theory, the goal is individuation—a state in which we have a sense of our autonomy and the autonomy of our partner, as well as a secure attachment (the assumption that abandonment is not imminent) to this partner. Our partners should be wanted, loved, desired, but not needed in order for us to feel whole and to function. The purpose of a partner is to enrich our life rather than to fill the missing piece in a fragile construction of self. In other words, only whole people can have whole relationships. If we depend on our partner to make us feel whole and soothe our own existential anxieties, then any problem he/she has will necessarily feel threatening, even if it has nothing to do with us. According to David Schnarch (1991), who has popularized this theory for couples, that state of affairs can be the death of intimacy—after all, how can you tell your partner all of your concerns and fears if you think that they will interpret these to be threats to the relationship and/or to them personally? The main message of interventions targeting individuation is, "It's not about you." *Yes!! → target of individuation*

Individuation is very relevant to couples dealing with painful intercourse. It is common for partners to present with concerns about what the pain means about the client's attraction or commitment to them, or for women to worry about how the pain makes their partners feel. This is a major stumbling block. It turns the pain into a symbol of relationship dysfunction when it most often is not, even if relationship dysfunction is present. An important component in therapy for GPPPD is the de-symbolization of the pain. The pain is the pain. It does not reflect negatively on the woman experiencing it and it does not reflect negatively on her partner. Any other interpretation is likely to make matters worse and impede progress. It is thus important for the therapist to encourage individuation and identify enmeshment when members of the couple interpret pain as a reflection of their own deficiencies.

object relations theory

Object-Relations theory: Individuation → autonomy of self + other / secure attachment.

Wanted, loved, desired but not needed in order for one to 'feel whole' & to function.

Managing partner reactions to the pain. Most partners who have solicitous reactions to their partners' pain believe they are doing the right and sensitive thing and most women are grateful for these solicitous reactions from their partners. The problem is that these types of reactions appear to make things worse for everyone. Educating couples about the impact of solicitousness can be very effective. Instructing partners on how to replace these solicitous reactions with facilitative ones is instrumental. Both the woman and her partner have to discuss and define the line between the encouraging/reinforcing of attempts at intercourse and the toleration of discomfort and the forcing of an activity too painful to hold any chance of pleasure. Negative partner reactions that involve hostility, anger, or passive aggressiveness clearly have to be targeted as these are very damaging.

Enhancing communication. The communication of sexual preferences has already been covered in this chapter, but it is central to also investigate and treat general communication deficits. If communication failures exist in other aspects of the relationship, they are likely to result in relationship conflict, which will inevitably trickle down to sexual interactions. If these sexual interactions are already complicated by pain, the result can be very damaging. Below are some transitions the therapist is encouraged to urge clients to make:

From mind-reading to asking. Individuals in romantic or marital relationships often engage in the dangerous practice of guessing what their partners are thinking or feeling. It is dangerous because it is often wrong and yet consequent behaviors are predicated on these faulty assumptions. A woman who experiences painful intercourse may be assuming that her partner is angry or hurt and act accordingly. Asking him how he feels may reveal a completely different set of emotions. It is easy to see how this misperception could confuse and create conflict. A simple question might have resulted in a more positive outcome or in conflict that is at least centered on reality rather than on erroneous pre-conceived notions. Clients often do not realize they do this and can easily be persuaded to desist, with immediate positive results.

From expecting mind-reading to requesting. The corollary of mind-reading a partner's thoughts and feelings is the expectation that they can read ours. It is very common to hear clients say, "If he really knew me or cared, he would know what I really wanted." It is simply not reasonable to expect others to know what we want, when often we do not even know ourselves. The tendency to expect that our partners be good mind-readers rather than request of them what we want reflects an idealization of intimacy as a state of pure, telepathic empathy. Individuals often report that they would have gladly granted a partner's request. Instead, their partners had assumed that they had passive-aggressively noted the desire and refused to comply. Teaching clients to make requests is relatively easy and effective. It is, however, dependent on an honest answer.

From lying to tactful truth-telling. The cessation of mind-reading is partially contingent on the person feeling that their partner will tell them the truth. Many individuals are afraid to tell the truth to their partners for fear of hurting their feelings. The repression of these truths, however, often results in more distress as truths tend to seep out in unexpected, equally hurtful ways or in even more damaging outbursts in which the truth is exaggerated by its long suffering repression. Couples struggling with painful intercourse often engage in this cycle of repression and aggression. A therapist can be instrumental in educating clients about the hazards of supposed repression, and educating clients how to speak a truth in tactful and constructive ways.

From character defamation to expressing how a behavior makes you feel. Confronting a partner about behaviors that are hurtful is always difficult (L'Abate, 2011). That is the origin of most arguments and couple conflict. Although nothing makes this type of interaction pleasant, some communication patterns definitely make it worse. A common destructive pattern is to say insulting things about the partner's character. For example, a husband who is very hurt by the facial expression of disgust made by his wife during intercourse might lash out and say, "You are so mean trying to make me feel terrible when we have intercourse, making those faces." It is easy to see how this would escalate. A much more constructive alternative would be something like, "I know that intercourse is difficult for you, but when you make faces indicating disgust, it makes me feel terrible inside." That statement is much more likely to be heard rather than defended against.

Re-establishing a sexual connection. As previously mentioned, it is very easy for couples struggling with painful intercourse to stop relating to each other sexually. Intercourse becomes increasingly problematic over time, and the sexual connection starts to fade. Although de-emphasizing intercourse and focusing on sensuality are useful tools on the road back to sexuality, they remain confined to discrete sexual episodes. Ideally, the re-establishment of a sexual connection can be greatly facilitated by infusing sexiness into the everyday. This can be a French kiss as you go out the door on your way to work or a neck massage from behind when you are chopping onions for dinner. Even when sexual intercourse happens at the end of the day, the foreplay starts the moment one wakes up. Satisfying sex tends to be preceded by sexy ways of relating to each other, even if there is no physical contact. Flirting should not just be reserved for strangers and acquaintances. Couples who have been together for a long time have a tendency to drop those sexy personas with each other. If sex has become problematic, as in the case of GPPPD, flirting can even be experienced as pressure to have sex. The therapist can help here. By de-emphasizing intercourse or, in some cases banning it for some time, the infusion of this quotidian sexiness can be divested of its performance threat.

Addressing the function of pain in the relationship. A crucial systems intervention in the treatment of GPPPD is to address the function of pain in the couple dynamic. Clients can easily list all the ways in which the pain has negatively impacted their relationship. Much more difficult to face, however, are the ways in which an improvement in symptoms may be threatening. It is critical to identify these potential secondary gain threats, as they will likely be a significant source of treatment resistance. Questions of relevance to both partners would be:

> How would your life change if you (she) no longer had pain with intercourse?
> Do you have fears about what might happen if the pain went away or improved?
> Can you think of any negative consequences to the resolution of symptoms?

A woman who is not attracted to her partner may fear that once the pain subsides, she loses her "legitimate" excuse for avoiding sex. An insecurely attached male partner may worry that once the problem resolves, his partner may leave him. He may need her to be "damaged" so that she does not turn elsewhere for partnership. Sometimes clients can directly answer these secondary gain questions and sometimes they cannot. The function of pain often becomes apparent when clients resist treatment components or demonstrate surprisingly little joy in significant improvements. It is important to be attentive to these unexpected developments.

Challenges to Therapy

There are many challenges in the treatment of GPPPD. Perhaps the greatest of these is the coordination of multiple health professionals in the treatment plan. This coordination can be complicated by the availability of such professionals, inter-disciplinary communication, and financial burden on the client. Clearly, treatment has to adapt to the constraints of any one case, but the optimal strategy is a concurrent interdisciplinary one (Binik & Meana, 2009). The emphasis is on the concurrent aspect of this treatment approach. In the past, when one discipline (e.g., medicine) failed to resolve the client's problem, the client would be referred to the next discipline (e.g., psychology), and so on. The concurrent model advocates for a treatment team (e.g., a gynecologist, sex therapist, physical therapist) working concurrently and collaboratively on the client's difficulty.

A second challenge is balancing people's beliefs in the importance of spontaneity in sex and the structured nature of the assigned exercises. The therapist must tread lightly here and resist the temptation to schedule sexual interactions. Sex cannot become homework—there is nothing sexy about homework. In addition, treatment for painful intercourse is often characterized by the "exhilaration/ disappointment roller coaster." The hope at the start of therapy, reinforced by early gains, can engender unbounded optimism about the eradication of symptoms. However, setbacks occur, improvements are adapted to, and the expectation of further improvement can rise substantially, sometimes unrealistically so. This can lead to feelings of disappointment and even resignation. It is wise for the therapist to be proactive and warn clients about this variable treatment course.

A third challenge is avoiding therapist-induced performance anxiety. When a therapist suggests or directs clients toward sexual exercises or activities, there is an inherent danger that clients will feel pressured by the therapist to engage in sex. This is generally unproductive and should be avoided. Non-adherence to exercises need to be discussed in terms of what the non-adherence signifies. Avoidance of sexual activity should be a topic that is explored in therapy with a total lack of judgment and a desire to truly understand why it persists.

The final challenge is the definition of treatment success. Although goals may be set at the start of therapy, clients will be secretly or openly revising these as they progress through treatment. One member of the couple may consider lack of pain to be the goal, while another may consider the treatment goal to be a certain intercourse frequency. Checking in with the expectations of both members of the couple can be helpful, although it does not always result in agreement. Ultimately, as in the treatment of any sexual dysfunction, the most important treatment outcome is sexual satisfaction, rather than frequency of intercourse or orgasm. Sometimes that is the only aspect of the sexual experience that sex therapy impacts and yet, ultimately, that is the only thing that matters—how happy individuals are with their experience, be that what it may.

→ most impt tx outcome : sexual satisfaction (not frequency)

Research and Future Directions

The last two decades have witnessed an unprecedented level of clinical and research attention to painful intercourse. After half a century of assumptions about the symbolic aspect of pain with intercourse, we are finally taking the pain seriously and investigating its properties and multiple etiologies. This shift in attention toward pain has been tremendously validating for women who suffer from these disorders, and highly productive from a basic science, etiologic perspective. We cannot, however, forget that this is a very special type of pain. Unlike most pains, it happens as a result of an interpersonal interaction, if only incidentally. It also happens in the context of a gendered and socio-culturally valued activity—sexual intercourse. This pain is thus necessarily complicated by questions of relationships, sexual politics, and femininity ideology (Curtin et al., 2011). A serious consideration of all factors is necessary in the treatment of GPPPD.

One important future direction for research and clinical practice in regard to painful sex is the consideration of intercourse pain in men. Having made GPPPD a strictly female sexual dysfunction in the *DSM-5* feels a little like a step backwards, as the *DSM-IV* did allow for the possibility of painful intercourse in men (heterosexual or gay). Data suggest that the prevalence of painful intercourse in men ranges from 5–15% (e.g., Clemens et al., 2005). A syndrome that results in male pelvic pain has been identified (Urological Chronic Pelvic Pain Syndrome [UCPPS]) and it encompasses a variety of urogenital pain symptoms (Shoskes, Nickel, Rackley, & Pontari, 2009). Initial studies on UCCPS indicate that patterns of sensitivity, neural activation, and pelvic floor muscle function in men with UCCPS are very similar to those of women with PVD (Davis et al., 2011). Additionally, painful intercourse has been identified in 12–14% of men who have sex with men (anodyspareunia: Damon & Rosser, 2005) and yet we know little about this population and their challenges with this problem. Individuals with disabilities are another group that needs more research and clinical attention. A number of chronic illnesses and their treatments can result in painful sex.

The last 20 years have evidenced a considerable research effort aimed at understanding the mechanisms and treatment of painful intercourse. The initial emphasis was on the properties of the pain and its sensory characteristics. This was a corrective and productive emphasis given the historical approach to painful intercourse as a somatic manifestation of psychosexual and relational problems. Now that GPPPD is recognized primarily as a pain disorder that interferes with sex, we must ensure that the research and clinical effort remain systems-focused and not lose sight of the fact that, regardless of etiology, any disorder that involves sexuality is likely to be significantly influenced by intra-psychic, interpersonal and societal/cultural factors.

References

American Psychiatric Association. (2000). *Diagnostic and statistical manual of mental disorders* (4th ed.). Washington, DC: Author.

American Psychiatric Association. (2013). *Diagnostic and statistical manual of mental disorders* (5th ed.). Washington, DC: Author.

Bergeron, S., Brown, C., Lord, M.J., Oala, M., Binik, Y.M., & Khalifé, S. (2002). Physical therapy for vulvar vestibulitis syndrome: A retrospective study. *Journal of Sex & Marital Therapy, 28*, 183–192. doi: 10.1080/009262302760328226

Bergeron, S., Rosen, N.O., & Pukall, C.F. (in press). Genital pain in women and men: It can hurt more than your sex life. In Y.M. Binik & K. Hall (Eds.), *Principles and practice of sex therapy*. New York: Guilford Press.

Binik, Y.M. (2010a). The DSM diagnostic criteria for vaginismus. *Archives of Sexual Behavior, 39*, 278–291. doi: 10.1007/s10508–009–9560–0

Binik, Y.M. (2010b). The DSM diagnostic criteria for dyspareunia. *Archives of Sexual Behavior, 39*, 292–303. doi: 10.1007/s10508–009–9563-x

Binik, Y.M., & Meana, M. (2009). The future of sex therapy: Specialization or marginalization? *Archives of Sexual Behavior, 38*, 1016–1027. doi: 10.1007/s10508–009–9475–9

Burri, A.V., Cherkas, L.M., Spector, T.D. (2009). The genetics and epidemiology of female sexual dysfunction: A review. *Journal of Sexual Medicine, 6*, 646–657. doi: 10.1111/j.1743–6109.2008.01144.x

Clemens, J.Q., Meenan, R.T., O'Keefe Rosetti, M.C., Gao, S.Y., & Calhoun, E.A. (2005). Incidence and clinical characteristics of National Institutes of Health Type III prostatitis in the community. *Journal of Urology, 174*, 2319–2322. doi: 10.1097/01.ju.0000182152.28519.e7

Comfort, A. (2009). *The joy of sex: The ultimate revised edition*. New York: Harmony Press.

Curtin, N., Ward, L. M., Merriwether, A., & Allison, C. (2011). Femininity ideology and sexual health in young women: A focus on sexual knowledge, embodiment, and agency. *International Journal of Sexual Health, 23*, 48–62. doi: 10.1080/19317611.2010.524694

Damon, W., & Rosser, B. R. (2005). Anosdyspareunia in men who have sex with men: Prevalence, predictors, consequences and the development of DSM diagnostic criteria. *Journal of Sex and Marital Therapy, 31*, 129–141. doi: 10.1080/009262305904777989

Dattilio, F. M., & Beck, A. T. (2013). *Cognitive-behavioral therapy with couples and families: A comprehensive guide for clinicians.* New York: The Guilford Press.

Davis, S. N. P., Morin, M., Binik, Y. M., Khalifé, S., & Carrier, S. (2011). Use of pelvic floor ultrasound to assess pelvic floor muscle function in urological chronic pelvic pain syndrome in men. *The Journal of Sexual Medicine, 8*, 3173–3180. doi: 10.1111/j.1743–6109.2011.02452.x

Desrochers, G., Bergeron, S., Landry, T., & Jodoin, M. (2008). Do psychosexual factors play a role in the etiology of provoked vestibulodynia? A critical review. *Journal of Sex and Marital Therapy, 34*, 198–226. doi: 10.1080/00926230701866083

Donaldson, R. L., & Meana, M. (2011). Early dyspareunia experience in young women: Confusion, consequences, and help-seeking barriers. *Journal of Sexual Medicine, 8*, 814–823. doi: 10.1111/j.1743–6109.2010.02150.x

Gentilcore-Saulnier, E., McLean, L., Goldfinger, C., Pukall, C. F., & Chamberlain, S. (2010). Pelvic floor muscle assessment outcomes in women with and without provoked vestibulodynia and the impact of a physical therapy program. *The Journal of Sexual Medicine, 7*, 1003–1022.

Gerber, S., Bongiovanni, A. M., Ledger, W. J., & Witkin, S. S. (2002). Defective regulation of the proinflammatory immune response in women with vulvar vestibulitis syndrome. *American Journal of Obstetrics and Gynecology, 186*, 696–700. doi: 10.1067/mob.2002.121869

Goldfinger, C., Pukall, C. F., Gentilcore-Saulnier, E., McLean, L., & Chamberlain, S. (2009). A prospective study of pelvic floor physical therapy: Pain and psychosexual outcomes in provoked vestibulodynia. *The Journal of Sexual Medicine, 6*, 1955–1968. doi: 10.1111/j.1743–6109.2009.01304.x

Harlow, B. L., & Stewart, E. G. (2005). Adult-onset vulvodynia in relation to childhood victimization. *American Journal of Epidemiology, 161*, 871–880. doi: 10.1093/aje/kwi108

Harlow, B. L., Wise, L. A., & Stewart, E. G. (2001). Prevalence and predictors of chronic lower genital tract discomfort. *American Journal of Obstetrics and Gynecology, 185*, 545–550. doi: 10.1067/mob.2001.116748

Hertlein, K. M., & Weeks, G. R. (2009). Toward a new paradigm in sex therapy. *Journal of Family Psychotherapy, 20*, 112–128.

Joannides, P. (2012). *The guide to getting it on! A book about the wonders of sex* (7th ed.). Waldport, OR: Goofy Foot Press.

Klaassen, M., & ter Kuile, M. M. (2009). Development and initial validation of the Vaginal Penetration Cognition Questionnaire (VPCQ) in a sample of women with vaginismus and dyspareunia. *Journal of Sexual Medicine, 6*, 1617–1627. doi: 10.1111/j.1743–6109.2009.01217.x

L'Abate, L. (2011). *Hurt feelings: Theory, research, and applications to intimate relationships.* New York: Cambridge University Press.

Landry, T., & Bergeron, S. (2011). Biopsychosocial factors associated with dyspareunia in a community sample of adolescent girls. *Archives of Sexual Behavior, 40*, 877–889. doi: 10.1007/s10508–010–9637–9

Masters, W. H., & Johnson, V. (1970). *Human sexual inadequacy.* Boston: Little, Brown.

Meana, M. (2012). *Sexual dysfunction in women.* Cambridge: Hogrefe Press.

Moyal-Barracco, M., & Lynch, P. J. (2004). 2003 ISSVD terminology and classification of vulvodynia: A historical perspective. *Journal of Reproduction Medicine, 49*, 772–777.

Öberg, K., Fugl-Meyer, A. R., & Fugl-Meyer, K. S. (2004). On categorization and quantification of women's sexual dysfunctions: An epidemiological approach. *International Journal of Impotence Research, 16*, 261–269. doi: 10.1038/sj.ijir.3901151

Payne, K. A., Binik, Y. M., Amsel, R., & Khalifé, S. (2005). When sex hurts, anxiety and fear orient toward pain. *European Journal of Pain, 9*, 427–436. doi: 10.1016/j.ejpain.2004.10.003

208

Pukall, C., Meana, M., & Fernandez, Y. (2010). Sexual dysfunctions and deviations. In D.L. Segal & M. Hersen (Eds.), *Diagnostic interviewing, 4th ed.* (pp. 283–314). New York: Springer.

Reissing, E.D., Armstrong, H.L., & Allen, C. (2013). Pelvic floor physical therapy for lifelong vaginismus: A retrospective chart review and interview study. *Journal of Sex and Marital Therapy, 39,* 306–320. doi: 10.1080/0092623X.2012.697535

Reissing, E.D., Binik, Y.M., Khalifé, S., Cohen, D., & Amsel, R. (2003). Etiological correlates of vaginismus: Sexual and physical abuse, sexual knowledge, sexual self-schema and relationship adjustment. *Journal of Sex and Marital Therapy, 29,* 47–59. doi: 10.1080/713847095

Rosen, N.O., Bergeron, S., Sadikaj, G., Glowacka, M., Delisle, I., Baxter, M.L. (2014). Impact of male partner responses on sexual function in women with vulvodynia and their partners: A dyadic daily experience study. *Health Psychology, 33*(8), 823–831.

Rosen, R., Brown, C., Heiman, J. Leiblum, S., Meston, C., Shabsigh, R., . . . D'Agostino, R.J. (2000). The Female Sexual Function Index (FSFI): A Multidimensional self-report instrument for the assessment of female sexual function. *Journal of Sex and Marital Therapy, 26,* 191–208. doi: 10.1080/009262300278597

Rosen, R.C., Riley, A., Wagner, G., Osterloh, I.H., Kirkpatrick, J., & Mishra, A. (1997). The International Index of Erectile Function (IIEF): A multidimensional scale for assessment of erectile dysfunction. *Urology, 49,* 822–830.

Rosenbaum, T.Y. (2007). Physical therapy management and treatment of sexual pain disorders. In S.R. Leiblum (Ed). *Principles and practice of sex therapy* (4th ed.) (pp. 157–177). New York: The Guilford Press.

Rosenbaum, T.Y. (2013). An integrated mindfulness-based approach to the treatment of women with sexual pain and anxiety: Promoting autonomy and mind/body connection. *Sexual and Relationship Therapy, 28*(1–2), 20–28. doi: 10.1080/14681994.2013.764981

Schnarch, D.M. (1991). *Constructing the sexual crucible: An integration of sexual and marital therapy.* New York: Norton.

Shoskes, D.A., Nickel, J.C., Rackley, R.R., & Pontari, M.A. (2009). Clinical phenotyping in chronic prostatitis/chronic pelvic pain syndrome and interstial cystitis: A management strategy for urologic chronic pelvic pain syndromes. *Prostate Cancer and Prostatic Diseases, 12,* 177–183. doi: 10.1016/j.eururo.2009.08.005

Smith, K.B., & Pukall, C.F. (2011). A systematic review of relationship adjustment and sexual satisfaction among women with provoked vestibulodynia. *Journal of Sex Research, 48,* 166–191. doi: 10.1080/00224499.2011.555016

Sullivan, M.J.L., Bishop, S.R., & Pivik, J. (1995). The Pain Catastrophizing Scale: Development and validation. *Psychological Assessment, 7,* 524–532.

Sullivan, M.J.L., Lynch, M.E., & Clark, A.J. (2005). Dimensions of catastrophic thinking associated with pain experience and disability in patients with neuropathic pain conditions. *Pain, 113,* 310–315. doi: 10.1016/j.pain.2009.06.031

Sungur, M. (2012). The role of cultural factors in the course and treatment of sexual problems: Failures, pitfalls and successes in a complicated case from Turkey. In S.K.S. Hall & C.A. Graham (Eds.). *The cultural context of sexual pleasure and problems: Psychotherapy with diverse clients* (pp. 307–332). New York: Routledge.

ter Kuile, M.M., & Reissing, E.D. (2014). Lifelong vaginismus. In: Y.M. Binik & K. Hall (Eds.), *Principles and Practice of Sex Therapy* (pp. 177–194). New York: Guilford Press.

van Lankveld, J.J.D.M., Granot, M., Weijmar Schultz, W.C., Binik, Y.M., Wesselman, U., Pukall, C.F., . . . Achtrari, C. (2010). Women's sexual pain disorders. *Journal of Sexual Medicine, 7,* 615–631.

Vlaeyen, J.W., & Linton, S.J. (2000). Fear-avoidance and its consequences in chronic musculoskeletal pain: A state of the art. *Pain, 85,* 317–332. doi: 10.1016/j.pain.2011.12.009

Winks, C., & Semans, A. (2002). *The good vibrations guide to sex: The most complete sex manual ever written* (3rd ed.). San Francisco: Cleiss Press.

Weeks, G., & Gambescia, N. (2009). A systemic approach to sensate focus. In K. Hertlein, G. Weeks, & N. Gambescia (Eds.), *Systemic sex therapy* (pp. 341–362). New York: Routledge.

Section 3

CONTEMPORARY ISSUES IN
SEX THERAPY

12

SEX THERAPY WITH LESBIAN AND GAY MALE COUPLES

Arlene Istar Lev and Margaret Nichols

It is undeniable that lesbian and gay people—at least in progressive western cultures—have made unprecedented social, political, and legal strides in the past few decades. Prior to that, same sex sexual desire was viewed as a perversion, and acting on these desires could make one a social pariah. Clandestine sexual experiences (the only ones really possible) could mean imprisonment, familial shame, unemployment, and community ostracism. Political and cultural upheaval has swept through civil life, and gay and lesbian couples have become increasingly mainstream, forming families sanctioned and supported by state governments.

Despite these massive social and political changes, however, there remains a lack of substantive research on same sex couples, much less on their sexuality. The Census Bureau only started collecting data on "unmarried partners" in 1990 and did not begin to analyze this data on same sex couples until 2000. According to this data there are an estimated 650,000 same sex couples in the United States (Gates, 2013), nearly evenly distributed between female and male couples. It can be assumed that many same sex couples did not reveal their status honestly in the census, and there are, of course, many more self-identified gay and lesbian persons who are not in defined coupled relationships, but likely having sexual relationships. About a quarter of these couples were legally married as of 2011 when the data was collected. It is likely that increasing numbers of same-sex couples will marry over the ensuing decades. The annual divorce rate for same sex couples currently appears to be about half that of different sex marriages, although this may change over time as gay and lesbian couples are in longer term legal partnerships.

Beyond demographic data, there is a small but growing body of research on how people in same-sex couples actually behave and function within their relationships. Blumstein and Schwartz broke ground in 1983 with their "American Couples" study comparing straight and gay married and unmarried couples and much of the research that has followed has validated the strengths and resiliencies of lesbian and gay couples (Bryant & Demian, 1994; Connolly, 2005; Gotta et al., 2011; Gottman et al., 2003; Kurdek, 2005; Peplau & Fingerhut, 2007; Solomon, Rothblum, & Balsam, 2005). Below we will examine some of this data in greater depth; however, decades of research have shown that lesbian and gay couples tend to have egalitarian relationships where power differentials are minimized. They express high levels of satisfaction, value intimacy, communication, and relational attunement, and have skills to resolve conflict constructively (see Ashton, 2011; Lev, in press).

There is, however, very little data on the sex lives of lesbian and gay people (Allen & Demo, 1995; Hunter, 2012) and the erotic lives of sexual minorities in general. Perhaps this shouldn't be surprising given the silence on all aspects of human sexuality. As Lev and Sennott have said, "Despite the commercial exploitation of sex in advertising and the popular media and the wide-spread proliferation of pornography, especially on the Internet, sexuality and eroticism remain inadequately explored areas in virtually all aspects of the social sciences and clinical research" (2012, p. 113). Although research is currently flourishing on issues related to marriage equality, same-sex parenting, and LGBTQ health disparities, the intimate lives of lesbians and gay men remains almost as secretive as it was when sodomy was illegal, and homosexuality was still a "dirty little secret."

Research on all aspects of human sexuality is complicated by funding and access to a representative sample of participants. When research involves the sexual lives of sexual minorities, the challenges are complicated by researcher bias, including the very ideological frameworks in which the studies are conducted (Riggs, 2011). Due to the pervasiveness of homophobia in mainstream culture and how it is internalized in LGBTQ subcommunities, studies of homosexual experience become falsely equated with constructs of homosexual persons. Risman and Schwartz (1988) say, "There is no felicitous way to talk about men or women with homosexual preferences and/or identities without labeling them and thus reifying homosexual desire into a type of human being" (p. 143). They suggest instead the use of the word homosexual as an adjective, rather than a noun, and nearly 25 years ago they advocated for research on the "sociology of sexual desire."

In this chapter we will focus explicitly on same sex sexuality, i.e., lesbian women and gay men. We will also be referring to the larger LGBTQ community, which includes lesbians, gay men, bisexual men and women, and gender nonconforming, transgender, transsexual, and queer identified people. The phrase LGBTQ has become ubiquitous, a term used to describe multiple overlapping communities of minority sexual orientations and gender identities. This can sometimes be useful and inclusive, for example when one is referring to public policy or community affiliation, but it can also overly conflate complex identities and become nearly meaningless, for example when someone refers to an "LGBTQ person," or an "LGBTQ relationship," or—for the purpose of this paper—"LGBTQ sexuality." We will attempt to use terminology carefully and purposely in this paper, recognizing the limitations of language, the quick pace and shifting of post-modern identities, and the rapid expanse of linguistic narratives to describe human sexual and gender identities.

Historically the term homosexual has been used interchangeably with gay/lesbian identity. However, many people in same-sex relationships are not "homosexuals" (as a noun), and identify as bisexual (being attracted to partners of both sexes) or pansexual (someone who is not limited in sexual attraction with regard to biological sex, gender identity, or gender expression). Bisexuals have been misunderstood in both mainstream and within LGBTQ cultures. A study rating attitudes of heterosexuals towards a multitude of stigmatized minorities and subgroups revealed that bisexual men and women were rated lower than all other groups besides injecting drug users (Herek, 2002). Within the LGBTQ community, bisexuals have historically been feared, mistrusted, and despised when they aren't completely invisible (Green, 2009; Nichols, 1994; Nichols, 2014).

This is especially salient, since the bulk of research on homosexuality has conflated bisexual people and their experiences into the data, masking important information about the fluidity of sexuality, and complexities of community affiliation and identity. Too often researchers have defined the term "gay couple" in a way that has rendered invisible the fact that one partner is "homosexual" and the other partner is "bisexual," as if these differences are meaningless in terms of community, identity, sexual proclivities, or interrelational dynamics. People who are bisexual have unique issues partnering in same-sex relationships due to the "mixed orientation" within the couple, including issues of identity management and community affiliation, with notable differences between men and woman (Brown, 2002). This is, of course, also true for heterosexual people in opposite-sex relationships, who are the focus of other chapters in this book.

Although specific focus on transgender people in relationships is outside the parameters of this article, it is important to understand that transgender and transsexual people can identify as heterosexual, gay/lesbian, or bisexual in identity, and some lesbian and gay couples (like some heterosexual couples) may have one or more transgender member/s. Whether or not the relationship is seen as "same-sex" can depend on multiple factors. The very concept of sexual orientation assumes the existence of two opposite sexes, a binary based in biological dimorphism which assumes that the biological similarity of the partners' bodies is the salient feature of the relationship. Male and female bodies are not, however, simply dichotomous. People with intersex conditions and those with "genderqueer" identities defy the binary; the very existence of transsexualism challenges the very stability of the sexed body (see Lev, 1998; Lev & Sennott, 2012; Lev, 2014; Malpas, 2012). "Same sex" sexuality might or might not be an attraction of two people born into the same bodies, and the words "same" and "sex," like the word homosexual, can often conflate and confuse, more than clarify. Although our focus is on lesbian and gay sexuality, identity, sexuality, and eroticism can be fluid because embodiment and gender identity itself can shift, and therefore influence sexual orientation.

In the past decade, as increasing options for sexual orientation and gender identity have emerged, the term "queer" has been reclaimed as a broad umbrella term to include LGBTQ peoples and community. Tilsen (2013) says that "to queer something is an emergent process of disrupting expected norms in such a way that new possibilities emerge and standard, unquestioned practices become open for interrogation" (p. 6). Iasenza (2010) says that the word queer speaks to "the potential fluidity and multidimensionality of same and other sex/gender experience in all people" (p. 292). In this chapter we will often use the term queer, when the terms gay or lesbian couple are too restrictive to describe the sexuality of the "same sex" couples we are describing.

We also look at sex therapy with same sex couples through the lens of the principles of systematic family and couples therapy. A systemic approach is the only appropriate theoretical stance when working with clients from marginalized groups. When the client's life experience and background is different from that of the "mainstream," it is important for the clinician to incorporate knowledge of that difference into their work (Diamond, Dickerson, & Blair, 2013). The therapist must have an understanding of how mainstream attitudes impact individuals, couples, and extended family and friend networks, and some knowledge of the communities where they live and among their various social groups (Parsons, Starks, DuBios, Grov, & Golub, 2011).

Hertlein and Weeks (2009) describe an Intersystem Approach to sex therapy that assesses client problems along five dimensions: individual/biological/medical; individual/psychological; dyadic; family-of-origin; and social/historical/religious/cultural. It is this approach we use in our chapter. We focus on social, historical, and cultural influences, looking at both the mainstream culture in which LGBTQ people must function as well as at the minority subculture that supports and validates queer people and sets its own norms for behavior and identity. We will consider the impact of "minority stress"—the macro and micro aggressions LGBTQ people are likely to face on a regular basis—but also the effect of peer standards and values (Meyer, 2003). Moreover, we consider how these forces filter down to the family-of-origin, "created family," the dyad, and the individual. The impact and interaction of cultural forces from two sources culture, make same sex oriented individuals and same sex dyads different from their mixed sex counterparts. In fact, same sex couples behave differently as dyads from their mixed sex counterparts.

Historical Context of Same Sex Couples

Historically, the social oppression and vilification of those who expressed same-sex desire was reflected in the new fields of psychiatry and sexology that emerged in the 1800s. In the mid-19th century, Western society began classifying people into distinct categories based on sexual orientation ("homosexual" and "heterosexual"); not surprisingly, this was also the same time period when the invention and codification of racial divisions began (Somerville, 2000). Sexual minorities became the target of medical, psychiatric, and legal interventions throughout the 19th century, resulting in criminalization, and abusive reparative therapies like shock treatment and chemical castration. Homosexuality as a pathology was not removed from the diagnostic manuals until 1973, with residual subcategories remaining until the printing of the *DSM-5* (American Psychiatric Association, 2013).

The birth of the field of sexology is marked by the 1886 publication of Kraft-Ebbing's Psychopathologia Sexualis, a compendium of "sexual deviance" that included behaviors ranging from same sex attraction to transgenderism to sado-masochism, as well as violent and nonconsensual activities like rape and pedophilia (Nichols, 2014). The history of the field of sex science, and then later that of sex therapy, is marked by ongoing tension between two opposing views of these aspects of human sexuality. The first, the view of Kraft-Ebbing, and later Freud, is that all sex and gender expressions that varied from heterosexual procreative sex were pathological. The second, exemplified by Hirschfeld and Kinsey, is that unconventional, non-standard sex acts and attractions are normal variations—statistically unusual but not inherently "diseased" or maladaptive.

The pathology paradigm has dominated both psychiatry and sexology until recently, but the activism that resulted in the removal of homosexuality in 1973 seems to have been just the beginning of a movement to de-pathologize sex and gender variance (Nichols, 2014; Silverstein, 2009). Many sex and gender diverse people, especially transgender people and those who practice BDSM (bondage/discipline/dominance/submission/sadism/masochism) are still diagnosed as mentally disturbed under certain conditions, even in the most recent edition of the *DSM*. Many of the categories of the original Kraft-Ebbings schema remain to this day, and many practitioners still subscribe to this model. This chapter is written from the perspective that sex and gender variation is "normal" unless it is nonconsensual, and that good, ethical, sex therapy requires practicing from a non-pathologizing model of mental health.

The pathological perspective has dominated not only psychiatry and psychiatric diagnosis, but also contemporary sexological research. The deviance model became incorporated into the clinical application of sexology and sex therapy. The early leaders of the field, Masters and Johnson and Helen Singer Kaplan, thought of homosexuality as less desirable than heterosexuality; Masters and Johnson purported to be able to "cure" it in some cases (1979) and Kaplan considered it a "disorder of desire" (1979). Both researchers played shameful roles in the AIDS epidemic of the 1980s, contributing to the stigmatization of gay men and societal paranoia about HIV transmission (Irvine, 2005). The deviance model still contributes to the social stigmatization of sex and gender minorities, and still dominates mainstream sexology research using ideological frameworks and static binary categories of gender and sexual orientation to describe phenomena that are in actuality complex, fluid, and interactional. For example, Bailey, a well-known modern researcher on sexual orientation and gender identity, has written that sex and gender presentations that do not lead directly to reproduction are a "developmental error" (Bailey, 1999, p. 884).

But more progressive researchers, who are frequently themselves sexual minorities, incorporate the "normal variation" model into their research. As a result, their studies—and conclusions—are richer, more nuanced, and more interesting. Instead of looking for the "etiology" of same sex attraction and nonconforming gender expression, these social scientists use the study of sex and gender variant people as an opportunity to re-examine and deconstruct the binaries of sex and gender (Riggs, 2011). For example, Diamond's (2008) research examined the ways in which sexual orientation can shift or change during the life course, and Beemyn and Rankin's (2011) studied the multiple expressions of gender-variant and transgender expression. Iasenza (2010) re-imagines how queer theory can influence sex therapy with opposite sex partners.

Within this historical context of oppression, it was inconceivable until recently for therapists to even formulate questions about same sex sexual satisfaction or potential sexual problems within a model that assumed same sex love was healthy. It is not surprising that the research is scant and that information about treating sexual dysfunction rarely includes special considerations of the issues of same sex couples.

The Impact of the Subcultural System on Same Sex Couples

A systemic approach necessitates understanding the impact of culture on couples: not only the dominant culture, but also the LGBTQ or queer subculture. For queer people, the LGBTQ community is not only a place of support and validation; it is also, for many, their only family (Weston, 1991). LGBTQ people occupy a distinct place among stigmatized minorities, for other people generally can depend on family-of-origin for support. Queer people have historically been rejected—or at least misunderstood—by their birth families. Thus many have chosen to live in neighborhoods and communities with other LGBTQ people, where they feel accepted. Others form networks of queer and queer affirming friends, partners, ex-partners, and children that assume new and creative forms of family and tribe. The queer community is an amorphous entity that includes organizations, openly queer businesses and professionals, and virtual (Internet) spaces and groups as well as physical neighborhoods filled with LGBTQ people and their allies. For a couple, this community often plays the same role of validation and support for the relationship that the mainstream culture plays for non-queer people (Lev, in press).

Sometimes the need for affiliation is very strong and can serve to conflate complex differences between the various sub-cultural groups. For example, the terms "lesbian" and "gay" are often used interchangeably, and linked together—as in "the lesbian and gay community"—the reality is the lesbians and gay men are sharply distinct subjects, forming vastly different communities, what Joan Nestle once referred to as "a fragile union" (Nestle, 1998). Some might argue the only thing that gay and lesbian people had in common was an oppressed minority status. And the alliance between those who are same sex oriented and bisexuals, transgender people, and other sex and gender variant people is even more tenuous and conflicted.

The LGBTQ subculture has changed rapidly and dramatically since the birth of the modern gay activist movement, widely considered to have begun in 1969. Behavior and values continue to evolve. For example, younger generations of lesbians and gay men have started what is referred to as the "Gayby Boom," whereas older people assumed being gay meant being childless (D'Augelli, Rendina, Grossman, & Sinclair, 2007). One of the most interesting aspects of change is the proliferation of new and ever-evolving identities in the queer subculture.

Among other things, the LGBTQ community (like all minority subcultures) determines how its members describe themselves, what labels they use, and what characteristics, behaviors, and traits are expected to accompany one's self-definition. Those who do not fit neatly into a category face subtle pressure to hide or suppress characteristics that do not conform. For example, people who we now call LGBTQ or queer called themselves "inverts" in the 19th and early 20th century, "homosexuals" in the mid 20th, "gays" and "lesbians" from the 1970s on. In pre-1969 lesbian culture, women were supposed to identify as either "butch" or "femme." Those who insisted on presenting as androgynous or did not want to play a particular relationship role were labeled "kiki" and viewed with suspicion. During the lesbian-feminist years that followed in the 1970s, the ethic reversed: lesbians who still called themselves butch or femme were denigrated by lesbian-feminists and androgyny was the expected norm. And in more contemporary queer subculture, there is still some pressure for bisexual people to label themselves gay or lesbian and suppress opposite sex attraction.

This concept is quite important, and it has gone virtually overlooked in the scientific literature until recently (Diamond, 2013b; Savin-Williams, 2014). Social science and sexology research on "gay" and "lesbian" people—with some notable exceptions, like HIV research—selects subjects based on self-identification but interprets findings as though they were measuring some essential quality of human nature, something ultimately grounded in genes and brain structures. In fact, self-labeled sexual orientation is only loosely correlated with same sex behavior, fantasy, and attractions (Diamond, 2013c). We are accustomed to assuming that there is a one-to-one correspondence between identity and some underlying biological reality—neuronal pathways, genes, and chromosomes. But the categories with which we identify ourselves and others are social constructs, even if it is those constructs ultimately derive from elements like erotic and romantic attractions, maybe even gender identity and expression, that are based in our bodies and brains. Identity labels are a clumsy attempt to take confusing, complex phenomenon and distill them into discrete categories.

A number of factors influence which identity labels queer people use and have used over time, but one of them is the pressure exerted by the dominant norms of the LGBTQ subculture (Tilsen, 2013). And the labels queer people use are the identities that are currently available and acceptable within the communities they live in and depend upon for support. When lesbians were "supposed to be" butches or femmes, that is how women identified. As "bisexual" becomes destigmatized among younger people, more people will self-label in that way. As the norms of LGBTQ culture change over time, the identity labels change, which means there is a strong generational cohort effect in the community. Clinicians working with same sex couples should be aware that the norms of behavior, expression, and even self-identification may be strikingly different for couples in their 20s than those in their 40s or 50s (Iasenza, 2010).

The LGBTQ community is ever-expanding. This means there is tremendous intersectionality (Diamond, 2008) in queer culture. Intersectionality refers to the overlap of different minority groups—for example, a black bisexual transwoman represents the intersection of race, gender, gender identity, and sexual orientation. People who "live" in places of great intersectionality often suffer minority stress from many sources. But the multi-layered experiences of their lives also gives them unique perspectives and life experiences. Hanne Blank (2012) writes about the "doxa," the cultural values that are so taken for granted that we consider them "truth" rather than values and norms. Most people are unaware of the "doxa" they have absorbed growing up and unaware that it has influenced them. But minorities—those with less power in society—are more likely to notice and question it, because the doxa of any given society usually includes negative assumptions about those with less power. People who are "intersectional" are aware of multiple "doxas," and are aware that the "truths" of different cultures clash. This can give them a unique objectivity and make them free to reject, accept, and blend or modify the rules for their own lives. They can invent new lifestyles and create new identities and modes of self—expression. Where there is intersectionality in a community there is dynamic change where minority groups overlap.

Further, the "queer" community is increasingly intersectional. The 21st century has seen the LGBTQ community truly become inclusive of sex and gender diverse minorities: asexuals, intersex people, members of the BDSM/fetish community, even polyamorous people talk of having an "orientation." The resulting community has become much more diverse than the sum of its parts. As Rothblum (2012) says, "it is important to view all dimensions of intersectionality as continuum. Sexuality itself is complex and multi-dimensional" (p. 265). The community is now "queer" in a 21st century sense, as Iasenza explains: "The term 'queer' has carried various meanings throughout history—a mid-20th century epithet for gay people, a reappropriated anthem for 1980's gay/lesbian activism, and a rejection of sex/gender binaries in more recent times." (p. 291). Iasenza is referring not only to the narrowness of the two-category system of sexual orientation, but to the reductionism of the two-gender gender system. The new "queer" community has rejected both models.

The rejection of sex binaries Iasenza cites has meant far more than an expansion to include those who self-label as bisexual. Savin-Williams (2005) and Tilsen (2013) found in their research that many young, queer people rejected labels entirely, identified as "queer," or used new identity labels like "pansexual." In addition, Lisa Diamond (2008) found that her subjects, young college women, changed identity labels frequently over a follow-up of more than a decade. They did not reject former labels nor rule out future change; they were using identity labels to describe their current attractions, behaviors, and most of all, their current partner arrangement, and not using them in the essentialist way we have come to take for granted. Diamond (2014) calls this attribute of her subjects' sexual orientation "sexual fluidity," and first believed that it and bisexuality were more characteristic of female sexuality. She has since come to reject that view, in a 2014 paper aptly titled, "I was wrong; Men are pretty darn fluid too." Savin-Williams' recent research on what he calls "mostly heterosexual men" (2014) demonstrates that men, when given the option of this non-heterosexual identity label, often readily adopt it. Savin-Williams' work is a further breakdown of traditional straight/gay sexual binary, showing that even three categories are not enough.

Diamond (2013a) is also researching the relationship between sexual attractions, romantic attractions, behaviors, and identity labels and finding lower than expected correlations between these variables for both men and women. There is increasing acknowledgement of and comfort with the fact that different elements of individual sexuality do not always go together, that the range of individual variations includes "lesbians who have sex with men, a gay man who fantasizes about women when having sex, heterosexual men who desire anal penetration" (Iasenza, 2010, p. 292). It is a mistake to assume that a self-identified lesbian or gay man has never had pleasurable sex with an opposite sex partner—or isn't doing so currently.

The 21st century rejection of gender categories that Iasenza notes has a complex and long historical background (Beemyn & Rankin, 2011). Throughout most of recorded history, same-sex sexual attraction and gender nonconformity have been considered to

219

be related, if not identical. Kraft-Ebbing and other early sexologists called homosexual attraction "sexual inversion"—same sex attracted people were considered to have an inborn "inversion" of gender traits, accounting both for nonconventional sex role presentation—effeminate males and masculine females—as well as the sexual attractions themselves. This tendency to conflate same sex attraction and gender continued until the 1970s when the conventional wisdom became that sexual orientation and gender identity and expression were totally unrelated. This belief is an oversimplification of what is a more complicated relationship (Lev, 2004); some lesbians and gay men are also quite gender nonconforming. Lesbians and gay men are well aware of the relationship between their orientation and gender nonconformity. Gay men recognize this in camp and drag, in calling each other "she" and "her," and lesbians reflect this in the terms "butch" and "femme" (Nestle, 1992). Lesbians eroticize gender nonconformity—the butch-femme dynamic is an erotic and relational one—but gay men still tend to denigrate femininity and eroticize hyper-masculinity, the ultimate in gender role conformity.

For younger queer people, however, the gender binary has already broken down, and it has blended with sexual orientation in interesting ways. Among those who consider themselves transgender, for example, the most commonly endorsed label for those under 35 is "genderqueer" and the most common labels for sexual orientation are "queer" or "pansexual" (Beemyn & Rankin, 2011; Kupfer, Nussbaum, & Mustanski, 2012; Nestle, Wilchins, & Howell, 2002). The well-documented increase in the proportion of FtM transmen in recent years started in the lesbian community, where an environment supportive of gender nonconformity provided a fertile ground for the exploration of gender identity. Beemyn and Rankin found that two-thirds of transmen identified as "butch" lesbians before identifying as transgender, and Lisa Diamond found 5 of her sample of over 80 women transitioned to a gender identity other than female by the 12 year mark (Diamond & Butterworth, 2008). Intersectionality of orientation and gender seem to be most pronounced currently in same sex female couples or couples where one partner is a bisexual/pansexual woman. There are many female couples comprised of two transwomen or a transwoman and a cisgendered queer woman, and many others are comprised of transmen and bisexual partners; many other couples are experiencing the transition of one partner. The breakdown of the gender binary is occurring on the physical level as well: some transgender people are comfortable having a body that differs from their gender expression or presentation, and eschew hormones and/or surgery. Others retain both male and female body features: a transwoman with breasts and a penis, a transman with a penis and a vagina.

Couple Relationship and Family Patterns

In the past 40 years the gay and lesbian liberation movement has successfully challenged homophobic assumptions about sexual deviance, family relationships, love, marriage, and family-building. It has been a massive social upheaval, perhaps one that is historically unprecedented, to have a despised, pathologized minority group become increasingly socially accepted and granted civil and legal rights.

However, with all the massive social changes, we must not lose sight of the intensity of both macro and microaggressions that LGBTQ people experience on a daily basis living in a homophobic and heteronormative culture. Heteronormativity as an ideology that is often unconscious, and that assumes everyone is heterosexual, while promoting traditional gender conventionality. Because heterosexual values are presumed to be superior to alternative forms of sexual orientation, gender expression, and family formation LGBTQ people are the recipients of institutionalized and personalized microaggressions due to their sexual orientation and/or gender expression. These include outright discrimination and bias, denial of their families, marginalization, and vilification of their sexual desires which manifests in lifelong psychological and emotional challenges (Meyer, 2003; Nadal et al., 2011; Nuttbrock, 2010; Sue, 2010). There is still a long way to go before same sex love is viewed as equal to opposite sex love, and it is within this context of oppression that lesbian and gay desires must take root.

Sexual desire is so central to the experience of being a lesbian or gay man that "coming out" to oneself is often triggered by the awareness of same sex attraction. It is the awaking of queer sexual desire that provokes lesbians and gay men to explore the ways they are different from those with more normative sexual feelings. In a world where difference was celebrated, same sex attraction would be no more problematic then having red hair or being very tall; in the world as it currently is manifest, same-sex desire requires one to make conscious choices about their behavior and identity. Unlike other minority issues— the color of one's skin or having a visible disability—there are choices involved: to act on one's desires or not, to hide or come out, either choice resulting in complex relational and emotional consequences. Knowing that one has "deviant" desires marks you, and even in these more progressive times, it is psychologically a process to make cognitive sense out of this difference, to embrace and move towards the subject of one's desire (Malpas, 2011).

For all the ways that sexuality is the central theme in coming out as lesbian or gay, it is also the most private parts of the experience. When lesbian and gay couples seek out counseling, like heterosexual couples, they often seek out general counseling for a variety of interpersonal and familial struggles (i.e., housework, parenting, communication); issues of intimacy and sexuality may be part of the challenges, but may not be the presenting problem. In the past, lesbian and gay people often sought out counseling to help them resist their homosexual desires, or cure them—this is becoming less common as same sex sexuality is increasingly sanctioned socially and legally. For lesbian and gay couples to seek out therapy to improve their sexual satisfaction, they have to first recognize and name that they are having sexual problems, be willing to reach out for help and trust they will not face discrimination from the therapist for being in a same sex relationship.

Historically, lesbian and gay couples have partnered within oppressive social circumstances, and outside of standard relational rules. Patterson et al. (1999) has said that "gay and lesbian couple relationships are . . . creative enterprises carried out under unconventional circumstances" (p. 339). In a world where dating and courtship patterns are carefully scripted along gender lines and heterosexual relationship patterns are carefully institutionalized (He makes the phone call and he makes the first sexual move; she makes herself available to him and she makes sure to sexually pleasure him), Steen & Schwartz, 2005) referred to same-sex relationships as "unscripted," and Blumstein and Schwartz (1983) describe same-sex relationships as "noninstitutionalized." Being outside of normative social institutions has often been painful for couples, when their long term relationships have not been recognized or honored. As same-sex marriage and queer families become increasingly normalized with formal and legal marriage ceremonies, it is possible that the norms that guide and maintain coupling will become more conventionally scripted and institutionalized. Patterson et al. (1999) suggested that "the act . . . of coming out as a couple becomes a device for gays and lesbians to claim the status, and increasingly, the benefits of couplehood by forcing social recognition of the significance of their relationships" (p. 342).

Despite the different circumstances of same sex couples they are, in general, similar to "opposite" sex couples in many ways (Gotta et al., 2011; Gottman et al., 2003; Kurdek,

2005; Peplau & Fingerhut, 2007; Solomon, Rothblum, & Balsam, 2005). They move through similar stages of family life (dating, falling in love, partnering, living together, and planning for children) as heterosexuals do (Ashton, 2011). Lesbian and gay couples describe a similarly high level of relationship quality as well as stability. They express equal satisfaction in their relationships and sex lives (Blair & Pukall, 2014).

But the data reveal a few important differences between same and different sex couples. Since Blumstein and Schwartz's groundbreaking work comparing heterosexually married, heterosexually unmarried, gay male and lesbian couples in 1983, a body of research has grown documenting these differences. According to recent census data, compared to different-sex couples, same sex couples are less likely to be raising children (20% vs. 44%), more likely to have a college degree (46% vs. 32%), and more likely to be in the labor force (82% vs. 69%). Individuals in same sex couples are also about 5 years younger and earn more money, perhaps because they are more likely to have college degrees (Gates, 2013). Because of the considerable overlap between the BDSM, polyamory, and gay communities (Richters et al., 2008; Barker, 2013), same sex dyads in sex therapy are more likely than mixed sex dyads to incorporate alternative sexual practices into their repertoire. Perhaps because many gay men and lesbians have relatively broad sexual practices, same sex couples have been found to "...take more time for each other and each other's feelings of pleasure, place less emphasis on rushing towards orgasm, and focus less on simultaneous orgasms" (Sandfort & de Keizer, p. 5).

The most striking difference between mixed and same sex couples found consistently in research, is that gay male and lesbian couples are more egalitarian in almost every way than male-female couples (Gotta et al, 2011; Solomon, Rothblum, & Balsam, 2005; Peplau, 2003). Same sex couples are more financially independent and more likely to contribute to the household equally. In mixed sex couples, women do more housework than men and the chores are more likely to be split along traditional gender lines, while same sex couples share housework equitably and do equal amounts of "feminine" versus "masculine" chores. Same sex couples have more equal levels of communication with each, contribute equally to the maintenance of the relationship, and have equal power in decision making. In other words, same sex couples are free of the gender stereotyping and power imbalances inherent in the still-sexist culture in which we live. In addition, they are better at resolving conflict than mixed sex couples. This research clearly demonstrates the effects of both sexual orientation and gender.

Sex therapists more familiar with working with mixed sex couples may find that these differences affect some aspects of their work. When relationship strife contributes to sexual dysfunction, the issues may be the same: money, household chores, and children. But the inherent, culturally ingrained assumptions about roles and power imbalances are absent and the partners are more likely to communicate well with each other; many same-sex relationships seem inherently more "fair"—and this may make the therapist's job easier. To the extent that sex drive is gender based, one finds different sexual problems and a different "spin" on them. Lesbians will most frequently present with absent or very low sexual frequency, but it will be common that both women are experiencing low desire in an otherwise well-functioning relationship. Gay male couples will frequently ask for help with issues around nonmonogamy. And you will rarely see couples where the desire is so discrepant that one partner never wants sex and the other wants it every day. And it is less common to see same-sex partners where one partner is "stuck" in an emotionally and financially dependent position relative to the other, although of course gender roles are not the only thing that produces dependency.

In heterosexual relationships, gender is likely a mediating factor in nearly all relational tasks including housework, childcare, employment consideration, and certainly sexual expectations. For same-sex couples, gender is a "relational task that is negotiated," so that the partners can become active participants in deciding how to divide the chores and responsibilities within their relationship (Lev & Sennott 2012). For many, if not most, gay and lesbian couples gender may not be a salient factor in their lives; for others gender identity, gender expression, and/or gender roles play an important part in their emotional and erotic expressions. It is important to remember that gender is different from sex, and that a couple can be a same-sex relationship, with opposite gender expressions and markers (Lev, 2004). Additionally, gender expressions may be opposite (i.e., butch/femme) but one should not assume that masculine and feminine gendered roles symbolized traditional power dynamics between the members of the couple (Lev, 2008). Apparent differences in gender presentation may not be reflected in relationship roles, for example a "butch" woman with a feminine-looking partner cannot be assumed to be taking on a "male" role, for example, even in clearly defined butch/femme lesbian couples femmes do not feel that they are solely responsible for the "wifely" housekeeping duties (Levitt, Gerrish, & Hiestand, 2003).

Same sex couples do not have the inherent imbalance that comes when the two partners have been socialized differently and have unequal access to power in the world outside the marriage. But this is not to say that all same sex couples are equally balanced in power; one partner may have more relationship power than the other by virtue of money, youth or attractiveness, or psychological dominance. But gender does not determine power differential the way it so often does in opposite-sex couples.

There are also differences between female and male dyads. Most research finds that male couples have the highest frequency of sexual activity and female couples the least, with mixed sex couples in between. Female couples report a broader range of sexual activities, and spend more time on any given sexual encounter than do mixed sex couples (Blair & Pukall, 2014; Holmberg & Blair, 2009; Nichols, 2006; Nichols, 1987). Research has long demonstrated that gay men are less likely to pursue monogamy in long term relationships (Blumstein & Schwartz, 1983; Bryant & Demian, 1994; Green & Mitchell, 2008; Peplau & Fingerhut, 2004). Solomon, Rothblum, and Balsam (2005) reported that nearly half of the gay men in their research reported sex outside of their primary relationship. Non-monogamy is however not associated with less couple satisfaction or commitment (LaSala, 2004). Gay male couples frequently have planned agreements about their outside sexual encounters, although research has also revealed that having an open relationship by agreement, does not necessarily mean that the partners will act upon it (Kurdek, 2004). Some gay male youth eschew non-monogamy and aspire to long-term monogamous relations (D'Augelli, Grossman, & Rendina, 2006); this may be one effect of the HIV epidemic (Gotta et al., 2011).

Lesbian Sexuality and Sex Therapy With Female Dyads

In a culture free of male dominance, what kind of sexuality would women want, practice, or experience.

(Nichols, 1987, p. 154)

Lesbian sexuality is born of female desire, which is impossible to completely separate from the foreground of patriarchy and woman-hating. Women's desire (heterosexual or homosexual) has rarely been the focus of research and lesbian desire has been viewed more as pornographic pleasure for the male gaze than as an act for the pleasure of the participants, i.e., images that are phallocentric and heterosexist (Teifer, 2001). Although lesbian sexuality has a long and passionate history, it cannot be separated from women's oppression; it has not been easy for women to come out of the closet and live openly as lesbians until the rise of the women's liberation movement. Certainly, butch-femme communities thrived (Kennedy & Davis; 1993) before this era, and the influence of the feminist movement has been mixed—fostering both greater freedom for women and sexual exploration, as well as sexual conflicts within this movement—for example, between anti-pornography and pro-sex activists.

While sexual freedom has never had the importance to queer women that it has to gay men, there is still an ethos of sexual openness and experimentation not found in heterosexual culture, nonetheless the lesbian community has fostered a strong sex radical movement unparalleled among heterosexual women (Nichols, 1987). Additionally, lesbians have always explored sensuality, erotic expression, gender dynamics, and other aspects of sexual play. Moreover, in recent years the queer women's community has struggled with the inclusion—and in some cases welcomed—transwomen and transmen and others on the gender spectrum, with the unique sexual concerns specific to trans* bodies. Thus lesbians in urban areas have usually been exposed to kinky sex, to polyamory, and to individuals transitioning between genders and exhibiting a wide range of gender expressions.

Blumstein and Schwartz's (1983) research, the first to really examine lesbian sex, revealed that lesbians had less frequent sex than other partnerships (gay men and heterosexual couples). They coined the term "lesbian bed death" inferring this lack of passion reflected an inability to maintain an ongoing sexual relationship within long term partnerships. Other researchers also found that lesbian couples had a lessening of sexual behavior and little or no genital contact (Hall, 1984; Loulin, 1984).

Nichols (2011) raises important questions about this phenomena. Do women have a biologically lower sex drive then men (i.e., if no men are present, pushing for more sex, will desire fade), or does this reflect female socialization, since women have learned to be sexually receptive and therefore do not know how to ask for or initiate sex? Or, she posits, is it possible that the problem is the actual questions we ask, i.e., the way we measure sexuality that is the problem, what Riggs (2011) referred to as "ideological frameworks." If sexual behavior is measured by penetration, or number of orgasms, or genital contact— perhaps researchers' phallocentric, heteronormative perspective is missing the actual passion and sexuality between women.

As noted earlier, lesbian couples have been noted to have egalitarian relationships, with high degrees of intimacy and communication and are skilled at conflict resolution. How do we resolve this discrepancy between these happy, but sexless, partnerships? Iasenza (2002) notes that lesbian sex may be less frequent and less genitally focused, but it is more sensual. Research has shown that lesbians spend more time on the average sexual encounter than do heterosexuals; using the measure of time spent on sex rather than sexual frequency, lesbians might be just as sexually satisfied (or perhaps more so) than their straight counterparts (Iasenza, 2002). Iasenza (1991) also found lesbians to be more sexually arousable and more sexually assertive than heterosexual women.

Although lesbian couples are more likely to be monogamous than gay men, female couples often openly discuss non-monogamy. Open communication is important to lesbians, even if they appear to be no more likely than heterosexual couples to actually practice it (Gotta et al., 2011; Solomon, Rothblum, & Balsam, 2005).

Gender has long been a salient area of exploration of lesbian couples (Laird, 1999). Butch/femme dynamics were the accepted norm before the beginning of lesbian-feminist communities in the 1970s (Nestle, 1992) and has remained a constant expression of sexual desire within postmodern communities (Levitt, Gerrish, & Hiestand, 2003; Loulin, 1990). Butch and femme are not merely "roles" that are "played" by lesbians, and are most certainly not a mimicking of heterosexual gender roles, but rather erotic expressions of sexual and gender identities that exist within lesbian communities. Russo and Owens-Reid (2014) wrote a blog post challenging the heterosexist assumptions about how gender works in lesbian relationship. They comment on the question often posited to lesbians, "If you like girls that look like boys, why don't you want to date boys?" with the retort, "If you like boys so much, why don't you want to date my girlfriend who 'looks like a boy'?" Their point is that "looking like a boy" is a particular lesbian erotic presentation (Loulin, 1990; Nestle, 1992), and has little to do with heterosexual posturing, or traditional gender identities, but speaks to a specific lesbian eroticism.

There has, however, been limited contemporary scholarship that challenges the enduring salience on gender dynamics in lesbian relationships. This invisibility in the research is a missed opportunity to raise questions about lesbian sexuality. What does the research reveal, as well as conceal, about female couples? Is it possible certain research tools privilege particular "kinds" of couples, i.e., those who are most out or educated, those who are white and privileged? Although there are broader options for relational dynamics available for lesbians today, butch/femme identities, female masculinity, femme expression, and the exploration of gender dynamics across sexual orientations, not only still exists in lesbian couples, but have continued to expand within the postmodern world.

Case Vignettes

Lisette and Rosa. Lisette casually mentioned that she and Rosa had a more active sex life in the summer than in the winter. When questioned, she shyly admitted that in the summer they tended to sleep in the enclosed porch, which felt more private than their bedroom which was above the landlady's bedroom. They often felt that she could hear them and this inhibited their already infrequent sex life. Upon exploration, Lisette shared that she once came up behind Rosa to hug her while she was doing the dishes, and Rosa froze and pushed her away. She was concerned that neighbors would see them embracing. Although this couple was legally married in the state in which they lived, and had been partners for years, they were still coping with layers of internalized homophobia that was particularly focused on behavior that could be interpreted sexually. This also manifested in the bedroom. Lisette admitted that she had a hard time telling Rosa what she liked. She said that sometimes she kept moving her body over, hoping that Rosa would understand where and how she wanted to be touched, but that Rosa just joked that they would fall off the bed if she kept moving. Lisette did not have the language to discuss her body parts, or her desires, in a way that felt empowering, and not "dirty." Working together in sex therapy, they were able to talk about these concerns, learn a mutually acceptable language to discuss their sexual desire, and become more playful sexually. This involved meeting with each of the women separately and completing a thorough sexual history, which included the values of their families about sexuality, how they learned to talk about body parts, and the individual narratives of their own coming out stories. Then the couple met together and shared their stories. Slowly (and very shyly), with support and encouragement in the consulting room, they began to verbalize how they would like to be touched, and what their visions for their sexual pleasure would look like. Sessions focused on topics like "getting caught," "being seen," and being visible as lesbian women—not just friends or even wives, but as erotic partners. Rosa began to explore and deconstruct messages received in her Catholic family about sexual desire, and Lisette shared how women's bodies were seen as "dirty" in her family. Ultimately, the women decided to buy their own home, so they didn't have to be so constrained by their landlady—a home with enough distance from the neighbors that Lisette joked, "We could even moan loudly and no one would hear."

Jo. Jo presented in therapy wearing masculine clothing, and sporting a short haircut. She was dating a woman she had met at work, and this was the woman's first sexual relationship with another woman. This had been a pattern for Jo. She enjoyed seducing straight woman, who found the sexual attention she gave them incredibly hot, but often struggled with ambivalence about her gender presentation. They liked her masculinity, but also often chided her about it. They could rarely commit to being in a relationship with another woman, and Jo had been left many times when her lovers were ready to "settle down" with a man. Jo thought that all "real lesbians" were butches, and since she was attracted to very feminine women, she felt "doomed" to never find a woman who really understood her and desired her. Jo explored how her gender was viewed within her family growing up, and how she was able to break away and develop her own sexual style. She saw being a lesbian as an act of "aloneness," and had been raised to believe in her religious and rejecting family, that if she continued to live "that way," she would never find a partner. Despite Jo's outward sexual presentation as a bold dyke, she lived with self-hatred and confusion about her gender, her sexuality, and her desire. In therapy, she was encouraged to explore what it would mean for her to find a femme lover, another lesbian who had a more feminine presentation, but was clearly interested in lesbian sexuality, and who respected and honored Jo's masculine sexual stance. Jo resisted the idea that such women could even be found, but through Internet chat rooms, butch/femme dating sites, and even a lesbian cruise, she was able to realize that she did not need to continue dating rejecting heterosexual women. It was a powerful healing to find a lesbian lover, who had no desire to be with a man, adored and enjoyed her masculine sexuality and saw their relationship as whole, and hot, and queer.

Gay Male Sexuality and Sex Therapy With Male Dyads

> Across the sweep of modern history, men such as these have risked their careers and reputations in order to have erotic contact with other men. . . . Is it surprising, then, that the erotic is so central to gay men's identities and culture?
>
> (Martin, 2006, p. 219)

There is much less research on woman to woman sexuality than there is on male to male, often referred to in the sexology literature as "MSM" (men who have sex with men, a term more behaviorally precise than "gay"). However, this research is narrow in focus. As Sandfort and de Keizer (2001) write: "Because sexual behavior is a major route of HIV transmission, and gay men constitute a major risk group in industrialized countries, a vast number of studies have been conducted... the research has been focused almost exclusively on safe versus unsafe sexual practices" (p. 3).

Sandfort and de Keizer (2001) summarize the research investigating sexual dysfunction in gay men. Most studies find higher overall rates of self-reported sexual dysfunction among gay men: 74% of gay men report some kind of sexual dysfunction, as compared to 30–50% of heterosexual men (McDonough, Bishop, Brockman, & Morrison, 2014). Bancroft et al. (2006) also reports that gay men have higher rates of anxiety about sex, and that gay men report more ED (erectile dysfunction) while heterosexual men report higher rates of RE (rapid ejaculation). Several studies have found that the most common sexual problem reported by gay male couples is the same as for mixed sex couples— discrepancies in desire for sex between partners—and that gay men report problems with sexual compulsivity less frequently. However, male dyads also report sexual problems rarely encountered in mixed sex or lesbian couples (Sandfort & de Keizer, 2001), such as aversion to anal sex and painful anal sex.

Clinicians working with male dyads must take into account the ways in which gay male sexual behavior is different from that of hetero men. Hart and Schwartz (2010) and Martin (2006) have outlined some of these differences. Although the percentage of gay male couples with non-monogamy agreements has declined from nearly 100% pre-AIDS epidemic to closer to 40–50% now (LaSala, 2001; Shernoff, 2006a; Parsons, Starks, Gamarel, & Grov, 2012; Solomon, Rothblum, & Balsam, 2005), clinicians are still quite likely to see this in the office, and to be called upon to help partners to negotiate such agreements or to help resolve conflicts over non-monogamy. Overall, gay men are more sexual than women or heterosexual men, both in frequency of sex and number of different partners. Therefore, therapists may need to examine their own internal norms about this abundant sexual activity to avoid developing negative judgments of gay male clients.

While same sex couples are, overall, more egalitarian than mixed sex couples, that does not mean that roles are equal in the bedroom. Especially when anal sex is practiced, two men may assume "active" or "passive" roles, which correspond to "top" and "bottom," or "insertor" and "insertee." Many men are flexible in their roles, but sometimes problems arise when both men prefer one role over the other. In addition, when erectile dysfunction is an issue, it is usually an issue for the anal sex "top," as the "bottom" can participate fully with a flaccid or partially erect penis.

Anal sex, however, is not directly analogous to penile-vaginal intercourse. The most common sexual acts among gay men are oral sex and mutual masturbation. Most mixed sex dyad sexual encounters assume penile-vaginal penetration, with oral sex, if present, part of "foreplay." Male dyads do not assume that anal sex will be included in every, or even any, sexual encounter (Hart & Schwartz, 2010).

HIV affects gay male sexuality tremendously, even though AIDS is no longer a death sentence. Prevention specialists have been frustrated by the fact that male to male sexual transmission has not only not been eradicated, it is on the rise, as condom use is by no means universal. In the United States, most new cases of HIV transmission occur among gay men, and the numbers are increasing (Centers for Disease Control, 2013). Unprotected anal intercourse (UAI), called "barebacking," is the mode of transmission, and it is common among gay men (Shernoff, 2006b). It is difficult to understand this without considering the sub-cultural system that influences gay men and male dyads, and without knowing some of the history of Gay Liberation. Early Gay Liberationists celebrated joyous, abundant, frequent sexuality among men. Free of constraints, some men in urban gay communities could amass hundreds, even thousands of sex partners. Sex became a way of sharing and connecting with other men, and for some gay men it was and is a spiritual, transcendent, personal, and communal experience. Sex became synonymous with liberation and gay identity for many men. This was so true that even after AIDS began to devastate the community in the 1980s, many gay men resisted the idea that HIV was spread sexually, as documented in plays, movies, and books like "The Normal Heart" and "And the Band Played On." For gay men, sex served and still continues to serve functions of intimacy and pleasure, but also of connection to community, gay pride, identity, ecstatic "peak" experiences, and spirituality.

Once the reality of sexual transmission was accepted, by the mid-1980s prevention efforts began, primarily funded by government money and including rigorous research (Mustanski & Parsons, 2014). Efforts focused on getting tested for HIV, using condoms, on reducing the number of different partners—and on "erotizicing" safe sex (Shernoff & Bloom, 1991). Rates of new infection dropped dramatically among gay men until the last decade, and now new infections are again on the rise. Prevention efforts have expanded beyond "safe sex" messages to include harm-reduction techniques like "serosorting," the practice of barebacking only with men of your own serostatus. This approach has had some success in reducing sexual transmission (Philip, Yu, Donnell, Vittinghoff, & Buchinder, 2010).

The latest prevention technique is called PrEP—Preexposure Prophylaxis, which involves taking small oral doses of antiretroviral drugs on a daily basis while still HIV negative. The CDC published guidelines for use in the United States on May 19, 2014 (Centers for Disease Control, 2014). PrEP reduces the risk of HIV transmission about 50% in gay men, even among those who are having unprotected anal sex. It is controversial for reasons ranging from the practical to the sex negative (Crary, 2014), and the debate currently divides the gay male community, as some AIDS activists and organizations advocate for its use as a harm-reduction technique, while others discourage its use. Mantell et al. (2014) found that half of gay men said that it was "very likely" that they themselves would use PrEP—but that many erroneously believe that PrEP works when taken only before sex. The same study found that nearly half of survey respondents believe PrEP will lead to a reduction in condom use, a major fear of those who deplore its use. Arguments against PrEP, marketed as "Truvada," include the fear that users who do not follow a consistent regiment will develop strains of HIV resistant to antiretroviral medications. Supporters of PrEP counter that rates of sexual transmission are rising among gay men because a significant number are already not using condoms, and that Truvada will protect those men currently engaging in "barebacking."

Recent research has shown that most seroconversions do not occur as a result of sex with multiple partners, but rather as a result of UAI between committed partners (Mustanski & Parsons, 2014). This is a finding of major importance, because most prevention efforts have been aimed towards men who are single or who are contracting HIV as a result of extra-dyadic sex. In fact, one study showed that like lesbians and heterosexuals, gay men value sex in the context of a committed relationship and sex with a sense of emotional and psychological connection over volume and variety of sex partners (Bourne et al., 2013). Therapists should be aware of this and, when appropriate, question male couples in sex therapy about their prevention efforts and knowledge of their own serostatus. Many couples have rules that require using condoms with extra-marital sex partners but not with each other, and are transmitting the virus between them when they believe themselves to be "safe."

Case Vignettes

Frank and Jarad. Frank and Jarad came to treatment for help restoring a sex life that had flagged after Frank discovered in a routine annual physical that he had seroconverted. Frank realized he had been deceived by an outside partner with whom he had an ongoing sexual relationship, who had claimed to be HIV negative. Frank had not transmitted the virus to Jarad, however, and Jarad was not angry at Frank for his mistake. Frank was diligent about taking the "cocktail" of drugs aimed at preventing his HIV from becoming active. However, the men's sex life with each other ceased after Frank's diagnosis, and Frank avoided sex outside the dyad as well. The therapist, after investigating the possibility that Frank's decreased sex drive was a side effect of the medications, determined that Frank was avoiding sex with Jarad for fear of "contaminating" Jarad. He was averse to outside sexual partners as well, wary of being deceived again. In therapy, Frank revealed feelings of deep shame and humiliation for having contracted HIV, and thoughts that his body was "toxic." Frank needed some individual sessions to work through these feelings. He was old enough to remember people dying of AIDS in the 1980s and 1990s, and during those years he had internalized the feelings that male bodies, especially the penis and semen, were "contaminated," feelings that were extremely common at the time (Shernoff & Bloom, 1991). EMDR and cognitive-behavioral reframing of his thoughts helped diminish the intensity of these negative feelings considerably. Jarad, for his part, was extremely patient, consistently re-assuring, and willing to wait over a year for Frank to be able to be sexual. This was easier for Jarad because, like many gay male couples, the men had an open relationship and Jarad occasionally had sexual encounters with others. In addition, in therapy the men learned the value of frequent and tender cuddling and physical contact. Slowly they were able to resume a sex life with each other, albeit more limited than it had been before. Moreover, Frank was never comfortable with having his own extra-marital sex again. He felt so deeply betrayed by the outside lover who had infected him that he could not feel open and free sexually with anyone but Jarad. Frank accepted this without bitterness, however. After his HIV infection, Frank never prioritized sex in his life quite as much as he had done before.

Alberto and James. Many gay men become connoisseurs of sex by virtue of experience and number of sex partners. This can sometimes work against them. Alberto and James had been in a monogamous marriage for 8 years, and gradually over the years James' interest in sex had declined. At the point they entered treatment, they rarely had sex, something which frustrated both men. When they attempted, James often had erectile problems. The quality of the rest of their relationship was high. James was 15 years older than Alberto and much more sexually experienced. His many casual sexual encounters had always followed a narrow and rigid sexual script; opportunities for sex had been so abundant for him that he simply rejected partners who did not match his criterion for sexual style. James' sexual "lovemap" involved being "seduced" by his partner in a particular way that involved finesse and subtlety. Alberto's sexuality was more expansive and flexible, but his natural style involved being boisterous, enthusiastic, and a little rough. Over the years, James had found this mismatch between his internal erotic script and Alberto's sexuality became increasingly important, and he grew less and less interested in sex. Alberto was dissatisfied with the infrequency of sex, but he also complained that the narrowness of James' interests left him bored. The therapist learned these things during individual sessions with each partner. After diagnosing the script discrepancies, the sex counselor held a couples session explaining that these "mismatches" existed and that therapy would consist of helping the men communicate their specific needs and learn how to fine-tune their sexual encounters. James and Alberto were also told that because of their different sexual desires, their sex together might never be as "hot" as sex had been outside the relationship. This was particularly hard for James to hear; he had spent many years accustomed to having easy access to "hot" sex through multiple partners, but he came to accept it. In general, however, the men understood the concept of a "mismatch" much more easily than many mixed sex couples would; gay men tend to have a pragmatic approach to sex. Getting the men to communicate their needs was fairly easy as well. They were encouraged to watch a variety of pornography together and discuss it afterwards, pointing out what they each found particularly arousing. What was more difficult was teaching Alberto to be more subtle and nuanced in his approach. It did not come naturally to him, and the therapist needed to do some "coaching" to help him develop finesse. But James ultimately responded to Alberto's attempts to seduce him in the way he desired. He was moved by Alberto's efforts, and that made it easier for him to "stretch" to expand his sexual repertoire to accommodate his partner's desire for novelty and experimentation.

Summary and Conclusions

A systemic approach to sex therapy with same sex couples involves considering the historical context of Western society's treatment of those who exhibit these desires, the current social and political climate, and the influence of the LGBTQ community on behavior, beliefs, and even identities of its members. The clinician should be aware of the great degree of intersectionality within the "queer" subculture and how this impacts the dyad, e.g., the couple may include one or more members who is transgender, practices BDSM, or is bisexual, and committed partners may have an agreement and rules about sexual and/or romantic relationships outside the dyad. Since gay and lesbian people are more likely than heterosexuals to be rejected by their families of origin, the primary support system of same sex couples may be "created families." Same sex couples "operate" differently from mixed sex couples in some ways, primarily in the more egalitarian nature of their relationships. Their sexuality is somewhat different, and the sexual practices of lesbian couples vary, in turn, from those of male dyads. While the problems of same sex couples are often similar to those of mixed sex, some specific sexual issues are different. By considering the systems context of same sex dyads, appreciating the particular stresses and pressures exerted by both the mainstream and the minority cultures, and understanding the ways lesbian and gay male relationships reflect those stresses and pressures, sex therapists increase their effectiveness working with same sex couples.

References

Allen, K.R., & Demo, D.H. (1995). The families of lesbians and gay men: A new frontier in family research. *Journal of Marriage and the Family, 57*, 111–127.

American Psychiatric Association. (2013). *Diagnostic and statistical manual of mental disorders* (5th ed.). Arlington, VA: American Psychiatric Publishing.

Ashton, D. (2011). Lesbian, gay, bisexual, and transgender individuals and the family life cycle. In M. McGoldrick, B. Carter, & N. Garcia-Preto (Eds.), *The expanded family lifecycle* (pp. 115–132). Boston, MA: Allyn and Bacon.

Bailey, J.M. (1999). Commentary: Homosexuality and mental illness. *Archives of General Psychology, 56*, 883–884.

Bancroft, J., Carnes, L., Janssen, E., Goodrich, D., & Long, J. (2006) Erectile and ejaculatory problems in gay and heterosexual men. *Archives of Sexual Behavior, 34*(3), 285–297.

Barker, M. (2013). Gender and BDSM revisited: Reflections on a decade of researching kink communities. *Psychology of Women Section Review, 15*(2), 20–28.

Beemyn, G., & Rankin, S. (2011). *The lives of transgender people*. New York: Columbia University Press.

Blair, K., & Pukall, C. (2014). Can less be more? Comparing the duration vs. frequency of Sexual encounters in same-sex and mixed-sex relationships. *Canadian Journal of Human Sexuality*. Published online July 7, 2014.

Blank, H. (2012). *Straight: A surprisingly short history of heterosexuality*. Boston: Beacon.

Blumstein, P., & Schwartz, P. (1983). *American couples: Money, work, sex*. New York: William Morrow.

Bourne, A., Hammond, G., Hickson, F., Reid, D., Schmidt, A., & Weatherburn, P. (2013). What constitutes the best sex life for gay and bisexual men? Implications for HIV prevention. *BMC Public Health*, *13*, 1083–1086.

Brown, T. (2002). A proposed model of bisexual identity development that elaborates on experiential differences of women and men. *Journal of Bisexuality*, *2*(4), 67–91.

Bryant, A. S. & Demian (1994). Relationship characteristics of American gay and lesbian couples: Findings from a national survey. *Journal of Gay and Lesbian Social Services*, *1*(2), 101–117.

Centers for Disease Control. (2013). *HIV in the United States: At a glance*. Retrieved from http://www.cdc.gov/hiv/pdf/statistics_basics_factsheet.pdf

Centers for Disease Control. (2014). Pre-Exposure Prophylaxis (PrEP). Retrieved from http://www.cdc.gov/hiv/prevention/research/prep/

Connolly, C. M. (2005). A qualitative exploration of resilience in long-term lesbian couples. *The Family Journal*, *13*, 266–280.

Crary, D. (2014) Truvada, HIV prevention drug, divides gay community. Retrieved from http://www.huffingtonpost.com/2014/04/07/truvada-gay-men-hiv_n_5102515.html

D'Augelli, A. R., Grossman, A. H., & Rendina, J. (May, 2006). *Lesbian, gay, and bisexual youth: Marriage and child-rearing aspirations*. Presentation at the Symposium of Contemporary Issues about LGBT-headed families. Philadelphia, PA.

D'Augelli, A. R., Rendina, H. J., Grossman, A. H., & Sinclair, K. O. (2007). Lesbian and gay youths' aspirations for marriage and raising children. *Journal of LGBT Issues in Counseling*, *1*, 77–98.

Diamond, L. (2008). *Sexual fluidity: Understanding women's love and desire*. Cambridge: Harvard University Press.

Diamond, L. M. (2013a). Links and distinctions between love and desire. In C. Hazan & M. Campa (Eds.), *Human bonding: The science of affectional ties* (pp. 226–250). New York: Guilford.

Diamond, L. M. (2013b). Sexual-minority, gender-nonconforming, and transgender youths. In D. Bromberg & W. O. Donohue (Eds.), *Handbook of child and adolescent sexuality: Developmental and forensic psychology* (pp. 275–300). Oxford: Elsevier Press.

Diamond, L. M. (2013c). Concepts of female sexual orientation. In C. Patterson & A. R. D'Augelli (Eds.), *The psychology of sexual orientation* (pp. 3–17). New York: Cambridge University Press.

Diamond, L. M. (2014, February). *I was wrong! Men are pretty darn sexually fluid too*. Austin, TX: Society for Personality and Social Psychology Preconference on Sexuality.

Diamond, L., & Butterworth, M. (2008). Questioning gender and sexual identity: Dynamic links over time. *Sex Roles*, *59*, 365–376.

Diamond, L., Dickenson, J., & Blair, K. (2013, November 16). Convergence and divergence among different measures of same-sex and other-sex sexuality. Paper presented at Annual Meeting of the Society for the Scientific Study of Sex. San Diego, CA.

Gates, G. (2013) *Same-sex and different-sex couples in the American Community Survey: 2005–2011*. California: Williams Institute.

Gotta, G., Green, R., Rothblum, E., Solomon, S., Balsam, K., & Schwartz, P. (2011). Heterosexual, lesbian, and gay male relationships: A comparison of couples in 1975 and 2000. *Family Process*, *50*, 353–376.

Gottman, J. M., Levenson, R. W., Gross, J., Frederickson, B. L., McCoy, K., Rosenthal, L., Ruef, A., & Yoshimoto, D. (2003). Correlates of gay and lesbian couples' relationship satisfaction and relationship dissolution. *Journal of Homosexuality*, *45*(1), 23–43.

Green, R.-J. (2009). From outlaws to in-laws: Gay and lesbian couples in contemporary society. In B. Risman (Ed.), *Families as they really are* (pp. 197–213, 488–489, 527–530). New York: Norton.

Green, R.-J., & Mitchell, V. (2008). Gay and lesbian couples in therapy: Minority stress, relation ambiguity, and families of choice. In A.S. Gurman (Ed.), *Clinical handbook of couple therapy* (4th ed., pp. 662–680). New York: Guilford Press.

231

Hall, M. (1984). Lesbians, limerance, and long-term relationships. In J. Loulin (Ed.), *Lesbian sex* (pp. 141–150). San Francisco: Spinsters Ink.

Hart, T., & Schwartz, D. (2010). Cognitive-behavioral erectile dysfunction treatment for gay men. *Cognitive and Behavioral Practice*, 17, 66–76.

Herek, G.M. (2002). Heterosexuals' attitudes towards bisexual men and women in the United States. *Journal of Sex Research*, 39(4), 264–274.

Hertlein, K., & Weeks, G. (2009). Toward a new paradigm in sex therapy. In K. Hertlein, G. Weeks, & N. Gambescia (Eds.), *Systemic sex therapy* (pp. 43–61). New York: Routledge,

Holmberg, D., & Blair, K. (2009). Sexual desire, communication, satisfaction, and preferences of men and women in same-sex versus mixed sex relationships. *Journal of Sex Research*, 46(1), 57–66.

Hunter, S. (2012). *Lesbian and gay couples: Lives, issues and practice*. Chicago, IL: Lyceum Books.

Iasenza, S. (1991). The relations among selected aspects of sexual orientation and sexual functioning in females. *Dissertation Abstracts International*. Ann Arbor: University Microfilms International (No. 9134752).

Iasenza, S. (2002). Beyond "lesbian bed death": The passion and play in lesbian relationships. *Journal of Lesbian Studies*, 6, 111–120.

Iasenza, S. (2010). What is queer about sex?: Expanding sexual frames in theory and practice. *Family Process*, 49(3), 291–308.

Irvine, J. (2005). *Disorders of desire: Sexuality and gender in modern American sexology*. Philadelphia: Temple University Press.

Kaplan, H. (1979). *Disorders of sexual desire and other new concepts and techniques in sex therapy* (Vol. 2). New York: Brunner Mazel.

Kennedy, E.L., & Davis, M. D. (1993). *Boots of leather, slippers of gold: The history of a lesbian community*. New York: Penguin Press.

Kupfer, L., Nussbaum, R., & Mustanski, B. (2012). Exploring the diversity of gender and sexual orientation identities in an online sample of transgender individuals. *Journal of Sex Research*, 49(2–3), 244–254.

Kurdek, L. A. (2004). Are gay and lesbian cohabiting couples *really* different from heterosexual married couples? *Journal of Marriage and Family*, 66(4), 880–900.

Kurdek, L. A. (2005). What do we know about gay and lesbian couples? *Current Directions in Psychological Science*, 14(5), 251–254.

Laird, J. (1999). Gender and sexuality in lesbian relationships. In J. Laird (Ed.), *Lesbians and lesbian families: Reflections on theory and practice* (pp. 47–90). New York: Columbia, 1999.

LaSala, M. (2001). Monogamous or not: Understanding and counseling gay male couples. *Families in Society: The Journal of Contemporary Human Services*, 82, 605–611.

LaSala, M. (2004). Monogamy of the heart: Extradyadic sex and gay male couples. *Journal of Gay and Lesbian Social Services*, 17(3), 1–24.

Lev, A. (in press). Resilience in lesbian and gay couples. In K. Skerrett & K. Fergus (Eds.). *Couple resilience across the lifespan: Emerging perspectives*. New York: Springer.

Lev, A.I. (1998). Invisible gender. *In the Family*, October, 8–11.

Lev, A. (2004). *Transgender emergence: Counseling gender-variant people and families*. New York: Taylor and Frances.

Lev, A. I. (2008). More than surface tension: Femmes in families. *Journal of Lesbian Studies*, 12(2–3), 127–144.

Lev, A. I. (2014). Understanding transgender identities and exploring sexuality and desire. In G. H. Allez (Ed). *Sexual diversity and sexual offending. Research, assessment and clinical treatment in psychosexual therapy* (pp. 45–59). London: Karnac.

Lev, A.I., & Sennott, S. (2012). Trans-sexual desire in different gendered bodies. In J. J. Bigner & J. L. Wetchler (Eds.), *Handbook of LGBT-affirmative couple and family therapy*. New York: Taylor & Francis.

Levitt, H.M., Gerrish, E. A., & Hiestand, K. R. (2003). The misunderstood gender: A model of modern femme identity. *Sex Roles*, 48(3/4), 99–113.

Loulin, J. (1984). *Lesbian sex*. San Francisco, CA: Spinster Ink.

Loulin, J. (1990). *The lesbian erotic dance: Butch, femme, androgyny and other rhythms.* San Francisco: Spinsters, Inc.

Malpas, J. (2011). Between pink and blue: A multi-dimensional family approach to gender nonconforming children and their families. *Family Process, 50*(4), 453–470.

Malpas, J. (2012). Can couples change gender? Couple therapy with transgender people and their partners. In J. J. Binger & J. L. Wetchler (Eds.), *Handbook of LGBT affirmative couple and family therapy.* New York: Routledge.

Mantell, J., Sandfort, T., Hoffman, S., Guidry, J., Masvawure, T., & Cahill, S. (2014). Knowledge and attitudes about Preexposure Prophylaxis among sexually active men who have sex with men and who participate in New York City Gay Pride events. *LGBT Health, 2*, 1–5.

Martin, J. (2006). Transcendence among gay men: Implications for HIV prevention. *Sexualities, 9*(2), 214–235.

Masters, W., & Johnson, V. (1979). *Homosexuality in perspective.* New York: Bantam Books.

McDonough, L., Bishop, C., Brockman, M., & Morrison, T. (2014). A systematic review of sexual dysfunction measures for gay men: How do current measures measure up? *Journal of Homosexuality, 61*(6), 781–816.

Meyer, I. H. (2003). Prejudice, social stress, and mental health in lesbian, gay, and bisexual populations: Conceptual issues and research evidence. *Psychological Bulletin, 129*(5), 674–697.

Mustanski, B., & Parsons, J. T. (2014). Introduction to special section on sexual health in gay and bisexual male couples. *Archives of Sexual Behavior, 43*(1), 17–20.

Nadal, K. L., Marie-Anne, I., Leon, J., Meterko, V., Wideman, M., & Wong, Y. (2011). Sexual orientation microaggressions: "Death by a thousand cuts" for lesbian, gay and bisexual youth. *Journal of LGBT Youth, 8*, 234–259.

Nestle, J. (1992). (Ed.) *The persistent desire: Femme-butch reader.* Los Angeles: Alyson.

Nestle, J. (1998). *A fragile union: New and selected writings.* San Francisco: Cleis Press.

Nestle, J., Wilchins, R., & Howell, C. (2002). *Genderqueer: Voices from beyond the sexual binary.* Los Angeles: Alyson Publications.

Nichols, M. (1987). What feminists can learn from the lesbian sex radicals. *Conditions Magazine, 4*, 152–163.

Nichols, M. (1994) Therapy with bisexual women. In. M. P. Mirkin (Ed.), *Women in context: Toward a feminist reconstruction of psychotherapy.* New York: Guilford.

Nichols, M. (2006) Sexual function in women with women: Lesbians and lesbian relationships. In I. Goldstein, C. Meston, S. Davis, & A. Traish (Eds.), *Women's sexual function and dysfunction* (pp. 307–313). New York: Taylor & Francis.

Nichols, M. (2011). Variations on gender and orientation in a first interview. In C. Silverstein (Ed.) *The initial psychotherapy interview: A gay man seeks treatment* (pp. 71–91). New York: Elsevier.

Nichols, M. (2014). Therapy with LGBTQ clients. In I. Binik & K. Hall (Eds.), *Principles and practice of sex therapy* (5th ed., pp. 309–333). New York: Guilford.

Nuttbrock, L., Hwahng, S., Bockting, W., Rosenblum, A., Mason, M., Macri, M., & Becker, J. (2010). Psychiatric impact of gender-related abuse across the life course of male-to-female transgender persons. *Journal of Sex Research, 47*(1), 12–23.

Parsons, J. T., Starks, T. J., DuBios, S., Grov, C., & Golub, S. A. (2011). Alternatives to monogamy among gay male couples in a community survey: Implications for mental health and sexual risk. *Archives of Sexual Behavior,* Online First—SpringerLink. Retrieved from http://www.springer-link.com/content/d656u4054241018k/

Parsons, J. T., Starks, T. J., Gamarel, K. E., & Grov, C. (2012). Non-monogamy and sexual relationship quality among same-sex male couples. *Journal of Family Psychology, 26*(5), 669–677. doi: 10.1037/a0029561

Patterson, D. G., Ciabattari, T., Schwartz, P., Adams, J. M., & Jones, W. W. (1999). The constraints of innovation: Commitment and stability among same-sex couples. In J. M. Adams & W. H. Jones (Eds.), *Handbook of interpersonal commitment and relationship stability* (pp. 339–359). New York: Springer.

Peplau, L. (2003). Human sexuality: how do men and women differ? *Current Direction in Psychological Science, 12*(2), 37–40.

Peplau, L. A., & Fingerhut, A. (2004). The paradox of the lesbian worker. *Journal of Social Issues, 60*(4), 719–735.

Peplau, L.A., & Fingerhut, A.W. (2007). The close relationships of lesbian and gay men. *Annual Review of Psychology, 58*, 405–424.

Philip, S.S., Yu, X., Donnell, D., Vittinghoff, E., & Buchinder, S. (2010). Serosorting is Associated with a decreased risk of HIV seroconversion in the EXPLORE study cohort. *Plos ONE, 5*, 1–7.

Richters, J., de Visser, R., Rissel, C., Grulich, A., & Smith, A. (2008). Demographic and psychosocial features of participants in bondage and discipline, "sadomasochism" or dominance and submission (BDSM): Data from a national survey. *Journal of Sexual Medicine, 5*(7), 1660–1668.

Riggs, D. (2011) Queering evidence-based practices. *Psychology and Sexuality, 2*(1), 87–98.

Risman, B. & Schwartz, P. (1988). Sociological research on male and female homosexuality. *Annual Review of Sociology, 14*, 125–147.

Rothblum, E. (2012). From invert to intersectionality: Understanding the past and future of sexuality. In R. das Nair & C. Butler (Eds.), *Intersectionality, sexuality, and psychological therapies: Working with lesbian, gay, and bisexual diversity* (pp. 263–268). New York: John Wiley & Sons.

Russo, K., & Owens-Reid, D. (2014). 13 things not to say to your lesbian friend. *Cosmopolitan* [weblog post]. Retrieved from http://www.cosmopolitan.com/sex-love/relationship-advice/things-not-to-say-to-your-lesbian-friend

Sandfort, R., & de Keizer, M. (2001). Sexual problems in gay men: An overview of empirical research. *Annual Review of Sex Research, 12*, 93–120.

Savin-Williams, R. (2005). *The new gay teenager*. Cambridge, MA: Harvard University Press.

Savin-Williams, R. (2014). An exploratory study of the categorical versus spectrum nature of sexual orientation. *Journal of Sex Research, 51*(4), 446–453. doi: 10.1080/00224499.2013.871691

Savin-Williams, R., & Rieger, G. (2013, November 17). Mostly heterosexual: Physiological and psychological Evidence for a 'new' sexuality. Paper presented at Annual Meeting of the Society for the Scientific Study of Sex. San Diego, CA.

Shernoff, M. (2006a). Negotiated nonmonogamy and male couples. *Family Process, 45*, 407–418.

Shernoff, M. (2006b). *Without condoms: Unprotected sex, gay men & barebacking*. New York: Taylor & Francis Group.

Shernoff, M., & Bloom, D.J. (1991). Designing effective AIDS prevention workshops for gay and bisexual men. *AIDS Education and Prevention, 3*, 31–46.

Silverstein, C. (2009). The implications of removing homosexuality from the DSM as a mental disorder. *Archives of Sexual Behavior, 38*(2), 161–163.

Solomon, S., Rothblum, E., & Balsam, K. (2005) Money, housework, sex and conflict: Same-sex couples in civil unions, those not in civil unions, and heterosexual married siblings. *Sex Roles, 52*(9/10), 561–575.

Somerville, S. (2000). *Queering the color line: Race and the invention of homosexuality in American culture*. Durham, NC: Duke University Press.

Steen, S., & Schwartz, P. (2005). Communication, gender, and power: Homosexual couples as a case study. In M.A. Fitzpatrick & A.L. Vangelisti (Eds.), *Explaining family interactions* (pp. 310–343). Thousand Oaks, CA: Sage.

Sue, D.W. (2010). *Microaggressions in everyday life: Race, gender, and sexual orientation*. New York: Wiley.

Tiefer, L. (2001). Feminist critique of sex therapy: Foregrounding the politics of sex. In P. J. Kleinplatz (Ed.), *New directions in sex therapy: Innovations and alternatives* (pp. 29–49). New York: Taylor and Francis.

Tilsen, J. (2013). *Therapeutic conversations with queer youth: Transcending homonormativity and constructing preferred identities*. New York: Jason Arsonson.

Weston, K. (1991). *Families we choose: Lesbians, gays, kinship*. New York: Columbia University Press.

13

SEXUAL COMPULSIVITY
Diagnosis, Assessment, and Treatment

David L. Delmonico and Elizabeth J. Griffin

Sexual addiction is thought to affect an estimated 6% of the adult population in the United States (Kafka, 2010), although there are no widespread studies to support this claim (Rosenberg, Carnes, & O'Connor, 2014). The efforts to understand, assess, and treat sexual addiction continue by both those who are directly impacted, as well as family members of sex addicts. Aside from the personal desperation that sex addicts often report, there are also public health concerns related to high frequency sexual behavior and the transmission of sexually transmitted diseases (Benotsch, Kalichman, & Pinkerton, 2001). This same study reported a moderate number of subjects (33%) who also used drugs as part of their pattern of behaviors. A study in New Zealand examined results from over 900 subjects and reported that while 13% of males and 7% of females report feeling their sexual thoughts, fantasies, and behaviors were out of control over the past year, only 4% of males and 2% of females felt that their behavior had significant negative consequences in their life (Skegg, Nada-Raja, Dickson, & Paul, 2010). Finally, Cooper, Delmonico, and Burg (2000) found similar results when surveying individuals who reported problematic sexual behavior on the Internet, with nearly 20% of subjects being at-risk for compulsive sexual behavior online, and 3% reporting both a combined Internet sex addiction and offline sexual addiction.

In addition to the personal distress and public health issues associated with sexual compulsion and/or addiction, such behaviors can also have a devastating impact on the couple and family system. Much of the literature examining the relationship between the pornography usage and sexual aggressiveness indicates there is an association between pornography consumption and sexual aggressiveness, higher acceptance of rape myths, increased difficulties in intimate relationships, and sexual perpepuation (Manning, 2006; Schneider, 2000b). Specifically, another study linked the number of hours of viewing pornography with increased importance on the sexual relationship and a reduced emphasis on the emotional portion of the relationship (Zillman & Bryant, 1988). On the other hand, at least one other study indicates that adolescents are not as susceptible as one may think to the effects of the sexually explicit material on their perceived view of women in a sexual scenario, thus challenging the notion that increases in viewing of sexually explicit material would contribute to distortions about women's intentions in sexual encounters (Peter & Valkenburg, 2011).

Given these estimates of the prevalence of sexual addiction among the general adult population, it is critical that clinicians be introduced to issues related to the diagnosis, assessment, and treatment of sexually addictive behaviors. In fact, the need for research and treatment consistency led to the creation of a specialized journal titled *Sexual Addiction and Compulsivity: The Journal of Treatment and Prevention.* Since the late 1990s this journal has been at the forefront of providing cutting-edge information to scholars and clinicians alike. This chapter summarizes many of the issues related to sexual addiction, presented in the context of the most current research in understanding, assessing, and treating sexual addiction.

Definition and Diagnosis of Sexual Addiction

unmanageable anxiety or addiction ?

One of the key issues is the controversy between sexual addiction and sexual compulsion (Bancroft & Vukadinovic, 2004). The main controversy is related to the motivation and underlying etiology of uncontrollable sexual behavior. Those who believe sexually uncontrollable behavior is the resolution of unmanageable anxiety fall in the sexual compulsion camp, whereas those in the sexual addiction camp believe one's uncontrollable sexual behavior is akin to other addictive disorders as described by the *DSM-5* (Hook et al., 2010). As the title of this chapter suggests, sexual addiction is an evolving construct and therefore its definition is a moving target. The bottom line is that there is no single, commonly accepted definition of sexual addiction.

The concept of sexual addiction does not appear in the latest version of the Diagnostic and Statistical Manual (*DSM-5*), despite the best efforts by various lobbying groups and support from clinicians (American Psychiatric Association, 2013). In the end, the DSM committee determined there was not enough empirical evidence to support the inclusion of such a construct in the manual (American Psychiatric Association, 2013). That said, the case presented to the DSM committee represented one of the most concerted efforts to define and measure the construct of what was termed *hypersexual disorder.* Although the American Psychiatric Association did not accept the diagnostic criteria, it represents the most current and descriptive thinking on how to operationalize the construct of sexual addiction and is therefore included in Figure 13.1 (Kafka, 2010).

The evolution of the construct of sexual addiction likely began as far back as the 1800s when psychiatrist Kraft-Ebing wrote that he witnessed the following in a client:

> an increased sexual appetite to such an extent that permeates all his thoughts and feelings, allowing no other aims in life, tumultuously, and in a rut-like fashion demanding gratification and resolving itself into an impulsive, insatiable, succession of sexual enjoyments. This pathological sexuality is a dreadful scourge for its victim, for he is in constant danger of violating the laws of the state and of morality, of losing his honor, his freedom and even his life.
>
> (Krafft-Ebing, 2012)

However, the term "sexual addiction" was not popularized until 1983 with the publication of *Out of the Shadows* (Carnes, 1983). The book used narrative format that described the cycle of addiction, resulting consequences, and subsequent emotional shame and desperation for those who engage in the seemingly out of control sexual behavior. In the book, Carnes introduced the idea of three "Levels" of sexual addiction depending on the behaviors engaged in as part of the addiction; however, since its publication, Carnes has rejected the notion that different types of behaviors indicated differing levels of sexual addiction. While the text is somewhat dated, and is mostly anecdotal, it remains a seminal work in the field and has been read by both professionals and lay persons who want to better understand sexual addiction.

A. Over a period of at least 6 months, recurrent and intense sexual fantasies, sexual urges, or sexual behaviors in association with three or more of the following five criteria:

A1. Time consumed by sexual fantasies, urges, or behaviors repetitively interferes with other important (non-sexual) goals, activities, and obligations.

A2. Repetitively engaging in sexual fantasies, urges, or behaviors in response to dysphoric mood states (e.g., anxiety, depression, boredom, irritability).

A3. Repetitively engaging in sexual fantasies, urges, or behaviors in response to stressful life events.

A4. Repetitive, but unsuccessful efforts to control or significantly reduce these sexual fantasies, urges, or behaviors.

A5. Repetitively engaging in sexual behaviors while disregarding the risk for physical or emotional harm to self or others.

B. There is clinically significant personal distress or impairment in social, occupational, or other important areas of functioning associated with the frequency and intensity of these sexual fantasies, urges, or behaviors.

C. These sexual fantasies, urges, or behaviors are not due to the direct physiological effect of an exogenous substance (e.g., a drug of abuse or a medication).

Specify if:

Masturbation
Pornography
Sexual Behavior with a Consenting Adult
Cybersex
Telephone Sex
Strip Clubs
Other:

Figure 13.1 Proposed *DSM-5* criteria for hypersexuality.

Since the introduction of the term "sexual addiction" in *Out of the Shadows*, there have been many other publications (e.g., books, journal articles, book chapters, etc.) dedicated to the topic. While there were many supporters of the concept of sexual addiction, the concept has also had a fair share of detractors, most of who disagree with the term "addiction," resulting in disagreement in the etiology, symptomology, assessment, and treatment of the disorder (Klein, 2002; Ley, 2012). Over the years, terms that have been commonly used to describe the phenomenon of out of control or excessive sexual behavior have included: don juanism, nymphomania, sexual compulsivity, sexual dependency, non-paraphilic related disorder, impulse control disorder, obsessive compulsive disorder, bi-polar disorder, impulse control disorder, sexual desire disorder, problematic sexual behavior, hypersexual disorder, and sexual addiction.

The American Psychiatric Association (APA) has also varied in its acceptance of the concept of sexual addiction. Although the APA has never used the term sexual addiction as a diagnosis, the *DSM-III* included the following description under the Psychosexual Disorder Not Otherwise Specified: "distress about a pattern of repeated sexual conquests with a succession of individuals who exist only as things to be used (Don Juanism and nymphomania)" (American Psychiatric Association, 1980, p. 283). Although this description was removed in the *DSM-III-R* and subsequent editions, the APA did entertain the idea of including hypersexual disorder in its latest edition, a signal that perhaps the APA will consider the concept in the future after more methodologically sound empirical studies are conducted.

At present, there is no official diagnosis for sexual addiction (or other similar constructs) in the Diagnostic and Statistical Manual. However, the construct is one that is the subject of a number of scientific inquires, peer-reviewed publications/presentations, and clinical case discussions in a variety of professional organizations. It is important to note, that while the concept of sexual addiction remains a topic of investigation there are still many professionals who oppose the use of this label. Some because they believe more evidence is needed before the construct can be officially labeled, while others feel the concept does not exist or is harmful to clients. Many, including the authors of this chapter, choose to use more behaviorally descriptive language to describe the constellation of behaviors that may be considered sexual addiction. For example, "out of control sexual behavior" or "problematic sexual behavior" are also used in place of the term sexual addiction. Use of such language helps to distance the theoretical association of terms like compulsivity and addiction. While the remainder of the chapter will use the term sexual addiction, it is important to take both the history, and current thinking about sexual addiction into consideration. Throughout this chapter, sexual addiction is conceptualized through the frame of the criteria for hypersexuality (see Kafka, 2010). The criteria created are the most evidenced based criteria to date, and represents much of what the sex addiction profession has discussed for the past three decades.

Cybersex

In today's digital age, cybersex has become one of the most frequently reported forms of sexual addiction, and the use of digital technologies for sexual purposes often accompanies many other forms of sexually addictive behavior. Cybersex includes both the viewing of pornography as well as sexual interactions with others using digital media. These sexual encounters with others online may either remain in the digital environment, or may be used to pursue sexual contact in the offline world. In any case, the intersection between sexual addiction and cybersex is one that continues to be researched and explored clinically (Carnes & Adams, 2002; Jones & Tuttle, 2012).

Cybersex problems cross all demographic boundaries. Research estimate that one of every three visitors to adult pornography web sites is likely to be female, and nearly 60% of those who use the search term *adult sex* on Internet search engines are female (Family Safe Media, Inc., 2010). Other groups, such as those under the age of 18, are also seeking sexual material online. The top search terms used by teens online include *teen sex* and *cybersex* (Family Safe Media, Inc., 2010). The average annual income for consumers of Internet pornography is a reported $75,000 plus. These statistics challenge our cultural assumptions about online sexual activity and who engages in it.

It is also important to recognize that not all online sexual activity should be viewed as having a negative impact on its consumers. Cooper, Delmonico, and Burg (2000) estimated that nearly 80% of those who engage in online sexual activity could be considered "recreational users," and do not self-report any significant problems related to their online behavior. Both youth and adults report using the Internet to research sexual information on issues such as preventing the spread of sexually transmitted infections, purchasing and reviewing options for contraception, exploring healthy sexuality, and so forth. However, for the 20% of individuals who struggle with problematic online sexual behavior, the consequences can be devastating and long lasting. While many studies differ on their idea about exactly how many hours or exact behaviors online would constitute problematic behavior (Jones & Hertlein, 2012), some individuals become compulsive with collecting and viewing pornography, others cross legal boundaries, while still others find themselves spending 10+ hours each day online in search of intimacy or romance. Of this 20% Cooper, Delmonico, and Burg (2000) suggested that only about 3–5% would likely be considered sexually addicts based on compulsivity measures as operationalized within the article. While it is impossible to cover all aspects of cybersex in this chapter, it is important to understand that sex addicts often use technology to engage in their addictive behavior. In order to learn more about cybersex, you may want to explore books or chapters dedicated to the topic (e.g., Carnes, Delmonico, & Griffin, 2000; Cooper, 2002; Edwards, Delmonico, & Griffin, 2011; Schneider & Weiss, 2001).

Sexual Addiction and Sexual Offense Behavior

Sexual Offense Awareness

Since sexually addictive behavior patterns may involve the crossing of boundaries with others as part of the acting out process, it is important to increase one's awareness of sexual offense issues. Sexual offenses commonly occur as the sexual addiction progress and individuals take higher and higher risks with their sexual behavior, resulting in legal boundaries being crossed. This may occur through behaviors such as exhibitionism, voyeurism, prostitution, etc. An additional common offense behavior is the possession of child pornography. While this may be an indicator of sexual interest in children, it may also be the result of compulsively viewing adult pornography that eventually progresses to the viewing of fetish pornography, and/or child pornography. Delmonico and Griffin (2013) published a text called *Illegal Images* directed towards helping professionals who want to understand more about their clients who view child pornography. Additionally, Delmonico and Griffin (1997) discuss the *Four Quadrant Model* that outlines the overlap between sexual addiction and sexual offense behavior.

Etiology of Sexual Addiction

Discussing the etiology of a disorder that has no official diagnosis in the *DSM-5* is difficult since the lack of an agreed upon criteria makes it difficult to study the phenomenon. Following the Intersystem Approach to conceptualizing the etiology of sexual addiction, there are three main areas for consideration: (1) individual biology/psychology, (2) interactions with others, especially intimate partners, and (3) intergenerational/family-of-origin issues (Weeks, 1994).

Individual/Biological

The advancement of technology over the past decade has drastically improved methods for examining brain processing. However, it should be noted that even with these significant advances in technology, there is still little understanding of how results from various types of brain scans may directly impact human behavior. The brain is far too complex to be reduced to images on a computer screen. This is best exemplified by the resulting divisions in the field of problematic sexual behavior as it relates to brain imaging.

There is a great deal of controversy regarding the role of neurochemistry and sexual addiction. There are researchers who subscribe to the belief that sexual addiction is primarily a neurobiological issue (e.g., Hilton & Watts, 2011; Milkman & Sunderwirth, 2009). Some argue that the neurochemistry has been problematic since birth, while others view problematic sexuality as a brain re-wiring issue that results from other environmental factors (e.g., trauma, association, reinforcement, etc.). Researchers such as John Money (1986) articulated the idea of a "love map" that is hardwired into the brain by a very early age, while others argue that brain plasticity is more common than once believed and that sexual desire, interest, and arousal can be changed over time.

Other arguments that support the neurochemistry and sexual addiction connection involves pharmacological research. Naficy, Samenow, and Fong (2013) discussed the use of psychotropic medications that appear to have significant impact on sexually addictive behaviors. Again, it is difficult to know exactly what is happening, or the order in which it is happening (e.g., decreased depression yields better sexual behavior management), but several studies demonstrate that the use of various medications can reduce sexually addictive thoughts and behaviors.

Opposing arguments include the fact that there is little evidence to suggest the brain is related to sexually addictive behaviors, and any identified brain differences in the research cannot be isolated to sex addicts and are likely to appear in control groups (e.g., Ley, Prause, & Finn, 2014; Steele, Staley, Fong, & Prause, 2013). Even previously accepted concepts, such as the assertion that sex addicts had impairment of their executive functioning in the brain, are being challenged. In a small sample, Reid, Karim, McCrory, and Carpenter (2010) provided evidence that the executive functioning for male sex addicts did not differ from the control group on self-reported measures of executive functioning.

While there may (or may not) be a connection between brain imaging and sexual behavior, the idea that brain structure or functioning *causes* problematic sexual behavior has no support. The most definitive statement that may be made is that there appears to be a relationship between the brain and sexual behavior, but we have yet to discover the true nature of this relationship. Even with today's current technology, it is impossible to know how much our sexuality is predestined versus neuropathways being formed and changed over time. Neuroscience research is the next frontier in understanding many behaviors, including the etiology of sexual addiction.

Individual/Psychological

Attachment theory has its roots back in the 1930s, but was formalized into an empirically supported, ethological-psychological theory of personality development, by Bowlby and Ainsworth in 1991 (Bretheron, 1992). Attachment theory asserts that our early infant/ child emotional connections to important figures cross time and space, and are critical to the future development of relationships in adulthood. Poor attachment may lead to a variety of social and emotional challenges. Flores (2004) linked attachment theory to the development of addictive behaviors in adulthood. While the focus of her text is on substance related issues, the context of how an individual may develop addictive behavior in response to an attachment-related disorder is well articulated. Zapf, Greiner, and Carroll (2008) examine attachment theory as a precursor to the development of male sexual addiction and conclude that male sex addicts differ significantly on attachment measures than their non-addicted counterparts.

It appears that attachment theory is a significant consideration in the etiology of sexual addiction. More research is needed in this area, but early indicators suggest that in part, understanding the early attachment patterns of sex addicts is an important strategy to conceptualizing, assessing, and treating the issue (Zapf, Greiner, & Carroll, 2008).

The Intersystem Approach suggests that the etiology of problematic behavior may be associated with interactions with significant others in one's life. Keane (2004) wrote about the development of desire disorders—including both sexual addiction and alcohol as primary examples. Sex addicts appear to have problems developing intimate relationships. Perhaps this is due to the attachment issues previously discussed, but whatever the reason, the inability to form emotionally invested romantic and non-romantic relationships results in some individuals attempting to connect with themselves and others in an unhealthy and addictive fashion. The etiology of sexual addiction may include desire disorders, or intimacy deficits resulting in problematic sexual behavior that is motivated by the need for connection and relationships.

In addition, certain individual characteristics have been associated with sexual addiction, including having obsessive thoughts, depression, interpersonal sensitivity, and psychotocism (Reid, Carpenter, & Lloyd, 2009). The interpersonal senstitivy is hypothesized to be associated with shame for one's behavior, while the depression may be explained as the emotional state precluding one's involvement in such behavior (Reid, Carpenter, & Lloyd, 2009).

Intergenerational/Environmental

In addition to the individual and interactional aspects, a neurobiology argument is that sexual addiction is primarily due to an event that occurs in an individual's environment, which remains unresolved in adulthood. Sexually addictive behaviors become a way to compensate for the environmental event. Such events often include childhood trauma or significant family dysfunction. The unresolved trauma often manifests in adulthood through intimacy and attachment issues (previously discussed)—which is then viewed as the foundation for developing sexually addictive behaviors. Reviewing the trauma literature reveals connections between childhood trauma and its impact on sexuality in adulthood (Briere, 1988; Van der Kolk, Perry, & Herman, 1991; Van der Kolk, 1989).

Intersystem Approach to Conceptualizing Sexual Addiction

Each of these three areas (individual, interactional, and intergenerational) are important considerations in conceptualizing the etiology of sexual addiction; however, rarely do they occur mutually exclusive of one another. Weeks (1994) described the Intersystem Approach as a comprehensive, empirically based clinical model that provides a theoretical framework for conceptualizing complex clinical issues. The Intersystem Approach may be particularly useful in conceptualizing sexual addiction given its systemic orientation and integration of a number of interdependent issues.

Many clinicians and researchers do not see the etiological explanations of sexual addiction as mutually exclusive; rather, they combine together to create a powerful drive to one's emotions and thoughts that results in the development of sexually addictive behaviors. In 2013, Bancroft discussed the neuropsychology of sexual arousal and desire, which included incentive motivations, inhibitory mechanisms, impaired inhibition, and negative mood states—all of which appear to have both a psychological and neuro-biological connection.

Van der Kolk (1989) discussed the compulsion to repeat the trauma and how this compulsion may manifest in a variety of maladaptive or addictive behaviors, including

241

sexual addiction. Further, the trauma experienced in childhood may cause neurobiological changes in the brain that may lead to sexually addictive behaviors. Therefore, it may not be the singularity factors that lead to sexual addiction, but rather the interaction of parts within the system that offer the most likely etiology for sexually addictive behavior (Hall, 2011; Katehakis, 2009; Van der Kolk, 2003).

Assessment

As with any addictive behavior, the assessment process is often complex and requires viewing the client as part of a larger eco-system that both contributes to and sustains their problematic sexual behavior. In order to develop accurate short term and long term goals, treatment plans must be based on a comprehensive assessment process that often spans several weeks.

Sexually addictive behaviors rarely stand alone and are often accompanied by a myriad of co-occuring issues and/or disorders. These may include sexual dysfunctions, medical issues, substance abuse, other behavioral addictions, depression, anxiety, attention deficit disorder, and post-traumatic stress, just to name a few.

The complex interweaving of the issues involved in sexual addiction can be difficult to determine and prioritize; therefore, the assessment process must include a variety of tools and techniques. For example, if standardized psychological instrumentation is not used, issues such as depression and anxiety may go unnoticed and untreated and thwart the efforts to manage an individual's sexual behavior. Personality disorders that could change the timing, scope, and direction of treatment could be missed and weeks or months may be wasted in treatment. The following paragraphs outline some of the critical components of a comprehensive evaluation for problematic sexual behavior. Several authors have written about the assessment process when sexual addiction diagnosis is being considered (e.g., Coleman, Raymond, & McBean, 2003; Schneider & Irons, 2001). The following sections compile and summarize the areas of the assessment that should be included for a comprehensive assessment for sexual addiction.

Initial Screening

It is important to remember that sexual health and deviance are often culturally and individually defined. Therefore, one purpose of an initial screening is to determine if further assessment and intervention is warranted. For example, clients often present for treatment because they are concerned about the frequency of their adult pornography use and accompanying masturbation and may have guilt over such behavior. Other common presenting problems include the partner who believes their partner is sexually addicted because they had an affair, or requested to engage in an "unusual" sexual practice (e.g., anal sex, use of sex toys, etc.). These are all examples of what is referred to as non-paraphillic sexual concerns and may or may not meet criteria for problematic sexual behavior. Each must be considered in the context of other information gathered during the initial screening, which may include frequency, intensity, and duration of the behavior. An initial interview should include questions that gather information that will help to distinguish between sexual concerns and problematic sexual behavior, including sexual addiction. Common questions may include:

"Have you made efforts to reduce the frequency of your sexual behavior?"
"Have you experienced any consequences as a result of your sexual behavior?"
"Do you find yourself thinking/planning sexual behavior constantly?"

It is important not to make judgments based on your own moral values, attitudes, and beliefs, but rather to use our current understanding of sexually addictive or compulsive sexual behavior.

In addition, the initial screening process should also include questions about possible co-occurring addictions. Carnes (1991) wrote that 83% of those with a sexual addiction reported other addictive behaviors. Addictions do not typically occur alone, but are often a complex myriad of rituals and behaviors that must be examined closely to allow for proper intervention (Schneider & Irons, 2001). Further, Carnes, Murray, and Charpentier (2005) discussed the concept of an "Addiction Interaction Disorder" where not only are there multiple addictions, but these addictions can become interdependent on one another, so that one becomes an integral part of a system of addictive behaviors.

Frequency and types of behavior alone are not indicators of sexual addiction. Schneider (2000a) suggested that counselors examine the history, frequency, sense of loss of control, level of obsession, and number/severity of life consequences to help ascertain if the sexual behavior has become addictive. Schneider (2004) discussed extensively the role and types of consequences that often accompany sexually addictive behaviors. Consequences can be grouped into three main areas: (a) physical (e.g., sexually transmitted infections, rape, physical injury, etc.), (b) psychological and emotional (e.g., depression, shame, marital discord, etc.), and (c) financial, legal, or employment (e.g., job loss, arrests, bankruptcy, etc.).

In addition to basic interview questions, there are several screening instruments and interviews that may be helpful in the initial screening process. The following sections discuss some of these instruments.

Sexual Interview/Instruments

Specific instruments used to gather a sexual history and assess for compulsive sexual behaviors should be included as part of a comprehensive evaluation. Examples of such instruments include the Sexual Addiction Screening Test (SAST) (Carnes, Green, & Carnes, 2010), the Hypersexual Behavior Inventory (Reid, Garos, & Carpenter, 2011), the Pornography Consumption Inventory (Reid et al., 2011), the Garos Sexual Behavior Index (Garos & Stock, 1998), and the Sexual Compulsivity Scale (Kalichman & Rompa, 2001). These instruments provide an initial screening for possible compulsive or addictive sexual behaviors. Other examples of instruments that can be used to further assess sexual behavior include the Sexual Dependency Inventory-Revised (Carnes, 2013), Multiphasic Sex Inventory (Nichols & Molinder, 1984), the Hypersexual Behavior Consequences Scale (Reid, Garos, & Fong, 2012), and the Internet Sex Screening Test (ISST) (Delmonico & Miller, 2003).

The comprehensive psych-social-sexual interview should address any issues that surfaced during other testing or assessment procedures. Often, questions from various instruments can serve to stimulate dialogue between the interviewer and interviewee. It is suggested that the interviewer review all pertinent and available data prior to starting the interview process since follow-up questions may be necessary during the interview. The sexual interview questions should seek to gather relevant sexual information and fill in gaps that are missing from other psychological and/or social areas. It is often useful to ask clients to complete a structured, written sexual history that includes a detailed account of all sexual behaviors since early childhood. This history can also assist in determining questions to ask during the interview. The interview should include questions to determine how the client's family-of-origin handled issues of sexuality. Perhaps the most difficult aspect of the interview is to ask personal, intimate, and sometimes uncomfortable questions. However, it is imperative to address issues such as fetishes, inappropriate sexual arousal, sexual offense behavior, cybersex usage, and unusual sexual practices.

Physical Issues

In most cases, a referral should be made for a complete physical examination by a physician familiar with problematic sexual behavior. Problematic sexual behaviors may sometimes be symptomatic of other underlying physiological diseases, such as dementia (Mendez & Shapira, 2013), traumatic brain injury (Simpson, Sabaz, & Daher, 2013), Tourette's syndrome (Krueger & Kaplan, 2000), Parkinson's Disease (Basson, 1996), and others.

Psychological Issues

In addition, a psychiatric referral may also be necessary to determine if any psychiatric issues could be addressed with psychotropic medication. When prescribed correctly, certain medications (e.g., anti-depressants, anti-anxiety medications, etc.) can also help individuals manage their sexually compulsive behavior. It is important to refer to a psychiatrist who understands nuances in prescribing medications that address problematic sexual behavior. Many times, clients need several months of stabilizing medications to allow them the full benefit of other therapies.

It is not uncommon for clients to have significant psychological conditions, resulting in a dual diagnosis with both sexual addiction and a mental health disorder. For that reason, clients should be given a number of psychological assessment instruments. These instruments may include personality measures (e.g., Minnesota Multiphasic Personality Inventory-2), depression (e.g., Beck Depression Inventory), anxiety (e.g., Beck Anxiety Inventory), measures of psychopathology (e.g., Millon Clinical Multiaxial Inventory-III), attention deficit (e.g., Test of Variable Attention), and psychopathy (e.g., Psychopathy Checklist-Revised). These instruments may be used to help determine if there are any underlying psychological or emotional disorders present. These tests should be administered in conjunction with a well-conducted psychosocial interview that covers topics such as family, past trauma, legal, occupational, educational, historical, and other relevant areas. It is not uncommon to have multiple diagnoses in this population of clients, and identification of these other diagnoses will be critical to treatment outcome. If the clinician is not trained to administer these instruments, a referral may be necessary to another clinician who is familiar with the assessments and their interpretations in cases of problematic sexual behavior and/or sexual addiction. Finally, if there is evidence of significant depression, a suicide lethality assessment should be performed using a standardized lethality instrument (e.g., Scale for Suicide Ideation).

Treatment Issues

Maintaining consistency with the Intersystem Approach in conceptualizing and assessing sexual addiction, the use of multiple treatment modalities are the most effective way to attain long-term wellness in this population. For example, encouraging a client to attend individual, group therapy, family/couple treatment, and a support group can address many of the etiological issues mentioned earlier. One way to conceptualize the treatment of sexually addictive behaviors is from various theoretical perspectives. Hall (2011) outlined how concepts from several mainstream theoretical perspectives can be used to treat sexual addiction, including psychodynamic, cognitive-behavioral, systemic, and transactional analysis. An alternate method of planning an Intersystem Approach to treatment is by considering the common topics typically addressed in the treatment of sexual addiction. The following paragraphs outline some of the common considerations in the treatment of sexual addiction, and include topics that can address the individual, interactional, and intergenerational aspects of sexual addiction.

Twelve-Step Support Groups

Whether or not you subscribe to the 12-Step model of addiction treatment, it is important to encourage attendance at some form of support group meetings to provide the extra support often needed by sexually addicted clients. There are multiple groups for 12-Step recovery from sexual behavior: Sexaholics Anonymous (SA); Sex Addicts Anonymous (SAA); Sexual Recovery Anonymous (SRA); Sexual Compulsives Anonymous (SCA); and Sex and Love Addicts Anonymous (SLAA). Encouraging client involvement in one of these fellowships will have long-lasting impact since attendance at these groups is free and will remain a valuable resource long after therapy has ended. Most support groups also offer the option of obtaining a "sponsor," someone with whom the individual develops a long and trusting relationship, and can assist the individual in their recovery efforts. This person can also serve as an accountability partner, an often essential key to the addiction recovery process. It is not likely that clients will be able to attend all modalities of treatment simultaneously; therefore, the preferred method includes group treatment, support group attendance, combined with individual sessions scheduled on a monthly or bi-monthly basis.

Stress and Anxiety Reduction

Sexually addictive behaviors can often be triggered by stress, depression, and anxiety. Most clinicians and researchers agree that a significant issue for sex addicts is emotional dysregulation (Adams & Robinson, 2001; Reid, Bramen, Anderson, & Cohen, 2014). This can be defined as an inability to appropriately manage one's emotions. It is often attributed to poor coping strategies, a lack of problem solving abilities, or poor social skills. Certain strategies (e.g., biofeedback, guided imagery, yoga, etc.) may be employed to help clients manage their stress and anxiety levels. Additionally, adding components of critical thinking, social problem solving, alternative coping strategies, can be useful in assisting clients to better manage their emotions. There are a number of workbooks that emphasize the cognitive behavioral strategies often useful in early recovery from sexual addiction. One such workbook is titled *Living a Life I Love* (Edwards & Coleman, 2009).

Relapse Prevention

As with any addictive disorder it is important that the client understands their addiction cycle, the triggers and rituals leading up to the addictive behavior, and steps that can be taken to interrupt the cycle. Basic psycho-educational modules around addictive and compulsive behaviors can be the foundation for future efforts in stopping negative behaviors. Clients may not always understand and integrate what they learn during these psycho-educational modules, but the hope is that they will remember the strategies discussed to prevent or reduce the impact of a relapse in the future. Relapse prevention is part of a larger context of "psychoeducational programming" that may include the nature of sexual addiction/disorders, family systems concepts, etc. (Weiss, 2004).

Celibacy (Sobriety) Contract

An initial goal in the treatment of sexual addiction should be eliminating or minimizing sexual acting out behavior. Similar to working with a client who attends therapy under the influence of alcohol or other drugs, the counselor will make little progress with a sexually addicted individual who is under the influence of their sexually compulsive behavior. One tool that can be helpful is the use of a "celibacy (sobriety) contract." While the re-introduction of sexually healthy behavior is the ultimate goal, a short period (30, 60, or 90 days) of abstinence from any form of sexual behavior can assist clients in focusing on the issues that arise when they are no longer self-medicating with their sexual behaviors. The introduction of a sobriety contract is dependent on the readiness of the client. Some clients respond well to the contract early in treatment, while others are too overwhelmed with the crisis to receive any benefit from brief celibacy. Clinical judgment must be used in determining the timing of a sobriety contract. Weiss (2004) discusses the importance of both a written sobriety plan (that defines what sobriety is for a particular client), as well as sexual sobriety planning with a sobriety contract.

Grief and Loss

Many sexual addicts have issues related to grief and loss that often surface when they begin to address their addictive behaviors. When the "drug of choice," (i.e., sex) has been removed, clients may have profound feelings of loss and confusion about how to cope with their newly discovered emotions. In many ways, giving up an addictive behavior that has been a significant coping strategy may be compared to experiencing other significant losses. Clinicians should be prepared to assist clients in the stages of grief and loss related to sobriety from sexual behaviors. In addition, grief and loss over one's sexual behavior can also serve as a trigger for other grief and loss issues the client may have failed to address in their history.

Trauma

An estimated 87% of sexual compulsives report some form of abuse or trauma in their history (Carnes, 1991). The sexually addiction patterns can often be associated with past trauma issues, which may have also interfered with a client's attachment and intimacy with others (Flores, 2004). Addressing such past trauma issues is a critical part of treating a sexual addiction; however, the timing about when to address such issues is critical. Some clients will use their past trauma to justify their current day behaviors, while others will be re-traumatized by the exploration of their past. Good clinical skills and knowledge/training about trauma are critical in this aspect of treatment. There has been some literature about using Eye Movement Desensitization and Reprocessing (EMDR) with sex addiction to address trauma issues (Cox & Howard, 2007). Although the case study design yielded promising results, more research is need to determine if this is a viable form of treatment for sexual addicts.

Spirituality

Addressing issues of spirituality (not necessarily religion) is an important and difficult task in treatment. Sex addicts often report that their spirituality has been significantly affected by their sexual acting out behaviors (Carnes, 1991). This may be due to the guilt and shame they experience as part of their sexual behavior patterns, or just a sense that they have "lost themselves" in their pattern of unhealthy sexual behaviors. Clients are often unaware of the impact sexuality plays in their spirituality until they begin the process of sobriety and recovery. However, the clinician's willingness to explore the connection between sexuality and spirituality often has profound impact on a sex addict's eventual recovery. May (2007) does a tremendous job of exploring the connection between addictions and spirituality, and his text is useful for both clinicians and clients who are struggling with their sexual addiction.

Sexual Health Plans

Clients need to be educated on healthy sexuality, and if relevant, the impact of past abuse issues on their sexual health. Many clients have a distorted view of what constitutes healthy sexuality. The therapy sessions can be utilized to help clients get clear on what values, attitudes, beliefs, boundaries, and behaviors they would include in their definition of healthy sexuality. An example of a technique that may help individuals get clear on their definition of healthy sexuality is the concentric circles exercise. Draw three circles, one each inside the other (like a bullseye). The client then places any sexual behaviors they are avoiding (known as their "bottom line behaviors") in the center circle. The second ring represents "yellow light" behaviors that may or may not be acceptable depending on your state of emotional or mental health. These yellow-light behaviors may include behaviors that are still being determined as healthy or unhealthy, and may include triggers that may lead towards bottom line behaviors. Finally, the outer circle includes healthy behaviors they know they can practice as part of their healthy sexuality. This exercise provides clients with a visual image of behaviors that are both healthy and unhealthy (Carnes, Delmonico, & Griffin, 2000).

Systemic Considerations

Early in the treatment process, it often becomes clear that the partner of the sex addict needs support, encouragement, and many times their own counseling. In addition to the issues to be managed by the identified patient, the revelation of sexually compulsive behavior within the context of a couple's relationship can have a deleterious effect on the non-involved partner. The trauma of the discovery of not just one but multiple transgressions in the relationship in addition to the discovery of the secrecy of their partner's addictive behavior may negatively impact the partner's self-esteem, self-image, sense of safety, and increase feelings of depression and anxiety (Schneider, 2000b). Due to the nature of the activities, many partners may also be reluctant to seek out support in this difficult time because of the shame involved in revealing their partner's compulsions, contributing to deeper feelings of isolation and pain. In many cases, the partner conceptualizes the betrayal as traumatic. To that end, a number of treatment strategies addressing trauma such as EMDR or Glass's (2002) PTSD approach to infidelity treatment may be warranted.

The timing of when to introduce couples counseling is critical, and will often only be successful when both members of the coupleship have addressed their own thoughts, feelings, and behaviors. Couples work is critical in the beginning phases of treatment when the problematic behaviors are discovered or disclosed. The therapist must carefully regulate the emotional climate of the sessions and support each in their understanding of the damage to the relationship. At other times, the individual partners might need more support in their respective therapies. If the couple manages to remain together, conjoint therapy can be the environment for establishing a healthier sexual relationship in which each partner is emotionally present. Laaser (2008) dedicated an entire book to individuals who have been sexually betrayed by their sexually addicted partners.

Other complex issues include when the sex addict and their partner have children. The issue of when, how, and why should the children be informed of the sexual addiction are complex. Corley and Schneider (2012) write about the issues associated with "disclosure" to family members and helps clinicians think through the professional, ethical, and clinical issues associated with disclosure. Again, this is a complex topic and often requires the sexual addict to have engaged in the treatment process for a considerable time before disclosing. Finally, couples therapy and family therapy will be essential to the overall healing of the sex addict and their family. The Intersystem Approach can assist in examining the system of each individual and the complex systems that formed when those individuals join together. It would behoove therapists-in-training to familiarize themselves with the literature regarding couples and family therapy with a sexually addicted client prior to embarking on this complex journey.

Case Example

Mark is a 38 year old married male. He and his wife sought counseling based on her concern of Mark's frequent masturbation and use of pornography. His wife, Ann, has reported that over the past several years Mark has become less sexual with her and that he admits to masturbating an average of twice per day. Mark has spent an undetermined amount of money on his pornography "collection." Mark did not dispute any information. Mark reported he has made several attempts to stop his masturbation and pornography use, but has been unsuccessful. Ann feels her emotional relationship with Mark has decreased significantly and that his relationship with their two children has been declining over the past two years. Ann has issued an ultimatum to Mark. His behavior must change in order for her to remain in the marriage.

The in-depth assessment begins with a comprehensive interview of Mark to gather information regarding relevant historical data and Mark's sexual history.

An initial screening interview with Mark, coupled with the Sexual Addiction Screening Test (SAST) revealed that Mark and Ann's concerns were founded. Mark scored at a level that indicated problematic sexual behavior on the SAST. Based on this information, Ann was referred to her own individual therapist who specialized in working with partners of sexual compulsives.

A more thorough assessment was conducted with Mark including personality assessments to determine if there were underlying psychological issues such as depression and anxiety, or personality disorders that should be considered in treatment. These results were followed up with instruments designed to specifically measure the presence and extent of depression and anxiety and to establish a baseline prior to the onset of therapy. Given the high levels of anxiety and depression, Mark was also assessed for suicidality using a standardized suicidality assessment. He was determined to be a low-level risk for suicide at this time. No other personality disorders were identified through psychological testing, nor any evidence of such disorders during the clinical interview. Interview questions regarding past and present behavior were used to screen for other possible addictive behaviors.

The assessment continued by screening Mark for cybersex use and sexual offense behaviors. Mark's detailed sexual history interview revealed that he has experienced fantasies of exposing himself to women in public places, but reports that he has not acted on these fantasies. Mark's legal history did not indicate any sexual crimes, including exhibitionism.

Based on this assessment, the following initial treatment plan was developed for Mark. Short term (first 3 months):

- Refer to primary care physician for a complete physical examination
- Refer to psychiatrist for medication evaluation to address depression, anxiety, and compulsive sexual behavior
- Refer to group therapy that would focus on sexually compulsive behaviors
- Introduce psycho-education modules on cycle awareness and relapse prevention
- Help Mark develop cognitive-behavioral strategies to minimize the compulsive sexual behavior (e.g., not carrying large amounts of cash for purchasing pornography or going to stores where he has bought pornography, use thought-stopping techniques, identify and change rituals around sexual behavior)
- Refer Mark to local support group for sexual compulsivity
- Secure a sponsor or one other trusted individual (other than partner) to confide in and use for support
- Implement a 90-day celibacy contract
- Assist Mark in developing a sexual health recovery plan

Mid-range goals (after 3 months)

- Explore grief and loss issues regarding giving up the behavior
- Explore family-of-origin and past trauma issues, if present
- Explore intimacy and attachment issues
- Implement victim empathy training as a strategy to prevent offense behavior
- Explore spirituality issues
- Refer for couples work (often, with a separate couples therapist)

Summary of Case

At first Mark was overwhelmed and resentful with the number and types of changes he needed to make in his life. It was not until he began to see the positive results of some the simple changes that he realized he could manage. Although Mark was challenged at times during his first 3 months, he was able to have more good days than bad. This is often the goal in the initial treatment phase. It is important not to expect perfection and understand that relapse is part of the change process (Prochaska, Norcross, & DiClemente, 1995).

As part of Mark's sexual health recovery plan, he and his wife agreed to a 90-day celibacy contract from all forms of sexual contact (including masturbation and pornography). The celibacy contract is one way to jump-start therapy and help clients understand the depth of their difficulties. It also helps break through any denial that remains. Mark experienced several lapses during this abstinence process. Mark was asked to record any relapses along with the thoughts, feelings, fantasies, and behaviors that he experienced throughout the day of the relapse. In this context, the relapses were re-framed in therapy as helpful events ("prolapses") to determine any triggers that might be contributing to using sex compulsively. Limiting the behavior to only several occasions helped bring out any problematic thinking that was contributing to Mark's compulsive sexual behavior. Mark also became involved in a 12-Step group as a form of support for continuing his newfound sexual health behaviors. He secured a sponsor whom he could trust to be open and honest about helping him improve his sexual health, relationships, and overall quality of life.

Notably, Mark's use of pornography and compulsive masturbation began to decrease as he learned to utilize his support network and continued in treatment. All went well until his fourth month of treatment when he experienced a major relapse. Again, the relapse was reframed into a learning experience and strategies were explored to prevent further behavioral binges.

Mark remained in treatment for approximately 24 months. During that time he attended weekly group sessions and individual sessions on bi-weekly basis. At the completion of his primary treatment, he continued with periodic individual sessions. During this time a number of issues were addressed including relationship and intimacy issues, past traumas (none were identifiable for Mark), spiritual issues, stress-reduction, and victim empathy training. Overall his progress was positive, with some rough spots along the way. Mark grieved the loss of his behavior throughout therapy and continued to struggle with the fact that he could not use sex as a coping strategy in the future. After his 90-day celibacy contract was over, Mark's sexual health plan allowed for occasional masturbation when not using it to medicate feelings of depression or anxiety. He continued to log his masturbation activity, including his thoughts, feelings, and fantasies before, during, and after the behavior. Mark and his partner entered into couples therapy with a separate therapist who specialized in marriage and family issues. He continued to modify his sexual health recovery plan as new issues arose in treatment, and other issues became less problematic.

Research and Future Directions

Similar to other addictions, the assessment and treatment of sexual addictions is often complex and challenging. Although there may be overlap with other addiction assessment and treatment issues, there are specific tools and techniques that counselors must employ in cases of sexual addiction. It is important for clinicians to participate in continuing education, training, and supervision that specifically includes sexual addiction. This chapter provides information regarding the initial assessment and intervention for sexual addiction, but unless counselors are trained in treating sexual addiction, referrals may be necessary.

The future of assessing, diagnosing, and treating sexual addiction is an unknown. Additional research that explores the etiologies discussed earlier in this chapter will be critical in determining the direction of the field. The *Diagnostic and Statistical Manual for Mental Health Disorders* (DSM) will likely not consider a diagnosis of sexual addiction (or any other form of problematic sexual behavior) until more research is available in this area. Neurobiological research will be an important line of inquiry—regardless of whether it is supportive of the concept of sexual addiction or negates it. For now, clinicians and researchers in this area must come together as a unified front and begin a systematic collection of data that can be analyzed in an objective, atheoretical fashion. In the meantime, clinicians must continue to assess and treat the issue of sexual addiction even in the face of a paucity of research. It appears that Evidence Based Practices (EBP) will continue to drive our treatment of disorders. In order to move the treatment of sexual addiction forward, systematic treatment protocols and outcome based research need to be conducted and replicated in order to add validity to the construct of sexual addiction.

References

Adams, K. M., & Robinson, D. W. (2001). Shame reduction, affect regulation, and sexual boundary development: Essential building blocks of sexual addiction. *Sexual Addiction & Compulsivity*, 8(1), 23–44. doi: 10.1080/10720160127559

American Psychiatric Association. (1980). *Diagnostic and Statistical Manual* (3rd ed.). Washington, DC: American Psychiatric Pub.

American Psychiatric Association (APA). (2013). *Diagnostic and statistical manual of mental disorders* (5th ed.). Washington, DC: Author.

Bancroft, J. (2013). Sexual addiction. In P.M. Miller (Ed.), *Principles of addiction: Comprehensive addictive behaviors and disorders* (pp. 855–861). San Diego, CA: Elsevier Academic Press, Inc.

Bancroft, J., & Vukadinovic, Z. (2004). Sexual addiction, sexual compulsivity, sexual impulsivity or what? Toward a theoretical model. *Journal of Sex Research*, 41(3), 225–234. doi: 10.1080/00224490409552230

Basson, R. (1996). Sexuality and Parkinson's disease. *Parkinsonism & Related Disorders*, 2(4), 177–185. doi: 10.1016/S1353-8020(96)00020-X

Benotsch, E., Kalichman, S. C., & Pinkerton, S. D. (2001). Sexual compulsivity in HIV-positive men and women: Prevalence, predictors, and consequences of high-risk behaviors. *Sexual Addiction & Compulsivity*, 8(2), 83–99. doi: 10.1080/1072016012756

Bretheron, I. (1992). The origins of attachment theory: John Bowlby and Mary Ainsworth. *Developmental Psychology*, 28, 759–775. doi: 10.1111/j.1469-7610.1995.tb02314.x

Briere, J. (1988). The long-term clinical correlates of childhood sexual victimization. *Annals of the New York Academy of Sciences*, 528(1), 327–334.

Carnes, P. J. (1983). *Out of the shadows*. Minneapolis: Compcare.

Carnes, P. J. (1991). *Don't call it love: Recovery from sexual addiction* (Reprint edition.). New York: Bantam.

Carnes, P. J. (2013). Sexual Dependency Inventory (v.4.0). Retrieved from http://www.iitap.com/resources/training-material/assessments

Carnes, P. J., & Adams, K. M. (2002). *Clinical management of sex addiction*. Philadelphia, PA: Routledge.

Carnes, P. J., Delmonico, D. L., & Griffin, E. J. (2000). *In the shadows of the net*. Center City, MN: Hazelden.

Carnes, P. J., Green, B., & Carnes, S. (2010). The same yet different: Refocusing the Sexual Addiction Screening Test (SAST) to reflect orientation and gender. *Sexual Addiction & Compulsivity*, 17(1), 30–30. doi: 10.1080/10720161003604087

Carnes, P. J., Murray, R. E., & Charpentier, L. (2005). Bargains with chaos: Sex addicts and addiction interaction disorder. *Sexual Addiction & Compulsivity*, 12, 79–120. doi: 10.1080/10720160500201371

Coleman, E., Raymond, N., & McBean, A. (2003). Assessment and treatment of compulsive sexual behaviour. *Minnesota Medicine*, 86, 42–47. doi: 10.1093/oxfordhb/9780195389715.013.0108

Cooper, A. (2002). *Sex and the Internet: A guide book for clinicians*. New York: Routledge.

Cooper, A., Delmonico, D. L., & Burg, R. (2000). Cybersex users, abusers, and compulsives: New findings and implications. *Sexual Addiction & Compulsivity*, 7(1–2), 5–30. doi: 10.1080/10720160008400205

Corley, M. D., & Schneider, J. P. (2012). *Disclosing secrets: An addicts guide for when, to whom, and how much to reveal*. Seattle, WA: CreateSpace Independent Publishing.

Cox, R. P., & Howard, M. D. (2007). Utilization of EMDR in the treatment of sexual addiction: A case study. *Sexual Addiction & Compulsivity*, 14(1), 1–20. doi: 10.1080/10720160601011299

Delmonico, D. L., & Griffin, E. J. (1997). Classifying problematic sexual behavior: A working model. *Sexual Addiction & Compulsivity*, 4(1), 91–104. doi: 10.1080/10720169708400133

Delmonico, D. L., & Griffin, E. J. (2013). *Illegal images: Critical issues and strategies for addressing child pornography use*. Holyoke, MA: NEAR Press.

251

Delmonico, D.L., & Miller, J.A. (2003). The Internet sex screening test: A comparison of sexual compulsives versus non-sexual compulsives. *Sexual & Relationship Therapy, 18*(3), 261–276. doi: 10.1080/1468199031000153900

Edwards, W., & Coleman, E. (2009). *Living a Life I Love: Healing sexual compulsivity, sexual addiction, sexual avoidance and other sexual concerns.* Self-Published: CreateSpace Independent Publishing Platform.

Edwards, W., Delmonico, D.L., & Griffin, E.J. (2011). *Cybersex unplugged: Finding sexual health in an electronic world.* Seattle, WA: CreateSpace Independent Publishing Platform.

Family Safe Media, Inc. (2010). Family Safe Media Pornography Statistics. Retrieved from http://www.familysafemedia.com/pornography_statistics.html

Flores, P.J. (2004). *Addiction as an attachment disorder.* New York: Jason Aronson Publishing.

Garos, S., & Stock, W.A. (1998). Measuring disorders of sexual frequency and control: The Garos sexual behavior index. *Sexual Addiction & Compulsivity, 5,* 159–177.

Glass, S. (2002). Couple therapy after the trauma of infidelity. In A. Gurman & N. Jacobson (Eds.), *Clinical handbook of couple therapy* (3rd ed.) (pp. 488–507) New York: Routledge.

Hall, P. (2011). A biopsychosocial view of sex addiction. *Sexual and Relationship Therapy, 26*(3), 217–228. doi: 10.1080/10720169808400160

Hilton, D.L., & Watts, C. (2011). Pornography addiction: A neuroscience perspective. *Surgical Neurology International, 2,* 19–27. doi: 10.4103/2152–7806.76977

Hook, J.N., Hook, J.P., Davis, D.E., Worthington, E.L., Jr, & Penberthy, J.K. (2010). Measuring sexual addiction and compulsivity: a critical review of instruments. *Journal of Sex & Marital Therapy, 36*(3), 227–260. doi: 10.1080/00926231003719673

Jones, K., & Hertlein, K.M. (2012). Four key dimensions in distinguishing Internet infidelity from Internet and sex addiction: Concepts and clinical application. *American Journal of Family Therapy, 40*(2), 115–125. doi: 10.1080/01926187.2011.600677

Jones, K.E., & Tuttle, A.E. (2012). Clinical and ethical conisderations for the treatment of cybersex addiction for marriage and family therapists. *Journal of Couple & Relationship Therapy, 11*(4), 274–290, doi: 10.1080/15332691.2012.718967

Kafka, M.P. (2010). Hypersexual disorder: A proposed diagnosis for *DSM-IV. Archives of Sexual Behavior, 39,* 377–400. doi: 10.1007/s10508–009–9574–7

Kalichman, S., & Rompa, D. (2001). The sexual compulsivity scale: Further development and use with HIV-positive persons. *Journal of Personality Assessment, 76,* 379–395. doi: 10.1207/S15327752JPA7603_0

Katehakis, A. (2009). Affective neuroscience and the treatment of sexual addiction. *Sexual Addiction & Compulsivity, 16*(1), 1–31.

Keane, H. (2004). Disorders of desire: Addiction and problems of intimacy. *Journal of Medical Humanities, 25*(3), 189–204.

Klein, M. (2002, August). Sex addiction: A dangerous clinical concept. *Electronic Journal of Human Sexuality, 5.* Retrieved from http://mail.ejhs.org/volume5/SexAddiction.htm

Krafft-Ebing, R.V. (2012). *Psychopathia Sexualis.* London, UK: Forgotten Books.

Krueger, R.B., & Kaplan, M.S. (2000). Disorders of sexual impulse control in neuropsychiatric conditions. *Seminars in Clinical Neuropsychiatry, 5,* 266–274.

Laaser, D. (2008). *Shattered vows: Hope and healing for women who have been sexually betrayed.* New York: Zondervan (Harper Collins) Publishing.

Ley, D.J. (2012). *The myth of sex addiction.* New York: Rowman and Littelfield Publishers.

Ley, D.J., Prause, N., & Finn, P. (2014). The emperor has no clothes: A review of the "pornography addiction" model. *Current Sexual Health Reports, 6*(2), 94–105.

Manning, J.C. (2006). The impact of internet pornography on marriage and the family: A review of the research. *Sexual Addiction & Compulsivity, 13*(2–3), 131–165. doi: 10.1080/10720160600870711

May, G.G. (2007). *Addiction and grace: Love and spirituality in the healing of addictions* (Reissue edition). San Francisco, CA: HarperOne.

Mendez, M.F., & Shapira, J.S. (2013). Hypersexual behavior in frontotemporal dementia: A comparison with early-onset Alzheimer's disease. *Archives of Sexual Behavior, 42*(3), 501–509. doi: 10.1007/s10508–012–0042–4

Milkman, H.B., & Sunderwirth, S.G. (2009). *Craving for ecstasy and natural highs: A positive approach to mood alteration.* Thousand Oaks, CA: Sage Publications.

Money, J. (1986). *Lovemaps.* Amherst, NY: Prometheus Books.

Naficy, H., Samenow, C.P., & Fong, T.W. (2013). A review of pharmacological treatments for hypersexual disorder. *Sexual Addiction & Compulsivity, 20*(1–2), 139–153. doi: 10.1080/10720162.2013.769843

Nichols, H.R., & Molinder, I. (1984). *Multiphasic sex inventory manual.* Tacoma, WA: Author.

Peter, J., & Valkenburg, P.M. (2011). The influence of sexually explicit Internet material and peers on stereotypical beliefs about women's sexual roles: Similarities and differences between adolescents and adults. *Cyberpsychology, Behavior and Social Networking, 14*(9), 511–517. doi: 10.1089/cyber.2010.0189

Prochaska, J.O., Norcross, J.C., & DiClemente, C.C. (1995). *Changing for good.* New York: Avon Books.

Reid, R.C., Bramen, J.E., Anderson, A., & Cohen, M.S. (2014). Mindfulness, emotional dysregulation, impulsivity, and stress proneness among hypersexual patients. *Journal of Clinical Psychology, 70*(4), 313–321. doi: 10.1002/jclp.22027

Reid, R.C., Carpenter, B.N., & Lloyd, T.Q. (2009). Assessing psychological symptom patterns of patients seeking help for hypersexual behavior. *Sexual and Relationship Therapy, 24*(1), 47–63. doi: 10.1080/14681990802702141

Reid, R.C., Garos, S., & Carpenter, B.N. (2011). Reliability, validity, and psychometric development of the hypersexual behavior inventory in an outpatient sample of men. *Sexual Addiction & Compulsivity, 18*(1), 30–51. doi: 10.1080/10720162.2011.555709

Reid, R.C., Garos, S., & Fong, T.W. (2012). Psychometric development of the hypersexual behavior consequences scale. *Journal of Behavioral Addictions, 1*(3), 115–122. doi: 10.1556/JBA.1.2012.001

Reid, R.C., Karim, R., McCrory, E., & Carpenter, B.N. (2010). Self-reported differences on measures of executive function and hypersexual behavior in a patient and community sample of men. *International Journal of Neuroscience, 120*(2), 120–127.

Reid, R.C., Li, D.S., Gilliland, R., Stein, J.A., & Fong, T. (2011). Reliability, validity, and psychometric development of the pornography consumption inventory in a sample of hypersexual men. *Journal of Sex & Marital Therapy, 37*(5), 359–385. doi: 10.1080/0092623X.2011.607047

Rosenberg, K.P., Carnes, P., & O'Connor, S. (2014). Evaluation and treatment of sex addiction. *Journal of Sex and Marital Therapy, 40*(2), 77–91. doi: 10.1080/0092623X.2012.701268

Schneider, J.P. (2000a). Compulsive and addictive sexual disorders in the family. *CNS Spectrums, 5*(10), 53–62.

Schneider, J.P. (2000b). Effects of cybersex addiction on the family: Results of a survey. *Sexual Addiction & Compulsivity, 7*, 31–58. doi: 10.1080/00224490109552104

Schneider, J.P. (2004). Understanding and diagnosing sex addiction. In R.H. Coombs (Ed.), *Handbook of addictive disorders: A practical guide to diagnosis and treatment* (pp. 197–232). Hoboken, NJ: John Wiley & Sons Inc.

Schneider, J.P., & Irons, R.R. (2001). Assessment and treatment of addictive sexual disorders: Relevance for chemical dependency relapse. *Substance Use & Misuse, 36*, 1795–1820. doi: 10.1081/JA-100108428

Schneider, J.P., & Weiss, R. (2001). *Cybersex exposed: Simple fantasy or obsession?* Center City, MN: Hazelden Information & Educational Services.

Simpson, G.K., Sabaz, M., & Daher, M. (2013). Prevalence, clinical features, and correlates of inappropriate sexual behavior after traumatic brain injury: A multicenter study. *Journal of Head Trauma Rehabilitation, 28*(3), 202–210. doi: 10.1097/HTR.0b013e31828dc5ae

Skegg, K., Nada-Raja, S., Dickson, N., & Paul, C. (2010). Perceived "out of control" sexual behavior in a cohort of young adults from the Dunedin multidisciplinary health and development study. *Archives of Sexual Behavior, 39*, 968–978. doi: 10.1007/s10508–009–9504–8

Steele, V. R., Staley, C., Fong, T., & Prause, N. (2013). Sexual desire, not hypersexuality, is related to neurophysiological responses elicited by sexual images. *Socioaffective Neuroscience & Psychology, 3*(0). doi: 10.3402/snp.v3i0.20770

Van der Kolk, B. A. (1989). The compulsion to repeat the trauma. *Psychiatric Clinics of North America, 12*(2), 389–411.

Van der Kolk, B. A. (2003). The neurobiology of childhood trauma and abuse. *Child and Adolescent Psychiatric Clinics of North America, 12*(2), 293–317. doi: 10.1016/S1056–4993(03)00003–8

Van der Kolk, B. A., Perry, J. C., & Herman, J. L. (1991). Childhood origins of self-destructive behavior. *American Journal of Psychiatry, 148*(12), 1665–1671.

Weeks, G. R. (1994). The intersystem model: An integrated approach to treatment. In G. R. Weeks & L. Hof (Eds.), *The marital relationship therapy casebook: Theory and application of the intersystem model* (pp. 3–34). New York: Routledge.

Weiss, R. (2004). Treating sex addiction. In R. H. Coombs (Ed.), *Handbook of addictive disorders: A practical guide to diagnosis and treatment* (pp. 233–272). Hoboken, NJ: John Wiley & Sons Inc.

Zapf, J. L., Greiner, J., & Carroll, J. (2008). Attachment styles and male sex addiction. *Sexual Addiction & Compulsivity, 15*(2), 158–175. doi: 10.1080/10720160802035832

Zillman, D., & Bryant, J. (1988). Pornography's impact on sexual satisfaction. *Journal of Applied Social Psychology, 18*, 438–453.

14

THE INTERPLAY BETWEEN MENTAL AND SEXUAL HEALTH

Kenneth Wayne Phelps, Ashley Blackmon Jones, and
Rebecca Ann Payne

Sexual health cannot be detached from mental health. Both are inextricably bound to quality of life and relational satisfaction. While vital to our overall well-being, these facets of health continue to share societal stigma, perpetuating misinformation and deterring from effective treatment. In a society that remains mostly silent with these clinical areas, the *Diagnostic and Statistical Manual of Mental Disorders, Fifth Edition* (DSM-5; American Psychiatric Association) (APA, 2013) continues to function as a voice for defining and studying their influence. Sexual dysfunctions, including disorders of arousal, desire, penetration pain, and orgasm, appear within the manual. These diagnoses of sexual functioning are certainly influenced by and influence other illnesses commonly treated by mental health and substance abuse professionals.

Moving beyond the classifications of the *DSM-5* (APA, 2013), it can be said that all individuals journeying toward their sexual potential navigate complex waters of personal vulnerability, relational fragility, and beliefs influenced by generational and cultural factors. This journey is rarely uneventful, as people are reminded of their psychological blind spots and conditioned responses. In the midst of this journey, many struggle with psychiatric disorders, such as depression or anxiety, while others may find themselves in the tailspin of addiction or the repetitive behaviors of obsessive compulsive disorder. For some, life brings forward echoes of trauma or somatic manifestations of psychological distress. Proper treatment, pharmacologic and/or psychotherapeutic, can go a long way in improving quality of life for those coping with mental illness. Unfortunately, psychotropic medication used to mend the struggles of the mind can at times worsen sexual functioning. Psychotherapeutic approaches have their own misgivings, as many disregard sexual health or the relational climate. Poor outcomes can often be avoided through use of proper psychoeducation, efficacious treatment modalities, and a comprehensive, biopsychosocial stance to care.

To provide care that facilitates satisfactory outcomes for individuals, couples, or families, systemic therapists must be armed with up-to-date knowledge of the bidirectional interplay of mental and sexual health. The purpose of this chapter is to do just that by: (1) reviewing the impact of various psychological symptoms (mood, anxiety, somatic, etc.) on sexual health; (2) discussing common effects of psychotropic medications, alcohol use, and illegal substances on sexual functioning; and (3) placing this knowledge within the consultation room of the biopsychosocial practitioner via case examples, therapeutic techniques, and collaborative treatment planning.

Symptom or Side effect

This last point of collaborative treatment planning may be especially important as a psychotherapist operating from the Intersystem Approach cannot practice in a silo. Discerning whether a sexual dysfunction accompanying a psychiatric illness may be a symptom of the illness, an unwelcome side effect of medication, predate the illness, or is attributable to other causal factors (e.g., substance abuse, medical diagnosis) can be a complex, but necessary process in treatment planning (Clayton, 2002; Clayton & Balon, 2009). This is best accomplished via a team of individuals utilizing the Intersystem Approach, considering the individual's biological vulnerabilities and psychological coping style, as well as the broader interactional and intergenerational systems (Weeks and Cross, 2004). While the below mentioned categories of psychological symptoms are presented separately for organizational purposes, it should be noted that co-occurrence of problems is typically the rule rather than the exception in clinical practice.

Depressive Disorders

Matt is a 35-year-old man who presented 6 months ago to an outpatient psychiatric office with complaints of worsening anhedonia, depressed mood, fatigue, decreased appetite, poor sleep, irritability, and feelings of worthlessness for the prior 4 weeks. He reported that he was having trouble completing work and recently received a below average evaluation from a supervisor. His partner, Tonya, has noticed his lack of interest in going out socially and in sexual activity. He reported that his relationship is strained and that he doesn't want to "drag Tonya down," but he just doesn't feel like doing anything. At that visit he was diagnosed with major depressive disorder, referred for psychotherapy, and started on a selective serotonin reuptake inhibitor (SSRI), an antidepressant medication.

At his follow up appointment, with combination pharmacotherapy and psychotherapy, Matt has seen drastic improvement in his depressive symptoms. When asked specifically about the symptoms he reported relating to intimacy, he reports that when he and his partner engage in sexual activity it "takes too long" and that he often doesn't "finish." Upon further exploration, he reports that he often terminates sexual activity before he is able to achieve orgasm and ejaculation, because of the length of time that it takes for him to complete sexual activity. Though he reports Tonya has been supportive, Matt frequently feels frustrated.

Symptoms

Prevalence: 35-70%

There are a number of psychiatric illnesses where depressed mood is a cardinal symptom (e.g., persistent depressive disorder, major depressive disorder, unspecified depressive disorder, bipolar disorder). Studies have estimated the prevalence of sexual dysfunction in major depressive disorder to be between 35% and 70% (Schweitzer, Maguire, & Ng, 2009). The case of Matt highlights two different aspects of depression and treatment. First, symptoms of major depressive disorder (MDD) commonly lead to sexual difficulty. For instance, Matt experienced decreased interest and pleasure in activities, feelings of worthlessness, fatigue, irritability, and amotivation. All of these symptoms can affect sexual functioning. Studies have also reported low libido and erectile dysfunction associated with depression (Zemishlany & Weizman, 2008). Additionally, sexual dysfunction can be a common side effect of antidepressant treatment. Patients may be more likely to be nonadherent or discontinue medications that cause sexual dysfunction (Schweitzer, Maguire, & Ng, 2009; LaTorre et al., 2013).

Antidepressant Pharmacotherapy

Neurotransmitters theorized to be involved in psychiatric illness and targeted in antidepressant treatment are also involved in sexual functioning, especially dopamine, serotonin, and norepinephrine (Zemishlany & Weizman, 2008). It has been reported in recent neuroscience literature that the mechanism of action for the sexual side effects of antidepressant treatment is associated with inhibition of dopamine release in the hypothalamus and mesolimbic pathway by serotonin (Bijlsma et al., 2013). Inhibition of libido, ejaculation, and orgasms has also been implicated with elevated levels of serotonin in the central nervous system (CNS) (Micromedex, 2013). Studies have suggested that the mechanism of action of the antidepressant agent is important. This is demonstrated by the lack of sexual side effects with bupropion (Wellbutrin) (due to the impact on norepinephrine and dopamine, not serotonin) and serotonergic agents that have a specific serotonin receptor activity (buspirone (Buspar) and vilazodone (Viibryd)) (Bijlsma et al., 2013).

Though still in use, older antidepressants, such as monoamine oxidase inhibitors (MAOIs) and tricyclic antidepressants (TCAs), have largely been replaced by selective serotonin reuptake inhibitors (SSRIs) and serotonin norepinephrine reuptake inhibitors (SNRIs). In a recent 2013 study, Gelenberg and colleagues examined sexual dysfunction in patients with depression who were treated with a SNRI and a SSRI. New-onset impairment of sexual functioning was most commonly reported during the first month of treatment. In patients with depression who achieved remission, sexual dysfunction was less likely to be reported than non-responders (Gelenberg et al. 2013).

While medication side effects are often an unwelcome byproduct to antidepressant treatment for most, there are instances where sexual side effects are utilized to help treat other sexual disorders. The prolonged time to orgasm and ejaculation with SSRIs can be used to treat premature ejaculation (Clayton & Shen, 1998, Micromedex, 2013). Decreased libido with SSRIs, among other treatment effects, has been used in the treatment of sexual offenders who have a paraphilic disorder (Garcia, Delavenne, Assumpcao, & Thibaut, 2013).

SSRIs are reported to cause sexual dysfunction in 30–70% of patients (Micromedex, 2013). Indeed, antidepressant medications that are primarily serotonergic, like the SSRIs, are the most common culprits of sexual side effects. In a 2009 meta-analysis, Serretti and Chiesa examined different antidepressant agents and their rates of sexual dysfunction. Sexual dysfunction as a result of antidepressant treatment had higher rates than placebo. Serretti and Chiesa also ranked different antidepressants according to their levels of impact on sexual dysfunction (from highest to lowest): sertraline (Zoloft), venlafaxine (Effexor), citalopram (Celexa), paroxetine (Paxil), fluoxetine (Prozac), imipramine (Tofranil), phenelzine (Nardil), duloxetine (Cymbalta), escitalopram (Lexapro), and fluvoxamine (Luvox). There were several medications examined that did not have a significant difference in rates of sexual dysfunction compared to placebo; three of these being mirtazapine (Remeron), nefazodone (Serzone, which is off the market), and bupropion (Wellbutrin) (Serretti & Chiesa, 2009).

An earlier study by Clayton and Shen explored the differing effects of psychotropic medications on the following phases of sexual response: (1) libido, (2) arousal, and (3) orgasm (Clayton & Shen, 1998). These researchers identified MAOIs and SSRIs as being associated with a lowered libido in both men and women, with no particular SSRI having lower rates of decreased sexual interest. Though there are case reports of decreased libido in women taking TCAs, this may be due to difficulty in achieving orgasm rather than decreased interest. For men, there is a reported discrepancy between what is noted in clinical practice (decreased libido) and what the evidence demonstrates (no decrease in libido). There is no significant evidence showing MAOIs, TCAs, and SSRIs cause problems with arousal in women. Much of the data on erectile dysfunction with TCAs, MAOIs, and SSRIs is limited to case reports in men. The most common sexual dysfunction associated with psychiatric medications in women is problems with delayed orgasm or inability to achieve orgasm. For men, TCAs and SSRIs both have demonstrated effects on orgasms. SSRIs can specifically cause anorgasmia or prolonged time to orgasm (Clayton & Shen, 1998).

Table 14.1 is a summary of SSRIs, SNRIs, and other medications used for the treatment of depression. Of note, many of these medications are also used for the treatment of anxiety. There are challenges in obtaining an accurate assessment of the incidence of sexual dysfunction in antidepressant treatment, as there are wide ranges reported in the literature, varied data collection methodologies, and lack of female population in study samples (Micromedex, 2013). Table 14.1 is taken from information obtained in Micromedex, a resource used by medical professionals to find detailed information about medications.

Upon further exploration, Matt reveals that he has no difficulty obtaining and maintaining an erection. He has nocturnal erections. He reports difficulty achieving orgasm and ejaculation with masturbation, which causes him frustration. Matt reports that his interest is improved from his initial presentation, but still less than what he would like. He also has developed some anxiety specifically around being able to achieve orgasm, since this has become a topic of discussion with Tonya.

Type of Sexual Dysfunction by Medication

Table 14.1 Antidepressants

Medication Generic (Trade) Mechanism of Action	Decrease Libido	Problems With Arousal	Problems With Orgasm/ Ejaculation
Fluoxetine (Prozac) SSRI	(1–11%)	Impotence (1–7%)	Abnormal Ejaculation (2–7%)
Paroxetine (Paxil) SSRI	M: (6–15%) F: (0–9%)	Impotence (2–9%)	Orgasm Disorder: F (2–9%) Abnormal Ejaculation (13–28%) appears to be dose dependent
Sertraline (Zoloft) SSRI	(up to 11%)	Impotence (1% +)	Abnormal Ejaculation (7–19%)
Citalopram (Celexa) SSRI	M: 3.8% F: 1.3%	Impotence (2.8%)	Disorder of Ejaculation (6.1%) Orgasm Incapacity: F (1.1%)
Escitalopram (Lexapro) SSRI	(3–7%)	Impotence (3%)	Disorder of Ejaculation (9–14%) Orgasm Incapacity: F (2–6%)
Fluvoxamine (Luvox) SSRI	Decreased: (IR: 2%, ER: 6%) 1 case report of increased	Impotence (IR = 2%)	Abnormal ejaculation (IR: 8%, ER: 10%) Orgasm Incapacity: (IR: 2%, ER: 5%)

Medication Generic (Trade) Mechanism of Action	Decrease Libido	Problems With Arousal	Problems With Orgasm/ Ejaculation
Venlafaxine (Effexor) SNRI	(1.1–8%)	Impotence (2.1–6%)	Abnormal Ejaculation (2.2–19%) Orgasm Disorder: F (2–5%)
Duloxetine (Cymbalta) SNRI	(4%)	ED (4–5%)	Abnormal Ejaculation (ejaculation d/o and failure) (2%) Delayed Ejaculation (3%)
Desvelafaxine (Pristiq) SNRI	3–6%	ED 3–11%	Abnormal Ejaculation Absence (up to 2%), Delayed (1–7%), Disorder (up to 5%) Orgasm Disorder (up to 3%) Orgasm Incapacity (up to 8%)
Mirtazapine (Remeron) Other			Orgasm Disorder: 1 case report of spontaneous orgasms: F Abnormal Ejaculation: 1 case report of ejaculation problems: M
Bupropion hydrobromide (Wellbutrin) Inhibits uptake of NE/DA	IR (3%); SR Increased		
Vilazadone (Viibryd) SSRI and partial agonist of 5HT1A	4%	ED 2%	Late Ejaculation 2% Orgasm Disorder 3%

Taken from Micromedex.

( ): incidence; M: male; F: female; ED: Erectile Dysfunction; IR: Immediate Release; SR: Sustained Release; NE: norepinephrine; DA: Dopamine.

Bipolar Disorders

Symptoms

Patients with bipolar disorder experience significant periods of hypomania or mania and depression. Changes in sexual activity can be significant manifestations of both manic and depressive symptoms. Individuals displaying manic symptoms show increased goal-directed activities, decreased need for sleep, racing thoughts, distractibility, and grandiosity. The most notable display of sexual problems in mania includes hypersexuality and associated risky behaviors that may put an individual at greater risk for contracting a sexual transmitted infection, having an unintended pregnancy, or being unfaithful in a monogamous relationship. Conversely, patients who are in a depressive episode of bipolar disorder may show significant amotivation, fatigue, and low desire, as discussed in the depressive symptom section (APA, 2013)

Pharmacologic Treatment of Bipolar

Providers can utilize a variety of pharmacological treatments for bipolar disorder. Mood stabilizers and antipsychotics are commonly used, but medications like antidepressants may also be used carefully for stabilization of symptoms, with close monitoring for manic symptoms.

Mood stabilizers. The term mood stabilizers refer to medications used in the treatment of psychiatric disorders, particularly bipolar disorders, including: lithium, valproic acid (Depakote), lamotrigine (Lamictal), and carbamazepine (Tegretol). These medications are not as highly implicated in sexual side effects as the antidepressants (Micromedex, 2013). Lithium has been implicated in decreased libido and impotence and carbamazepine has been reported to cause impotence (Micromedex, 2013). In men with bipolar disorder who were taking lithium and other medications, erectile dysfunction was reported (Clayton & Shen, 1998).

Thorazine

Antipsychotics. Antipsychotics can be used for acute mania and for maintenance treatment of bipolar disorder. Chlorpromazine (Thorazine) is a typical antipsychotic that is approved for the use of bipolar disorder in adults. The atypical antipsychotics—aripiprazole (Abilify), quetiapine (Seroquel), risperidone (Risperdal), olanzapine (Zyprexa), lurasidone (Latuda), and ziprasidone (Geodon)—have FDA approval for use in bipolar disorder. Abilify and Seroquel XR also have approved indications for adjunctive treatment in depression and Zyprexa for use in depression with fluoxetine. Seroquel XR and Latuda have a specific indication for bipolar depression (Micromedex, 2013).

Antipsychotics have been shown in the literature to be associated with sexual dysfunction, but more studies are needed (LaTorre et al., 2013; Micromedex, 2013). Antipsychotic-induced sexual dysfunction treatments were examined in a recent Cochrane review, which highlighted the lack of studies regarding treatment (Schmidt, Hagen, Kriston, Soares-Weiser, Maayan, & Berner, 2012). Antipsychotics vary in the specifics of their mechanisms of action, but many block dopamine and alpha adrenergic receptors, and have antihistaminic and anticholinergic properties, which can lead to sexual dysfunction (LaTorre et al., 2013; Micromedex, 2013). These properties can cause many different effects, depending on the target receptor, including sedation, decreased peripheral vasodilation, and elevated prolactin (LaTorre et al., 2013). Some studies suggest that elevated levels of prolactin, which can be caused by antipsychotic medication, have been associated with an increase in sexual dysfunction (LaTorre et al., 2013).

Reports of the rate of sexual dysfunction are variable. The overall rate of decreased libido with antipsychotics is about 38%, with high doses of the low potency antipsychotics being the most common cause. For women, antipsychotics have been reported to decrease libido, especially in ages 60–70 years old, and also to cause anorgasmia or delayed orgasm. For men, they have been associated with erectile dysfunction and orgasmic disorder (Clayton & Shen, 1998)

Anxiety Disorders and Associated Diagnoses

Symptoms

While sexual activity carries with it a certain amount of necessary anxiety—as a close cousin of excitement and arousal—many individuals suffer with debilitating anxiety that may actually inhibit functioning. Foundational research in the 1980s first documented higher rates of sexual problems among those with anxiety disorders (Kaplan, 1988). Whether the restlessness and worrisome thoughts of generalized anxiety disorder (GAD) or social isolation of agoraphobia, it is not surprising that anxiety and sexual problems often co-occur.

One of the most widely discussed anxieties of sexual activity is performance-based anxiety, which has been associated strongly with social phobia (SP) or social anxiety disorder in the literature (Heimberg & Barlow, 1988; Zemishlany & Weizman, 2008). Fear of humiliation and rejection in social situations are a key component of SP, which can lead to the pursuit of perfectionism when it comes to sexual activity. Striving for the perfect arousal or orgasm may decrease sexual functioning as it detracts from psychological pleasure and the relational experience. For example, a male may become hypervigilant about obtaining or sustaining an erection, leading to loss of his erectile capacity from anxious thoughts. A woman may feel pressured by her partner to attain orgasm, but in doing so loses the intimate, loving mindset needed to shed her inhibitions. Women with clinical anxiety have been shown to have more difficulty with obtaining and enjoying orgasm (Labbatte, Grimes, & Arana, 1998). Beyond pursuing perfection, individuals with SP had documented fewer sexual relationships, impairments in subjective satisfaction, lowered desire and arousal, and men were more likely to seek out prostitution to meet their needs (Bodinger et al., 2002).

When other diagnoses have been explored, obsessive compulsive disorder (OCD), post-traumatic stress disorder (PTSD), and panic disorder (PD) have often been associated with sexual difficulties. PTSD, recently grouped under Trauma and Stressor-Related Disorders in the *DSM-5* (APA, 2013), was found to be a significant risk factor for sexual problems among combat veterans, including erectile dysfunction and premature ejaculation (Letoureneau, Schewe, & Frueh, 1997). For many, the traumatic event suffered may include sexual violence leading to intrusion symptoms during sex, persistent avoidance of intimate activity, negative cognitions of self, and even dissociation.

Tabitha is a 20-year-old female who was sexually molested by her father from 10–12 years old. Tabitha was involved in treatment shortly after the discovery of the abuse. Showing progress, she eventually discontinued therapy around 14 years old. She recently had a relapse in symptoms, finding herself triggered throughout her day by sights, sounds, and smells. She also has recent difficulty sleeping due to nightmares of her father's violence for which she has tried taking melatonin without improvement. This worsening of functioning occurred in the context of starting her first consensual sexual relationship with partner of two years, Keith. After their first sexual encounter Tabitha cried and had intrusive thoughts that she was "dirty" and "was just there for his pleasure." On their second attempt at intercourse, Tabitha felt extremely anxious and noticed profound pain with penetration. Since this encounter, Tabitha finds herself more tearful and low, whereas Keith has been more withdrawn due to not wanting to pressure Tabitha. Their overall intimate bond and nonsexual touching has decreased over the last few months.

The avoidance symptoms that may occur in individuals coping with PTSD may be mirrored in unique ways in persons dealing with OCD. OCD sufferers have more difficulty reaching orgasm and may be sexually avoidant (Aksaray et al., 2001; Fontenelle et al., 2007). This is not surprising when considering contamination fears or rituals that may interfere with foreplay or sexual acts. A unique part of OCD includes sexual obsessions that are egodystonic, causing significant fright and often misconstrued by professionals as a sexual fantasy, sexual identity crisis, or paraphilia (Buehler, 2011). The anxiety experienced when refraining from a compulsion can manifest into panic-like symptoms. Panic attacks, including those with panic disorder, have their own negative impact on sexual functioning (Clayton & Balon, 2009).

Body dysmorphic disorder (BDD), now classified as an obsessive compulsive disorder by *DSM-5*, is diagnosed when an individual is preoccupied with an imagined or minor flaw in one's appearance, which is accompanied by repetitive behavior or mental acts in response to the preoccupation (APA, 2013). Most commonly, individuals have concerns about facial features, skin, hair, breasts, and genitalia (Phillips, 2002). The preoccupation and associated response, whether an act or thought pattern, are time consuming; yet despite this, most individuals exhibit little to no insight into this illness. Though few studies exist about this disorder or its impact on sexual dysfunction, demographic data from extant literature found the majority of individuals with BDD are unmarried and have never been married. Often, these individuals are self-conscious about the either minor or nonexistent flaw to the extent they feel ashamed and avoid engaging in sexual relationships (Phillips, 2002).

Pharmacologic Treatment of Anxiety

Treatment to alleviate anxiousness around sexual activity or to treat individuals with a pre-existing anxiety disorder that interferes with sexual functioning can improve one's sexual health. Unfortunately, some pharmacologic treatments for anxiety may cause significant sexual side effects. The most common pharmacological treatments for anxiety disorders include SSRIs, SNRIs, and benzodiazepines. Other medications (some off-label), like TCAs, hydroxyzine, and gabapentin are also used.

Many SSRIs are approved by the U.S. Food and Drug Administration for the treatment of anxiety. These medications are commonly used to treat depression, and the information regarding sexual dysfunction due to these medications is discussed in the previous section. Benzodiazepines are also utilized in the treatment of anxiety in some patients, and can be prescribed for as needed use or for daily use. Sometimes these medications are prescribed for short term relief while an SSRI/SNRI begins to work, and other times they are continued long term. Benzodiazepines work through GABA receptors and patients can develop a physiological dependence, causing tolerance and withdrawal symptoms if the medication is not carefully tapered under medical supervision. Benzodiazepine withdrawal can occur if the medication is abruptly discontinued or the dose is quickly decreased. Patients with benzodiazepine withdrawal may experience symptoms such as tremors, restlessness, anxiety, insomnia, sweating, nausea, hallucinations, psychosis, seizures, or even death (Raj & Sheehan, 2004; Mariani, Smith, Wesson, & Sabnani, 2007). It is important that if a sexual adverse effect occurs and the patient desires to stop the medication, they work closely with their healthcare provider to do this safely, and avoid rebound anxiety or potentially serious withdrawal symptoms, Some examples of commonly prescribed benzodiazepines are alprazolam (Xanax), clonazepam (Klonopin), lorazepam (Ativan), and diazepam (Valium). Some examples of commonly prescribed benzodiazepines are alprazolam (Xanax), clonazepam (Klonopin), lorazepam (Ativan), and diazepam (Valium). Benzodiazepines act as a central nervous system (CNS) depressant, which can cause a decrease in libido (Micromedex, 2013).

Another medication utilized for treatment of anxiety is hydroxyzine (Vistaril). This medication is an antihistamine and can be taken on an as needed basis or scheduled. Hydroxyzine is not known to be associated with physiological dependence, tolerance, or withdrawal. It has antihistaminic, anticholinergic, and CNS sedating properties. Anticholinergic agents can adversely affect erections and antihistaminic and CNS depressant medications can potentially cause sexual dysfunction (Micromedex, 2013).

Type of Sexual Dysfunction by Medication

Table 14.2 Anti-anxiety

Medication	Decrease Libido	Problems With Arousal	Problems With Orgasm
Buspirone (Buspar)			Orgasm Incapacity- 1/10 when added to fluoxetine. Uncertain cause.
Alprazolam (Xanax)	(6–14.4%)		
Diazepam (Valium)	Reports of libido changes		
Clonazepam (Klonopin)	Reports of increased and decreased		
Lorazepam (Ativan)			
Hydroxyzine (Vistaril)	Antihistamines have been documented as causing sexual dysfunction		

Taken from Micromedex.

Somatic Disorders

Somatic symptom disorder occurs when an individual has one or more somatic symptoms (whether a medical diagnosis is present or not) that is distressing, disrupts daily life, and has excessive thoughts, feelings, or behaviors related to said somatic symptom(s) for at least 6 months (APA, 2013). The hallmark of this disorder is the distress caused by the symptom and the persistent and excessive time spent focusing on the symptom, which can manifest in a number of ways. Individuals may have persistent thoughts about the brevity or seriousness of the symptom, be persistently highly anxious about the symptom or their health in general, or substantially invest their time in matters related to the symptom (APA, 2013). The diagnosis of somatic symptom disorder is new in the *DSM-5* and there are no known studies examining sexual dysfunction for individuals with this diagnosis. However, after understanding the concepts of this disorder and longstanding treatment of the broader conceptualization of somatization, one can hypothesize several potential areas of sexual dysfunction.

Sexual intercourse between partners in a relationship may be limited if one partner suffers with somatic symptom disorder. For example, if pain is the predominant somatic symptom, the affected partner may be disinterested in sex or fear sex, concerned the act could exacerbate existing complaints. This disinterest may be discouraging to the asymptomatic partner, increasing likelihood of dissatisfaction and relationship discord. The preoccupation that accompanies a somatic symptom disorder may be thoroughly time consuming for the affected partner, leaving little time or interest in sexual relationships. If pelvic pain is present, a woman may be quite reluctant to engage in any type of intimacy with her partner, not just sex. Further information would be needed to explore whether diagnostically this individual would more likely be experiencing genito-pelvic pain/penetration disorder, which can often be effectively treated in clinical practice. Those with somatic symptom disorder may be prescribed medications, such as opioids or SSRIs that also affect libido and sexual function.

Eating Disorders

Eating disorders include anorexia nervosa (AN), bulimia nervosa (BN), binge eating disorder, other specified eating disorders, and unspecified eating disorders (APA, 2013). Eating disorders are characterized by fear of gaining weight, attempts to thwart any weight gain no matter the method, and an unrealistic, distorted perception of body weight or shape. Studies have shown high rates of sexual disturbance among individuals with eating disorders, compared to a peer group without pathology (Segraves, 2010). One team of investigators found that 80% of women with eating disorders reported sexual disturbance (Zemishlany & Weizman, 2008). More specifically, patients with eating disorders report lower libido and endorse more negative affect during sexual intercourse compared to normative peers (Powers, 2002). Sex is often considered with disgust or even aversion and sexual behavior is often inhibited in individuals with eating disorders (Zemishlany & Weizman, 2008). Psychiatric conditions such as mood disorders or personality disorders frequently co-occur with eating disorders. The comorbid psychiatric disorder itself and the treatments for these conditions (i.e., SSRIs) can also impact sexual function.

Substance Use Disorders

Drug and alcohol use disorders can have significant deleterious effects on sexual health and negatively impact relationships. As a sex therapist, it is important to be familiar with not only substance use disorders, but also problematic behaviors that may stem from use that do not meet criteria for a diagnosis. It is imperative to take a thorough substance use history from each partner when working with a couple with sexual dysfunction, as substance use is a known contributor to sexual dysfunction (Substance Abuse and Mental Health Services Administration, 2012).

Taking a thorough substance use history from each partner should include information on: drug or drink of choice, quantity, frequency, symptoms experienced if the substance is not available, how long the substance has been used, and sequelae of use (i.e., blackouts, arrests). The National Institute on Alcohol Abuse and Alcoholism (NIAAA, 2013) has outlined guidelines for moderate or "at-risk" drinking patterns, which can be a useful resource to help quantify drinking. Additionally, it is important to obtain information about the development of the drinking or drug use. The etiology of substance use is quite variable and often multifactorial. Psychiatric and substance use disorders are highly comorbid and frequently intertwined such that it can be difficult to discern the presenting symptom. For example, an individual with MDD may turn to cocaine or another stimulant for the euphoria to alleviate low affect. Individuals with SP may find that drinking alcohol acts as a "social lubricant," allowing them to interact socially with others with more ease (Morris, Stewart, & Ham, 2005).

Just as alcohol and drugs can be used to cope with an untreated psychiatric problem, individuals may use drugs and alcohol to facilitate relationships and enhance sexual performance. Alcohol may lower one's inhibition and anxiousness regarding sexual intercourse via modulating neurotransmitters like dopamine and transiently increasing luteinizing hormone (Crenshaw & Goldberg, 1996). Partners may drink anticipating an increase in sexual arousal or to experience an increase in sexual arousal (Crenshaw & Goldberg, 1996; George et al., 2011). Expectancy effects of alcohol play a large role in one's sexual response, though the exact function of expectancy has not yet been clearly delineated. Marijuana at low doses has been reported to enhance sexual function through disinhibition, relaxation, altered time and touch perception, increased sensuality, and increased eroticism (Crenshaw & Goldberg, 1996). Generally, partners may experience perceived benefits from low doses or amounts of substance use. However, as either one or both partners increase use to moderate or heavy amounts or more frequent use, sexual dysfunction is likely to occur as a result of physiological and psychological effects.

Problematic substance use can lead to prominent psychological distress, in particular stemming from discord within the relationship as a result of the use. Men with alcohol use disorders may be more aggressive when under the influence, both verbally and physically, which in turn impacts relationships (Crenshaw & Goldberg, 1996). Couples may continue to encounter similar problems even when the partner using seeks treatment and is in recovery; trust must be rebuilt, self-esteem must rebound for both partners, and return to a healthy sexual relationship may take time and may not return to premorbid functioning.

Alcohol

Physiologically, substances have a significant impact on sexual function and health. Alcohol can diminish sexual responsiveness at levels of intoxication (0.06 blood alcohol level or above) (Crenshaw & Goldberg, 1996) in both men and women. Women experience less vaginal lubrication, but may continue to be more subjectively receptive to sex (Beckman & Ackerman, 1995), which may result in undesired behaviors or being taken advantage of sexually. Moderate alcohol consumption can result in inability of either partner to perform sexually; males are unable to get or sustain an erection and both men and women are unable to achieve orgasm. Sexual desire may be diminished, though this is controversial and appears to be different for men and women. Some studies note alcohol may increase women's sexual desire and may only lead to changes in sexual behavior in a minority of women, while others note decreased desire for both men and women with moderate alcohol consumption (Beckman & Ackerman, 1995; George et al., 2011; Miller & Gold, 1988; Peugh & Belenko, 2001). Chronic medical conditions such as cirrhotic liver, gynecomastia, and neuropathies can develop from continued alcohol use that could also impact sexual desire and function.

Marijuana

Marijuana is the most commonly used illicit drug in the United States. In surveys conducted in the 1960s and 1970s, individuals reported that marijuana increased sexual desire, enhanced the quality of orgasm, increased the sensation of touching and physical closeness, and increased sexual pleasure and satisfaction for both men and women (Halikas, Weller, & Morse, 1982). With chronic use, however, partners may be less interested in sexual relations with their partner and more interested in experiencing the high or euphoria associated with marijuana use. Additionally, sexual performance may be dampened with marijuana intoxication. Several studies have found that individuals experience decreased ability to achieve orgasm and dyspareunia with use of marijuana (Crenshaw & Goldberg, 1996; Johnson, Phelps, & Cottler, 2004; Smith et al., 2010). Marijuana has known effects on reproductive function with decreased luteinizing hormone and testosterone, as well as decreased sperm count and impaired motility (Fronczak, Kim, & Barqawi, 2012). There is a need for more information regarding the sexual consequences, both psychological and physiological, of marijuana use given its incidence and prevalence.

Opioids

Opioids, including heroin, methadone, and opioid medications or prescription pain killers, are now the second most commonly abused drug in the United States, next to marijuana (National Survey on Drug Use and Health (NSDUH), 2012). Abuse and dependence on opioid medications has risen dramatically in the last decade (Compton & Volkow, 2006). Opioids used to achieve adequate pain control can certainly lead to improved quality of life. If one partner suffers from a pain syndrome, sexual intercourse could be impossible or not pleasurable. The use of opioids can be helpful in providing relief; however, opioids have a well-known impact on sexual health and function. Opioids inhibit hormones in the neuroendocrine system (GnRH and LH) that result in decreased testosterone levels and diminished spermatogenesis. Opioids can decrease libido and delay orgasm and/or ejaculation, which could benefit men with premature ejaculation (Crenshaw & Goldberg, 1996). Long term opioid use has been linked with hypogonadism and an increased risk of erection problems (Ramsey, 2013).

Stimulants

Stimulants, which encompass cocaine, methamphetamines, and amphetamines, are known for inducing euphoria. Other effects include autonomic nervous system activation leading to increased heart rate and blood pressure as a result of vasoconstriction, and psychological effects such as paranoia leading to hostility and aggression. Stimulants can have a variety of effects on sexual function. Individuals intoxicated on stimulants may experience an increase in sexual desire and libido, but have inhibition of orgasm (Crenshaw & Goldberg, 1996). Additionally, the euphoria associated with use may surpass sexual pleasure, leading to disinterest in intimacy with one's partner. With continued use of stimulants, individuals may experience impotence and/or anorgasmia (Crenshaw & Goldberg, 1996).

Substances other than those noted above have clear implications on sexual health and lead to sexual dysfunction. For the purposes of this chapter, a brief overview was provided, but was not meant as a comprehensive review of each substance of abuse. It is important to consider and ask about other substances, such as anabolic androgens, designer drugs, inhalants, nicotine, "club drugs," and caffeine, that will not be explored further in this chapter. Cigarette smoking is a clear contributor to sexual dysfunction, primarily through vasoconstriction of vessels in the pelvic area, atherosclerosis, and effect on hormones, eventually leading to impotence (Crenshaw & Goldberg, 1996). "Club drugs," such as methylenedioxymethamphetamine (MDMA), also known as "Ecstasy," ketamine, a dissociative anesthetic, and gamma hydroxyl butyrate (GHB), a precursor of GABA which is an inhibitory neurotransmitter, are known for increasing interpersonal relatedness and may be used specifically in anticipation of an expected sexual encounter. A comprehensive review of the sexual side effects of prescription medications outside the classes noted earlier is also beyond the scope of the chapter. All too often, particularly in the case of chronic illness, individuals may see different physicians for different conditions. The interactions between multiple prescribed medications and the subsequent sexual side effects may be unknown, yet have a powerful influence on sexual health and functioning.

Ray and Nancy are a couple in their mid-40s. They have two adolescent sons and both work full time; Ray is a teacher and coach and Nancy is an administrative assistant. Several years ago, Nancy was in a motor vehicle accident in which she sustained several fractures of her vertebrae in the cervical spine. At the time, she underwent surgery and the vertebrae were stabilized. She was put on prescription pain killers and over the years, her use has

Table 14.3

Drug	Main Effect
Alcohol	• decreased sexual responsiveness-decreased vaginal lubrication-inability to achieve/sustain erection
Marijuana	• decreased ability to achieve orgasm-dyspareunia
Opioids	• decreased libido-delay orgasm/ejaculation
Stimulants	• inhibit orgasm-impotence
Cigarettes	• impotence

escalated. Ray and Nancy are referred to you from Ray's primary care physician for help with "intimacy issues." Ray feels that he carries the burden of responsibility at home, as Nancy often comes straight home from work and goes to bed after having taken a number of painkillers, rising to return to work in the morning. He is responsible for cooking meals, transporting their sons to afterschool practices, and doing the cooking, cleaning, laundry, grocery shopping, and bill paying around the house. He is worried about her losing her job as she frequently misses work, and is concerned about how they would manage financially should that happen. He and Nancy have attempted to have intercourse, but Ray is unable to sustain erection long enough to achieve orgasm. He has asked her to be more responsible around the house and recognizes the role that plays in his diminished desire for intimacy, but feels guilty in doing so because she frequently refers to the accident and the pain she sustained from it.

Other Psychiatric Disorders

While this chapter was meant to cover the most common diagnoses and medications seen in clinical practice, a number of other psychiatric disorders can influence sexual functioning, including psychotic disorders, cognitive disorders, and personality disorders. The prevalence of sexual activity among patients with mental illness ranges between 44% and 80%; however, how mental illness impacts sexual relations and relationships has not been thoroughly investigated with the exception that certain classes of medications can cause sexual dysfunction and sexual dysfunction is more common in those with psychiatric disorders compared to the general population (Ecklund & Ostman, 2010).

Patients with psychotic disorders may have symptoms that interfere with sexual relationships. Positive symptoms, such as significant paranoia and auditory or visual hallucinations may lead to avoidance of personal relationships. The partner may notice the patient responding to internal stimuli and be fearful, resulting in distancing themselves from the patient. Alternately, patients may exhibit negative symptoms such as isolation, amotivation, and inability to respond appropriately to social cues, again leading to either disinterest or inability to build interpersonal relationships. People with psychotic disorders who are taking antipsychotics, may experience sexual side effects such as sedation, decreased peripheral vasodilation, and elevated prolactin (LaTorre et al., 2013), as discussed in the earlier section on bipolar disorder. Elevated prolactin, can lead to amenorrhea and thus infertility, in women and galactorrhea in both men and women (Marken, Haykal & Fisher, 1992). Some antipsychotic medications, namely typical antipsychotics and risperidone, are thought to be more egregious offenders in terms of prolactin elevation compared to other antipsychotic medications (Cookson, Hodgson, & Wildgust,

2012). Additional side effects of antipsychotics include both metabolic problems, weight gain, glucose intolerance with increased likelihood for the development of diabetes, and hypercholesterolemia (Guenette et al., 2013) and motoric symptoms, such as extrapyramidal symptoms, Parkinsonian symptoms, and tardive dyskinesia (Kane & Correll, 2010). Metabolic side effects with resulting weight gain and additional medical comorbidities can result in fatigue and overall poor health, leading to lower self-esteem, poor self-image, and increased sexual inhibition, which can impact sexual relationship. Motor side effects, whether acute such as with extrapyramidal symptoms like muscle rigidity or torticollis, or chronic such as tardive dyskinesia with involuntary movements of muscle groups, can be significantly distressing when attempting to engage or engaging in a sexual relationship.

A clinical concern for many practitioners includes inappropriate sexual behaviors (e.g., touching others, excessive masturbation, self-exposure) involved in patients with cognitive disorders, such as dementia. Estimates of inappropriate sexual behaviors in individuals with dementia, regardless of etiology-whether Alzheimer's, vascular, or Lewy body, range between 7–25% (Black, Muralee, & Tampi, 2005). There are several classes of medications that have been studied to target these behaviors, including antidepressants, antipsychotics, mood stabilizing agents, hormone modulators such as estrogens, antiandrogens, and gonadotropin releasing hormone analogues, and cholinesterase inhibitors. The efficacy of these agents on reducing or resolving inappropriate sexual behaviors in patients with dementia remains largely unknown at this time, as studies have been small and include primarily case reports or case series (Ozkan, Wilkins, Muralee, & Tampi, 2008).

A final diagnostic area worth mentioning are the personality disorders, previously Axis II in the *DSM-IV-TR*. The interpersonal gymnastics required by partners of patients with a personality disorder may make overall relational functioning, as well as sexual health suffer. Many of the personality disorders have significant interpersonal behaviors that may impact relationships, including sexual ones. Personality disorders included in Cluster A, known as the "odd" cluster, include schizotypal, schizoid, and paranoid personality disorders. In general, patients with Cluster A personality disorders exhibit a range of behaviors and affects such as suspiciousness, distrust of others, restricted affect, and even odd or unusual behaviors that greatly effects their ability to form and maintain interpersonal relationships. Cluster B personality disorders, also known as the "dramatic" cluster of personality disorders, include antisocial, borderline, histrionic, and narcissistic personality disorders. These disorders are characterized by pathologic emotional responsiveness, which can include inability to experience empathy and difficulty with emotional regulation and impaired ability to self-soothe, which results in lifelong interpersonal difficulties. One study demonstrated that about half of men in relationships with women with borderline personality disorder have a personality disorder themselves, further complicating relationship dynamics. These relationships were characterized by frequent relationship instability with separation on average every 6 months (Bouchard, Sabourin, Lussier, & Villeneuve, 2009). Cluster C personality disorders, also known as the "anxious" cluster, and includes avoidant, obsessive compulsive (OCPD), and dependent personality disorders. Individuals with avoidant personality disorder may desire relationships, but anxiousness about how they are perceived by others dominates and impedes or prohibits them from doing so. Individuals with OCPD may exhibit a restricted range of affect and be controlling, while the dependent personality disordered patient may exhibit a strong fear of abandonment or separation, resulting in clingy and submissive interactions within a relationship (Hensley & Nurnberg, 2002).

The Intersystem Approach to Mental and Sexual Health

The interplay between mind and body is frequently seen for those experiencing a mental illness as they traverse relational and sexual terrain. The intersystem model allows conceptualization from individual, couple, and intergenerational systems (Weeks, 1977; Weeks & Cross, 2004). This is necessary as the impact of diagnosed mental illness or subthreshold symptoms of psychological distress have a ripple effect on the person and their interpersonal network. As patients or clients work with providers to select treatment options that meet their unique needs, consideration of intervention at all these levels is necessary for the systemic therapist.

Individual System

The individual coping with mental illness or addiction needs effective biopsychosocial intervention. Multiple psychotropic options have been outlined in this chapter thus far. Upon reading the material, the systemic therapist is left with the questions: What is my role in discussing medications with a patient? What should I do if a patient directly inquires about a side effect? How should I handle knowledge of a patient's nonadherence? These are valid and necessary questions for psychotherapists to ask themselves when thinking about the biological portion of the biopsychosocial approach.

To answer some of these questions, it may be helpful to provide a brief story. One of the authors previously worked in a sporting store while in college. He worked primarily in the running shoe and athletic equipment portion of the store, rather than hunting, fishing, or watersport departments. Since departments were closely placed, customers would often enter his department inquiring about specific fishing reels or watersports equipment. Rather than dismissing the question or attempting to provide thorough but possibly inaccurate information, he would ensure he understood their question, provide a small piece of information, and walk the individual back to the correct department so the appropriate associate could answer their question. In our perspective, this is how effective teams work in healthcare. Thus, if the patient with persistent depressive disorder inquires about lowered desire as a possible side effect of their antidepressant, the prudent therapist may inform the patient that, "Low desire can be a side effect of some antidepressants. I would recommend that you call your medical provider after our appointment or make a note to discuss this at your next visit. You should stay on your medication as prescribed unless this is discussed directly with your doctor." Utilizing skills in patient agency from the subspecialty of medical family therapy would be particularly relevant during this conversation (McDaniel, Doherty, & Hepworth, 2013). A direct phone call to the provider to outline the patient's concerns would also be advantageous. Exploration into other reasons for lowered desire (e.g., cognitive distortions, current relational functioning, impact of disorder, messages from family-of-origin or culture) would be warranted and encompassed in the psychosocial dimension of the biopsychosocial formulation.

For most diagnosable psychiatric disorders, cognitive behavioral therapy (CBT) is the gold standard for treatment due to the extensive research base (Beck, 1995). CBT focuses on identifying maladaptive thought patterns that may lead to problems in the emotional, behavioral, or interpersonal realms (Beck, 1995). CBT utilizes collaborative empiricism and Socratic questioning to co-explore an individual's thoughts, helping them question and challenge their previously held conclusions about self, other, or the world (Beck, 1995). For instance, a male with performance anxiety and diagnosed social anxiety might work collaboratively with a therapist to challenge the thought "If I lose my erection, my wife will think I am useless and not want to be with me." By introduction of counter-evidence to this thought distortion, the person begins to have a more balanced view of himself, their sex life, and his wife's view of him. Assimilating information from Metz and McCarthy's Good Enough Sex Approach (2011) can also be helpful for individuals with sexual-based cognitive distortions, as it shows that even among the most sexually satisfied couples there are unsatisfying or dysfunctional sexual encounters. While CBT is often individual based therapy, clinicians have applied these techniques in a more systemic fashion to couples and families negotiating a wide array of presenting problems (Epstein & Baucom, 2002).

Sex and relational therapists are commonly recommending mindfulness based approaches for co-occurring mental and sexual concerns (Buehler, 2011). The advent of mindfulness has been a key proponent of dialectical behavioral therapy (Linehan, 1993). A core part of mindfulness involves focusing on the breath (and overall bodily sensations) as a means of being present-focused. While many individuals use diaphragmatic breathing as a reactive strategy to anxious distress, it is perhaps most effective when used proactively. For example, an individual who becomes nervous during sensate focus activities should not wait until the onset of distress to begin breathing, but rather engage in relaxed, "belly breathing" prior to beginning the touching exercise. Of course, these and other sex therapy techniques have to be considered with the social or interactional system in mind.

Couple System

Addressing the sexual needs of those with mental illness or substance use goes beyond asking symptom-oriented questions to broader inquiry about the impact of symptoms on the relationship, as well as reciprocally the impact of the relationship on the person's symptoms. For instance, how does a person with comorbid alcohol use disorder and bipolar disorder remain emotionally engaged with their partner? Are their episodes of mania or depression contributing to relational distance, low desire, or hypersexuality in or out of the relationship? Do arguments between the couple ever trigger distancing, nonadherence to medication, or drinking binges? Answers to these questions can provide a more thorough picture of the presenting problems.

A number of helpful relational approaches have emerged that can be quite useful when treating couples on the brink of separation. Enhanced CBT for couples was referenced earlier as an approach to care that challenging problematic thoughts within the relationship (Epstein & Baucom, 2002). Additionally, Frank Dattilio (1993, 2013) has been a leader in the application of cognitive-behavioral techniques for couples. In these approaches, members of the couple work to challenge faulty assumptions and expectations via cognitive techniques, while simultaneously creating increased attunement via new behavioral patterns and emotional responses. Another approach that holds enormous benefit is Emotionally Focused Couples Therapy (EFT), which has been proven efficacious in a number of clinical studies (Johnson, 2002, 2004). Of note, EFT has been particularly helpful when one member of a couple is suffering from depression or trauma related symptoms. EFT works by helping couples externalize their symptomatic cycle while exploring underlying primary emotions and attachment needs. As individuals identify longings and express past hurts or fears, they build a stronger attachment bond, which is proposed to also improve their sexual relationship (Johnson, 2002). A final area of interactional focus for the Intersystem practitioner draws from the power of group therapy approaches or interventions, such as Alcoholics Anonymous or Narcotics Anonymous. Individuals and families navigating addiction can find a community through these and other group settings where their unique narrative can be shared and altruistic benefits can be gained.

Intergenerational System

An Intersystem Approach to sexual health would not be complete without consideration of beliefs, sexual scripts, or trauma narratives passed down through generations (Weeks, 1977; Weeks & Cross, 2004). As youth, we internalize messages from our family-of-origin, community, and broader culture. As we explore the inner dialogue of the patients and couples we treat, the roots of these messages tell us something valuable about the person's current defense mechanisms and psychological functioning. Some beneficial questions as they pertain to psychiatric illness and sexual health include: What was the feeling toward discussions of mental well-being or sex in your family growing up? Did family members talk about things like depression, anxiety, or substance use? If individuals had mental health problems, did they seek treatment or keep this silent? What was this emotional climate in your family? Share with me some of the early dialogue about sex that you received from family or other elders during your upbringing. How did family members respond or not respond to your questions about sex or the bodily changes of puberty? Were you exposed to any environmental stressors, such as poverty, trauma, violence, etc.?

Final Clinical Pearls

Work It Up

As with any thorough assessment, other causes of sexual dysfunction must be worked up and ruled out. There are many organic causes that can present with sexual dysfunction, aside from symptoms of a psychiatric illness or adverse effects from medications, including medications used to treat non-psychiatric medical conditions. It may not be a single cause, but a multitude of things contributing to the sexual difficulties.

Ask and You Shall Receive

When it comes to sexual complaints or concerns patients may not volunteer this information. Obtaining a detailed sexual history is crucial. Excluding a sexual history or failing to ask about sexual dysfunction leaves the practitioner with an incomplete biopsychosocial assessment; thus, treatment planning and outcomes may suffer. It is typically best to begin by asking broad, open-ended questions and then proceeding to a more specific and detailed line of questioning.

Give Me All the Details

When examining sexual side effects, utilize questions that help define the specific nature of the problem. Assess for sexual dysfunction along the sexual response cycle: desire, excitement, plateau, orgasm, resolution. Additionally, there could also be relational problems irrelevant to medication in the resolution phase, due to the absence of afterplay (e.g., touching, holding, or talking post sexual activity). As the cases highlight, symptoms of psychiatric illness and side effects of treatment can affect one or several of these areas.

Let's Talk About Sex

Being comfortable asking questions about sexual activity and dysfunction will in turn make the patient or couple feel more comfortable discussing these intimate topics. Develop your own style and make it a routine part of your interview. Link questions about mental

271

health to sexual health: "So you've mentioned how your anxiety makes it hard to settle down after work. How has your anxiety influenced your ability to be sexual?" This broad linking question helps to introduce the dialogue about sexual health. Follow up questions should elicit more detail, such as "Are you having trouble obtaining or maintaining an erection?", "Do you ejaculate sooner than you would like?", or "Are you able to achieve orgasm during sexual activity?" Patients will feel more at ease and you will be conveying your interest in helping them in all areas of their life.

Don't Hesitate, Collaborate!

Collaboration with other providers is the ideal treatment plan for a patient having sexual dysfunction. Other providers may not be aware of the sexual health problem that a patient is having. Primary care providers and psychiatrists can help evaluate and rule out medical causes of sexual dysfunction and can examine medication regimens for potential dose changes, medication switches, or interventions that may help with sexual dysfunction. Utilizing a team approach, with the patient included, and working together to establish specific treatment goals, will benefit the patient or couple, ideally working towards problem resolution.

While necessary in today's healthcare landscape, collaboration can be difficult to achieve. Medical and mental health providers are often pressed for time, which makes it challenging to effectively discuss cases. Additionally, these two camps (medical and psychosocial) are often trained using different languages and styles of communication. This can create a breeding ground for misunderstandings or conflicting plans for care. One solution for this dilemma is the furthering of systems that support integrated care (or colocated care at the least). In these systems, providers are consistently networking and sharing patient care responsibilities, making case consultation the norm rather than the exception. Even from afar, therapists and medical providers can make concerted efforts to build relationships that support collaboration. Ultimately, greater functionality of the treatment team may isomorphically translate to healthier relationships for patients and couples, as they feel more knowledgeable and supported in their journey.

References

Aksaray, G., Yelken, B., Kaptanoglu, C., Oflu, S., & Ozaltin, M. (2001). Sexuality in women with obsessive compulsive disorder. *Journal of Sex and Marital Therapy, 27,* 273–277.

American Psychiatric Association (APA). (2013). *Diagnostic and statistical manual of mental disorders* (5th ed.). Washington, DC: Author.

Beck, J. (1995). *Cognitive therapy: Basics and beyond.* New York: The Guilford Press.

Beckman L. J., & Ackerman K. T. (1995). Women, alcohol, and sexuality. *Recent Developments in Alcoholism, 12,* 267–285.

Bijlsma, E., Chan, J., Olivier, B., Veening, J., Millan, M., Waldinger, M., & Oosting, R. (2013). Sexual side effects of serotonergic antidepressants: Mediated by inhibition of serotonin on central dopamine release? *Pharmacology, Biochemistry and Behavior.* Manuscript submitted for publication.

Black B., Muralee S., & Tampi R.R. (2005). Inappropriate sexual behaviors in dementia. *Journal of Geriatric Psychiatry and Neurology, 18*(3), 155–162. doi: 10.1177/0891988705277541

Bodinger, L., Hermesh, H., Aizenberg, D., Valevski, A., Marom, S., Shiloh, R., . . . Weizman, A. (2002). Sexual function and behavior in social phobia. *Journal of Clinical Psychiatry, 63,* 874–879. doi: 10.4088/JCP.v63n1004

Bouchard, S., Sabourin, S., Lussier, Y., & Villeneuve, E. (2009). Relationship quality and stability in couples when one partner suffers from borderline personality disorder. *Journal of Marital and Family Therapy, 35,* 446–455. doi: 10.1111/j.1752–0606.2009.00151.x

Buehler, S. (2011). *Sex, love, and mental illness: A couple's guide to staying connected*. Santa Barbara, CA: Praeger.

Clayton, A. H. (2002). *Women's mental health: A comprehensive textbook*. In S. G. Kornstein & A. H. Clayton (Eds.), New York: The Guilford Press.

Clayton, A.H., & Balon, R. (2009). The impact of mental illness and psychotropic medications on sexual functioning: The evidence and management. *Journal of Sexual Medicine, 6*, 1200–1211. doi: 10.1111/j.1743-6109.2009.01255.x

Clayton, D., & Shen, W. (1998). Psychotropic drug-induced sexual function disorders: Diagnosis, incidence and management. *Drug Safety, 29*(4), 299–312.

Compton, W.M., & Volkow, N.D. (2006). Major increases in opioid analgesic abuse in the United States: Concerns and strategies. *Drug and Alcohol Dependence, 83*, 103–107.

Cookson, J., Hodgson R., & Wildgust H.J. (2012). Prolactin, hyperprolactinemia and antipsychotic treatment: A review and lessons for treatment of early psychosis. *Journal of Psychopharmacology, 26*(5), 42–51. doi: 10.1177/0269881112442016

Crenshaw, T.L. & Goldberg, J. P. (1996). *Sexual pharmacology: Drugs that affect sexual function*. New York: W. W. Norton & Company, Inc.

Dattilio, F.M. (1993). Cognitive techniques with couples and families. *The Family Journal, 1*, 51–65.

Dattilio, F.M. (2013). *Cognitive-behavioral therapy with couples and families: A comprehensive guide for clinicians*. New York: The Guilford Press.

Ecklund M., & Ostman M. (2010). Belonging and doing: Important factors for satisfaction with sexual relations as perceived by people with persistent mental illness. *International Journal of Social Psychiatry, 56*(4), 336–347.

Epstein, N.B., & Baucom, D.H. (2002). *Enhanced cognitive-behavioral therapy for couples: A contextual approach*. Washington, DC: American Psychological Association.

Fontenelle, L.F., de Souza, W.F., de Menezes, G.B., Mendlowicz, M.V., Miotto, R.R., Falcao, R., ... Figueira, I. L. (2007). Sexual function and dysfunction in Brazilian patients with obsessive compulsive disorder and social anxiety disorder. *Journal of Nervous Mental Disorders, 195*, 254–257. doi: 10.1097/01.nmd.0000243823.94086.6f

Fronczak, C.M., Kim, E.D., & Barqawi, A.B. (2012). Insults of illicit drug use on male fertility. *Journal of Andrology, 33*, 515–528. doi: 10.2164/jandrol.110.011874

Garcia, F.D., Delavenne, H.G., Assumpcao, A.F., & Thibaut, F. (2013). Pharmacologic treatment of sex offenders with paraphilic disorder. *Current Psychiatry Reports, 15*(5):356.

Gelenberg, A.J., Dunner, D.L., Rothschild, A.J., Pedersen, R., Dorries, K.M., & Ninan, P.T. (2013). Sexual functioning in patients with recurrent major depressive disorder enrolled in the PREVENT study. *The Journal of Nervous and Mental Disease, 201*(4), 266–273. doi: 10.1097/NMD.0b013e318288d298

George W.H., Davis, K.C., Helman, J.R., Norris, J., Stoner, S.A., Schacht, R.L., ... Kajumulo, K. F. (2011). Women's sexual arousal: Effects of high alcohol dosages and self-control instructions. *Hormones and Behavior, 59*(5), 730–738. doi: 10.1016/j.yhbeh.2011.03.006

Guenette, M.D., Hahn, M., Cohn, T.A., Teo, C., & Remington G.J. (2013). Atypical antipsychotics and diabetic ketoacidosis: A review. *Psychopharmacology, 226*, 1–12. doi: 10.1007/s00213-013-2982-3

Halikas, J., Weller, R., & Morse, C. (1982). Effects of regular marijuana use on sexual performance. *Journal of Psychoactive Drugs, 14*, 59–70.

Heimberg, R.G., & Barlow, D.H. (1988). Psychosocial treatments for social phobia. *Psychosomatics, 29*, 27–37.

Hensley, P.L., & Nurnberg, H.G. (2002). Personality disorders. In S. G. Kornstein & A. H. Clayton (Eds.), *Women's mental health: A comprehensive textbook* (pp. 323–343). New York: The Guilford Press.

Johnson, S. (2002). *Emotionally focused couple therapy with trauma survivors: Strengthening attachment bonds*. New York: The Guilford Press.

Johnson, S. (2004). *The practice of emotionally focused couple therapy* (2nd ed.). New York: Brunner-Routledge.

Johnson, S. D., Phelps, D. L., & Cottler, L. B. (2004). The association of sexual dysfunction and substance use among a community epidemiological sample. *Archives of Sexual Behavior, 33*(1), 55–63. doi: 10.1023/B:ASEB.0000007462.97961

Kane, J. M., & Correll C. U. (2010). Pharmacologic treatment of schizophrenia. *Dialogues in Clinical Neuroscience, 12*(3), 345–357. doi: 10.1038/mp.2012.47

Kaplan, H. S. (1988). Anxiety and sexual dysfunction. *Journal of Clinical Psychiatry, 49,* 21–25.

Labbatte, L. A., Grimes, J. B., & Arana, G. W. (1998). Serotonin reuptake antidepressant effects on sexual function in patients with anxiety disorders. *Biological Psychiatry, 43,* 904–907.

LaTorre, A., Conca, A., Duffy, D., Giupponi, G., Pompili, M., & Grozinger, M. (2013). Sexual dysfunction related to psychotropic drugs: A critical review part II: Antipsychotics. *Pharmacopsychiatry, 46*(60), 201–208. doi: 10.1055/s-0033–1347177

Letoureneau, E. J., Schewe, P. A., & Frueh, B. C. (1997). Preliminary evaluation of sexual problems in combat veterans with PTSD. *Journal of Traumatic Stress, 10,* 125–132. doi: 10.1002/jts. 2490100112

Linehan, M. M. (1993). *Cognitive-behavioral treatment of borderline personality disorder.* New York: The Guilford Press.

Mariani, J. J., Smith, D. E., Wesson, D. R., & Sabnani, S. A. (2007). Alcohol and other supressant drugs. In Glen O. Gabbard (Ed.), *Gabbard's treatment of psychiatric disorders* (4th ed.). Arlington, VA: American Psychiatric Publishing.

Marken, P., Haykal R., & Fisher, J. (1992). Therapy review: Management of psychotropic-induced hyperprolactinemia. *Clinical Pharmacy, 11*(10), 851–856.

McDaniel, S. H., Doherty, W. J., & Hepworth, J. (2013). *Medical family therapy and integrated care* (2nd ed.). Washington, DC: American Psychological Association.

Metz M. E., & McCarthy, B. W. (2011). *Enduring desire: Your guide to lifelong intimacy.* New York: Routledge.

Micromedex. (2013). Each drug by name, including DRUGDEX Evaluations. Drug Consults "Drug-Induced Sexual Dysfunction." Retrieved from http://www.micromedexsolutions.com/ micromedex2/4.24.0/WebHelp/Document_help/Drug_Eval_document.htm

Miller, N. S., & Gold, M. S. (1988). The human sexual response and alcohol and drugs. *Journal of Substance Abuse Treatment, 5*(3), 171–177.

Morris, E. P., Stewart, S. H., & Ham, L. S. (2005). The relationship between social anxiety disorder and alcohol use disorder: A critical review. *Clinical Psychology Review, 25*(6), 234–260. doi: 10.1016/j.cpr.2005.05.004

National Institute on Alcohol Abuse and Alcoholism (NIAAA). (2013). *Moderate & binge drinking.* National Institute on Alcohol Abuse and Alcoholism.

National Survey on Drug Use and Health (NSDUH). (2012). National Survey on Drug Use and Health. Retrieved from https://nsduhweb.rti.org/respweb/homepage.cfm

Ozkan B., Wilkins K., Muralee S., & Tampi R. R. (2008). Pharmacotherapy for inappropriate sexual behavior in dementia: A systematic review of literature. *American Journal of Alzheimer's Disease and Other Dementias, 23*(4), 344–354. doi: 10.1177/1533317508318369

Peugh, J., & Belenko, S. (2001). Alcohol, drugs and sexual function: A review. *Journal of Psychoactive Drugs, 33*(3), 223–232.

Phillips, K. A. (2002). Body dysmorphic disorder. In S. G. Kornstein & A. H. Clayton (Eds.), *Women's mental health: A comprehensive textbook* (pp. 295–306). New York: The Guilford Press.

Powers, P. S. (2002). Eating disorders. In S. G. Kornstein & A. H. Clayton (Eds.), *Women's mental health: A comprehensive textbook* (pp. 244–262). New York: The Guilford Press.

Raj, A., & Sheehan, D. (2004). Benzodiazepines. In A. F. Schatzberg & C. B. Nemeroff (Eds.), *The American psychiatric publishing textbook of psychopharmacology* (3rd ed.) (pp. 378–379). Washington, DC & London, England: American Psychiatric Publishing, Inc.

Ramsey, S. (2013). Opioids for back pain are linked to increased risk of erectile dysfunction. *British Medical Journal, 346,* f3223. doi: 10.1136/bmj.f3223

Schmidt, H. M., Hagen, K. L., Kriston, L., Soares-Weiser, K., Maayan, B., & Berner, M. (2012). Management of sexual dysfunction due to antipsychotic drug therapy: Review. *The Cochrane Library, 11,* 1–66. doi: 10.1002/14651858.CD003546.pub3

Schweitzer, I., Maguire, K., & Ng, C. (2009). Sexual side effects of contemporary antidepressants: Review. *Australian and New Zealand Journal of Psychiatry, 43*, 795–808. doi: 10.1080/00048670903107575

Segraves, R. T. (2010). Encompassing sexual medicine within psychiatry: Pros and cons. *Academic Psychiatry, 34*, 328–332. doi: 10.1176/appi.ap.34.5.328

Serretti, A., & Chiesa, A. (2009). Treatment-emergent sexual dysfunction related to antidepressants: A meta-analysis. *Journal of Clinical Psychopharmacology, 29*, 259–266. doi: 10.1097/JCP.0b013e3181a5233f

Smith, A. M., Ferris, J. A., Simpsom, J. M., Shelley, J., Pitts, M. K., & Richter, J. (2010). Cannabis use and sexual health. *The Journal of Sexual Medicine, 7*(2Pt1), 787–793. doi: 10.1111/j.1743–6109.2010.02198.x

Substance Abuse and Mental Health Services Administration. (2012). Results from the 2011 National Survey on Drug Use and Health (NSDUH): Summary of National Findings, NSDUH Series H-44, HHS Publication No. (SMA) 12–4713. Rockville, MD: Substance Abuse and Mental Health Services Administration.

Weeks, G. (1977). Toward a dialectical approach in intervention. *Human Development, 20*, 277–292.

Weeks, G., & Cross, C. (2004). The intersystem model of psychotherapy: An integrated systems approach. *Guidance and Counseling, 19*, 57–64.

Zemishlany, Z., & Weizman, A. (2008). The impact of mental illness on sexual dysfunction. *Advanced Psychosomatic Medicine, 29*, 89–106.

15

SEX THERAPY
A Panoramic View

Gerald R. Weeks, Nancy Gambescia, and Katherine M. Hertlein

A Look Behind: Where We've Been

Masters and Johnson (1966; 1970), pioneers in the field of sex therapy, underscored the idea that there is no such thing as an uninvolved partner in the treatment of sexual dysfunctions. Their notion of couples sex therapy, however, was asystemic. In other words, while the partners were in the clinical setting jointly, they together were not considered the unit of treatment. In fact, one partner was viewed as the identified patient while the other partner functioned as a co-therapist facilitating the completion of treatment assignments at home.

Following the lead of the early marital therapists, sex therapists eventually recognized that the couple, rather than the individual client, was the focal point of treatment. This concept continues to be indispensable to contemporary sex therapy, but is inefficiently emphasized in the clinical literature (see Binik & Hall, 2014; Leiblum, 2007; Kleinplatz, 2001; Woody, 1992). Recently, sex therapy texts have begun to recognize the systemic aspects of the couple's relationship, the interplay between relationship and sexual dynamics, and the reciprocal nature of sexual dysfunctions on the relationship and relationships on sexual functioning (Weeks, 2004; Weeks & Fife, 2014; Weeks & Gambescia, 2002; Weeks & Hof, 1987).

Lack of a Systemic Focus in Sex Therapy

Throughout most of the history of sex therapy, having the couple in the office together did not necessarily promote a systemic understanding of the many factors that contributed to and maintained their sexual problems. The individual, relational, familial, environmental, and social issues operating within the couple's intimate relationship were rarely recognized or addressed (Gurman & Fraenkel, 2002). The deceptive aspect of asystemic treatment was the belief that therapists were actually conducting couples therapy despite the reliance on individual behavioral interventions and the lack of formal training in couple processes and case conceptualization.

Emily Mudd, distinguished sex counselor, educator, researcher, and founder of The Marriage Council of Philadelphia, noted the absence of a systemic focus in the work of Masters and Johnson (Weeks, personal communication, 1992). Mudd recognized that Masters and Johnson did not clearly view the couple as the recipient of treatment, despite her work to educate them. Unfortunately, they were already so attached to their behavioral approach they were unable to master the art of being able to conceptualize the couple systemically.

masters + Johnson - behavioral approach

Behavioral Concentration in Sex Therapy

The therapeutic approach of Masters and Johnson (1970) and other leading sex therapists (Heiman & LoPiccolo, 1988; Kaplan, 1974; Leiblum, 2007; Leiblum & Rosen, 2000a; Rimm & Masters, 1974) was primarily behavioral. Their treatment centered on the correction of problems such as faulty learning, lack of education, misinformation, negative sexual attitudes, and paucity of sexual experience. Kaplan (1974) recognized and addressed interactional problems in the couple and the negative impact of couple conflict on sexual satisfaction. Also, she introduced the idea of using psychodynamic treatment for sexual problems that were refractory to behavioral approaches. This "bypass" technique was employed for most cases; relational issues were circumvented and sexual problems were addressed initially (p. 168).

Kaplan also discussed the use of incremental homework assignments to reduce sexual anxiety, increase sexual performance, and enhance sexual pleasure (as discussed in Gambescia & Weeks, 2006). Treatment protocols emphasized education, permission, communication training, and the use of cognitive and behavioral techniques. Various highly regarded sex therapy texts used the same behaviorally oriented principles and techniques, including homework assignments (Leiblum, 2007; Leiblum & Rosen, 2000a; LoPiccolo & LoPiccolo, 1978; Wincze & Carey, 1991). In general, there was little appreciation of the numerous systemic factors that could precipitate and maintain sexual problems.

Bifurcation of Marital and Sex Therapy

Although the conjoint format was used in both marital and sex therapy, the two fields were never integrated in the early decades of sex therapy. Marital therapy concentrated on the relational issues and sex therapy addressed sexual problems. This identity problem obstructed and continues to limit the development of the field of sex therapy (Binik & Meana, 2009; Schover & Leiblum, 1994). This unnatural bifurcation did not go unnoticed by Masters and Johnson (1970), Leiblum (2007), and Borrelli-Kerner and Bernell (1997). The latter publication highlighted the lack of intersection between the two fields noting that sex therapy was "short term, ten- to twenty-session, goal-directed treatment specifically designed to ameliorate sexual symptoms." For the most part, other dynamics were considered only when they affected the sexual arena.

To a large extent, the gulf between the fields of marital and sex therapy continues to exist. Gurman and Fraenkel (2002), in a review of couple therapy, they note "the worlds of the 'marital' or 'couple' therapist and 'sex therapist' seem rarely to intersect" (p. 239). In our experience, the difference between sex and couple therapies is one of timing of the focus. In other words, there are times when the couple needs to discuss problems in the relationship in order to move on to the treatment of the sexual problems.

A Look Around: Where We Are

A Shift in Perspective: The Need for Integration in Sex Therapy

Contrary to the earlier perspectives about the nature of sexual problems and their associated treatments, we view sex therapy as a unique subset of couple therapy. In most instances, sex therapy involves working with the couple and, regardless of the presentation; the couple (rather than one partner) is the recipient of treatment. We have found, time after time, that partners in treatment will reveal co-occurring sexual problems in addition to the relational and individual emotional difficulties they are experiencing. A problematic sexual relationship might have emergent implications for couples; thus, they might not want to consider underlying relationship problems. Their relationship cannot be ignored when dealing with sexual problems (Crowe, 1995; Weeks, 2004). In effect, relationship dynamics become embedded in the couple's sexual system and vice versa.

Weeks and Hof (1987) argued that sex therapy and couple therapy must be viewed from an integrative perspective. Their text, *Integrating Sex and Marital Therapy*, was the first to conceptualize sexual problems from a systems perspective contending that in sex therapy the partners must be treated as a couple rather than focusing on a symptomatic partner. This view of sex therapy was later expanded in texts on the treatment of erectile dysfunction and hypoactive sexual desire (Weeks & Gambescia, 2000; 2002). One of the most significant contributions within the work of Weeks and Gambescia (2000; 2002) was the directive that sex therapists attend to the three components that constitute Sternberg's (1986; 1999) triangle of love: commitment, intimacy, and passion. For instance, a fear of intimacy or lack of commitment can significantly impact the sexual relationship. Gehring (2003) supported this contention, as he found that a couple's sexuality is better expressed under circumstances when the partners embrace intimacy in their relationship. More recent research continues to emphasize the critical connection between sexual and relationship satisfaction with communication serving as the mediating variable (Mark & Jozkowski, 2013; Schwartz & Young, 2009). It is necessary for sex therapists and couple therapists to have the ability to work with all three aspects of the love triangle because each is important to the maintenance of a nourishing relationship.

Perhaps the most noteworthy paradigm shift in the field of sex and marital therapy was the introduction of the Intersystem Approach described by Weeks (1989; 1994; 2004) and explained in an earlier chapter in this volume. This approach attends to the biological, psychological, familial, socio-cultural, and environmental factors operating in the lives of couples experiencing sexual problems. Rather than believing the sexual dysfunction is one partner's problem, this integrative approach uses a systemic lens, which views the dysfunction within the context of the couple relationship and larger aspects of the system. The result is a more comprehensive and less restrictive treatment modality. More recently, others recognized the advantages of using a systemic bio-psycho-social model (Jones, Meneses da Silva, & Soloski, 2011); however their sexological systems theory lacks any integrational constructs that would unify the different parts of their model, a component that is addressed within the context of the Intersystem Approach. Another trend in the field of sexology was the medicalization of sexual problems with an emphasis on integrating medical and psychological treatments in sex therapy (see Leiblum, 2007; Rosen, 2007; Rosenbaum, 2007).

Binik and Meana (2009) published an article highly critical of the isolation and independence of sex therapy as a profession and practice. They believe the field of sex therapy is stagnating because it is not part of a larger field. The rationale presented is centered, to some degree, on the notion that typically therapies are based on a theoretical framework such as cognitive theory. As a profession, we do not have eating therapy, depression therapy, anxiety therapy, and so on. They argued that sex therapy does not have a theory, a unique set of practices, or studies showing its efficacy. In fact, they did a detailed analysis of the interventions used in sex therapy which showed they could all fall within the broader categories of cognitive restructuring, emotional regulation, stimulus control, desensitization, behavior activation, or relationship skill building (p. 1022). This critique offered a highly compelling argument that sex therapy, as an independent "brand" of therapy, should be integrated with psychotherapy.

On the other hand, Pukall (2009) agreed with the stance taken by Binik and Meana (2009) that sex therapy is not unique from other types of psychotherapies; she argued that what makes sex therapy unique is because "it deals with sex" (p. 1040). Basically, she contended that most psychologists and couple and family therapists are not comfortable dealing with sexual issues nor do they have enough training in sexology and the treatment programs for various sexual dysfunctions. While we believe this last statement is true, it is also unfortunate. *Have we as therapists created a separate field of therapy simply because we are not comfortable dealing with sex?* Based on our experience in training hundreds of therapists we believe this is exactly the case. Many general psychotherapy practitioners elect to become a sex therapist after they have received their training and licensure. For this reason, no matter how strongly one might argue that sex therapy should not be an independent field, we do not think it will disappear.

Acknowledgment of the Interplay Between Biology and Sexuality in Sex Therapy

Therapists are becoming increasingly aware of the undeniable interaction between certain medications and sexual functioning; yet, until the mid 1990s, the primary source of information related to this relationship was the *Physician's Desk Reference*. In 1996, Crenshaw and Goldberg published a revolutionary text focusing specifically on the biochemistry of sex and the effects that various medications have on sexual functioning. The introductory chapters of *Sexual Pharmacology* (Crenshaw & Goldberg, 1996) reviewed the research on what is known about the biochemical process in sexual functioning. The remainder of the volume examined studies performed by others in the field and original research conducted by the authors. The sexually detrimental sexual side effects of some of the major classes of medications were included, such as anti-depressants, anti-anxiety medications, and anti-hypertensive medications. Whenever possible these authors presented alternative pharmacotherapy that would have fewer or no sexual side effects or suggest the client speak to their doctor about how to better manage medication. An implicit goal of the volume was to advocate the development of medications with fewer sexual side effects and antidotes for those medications with sexual side effects (Crenshaw & Goldberg, 1996). Today there are several additional texts that focus on medications and their effect on sex such as Ashton (2007) and Seagraves and Balon (2003). The latter publication contains a special chapter dealing with sexual pharmacology.

Medicalization of Sex Therapy

Common sexual problems were frequently discussed and treated through psychotherapy until 1998, when Pfizer Pharmaceuticals released the drug sildenafil (Viagra), a mild vasodilator which proved to be effective in the treatment of many cases of erectile dysfunction (ED). Because of the medicalization of treating ED, an evolution in the field of sex therapy occurred. Many men experiencing sexual dysfunction today often seek medications over psychotherapy to resolve sexual problems (Weeks & Gambescia, in press). The release of Viagra was followed by production and approval of similar oral medications for ED, vardenifil (Levitra) and tadalafil (Cialis). These oral agents, called phosphodiesterase type 5 inhibitors (PDE5 inhibitors), help to promote and restore erectile functioning to many men by facilitating the physical component of erection. Globally, millions of men consume these relatively safe and effective medications as they are considered the first line of defense in the treatment of ED (Shamloul & Ghanem, 2013). PDE5 inhibitors can be

PDE-5's — treat ED

successful in promoting penile tumescence, yet they should not be considered a miraculous course to a satisfying sex life. They are not aphrodisiacs; thus, the man must have interest and desire for sexual activity for the oral agents to be effective.

Although successful in many cases, our clinical experience shows that PDE5 inhibitors cannot always "fix" sexual dysfunction, since erection is a physical outcome of psychological processes. If relationship problems are present, or the man lacks comfort, desire, or confidence, he may still have erectile difficulties while taking PDE5 inhibitors. Further, bypassing psychological treatment often circumvents the partner's issues, needs, and contributions to the problem. In fact, the noncompliance rate for oral medications indicates that the man might rather avoid sex with his partner due to chronic preexisting relational problems (Carvalheira, Pereira, Maroco, & Forjaz, 2012; Klotz, Mathers, & Sommer, 2005). Additionally, the partner is often left out of decisions about treatment and can be startled by the man's new interest in and capacity for erections. Often physicians do not have the time or training to discuss the man's psychological or relational issues. Further, the psychological/relational assessment is still seldom included in the clinical evaluation of disorders such as ED in medical settings.

The shift toward medicalization has significant implications, both positive and negative, for society and couples. Drug companies, for example, bear the burden of demonstrating that medications are effective, leading to renewed interest in the refinement of the etiology and definitions of the various dysfunctions as well as the development of assessment instruments to measure the effects of the medical interventions. Women's sexual medical complaints are also being taken more seriously. Previously, physicians would often attribute pain symptoms in women to psychogenic causes rather than organic problems (Binik, Bergeron, & Khalifé, 2000; Bergeron, Rosen, & Pukall, 2014), resulting in frequent misdiagnoses, referrals to therapists who knew little of these disorders, and subsequently an inability to receive the appropriate treatment (LoPiccolo, 1978). Currently, conditions involving painful sexual activity (genito-pelvic pain/penetration disorders) are receiving more attention in terms of accurate diagnosis and treatment (American Psychiatric Association, 2013). Further, treatment is directed to the comorbidity between physiological, psychogenic, and relational constituents of such problems (Basson, 2012; Binik, 2010a; 2010b; LoFrisco, 2011; Meana, 2009; Stephenson & Metson, 2012; Rosenbaum, 2013). In addition to pain disorders, pharmaceutical companies recognize the need for medications that will improve female functioning, especially the lack of sexual desire. Numerous treatments to help restore sexual desire for women are being investigated, yet none appear to be promising due to the complicated nature of female sexual interest and arousal.

Greater Openness Regarding Sexuality and Sexual Problems

The use of oral PDE5 inhibitors has contributed to a number of profound changes in treatment and public perceptions of erectile dysfunction (ED) (see, for example, Sae-Chul & Sook, 2006; Shamloul & Ghanem, 2013). Since oral remedies are the mainstay of treatment for ED, the shroud of secrecy related to ED and its treatment has been removed. Pharmaceutical advertising of the oral agents on television and major sporting events has promoted an era of greater openness regarding sexual problems in general. The public consciousness regarding sexuality, sexual function, and dysfunction is raised concurrent with an increased interest in medical and psychological treatments. Problems that were rarely discussed in the past, such as a couple's sexual intimacy, are gradually becoming a part of the standard physical examination. Additionally, because ED can be a harbinger of underlying physical disease processes and is associated with increased stress in men, physicians now inquire about sexual functioning as a natural part of the overall examination (Simopoulos & Trinidad, 2013). This greater candor regarding sexuality may inspire people to seek out treatment who otherwise would not have disclosed their issues to a physician or psychotherapist. We are in an era of increasing communication between the couple regarding their sexual lives, difficulties, and solutions.

The Incorporation of Technology Into Our Sexual Lives

Increasing advances in electronic, digital, and other technological products, such as the Internet, have had a significant effect on sexuality (Agusta & Duran, 2012; Hertlein, 2012; Schneider, Weiss, & Samenow, 2012). In addition to the billions of people with access to the Internet via personal computers, there are many who have entry via cell phones and small wireless devices. Effectively, anyone with access to the Internet can search the web and find almost any source of information or education, as well as other partners, thus introducing another problem into a couple's relationship. Countless Internet sites provide information regarding sexual function, dysfunction, and sexually transmitted illnesses. For example, the Kinsey Institute (2007) provides a list on their website of online sexuality-related resources, as does the Sexuality Information and Education Council of the United States (SIECUS, www.siecus.org) and a host of other sites.

Increasingly, therapists are using programs such as Face Time and Skype to conduct cyber-psychotherapy sessions although the ethics of online psychotherapy are hotly debated. Online therapy is becoming a more common and effective way to provide treatment in a digital age, particularly with the treatment of depression, panic disorder, and other behaviorally based presenting problems (Andersson et al., 2011; Blankers, Koeter, & Schippers, 2011; Wooton et al., 2011). Marriage and family therapists, however, are slow to acknowledge the use of technology in their practices (Hertlein, Blumer, & Smith, 2014), thus potentially rendering intervention effectiveness.

Sexual Compulsivity

The Internet also provides an unimaginable variety of sexually explicit pictures, writings, and other material whose primary purpose is to produce sexual arousal. In some cases, the results of the integration of technology in a couple's sex life can produce benefits and increase intimacy in a couple; it can also, however, serve as a detriment in couple's lives (Hertlein & Ancheta, 2014). Pornographic information is readily available, affordable, and accessible to the consumer. Without leaving the home, individuals can anonymously engage in sexually explicit viewing or locate those who want to meet for sexual liaisons. The many venues of cybersex (engaging in sexually explicit chat and behaviors facilitated by the Internet) have contributed to problematic Internet usage with regard to sexuality (Hertlein & Nelson, 2006; Gerson, 2011; Schneider, 2003). For many, cybersex has replaced or added to traditional forms of compulsive sexual behavior such as using print pornography or engaging in sex with prostitutes. Such conduct is damaging to the compulsive user, their partners, and families. Many sexually compulsive Internet users have lost or damaged their relationships because their partner views their behavior as a form of infidelity or a breach of the relationship contract (Cohn, 2014). Internet compulsivity can also interfere with occupational functioning and result in loss of employment. Additionally, Internet sex has promoted the exploitation and victimization of children by sexual predators, who, while anonymous, pose in a variety of ostensibly safe pretenses.

A more complete discussion of this topic can be found in Rosenberg, Carnes, and O'Connor (2014), and the journal, *Sexual Addiction & Compulsivity.*

One of the more recent theoretical developments with regard to the Internet and sexuality (and, more specifically, its role in sex therapy) is the introduction of the Couple and Family Technology framework (Hertlein, 2012; Hertlein & Blumer, 2014). This framework identifies the ways in which computers and new technology/media influence our relationships. With regard to sexuality, the rules and boundaries of relationships become more flexible—in both helpful and problematic ways. It provides, for example, an equal playing field for both partners in regard to their ability to initiate sexual interactions since to do so is relatively easy and inexpensive. On the other hand, it also provides ways in which couples can engage in sexual interactions with others outside of their relationship. Sex therapists would be well advised to consider this type of framework in their practice as a way to attend to both the specific sexual issues as well as unique couple issues that emerge within the context of sex therapy in a digital age.

Special Populations

Therapists today have the obligation and duty to recognize, become comfortable with, and expand their competency in working with unique groups of individuals with sexual issues. As different groups grow and emerge, clinical and empirical data are becoming more available to the practitioner and client. Additionally, as the American population ages, individuals are enjoying sex into their later years, whether partnered or alone. Aging is replete with normative challenges and specific sexual issues (Muzacz & Akinsulure-Smith, 2013; Shaw, 2012; Trudel, Turgeon, & Piche, 2010; Wang et al., 2014).

Other marginalized groups expressing recognition and desire for help with sexual needs include but are not limited to: the physically and psychologically disabled (Burns, Hough, Boyd, & Hill, 2010; Rushbrooke, Murray, & Townsend, 2014; Verschuren et al., 2010); LGB (lesbian, gay, bisexual) and other gender-kinky individuals (Iasenza, 2010; Nichols & Shernoff, 2007); and transgender and other gender nonconforming persons (Lev & Sennott, 2012).

Ageism. Americans are living longer and enjoying active lives; therefore, a rapidly growing sexual minority is older individuals. The idea that one's sex life ends at 50 is no longer an accepted one. For instance, 50-year-old men and women are only at the midpoint of their sexual longevity (Davis, 2007) and sexuality is considered an important part of life in older adults (Shaw, 2012; Wang et al., 2014). Therapists are encouraged to help clients over 50 realize that their sexuality can be replete with continued exploration, enjoyment, and gratification (Heiman et al., 2011). Because people are living longer healthier lives, the therapist must address normative age-related changes in sexual function such as delayed erection and prolonged refractory periods for men, and the progressive vagina atrophy or thinning of the vaginal lining for women (Trudel, Turgeon, & Piche, 2010). In some of these cases penile-vaginal intercourse is not possible or desired, yet the couple can be helped to explore other avenues for expressing and enjoying sexuality.

Additionally, attention is now being directed to developing standards of care for aging LGBT older adults and their families (Kuyper & Vanwesenbeeck, 2011). One key to helping clients think more positively about sexuality and aging is for therapists to re-evaluate their own beliefs and focus more on the positive aspects of what their clients can and are able to achieve in their present situation. Therapists can help with expanding the sexual repertoire, deemphasizing coitus as a goal in itself, focusing on sensuality as a mechanism for intimacy, and reframing sex to accommodate the physical adjustments of aging

(Meana, Lykins, Spicer Rakipi, & Weeks, 2006). This kind of clinical work utilizes a comprehensive approach, characteristic of all sex therapy, including cognitive, behavioral, relational, and medical aspects of treatment.

Chronic illness and disability. Sexual expression is an essential element of life for all persons yet chronically ill and disabled individuals can struggle with various aspects of the sexual experience. Sex therapists today must acquire the knowledge and demonstrate the sensitivity necessary to modify current techniques and approaches when treating those in these special populations such as intellectual disabilities (Rushbrooke, Murray, & Townsend, 2014), physical infirmities (Burns, Hough, Boyd, & Hill, 2010; Verschuren et al., 2010), and chronic pain (Bergeron, Rosen, & Pukall, 2014). There is a tremendous need to examine issues such as: the lack of privacy, body image concerns, sex education, sexual function and reproduction, and dealing with stereotypes and prejudices. It is important for therapists not to label those with disabilities as sexually dysfunctional based on their own preconceptions of what is and what is not functional. In a book targeted toward the general population, Joannides (2009) addresses this issue by including a chapter outlining ideas to enhance one's sex life when one partner is affected by disability. Other texts (Kaufman, Silverberg, & Odette, 2007) and websites are targeted to promoting enjoyable sexual intimacy through information on expectations, performance, capacity, positions, aids, etc. The treatment of chronic illness and disability must utilize a multidisciplinary approach, which includes contributions from the field of relationship/sex therapy.

Lesbian, gay, and bisexual and transgender individuals. The general category of homosexuality was eliminated from the *DSM-III* (Diagnostic and Statistical Manual of Mental Disorders) in 1973 and replaced with the designation ego-dystonic homosexuality (American Psychiatric Association, 1973). In 1987 any reference to homosexuality was deleted from the publication of the *DSM-III-R* (American Psychiatric Association, 1980; 1987). This began a trend towards greater acceptance of sexual minority groups. Nonetheless, the *DSM-5* continues to pathologize gender non-conformity by retaining the diagnosis, gender dysphoria, a fiercely debated decision (American Psychiatric Association, 2013). Regardless, individuals who identify as transgender or gender nonconforming are more visible on the Internet and in the real world, yet they continue to be marginalized and misunderstood (Lev & Sennott, 2012). Recently, there is an emergence of scholarly literature regarding the treatment of transgender people, affirmation of their choices, support of their families, and the individual nature of this transition (Ehrensaft, 2011; Krieger, 2011; Malpas, 2012; McGeorge & Carlson, 2011; Rankin & Beemyn, 2011). It is the obligation of the therapist to provide a safe environment when working with sexual issues, especially with marginalized populations (Iasenza, 2010; Smith, Shin, & Officer, 2012). This involves self-awareness, self-education, and clinical competency. Potential barriers to obtaining sexual information such as countertransference issues, sexual anxiety, fear, and ignorance in the therapist must be recognized and corrected. Further, an appreciation of the multidimensionality of sex and gender must be engendered. Fundamentally, the therapist must work to tolerate and accept incongruities and paradoxes in sexual behavior and to question heteronormative preconceptions about normal (McGeorge & Carlson, 2011; Tilsen, 2013).

LGB (lesbian, gay, bisexual) and other gender-kinky individuals have been particularly vulnerable to the effects of social oppression, discrimination, and prejudice due to their sexual orientation, expression, and preferences (McGeorge & Carlson, 2011). Often, they suffer from internalized shame, guilt, and homophobia, all of which can interfere with sexual intimacy. While research has shown that LGB clients have many of the same types of sexual problems experienced by heterosexual individuals (Kuyper &

Vanwesenbeeck, 2011), these couples often request treatment for difficulties specific to their preferred sexual practices (Nichols & Shernoff, 2007). Because LGB lifestyles and sexual practices are frequently misjudged, therapists unintentionally impose a limiting heterosexist template on assessment and treatment of their sexual concerns (McGeorge & Carlson, 2011) and tend to pathologize their variances.

Transgender individuals, unlike LGB sexual minorities, struggle with issues related to core gender identity (as a male or a female) rather than that of sexual orientation (the genders to which one's feelings, thoughts, fantasies, and attraction are focused). The therapist must recognize that gender non-conformity is not necessarily an illness. Transgender clients and their loved ones must be helped to cope with the integration of their changing identities and roles. Often, medical treatments such as hormone therapy and surgery are sought to modify one's gender presentation and the therapist will be required to collaborate with other health care providers to achieve a gender transition. Standards of care for transgender and gender non-conforming people were established by the World Professional Association for Transgender Health (2012; Lev, 2004) formerly known as the Harry Benjamin International Gender Dysphoria Association ("Special," 2001; Coleman et al., 2012). The American Psychological Association (APA) proposed major guidelines that require that therapists understand their own and society's attitudes toward sexual minorities (Butler, 2009). Also, the American Counseling Association published competencies for counseling transgender clients (2010). Finally, Good Practice guidelines were released in 2013 in England for the assessment and treatment of adults with gender dysphoria (Wylie et al., 2014). Therapists must understand and be respectful of LGBT relationships, families, challenges, and circumstances. When needed, therapist must seek consultation or make the appropriate referrals.

The paraphilias. There is a great deal of information in the *DSM-IV-TR* (American Psychiatric Association, 2004) concerning the diagnosis of paraphilia-related disorders, yet there is little research and empirical evidence about treatment outcomes (Kafka, 2007). The *DSM-5* (American Psychiatric Association, 2013) uses the term, paraphilic disorders, and separates "atypical" sexual interests into two categories: behaviors and disorders. The term, disorders, indicates a level of personal distress associated with the atypical or paraphilic behaviors for the individual or the partner, not merely distress related to societal disapproval. There is significant controversy regarding this distinction and other aspects of paraphilic behavior (Balon, 2013). The *DSM-5* chapter on paraphilic disorders includes eight conditions: exhibitionistic disorder, fetishistic disorder, frotteuristic disorder, pedophilic disorder, sexual masochism disorder, sexual sadism disorder, transvestic disorder, and voyeuristic disorder. Such disorders typically involve atypical sexual urges, fantasies, and/or behaviors with non-human objects, children, non-consenting adults, or engaging in the humiliation or suffering of oneself or another person (American Psychiatric Association, 2013).

As stated, the *DSM-5* revised the names of these disorders to differentiate between the behavior itself and the disorder stemming from that behavior; thus, engaging in the behavior is not viewed as pathological unless there is personal or interpersonal distress. Many therapists prefer not to pathologize sexual behaviors involving willing adults, even if the behavior might be considered socially inappropriate, variant, or kinky (Kelsey, Stiles, Spiller, & Diekhoff, 2013; Nichols, 2006; Nichols & Shernoff, 2007; Wright, 2010). Therapists are encouraged to seek available information about treatment, encourage clients to communicate with their providers and partners, have positive attitudes, and focus on the outcomes that are possible (Gill & Hough, 2007). Ultimately there appears to be a great need for more research and literature relating to paraphilias and paraphilic disorders in order to establish a wider range of competencies as to how these persons are best effectively treated.

Emerging groups. Asexual individuals, though only making up a small proportion of the population, are an example of an evolving sexual minority group. These individuals typically report the absence of a traditional sexual orientation; thus asexuality is an intrinsic component of their self-identity. This group is coming forth as a unified political and social force believing the absence of sexual feelings or attraction to other males or females is a natural state. A great deal of variation exists among asexual persons in terms of intimate contact with others and feelings of arousal (Poston & Baumle, 2010; Van Houdenhove, T'Sjoen, & Enzlin, 2014). Exploring the meaning of the term, asexual, for each client is necessary as there are many subcategories within this group (Bogaert, 2004; Chasin, 2011). The research is inconclusive to date; but some consider that asexual individuals are not necessarily suffering from a sexual disorder such as the lack of desire because they are not in distress (Brotto et al., 2010). It is the responsibility of the therapist to understand rather than judge and to inform themselves and their clients of the most recent information regarding asexuality (see Bogaert, 2012).

Theoretical Gaps in Sex Therapy

Since its inception, the field of sex therapy has grown considerably in the understanding of etiology of sexual problems, evidence-based general treatment principles, and existing and potential medical therapies. Sex therapy today continues to evolve in numerous directions leaving large gaps in our current treatment approaches. Binik and Meana (2009) attest to the absence of a theoretical foundation for sex therapy and the preponderance of stereotypical assumptions, gender biases, and an ever-increasing biological orientation. Fraser and Solovey (2004) concur that historically, the field of sex therapy has often circumvented cultural, contextual, and interpersonal issues while over-focusing on performance oriented sex.

Additionally, there is an absence of a unified theoretical orientation for sex therapy. In a special issue of the *Journal of Sex Research*, Wiederman (1998) observed that the field of sex therapy has been dominated by techniques that are not theoretically grounded. In the early days of sex therapy, it was often sufficient to provide the clients with psycho-education and simple techniques. As the public became more educated, the "easy" cases decreased leaving therapists with many puzzling and difficult cases to treat (Wiederman, 1998). For example, Masters and Johnson (1970) claimed that delayed ejaculation was an easy problem to treat and had a high success rate. In our experience, this problem ranks as one of the most complex and difficult.

Weiss (1998) also noted that sex therapy has been largely atheoretical, providing a detailed list of 39 distinctive theoretical structures in psychology and the application of some of these techniques to sex therapy. Unfortunately, none of these theories has been consistently adopted, has explanatory power, or has been scrutinized empirically in this field. The most recent model to appear in this field has been sexual script theory, which asserts that the subjective understanding of an individual's sexuality determines preferences in sexual behavior (Kimmel, 2007; McCormick, 2010). Unfortunately, Gagnon (1990), the proponent of the theory, was unable to demonstrate how sexual scripts are internalized and reinforced.

It seems that sex researchers have not demonstrated a great deal of interest in how systems theory could be applied to sex therapy and such application has been rare. For instance, Jurich and Myers-Bowman (1998) were only able to locate seven research articles based on systems theory in sex therapy from 1974 to 1995. Clearly, not much has changed in the field of sex therapy in terms of new treatment approaches based on new theoretical approaches. In one of the prevailing texts in the field (Binik & Hall, 2014) there is no discussion about the lack of theory development in the field or theory in sexual science or sex therapy.

Looking Ahead: Future Directions

The Effect of Increased Medicalization

The current research on the treatment of sexual dysfunctions conducted by pharmaceutical companies has both positive and negative implications for the future of sex therapy. First, pharmaceutical companies will continue to provide the impetus for research in sexual physiology and neurological processes because producing drugs that facilitate erections or assist with orgasms involves a detailed understanding of the physiological mechanisms. Conversely, however, as medicalization continues, drug companies will likely spend more research dollars on developing new medications rather than exploring alternative psychological treatment methods. Drug companies have no incentive to find new therapeutic approaches. This trend clearly has influenced the public's proclivity for rapid, effortless, medical solutions for sexual problems. It is likely that funding agencies may also shift in the direction of medical solutions, leading to decreased funding for psychologically oriented sex research and sex therapy. Alternately, based on many of the chapters in this volume (and, most notably, the chapter on low desire), the primary factors affecting sexual desire are clearly relational and contextual, which cannot be addressed by pharmaceutical intervention.

Throughout this chapter, we gave examples of the role of unrealistic expectations in a man's preference for medication and the disinclination to recognize and address the psychological, relational, and other etiologic factors in sexual dysfunctions such as ED. The use of medical therapy alone without the benefit of psychotherapy can have detrimental effects on his partner, the relationship, and the man's self-esteem (see chapter on ED). Sexual functioning involves more than physiological tumescence. Augmenting erections does not correct insidious and pervasive individual, relational, and contextual issues such as anxiety, depression, and lack of desire for the partner. Additionally, the use of medications may increase desire and/or enhance a man's ability to perform, but may not increase the partner's desire or interest in sex. Sudden performance changes in the man will offset a functional (albeit less than optimal) sexual homeostasis and can inflame the underlying relational dissatisfaction.

The interplay of psychological and organic factors sustaining ED, low desire, and other sexual difficulties suggests that a comprehensive treatment approach is more favorable than a strictly medical approach (Weeks & Gambescia, 2000; 2002). In our text on ED, we demonstrated that even though the problem might have a strictly medical basis there are significant psychological ramifications. Despite burgeoning medical advances in the field, sexual functioning remains a relational issue that almost always affects the partnership. Thus, there is a need for greater integration in the field of sex therapy and medical treatment. The role of the therapist, therefore, must expand and adapt to the challenges of multiple modalities being used to treat some sexual problems.

Infusing Theory Into Practice

Based on our review of the literature from 2009 forward, the field of sex therapy has not developed a strong theoretical basis nor does there appear to be any serious attempts to do so. Instead, therapists are still working from a limited theoretical foundation and generally use behaviorally oriented techniques in an eclectic fashion. We believe we have presented the only metatheoretical basis for sex therapists to use in their treatment. We propose that any theories that eventually gain dominance will need to be integrative in nature in order to attend to all of the aspects of sexuality and factors which affect a couple's sexual life. The development of such a theory will be challenging for a field that operates in isolation from theoretically based approaches to therapy.

Armstrong (2006) proposed that revitalizing a humanistic approach to sexuality and sex therapy would benefit the field of sex therapy. In this approach, it is necessary to understand and treat the individual(s) in their interpersonal and experiential contexts. Tiefer (2006) agreed that there is a need for those involved in the field of sex therapy to have a stronger philosophical foundation when approaching individual's struggles with sexually related issues. She asserts that revamping the humanistic approach to sexuality will prevent the field of sex therapy from having a focus that is too narrow or commercialized. In summary, the fields of sex research, human sexuality, and sex therapy are in need of much more theoretical grounding, debate, treatment development, and research.

Developing and Utilizing Integrative Approaches

Our review of recent publications reflects an increasing emphasis on medical issues and basic science and fewer systemically conceived interventions (Binik & Meana, 2009; Binik & Hall, 2014; Leiblum, 2007). Further, sex and marital therapy continue to be regarded as separate entities, and increasing medical advances widens this divide. We believe the primary future direction for sex therapy is in the development of integrative and multidisciplinary treatment.

We have argued for the application of a comprehensive, integrative approach to the assessment and treatment of sexual dysfunctions that will bridge the gap between marital and sex therapies and provide a systemic rather than individualistic methodology. The Intersystem Approach developed by Weeks (1989; 1994; 2004; 2005) provides such an innovation as it incorporates four major foci: (1) the medical, social, and psychological issues related to the individual partners, (2) interactional (couple) dynamics, (3) family-of-origin considerations, and (4) the larger societal/cultural issues impinging on the couple. Each domain of focus is clearly identified. Additionally, integrational constructs cut across and tie together the domains to complete the theory. Over the past 20 years, the Intersystem Approach has added significantly to the existing clinical literature on general psychotherapy (Weeks & Cross, 2004), couple and sex therapy (Weeks & Fife, 2014; Weeks & Hof, 1987; 1995; Weeks & Treat, 2001), specific sexual dysfunctions (Weeks & Gambescia, 2000; 2002), and infidelity (Weeks, Gambescia, & Jenkins, 2003). We welcome new discoveries that are being made in neuroscience, biology, physiology, or the medical aspects of sexuality as these can be integrated into the Intersystem perspective. Thus, we believe there is considerable room for psychotherapeutic advancement in the field of sex therapy, especially for systems-oriented therapists.

We expect that the field of sex therapy will continue to produce sparse clinical and research data that concentrates on behaviorally oriented treatment, which is still the normative approach to treatment. Nevertheless, we fear that the field will continue to become more divided because the training of the members of each camp, AASECT (American Association of Sexuality Educators, Counselors and Therapists) and AAMFT (American Association of Marriage and Family Therapy), will not be able to transcend their professional experience, training, and perceived scope of practice. The behaviorists will continue to be behaviorists and systems thinkers will continue to be systems thinkers with little overlap or interest in the others' approach. We believe that Intersystem theory best explains the interlocking nature of sexual dysfunction and has been theoretically and clinically demonstrated in cases of erectile dysfunction and lack of sexual desire (Weeks & Gambescia, 2000; 2002). Clinicians who share the common goal of treating intimate relationships should be amenable to assimilating new information, regardless of the problem. This knowledge would include an understanding of the major sexual dysfunctions and sexual difficulties such as partner choosing an inconvenient time, too little foreplay or after play, desire for different sexual practices, and dealing with the normal discrepancies of frequency and desire.

Education/Training Implications

Coupled with the momentum of the traditional behavioral approach, the Intersystem Approach is beginning to gain more support since the publication of our two volumes in 2009 (Hertlein, Weeks, & Gambescia, 2009; Hertlein, Weeks, & Sendak, 2009). Despite this, many therapists may not use the Intersystem Approach because they perceive it as too complex. In effect, this approach merely organizes what the therapist should already be doing: attending to the many issues related to the individual, relationship, family-of-origin, and factors associated with larger systems in which the couple and the individuals are embedded. A therapist practicing from an integrative perspective needs to be well trained in the modalities of individual, couple, and family therapy. This training represents a significant investment and dedication to systemic thinking, an appreciation of the interaction of all of the components of sexual problems. Most graduate programs for training marital and family therapists have recognized the value in utilizing such an integrative approach, but sex therapy has not developed multiple methods for dealing with sexual problems.

Additionally, physicians generally lack comfort, education, and knowledge of psychological treatment modalities in the assessment and treatment of sexual dysfunctions, expressions, variations, etc. They must learn that the etiology of a sexual problem can frequently be an interaction between biological and psychological factors. Unfortunately, few physicians receive formal training in couple and sex therapy. Moreover, few psychiatry residency programs are committed to teaching about this vital and often overlooked aspect of the human experience. Sexual issues are important to the individual at all stages of the life cycle, and sexual functioning is a lifelong capacity. Research indicates that sexual and relationship satisfaction are correlated and fostered by communication. Sexual problems are common and often embedded in the dynamics of relationship. Additionally, disruptions in sexual functioning can be the harbinger of an underlying medical disorder.

Physician Curricula must underscore the concept that the couple is the unit for understanding partnered sexual problems (Levine & Scott, 2010). Further, instruction in sexual interviewing of the individual or couple must be provided for physicians in training (Maurice, 1999). Such information will encourage appropriate referrals to be made on behalf of individuals and couples experiencing sexual problems and likely reduce the dependence on medical solutions or the perception that there is a medical solution for every sexual problem. Medical practitioners who recognize the psychogenic and relational risk factors for sexual problems often admit that they do not have the time or training to address these issues, yet they do not consult with a sex therapist unless the therapist has made an effort to forge a relationship. Coordinated treatment between medical and psychological practitioners is a step towards reducing feelings of failure, anxiety, and hopelessness in individuals and partners experiencing problems with sexual intimacy.

New Approaches

Aside from the Intersystem Approach, there have been only a few novel approaches for sexual problems that have been published since the publication of the last volume of *Systemic Sex Therapy* in 2009. Prior to that, Daines and Hallam-Jones (2007) developed a multifaceted intervention sex therapy (MIST) approach, in which two or more of the main components of sex therapy may be used either sequentially or in a fully integrated way: (1) medical and physical treatment, (2) behaviorally oriented sex therapy, (3) psychodynamic therapy, and (4) cognitive behavioral therapy. From our perspective, this approach is not systemic but more akin to an eclectic approach to therapy where two or more therapeutic approaches are utilized. Jones, da Silva, and Soloski (2011) published an article called sexological systems theory, which was based on an ecological/bio-psycho-social model. The major shortcoming of this model is the lack of theoretical integration and lack of specificity regarding the domains of behavior that need to be assessed and treated.

Barker (2011) applied existential therapy principles to sex therapy. This theory stresses the importance of not using labels or diagnosis in treating sexual problems, but to keep the focus on mutual pleasure. In addition, there are three other foci of treatment: the clients lived experience, the multiple meanings of sex, and the dimensions of existence. The lived experience refers to the client's worldview and what is meaningful to them. Secondly, sex can have multiple meanings contingent upon the function it serves at different times. Finally, in an existential approach, mind and body are viewed as one; thus, sexual problems always involve both a mental and physical dimension. Due to the anti-diagnostic view of this approach we doubt it will gain much traction. The therapeutic community at large is trained to think diagnostically and insurance reimbursement is dependent on making a diagnosis.

The latest psychotherapeutic theory to be applied to sexual problems is mindfulness, a meditative practice which originates in Buddhism. It promotes awareness of thoughts, feelings, bodily sensations, a non-judgmental process, and the lack of a goal orientation (Lazaridou & Kalogianni, 2013). Several studies have applied mindfulness to different aspects of sexuality. Brotto, Basson, and Luria (2008) conducted a simple study using only three 90-minute sessions spaced at 2-week intervals. Mindfulness in their study was described as the practice of relaxed wakefulness. The women reported an increase in sexual desire and arousal, especially women who had a history of sexual abuse. Mindfulness was also used to treat sexual pain and anxiety. Rosenbaum (2013) used this approach with women who experienced vaginismus and dyspareunia. She proposed that mindfulness would facilitate a better mind/body connection thereby helping women relax. Her article was simply a description of the clinical process and not an outcome-based study. Sommers (2013) published an article describing the use of mindfulness therapy in a few case studies and reviewed some empirical studies on mindfulness therapy in lovemaking and life. He believes that mindfulness has two core principles. The first is to be focused in the present or to stay in the here-and-now. The second principle is to be absorbed in the process that is taking place. The client is to simply be fully immersed in the experience at hand, and not focused on a goal. Finally, Brotto, Mehak, and Kit (2009) applied the practices of mindfulness and yoga in a qualitative study. They offer that those who practice yoga experience the benefits from a greater mind-body connection, and ultimately enjoy more satisfying sexuality. Brotto, Mehak, and Kit (2009) hope to invite more rigorous empirical validation of the positive effects of yoga on sexual functioning.

Mindfulness involves being open to new ideas and novelty, developing an ability to focus, and be more self-aware. The use of mindfulness therapy in resolving sexual problems is supported by several studies but lacked methodological rigor. Nonetheless, these preliminary studies do suggest that mindfulness may play a much larger role in sex therapy in the future.

Research

The trend in research in psychotherapy has shifted toward demonstrating that treatment programs are effective or in developing evidence-based treatments. Unfortunately, the outcome research in sex therapy is still relatively limited in depth (Binik & Hall, 2014; Schover & Leiblum, 1994). This fact is somewhat surprising, given the reliance on behavioral methods frequently utilized in sex therapy and the propensity for behaviorally oriented approaches to be empirically validated. In addition, the reliance on behavioral strategies makes less sense when research in sexual problems supports the contention that dysfunctions emerge from the various dimensions outlined in the Intersystem Approach. It is imperative that the field of sex therapy continues to test the effectiveness of the models or the critical components of treatment for the various problems or disorders. Evidence-based theory driven research is the new gold standard in psychological research and should apply equally to sex therapy research.

There are two major ways researchers approach psychotherapy research. The traditional method is to investigate whether a particular treatment program is effective (Lambert, 2013). The second is to investigate what researchers call the "common factors" approach, which identifies the factors or collective factors across each model that contribute to effective treatment. Sex therapy has, thankfully, not been excluded from this analysis although this type of method is rare in sex therapy research. Donahey and Miller (2000) cite the role of extra-therapeutic factors as being a significant component in therapy, stating: "By being mindful of the significant role that client strengths, capabilities, resources, social supports, and the fortuitous events that weave in and out of client's lives play in everyday practice, sex therapists can enhance their contribution to treatment outcome" (p. 222). Further, they highlighted the importance of the relationship between the client and therapist, explored the role of hope and expectancy and its impact on the sex therapy process, and provided strategies to help a therapist determine appropriate model or technique selection. A literature review post 2000 failed to find any articles that focused on common factors research in sex therapy. Common factors research topics along this line might include testing the degree to which the extra-therapeutic factors shift outcome based on the nature of a couple's presenting problem, the role of the therapist-client relationship in sex therapy with same sex couples, or how a couple's sense of failure in sexual functioning mitigates their feelings of hope and expectancy, thus altering the therapeutic outcome. Incorporating the common factors approach into sex therapy is all but undiscovered territory. In Weeks and Fife's (2014) book on couple therapy the reader can find a comprehensive review of common factors shown to improve the outcome of couple therapy. We suspect many of these factors will apply to sex therapy since it involves couples therapy, especially when approached from the Intersystem perspective.

Hawton (1992) may have foretold the story when he asked whether sex therapy research had withered on the vine. The dearth of sex therapy research has historically been abysmal. Heiman and Meston reviewed the research literature in 1997 and found that only a few treatments met the criteria for being evidence-based. Keep in mind this research was not done using *DSM-5* clinical labels or diagnostic criteria. They found that the treatments for Primary Female Orgasmic Disorder and Erectile Dysfunction were "well established" and the treatments for Secondary Female Orgasmic Disorder, Vaginismus, and Premature Ejaculation were probably effective. They also noted that many studies were poorly designed with lack of control groups, treatment protocols, and measurements of sexual satisfaction (Heiman & Meston, 1997).

The efficacy of psychological interventions for sexual dysfunctions was investigated by Fruhauf et al. (2013). They performed a meta-analysis that combined and contrasted data from many studies, attempting to find common themes and trends. This study used fairly high inclusion criteria. Fruhauf et al. (2013) found that psychological interventions were effective in improving symptom severity and sexual satisfaction with Female Orgasmic Disorder and Female Hypoactive Sexual Desire Disorder. They also discussed the lack of rigor in the design of many studies showing positive results of questionable validity. It is interesting to note this study was published in 2013 but they did not include any studies published after 2009.

In a chapter on the deficits in sex therapy, Meana, Hall, and Binik (2014) also reviewed the overall state of sex therapy and stated there is a need for more evidence-based studies. They noted that pharmacological treatments have received considerable research attention perhaps because of the availability of funding from drug companies and the ease with which such studies can be performed. However, they found that psychotherapy studies were lacking.

The clear emphasis of the fifth edition of the *Principle and Practices of Sex Therapy* book (Binik & Hall, 2014) is on evidence-based practices for the major sexual dysfunctions. While we agree that evidence-based practices would be ideal for all the techniques for all the major dysfunctions, this is not a realistic case. Because of the emphasis on evidence-based treatment, many of the treatment principles are general and specific techniques that once appeared in the literature are absent. How did we ever do any kind of therapy before the advent of the concept of evidence-based practices? In comparison, sex therapy is a young and very small field relative to its social science siblings such as psychology and many practitioners are not researchers. We may find that the treatments currently lacking evidence-based treatments will be confirmed in the future. We believe that clinical practice always runs ahead of clinical research. We do not sit on our hands until a researcher tells us something works. As practitioners we live in a real world lab, and over the years develop a sense of what works, when, and with whom. Researchers then try to confirm what clinicians have been doing. Practitioners and clients will not be deterred from doing therapy as long as the clients seek help and the practitioner can fulfill some of the requirements of common factors research in couple's therapy (Weeks & Fife, 2014). For example, as long as the therapist can offer a credible explanation and treatment plan from a systemic view couples are likely to continue treatment. As practitioners we cannot and should not ignore our clinical experience and the success of our clients pending a research telling us what might work best. Therapy has always been a trial and error endeavor (Gambescia & Weeks, 2007). If one technique or approach isn't working, we try something else. Researchers may end up giving up a precise roadmap to the best methods of doing sex therapy, but in the meantime we can still use a less precise roadmap that will usually get us to the same destination with what may be some unnecessary detours and roads that aren't as direct.

In sum, the field of sex therapy is severely lacking research of the same quality found in the top-tier psychology and marriage and family therapy journals, especially when trying to discover which techniques, methods, and strategies are most effective in treatment protocols.

The Way Forward

This text represents a major comprehensive effort to change the paradigm for the field of sex therapy and its application to a wide spectrum of sexual problems. The field of sex therapy has become isolated and insulated from other mental health fields such as psychology and marriage and family therapy in which it is embedded. Unfortunately, traditional sex therapists would rather not embrace the context of the field. The intervention strategies in this book are based on a metatheory or metaframework that stresses integration, systemic thinking, and coordination of treatment modalities drawn from many different disciplines. The field of sex therapy needs to be revitalized through much more theory building within the field of sex therapy, bridging the gap with other disciplines involved in psychotherapy, and theory-based research. We propose that sex therapy be considered an evolving field that can grow through the Intersystem Approach. The Intersystem Approach provides a blueprint for the future. The theory embraces an understanding of sexuality and sex therapy at multiple levels and excludes nothing that has value for us as therapists and the consumer who expects to be treated as a whole person rather than a mirror reflecting the fragmentation within our field.

References

Agusta, J., & Duran, E. (2012). Sexting: Research criteria of a globalized social phenomenon. *Archives of Sexual Behavior, 41*, 1325–1328. doi: 10.1007/s10508–012–0038–0

American Counseling Association. (2010). American Counseling Association competencies for counseling with transgender clients. *Journal of LGBT Issues in Counseling, 4*, 135–159.

American Psychiatric Association. (1973). *Diagnostic and statistical manual of mental disorders* (3rd ed.). Washington, DC. Author.

American Psychiatric Association. (1980). *Diagnostic and statistical manual of mental disorders* (3rd ed.). Washington, DC. Author.

American Psychiatric Association. (1987). *Diagnostic and statistical manual of mental disorders* (3rd ed., rev.). Washington, DC. Author.

American Psychiatric Association. (2004). *Diagnostic and statistical manual of mental disorders* (3rd ed., rev.). Washington, DC. Author.

American Psychiatric Association. (2013). *Diagnostic and statistical manual of mental disorders* (5th ed.). Washington, DC: Author.

Andersson, G., Estling, F., Jakobsson, E., Cuijpers, P., & Carlbring, P. (2011). Can the patient decide which modules to endorse? An open trial of tailored Internet treatment of anxiety disorders. *Cognitive Behaviour Therapy, 40*, 57–64. doi: 10.1080/16506073.2010.529457

Armstrong, L. (2006). Barriers to intimate sexuality; Concerns and meaning-based therapy approaches. *The Humanist Psychologist, 34*(3), 281–298. doi: 10.1207/s15473333thp3403_5

Ashton, A. (2007). The new sexual pharmacology: A guide for the clinician. In S. Leiblum (Ed.), *Principles and practice of sex therapy* (4th ed.) (pp. 509–542). New York: Guilford.

Balon, R. (2013). Controversies in the diagnosis and treatment of paraphilias. *Journal of Sex & Marital Therapy, 39*, 7–20. doi: 10.1080/0092623X.2012.709219

Barker, M. (2011). Existential sex therapy. *Sexual and Relationship Therapy, 26*(1), 33–47.

Basson, R. (2012). The recurrent pain and sexual sequelae of provoked vestibulodynia: A perpetuating cycle. *Journal of Sexual Medicine, 9*(8), 2077–2092.

Bergeron, S., Rosen, N., & Pukall, C. (2014). Genital pain in women and men: It can hurt more than your sex life. In Y. Binik & K. Hall (Eds.), *Principles and practice of sex therapy* (5th ed., pp. 159–176). New York: Guilford.

Binik, Y. M. (2010a). The DSM diagnostic criteria for dyspareunia. *Archives of Sexual Behavior, 39*(2), 292–303. doi: 10.1007/s10508–009–9563-x

Binik, Y. M. (2010b). The DSM diagnostic criteria for vaginismus. *Archives of Sexual Behavior, 39*(2), 278–291. doi: 10.1007/s10508–009–9560–0

Binik, Y. M., Bergeron, S., & Khalifé, S. (2000). Dyspareunia. In S. R. Leiblum (Ed.), Principles and practice of sex therapy (4th ed., pp. 154–180). New York: The Guilford Press.

Binik, Y.M., & Hall, K. (Eds.). (2014). *Principles and practices of sex therapy* (5th ed.) (pp. 551–558). New York: Guilford.

Binik, Y. M., & Meana, M. (2009). The future of sex therapy: Specialization or marginalization? *Archives of Sexual Behavior, 38*(6), 1016–1027. doi: 10.1007/s10508–009–9475–9

Blankers, M. B., Koeter, M. W. J., & Schippers, G. M. (2011). Internet therapy versus internet self-help versus no treatment for problematic alcohol use: A randomized controlled trial. *Journal of Consulting and Clinical Psychology, 79*(3), 330–341. doi: 10.1037/a0023498

Bogaert, A. F. (2004). Asexuality: Prevalence and associated factors in a national probability sample. *Journal of Sex Research, 41,* 279–287.

Bogaert, A. F. (2012). *Understanding asexuality.* Littlefield, UK: Rowman & Littlefield publishers.

Borrelli-Kerner, S., & Bernell, B. (1997). Couple therapy of sexual disorders. In R. S. Charlton (Ed.), *Treating sexual disorders* (pp. 165–199). San Francisco: Jossey-Bass.

Brotto, L. A., Basson, R., & Luria, M. (2008). A mindfulness-based group psychoeducational intervention targeting sexual arousal disorder in women. *Journal of Sexual Medicine, 5*(7), 1646–1659. doi: 10.1111/j.1743–6109.2008.00850.x

Brotto, L. A., Knudson, G., Inskip, J., Rhodes, K., & Erskine, Y. (2010). Asexuality: A mixed methods approach. *Archives of Sexual Behavior, 39,* 599–618.

Brotto, L. A., Mehak, L., & Kit, C. (2009). Yoga and sexual functioning: a review. *Journal of Sex and Marital Therapy, 35*(5), 378–390. doi: 10.1080/00926230903065955

Burns, S. M., Hough, S., Boyd, B., & Hill, J. (2010). Men's adjustment to spinal cord injury: The unique contributions to conformity to masculine gender norms. *American Journal of Men's Health, 4*(2), 157–166. doi: 10.1177/1557988309332690

Butler, C. (2009). Sexual and gender minority therapy and systemic practice. *Journal of Family Therapy, 31*(4), 338–358. doi: 10.1111/j.1467–6427.2009.00472.x

Carvalheira, A. A., Pereira, N. M., Maroco, J., & Forjaz, V. (2012). Dropout in the treatment of erectile dysfunction with PDE5: A study on predictors and a qualitative analysis of reasons for discontinuation. *Journal of Sexual Medicine, 9*(9), 2361–2369. doi: 10.1111/j.1743–6109.2012.02787.x

Chasin, C. J. (2011). Theoretical issues in the study of asexuality. *Archives of Sexual Behavior, 40,* 713–723. doi: 10.1007/s10508–011–9757–x

Cohn, R. (2014). Calming the tempest, bridging the get gorge: Healing in couples ruptured by sex addiction. *Sexual and Relationship Therapy, 29*(1), 76–86. doi: 10.1080/14681994.2013.869314

Coleman, E., Bockting, W., Botzer, M., Cohen-Kettenis, P., DeCuypere, G., Feldman, J., Fraser, L., . . . Zucker, K. (2012). Standards of care for the health of transsexual, transgender, and gender-nonconforming people, version 7. *International Journal of Transgenderism, 13*(4), 165–232. doi: 10.1080/15532739.2011.700873

Crenshaw, T., & Goldberg, G. (1996). *Sexual pharmacology.* New York: W.W. Norton.

Crowe, M. (1995). Couple therapy and sexual dysfunction. *International Review of Psychiatry, 7,* 195–204.

Daines, B., & Hallam-Jones, R. (2007). Multifaceted intervention sex therapy (MIST). *Sexual and Relationship Therapy, 22*(3), 339–350.

Davis, L. (2007). Golden sexuality: Sex therapy for seniors. In L. Vandecreek, F. Peterson, Jr., & J. Bley (Eds.), *Innovations in clinical practice: Focus on sexual health* (pp. 261–273). Sarasota, FL: Professional Resource Press.

Donahey, K. M., & Miller, S. D. (2000). Applying a common factors perspective to sex therapy. *Journal of Sex Education and Therapy, 25,* 221–230.

Ehrensaft, D. (2011). *Gender born, gender made: Raising healthy gender-nonconforming children.* New York: The Experiment.

Fraser, J., & Solovey, A. (2004). A catalytic approach to brief sex therapy. In S. Green & D. Flemons (Eds.), *Quickies; the handbook of brief sex therapy* (pp. 189–212). New York: W.W. Norton.

Fruhauf, S., Gerger, H., Schmidt, H., Munder, T., & Barth, J. (2013). Efficacy of psychological interventions for sexual dysfunctions: A systematic review and meta-analysis. *Archives of Sexual Behavior, 42,* 915–933. doi: 10.1007/s10508–012–0062–0

Gagnon, J. (1990). The explicit and implicit use of the scripting perspective in sex research. *Annual Review of Sex Research, 1,* 1–43.

293

Gambescia, N., & Weeks, G. R. (2006). Erectile dysfunction. In J. Fisher & W. O'Donohue. (Eds.), *Practitioner's guide to evidence based psychotherapy* (pp. 284–290). New York: Springer Publishers.

Gambescia, N., & Weeks, G. R. (2007). Sexual dysfunction. In N. Kazantzis & L. L'Abate (Eds.), *Handbook of homework assignments in psychotherapy: Research, practice, prevention* (pp. 351–369). New York: Springer.

Gehring, D. (2003). Couple therapy for low sexual desire: A systemic approach. *Journal of Sex & Marital Therapy, 29*, 25–38. doi: 10.1080/713847099

Gerson, M. (2011). Cyberspace betrayal: Attachment in an era of virtual connection. *Journal of Family Psychotherapy, 22*(2), 148–156. doi: 10.1080/08975353.2011.578039

Gill, K., & Hough, S. (2007). Sexual health of people with chronic illness and disability. In L. VandeCreek, F. Peterson, Jr., & J. Bley (Eds.), *Innovations in clinical practice: Focus on sexual health* (pp. 223–243). Sarasota, FL: Professional Resource Press.

Gurman, A. S., & Fraenkel, P. (2002). The history of couple therapy: A millennial review. *Family Process, 41*(2), 199–260. doi: 10.1111/j.1545–5300.2002.41204.x

Hawton, K. (1992). Sex therapy research: Has it withered on the vine? *Annual Review of Sex Research, 3*, 49–72.

Heiman, J. R., Long, J. S., Smith, S. N., Fisher, W. A., & Sand, M. S. (2011). Sexual satisfaction and relationship happiness in midlife and older couples in five countries. *Archives of Sexual Behavior, 40*, 741–753. doi: 10.1007/s10508–010–9703–3

Heiman, J., & LoPiccolo, J. (1988). *Becoming orgasmic*. New York: Prentice Hall.

Heiman, J. & Meston, C. M. (1997). Empirically validated treatment for sexual dysfunction. *Annual Review for Sex Research, 8*, 148–194.

Hertlein, K. (2012). Digital dwelling: Technology in couple and family relationships. *Family Relations, 6*(3), 374–387. doi: 10.1111/j.1741–3729.2012.00702.x

Hertlein, K. & Ancheta, K. (2014). Advantages and disadvantages of technology in relationships: Findings from an open-ended survey. *The Qualitative Report, 19*(22), 1–11. http://www.nova.edu/ssss/QR/QR19/hertlein22.pdf

Hertlein, K. M., & Blumer, M. (2014). *The couple and family technology framework: Intimate relationships in a digital age*. New York: Routledge.

Hertlein, K. M., & Blumer, M. L. C., & Smith, J. (2014). Marriage and family therapists' use and comfort with online communication with clients. *Contemporary Family Therapy, 36*, 58–69.

Hertlein, K. M., & Nelson, T. (2006, October). Designing an Internet infidelity treatment framework. Workshop presentation at the annual meeting of the American Association for Marriage and Family Therapy Conference, Austin, TX.

Hertlein, K. M., Weeks, G. R., & Gambescia, N. (Eds.) (2009). *Systemic sex therapy*. New York: Routledge: Taylor & Francis Group, LLC.

Hertlein, K. M., Weeks, G. R., & Sendak, K. S. (2009). *A clinican's guide to systemic sex therapy*. New York: Routledge: Taylor & Francis Group, LLC.

Iasenza, S. (2010). What's queer about sex: Expanding sexual frames in theory and practice. *Family Process, 49*(3), 291–308. doi: 10.1111/j.1545–5300.2010.01324.x

Joannides, P. (2009). *The guide to getting it on* (6th ed.). Waldport, OR: Goofy Foot Press.

Jones, K., Barkerda, A., Silva, M. & Soloski, K. (2011). Sexological Systems Theory: An ecological model and assessment approach for sex therapy. *Sexual and Relationship Therapy, 26*(2), 127–144. doi: 10.1080/14681994.2011.574688

Jones, K., Meneses da Silva, A., & Soloski, K. L. (2011). Sexological systems theory: A developmental model and assessment approach for sex therapy. *Journal of Sexual and Relationship Therapy, 26*(2), 127–144, doi: 10.1080/14681994.2011.574688

Jurich, J., & Myers-Bowman, K. (1998). Systems theory and its application to research on human sexuality. *Journal of Sex Research, 35*, 72–87.

Kafka, M. (2007). Paraphilia-related disorders: The evaluation and treatment of nonparaphilic hypersexuality. In S. Leiblum (Ed.), *Principle and practice of sex therapy* (4th ed.) (pp. 442–476). New York: Guilford.

Kaplan, H. (1974). *The new sex therapy: Active treatment of sexual dysfunctions*. New York: Times Books.

Kaufman, M., Silverberg, C., & Odette, F. (2007). *The ultimate guide to sex and disability: For all of us who live with disabilities, chronic pain & illness*. San Francisco, CA: Cleis Press, Inc.

Kelsey, K., Stiles B.L., Spiller L., & Diekhoff G.M. (2013). Assessment of therapists' attitudes towards BDSM. *Psychology & Sexuality, 4*(3), 255–267. doi: 10.1080/19419899.2012.655255

Kimmel, M. (Ed.). (2007). *The sexual self: The construction of sexual scripts*. Nashville, TN: Vanderbilt University Press.

Kinsey Institute. (2007). *Sexuality information links*. Retrieved from http://www.indiana.edu/~kinsey/resources/sexlinks.html

Kleinplatz, P. (Ed.). (2001). *New directions in sex therapy: Innovations and alternatives*. Philadelphia: Taylor & Francis.

Klotz, T., Mathers, M., & Sommer, F. (2005). Why do patients with erectile dysfunction abandon effective therapy with sildenafil (Viagra)? *International Journal of Impotence Research, 17*, 2–4.

Krieger, I. (2011). *Helping your transgender teen: A guide for parents*. New Haven, CT: Genderwise Press.

Kuyper, L., & Vanwesenbeeck, I. (2011). Examining sexual health differences between lesbian, gay, bisexual, and heterosexual adults: The role of sociodemographics, sexual behavior characteristics, and minority stress. *Journal of Sex Research, 48*(2/3), 263–274. doi: 10.1080/00224491003654473

Lambert, M. (2013). *Bergin and Garfield's handbook of psychotherapy and behavioral change* (6th ed.). Hoboken, NJ: Wiley and Sons.

Lazaridou, A., & Kalogianni, C. (2013). Mindfulness and sexuality. *Sexual and Relationship Therapy, 28*(1–2), 29–38.

Leiblum, S. (2007). *Principles and practice of sex therapy* (3rd ed.). New York: Guilford.

Leiblum, S., & Rosen, R. (2000a). *Principles and practice of sex therapy* (3rd ed.). New York: Guilford.

Leiblum, S., & Rosen, R. (2000b). Introduction: Sex therapy in the age of Viagra. In S. Leiblum & R. Rosen (Eds.), *Principles and practice of sex therapy* (3rd ed.) (pp. 1–16). New York: Guilford.

Lev, A.I. (2004). *Transgender emergence: Therapeutic guidelines for working with gender-variant people and their families*. Binghamton, NY: The Hayworth Clinical Practice Press.

Lev, A., & Sennott, S. (2012). Understanding gender nonconformity and transgender identity: A sex positive approach. In P. Kleinplatz (Ed.), *New directions in sex therapy: Innovations and alternatives* (pp. 321–336). New York: Routledge.

Levine, S., & Scott, D. (2010). Sexual education for psychiatric residents. *Academic Psychiatry, 34*(5), 349–352. doi: 10.1176/appi.ap.34.5.349

LoFrisco, B.M. (2011). Female sexual pain disorders and cognitive behavioral therapy. *Journal of Sex Research, 48*(6), 573–579. doi: 10.1080/00224499.2010.540682

LoPiccolo, J. (1978). Direct treatment of sexual dysfunction. In J. LoPiccolo & L. LoPiccolo (Eds.), *Handbook of sex therapy* (pp. 1–17). New York: Plenum.

LoPiccolo, J., & LoPiccolo, L. (1978). *Handbook of sex therapy*. New York: Plenum.

Malpas, J. (2012). Can couples change gender? Couple therapy with transgender people and their partners. In J.J. Binger & J.L. Wetchler (Eds.), *Handbook of LGBT affirmative couple and family therapy*. New York: Routledge.

Mark, K., & Jozkowski, K. (2013). The mediating role of sexual and nonsexual communication between relationship and sexual satisfaction in a sample of college-age heterosexual couples. *Journal of Sex & Marital Therapy, 39*(5–6), 410–427. doi: 10.1080/0092623X.2011.644652

Masters, W.H., & Johnson, V. (1966). *Human sexual response*. Boston: Little, Brown.

Masters, W.H., & Johnson, V. (1970) *Human sexual inadequacy*. Boston: Little, Brown.

Maurice, W. (1999). *Sexual medicine in primary care*. St. Louis: Mosby, Inc.

McCormick, N.B. (2010). Sexual scripts: Social and therapeutic implications. *Sexual & Relationship Therapy, 25*(1), 96–120. doi: 10.1080/14681990903550167

McGeorge, C., & Carlson, T.S. (2011). Deconstructing heterosexism: Becoming an LGB affirmative heterosexual couple and family therapist. *Journal of Marital and Family Therapy, 37*(1), 14–26. doi: 10.1111/j.1752–0606.2009.00149.x

Meana, M. (2009). Painful intercourse: Dyspareunia and vaginismus. In K. Hertlein, G. Weeks, & N. Gambescia (Eds.), *Systemic sex therapy* (pp. 237–263). New York: Routledge.

Meana, M., Hall, K., & Binik, Y. (2014). Sex therapy in transition. In Y. Binik & K. Hall (Eds.), *Principles and practices of sex therapy* (5th ed., pp. 551–558). New York: Guilford.

Meana, M., Lykins, A., Spicer Rakipi, R., & Weeks, G. (2006). Sexual functioning in a non-clinical sample of partnered lesbians. *Journal of Couple & Relationship Therapy, 5*(2), 1–22. doi: 10.1300/J398v05n02_01

Muzacz, A.K., & Akinsulure-Smith, A.M. (2013). Older adults and sexuality: Implications for counseling ethnic and sexual minority clients. *Journal of Mental Health Counseling, 35*(1), 1–14.

Nichols, M. (2006). Psychotherapeutic issues with 'kinky' clients: Clinical problems, yours and theirs. In P. J. Kleinplatz, & C. Moser (Eds.), *Sadomasochism: Powerful pleasures* (pp. 281–300). New York: Harrington Park Press.

Nichols, M., & Shernoff, M. (2007). Therapy with sexual minorities: Queering practice. In S. Leiblum (Ed.), *Principles and practice of sex therapy* (4th ed., pp. 379–415). New York: Guilford.

Physician's Desk Reference. (1996). *Physician's desk reference* (50th ed.). New Jersey: Thompson PDR.

Poston, Jr., D.L., & Baumle, A.K. (2010). Patterns of asexuality in the United States. *Demographic Research, 23*, 509–530. doi: 10.4054/DemRes.2010.23.18

Pukall, C.F. (2009). Sex therapy is special because it deals with sex. *Archives of Sexual Behavior, 38*(6), 1039–1040. doi: 10.1007/s10508–009–9468–8

Rankin, S., & Beemyn, B. (2011). *The lives of transgender people*. New York: Columbia.

Rimm, D., & Masters, J. (1974). *Behavior therapy: Techniques and empirical findings*. Oxford: Academic Press.

Rosen, R. (2007). Erectile dysfunction: Integration of medical and psychological approaches. In S. Leiblum (Ed.), *Principles and practice of sex therapy* (4th ed.) (pp. 277–310). New York: Guilford.

Rosenbaum, T. (2007). Physical therapy management and treatment of sexual pain disorders. In S. Leiblum (Ed.), *Principles and practice of sex therapy* (4th ed.) (pp. 157–180). New York: Guilford.

Rosenbaum, T.Y. (2013). An integrated mindfulness-based approach to the treatment of women with sexual pain and anxiety: Promoting autonomy and mind/body connection. *Sexual and Relationship Therapy, 28*(1–2), 20–28. doi: 10.1080/14681994.2013.764981

Rosenberg, K., Carnes, P., & O'Connor, S. (2014). Evaluation and treatment of sex addiction. *Journal of Sex & Marital Therapy, 40*(2), 77–91.

Rushbrooke, E., Murray, C., & Townsend, S. (2014). The experiences of intimate relationships by people with intellectual disabilities: A qualitative study. *Journal of Applied Research in Intellectual Disabilities*, January 30. doi: 10.1111/jar.12091

Sae-Chul, K., & Sook, P. (2006). Five years after the launch of Viagra in Korea: Changes in perceptions of erectile dysfunction treatment by physicians, patients, and the patients' spouses. *Journal of Sexual Medicine, 3*(1), 132–137.

Schneider, J. (2003). The impact of compulsive cybersex behaviours on the family. *Journal of Sexual and Relationship Therapy, 18*(3), 329–354.

Schneider, J., Weiss, R., & Samenow, C. (2012): Is it really cheating? Understanding the emotional reactions and clinical treatment of spouses and partners affected by cybersex infidelity, sexual addiction & compulsivity: *The Journal of Treatment & Prevention, 19*(1–2), 123–139.

Schover, L., & Leiblum, S. (1994). Commentary: The stagnation of sex therapy. *Journal of Psychology & Human Sexuality, 6*, 5–30.

Schwartz, P., & Young, L. (2009). Sexual satisfaction in committed relationships. *Sexuality Research & Social Policy, 6*(1), 1–17.

Seagraves, R., & Balon, R. (2003). *Sexual pharmacology: Fast facts*. New York: W.W. Norton.

Shamloul, R. & Ghanem, H. (2013). Erectile dysfunction. *The Lancet, 381*(9861), 153–165.

Shaw, J. (2012). Approaching sexual potential in relationship: A reward of age and maturity. In P. Kleinplatz (Ed.), *New directions in sex therapy: Innovations and alternatives* (pp.175–194). Philadelphia: Brunner-Routledge.

Simopoulos, E.F., & Trinidad, A.C. (2013). Male erectile dysfunction: integrating psychopharmacology and psychotherapy. *General Hospital Psychiatry, 35*(1), 33–38.

Smith, L. C. Shin, R. Q., & Officer, L. M. (2012). Moving counseling forward on LGB and transgender issues: Speaking queerly on siscourses and microaggressions. *The Counseling Psychologist*, 40(3), 385–408.

Sommers, F. G. (2013). Mindfulness in love and love making: A way of life. *Sexual and Relationship Therapy*, 28(1–2), 84–91.

Special: Harry Benjamin international gender dysphoria association's the standard of care for gender identity disorders—Sixth version. (2001). *International Journal of Transgenderism*, 5, 1.

Stephenson, K. R., & Meston, C. M. (2012). Consequences of impaired female sexual functioning: Individual differences and associations with sexual distress. *Sexual and Relationship Therapy*, 27(4), 344–357.

Sternberg, R. (1986). A triangular theory of love. *Psychological Review*, 93(2), 119–135.

Sternberg, R. (1999). *Love is a story: A new theory of relationships*. Oxford: Oxford University Press.

Tiefer, L. (2006). Sex therapy as a humanistic enterprise. *Sexual and Relationship Therapy*, 21, 359–375.

Tilsen, J. (2013). *Therapeutic conversations with queer youth: Transcending homonormativity and constructing preferred identities*. New York: Jason Aronson, Inc.

Trudel, G., Turgeon, L., & Piche, L. (2010). Marital and sexual aspects of old age. *Sexual and Relationship Therapy*, 25(3), 316–341.

Van Houdenhove, E., T'Sjoen, G., & Enzlin, P. (2014). Asexuality: Few facts, many questions. *Journal of Sex and Marital Therapy*, 40(3), 175–192.

Verschuren, J. A., Enzlin, P., Dijkstra, P. U., Geertzen, J. B., & Dekker, R. (2010). Chronic disease and sexuality: A generic conceptual framework. *Journal of Sex Research*, 47(2/3), 153–170. doi: 10.1080/00224491003658227

Wang, V., Depp, C. A., Ceglowski, J., Thompson, W. K., Rock, D., & Jeste, D. V. (2014). Sexual health and function in later life: A population-based study of 606 older adults with a partner. *American Journal of Geriatric Psychiatry*. March 19. doi: 10.1016/j.jagp.2014.03.006

Weeks, G. (Ed.). (1989). *Treating couples: The intersystem model of the marriage council of Philadelphia*. New York: Brunner/Mazel.

Weeks, G. (1994). The intersystem model: An integrative approach to treatment. In G. Weeks and L. Hof (Eds.), *The marital-relationship therapy casebook* (pp. 3–34). New York: Brunner/Mazel.

Weeks, G. (2004). Integration in sex therapy. *Sexual and relationship therapy*, 19, S11–S12.

Weeks, G. (2005). The emergence of a new paradigm in sex therapy: Integration. *Sexual and Relationship Therapy*, 20, 89–103.

Weeks, G., & Cross, C. (2004). The intersystem model of psychotherapy: An integrative systems treatment approach. *Guidance and Counseling*, 19, 57–64.

Weeks, G., & Fife, S. (2014). *Couples in treatment: Techniques and approaches for effective practice* (3rd ed.). New York: Routledge.

Weeks, G., & Gambescia, N. (2000). *Erectile dysfunction: Integrating couple therapy, sex therapy, and medical treatment*. New York: W.W. Norton.

Weeks, G., & Gambescia, N. (2002). *Hypoactive sexual desire: Integrating sex and couple therapy*. New York: W.W. Norton.

Weeks, G., & Gambescia, N. (in press). Couple therapy and the treatment of sexual problems: The Intersystem Approach. In A. Gurman, J. Lebow, & D. Snyder, *Clinical handbook of couple therapy (5th edition)*. New York: Guilford.

Weeks, G., Gambescia, N., & Jenkins, R. (2003). *Treating infidelity*. New York: W.W. Norton.

Weeks, G., & Hof, L. (1987). *Integrating sex and marital therapy*. New York: Brunner/Mazel.

Weeks, G., & Hof, L. (1995). *Integrative solutions: Treating common problems in couples therapy*. New York: Brunner/Mazel.

Weeks, G., & Treat, S. (2001). *Couples in treatment: Techniques and approaches for effective practice* (2nd ed.). New York: Brunner/Routledge.

Weiss, D. (1998). Conclusion: The state of sexual theory. *Journal of Sex Research*, 35, 100–114.

Wiederman, M. (1998). The state of theory in sex therapy. *Journal of Sex Research*, *35*, 88–99.

Wincze, J. P., & Carey, M. P. (1991). *Sexual dysfunction*. New York: Guilford.

Woody, J. D. (1992). *Treating sexual distress*. Thousand Oaks, CA: Sage.

Wooton B. M., Titov, N., Dear, B. F., Spence, J., & Kemp, A. (2011). The acceptability of internet-based treatment and characteristics of an adult sample with obsessive compulsive disorder: An internet survey. *PLoS ONE*, *6*(6), e20548. doi: 10.1371/journal.pone.0020548

World Professional Association for Transgender Health. (2012). Standards of care for the health of transsexual, transgender, and gender non-conforming people. Retrieved from http://www.wpath.org/uploaded_files/140/files/Standards%20of%20Care,%20V7%20Full%20Book.pdf

Wright, S. (2010). Depathologizing consensual sexual sadism, sexual masochism, transvestic fetishism, and fetishism. *Archives of Sexual Behavior*, *39*(6), 1229–1230. doi: 10.1007/s10508-010-9651-y

Wylie, K., Barrett, J., Besser, M., Bouman, W., Bridgman, M., Clayton, A., . . . Ward, D. (2014). Good practice guidelines for the assessment and treatment of adults with gender dysphoria. *Sexual and Relationship Therapy*, *29*(2), 154–214.

16

EPILOGUE

A Personal Note on Being a Sex Therapist

Gerald R. Weeks, Nancy Gambescia, and Katherine M. Hertlein

Prior to the publication of the original edition of this text, we had not yet seen a book, chapter, or article dealing with what it means to be a sex therapist. Hopefully, we have contributed to a greater understanding of our work through several discussions within this updated text that address this issue. The purpose of this volume has been to introduce the beginning therapist to the field of sex therapy and to introduce all therapists to a systems view of sex therapy. We want to encourage therapists to embrace sexual issues in treatment and to understand the complex interplay between the various systems contributing to a sexual problem. With the medicalization of psychotherapy and the increased focused on integrative approaches, this is a time for us as sex therapists to redefine our roles.

The field of sex therapy is also met with challenges. Whether it be the deficit in the clarity of the designation, barriers in training, or other factors, training exclusively in sex therapy does not lead one to a certification; yet we understand that licensure is the first step to become qualified to practice. We also know that the number of sex therapists, like most professionals, will diminish in numbers over the next few years as the baby boomers in this field retire. Though sex therapy practitioners are frequently credentialed as psychotherapists, psychiatrists, physicians, social workers, and other mental health professionals, many do not understand the function of a sex therapist. Further, sex therapy is also looked on with suspicion by the general public and frequently put under much scrutiny. It is accorded low status among researchers who fail to understand the rigors of doing sex research and therapy. For these and many other reasons having to do with the personality of the clinician, few therapists pursue becoming a sex therapist. Our wish is to see that national sex therapy organizations recruit more members, start mentoring programs, maintain strict credentialing, and provide certification. These processes would eliminate ambiguity, regulate training and clinical experience, legitimize the reputation of the sex therapist, and grant the field the recognition it deserves. Only then will the public be assured that the practitioner has completed specific requirements that ensure a particular standard of care.

Combined with these challenges, being a sex therapist also means additional training beyond one's terminal degree and additional expense. So the question becomes: why do some therapists choose to enter and remain in this field? Part of the reason may be that sex is intrinsically interesting and a curiosity. Sexual behavior is expressed in an almost infinite variety of ways which reflect one's culture, family values, psychology, and biology.

Once past the newness of the field, the clinician finds they have entered a world where few venture; sexual behavior is the most unique, personal, and hidden part of self. While over the course of their career, all therapists hear the phrase, "I have never told anyone this. . . ," sex therapists hear it every day. Our clients invite us into the most intimate part of their life, with some hesitation, and depending on how we respond; they may invite us to understand that part of themselves completely. It is the ultimate privileged position for us to share in their vulnerability and naked truth about their sexuality. Our clients' sexuality is but one piece of the overall puzzle in their lives that remains in the background. It is the one area of their life where their pain, regret, grief, inhibitions, prohibitions, and many other feelings are now allowed expression directly.

Sex is one of the great joys of life that bonds couples together and can allow the individual to feel free to pursue sexual happiness, wholeness as a person, and freedom. In spite of the fact that what we do remains invisible to all but our clients, the effect is profound and the personal rewards transcend attempts at verbalization. We open ourselves to resonate with our clients sexuality and in so doing reap the same rewards.

INDEX

abandonment, fear of 132, 268
Abilify 260
absent/low desire in men 126, 132; cognitive
distractions and 133; and sexual trauma 134
absent/low desire in women 125–6; acquired
127; clinical assessment 129; and cognitive
distraction 133; comprehensive studies
consistent with the Intersystem Approach
134–5; conclusion 146; in conjunction with
other sexual dysfunctions 126; definition
126–8; diagnostic criteria 126–7; empirical
tools for assessment 131; etiology 131–4;
general 127; Intersystem framework 131;
lifelong 127; models of sexual desire 128–9;
prevalence 126; relapse prevention 145;
research 145–6; situational 127; theoretical
model of treatment 129–131; treatment
strategies 135–45; see also female sexual
interest/arousal disorder
absent/low desire in women risk factors:
environmental 129–30, 131, 133–4;
interactional 133; intergenerational 130,
133–4; physical 131; psychological 131–2
absent/low desire in women treatment:
addressing affect 139; addressing pessimism
and skepticism 136; clinical assessment 129;
cognitive work 139–40; communication
140; correcting unrealistic expectations
138; creating an erotic environment 143;
establishing treatment goals 138; family-of-
origin issues 143; implementing goals
138; indications and contraindications
135–6; lowering response anxiety 138–9;
maintaining a systemic focus 137; medical
therapies 144–5; psychoeducation 140;
responsibility for sexual intimacy 137; setting
priorities 137–8; systemic homework 140–1;
treating other sexual dysfunctions 141; using
sensate focus 136–7; working with conflict

and anger 142–3; working with fears of
intimacy 141–2
abuse: child sexual (CSA) 58–8; emotional
136; history of 246; physical 136, 193;
psychological 193; sexual 7, 11, 24, 76, 132,
136, 156, 193, 194, 289; substance 242;
see also substance use disorders
ACTIS venous flow controller 80
acute stress disorders 11
addictive behaviors 242, 245, 255; see also
sexual addiction
addictive disorders 236
affection, emphasizing 198
ageing: and absent/low desire in women 136;
effect on delayed ejaculation 108–10; effect
on female arousal problems 153; and genito-
pelvic pain/penetration disorder 192; and the
LBGT population 282; and sexuality 282
agoraphobia 261
AIDS 216, 227–8
Alcoholics Anonymous 270
alcohol issues: "at risk" drinking patterns
264; delayed ejaculation 111; premature
ejaculation 92
alcohol use disorders 264–5, 267, 270
alprazolam (Xanax) 262, 263
alprostadil 97–8
Alzheimer's disease 75, 268
amantadine 110
amenorrhea 267
American Association for Marriage and Family
Therapy (AAMFT) 5, 25, 34, 48, 287
American Association of Sexuality Educators,
Counselors and Therapists (AASECT) 23,
24, 25, 28, 35, 48, 287
American Counseling Association (ACA) 48;
on counseling transgender clients 284
American Psychiatric Association (APA): on
sexual disorders 18, 236, 237; on sexual

301

obsessive compulsive disorders (OCD) 111,
132, 255, 261–2
obsessive compulsive personality disorder
(OCPD) 268
obsessiveness, and delayed ejaculation 118
obsessive thoughts 241
olanzapine (Zyprexa) 260
online therapy 281
opiates 92
opioids 263, 266, 267
oral contraceptives 192
oral opioid analgesics 97
oral sexual contacts 6, 227
orgasm(s): categories of 171; clitoral vs. vaginal
171, 175; delayed/absent 37; female 10, 11;
male 108–9; multiple 9
orgasmic disorders 152, 158; caused by
antipsychotic medications 260; *see also*
anorgasmia; female orgasmic disorder
orgasmic function 61; and ageing 7
Out of the Shadows (Carnes) 236–7

pain: chronic 92, 193; ejaculatory 92; fear of
8, 193; genito-pelvic 92, 136, 263; impact
of on relationship 205; perineal 92; and
physiological processes 198; treating and
demystifying 197; *see also* genito-pelvic pain/
penetration disorder
Pain Catastrophizing Scale (PCS) 196
pain diary 197, 199
pain disorders 280
painful intercourse *see* genito-pelvic pain/
penetration disorder
pain killers, prescription 266
panic attacks 261
panic disorder 261, 281
pansexuality 214, 219
paradoxical strategies 145
paranoia 267
paranoid personality disorder 268
paraphilia-related disorders 284
paraphilias 6, 24
paraphilic behavior 21
paraphilic disorder 257
parentification 134
Parkinson's Disease 75, 92, 242
paroxetine (Paxil) 96, 257, 258
partnered sex, and erectile disorder 76
partner sexual disinterest 81, 133
passion 42, 45–6, 278
Paxil 21, 96
PDE5i (phosphodiesterase type 5 inhibitor) 19,
20, 98, 167, 279; discontinuation of use 81;
see also Cialis; Levitra; Viagra

pedophilic disorder 284
pelvic floor abnormalities 193
pelvic floor biofeedback 199
pelvic inflammatory disease 192
pelvic trauma 111
penile fibrosis 80
penile hypersensitivity 92
penile hypoanesthesia 97
penile injections 80
penile prosthesis 80–1
penis 21; manual or vibratory stimulation of 110;
response of 9; *see also* erectile disorder (ED)
penis envy 11
perfectionism 261
performance anxiety 75, 112, 120; and female
orgasmic disorder 173, 179, 186; and social
phobia or social anxiety disorder 261;
therapist-induced 206
perineum, pain in 92
peripheral vascular disease 156
persistent depressant disorder *see* depression;
depressive disorders
persistent genital arousal disorder 153
personality disorders 37, 264, 268
pessimism, and absent/low desire in women 136
Peyronie's disease 74
pharmacotherapy *see* antidepressant
medications; medications; medications for
treatment
phenelzine (Nardil) 257
Phosphodiesterase type 5 (PDE5) inhibitors 79
physical abuse 136, 193
physical attraction, lack of 63, 66, 135
physical examinations 61, 95, 96, 249
physical infirmities 283
physical therapy 117, 198–9
physical treatment 287
physicians 299; training for 22, 24, 288–9
Physician's Desk Reference 279
physiology, of sexuality and sexual response
8–9, 24, 32
playfulness and levity 120, 201
politics, effect on absent/low desire in women 130
pornography 63, 66, 248, 250; fetish 239;
Internet 8, 27, 238–9, 281; print 281; and
sexual addiction 235
postmodern systemic therapy 154–5
posttraumatic stress disorder (PTSD) 11, 156,
247, 261; and sexual addiction 242
power issues 25, 27, 76, 93, 136
pregnancy, fear of 111–12
premature ejaculation (PE) (early ejaculation)
8, 41, 90, 290; assessment 95–6; case study
101–2; comorbidity with ED 98; defined

sociocultural factors and norms 76, 278;
affecting delayed ejaculation 113; effect on
absent/low desire in women 130; in female
orgasmic disorder 175; and premature
ejaculation 94–5; and sexuality 38, 77, 134
socioeconomic status issues: and genito-
pelvic pain/penetration disorder 192; and
premature ejaculation 94; and sexuality 38
sociology, and sex therapy 22
solo sex 134, 143; *see also* masturbation
somatic disorders 263
somatic hypervigilance 193
spinal cord injuries 75, 111
spirituality, and sexual addiction treatment 249
SSRIs *see* selective serotonin reuptake inhibitors
Staxyn 98
steroids, topical 197
stimulants, effects of 266–7
stop-start method 98–9
stress 48, 64; and absent/low desire in women
127, 136; and female orgasmic disorder 173;
and female sexual interest/arousal disorder
168; psychosocial 92; reduction of 245; and
sexual addiction 245; and sexual arousal 85;
see also posttraumatic stress disorder
subjective sexual arousal disorder 153
substance abuse 242
Substance/Medication-Induced Sexual
Dysfunction 57, 108
substance use disorders: alcohol 265, 267;
marijuana 264, 265, 267; and sexual
dysfunction 264–5
suicide lethality assessment 244
support groups 270; for sexual addiction 244,
245, 250
surgery/surgical procedures: for transgender
individuals 284l for treatment of genito-
pelvic pain/penetration disorder 197, 198
surrogate partner therapy 26
swinging 63
systemic illness 75
systems theory 33, 34, 287; and female
orgasmic disorder 177; sexological 278, 289

tadalafil (Cialis) 98, 279
tardive dyskinesia 268
technology, and sexual lives 281
TEMPE (topical eutectic mixture for PE) 97
temperament 37
Test of Variable Attention 244
testosterone 21, 68, 131; effect of opioids
on 266; low levels of 57–8, 61, 144;
and marijuana use 265; and premature

ejaculation 92; and sexual appetite 144;
sublingual 167
theory, future of in sex therapy 49–50
Theory of Interaction 38–41; interactional
components of 40–1; intrapsychic
components of 40
therapeutic reframe 137
therapists: flexibility of 3–4, 12–13; legal
issues 4
therapy: online 281; surrogate partner 26; *see
also* couple therapy; family therapy; group
therapy for sexual addiction; marital therapy;
mindfulness-based therapies; physical
therapy; postmodern systemic therapy
Thorazine 260
thyroid dysfunctions, and absent/low desire in
women 131
thyroid problems 173
thyroid stimulating hormone (TSH), and PE 92
tibolone 167
Tiefer, Leonore 22
Tofranil 257
topical anesthetics 97
torticollis 268
touching: genital 197; inappropriate sexual 9;
of others 268
Tourette's syndrome 244
tourniquets 80
training: for counseling 24; implications for
288–9; sexology 26, 27; sexuality 34
tramadol 97
tranquilizers 75; and delayed ejaculation 108
transgender individuals 215–16, 283–4; in
same-sex relationships 220
transgenerational dynamics 76
transvestic disorder 284
trauma: childhood 241; emotional 76, 132;
history of 113, 246, 255, 261; pelvic
111; sexual 56, 76, 134, 156; and sexual
addiction 241, 246; treatment for 270
Trauma and Stressor-Related Disorders 261
traumatic brain injury 92, 244
triangle of love 278
Triangular Theory of Love 42
tricyclic antidepressants (TCAs) 97, 257, 262
triggers, for sexual addiction 245
trust, development of 120
truth-telling 204
Truvada 228
twelve-step support groups 245

unemployment 173
"unmarried partners" *see* same-sex couples

√7/6 7/8	**Basics of Sex Therapy and the Intersystems Approach** 1. Check in 2. Discussion of reading 3. Clinical presentations 4. Group case consultations	Hertlein et al. ch. 1-3 ✓ **Due:** Personal Therapy Verification, if on weekly therapy track or other, as needed
√7/13 7/15	**Treatment of Male Hypoactive Sexual Desire Disorder, Erectile Disorder, Premature Ejaculation, & Delayed Ejaculation** 1. Check in 2. Discussion of reading 3. Clinical presentations 4. Group case consultations	Hertlein et al. ch. 4-7 ✓
√7/20 7/22	**Treatment of Absent/Low Desire & Inhibited Arousal in Women** 1. Check in 2. Discussion of reading 3. Clinical presentations 4. Group case consultations	Hertlein et al. ch. 8-9 ✓
√7/27 7/29	**Treatment of Female Orgasmic Disorder & Painful Intercourse** 1. Check in 2. Discussion of reading 3. Clinical presentations 4. Group case consultations	Hertlein et al. ch. 10-11 ✓
8/3 8/5	**Sex Therapy for Other Sexual Disorders** 5. Check in 6. Discussion of reading	Binik & Hall ch. 9-13